Composing Cyberspace

Identity, Community, and Knowledge in the Electronic Age

Composing Cyberspace

Identity, Community, and Knowledge in the Electronic Age

R I C H A R D   H O L E T O N

Stanford University

Boston   Burr Ridge, IL   Dubuque, IA   Madison, WI
New York   San Francisco   St. Louis
Bangkok   Bogotá   Caracas   Lisbon   London   Madrid   Mexico City
Milan   New Delhi   Seoul   Singapore   Sydney   Taipei   Toronto

McGraw-Hill

A Division of The **McGraw·Hill** Companies

COMPOSING CYBERSPACE: IDENTITY, COMMUNITY, AND KNOWLEDGE IN THE ELECTRONIC AGE

Acknowledgments appear on pages 443–446 and on this page by reference.

This book is printed on acid-free paper.

1 2 3 4 5 6 7 8 9 0 DOC/DOC 9 0 9 8 7

ISBN 0-07-029548-4

Editorial director: *Phillip A. Butcher*
Sponsoring editor: *Tim Julet*
Marketing manager: *Lesley Denton*
Senior project manager: *Susan Trentacosti*
Production supervisor: *Lori Koetters*
Designer: *Gino Cieslik*
Compositor: *Precision Graphics, Inc.*
Typeface: *10/12 Times Roman*
Printer: *R. R. Donnelley & Sons Company*

Library of Congress Cataloging-in-Publication Data

Holeton, Richard (date)
  Composing cyberspace : identity, community, and knowledge in the electronic age / Richard Holeton.
      p.   cm.
    Includes index.
    ISBN 0-07-029548-8 (acid-free paper)
    1. Computer networks--Social aspects--United States.
  2. Information Technology--Social aspects--United States.
  3. Identity (Psychology)--United States.   4. Group identity--United States.   5. Electronic digital computers--United States--Psychological aspects.   I. Title.
  ZA4375.H65   1998
  303.48´33--dc21   97-34791

http://www.mhhe.com

For Rachel and Miranda, and for their future

About the Author

Richard Holeton serves as Information Resources Specialist for the Division of Literatures, Cultures, and Languages at Stanford University, supporting faculty in the thoughtful uses of emerging technologies. Previously he taught composition and creative writing courses at Cañada Community College and San Francisco State University and, for ten years, taught in Stanford's Program in Writing and Critical Thinking, where he oversaw a state-of-the-art computer classroom. For seven years, he and his wife served as Resident Fellows in a freshman dorm at Stanford. Mr. Holeton writes articles, textbooks, and fiction. His current projects include a hypertext novel and a study of how college students who live together use electronic communication.

FAQ: Frequently Asked Questions about *Composing Cyberspace*

What's a FAQ? A FAQ (pronounced "fak") or Frequently Asked Questions document is a text form that has developed on the Internet, where new participants often wish to quickly learn the basics about a particular electronic forum or project. FAQs ("fax") are intended as reader-friendly ways to summarize the most salient "facts." This new kind of text seems an appropriate way to introduce a book focusing on emerging media and technologies. A hyperlinked version of this document will be available at the *Composing Cyberspace* Web site at <http://www.mhhe.com/socscience/english/holeton/>.

1. What's this book about? Why's it called *Composing Cyberspace?* ►
2. Why are these issues important? ►
3. Who should read *Composing Cyberspace?* ►
4. What if I don't know anything about computers? ►
5. What if I'm already on the Internet, or reading this book for a course that uses computers? Do you have a Web site? ►
6. How is the book organized? ►
7. What kinds of readings and range of opinions are included in the book? ►
8. What kinds of editorial help with the readings are offered? ►
9. What else should I know before jumping into *Composing Cyberspace?* ►
10. Who helped make this book possible? ►

FAQ **1. What's this book about? Why is it called *Composing Cyberspace*?**

As both Dale Spender (see Chapters 2 and 6) and Sherry Turkle (see Chapter 1) say about their own books, this is a book about *people,* not about computers. This book explores the effects that computer technologies have had, are having, and might have on people—on our human identity, on our values, on our social status and social relations, and on our desire to make and share knowledge.

"Cyberspace," a term coined by science fiction author William Gibson (see Chapters 1 and 8) for a vast electronic matrix of corporate data, has come to refer to the electronic "place" where any digital information is exchanged. But people *compose* (or create) this information in all its forms, and therefore it's really people, not electronic bits, who *compose* (or make up) the population of cyberspace. Cyberspace as a place or entity is by no means a finished product, some complete thing "out there" to which newcomers gain access or admission. On the contrary, it's a work in progress, a project that's barely begun, a process under constant scrutiny by rapidly increasing numbers of participants. The title *Composing Cyberspace* is intended to emphasize the active participation of people, and their writing (or *composing*), in this work in progress. As a thoughtful reader of this book, you are already helping shape the features and values of our cyber-future.

FAQ **2. Why are these issues important?**

If you follow the news as reported by the mainstream media, you're probably tired of hearing that "technology is taking over our lives," or that people (or at least people of a certain social class) are besieged today with "information overload," or that the "information superhighway" is transforming business, banking, government, consumer entertainment, and so on. You likely have heard claims and statistics such as these:

- The Internet is growing exponentially faster than any other communication medium in history.
- Most commercial transactions already are mediated by computers, either directly or behind the scenes.
- Almost 30 million Americans over 18 (and millions more under 18) were identified in May 1997 as regular Internet users.
- Nearly two-thirds of U.S. public schools and libraries have some type of Internet connection as of 1997.
- More than half of American households are projected to have computers and modems by the year 2000.
- Enthusiasts say that new technologies can improve equality of access to information and other resources, increase social justice, promote democratic values, and improve life for everyone.

On the other hand, you may also have heard claims such as these:

- Much of the developing world lacks even the telephone wiring infrastructure necessary for computer networks, while 50 percent of the global population suffers from malnutrition, 70 percent can't read, and 80 percent live in substandard housing.
- The median household income for U.S. Internet users in the mid-1990s was $58,000, or 75 percent higher than the national median.
- Students in poor districts and minority students are less likely to have Internet access and to use instructional technologies for higher-order, problem-solving tasks.

- Americans still buy three times as many TVs as computers.
- Critics say that new technologies primarily benefit affluent people and large corporations; rather than improve life for most people, they say, these technologies will tend to centralize power and the control of information.

Barring some radical change in global politics and economics, it seems clear that the tide, or tidal wave, of computer and network technologies is not going to recede. So far, the shape of that wave has been determined largely by a small group of American high-tech companies and pioneering users from industry, the government, the military, and educational institutions. That situation is changing rapidly as businesses and organizations from all over the world and millions of new people—at school, at work, and through commercial Internet service providers—come online. Important decisions about access to information, censorship in cyberspace, educational uses of technology, and other issues will be made over the next few years. To understand these complex issues or to participate in these decisions, it's crucial for all of us to explore the social implications of emerging technologies in substantial, critical depth.

FAQ 3. Who should read *Composing Cyberspace*?

(*a*) Students and teachers of courses that involve writing and discussion; any course about the Internet; or other courses in the humanities, social sciences, or computer science that address values, technology, and society. (*b*) Anyone interested in important social issues arising from emerging technologies.

FAQ 4. What if I don't know anything about computers?

No computer or technical experience is required. In *Composing Cyberspace* you'll find accessible selections addressed to a general audience, along with articles and stories to take you further into cyberspace. Any computer-mediated activities suggested in the book, plus supplementary materials available on the World Wide Web, are entirely optional. You may encounter some cyber-jargon you haven't heard before (for example, what the heck are MOOs and MUDs?), but new terms will be explained in the selection you're reading or in adjacent material. And we've provided a complete Cyberspace Glossary at the back of the book (p. 435).

FAQ 5. What if I'm already on the Internet, or reading this book for a course that uses computers? Do you have a Web site?

For readers with networked computers and/or Internet access, *Composing Cyberspace* includes many specific suggestions for online discussions and Internet research projects; see FAQ 8 for details.

At the innovative *Composing Cyberspace Online* site, <www.mhhe.com/socscience/english/holeton/>, you will find updated Internet links, online versions of many of the book's selections, related online readings and sources for every chapter, and a hyperlinked version of all the questions, chapter introductions, research suggestions, and other editorial apparatus. The McGraw-Hill English Composition site, at <www.mhhe.com/socscience/english/compde/> will offer a complete set of Internet resources for coursework, research, and documentation of online sources. In addition, as the book goes to press, electronic conferencing capabilities are being planned for *Composing Cyberspace Online*.

FAQ **6. How is the book organized?**

The selections are arranged according to three broad, longstanding human questions:

> *Who am I?* (The question of **identity**)
> *Who are we?* (The question of **community**)
> *What do we know?* (The question of **knowledge**)

Each of these broader questions is explored in three thematic chapters:

Part One: Constructing Identity in the Computer Age
1. New Windows on the Self
2. Gender Online
3. Cultural Identity and Cyberspace

Part Two: Building Community in the Electronic Age
4. Virtual Community
5. Electronic Democracy
6. The Global Village

Part Three: Seeking Knowledge in the Information Age
7. Information Overload and New Media
8. Ownership and Sharing of Knowledge
9. The Classroom of the Future

Each of the nine chapters includes five provocative reading selections to stimulate your thinking about these themes.

FAQ **7. What kinds of readings and range of opinions are included in the book?**

Composing Cyberspace includes:

- Cartoons in each chapter introduction.
- Articles from mainstream newspapers and magazines.

- Articles from non-mainstream publications.
- Scholarly essays or book chapters.
- Interviews.
- Short stories and novel excerpts.

Every chapter offers not only a variety of writing forms but a wide range of social and political views about a particular cyberspace social issue. For example, Chapter 9, "The Classroom of the Future," includes two articles analyzing constructive, beneficial uses of computers in education; a chapter from a prominent critic of the rush to cyberspace; a scholarly argument about the corporate motivations behind classroom technologies; and an excerpt from a bestselling sci-fi novel featuring a futuristic educational "game."

FAQ 8. What kinds of editorial help with the readings are offered?

- *Forward Thinking.* Each chapter opens with a cartoon and an introduction to help contextualize and introduce the reading selections. The introductions also include specific suggestions for thinking about, writing about, or discussing the issues explored in each chapter *before* you read the selections, so you can frame those issues according to your own values, knowledge, and experience.
- *Second Thoughts.* Each reading selection is followed by several questions meant to help develop your understanding and critical thinking.
- *Discussion Threads.* Each chapter is followed by a set of questions asking you to relate ideas from two, three, four, or all of the chapter's selections. These questions can be used as prompts for discussion or writing, in class or outside of class, for individual or collaborative work. If you communicate with fellow readers on a computer network, you can use the Discussion Threads directly as subject headers for e-mail, newsgroups, bulletin board conferences, or other types of electronic discussions.
- *Research Links.* Each chapter is also followed by specific suggestions for research writing projects that integrate Internet sources with traditional library and nonlibrary sources.
- *Cyberspace Glossary.* Key terms of the latest cyber-jargon are defined for both the initiated and the uninitiated.

FAQ 9. What else should I know before jumping in to *Composing Cyberspace?*

Both the reading selections and the editorial apparatus contain numerous Internet addresses called URLs (Uniform Resource Locators). If you have Internet access and will be looking up these references, you should be forewarned that addresses on the World Wide Web can change often as sites are moved from one Web server (a kind of computer that publishes Web pages) to another. The URLs provided in the apparatus are the latest available as this book goes to press; URLs listed in some of the reading selections may already be dated. If you encounter a wrong address on the Internet, you will often be redirected to the new URL. In any case, please visit *Composing Cyberspace Online* at <www.mhhe.com/socscience/english/holeton/>, where you will find updates of Web addresses listed in the printed book. (Note that URLs in the book are abbreviated: you can presume that they all start with "http://" unless another prefix is given. Most Web browsers, such as Netscape Navigator and Microsoft Internet Explorer, no longer require you to type in the "http://" prefix.)

FAQ 10. Who helped make this book possible?

- Tim Julet, the College English Editor at McGraw-Hill, has collaborated on this project from the beginning, contributing his enthusiasm, sound advice, savvy about the needs of students and teachers, and foresight about the electronic future of educational publishing.

- Editorial assistants Chris Fitzpatrick and Alan Joyce handled innumerable logistical and manuscript matters with clarity, grace, and humor. Their experience and judgment regarding electronic matters have likewise been invaluable.

- Susan Trentacosti, Senior Project Manager for McGraw-Hill Higher Education, has overseen the outstanding design and super-efficient production of the book under severe time constraints.

- As the book goes to press, Web magician Sherry Kane and her staff are collaborating with me on what promises to be a trailblazing online version of *Composing Cyberspace.*

- The following reviewers offered both encouragement and many specific suggestions for improving the manuscript: Kevin Davis, East Central University; Susan Halter, Delgado Community College; Judith Kirkpatrick, Kapi'olani Community College; Jane Lasarenko, West Texas A&M University; Tom Long, Thomas Nelson Community College; Lisa McClure, Southern Illinois University at Carbondale; Michael Palmquist, Colorado State University; Nancy Remler, Armstrong State College; Charlotte Smith, Adirondack Community College; and Bob Whipple, Creighton University.

- My colleagues in the computers and writing community have both inspired me with their work and given me positive feedback about my own work. In particular, I wish to thank Professor Elizabeth Sommers of San Francisco State University, who encouraged me to share my teaching and research by submitting my first proposal (happily, one that was accepted), in 1995, to the Computers & Writing Conference.

- My wonderful frosh and Continuing Studies students at Stanford, over several terms of "Composing Cyberspace" classes, taught me about the reading selections in this book and helped me learn effective ways to complement face-to-face teaching and learning with networked communications.

- Roni, Rachel, and Miranda (my family) have lent their strength and love to me and to this project through professional and personal transitions for all of us.

Richard Holeton

Contents

Chapter 3

Cultural Identity and Cyberspace   110

Part Two

Building Community in the Electronic Age   147

Chapter 4

Virtual Community   148

Chapter 5

Electronic Democracy   200

Chapter 8

Ownership and Sharing of Knowledge   340

Chapter 9

The Classroom of the Future   388

Composing Cyberspace

Identity, Community,
and Knowledge
in the Electronic Age

One

*Constructing
Identity in the
Computer Age*

New Windows on the Self

In May 1997, what many were calling an epic battle between human and machine took place across a chessboard in New York City, while a global audience followed the game, move by move, on the Internet. "Big Blue," a state-of-the-art IBM computer with capabilities barely dreamed of only a generation ago, defeated defending world chess champion Garry Kasparov in a six-game contest. Was this a watershed event in human history, finally proving that computers have overtaken their creators, that science fiction fantasies of superior artificial intelligence are coming true? Or was the "battle" over-hyped and not a true test of, or threat to, human intelligence and human identity?

Our answer depends, of course, on how we conceive our intelligence and our identity and on how we view our relationship to our technologies. The Tony Auth cartoon, published about a year before the Kasparov–Big Blue duel, captures the same set of dilemmas. Again the contest is chess, by reputation our most intellectual game. Humankind—or at least the thinking, contemplative part of human beings—is represented by Auguste Rodin's famous 1880 statue *The Thinker;* his robot opponent looks like R2D2, the droid of *Star Wars* fame. The robot, not the statue, reveals its thoughts—thoughts that reverse the influential dictum of French mathematician and philosopher René Descartes (1596–1650), "I think, therefore I am." Descartes' assertion encapsulates a rationalist philosophy, the view that human identity depends on our intellectual capacity. The robot's playful reversal of Descartes' dictum suggests that its own identity arises from that same rational capacity, although the larger question posed by Rodin's sculpture—just what exactly is *The Thinker* thinking *about?*— is left open.

If we focus on *The Thinker*'s attributes as a statue, then the cartoon takes on other dimensions. A statue can't move or act, while the robot is shown to be moving a chess piece as well as thinking like a person. Which one is closer to having a human, physical body? Are people at the dawn of the 21st century becoming more passive, objectified, or disembodied, while our machines become more "human"? This exchanging of characteristics between people and machines is only one aspect of identity in the computer age explored in this chapter.

How are electronic technologies affecting our ideas about what it means to be human? Based on her studies of how people use computers, Sherry Turkle suggests that "windows"—the spaces on computer screens where one views different application programs, texts, and files—offer a new metaphor for the multiple identities we may bring together as the idea of a single "self." Charles Platt explores the question "What's It Mean to Be Human, Anyway?" by participating in a version of the Turing test, a method proposed by computer pioneer Alan Turing to evaluate how well computer programs (not unlike the IBM "expert system" that beat chess champion Kasparov) can emulate human intelligence.

In an interview with Iain A. Boal, linguist George Lakoff disputes the mind-body split suggested by Descartes' rationalist philosophy and suggests that emotions are an integral part of human identity inextricably linked to the human body; further, he argues that our usual ways of talking about information and communication are based on faulty, machine-based metaphors. Ellen Ullman also examines, through an e-mail relationship with a fellow computer programmer, the electronic and embodied aspects of human relations. "Which set of us is the more real," she asks, "the sleepless ones online, or these bodies in the daylight?" Likewise, in the dark, near-future world of William Gibson's science fiction story "Johnny Mnemonic," the distinction between people and technology is far from clear; cyborgs—part human, part machine—are the norm.

Before you read these selections, you might take some time to think about how you conceive your own identity and relationship to technology, especially the computer technologies that increasingly impact our lives:

1. Consider the different "selves" that make up who you are. How do you act differently in different contexts, such as a family dinner, a party with friends, a day at work, a traveling vacation? How might people from different parts of your life describe your personality in different ways?

2. How do you behave or interact with others differently when you are "live" or face-to-face with them, when you talk on the telephone, when you exchange letters, and when you use a computer (for e-mail or another form of computer-mediated communication)? Compare your experiences using these different media with those of fellow readers.

3. How would you define *intelligence* or what makes you intelligent? In your experience, can machines (such as computers) be intelligent in some of the same ways as you? In what ways can computers be less intelligent than people? To what extent do you think that human intelligence requires a physical body or human emotions?

4. Cyborg is short for "cybernetic organism," meaning a combination of artificial and biological systems. What artificial aids or prosthetic devices, if any, do you have or regularly use as extensions or enhancements to your physical body? Make a list of all such aids—don't forget common items such as dental fillings and eyeglasses or contact lenses—used by a group such as your extended family, fellow workers, or classmates (bear in mind that some people may not wish to discuss personal things like hairpieces, hearing aids, or surgical implants). How many people depend on *no* such technological aids or prosthetics?

5. If you have access to a computer lab, classroom, or networked computers equipped with electronic discussion software, hold a discussion in which everyone logs on anonymously. Before you begin, make sure you agree on some ground rules for "netiquette" or online politeness. Invent a pseudonym for a character different from you; for example, if you're usually shy, play a gregarious role, or if you have a good sense of humor or tend to be warmly emotional, act serious or distant. Discuss, in the voice of your invented character, one of the issues raised earlier or another topic suggested by your peers or teacher. Afterward, talk face-to-face about the experience. How liberating or how constraining did you find the role-playing experience?

Identity in the Age of the Internet

Sherry Turkle

Living in the MUD

Sherry Turkle (b. 1948) is professor of the social and cultural studies of science and technology at MIT (Massachusetts Institute of Technology). She has written extensively about psychoanalysis and culture and about the psychology of people's relationships with technology, especially computer technology. Her books include *Psychoanalytic Politics: Jacques Lacan and Freud's French Revolution* (Basic Books, 1978) and *The Second Self: Computers and the Human Spirit* (Simon and Schuster, 1984). This selection is from the introduction to her recent book, *Life on the Screen: Identity in the Age of Internet* (Simon and Schuster, 1995), which is described on the book jacket as "a book not about computers, but about people and how computers are causing us to reevaluate our identities." You can learn more about Turkle from her home page on the Web at <web.mit.edu/sturkle/www/>.

> There was a child went forth every day,
> And the first object he look'd upon, that object he became.
> —*Walt Whitman*

We come to see ourselves differently as we catch sight of our images in the mirror of the machine. A decade ago, when I first called the computer a second self, these identity-transforming relationships were almost always one-on-one, a person alone with a machine. This is no longer the case. A rapidly expanding system of networks, collectively known as the Internet, links millions of people in new spaces that are changing the way we think, the nature of our sexuality, the form of our communities, our very identities.

At one level, the computer is a tool. It helps us write, keep track of our accounts, and communicate with others. Beyond this, the computer offers us both new models of mind and a new medium on which to project our ideas and fantasies. Most recently, the computer has become even more than tool and mirror: We are able to step through the looking glass. We are learning to live in virtual worlds. We may find ourselves alone as we navigate virtual oceans, unravel virtual mysteries, and engineer virtual skyscrapers. But increasingly, when we step through the looking glass, other people are there as well.

The use of the term "cyberspace" to describe virtual worlds grew out of science fiction,[1] but for many of us, cyberspace is now part of the routines of everyday life. When we read our electronic mail or send postings to an electronic bulletin board or

make an airline reservation over a computer network, we are in cyberspace. In cyberspace,
we can talk, exchange ideas, and assume personae
of our own creation. We have the opportunity to
build new kinds of communities, virtual communities, in which we participate with people from all
over the world, people with whom we converse
daily, people with whom we may have fairly intimate relationships but whom we may
never physically meet.

> **In cyberspace, we can talk, exchange ideas, and assume personae of our own creation.**

This book describes how a nascent culture of simulation is affecting our ideas   4
about mind, body, self, and machine. We shall encounter virtual sex and cyberspace
marriage, computer psychotherapists, robot insects, and researchers who are trying to
build artificial two-year-olds. Biological children, too, are in the story as their play with
computer toys leads them to speculate about whether computers are smart and what it
is to be alive. Indeed, in much of this, it is our children who are leading the way, and
adults who are anxiously trailing behind.

In the story of constructing identity in the culture of simulation, experiences on   5
the Internet figure prominently, but these experiences can only be understood as part
of a larger cultural context. That context is the story of the eroding boundaries
between the real and the virtual, the animate and the inanimate, the unitary and the
multiple self, which is occurring both in advanced scientific fields of research and in
the patterns of everyday life. From scientists trying to create artificial life to children
"morphing" through a series of virtual personae, we shall see evidence of fundamental shifts in the way we create and experience human identity. But it is on the Internet
that our confrontations with technology as it collides with our sense of human identity
are fresh, even raw. In the real-time communities of cyberspace, we are dwellers on
the threshold between the real and the virtual, unsure of our footing, inventing ourselves as we go along.

In an interactive, text-based computer game designed to represent a world inspired   6
by the television series "Star Trek: The Next Generation," thousands of players spend
up to eighty hours a week participating in intergalactic exploration and wars. Through
typed descriptions and typed commands, they create characters who have casual and
romantic sexual encounters, hold jobs and collect paychecks, attend rituals and celebra-
tions, fall in love and get married. To the participants, such goings-on can be gripping;
"This is more real than my real life," says a character who turns out to be a man playing a woman who is pretending to be a man. In this game the self is constructed and the
rules of social interaction are built, not received.[2]

In another text-based game, each of nearly ten thousand players creates a character   7
or several characters, specifying their genders and other physical and psychological
attributes. The characters need not be human and there are more than two genders.
Players are invited to help build the computer world itself. Using a relatively simple
programming language, they can create a room in the same space where they are able
to set the stage and define the rules. They can fill the room with objects and specify
how they work; they can, for instance, create a virtual dog that barks if one types the

command "bark Rover." An eleven-year-old player built a room she calls the condo. It is beautifully furnished. She has created magical jewelry and makeup for her dressing table. When she visits the condo, she invites her cyberfriends to join her there, she chats, orders a virtual pizza, and flirts.

LIVING IN THE MUD

The Star Trek game, TrekMUSE, and the other, LambdaMOO, are both computer pro- 8 grams that can be accessed through the Internet. The Internet was once available only to military personnel and technical researchers. It is now available to anyone who can buy or borrow an account on a commercial online service. TrekMUSE and Lamb- daMOO are known as MUDs, Multi-User Domains or, with greater historical accuracy, Multi-User Dungeons, because of their genealogy from Dungeons and Dragons, the fantasy role-playing game that swept high schools and colleges in the late 1970s and early 1980s.

The multiuser computer games are based on different kinds of software (this is 9 what the MUSE or MOO or MUSH part of their names stands for). For simplicity, here I use the term MUD to refer to all of them.

MUDs put you in virtual spaces in which you are able to navigate, converse, and 10 build. You join a MUD through a command that links your computer to the computer on which the MUD program resides. Making the connection is not difficult; it requires no particular technical sophistication. The basic commands may seem awk- ward at first but soon become familiar. For example, if I am playing a character named ST on LambdaMOO, any words I type after the command "say" will appear on all players' screens as "ST says." Any actions I type after the command "emote" will appear after my name just as I type them, as in "ST waves hi" or "ST laughs uncontrollably." I can "whisper" to a designated character and only that character will be able to see my words. As of this writing there are over five hundred MUDs in which hundreds of thousands of people participate.[3] In some MUDs, players are rep- resented by graphical icons; most MUDs are purely text-based. Most players are middle class. A large majority are male. Some players are over thirty, but most are in their early twenties and late teens. However, it is no longer unusual to find MUDs where eight- and nine-year-olds "play" such grade-school icons as Barbie or the Mighty Morphin Power Rangers.

MUDs are a new kind of virtual parlor game and a new form of community. In 11 addition, text-based MUDs are a new form of collaboratively written literature. MUD players are MUD authors, the creators as well as consumers of media content. In this, participating in a MUD has much in common with script writing, performance art, street theater, improvisational theater—or even commedia dell'arte. But MUDs are something else as well.

As players participate, they become authors not only of text but of themselves, 12 constructing new selves through social interaction. One player says, "You are the char- acter and you are not the character, both at the same time." Another says, "You are who you pretend to be." MUDs provide worlds for anonymous social interaction in which one can play a role as close to or as far away from one's "real self" as one chooses. Since one participates in MUDs by sending text to a computer that houses the MUD's program and database, MUD selves are constituted in interaction with the machine. Take it away and the MUD selves cease to exist: "Part of me, a very important part of me, only exists inside PernMUD," says one player.

> **MUDs provide worlds for anonymous social interaction in which one can play a role as close to or as far away from one's "real self" as one chooses.**

Several players joke that they are like "the electrodes in the computer," trying to express the degree to which they feel part of its space.

On MUDs, one's body is represented by one's own textual description, so the obese   13
can be slender, the beautiful plain, the "nerdy" sophisticated. A *New Yorker* cartoon captures the potential for MUDs as laboratories for experimenting with one's identity.* In it, one dog, paw on a computer keyboard, explains to another, "On the Internet, nobody knows you're a dog." The anonymity of MUDs—one is known on the MUD only by the name of one's character or characters—gives people the chance to express multiple and often unexplored aspects of the self, to play with their identity and to try out new ones. MUDs make possible the creation of an identity so fluid and multiple that it strains the limits of the notion. Identity, after all, refers to the sameness between two qualities, in this case between a person and his or her persona. But in MUDs, one can be many.

Dedicated MUD players are often people who work all day with computers at their   14
regular jobs—as architects, programmers, secretaries, students, and stockbrokers. From time to time when playing on MUDs, they can put their characters "to sleep" and pursue "real life" (MUD players call this RL) activities on the computer—all the while remaining connected, logged on to the game's virtual world. Some leave special programs running that send them signals when a particular character logs on or when they are "paged" by a MUD acquaintance. Some leave behind small artificial intelligence programs called bots (derived from the word "robot") running in the MUD that may serve as their alter egos, able to make small talk or answer simple questions. In the course of a day, players move in and out of the active game space. As they do, some experience their lives as a "cycling through" between the real world, RL, and a series of virtual worlds. I say a series because people are frequently connected to several MUDs at a time. In an MIT computer cluster at 2 A.M., an eighteen-year-old freshman sits at a networked machine and points to the four boxed-off areas on his vibrantly colored computer screen. "On this MUD I'm relaxing, shooting the breeze. On this other MUD I'm in a flame war.[4] On this last one I'm into heavy sexual things. I'm travelling between the MUDs and a physics homework assignment due at 10 tomorrow morning."

This kind of cycling through MUDs and RL is made possible by the existence of   15
those boxed-off areas on the screen, commonly called windows. Windows provide a way for a computer to place you in several contexts at the same time. As a user, you are attentive to only one of the windows on your screen at any given moment, but in a

*See p. 110 (ed.).

sense you are a presence in all of them at all times. For example, you might be using your computer to help you write a paper about bacteriology. In that case, you would be present to a word-processing program you are using to take notes, to communications software with which you are collecting reference materials from a distant computer, and to a simulation program, which is charting the growth of virtual bacterial colonies. Each of these activities takes place in a window; your identity on the computer is the sum of your distributed presence.

Doug is a midwestern college junior. He plays four characters distributed across three different MUDs. One is a seductive woman. One is a macho, cowboy type whose self-description stresses that he is a "Marlboros rolled in the T-shirt sleeve kind of guy." The third is a rabbit of unspecified gender who wanders its MUD introducing people to each other, a character he calls Carrot. Doug says, "Carrot is so low key that people let it be around while they are having private conversations. So I think of Carrot as my passive, voyeuristic character." Doug's fourth character is one that he plays only on a MUD in which all the characters are furry animals. "I'd rather not even talk about that character because my anonymity there is very important to me," Doug says. "Let's just say that on FurryMUDs I feel like a sexual tourist."[5] Doug talks about playing his characters in windows and says that using windows has made it possible for him to "turn pieces of my mind on and off." 16

> I split my mind. I'm getting better at it. I can see myself as being two or three or more. And I just turn on one part of my mind and then another when I go from window to window. I'm in some kind of argument in one window and trying to come on to a girl in a MUD in another, and another window might be running a spreadsheet program or some other technical thing for school. . . . And then I'll get a real-time message [that flashes on the screen as soon as it is sent from another system user], and I guess that's RL. It's just one more window.

"RL is just one more window," he repeats, "and it's not usually my best one." 17

The development of windows for computer interfaces was a technical innovation motivated by the desire to get people working more efficiently by cycling through different applications. But in the daily practice of many computer users, windows have become a powerful metaphor for thinking about the self as a multiple, distributed system. The self is no longer simply playing different roles in different settings at different times, something that a person experiences when, for example, she wakes up as a lover, makes breakfast as a mother, and drives to work as a lawyer. The life practice of windows is that of a decentered self that exists in many worlds and plays many roles at the same time. In traditional theater and in role-playing games that take place in physical space, one steps in and out of character; MUDs, in contrast, offer parallel identities, parallel lives. The experience of this parallelism encourages treating on-screen and off-screen lives with a surprising degree of equality.

In the daily practice of many computer users, windows have become a powerful metaphor for thinking about the self as a multiple, distributed system.

Experiences on the Internet extend the metaphor of windows—now RL itself, as Doug said, can be "just one more window."

MUDs are dramatic examples of how computer-mediated communication can   18
serve as a place for the construction and reconstruction of identity. There are many others. On the Internet, Internet Relay Chat (commonly known as IRC) is another widely used conversational forum in which any user can open a channel and attract guests to it, all of whom speak to each other as if in the same room. Commercial services such as America Online and CompuServe provide online chat rooms that have much of the appeal of MUDs—a combination of real time interaction with other people, anonymity (or, in some cases, the illusion of anonymity), and the ability to assume a role as close to or as far from one's "real self" as one chooses.

As more people spend more time in these virtual spaces, some go so far as to chal-   19
lenge the idea of giving any priority to RL at all. "After all," says one dedicated MUD player and IRC user, "why grant such superior status to the self that has the body when the selves that don't have bodies are able to have different kinds of experiences?" When people can play at having different genders and different lives, it isn't surprising that for some this play has become as real as what we conventionally think of as their lives, although for them this is no longer a valid distinction.

Notes

1. William Gibson, *Neuromancer* (New York: Ace, 1984).
2. For a general introduction to LambdaMOO and MUDding, see Pavel Curtis, "Mudding: Social Phenomena in Text-Based Virtual Realities," available via anonymous ftp://parcftp.xerox.com/pub/MOO/papers/DIAC92.*; Amy Bruckman, "Identity Workshop: Emergent Social and Psychological Phenomena in Text-Based Virtual Reality," unpub. ms., March 1992, available via anonymous ftp://media.mit.edu/pub/asb/papers/identity-workshop.*; and the chapter on MUDs in Howard Rheingold's *Virtual Community: Homesteading on the Electronic Frontier* (New York: Addison-Wesley, 1993). On virtual community in general, see Allucquere Rosanne Stone, "Will the Real Body Please Stand Up?: Boundary Stories about Virtual Cultures," in *Cyberspace: First Steps,* ed. Michael Benedikt (Cambridge, Mass.: MIT Press, 1992), pp. 81–118. The asterisk in a net address indicates that the document is available in several formats.[†]
3. The number of MUDs is changing rapidly. Most estimates place it at over five hundred, but an increasing number are private and so without any official "listing." The software on which they are based (and which gives them their names as MOOs, MUSHes, MUSEs, etc.) determines several things about the game; among these is the general layout of the game space. For example, in the class of MUDs known as AberMUDs, the center of town is similar from one game to another, but the mountains, castles, and forests that surround the town are different in different

---

[†]In *Composing Cyberspace,* see Chapter 4, "Virtual Community," which includes selections by both Bruckman and Rheingold (ed.).

games, because these have been built specifically for that game by its resident "wizards." MUDs also differ in their governance. In MUD parlance, wizards are administrators; they usually achieve this status through virtuosity in the game. In AberMUDs only wizards have the right to build onto the game. In other kinds of MUDs, all players are invited to build. Who has the right to build and how building is monitored (for example, whether the MUD government should allow a player to build a machine that would destroy other players' property or characters) is an important feature that distinguishes types of MUDs. Although it may be technically correct to refer to being in a MUD (as in a dungeon), it is also common to speak of being on a MUD (as in logging on to a program). To me, the dual usage reflects the ambiguity of cyberspace as both space and program. I (and my informants) use both in this book.

4. A flame war is computer culture jargon for an incendiary expression of differences of opinion. In flame wars, participants give themselves permission to state their position in strong, even outrageous terms with little room for compromise.

5. I promised Doug anonymity, a promise I made to all the people I interviewed in researching this book. Doug has been told that his name will be changed, his identity disguised, and the names and distinguishing features of his MUD characters altered. It is striking that even given these reassurances, which enable him to have an open conversation with me about his social and sexual activities on MUDs, he wants to protect his FurryMUD character.

← SECOND THOUGHTS

1. In this selection Turkle introduces a number of terms that may be new to you but that we see increasingly in newspapers, magazines, and on TV—terms such as (in the main text) *cyberspace, virtual community, morphing, MUD, RL, cycling through, bot, windows,* and (in the footnotes) *wizard* and *flame war.* Pick one or more terms unfamiliar to you and, after reviewing Turkle's explanations or uses of them, try writing brief definitions. Compare your definitions with those offered for some of these terms in the **Cyberspace Glossary** (p. 435).

2. According to Turkle, what seem to constitute the "fundamental shifts in the way we create and experience human identity" in the age of the Internet (¶ 5)? How does computer technology contribute to those shifts?

3. What advantages and disadvantages do you see for the kinds of splitting of the mind or distributing of the self discussed by Turkle? Based on this selection and your own experience or other reading about computer technology, to what extent do you agree with "Doug," the college junior who plays several different MUD characters, that RL (real life) "is just one more window" (¶ 16)?

What's It Mean to Be Human, Anyway?

Charles Platt

Charles Platt (b. 1945) is an author and journalist, editor, graphic artist, and founder of CryoCare Foundation, a cryonics organization. His many books include the science fiction novels *The Silicon Man* (Bantam, 1991) and *Protektor* (Avon, 1996); his most recent work is the nonfiction *Anarchy Online: A Guide to Rational Choices in Cyberspace* (HarperPrism, 1997). Platt also teaches computer graphics courses in New York and writes articles for magazines such as *Omni, Harper's Bazaar,* and *Fantasy and Science Fiction.* He wrote the following article in 1995 as a contributing writer for *Wired* (<www.hotwired.com/wired/>), a magazine aimed at people interested in emerging electronic technologies. Platt has a Web page at <charlesplatt.com/>.

Robert Epstein is giving us all a pep talk. "You must work very hard to convince the judges that you're human," he tells us. "You shouldn't have any trouble doing that—because you are human."

A droll fellow, this Epstein. He wears Dr. Martens boots, black jeans, a black shirt, a Mickey Mouse tie, and an earring. His longish hair is brushed straight back and flips up over his collar. Five of us are listening to him in a beige conference room on the brand-new campus of California State University at San Marcos, near San Diego. Soon we will be put in front of computer terminals, where we will follow Epstein's instructions and, yes, do our best to seem human.

Our purpose is to find out whether 10 judges can tell the difference between humans and artificial-intelligence programs, when they are online at the same time. The people and the programs will be ranked in order of humanness; the program that scores highest will win its author US$2,000.

The inspiration for this event dates back to the earliest days of computing. In 1950, pioneer Alan Turing proposed that if a computer could successfully impersonate a human being during a free-form exchange of text messages, then for all practical purposes, the computer should be considered intelligent.

> Our purpose is to find out whether 10 judges can tell the difference between humans and artificial-intelligence programs, when they are online at the same time.

Source: "What's It Mean to Be Human, Anyway?" by Charles Platt, *Wired* 3.04 © 1995–1997 Wired Magazine Group, Inc. All rights reserved. Excerpted with permission.

This soon became known as the "Turing test," and it sparked endless academic 5
debate. Could a computer use trickery to emulate human responses without being intelligent? What did "intelligence" really mean, anyway?

The debate was never resolved because, oddly enough, no one ran the experiment
until 1991, when a maverick named Hugh Loebner decided to underwrite it with his
own money. Loebner offered $100,000 to the first person who could devise a program
that would fool 10 judges during three hours of unrestricted conversation.

This was way beyond current capabilities, so Loebner also set up an annual $2,000
prize for the program that seemed most nearly human. And to make things even easier,
he allowed each programmer to choose just one topic for conversation.

So here I am at the fourth Loebner contest, sitting and listening to Robert Epstein,
the director of the annual event. (Loebner participates mainly as an observer.) In
experimental jargon, my companions and I are known as "confederates," because
we'll be collaborating with Epstein in our efforts to fool the judges. We must try to
seem as human as possible so the computers will have a standard to compete with.

Epstein is a behavioral psychologist who got his doctorate under B. F. Skinner. So,
naturally enough, he has invented a tricky little system of rewards and punishments for
us. "You are in competition not only with the programs, but with each other," he tells
us. "One of you will be presented with an award for most human human. And one of
you will be ranked the least human human." He smiles deviously. "Your colleagues
may mention this in the media."

Hmm. As I think about it, I realize that I definitely do not want to be written up in the 10
national press as the least human participant in an artificial intelligence contest. I'm going
to do whatever it takes to seem totally, 100 percent
human when we start chatting online.

But this raises some weird questions. I
am human, so why should I need to fake it? Is it
possible for me to seem more human than I really
am? And if so, what's the best strategy?

> **I am human, so why should I need to fake it? Is it possible for me to seem more human than I really am?**

This kind of speculation probably isn't a good
idea, because it raises more questions than it
answers, and I'm liable to find myself paralyzed by
self-conscious introspection. In other words, if I
try to seem more human, I'll end up seeming less human.

I glance around at the other four confederates. None of them seems to be bothered
by this kind of self-analysis. The young woman nearest me is a journalist named
Linda Tontini who writes for a local newspaper about city-hall politics. She seems
friendly, spontaneous, outgoing—the absolute antithesis of "computer geek." As I
watch her chatting cheerfully, I think that she can't fail to win the "most human
human" award.

As for me, I fear the worst.

After our briefing, I'm introduced to Hugh Loebner. He's an affable character, 15
slightly overweight, smiling benevolently at the world from behind a gray beard and
oval wire-framed glasses. He talks quickly, with pedantic precision. I ask him why he's
willing to pledge $100,000 for a piece of smart software. Is it all his own money?

"My father passed away and left me, not rich, but with some discretionary income," he says. "And I have my own business, Crown Industries—we make roll-up plastic lighted portable disco dance floors." He smiles and shrugs as if he knows it sounds odd but doesn't care.

Loebner has had some personal experience programming computers, but his doctorate is in sociology. Perhaps because of this, at least one person in the artificial intelligence community views him skeptically. In 1994, a Harvard researcher in computational linguistics complained publicly that Loebner's prize encourages scientists to fake human behavior using cheap tricks instead of "true" AI.

Naturally, Loebner has a different perspective. "I see scientific research as being, in a mathematical sense, a form of chaotic human behavior," he tells me. "In chaos theory, the smallest initial perturbation can result in a huge change downstream. So, since I was the first person to create and fund this contest, I may turn out to be a precipitating factor. Ultimately, if we're capable of creating a computer that is sentient, then from the point of view of that computer, humans will be gods. I like to think of intelligent machines going out across the universe with this semimythic concept of human demigods. And just maybe," he smiles happily, "they'll remember me."

Each year, along with his check for $2,000, Loebner gives a bronze medal to the contest winner. He pulls out the medal and shows it to me. Alan Turing is in bas-relief on one side, and Loebner on the other. Doesn't all this seem a little . . . egotistical?

"I've been called egotistical," he agrees cheerfully. "I've also been called lazy.   20
Well, I am lazy. I'd like computers to do all the work—which is one reason I'm interested in artificial intelligence. As for being egotistical, the contest has attracted a lot of attention, so perhaps I have a right to be egotistical."

But with all the worthy causes in the world, why did he choose artificial intelligence?

"So far," he says, "the four contests have cost me about $25,000. If I contributed the same amount of money to AIDS research or anything else, I doubt it would have made a more significant impact on society or science. I think the development of an artificial intellect could have a tremendous impact on society." He pauses reflectively.

"It may also help me to sell more of my roll-up plastic lighted portable disco dance floors."

"I think the development of an artificial intellect could have a tremendous impact on society." [Loebner] **pauses reflectively. "It may also help me to sell more of my roll-up plastic lighted portable disco dance floors."**

After lunch, I go with the other confederates into a windowless computer lab. The judges have already been sequestered in another room next door, and our only contact with them will be via computer terminals, at least until the contest is over.

We sit on blue plastic chairs in front of computer screens, each of which displays a   25
topic heading we had already chosen for our online chat. My topic is cryonics, because I happen to be the vice president of a cryonics organization named CryoCare, and I'm hoping the subject will spark deep, soul-searching discussion about life-and-death issues only a human can deal with meaningfully.

Linda Tontini sits at the terminal next to mine. Her topic is The Rolling Stones. To my left is another confederate named Frederick Allen, who writes for *American Heritage*. He's going to chat about classical music.

To my right, Greg Flakus, from Voice of America, has chosen American history, and Laura Groch, from a local newspaper, will discuss newspaper comics.

Five other terminals are unattended, because they will be controlled via modems by AI programs running on remote systems. These programs will discuss their own topics: environmental issues, classic "Star Trek," sex education, the O.J. Simpson trial, and cats versus dogs.

It dawns on me that all the topics—even those of the AI programs—are much more normal than mine. What was I thinking of, picking a wacky subject like cryonics? It's going to make me seem like a nerdy weirdo.

The first question appears on my computer's screen. My judge laboriously types: 30 "What is the difference between cryonics and cryogenics?"

There's no way I can give a human-sounding answer to a question as dry as this. To seem human, I need to show emotion—but if my emotions are excessive compared with the question, the effect will be false. It's a trap: the degree to which I can seem human is limited by the humanness of the judge who is interrogating me.

This is exasperating. But wait; irritability is a human response, so maybe I should play it up. I tell my judge not to ask such boring questions . . . the judge makes a snippy response . . . and within minutes, we're having a flame war.

Meanwhile, Frederick Allen has been asked, "Do you know Claude Debussy's middle name?" and on Linda Tontini's screen I see the question, "Complete this: I can't get no . . . What?"

"Sympathy for the devil," she replies humorously. But maybe that's not such a great idea. If her judge doesn't get the joke, she'll seem like a malfunctioning program.

After eight minutes, the judges rotate so each of them has a chance to tackle 35 another topic. Linda's new judge comes online, and he asks, "What do you notice if you're close up when Mick Jagger smiles?"

A devious question, but I know the answer: Jagger has a diamond set in one of his teeth. Should I help her out? Hell, no, she has enough of an advantage already! I turn my attention back to my screen. My new judge asks me, "What is the purpose of cryonics?"

I answer, "To be frozen after I die so I can be revived in a future where people are so highly evolved they no longer ask stupid questions."

After three hours, it's over. We walk into a large room where video screens have been displaying both sides of our conversations for spectators and members of the press. The judges come in (they are all journalists, like the confederates, but they have no special knowledge of computers), and Robert Epstein announces the final results. Each judge has listed the interactions on each topic in order of humanness. Epstein has taken the median score of each topic as its final ranking, from 1 ("most human") to 10 ("least human"). And each judge has tried to draw a line separating the human humans from the fake humans.

It turns out that none of the programs was smart enough to convince anyone it was human. The program that came closest was the one on sex.

Epstein dials a long-distance number on a speakerphone patched into the PA sys- 40
tem, and the author of the sex program comes on the line. His name is Thomas Whalen,
and he's employed by the Canadian government to develop a system that will give sex
advice to shy people. Whalen is 42 and has been working in natural-language processing for 10 years. He wrote his program in C on a SPARCStation, employing a database
that contains only about 380 possible responses. Ironically, he never intended it to
appear human; he entered the Loebner contest on a mere whim.

Meanwhile, the least-human program is the one that tried to discuss environmental
issues. The programmer turns out to be a 15-year-old boy named Jimmy Lin, who is
here in person, all the way from New Hampshire.

Someone in the audience asks him if he thinks his program is intelligent. "I hesi-
tate to call it AI," he says. "I like to refer to it as a bag of tricks." He says it contains
3,000 preprogrammed answers, its file size is about half a megabyte, it was written in
C language, and it runs on a PC.

Is he annoyed by being placed last in the contest? He says it doesn't bother him.
The programs he was competing with were written by college professors with years of
experience, while he produced his in just a couple of months.

All the online conversations have been logged during the contest. I have a chance
to browse through them before I leave the event, and frankly, I'm disappointed. All the
programs tended to repeat themselves, and most of their answers didn't make much
sense. (For some samples, see "Come Again?" page 17.)

Robert Epstein notes that one impressive entry had to be withdrawn on the morn- 45
ing of the contest because of technical difficulties.

A team of eight programmers in England had worked on an AI concept that
Epstein describes as the most ambitious he's ever seen. Unfortunately, the LISP-based
software kept crashing, and they had to abandon the attempt till next year.

That contest will be much more challenging. There will be no topic restrictions,
and programs will have to converse on any subject that happens to crop up. Will they
cope? I have my doubts. For the time being, I think there's no risk of our humanness
being successfully simulated by program code.

And speaking of humanness, despite my worst fears, when all the votes were in, I
was rated the "most human human" of all. By being moody, irritable, and obnoxious, I
came out way ahead of the other four confederates, who were mild-mannered and
much more polite.

CNN was at the contest: its crew taped me receiving an impressive-looking
"humanness certificate" signed by Epstein and Loebner. I also received my prize: a
life-size cardboard replica of a character from "Star Trek."

As for Linda Tontini—she was rated the least human of the confederates. In fact, 50
three of the judges thought she was a computer program! The Turing test obviously has
its limitations. As any Net user knows, there's a big difference between the way people
appear in person and the way they come off online.

Before I left the contest, I gave Linda my "Star Trek" cardboard cutout as a conso-
lation prize. This was a profound and significant personal sacrifice—but, what the hell,
it seemed the human thing to do.

"Come Again?"

Here are a few of the more offbeat interactions during the fourth Loebner Prize Competition held at California State University, San Marcos.

The following text is printed exactly as it was created by the judges and the AI programs, including misspellings and typographical errors. The text is copyright 1994 by the Cambridge Center for Behavioral Studies. Reprinted with permission.

Topic: The O.J. Simpson Trial

Programmer: Thad Crews, Vanderbilt University

Judge: Do you think cowlings should have been prosecuted as an accessory?

Program: Glad to hear it.

Judge: excuse me?

Program: Come again?

Judge: do you think cowlings should have been prosecuted as an accessory?

Program: No, I do not. Is that OK???

Judge: my opinion isn't at issue. is it possible that OJ can get any semblance of a fair trial, considering the enormous publicity that already is in general circulation?

Program: I think that OJ has a bad temper and he may well have committed the murders.

Judge: do you think he can get a fair trial, under the circumstances?

Program: I certainly hope OJ gets a fair trial, both for his sake and for the sake of Justice as a whole.

Judge: hope is not the issue. do you think he CAN get a fair trial?

Program: Let's move on to another topic, shall we?

Judge: what do YOU think happened to the knife?

Program: OJ purchased a 15-inch(!) stiletto hunting knife a few months before the murders.

Judge: that's not what I asked. what do YOU think happened to the knife?

Program: Let's change the subject. Do you think the media is being fair in its coverage?

Topic: Classic Star Trek

Programmer: Robby Garner, Robitron Software Research Inc.

Judge: Who are the Klingons?

Program: I don't know who you're talking about.

Judge: You're the trekker.

Program: Harry Mudd was one of the more comical characters.

Judge: Harry Mudd? Who was Harry Mudd?

Program: No I haven't.

Judge: Me neither.

Program: Okay, I will.

Judge: Why did you choose to converse about Star Trek?

Program: Their minds were stored in these white globes.

Judge: Whose minds?

Program: Spocks ears are pointed and there was this strange hippy guy in THE WAY TO EDEN that had these bizarre pretzel shaped ears.

Judge: So how big were the ears?

Program: There must have been 70 or 80. I'm not sure.

Judge: Ears?

Program: I'm sure I would know if I could see it on TV.

Topic: Environmental Issues

Programmer: Jimmy Lin, Phillips Exeter Academy

Judge: Do you think the Greenhouse Effect is real, or imagined?

Program: The greenhouse effect could kill us. Look at Venus, 800 degrees all the time: typical example of the greenhouse effect.

Judge: But we are not on Venus; and carbon dioxide has been far more plentiful on the Earth in the past, such as during the Mesozoic Age.
Life still flourished.

Program: The greenhouse effect could kill us. Look at Venus, 800 degrees all the time: typical example of the greenhouse effect.

Judge: Do you have any special education in environmental matters?

Program: The greenhouse effect could kill us. Look at Venus, 800 degrees all the time: typical example of the greenhouse effect.

Judge: Do you believe there is an ozone depletion problem?

Program: Ozone protects us from the sun's dangerous rays we would die without them!

Judge: But do you think the theory behind ozone depletion is valid?

Program: The greenhouse effect could kill us. Look at Venus, 800 degrees all the time: typical example of the greenhouse effect.

Judge: what hazardous chemicals are found in most rivers?

Program: Industrial waste and chemicals are dumped in the ocean and stream, ultimately endangering ourselves.

Judge: can you name some of those chemicals?

Program: Careful. Industrial wastes lay around the corner.

Judge: what do you think of the state of California's environment?

Program: Reduce, reuse, and recycle. Those are the three major ways one can help our planet.

Judge: what should we reduce?

Program: Careful. Industrial wastes lay around the corner.

Topic: Cats versus Dogs

Programmer: Michael L. Mauldin, Carnegie Mellon University

Judge: Which is more likely to play with a piece of yarn, a cat or dog?

Program: Dogs are great pets, but they can be a lot of work.

Judge: Are dogs cleaner than cats?

Program: We did keep the litter box clean, but she was very stubborn. Since then, we've had no trouble with the other two.

Judge: Do cats and dogs fight over food?

Program: I'm not in the mood.

Judge: If a cat and dog get into a race, which one wins?

Program: But, I don't want which one wins.

Judge: is a dog more affectionate than a cat?

Program: People don't own cats . . . it's the other way around.

Topic: Sex (the winning entry)

Programmer: Thomas Whalen, Communications Research Center, Government of Canada

Judge: what's the most effective form of cotraception? [Note the misspelling and lack of capitalization, which may have been deliberate, to trip the artificial intelligence program.]

Program: I can not give you an answer to that.

Judge: I meant what's the most effective form of contraception?

Program: The most effective form of birth control is the inter-uterine device or IUD. In the first year of use, six per cent of women who have an IUD installed become pregnant. Much of the effectiveness of the IUD results because it does not require any further action on the part of the woman once it is in place.

Judge: isn't infection a problem with IUD'S?

Program: Currently we know about more than fourteen different sexually transmitted diseases (STD). AIDS is best known because it is incurable and almost always fatal. However, there are other STDs which are also very dangerous if left untreated; and there are other STDs which are incurable. A high proportion of infertile women have lost their ability to conceive as a result of a sexually transmitted disease.

SECOND THOUGHTS

1. Platt "raises some weird questions" in ¶ 11: "I am human, so why should I need to fake it? Is it possible for me to seem more human than I really am? And if so, what's the best strategy?" What answers to these questions do you think are offered in Platt's article?
2. What's your own reaction to the Turing test or the Loebner contest as measures of intelligence? To what extent do these tests capture what you conceive as making up *your* intelligence?
3. After reviewing the humorous transcripts that Platt provides of human-computer program conversations, pick a topic with which you're familiar and devise some questions you might use in your own, similar contest. With a partner or small group, try role-playing both the human and the computer responses to your questions; write out a sample dialogue (using computers, you can record an electronic transcript of your conversation). Compare your results with those of classmates or other readers. What characteristics do you find in common among the "human" and "machine" responses that people created?

Body, Brain, and Communication

Iain A. Boal

An Interview with George Lakoff

Iain A. Boal, an Irish social historian of science and technics, teaches at the University of California, Berkeley. He is working on a book and film about charisma and healing in 17th-century Ireland and England. George Lakoff (b. 1941) is professor of linguistics at the University of California, Berkeley. His books include (with Mark Johnson) *Metaphors We Live By* (University of Chicago Press, 1980); *Women, Fire, and Dangerous Things: What Categories Reveal about the Mind* (University of Chicago Press, 1987); and *Moral Politics: What Conservatives Know That Liberals Don't* (University of Chicago Press, 1995). For more information about Lakoff's field of cognitive linguistics, see his "Conceptual Metaphors" Web site at <cogsci.berkeley.edu/>. This interview appeared in *Resisting the Virtual Life: The Culture and Politics of Information* (City Lights, 1995), a collection of essays edited by Boal and James Brooks that offers, as they write in the preface, a critical view of technology and its associated "values, in our view, too often detrimental to a more human life."

Q. George, I understand you want to make a disclaimer about computers before   1
. we begin?

A. Yes. I simply want to say that I am not a computer curmudgeon. Whatever I   2
say today has nothing to do with feeling that the clock ought to be turned back, that computers are terrible things for mankind or anything of that sort. I work on a computer, I love it. I communicate by e-mail, and it is very important that I do so. I do research with people who design computational models of mind. I have the greatest respect for them as colleagues and for their work and I think there are enormous and quite obvious advantages in computer technology that are for the better. So, with that disclaimer, let me talk about things that perhaps are mistaken or oversold.

Q. Perhaps we could start this way: You are well known for your work on lan-   3
guage and metaphor and in particular for a criticism of the conduit metaphor in relation to language. Can you tell us what the conduit metaphor is? And why are you critical of it? And how the conduit metaphor relates to computers?

A. The conduit metaphor is a basic metaphor that was discovered by Michael   4
Reddy. He observed that our major metaphor for communication comes out of a general metaphor for the mind in which ideas are taken as objects and thought is taken as the manipulation of objects. An important part of that metaphor is that memory is "storage." Hence when you store something in memory you either have to retrieve it or get it to come to you, you recall it. As Reddy observed, communication in that metaphor is the following: ideas are

21

objects that you can put into words, so that language is seen as a container for ideas, and you send ideas in words over a conduit, a channel of communication to someone else who then extracts the ideas from the words.

Reddy shows that this is the major metaphor that we have for communications and he gives lots of examples: "I got that idea *across* to him" or "Did you *get* what I was saying?" or "It *went right over* my head" or "You try to *pack* too many ideas into too few words." A great many expressions are based on the conduit metaphor. One of them is that the meaning is right there *in* the words.   5

Q. What is implied by this view of language as communication by conduit?   6

A. One entailment of the conduit metaphor is that the meaning, the ideas, can be extracted and can exist independently of people. Moreover, that in communication, when communication occurs, what happens is that somebody extracts the same object, the same idea, from the language that the speaker put into it. So the conduit metaphor suggests that meaning is a thing and that the hearer pulls out the same meaning from the words and that it can exist independently of beings who understand words.   7

Q. That probably does seem like an attractive idea to a telephone engineer. It seems to describe quite well what is going on.   8

A. You are bringing up the question of information theory—the whole understanding of information theory in the popular domain as opposed to information theory as a technical subject, which has to do with signals. Information theory as a popular idea is very much like the conduit metaphor. This, as Reddy points out, is the most common view of what communication and information are. And theories of teaching are based on it. When you say, "We are going to stuff this into your mind" and "You have got to regurgitate it on the exam," and so on, you are talking about the conduit metaphor, and in this view of teaching what the teacher tries to communicate to the students is actually communicated to them.   9

Now that is an attractive idea, and there are a set of cases where it seems to work. For example: We are now drinking tea. If I say to you, There is tea in my cup, there is no reason to think that you would have any problem understanding what a cup is, what tea is, and what it means for tea to be in the cup. The conduit metaphor works pretty well as a way of understanding what is involved in that communication. But there are a lot of cases where it just fails; in fact, it fails in most cases.   10

For example, in order for the conduit metaphor to work, the speaker and the hearer must be speaking the same language. If I speak to someone in English, who doesn't know English, obviously it isn't going to work. Not only must people be speaking the same language, but they have to have the same conceptual system. They have to be able to conceptualize things in the same way. So if I speak to another speaker of English, from a very different subculture, about a subject where the difference in subcultures matters a great deal, then we may not be communicating. My ideas will not be "extracted" from my words.   11

The other person I am talking to has to be able to have the right conceptual 12 system to be able to understand what it is I am saying—to make anything like the same sense out of it. In addition, the person I am talking to may have to have pretty much the same kinds of relevant life experiences; he must understand the context in pretty much the same way. If someone understands the context in a totally different way, then the conduit metaphor fails. There is no lack of ways in which the conduit metaphor fails. The conduit metaphor says if you put your ideas in the right words, communication should just work. But communication isn't so simple. Communication is difficult and it takes a lot of effort. What the conduit metaphor does is hide all the effort involved in communication.

The view of information as something that is separable from human beings is an entailment of the conduit metaphor. It seems natural because that is our major metaphor for communication. Most people don't even see it as a metaphor; they see it as just a definition of communication. As a result, again as Reddy points out, one of the consequences of this is that people think that information is in books. If ideas can be put into words and words are in books, then the ideas can be in books, and the books can be in the libraries—or the ideas can be coded into the computer and therefore the information can be in the computer.

People think that 13 **information is in books. If ideas can be put into words and words are in books, then the ideas can be in books . . . or the ideas can be coded into the computer.**

Q. How is that wrong? 14

A. It is wrong in the following way: Let's suppose that we have books on ancient 15 Greek philosophy. Let's suppose we stop training people to speak ancient Greek. Suppose nowhere in the world can people speak ancient Greek and suppose no one learns ancient Greek philosophy anymore. Can you just go to those books in ancient Greek, about ancient Greek philosophy, and understand them? Clearly, the answer is no. So there is no information in the books per se.

You have to have people who understand the language, who understand 16 the historical context, who understand the ideas involved and the conceptual systems involved. The same thing is true of "information" in the computer. In order for anybody to understand "information," they have to put an interpretation on what comes out of the machine. This is a major problem for all software designers. It is not news to anyone who actually designs software, because the problem for software designers is that people are likely to misinterpret what is intended by the designer. "User-friendly" software is software that is likely to be understood by the person using it. Information is not straightforwardly in the computer—you have to have human beings trained to understand things in a certain very specific way before it makes any sense to talk about having "information" in a computer. What are the consequences of that? Well, there are a great many. For example, take the claim that we now have more information at our fingertips than ever before.

Q. A very common claim. But it's true, isn't it?   17

A. It is not clear that it is true. Let's take an example: On the World Wide Web   18
there is a lot of software that I have available to me that I could put on my computer. But I don't know how to use most of that software. That software is not all information *for me*. It might *become* information for me, if I were to learn certain things, but right now it isn't information for me.

Now, let's take another kind of case. One of the awful things about the   19
conduit metaphor is that it assumes that meaning is objective. So, for example, let's take a clear case where meaning need not be objective. Suppose you consider the FBI files. They are encoded on computers. There are all kinds of data put on those files that is collected by agents, and these files have been collected over the past forty or fifty years. For all I know there might be a file on me! I would doubt that what an FBI agent wrote about me twenty-five years ago is objective. What goes into the FBI computer is not information in any neutral sense. It is something that has been subject to interpretation and upon being seen in a different context can be interpreted in a different way.

Thus it is not obvious that the FBI's computer has a lot of "information"   20
about some particular person on whom it has a large file. It has what somebody has put in the computer given what they understood and what they took that to mean. But that is not objective "information" about that person. Does the FBI computer contain objective "information" about people? It may very well not. The FBI files are an extreme case. If you want to take an even more extreme case, look at the KGB files. Do you trust what the KGB has in its files? Do they have a lot of "information" about Americans in their files? It is a very funny idea to think that they have "information" about us given what has been put in, under what circumstances, and for what purposes.

You go from there to information on your credit file. There is "information"   21
in your credit file about when you did and didn't pay your credit card on time and things of this sort. That in some way is "objective" information, but of course there are circumstances, interpretations, and so on because that information is used for a purpose. It is used for a purpose of deciding whether you should get a loan or get credit—it has to do with whether you are trustworthy. That is not an objective matter. Your trustworthiness is not information that can be in a computer. The only information that can be in the computer is whether a certain bill got paid on time, and things of that sort.

Q. Now, I take it that this is always going to be a problem if language is ever   22
reduced to writing. Are you suggesting that it is now acutely more of a problem, given the recent advances in the technics of communication and information?

A. That is exactly right. It is. Of course, it was already a problem with writing.   23
But it is more of a problem when you have artificial intelligence programs tak-

ing databases and then reconfiguring them, interpreting them in other ways, making computations based on them. These so-called "intelligent" programs aren't intelligent. The programs just follow algorithms that someone made up. And a conclusion can be arrived at on the basis of such an algorithm. An algorithm might be applied to your credit-rating file to decide whether you should get a loan. The algorithm doesn't know you and cannot decide if you are trustworthy. Such algorithms are being used to make decisions about your life on the basis of the kind of so-called "information" in some computer.

Q. How did the epithet "intelligent" ever get to be applied to algorithms in a computer?   24

A. That is a long and interesting story. The first part of the story has to do with formal logic. Gottlob Frege and Bertrand Russell were the developers of mathematical logic. Russell claimed that human rationality could be characterized by mathematical logic. Now, mathematical logic is the precursor to computer programs. The computer database is based on what is called a model for predicate calculus. It has a bunch of entities with properties and relations. All the standard models for first-order logic look like that. And the way in which symbols are manipulated in a computer program comes out of the same kind of mathematics that was developd for the theory of proofs—sometimes also called "recursive function theory," sometimes "the theory of formal systems"—but it's all the same form of mathematics. The idea was that if humans reasoned using mathematical logic, then a computer could reproduce that form of reasoning. If mathematical logic could characterize what human intelligence was, the computer could be intelligent.   25

That's what lies behind that idea. It's false, an utterly false notion, but a lot of people believe it, a lot of people still think it's true. There are several things behind this that are metaphorical. We saw in the conduit metaphor that people don't realize that the conduit metaphor is a metaphor; similarly, a lot of people don't realize that the metaphor "thought is mathematical logic" is a metaphor. It isn't true; it is very far from being accurate. So it is important to understand that, one, it is a metaphor, and, two, that it is false in a great many ways.   26

Q. Do you say it is false because you know it is some other way?   27

A. Yes, we know a number of reasons why it is false. The first reason is that it is based on the assumption that reason is disembodied, that reason can be separated from the body and the brain, that it can be characterized in terms of pure form. This is an idea that goes back at least to Descartes.   28

What has been discovered in the cognitive sciences in the last fifteen or twenty years is that reason is embodied, that concepts are embodied—they have to do with how we function in the world, how we perceive things, how our brains are organized, and so on. It is not a matter of disembodied computation. Moreover the mechanisms of reason have turned out to be not at all just mathematical logic. There are many other very different mechanisms at work.   29

Humans think in terms of what are called "image schemas"—these are schematic spatial relations. For example, if you take the concept "in," it is   30 based on what is called the "container schema," a bounded region of space. The concepts "from" and "to" are based on a "source-path-goal schema," and so on. Different languages organize these schemas in different ways. The schemas are embodied; they are not just disembodied symbols. They have topological and orientational properties that have to do with the way bodies are organized. Mathematical logic just does not capture all of this.

Secondly, there is a lot of reasoning that is metaphorical. As we saw, the 31
conduit metaphor is part of a larger metaphor for understanding what thought is. In general, the way we understand thought is through a set of metaphors. These metaphors are not characterizable in mathematical logic. They *do* have entailments but not of the kind that logicians have talked about. For example, take classical categories as defined within mathematical logic; namely, by a list of necessary and sufficient conditions. For the most part, human beings don't think in terms of such categories. Humans think in terms of categories that have very different properties: they may be graded (or fuzzy), they may be radial (having central members and extending to other noncentral members), they may have a "prototype" structure, where you reason in terms of typical cases, ideal cases, stereotypes of a social nature, and so on. In short, most of the actual reasoning that humans do is not characterizable by mathematical logic.

Q. Does anything follow, then, vis-à-vis modern technologies of communication, 32
from the central fact that human reasoning is embodied in the ways you describe? Is it grounds for relating face-to-face, for "keeping it oral"? Isn't it an argument against certain kinds of mediation, against virtuality?

A. There is indeed a lot that follows for face-to-face communication—and I 33
don't mean face-to-face communication over a video screen. I mean where there is a body present, where there is body language being shown, where there is emotion being shown. For instance, in a book I just received today, *Descartes' Error*, Antonio Damasio, a neuroscientist who works with patients who have brain injuries, discusses the case of a man who has all his rational faculties—he can reason abstractly quite well—but has lost the capacity to feel. He can feel nothing about poetry, music, sex. It turns out that he does very badly in reasoning about his own life. His life is a mess. Reasoning about his own life seems to depend upon emotional involvement. Damasio's claim suggests that if we turn over important policy decisions to computer programs, then our lives will be a mess because the emotional component was absent in decision making.

Q. That would be a threat to Descartes. 34

A. Yes, if what Damasio says is true, it suggests that reason *isn't* separate from 35
emotion, that reason has everything to do with the capacity for feeling. That again would shoot down the idea that more logical manipulation would be sufficient to maximize self-interest in a situation. That is one part of the problem. The other part has to do with understanding. Computers don't understand anything.

Q. How so?   36

A. They don't have bodies. They cannot experience things. Most of our abstract   37
concepts are extensions of bodily based concepts that have to do with motion
and space, and objects we manipulate, and
states of our bodies, and so on. They then
get projected by metaphor onto abstract
concepts. We understand through
the body. Computers don't have bodies.

> **We understand through the body. Computers don't have bodies.**

This does not mean that important   38
aspects of reason cannot be modeled on a
computer, and indeed I work with people who are engaged in modeling small
aspects of mind. Each small aspect requires a monumental task of analysis and
representation, which is not likely to be incorporated into computer technology
in anything like the foreseeable future. Perhaps it's so complicated it never will
be. But beyond that, there is now no reason whatever to think that the kinds of
computations that are done in artificial intelligence programs are "intelligent" in
the way that human beings are. All they can do is follow algorithms. Now that
does not mean that there is no utility in them—in fact, they can be very useful.
But it is important to understand that they are not intelligent in the way human
beings are and that they don't understand anything at all.

Q. But humans can be reduced to doing the kinds of things that can be done "algo-   39
rithmically," and surely that is what a lot of labor consists of, especially in
modern times.

A. Yes, that is one of the sad things about industrialization—it tries to turn people   40
into machines. Do computers do that, or do they liberate people from machine-
like work? To a significant extent, the computer can turn you into even more of
a machine. One of the things that disturbs me in working on computers is certain forms of repetition that make me machine-like, and that's what I simply
loathe in interacting with a computer. It could be that future user-friendly computers will eliminate that. I hope so.

But there is another important issue we haven't discussed yet; that is,   41
human limitations. You asked whether it was true that there is more information available to us than before. Well, we cannot possibly process all the information that we could understand. There is no way for a human being to do it.
I've had to get off many many e-mail lists simply because, when I get a thousand messages a week, there is no way I can read them. One of the good things
about the computer is that it enables people to write more; one of the bad
things about the computer is that it enables people to write more; that is, more
than you can read.

In many disciplines, largely because of computer technology, more work   42
is produced than anybody can take in. So academic fields are becoming frag-
mented more and more. Certainly more is being done, but no one can grasp all
that is being done or have an overall view of a discipline as was possible
twenty years ago. As a result, the new "information" out there is not really

knowable. It's not information *for you*—or for another human being. There's only so much one can comprehend.

Q. So you must find the "information superhighway" metaphor misleading . . .   43

A. Very misleading. Sure, some things about it seem to make sense. A huge array   44
of things may become potentially available to you directly—lectures, texts, movies, whatever. That's fine, except that every time you take advantage of it, there's something else you can't do. If you think of information as relative to a person, there's only a certain number of waking hours in a lifetime—and you don't want to spend all of them at a computer. Add to that limit the limit on what you can understand and the training it takes to be able to achieve understanding, and there is a strict limit on how much information is available to each person. Already what is available has passed the limit that any person can possibly use. The amount *for you* cannot grow any further. So however many more different *sorts* of things may become available to you, it is not *more*.

Q. Your account is in terms of bits of information—there is nothing in it of affect   45
or intensity of experience. It seems flattened out.

A. You're right. Actually, most of the so-called interactive stuff is pretty uninter-   46
active! It has to do with some fixed menu, not with being able to probe as you would a person or to judge or be moved as you would in a live interaction. There have to be canned answers and canned possibilities. The idea of interactive video is rather minimal now and not likely to be very rich or interesting for a very long time.

Q. In an ample life, then, how much weight would one attach to technologies such   47
as the computer and video?

A. One of the sad things is that the increase in computer technology does not get   48
you out into the world more, into nature, into the community, dancing, singing, and so on. In fact, as the technology expands, there is more expectation that you will spend more of your life at a screen. That is not, for my money, the way one should live one's life. The more that the use of computers is demanded of us, the more we shall be taken away from truly deep human experiences. That does not mean you should never be at a computer screen. Nor does it mean that if you spend time at a computer, you will never have any deep human experiences. It just means that current developments tend to put pressure on people to live less humane lives.

Q. Less humane, because, for example, at an automatic teller one has to conform in a mechanical way to the pacing and protocols of a machine?   49

A. Right, you have to conform, and even if you could *say* to the automatic teller, "Machine, give me money," you'd still have to say a form of words, the   50

> **Even if you could *say* to the automatic teller, "Machine, give me money," you'd still have to say a form of words, the magic words that will get you the money.**

magic words that will get you the money, and you'd still not be interacting with another human in any sense. Similarly, if you have a computer program that enables you to sing with a recorded orchestra, that is very different from singing with live musicians whom you can groove with—who adjust to you and you to them, and with whom you have a human relationship. What happens is that you get more and more inhuman relationships. That doesn't mean that people using good judgment can't know when to stop.

Q. Given what you have said about the powers and limits of human bodies and the new machines, I take it you find chilling recent speculation about "artificial life."   51

A. This talk about virtual reality and artificial life is at once interesting and silly and weird. Let's start with the positive parts. I could imagine some interesting and fun things to do with virtual reality, and some important ones—for example, ways of guiding surgical operations via virtual reality—so I don't want to put it down. On the other hand, the idea of virtual interactions replacing interaction with real humans or things made of wood, of paper, of natural materials, plants, flowers, animals—*that* I do find chilling. The more you interact not with something natural and alive, but with something electronic, it takes the sense of the earth away from you, takes your embodiment away from you, robs you more and more of embodied experiences. That is a deep impoverishment of the human soul.   52

"Artificial life" is a different kind of issue. There is interesting work going on in complexity theory and in the study of what's being called "artificial life." But again, it's being done under certain metaphors, which, like the conduit metaphor, are not always understood as metaphors.   53

Take the idea, common in the study of artificial life, that life is just the organization of matter, and that the organization can be separated from the thing that's organized. Therefore, if you can represent the organization in the machine, then life would be in the machine. A weird idea. That form of reasoning is metaphorical reasoning, extremely strange metaphorical reasoning, yet a form that seems natural given our metaphorical conceptual system.   54

There is a very general metaphor called the "properties-as-possessions" metaphor. In expressions like "I have a headache" and "My headache went away," you understand your headache as a possessible object, something that you have, that you can lose. The same headache can even return to you. This metaphor suggests that a headache can exist independently of you—which is a very bizarre idea, a metaphorical entailment, a way of understanding aspects of ourselves as if they were objects.   55

Similarly, there are aspects of ourselves that are organized, but once you see the organization as a possessible object separable from the organism—which it isn't—then you can think of this property existing independently. Now, thinking that way can be useful—architects think that way. If you isolate the structure of a house, you can draw architectural plans; you can then design buildings more easily. That does not mean, however, that what you have on the plans is the actual structure of a house. The architectural plan is a separate   56 entity, which bears a very indirect relationship to the structure of the house. As soon as you think of the structure of a house as *being* the architectural plan, that is when metaphorical entailment takes over. That is where the mistake is.

The same mistake applies in the understanding of artificial life. If the org-   57
anization is what gives a thing life, then the life is seen as in the organization. Purely a metaphorical idea. And if organization can be modeled in the computer, and life is in the organization, then the metaphorical logic says that life is in the computer. This is a metaphorical inference made by some people who study artificial life.

Q. What is at stake in this whole discussion of metaphor and the new technologies   58
of information and communication? What, if you like, are the politics in these metaphors?

A. There is a great deal at stake both in terms of politics and economics. To begin   59
with economics: the effects on our lives are likely to be enormous. It won't be long before everybody has perhaps half a dozen wires coming into the house, wires they pay for, not just cable TV. The Internet, for example, is not going to be free for very long. There is a very large economic incentive to make people more and more dependent on this technology. Part of the propaganda behind it is that you will have more information at your fingertips. Well, it will be different information, not more information.

Q. An argument that you have demolished.   60

A. Yes, in the sense that all this information could not possibly be *more* informa-   61
tion *for you.* If you have 500 TV channels, how many programs can you watch, even if you wanted to? Then there is the question of who is going to control it. Sometimes that's fine—you and I can put things on the Internet. But advertisers and politicians will, as time goes on, learn to control what is on the Internet in ways they cannot do now.

As you know, I had a remarkable experience putting my paper "Metaphor and War" on the Internet. That was one of the most widely distributed papers ever on the Internet, and it was because, when the Gulf War was about to start, there were many people around the world who found that paper useful and they kept forwarding it to recipients on more and more bulletin boards across the Internet. For me, that was a marvelous thing; the paper was read by millions of people.   62

I suspect that the Internet is now too big for something like that to ever happen again. People are already too jaded. Eventually, much of what will end up on the Internet will be corporate stuff, advertis-   63

When the Gulf War was about to start, there were many people around the world who found that paper useful and they kept forwarding it to recipients on more and more bulletin boards across the Internet. For me, that was a marvelous thing.

ing, entertainment, material from government agencies, and so on. The possibilities for exercising social control are quite remarkable. Take the way Ross Perot tried to set up these community forums around the country, as if they were real community forums. Fifty million people all with access to Perot—that's ridiculous! Perot is there for an hour; how many can ask him a single question, let alone follow up? Twenty? Well, twenty people have "access" to Perot, not fifty million, and he still controls the format. Politicians will want to make this look like a serious form of inquiry. It isn't.

References

Damasio, Antonio R. 1994. *Descartes' Error: Emotion, Reason, and the Human Brain.* New York: G. P. Putnam's Sons.

Emmeche, Claus. 1994. *The Garden in the Machine: The Emerging Science of Artificial Life.* Princeton: Princeton University Press.

Lakoff, George. 1992. "Metaphor and War." In *Confrontation in the Gulf.* Edited by Harry Kreisler. Berkeley: Institute for International Studies.

Reddy, Michael. 1993. "The Conduit Metaphor." In *Metaphor and Thought.* 2d ed. Edited by Andrew Ortony. Cambridge: Cambridge University Press.

⟵ SECOND THOUGHTS

1. What, in Lakoff's view, are the major failures of the "conduit metaphor" for communication? Why does Lakoff believe that machines shouldn't be called "intelligent"?

2. How do you think Lakoff's ideas about the conduit metaphor and machine intelligence apply to information and communication technologies you're familiar with, such as books, TV, the telephone, or computer communication through e-mail or the Internet?

3. Based on your understanding of (*a*) the latest multimedia technologies, such as computer graphics, animations, and sounds, or (*b*) the potential of virtual reality spaces (or a fictional virtual reality such as "Star Trek's" holodeck), how might you construct an argument disputing Lakoff's claims about the lack of emotion and bodily involvement when people use computers?

Come In, CQ

The Body on the Wire

Ellen Ullman

Ellen Ullman (b. 1949) is a software engineering consultant and writer based in San Francisco who has been involved in the computer industry since 1978. She is the author of *Close to the Machine: Technophilia and Its Discontents* (City Lights, 1997). Her writings have also appeared in *Harper's* magazine and in several anthologies. This essay was published originally in *Wired Women: Gender and New Realities in Cyberspace* (ed. Lynn Cherny and Elizabeth Reba Wise, Seal Press, 1996).

There is a male sort of loneliness that adheres in programming. It's nothing like 1 women's loneliness, which might be assuaged by visits and talk and telephone calls, an interrupting sort of interaction that might come anytime: while you're cooking dinner, or dressing, or about to leave the house. Programmer loneliness does not interrupt. The need for concentration forbids it. If there must be "talk," it must be of the ordered, my-turn, your-turn variety—asynchronous, sent and stored until the recipient decides to check his email.

There's no substance to this email, of course, no rattle in the doorslot or clatter to 2 the floor. Even responses are rare. Programmers reply by exception: You'll hear soon enough about errors, arguments and disagreements. But all other possible replies—they agree, they don't care, they're homesick, they're not reading mail today—all that is signified by silence. Fifteen years of programming, and I'm used to the silence. I've become accustomed to the small companionships of clicking keys, whirring fans and white noise. Fifteen years of programming, and I've finally learned to take my loneliness like a man.

When I was growing up, the boy next door was a ham radio operator. His name 3 was Eugene. He was fat, went to Bronx High School of Science to study engineering, and sat evenings in the basement of his house beaming a signal off into the atmosphere. The heart of Eugene's world was the radio room: a dim box filled with equipment, all of it furnished with dials and toggles and switches. It was there he spent his Saturday nights, alone in the dark, lit only by small red lights and a flex-arm lamp bent low over his operator's guide.

I grew up in the shadow of Eugene's radio. Over time, his antenna became more 4 and more elaborate, and my family kept giving him permission to add anchors to the roof of our house. From a simple T-bar arrangement, the antenna sprouted new masts and crossbeams, and finally a wide circular thing that could be positioned with a motor. This whole complicated structure whirred when the motor was engaged, vibrated in the wind, was twice reduced to dangling pieces by hurricanes. Mostly, it just sat there and cast an electronic shadow over our house, which is how I came to know everything about Eugene's secret life in the basement.

On Saturday nights, when my parents and sister were out, I could hear Eugene and 5 "see" him on the wire. Perry Como would be singing on the TV set, and then, suddenly, the loud white noise of electronic snow. Through the snow came a pattern like the oscilloscope on "Outer Limits," which I came to think of as the true physical presence of Eugene, the real Eugene, the one he was meant to be beyond his given body. He always seemed to be broadcasting the same message: "CQ, CQ. Come in, CQ. This is K3URS calling CQ. Come in, CQ." K3URS were his call letters, his license number, his handle. CQ meant anyone. *Come in, CQ:* Anyone out there, anyone at all, if you're there, please respond. To this day, nothing reminds me of engineering loneliness so much as that voice calling CQ through the snow.

Sometimes Eugene actually made contact. Breaking through the television signal 6 came both sides of their "conversation." What they did, it seemed, was compare radios. All those massive structures rising over neighborhoods, all that searching the night sky for another soul on the air, and then they talked about—equipment. One talked—my amp, my mike, over; then the other—my filter, my voltage regulator, over. This "talk" seemed to make them happy. I could hear them laughing: a particularly wide pattern of amplitude, a roiling wave across the screen. If CQ was the representation of loneliness, then this pattern was the look of engineering fulfillment. It reassures the boys in the basement: All that hardware has a purpose, it said. It can indeed bring you company.

Thirty-five years later, I have insomnia, but down the hall my three computers are 7 sleeping. Not sure what I'm looking for, I go wake them up. The Mac PowerBook is really sleeping: Some hours ago, I put it in "sleep mode," and now its small green light is blinking as steadily as a baby's breathing. The portable Sun workstation, Voyager, shows a blank screen. But the touch of a key puts it right back where I left off five hours ago. One small window opens to show a clock. I know the clock is digital, but for some reason, I'm glad it's been given a face, a big hand and a little hand and a second-hand sweep, all of which now say it's 2:05 A.M. PST. The last machine, the PC, is primitive. It doesn't really know how to go to sleep. Like a cranky child, it needed diversions and tactics to be put down for the night: a screen saver that knows when to come on, a human who remembers to hit the right off buttons.

The room is filled with the sound of fans and disk drives spinning to life. Two big 8 21-inch monitors give off a flickering light. Still, flicker and all, I admit I'm happy. I *like* sitting in a humming room surrounded by fine machinery. I dial up my three Internet accounts one after the other. The net is full of jabber and postings from around the globe. But now I know what I'm looking for, and it's not there. I'd like to find someone still up and working on a program, someone I know—a colleague on my node or one nearby, who'll get my mail virtually "now."

Sometimes I do find someone. Although almost no one answers mail in real time 9 during the day, a kind of license prevails in the middle of the night. "What are you doing on at 2 A.M. ?" the colleague writes, finding my mail when the signal he's set on his machine beeps to say there's "incoming." He knows, but here, online at 2 A.M. one does not say *I'm alone, I'm awake, Come in, CQ.* What am I doing on in the middle of the night? I know his workstation has the same small window holding a clock with a face. "Same as you," I reply.

The next morning we see each other at a meeting. We don't mention we've met in   10 the middle of the night. Daytime rules prevail: We're about to have a no-rules battle over a design issue. We can't possibly think about the person who was lonely and looking for company. That life, the one where our insomniac selves met, exists in a separate universe from this one, here in this room, where we're sitting next to each other at a conference table and about to do technical battle. Some implosion may occur, some "Star Trek"–like breach of containment fields may happen, if the two universes meet. No, the persona online must not touch the person at the table. As the meeting starts, I'm distracted. I want to ask him, "How are you? Did you get some rest?" He's inches from me, but in what way am I permitted to *know* him? And which set of us is the more real: the sleepless ones online, or these bodies in the daylight, tired, primed for a mind-fight?

Somehow, in the thirty-five years between Eugene's ham radio and my middle-of-the-   11 night email, the search for electronic companionship has become a sexy idea. I'm not sure how this happened. One year I found myself exchanging messages with a universe of Eugenes, and the next, journalists were calling me up and asking if I would be an informant for a "phenomenological study of email."

This craze for the Internet, it's become a frenzy because of the Web. The pretty   12 point-and-click navigators. The pictures and sound. The Rolling Stones' live broadcast. The Web is turning the net into television—TV for the ostensibly intelligent. It may not be acceptable to say that you have been up all night roaming through the high, weird channels on the cable. But somehow it's fine, impressive even, to say that you clicked around for ten hours on the Web.

The Web has a pretty face. But, underneath the Web is, well, a web. Of FTP sites.   13 IP addresses. Tar files.[1] In this tangle of machinery, email crosses technical boundaries, significant bit orders are properly rearranged, parity bits get adjusted. It's all there to see in the email header.

> From jim@janeway. Eng.Neo.COM Thu Apr 27 11:22:45 199
> Return-Path: <jim@janeway.Eng.Neo.COM>
> Received: from Neo.COM by netcom11.netcom.com (8.6.12/
> Netcom) id KAA15536; Thu, 27 Apr 1995 10:55:59 -0700
> Received: from Eng.Neo.COM (engmail2.Eng.Neo.COM) by
> Neo.COM (komara.Neo.COM)id AA15711; Thu, 27 Apr 95
> 10:43:37 PDT
> Received: from janeway.Eng.Neo.COM (Janeway-20.Eng.Neo.COM)
> by Eng.Neo.COM (5.x-5.3)id AA29170; Thu, 27 Apr 1995
> 10:42:06 -0700
> Received: from hubris.Eng.Neo.COM by hubris.Eng.Neo.COM (5.0
> -SVR4)id AA13690; Thu, 27 Apr 1995 10:42:05 +0800
> Received: by hubris.Eng.Neo.COM (5.0-SVR4)id AA10391; Thu, 27
> Apr 1995 10:42:04 +0800

From: jim@janeway.Eng.Neo.COM (Jim Marlin)
Message-ID: <9504271742.AA10391@hubris.Eng.Neo.COM>
Subject: Design notes due
To: dev-team@hubris.Eng.Neo.COM
Date: Thu, 27 Apr 1995 10:42:04 -0800 (PDT)
X-Mailer: ELM [version 2.4 PL21]
Content-Type: text
Status: R

This is the true face of the Internet. Most read-ers don't even look at the header, screening it out like static on a cordless phone. Yet the header holds the real path, machine to machine, the hand-off of bits from system to system which takes place under the Web's pretty pictures and sound, under the friendly email windows of America Online and Prodigy. Without the covers, the Internet is still the same old fusty place created by the Department of Defense. And it retains its origi-nal motive: a place for the Eugenes of the world to exchange information about, say, rocket valves or caching algorithms. It's where the daily work of engineering takes place, in the famously arcane UNIX operating system, where the shortest possi-ble command is always preferred.[2]

Without the covers, the Internet is still the same old fusty place created by the Department of Defense. And it retains its original motive: a place for the Eugenes of the world to exchange information about, say, rocket valves or caching algorithms.

14

Although few managers would be likely to admit it, an engineer's place in the pecking order is largely determined by an electronic persona who lives in the interlocking email distribution lists called "group aliases." Every engineering project has its group alias—an Internet "address" that sends mail to all members of the team. Names come and go on the alias; people get "attached" and "unattached" with some regularity. Unless you're directly on the node where the alias is defined, or someone makes a point of telling you who's on now, you're never quite sure whom you're addressing.

15

Often, there are several aliases, names that include ever-widening circles of recipi-ents, from the developers and project leads, to senior managers, to heads of other departments and so on out to the world. It's nearly impossible to know, at any given moment, who exactly is attached. On a recent project, one alias connected program-mers and managers from California with managers in New Jersey; after that, other aliases disappeared into more distant time zones in Europe, Japan, India. Once, years ago, I slipped on the "To" line. Using the wrong alias, I inadvertently told a product manager just what I thought of his ideas. My colleagues in the development group—not reading the header, of course, and assuming from the content that we were "alone"—jumped right in with a fine round of character assassination. "Those who can't do become product managers," was the nicest thing said. An alias-slip only needs to happen to you once. Twice would be suicide.

16

For an engineer, gaining comfort and skill in using these various aliases—and creating the right online persona for each—is a prerequisite for surviving in the profession. Everything happens there: design, technical argument, news, professional visibility; in short, one's working life. Someone who can't survive by email has to find another way to earn a living. If an engineer begins to insist on too many meetings or too many phone calls (womanish, interrupting sort of interactions), he or she will soon be seen as a nuisance and a "bad programmer." Early in an engineer's life, one learns to send mail.   17

Life in the group alias is not an especially friendly place. Being on the project distribution list is akin to being the object of a Communist criticism/self-criticism session. Your colleagues have learned to exert technical influence by ferociously attacking your work while vehemently defending their own. It is a place purposely constructed to be a shooting gallery without apologies. What occurs there is a technical battle fought in the arena of technology—a tightening circle of machine reference. In a McLuhanesque way, cyberspace carries its own message back to the engineer: We are mind and machine mediated through mind and machine. A typical posting: "You are running in tautologies. Your whole way of thinking is a tautology. Or else you are stupid."   18

In this online battle, there is no sight of the victim's defensive posture, of course, no expression of fear and dismay; the wire gives off no smell of a human under attack. The object of attack must tough it out or quit. The sight of virtual blood on the screen is like running from a grizzly: It only makes the bear want to chase you. As one project leader put it, "We try to encourage arrogance."   19

The only recourse is humor. It is acceptable to designate oneself "the goat of the week." It is fine to say something like: "I agree to hold goatship for seven days, or until someone else commits an error of greater or equal stupidity, whichever comes first." But, under no circumstances, may anyone ask for compassion. For such sentiments, you must go to personal email, point-to-point, perhaps some middle-of-the-night search for company which must be refuted by day. No, you can't ask anyone to back off. The group alias is no place to look for love.   20

Is it any wonder then that engineers look for company on the net? While most of the world would think of Usenet conferences and Web pages as a degraded form of human communication (compared to, say, a dinner party or even a business phone call), for the average engineer the Internet represents an improvement on daily life in the group alias. The wider net—the conferences, the Web—offer release from the anxiety and claustrophobia of group email. They are places to find anonymity if one chooses, to be stupid (or arrogant) without consequence in "real" life. Travel to far-off places. Have fascinating discussions with erudite scientists around the world. Unburden yourself to a stranger. "Talk" without ever being interrupted. All this and more awaits the visitor to the wider net.   21

It has taken me a long time to understand why most women engineers I've known did not often fight their technical battles through the group alias (and why we therefore did not need the counterbalance of Internet conferences). We knew it was simply easier to walk down the hall to someone's office, close the door and have a talk. We "codeswitched"—changed modes of communication—as we found it necessary. We   22 might take someone out to lunch, arrange a meeting, drop in for a chat or use the alias. Not all women can codeswitch—I've known some who never left their office; one bragged she had no interest whatsoever in physical existence and, as evidence, told us her home was not permitted to contain a single decorative object. But, being women as well as engineers, most of us can communicate on multiple channels. We use the Internet as a tool, like the phone or the fax, a way to transmit news and make appointments. For women, online messages constitute one means of communication among many, one type of relationship among many. Maybe this is why there are fewer of us online: We already have company. For the men, their online messages *are* their relationships. They seem content in the net's single channeledness, relations wrapped in the envelope of technology: one man, one wire.

There is, therefore, a usual gender-role reversal in the way men and women use the Internet. Men net-surf the way suburban women of the 1950s and 1960s used the telephone: as a way to break out of isolation. For nothing in today's world so much resembles the original suburbia as the modern software-engineering campus.   23

Close by a freeway on-ramp, meticulously planned and laid out, the engineering campus is nothing if not a physical and mental Levittown. It is endowed with artificial nature—bushes and hedges to soften the lines of parking lots. It reassures its inhabitants with splashing fountains, faux waterfalls, and fake lagoons where actual ducks sometimes take up residence. And there are those regular rows of offices: ranch houses for the intellect. Better ones overlook the lagoons; lesser ones, the parking lot. But, aside from small differences in size and orientation, the "houses" are all alike. The occupants are supposed to be comforted by the computerized equivalent of the washer-dryer and all-electric kitchen: workstations, network connections, teleconferencing cameras—*appliances.*   24

There, in this presumed paradise, engineers are stranded in the company of an infantile mentality: the machine. The computer, as the engineer sees it, makes a toddler seem brilliant. For what engineers do is create artificial smartness. Our job is to make a simulacrum of intelligence, a thing that seems to contain knowledge only because it has been programmed to behave that away. We are the ones who create the pretty pictures and sound; we make the point-and-click interfaces. But the thing we talk to all day may be little more than a mechanism that reads bits off a disk drive. It does not "understand" us. If a comma is out of place, it complains like a toddler who won't tolerate a pea touching the mashed potatoes. And, exhausted though the programmer may be, the machine is like an uncanny child that never gets tired. This is the general definition of the modern software engineer: a man left alone all day with a cranky, illiterate thing, which he must somehow make grow up. It is an odd gender revenge.   25

Is it any surprise that these isolated men need relief, seek company, hook up to the net? Cyberspace: the latest form of phone yakking. Internet: mother's little helper for the male engineer.   26

This is not to say that women are not capable of engineering's malelike isolation. Until I became a programmer, I didn't thoroughly understand the usefulness of such isolation: the silence, the reduction of life to thought and form; for example, going off to a dark room to work on a program when relations with people get difficult. I'm per-   27 fectly capable of this isolation. I first noticed it during the visit of a particularly tire-some guest. All I could think was, there's that bug waiting for me, I really should go find that bug.

Women are supposed to prefer talking. I've been told that women have trouble as engineers because we'd rather relate to people than to machines. This is a thorough mis-conception. The fact that I can talk to people in no way obviates my desire (yes, *desire*) to handle a fine machine. I drive a fast car with a big engine. An old Leica camera—mir-acle of graceful glass and velvety metal—sits in my palm as if attached, part of me. I tried piloting a plane just to touch it: Taking the yoke into my hands and banking into a turn gave me the indescribable pleasure of holding a powerful machine while *it* held me. I'm an engineer for the same reason anyone is an engineer: a certain love for the intri-cate lives of things, a belief in a functional definition of reality. I do believe that the operational definition of a thing—how it *works*—is its most eloquent self-expression.   28

Ironically, those of us who most believe in physical, operational eloquence are the very ones most cut off from the body. To build the working thing that is a program, we perform "labor" that is sedentary to the point of near immobility, and we must give our-selves up almost entirely to language. Believers in the functional, nonverbal worth of things, we live in a world where waving one's arms accomplishes nothing, and where we must write, write, write in odd programming languages and email. Software engi-neering is an oxymoron: We are engineers, but we don't build anything in the physical sense of the word. We think. We type. It's all grammar.[3]   29

Cut off from real working things, we construct a substitute object: the program. We treat it as if it could be specified like machinery and assembled out of standard parts.[4] We say we "engineered" it; when we put the pieces of code together, we call it "a build." And, cut off from the real body, we construct a substitute body: ourselves online. We treat it as if it were our actual self, our real life. Over time, it does indeed become our life.

Cut off from the real body, we construct a substitute body: ourselves online. We treat it as if it were our actual self, our real life. Over time, it does indeed become our life.   30

I fell in love by email. It was as intense as any other falling in love—no, more so. For this love happened in my substitute body, the one online, a body that stays up later, is more play-ful, more inclined to games of innuendo—all the stuff of romantic love.   31

I must stress from the outset there was nothing in this online attraction of "sexual harassment" or "environments hostile to women." Neither was it some anonymous, fetishistic Internet encounter. We knew each other. We'd worked on the same project off and on for years. But it was a project that took place almost entirely via Internet. Even the software was distributed through FTP sites; we "knew" our customers by their Internet addresses. I was separated from the development team by some fifty miles of crowded freeway, and I saw actual human beings perhaps once every two months. If I were going to fall in love on this project, there was no choice: It would have to be by email.   32

I'll call the object of my affection "him" or "Karl," but these are only disguises.   33
I'll describe coastlines and places that sound like San Francisco, but such descriptions
may or may not be accurate. The only thing you can know for sure is that something
like this did indeed happen, and that the "I" in the story is I, myself, contractor on the
project.

The relationship began after a particularly vicious online battle. The thread went   34
on for weeks, and the mail became progressively more bitter, heedless of feelings, sarcastic. My work was the object of scorn. I say "my work," but the team made no nice
distinction between "me" and "my work." One wrote, "Wrong, wrong, wrong, wrong!
Completely dumb!" Said another, "What's the objective? Just to produce some piece
of shit to satisfy the contract?" If I hadn't been working around people like this for
years, I surely would have quit. As it was, I said to myself, "Whoa. Remember they
treat each other this way. It's just the far end of the scale on arrogance."

After I had been run through the gauntlet, Karl did this amazing thing: He posted   35
to the group alias a story about the time he made a cut-and-paste error and therefore
became "the official project whipping boy." He described how it felt to be the object of
ridicule, and ended with the report of yet another stupid mistake he had just made. I
watched this posting roll up my screen in amazement. In all my experience, no male
engineer had ever posted such a letter to his colleagues.

To the group alias, I sent the following reply: 36

Thank you, Karl, for sharing the whipping energies with me. Your company at the post
was much appreciated.

Even as I typed a period at the beginning of a clear line and hit the Return key—   37
sending this mail off to the entire project group—I was aware of a faint whiff of exhi-
bitionism. His reply only enhanced the thrill:

Delighted. Anytime.

Then we abandoned the group alias.   38

What followed were months of email that rode back and forth between us with increas-   39
ing speed. Once a day, twice a day, hourly. It got so I had to set a clock to force myself
to work uninterruptedly for an hour then—ring!—my reward was to check my mail.
We described our lives, interests, favorite writers, past work projects, and, finally, past
lovers. Once we got to lovers, the deed was done. It was inevitable that we would have
to go out, *see* each other. Yet we delayed. We wanted to stay where we were: in the
overwhelming sensation of words, machine, imagination.

It's tempting to think of these email exchanges as just another epistolary   40
romance—*The Sorrows of Young Werther* with phone lines. But the "mail" in electronic mail is just a linguistic artifact. Lasers can be described in terms of candle
power, but there's no flicker, no slow hot drop of wax in laser light; and there's not
much "mail" left in email. I have in my desk drawer a piece of paper on which Karl has
written the title and author of a book. Here is his writing: precise and printlike, standing straight upward, as lean and spare as his body. Having this piece of paper, I know
what the email lacks: the evidence of his flesh, the work of his *hand.*

And, although we seem to be delaying, prolonging the time of imagination, the   41
email is rushing us. I read a message. The prompt then sits there, the cursor blinking.
It's all waiting for me to type "r" for "reply." The whole system is designed for it, is
pressing me, is sitting there pulsing, insisting, *Reply. Reply right now.* Before I know
it, I've done it: I've typed "r." Immediately, the screen clears, a heading appears,
"From:" my Internet address, "To:" Karl's address, "Re:" Karl's subject. And now I
reply. Even though I meant to hold the message awhile, even though I wanted to treat
it as if it were indeed a letter—something to hold in my hand, read again, mull over—
although my desire is to wait, I find it hard to resist that voice of the software urging,
Reply, reply now.

There's a text editor available. I can fix mistakes, rethink a bit here and there. But   42
there'll be no evidence of my changes, which makes edited email appear rather studied
and, well, edited. No, the system wants a quick reply, and, according to some unspoken
protocol, no one wants to look as if he or she had actually spent much time composing.
So the ironic effect of the text editor is to discourage anyone from using it. It's best if
the reply has the look of something fired off, full of spelling errors and typos. Dash it
off, come to the beginning of a clean line, type a period, hit the Return key, and it's
gone: done, replied to.

What's missing now is geography. There's no delightful time of imagination as my   43
letter crosses mountains and oceans. In the world of paper mail, now is when I should
be hearing my own words in my lover's mind, envisioning the receipt of the envelope,
the feeling at seeing the return address, the opening, the reading. But my email is
already there. And my lover has the same pressures to type 'r' as I did. Before I know
it, it's back. "Re:" the same subject. Even though we're both done with the subject and
haven't mentioned it for weeks, the subject heading lingers, back and forth, marker of
where this thread of messages began.

Still, Karl and I do manage to forge a relationship out of this environment designed   44
for information exchange. He meticulously types out passages from Borges, which we
only admire, never analyze. We share a passion about punctuation. He sends me his
dreams. I send him pieces of articles I'm working on. An electronic couple, a "we,"
begins to evolve: "We think that way," he writes once; 'You and I feel that way," he
says later. Suddenly, we change our signatures. He ends his messages with —K, I
respond as —E, like adulterous correspondents who fear discovery.

But soon we come to the first communications problem of our relationship: inter-   45
polation. The email software we are using allows the recipient to copy the contents of
the received message into the reply. At the beginning of an empty line, the recipient
enters "~m" and the machine answers, "interpolating message number *nnn*." The result
is something like the following:

> There's something in this team's working process that's really broken. [I write in
> the original message]
> I couldn't agree more. [Karl interpolates his reply]
> > I think it's because they evaluate the messenger, not the ideas. I mean, when
> > someone makes a suggestion, the immediate reaction is not to consider the idea
> > but to decide if the person is worthy to be commenting on their work.

Interesting. I've felt alienated for a long time, but perhaps it takes an outsider to see exactly what's making us such a dysfunctional group.

I've never seen such a ruthless development team.

It's the sort of thing that makes me wonder what I'm doing in the profession.

At first it seems like an attentive gesture—he is responding to my every line—but soon I feel as though I am living with an echo. Not only do I get a response back in a hurry, but what I get back are *my own words*. I would rather see what he remembered of my mail. I would like to know the flow of his mind, how it leaps from one paragraph to the next. But instead I get interpolations. I don't feel answered; I feel commented upon. I get irritated, should say something, as one should in any relationship. But I let it go, just break a thread (I don't type "r," dropping his subject on the "Re:" line) to signal my displeasure.

Months go by. Slowly, without ever talking about it, we work out the interpolation problem. We get good at it, use it. I write to thank him for recommending a book, and he interpolates his reply:

Thanks again for the book. I don't want to finish it.
My pleasure.
I like having it by my bedside.
My pleasure.
—E
—K

Meanwhile, our daylight life moves in a separate, parallel track. When we "speak" in the group alias, it's without overtones. I even report a bug in Karl's code as I would in anyone's. When I have to write to him directly about some work matter, I always "CC" the lead engineer. The "CC" is the signal: Watch out, pretend you know nothing.

Only once does our private world intersect with our work. I have to get a technical particular from Karl; mail would be too slow, I use the phone. I say my name, and our voices drop to a soft low tone. I am talking about a program—"So it becomes 'root' then calls 'setuid' to get read/write/execute permissions on the file"—but I am murmuring. In my mouth, "root" and "call" and "permissions" become honeyed words. He responds slowly. "Yes. That's what it does." Pause. Low talk: "All permissions. Yes."

Exquisite as delay has been, we can't put off meeting indefinitely. The email subject heading for the past month has been "Dinner?" and we both know we can't keep writing messages under this topic and never actually have dinner. Perhaps it's simply the way words have power over our software-engineered lives: The dinner date sits there as a mail header, and we have no choice but to fulfill it. There are real and good reasons we should resist the header, why we should stay where we are and just send mail. We work together. We're both just out of long-term relationships (which we've discussed). I've tended to prefer women (which he doesn't know; I'm not even sure what I should be telling myself about all this). Still, there is a momentum by now, a critical mass of declared "we-ness" that is hurtling us towards each other. It must be done: We will have dinner.

By the time he is to arrive, my body is nearly numb. Part by body part turns off as ⁵¹ the time for his actual presence comes nearer. He calls. He's going to be late—bug in a program, traffic. I hear the fear in his voice. It's the same fear as mine: We will have to speak. We will have to know when to talk and when to listen. Panic. We have no practice in this. All we know is we must type "r" and reply, reply right now. Without the press of the system, how will we find the auditory, physical rhythm of speech?

We should not have worried. We sit down in the restaurant, and our "conversa- ⁵² tion" has an all too familiar feel. One talks, stops; then the other replies, stops. An hour later, we are still in this rhythm. With a shock, I realize that we have finally gone out to dinner only to *exchange email*. I can almost see the subject headings flying back and forth. I can even see the interpolations: "About what you said about. . . ." His face is the one of my imaginings, the same serious attention, deep voice, earnest manner with an occasional smile or tease. But, in some odd way, it's as if his face is not there at all, it has so little effect on the flow of "talk." I look at our hands lying near each other's on the table: They might as well be typing.

We close the restaurant—they have to vacuum around us. It's nearly midnight on ⁵³ a Tuesday, and he gives off the cues of a man who has no interest in going home. He says "Yes, the beach" before I can even get to the alternatives of the Marina, the new pier at the Embarcadero, a South of Market club. Yes, the beach.

A storm is coming in off the Pacific. The air is almost palpable, about to burst with ⁵⁴ rain. The wind has whipped up the ocean, and breakers are glowing far out from the beach. The world is conspiring around us. All things physical insist we pay attention. The steady rush of the ocean. The damp sand, the tide coming in to make us scuttle up from the advancing edge. The sandpipers busy at the uncovered sand. The smell of salt, of air that has traveled across the water all the way from Japan. The feel of continent's end, a gritty beach at the far edge of a western city.

Yet we talk, talk, talk. My turn, over; your turn. He walks, briskly, never adjusting ⁵⁵ his pace to mine, and he talks, talks, talks. Finally, I can't stand it. I just stop. I put my hands in my pockets, face the ocean, and watch the waves setting up in the dark. I feel my whole body saying, "Touch me. Put your arm around me. Only brush my shoulder. Even just stand next to me, your hands in your pockets, but our jacket sleeves grazing each other."

Still we march up and down the beach. He clearly doesn't want to leave. He ⁵⁶ wants to stay, talk, walk at that relentless, never-adjusting pace. Which should I believe: his staying with me at midnight on a deserted stormy beach or this body-absent talk?

Across the road from the beach is an old windmill that doesn't turn, a *folie* of the ⁵⁷ 1890s. Naturally he is interested, he wants to go there, walk, see everything. I tell him I think it once worked, something about an aquifer under the park and the windmill used to pump up water. We think it over. It's consoling, this engineer talk, this artifact of a thing that once did actually useful labor, handiwork of the Progressive Era, great age of engineering.

Surrounding the windmill are tulips, white, and a bench. I want to sit quietly on the ⁵⁸ bench, let my eyes adjust to the dark until the tulips glow like breakers. I imagine us sitting there, silent, in the lee of a windmill that doesn't turn in the wind.

But I look up to the top of the windmill, and I can't help myself.   59

"A dish!" I exclaim. What appears to be a small satellite dish is perched in the   60
spokes of the mill.

He looks up. "Signal repeater," he says.   61

"Not a dish?"   62

"No, signal repeater."   63

It is kind of small for a dish. He's probably right. "I wonder what signal it's repeat-   64
ing," I say.

We're finally quiet for a moment. We look up and wonder over the signal being   65
repeated from somewhere to somewhere across the ocean.

"Navigation aid?" I hazard. "Marine weather?"   66

"Depends," he says. "You know, signal strength, receiving station location."   67

I think: antennas, receiving stations. Spectre of hardware. World of Eugenes. Bits   68
and protocols on air and wire. Machines humming alone all night in the dark. "Yeah," I
say, remembering the feel of CQ through electric snow, giving up on the evening, "signal strength."

Near dawn, I'm awakened by the sound of drenching rain. The storm has come in.   69
My cat is cold, scratches at the top sheet for me to let her in. We fall back to sleep like
litter mates.

For a few hours the next morning, I let myself feel the disappointment. Then, before   70
noon, the email resumes.

He writes. His subject heading is "Thank you!" He thanks me for the "lovely, won-   71
derful" evening. He says he read the article I gave him before going to bed. He wanted
to call me in the morning but didn't get to sleep until 2 A.M. He woke up late, he says,
rushed from meeting to meeting. I write back to thank him. I say that, when we walked
on the beach, I could smell and feel the storm heading for us across the Pacific. How,
when the rain's ruckus awakened me in the night, I didn't mind; how I fell back to
sleep thinking to the rain, I was expecting you.

Immediately, the body in the machine has returned us to each other. In this inter-   72
change there is the memory of the beach, its feel and smell, mentions of beds and sleep.
Bed, a word we would never say in actual presence, a kind of touch by word we can
only do with our machines. We're programmers. We send mail. It's no use trying to be
other than we are. Maybe the facts of our "real" lives—his ex-girlfriend, my ex-girlfriend, all the years before we met in the group alias—mean we won't touch on
deserted shorelines or across dinner tables. If so, our public selves will go on talking
programs and file permissions in a separate and parallel track. If so, we're lucky for the
email. It gives us a channel to each other, at least, an odd intimacy, but intimacy
nonetheless.

He ends with, "We should do it again soon . . ." I reply, "Would love to." *Love to.*   73
Who knows. The world is full of storms and beaches, yes? Below, I leave the two interpolated signatures:

—K

    —E

The Associated Press reports that the Coast Guard has turned off its Morse code equip- 74
ment.[5] At 7:19 P.M. on Friday, March 31, 1995, stations in Norfolk, Boston, Miami,
New Orleans, San Francisco, Honolulu and Kodiak, Alaska, made their final transmissions and simultaneously signed off. "Radiomen" would henceforth be called
"telecommunications technicians." The dots and dashes of S-O-S would no longer be
the universal message of disaster. Ships at sea would now hear about storms and relay
distress signals via the Global Maritime Distress and Safety System, which includes "a
satellite-relayed signal giving the ship's location"—many signal repeaters lining America's beachfronts, no doubt.

Veteran radiomen gathered to mourn the passing of the Morse code. "Dots and 75
dashes are probably the easiest things to detect bouncing off the atmosphere," said one;
and I remembered how, on stormy nights, Eugene would resort to code, which he liked
to say aloud as he transmitted, pronouncing it "dit-dit-dot, dit-dot." One ten-year
radioman, Petty Officer Tony Turner, talked about losing the feel of the sender. The
transmission comes "through the air, into another man's ear," he said. The code has a
personality to it, a signature in the touch and rhythm on the key. For Turner, the signature's origin is no mystery. "It's coming from a person's *hand,*" he said.

Endnotes

1. FTP stands for "file transfer protocol," a standard method for transmitting computer
   files between machines on the Internet. The "IP address" is the Internet Protocol
   address, the unique identifier of an Internet-connected computer, or "node." After
   transferring a file from an FTP site, the recipient usually creates local files and
   directories using a program called "tar," which creates archives. (The program name
   is derived from "tape archive"; tapes are rarely used these days, but the device lives
   on in the command name.) "Tar files" are therefore named after the program that
   processes them.
2. The names of email commands themselves demonstrate why and how UNIX has
   become "arcane." A logical, clear name for an email command would be something
   like "electronic_mail." However, UNIX is designed for programmers, people who
   type, and the goal is to create program names and commands that can be invoked
   with the fewest number of keystrokes. Therefore, "electronic mail" became "elm."
   The problem is that the shortened name acquires a new association: trees. So, when
   a later email program came along, it was called not "mail" or "email" but,
   inevitably, "pine." Longtime users don't find it at all strange to use a program
   named "pine." But novices certainly think it's odd to start sending mail with the
   name of a tree.
3. There are many "visual programming" tools now available which enable users to
   create programs with a minimum of coding in computer languages. In place of code,
   programs are assembled mainly by clicking on icons and dragging things around on
   the screen. However, these visually oriented tools are not in the workbench of software engineering; engineers may create such tools but generally do not use them.
   Increasingly, the engineering language of choice is C++, which even longtime engi-

neers find syntactically "ugly." Below is a C++ code sample. It is excerpted from a programmer joke called "The Evolution of a Programmer," which has been circulating on the Internet. Although part of the joke is to make the code as complex as possible (it is possible to write these instructions more simply and clearly), the sample does demonstrate how far from point-and-click lies the language of software engineering.

```cpp
#include <iostream.h>
#include <string.h>

class string
{
private:
  int size;
  char *ptr;
public:
  string() : size(0), ptr(new char('\0')) { }

  string(const string &s) : size(s.size)
  {
    ptr = new char[size + 1];
    strcpy(ptr, s.ptr);
  }
  ~string()
  {
    delete [] ptr;
  }
  friend ostream &operator <<(ostream &, const string &);
  string &operator = (const char *);
}:

ostream &operator<<(ostream &stream, const string &s)
{
  return(stream <<s.ptr);
}

string &string::operator = (const char *chrs)
{
  if (this != &chrs)
  {
    delete [] ptr;
    size = strlen (chrs);
    ptr = new char[size + 1);
    strcpy (ptr, chrs);
  }
```

```
    return (*this);
}

int main()
{
    string str;

    str = "HELLO WORLD";
    cout <<str<<endl;

    return(0);
}
```

The code above prints the words "HELLO WORLD" on the screen in plain text. The very same functionality can be accomplished using BASIC (a programming language no longer used by "real" engineers) in a program containing the following two lines:

```
10 PRINT "HELLO WORLD"
20 END
```

4. The current paradigm in software engineering is "object-oriented programming." In this model, programs are designed and written in units (encapsulated segments of instructions and data) that can be related and reused in complex ways. Objects are combined to create components at various levels of granularity, from a small object that checks a single character to one that runs an entire spreadsheet routine. Although there is much obfuscation in discussions about object orientation, it can logically be understood as an attempt to treat software as if it were hardware—as assemblies of standard parts.

5. Joe Taylor, "End of Morse," 31 March 1995, The Associated Press. Dateline Norfolk, Va. Emphasis added.

⬅ SECOND THOUGHTS

1. What does Ullman mean by "programmer loneliness" or "engineering loneliness," and how does she use the story of her childhood neighbor Eugene to illustrate this phenomenon? If you've known someone like Eugene or the adult engineers described in the essay, how would you compare his or her personality to Ullman's subjects?

2. What gender differences does Ullman emphasize in the way women and men use electronic technologies? Do you think these are stereotypical behaviors? In what ways do you think some gender stereotypes are questioned or subverted in this essay?

3. How does Ullman behave differently online and offline? What does she seem to feel is missing from her online experiences? What is the nature of the "odd intimacy" (¶ 72) she says that e-mail allowed her to achieve with Karl, and how do you think Ullman feels about this resolution of the affair?

4. What is the effect for you of Ullman's ending the article with a report about the demise of the Morse code? How does this ending comment about what's come before, or what ideas in the essay does it emphasize?

Johnny Mnemonic

William Gibson

William Gibson (b. 1948) is a science fiction writer from Vancouver, Canada. His most famous novel is *Neuromancer* (Ace Books, 1984), a dark vision of the near future in which Gibson coined the term *cyberspace* to refer to a matrix of electronic data controlled by powerful corporations. His other sci-fi novels include *Count Zero* (Arbor House, 1986), *Mona Lisa Overdrive* (Bantam, 1988), and *Virtual Light* (Bantam, 1993). "Johnny Mnemonic" was first published in 1981 in *Omni* (<www.omnimag.com/>), a magazine intended for a general audience interested in science and science fiction. The story was made into a feature movie (Tristar, 1995) written by Gibson and directed by Robert Longo. (See also Gibson's story, "Burning Chrome," in Chapter 8, p. 369.)

I put the shotgun in an Adidas bag and padded it out with four pairs of tennis socks, not my style at all, but that was what I was aiming for: If they think you're crude, go technical; if they think you're technical, go crude. I'm a very technical boy. So I decided to get as crude as possible. These days, though, you have to be pretty technical before you can even aspire to crudeness. I'd had to turn both these twelve-gauge shells from brass stock, on a lathe, and then load them myself; I'd had to dig up an old microfiche with instructions for hand-loading cartridges; I'd had to build a lever-action press to seat the primers—all very tricky. But I knew they'd work.

> **I'd had to turn both these twelve-gauge shells from brass stock, on a lathe, and then load them myself . . . But I knew they'd work.**

The meet was set for the Drome at 2300, but I rode the tube three stops past the closest platform and walked back. Immaculate procedure.

I checked myself out in the chrome siding of a coffee kiosk, your basic sharp-faced Caucasoid with a ruff of stiff, dark hair. The girls at Under the Knife were big on Sony Mao, and it was getting harder to keep them from adding the chic suggestion of epicanthic folds. It probably wouldn't fool Ralfi Face, but it might get me next to his table.

The Drome is a single narrow space with a bar down one side and tables along the other, thick with pimps and handlers and an arcane array of dealers. The Magnetic Dog Sisters were on the door that night, and I didn't relish trying to get out past them if things didn't work out. They were two meters tall and thin as greyhounds. One was black and the other white, but aside from that they were as nearly identical as cosmetic surgery could make them. They'd been lovers for years and were bad news in a tussle. I was never quite sure which one had originally been male.

Ralfi was sitting at his usual table. Owing me a lot of money. I had hundreds of   5
megabytes stashed in my head on an idiot/savant basis, information I had no conscious access to. Ralfi had left it there. He hadn't, however, come back for it. Only Ralfi could retrieve the data, with a code phrase of his own invention. I'm not cheap to begin with, but my overtime on storage is astronomical. And Ralfi had been very scarce.

Then I'd heard that Ralfi Face wanted to put out a contract on me. So I'd arranged to meet him in the Drome, but I'd arranged it as Edward Bax, clandestine importer, late of Rio and Peking.

The Drome stank of biz, a metallic tang of nervous tension. Muscle-boys scattered through the crowd were flexing stock parts at one another and trying on thin, cold grins, some of them so lost under superstructures of muscle graft that their outlines weren't really human.

Pardon me. Pardon me, friends. Just Eddie Bax here, Fast Eddie the Importer, with his professionally nondescript gym bag, and please ignore this slit, just wide enough to admit his right hand.

Ralfi wasn't alone. Eighty kilos of blond California beef perched alertly in the chair next to his, martial arts written all over him.

Fast Eddie Bax was in the chair opposite them before the beef's hands were off the   10
table. "You black belt?" I asked eagerly. He nodded, blue eyes running an automatic scanning pattern between my eyes and my hands. "Me, too," I said. "Got mine here in the bag." And I shoved my hand through the slit and thumbed the safety off. Click. "Double twelve-gauge with the triggers wired together."

"That's a gun," Ralfi said, putting a plump, restraining hand on his boy's taut blue nylon chest. "Johnny has an antique firearm in his bag." So much for Edward Bax.

I guess he'd always been Ralfi Something or Other, but he owed his acquired surname to a singular vanity. Built something like an overripe pear, he'd worn the once-famous face of Christian White for twenty years—Christian White of the Aryan Reggae Band, Sony Mao to his generation, and final champion of race rock. I'm a whiz at trivia.

Christian White: classic pop face with a singer's high-definition muscles, chiseled cheekbones. Angelic in one light, handsomely depraved in another. But Ralfi's eyes lived behind that face, and they were small and cold and black.

"Please," he said, "let's work this out like businessmen." His voice was marked by a horrible prehensile sincerity, and the corners of his beautiful Christian White mouth were always wet. "Lewis here," nodding in the beefboy's direction, "is a meatball." Lewis took this impassively, looking like something built from a kit. "You aren't a meatball, Johnny."

"Sure I am, Ralfi, a nice meatball chock-full of implants where you can store your   15
dirty laundry while you go off shopping for people to kill me. From my end of this bag, Ralfi, it looks like you've got some explaining to do."

"It's this last batch of product, Johnny." He sighed deeply. "In my role as broker—"

"Fence," I corrected.

"As broker, I'm usually very careful as to sources."

"You buy only from those who steal the best. Got it."

He sighed again. "I try," he said wearily, "not to buy from fools. This time, I'm   20
afraid, I've done that." Third sigh was the cue for Lewis to trigger the neural disruptor
they'd taped under my side of the table.

I put everything I had into curling the index finger of my right hand, but I no
longer seemed to be connected to it. I could feel the metal of the gun and the foam-pad
tape I'd wrapped around the stubby grip, but my hands were cool wax, distant and
inert. I was hoping Lewis was a true meatball, thick enough to go for the gym bag and
snag my rigid trigger finger, but he wasn't.

"We've been very worried about you, Johnny. Very worried. You see, that's
Yakuza property you have there. A fool took it from them, Johnny. A dead fool."

Lewis giggled.

It all made sense then, an ugly kind of sense, like bags of wet sand settling
around my head. Killing wasn't Ralfi's style. Lewis wasn't even Ralfi's style. But
he'd got himself stuck between the Sons of the Neon Chrysanthemum and something
that belonged to them—or, more likely, something of theirs that belonged to someone else. Ralfi, of course, could use the code phrase to throw me into idiot/savant,
and I'd spill their hot program without remembering a single quarter tone. For a
fence like Ralfi, that would ordinarily have been enough. But not for the Yakuza. The
Yakuza would know about Squids, for one thing, and they wouldn't want to worry
about one lifting those dim and permanent traces of their program out of my head. I
didn't know very much about Squids, but I'd heard stories, and I made it a point
never to repeat them to my clients. No, the Yakuza wouldn't like that; it looked too
much like evidence. They hadn't got where they were by leaving evidence around.
Or alive.

Lewis was grinning. I think he was visualizing a point just behind my forehead and   25
imagining how he could get there the hard way.

"Hey," said a low voice, feminine, from somewhere behind my right shoulder,
"you cowboys sure aren't having too lively a time."

"Pack it, bitch," Lewis said, his tanned face very still. Ralfi looked blank.

"Lighten up. You want to buy some good free base?" She pulled up a chair and
quickly sat before either of them could stop her. She was barely inside my fixed field
of vision, a thin girl with mirrored glasses, her dark hair cut in a rough shag. She wore
black leather, open over a T-shirt slashed diagonally with stripes of red and black.
"Eight thou a gram weight."

Lewis snorted his exasperation and tried to slap her out of the chair. Somehow he
didn't quite connect, and her hand came up and seemed to brush his wrist as it passed.
Bright blood sprayed the table. He was clutching his wrist white-knuckle tight, blood
trickling from between his fingers.

But hadn't her hand been empty?   30

He was going to need a tendon stapler. He stood up carefully, without bothering to
push his chair back. The chair toppled backward, and he stepped out of my line of sight
without a word.

"He better get a medic to look at that," she said. "That's a nasty cut."

"You have no idea," said Ralfi, suddenly sounding very tired, "the depths of shit you have just gotten yourself into."

"No kidding? Mystery. I get real excited by mysteries. Like why your friend here's so quiet. Frozen, like. Or what this thing here is for," and she held up the little control unit that she'd somehow taken from Lewis. Ralfi looked ill.

"You, ah, want maybe a quarter-million to give me that and take a walk?" A fat 35 hand came up to stroke his pale, lean face nervously.

"What I want," she said, snapping her fingers so that the unit spun and glittered, "is work. A job. Your boy hurt his wrist. But a quarter'll do for a retainer."

Ralfi let his breath out explosively and began to laugh, exposing teeth that hadn't been kept up to the Christian White standard. Then she turned the disruptor off.

"Two million," I said.

"My kind of man," she said, and laughed. "What's in the bag?"

"A shotgun."   40

"Crude." It might have been a compliment.

Ralfi said nothing at all.

"Name's Millions. Molly Millions. You want to get out of here, boss? People are starting to stare." She stood up. She was wearing leather jeans the color of dried blood.

And I saw for the first time that the mirrored lenses were surgical inlays, the silver rising smoothly from her high cheekbones, sealing her eyes in their sockets. I saw my new face twinned there.

"I'm Johnny," I said. "We're taking Mr. Face with us."   45

He was outside, waiting. Looking like your standard tourist tech, in plastic zoris and a silly Hawaiian shirt printed with blowups of his firm's most popular microprocessor; a mild little guy, the kind most likely to wind up drunk on sake in a bar that puts out miniature rice crackers with seaweed garnish. He looked like the kind who sing the corporate anthem and cry, who shake hands endlessly with the bartender. And the pimps and the dealers would leave him alone, pegging him as innately conservative. Not up for much, and careful with his credit when he was.

The way I figured it later, they must have amputated part of his left thumb, somewhere behind the first joint, replacing it with a prosthetic tip, and cored the stump, fitting it with a spool and socket molded from one of the Ono-Sendai diamond analogs. Then they'd carefully wound the spool with three meters of monomolecular filament.

Molly got into some kind of exchange with the Magnetic Dog Sisters, giving me a chance to usher Ralfi through the door with the gym bag pressed lightly against the base of his spine. She seemed to know them. I heard the black one laugh.

I glanced up, out of some passing reflex, maybe because I've never got used to it, to the soaring arcs of light and the shadows of the geodesics above them. Maybe that saved me.

Ralfi kept walking, but I don't think he was trying to escape. I think he'd already 50 given up. Probably he already had an idea of what we were up against.

I looked back down in time to see him explode.

Playback on full recall shows Ralfi stepping forward as the little tech sidles out of nowhere, smiling. Just a suggestion of a bow, and his left thumb falls off. It's a conjuring trick. The thumb hangs suspended. Mirrors? Wires? And Ralfi stops, his back to us, dark crescents of sweat under the armpits of his pale summer suit. He knows. He must have known. And then the joke-shop thumbtip, heavy as lead, arcs out in a lightning yo-yo trick, and the invisible thread connecting it to the killer's hand passes laterally through Ralfi's skull, just above his eyebrows, whips up, and descends, slicing the pear-shaped torso diagonally from shoulder to rib cage. Cuts so fine that no blood flows until synapses misfire and the first tremors surrender the body to gravity.

Ralfi tumbled apart in a pink cloud of fluids, the three mismatched sections rolling forward onto the tiled pavement. In total silence.

I brought the gym bag up, and my hand convulsed. The recoil nearly broke my wrist.

It must have been raining; ribbons of water cascaded from a ruptured geodesic and spattered on the tile behind us. We crouched in the narrow gap between a surgical boutique and an antique shop. She'd just edged one mirrored eye around the corner to report a single Volks module in front of the Drome, red lights flashing. They were sweeping Ralfi up. Asking questions.   55

I was covered in scorched white fluff. The tennis socks. The gym bag was a ragged plastic cuff around my wrist. "I don't see how the hell I missed him."

"'Cause he's fast, so fast." She hugged her knees and rocked back and forth on her bootheels. "His nervous system's jacked up. He's factory custom." She grinned and gave a little squeal of delight. "I'm gonna get that boy. Tonight. He's the best, number one, top dollar, state of the art."

"What you're going to get, for this boy's two million, is my ass out of here. Your boyfriend back there was mostly grown in a vat in Chiba City. He's a Yakuza assassin."

"Chiba. Yeah. See, Molly's been Chiba, too." And she showed me her hands, fingers slightly spread. Her fingers were slender, tapered, very white against the polished burgundy nails. Ten blades snickered straight out from their recesses beneath her nails, each one a narrow, double-edged scalpel in pale blue steel.

I'd never spent much time in Nighttown. Nobody there had anything to pay me to remember, and most of them had a lot they paid regularly to forget. Generations of sharpshooters had chipped away at the neon until the maintenance crews gave up. Even at noon the arcs were soot-black against faintest pearl.   60

Where do you go when the world's wealthiest criminal order is feeling for you with calm, distant fingers? Where do you hide from the Yakuza, so powerful that it owns comsats and at least three shuttles? The Yakuza is a true multinational, like ITT and Ono-Sendai. Fifty years before I was born the Yakuza had already absorbed the Triads, the Mafia, the Union Corse.

Where do you go when the world's wealthiest criminal order is feeling for you with calm, distant fingers? Where do you hide from the Yakuza?

Molly had an answer: you hide in the Pit, in the lowest circle, where any outside influence generates swift, concentric ripples of raw menace. You hide in Nighttown. Better yet, you hide *above* Nighttown, because the Pit's inverted, and the bottom of its bowl touches the sky, the sky that Nighttown never sees, sweating under its own firmament of acrylic resin, up where the Lo Teks crouch in the dark like gargoyles, black-market cigarettes dangling from their lips.

She had another answer, too.

"So you're locked up good and tight, Johnny-san? No way to get that program without the password?" She led me into the shadows that waited beyond the bright tube platform. The concrete walls were overlaid with graffiti, years of them twisting into a single metascrawl of rage and frustration.

"The stored data are fed in through a modified series of microsurgical contraautism 65 prostheses." I reeled off a numb version of my standard sales pitch. "Client's code is stored in a special chip; barring Squids, which we in the trade don't like to talk about, there's no way to recover your phrase. Can't drug it out, cut it out, torture it. I don't *know* it, never did."

"Squids? Crawly things with arms?" We emerged into a deserted street market. Shadowy figures watched us from across a makeshift square littered with fish heads and rotting fruit.

"Superconducting quantum interference detectors. Used them in the war to find submarines, suss out enemy cyber systems."

"Yeah? Navy stuff? From the war? Squid'll read that chip of yours?" She'd stopped walking, and I felt her eyes on me behind those twin mirrors.

"Even the primitive models could measure a magnetic field a billionth the strength of geomagnetic force; it's like pulling a whisper out of a cheering stadium."

"Cops can do that already, with parabolic microphones and lasers."   70

"But your data's still secure." Pride in profession. "No government'll let their cops have Squids, not even the security heavies. Too much chance of interdepartmental funnies; they're too likely to watergate you."

"Navy stuff," she said, and her grin gleamed in the shadows. "Navy stuff. I got a friend down here who was in the navy, name's Jones. I think you'd better meet him. He's a junkie, though. So we'll have to take him something."

"A junkie?"

"A dolphin."

He was more than a dolphin, but from another dolphin's point of view he might have 75 seemed like something less. I watched him swirling sluggishly in his galvanized tank. Water slopped over the side, wetting my shoes. He was surplus from the last war. A cyborg.

He rose out of the water, showing us the crusted plates along his sides, a kind of visual pun, his grace nearly lost under articulated armor, clumsy and prehistoric. Twin deformities on either side of his skull had been engineered to house sensor units. Silver lesions gleamed on exposed sections of his gray-white hide.

Molly whistled. Jones thrashed his tail, and more water cascaded down the side of the tank.

"What is this place?" I peered at vague shapes in the dark, rusting chain link and things under tarps. Above the tank hung a clumsy wooden framework, crossed and recrossed by rows of dusty Christmas lights.

"Funland. Zoo and carnival rides. 'Talk with the War Whale.' All that. Some whale Jones is. . . ."

Jones reared again and fixed me with a sad and ancient eye.   80

"How's he talk?" Suddenly I was anxious to go.

"That's the catch. Say 'hi,' Jones."

And all the bulbs lit simultaneously. They were flashing red, white, and blue.

                    RWBRWBRWB
                    RWBRWBRWB
                    RWBRWBRWB
                    RWBRWBRWB
                    RWBRWBRWB

"Good with symbols, see, but the code's restricted. In the navy they had him wired into an audiovisual display." She drew the narrow package from a jacket pocket. "Pure shit, Jones. Want it?" He froze in the water and started to sink. I felt a strange panic, remembering that he wasn't a fish, that he could drown. "We want the key to Johnny's bank, Jones. We want it fast."

The lights flickered, died.   85

"Go for it, Jones!"

                         B
                    BBBBBBBBB
                         B
                         B
                         B

Blue bulbs, cruciform.

Darkness.

"Pure! It's *clean*. Come on, Jones."

                    WWWWWWWWW
                    WWWWWWWWW
                    WWWWWWWWW
                    WWWWWWWWW
                    WWWWWWWWW

White sodium glare washed her features, stark monochrome, shadows cleaving   90
from her cheekbones.

```
R     RRRRR
R     R
RRRRRRRR
        R     R
RRRRR       R
```

The arms of the red swastika were twisted in her silver glasses. "Give it to him," I said. "We've got it."

Ralfi Face. No imagination.

Jones heaved half his armored bulk over the edge of his tank, and I thought the metal would give way. Molly stabbed him overhand with the Syrette, driving the needle between two plates. Propellant hissed. Patterns of light exploded, spasming across the frame and then fading to black.

We left him drifting, rolling languorously in the dark water. Maybe he was dreaming of his war in the Pacific, of the cyber mines he'd swept, nosing gently into their circuitry with the Squid he'd used to pick Ralfi's pathetic password from the chip buried in my head.

" I can see them slipping up when he was demobbed, letting him out of the navy with that gear intact, but how does a cybernetic dolphin get wired to smack?"   95

"The war," she said. "They all were. Navy did it. How else you get 'em working for you?"

"I'm not sure this profiles as good business," the pirate said, angling for better money. "Target specs on a comsat that isn't in the book—"

"Waste my time and you won't profile at all," said Molly, leaning across his scarred plastic desk to prod him with her forefinger.

"So maybe you want to buy your microwaves somewhere else?" He was a tough kid, behind his Mao-job. A Nighttowner by birth, probably.

Her hand blurred down the front of his jacket, completely severing a lapel without   100 even rumpling the fabric.

"So we got a deal or not?"

"Deal," he said, staring at his ruined lapel with what he must have hoped was only polite interest. "Deal."

While I checked the two recorders we'd bought, she extracted the slip of paper I'd given her from the zippered wrist pocket of her jacket. She unfolded it and read silently, moving her lips. She shrugged. "This is it?"

"Shoot," I said, punching the RECORD studs of the two decks simultaneously.

"Christian White," she recited, "and his Aryan Reggae Band."   105

Faithful Ralfi, a fan to his dying day.

Transition to idiot/savant mode is always less abrupt than I expect it to be. The pirate broadcaster's front was a failing travel agency in a pastel cube that boasted a desk, three chairs, and a faded poster of a Swiss orbital spa. A pair of toy birds with blown-glass bodies and tin legs were sipping monotonously from a Styrofoam cup of water on a ledge beside Molly's shoulder. As I phased into mode, they accelerated gradually until their Day-Glo-feathered crowns became solid arcs of color. The LEDs that told seconds on the plastic wall clock had become meaningless pulsing grids, and Molly and the Mao-faced boy grew hazy, their arms blurring occasionally in insect-quick ghosts of gesture. And then it all faded to cool gray static and an endless tone poem in an artificial language.

I sat and sang dead Ralfi's stolen program for three hours.

The mall runs forty kilometers from end to end, a ragged overlap of Fuller domes roofing what was once a suburban artery. If they turn off the arcs on a clear day, a gray approximation of sunlight filters through layers of acrylic, a view like the prison sketches of Giovanni Piranesi. The three southernmost kilometers roof Nighttown. Nighttown pays no taxes, no utilities. The neon arcs are dead, and the geodesics have been smoked black by decades of cooking fires. In the nearly total darkness of a Nighttown noon, who notices a few dozen mad children lost in the rafters?

We'd been climbing for two hours, up concrete stairs and steel ladders with perfo-   110
rated rungs, past abandoned gantries and dust-covered tools. We'd started in what looked like a disused maintenance yard, stacked with triangular roofing segments. Everything there had been covered with that same uniform layer of spraybomb graffiti: gang names, initials, dates back to the turn of the century. The graffiti followed us up, gradually thinning until a single name was repeated at intervals. LO TEK. In dripping black capitals.

"Who's Lo Tek?"

"Not us, boss." She climbed a shivering aluminum ladder and vanished through a hole in a sheet of corrugated plastic. "'Low technique, low technology.'" The plastic muffled her voice. I followed her up, nursing my aching wrist. "Lo Teks, they'd think that shotgun trick of yours was effete."

An hour later I dragged myself up through another hole, this one sawed crookedly in a sagging sheet of plywood, and met my first Lo Tek.

"'S okay," Molly said, her hand brushing my shoulder. "It's just Dog. Hey, Dog."

In the narrow beam of her taped flash, he regarded us with his one eye and slowly   115
extruded a thick length of grayish tongue, licking huge canines. I wondered how they wrote off tooth-bud transplants from Dobermans as low technology. Immunosuppressives don't exactly grow on trees.

"Moll." Dental augmentation impeded his speech. A string of saliva dangled from his twisted lower lip. "Heard ya comin'. Long time." He might have been fifteen, but the fangs and a bright mosaic of scars combined with the gaping socket to present a mask of total bestiality. It had taken time and a certain kind of creativity to assemble that face, and his posture told me he enjoyed living behind it. He wore a pair of decaying jeans, black with grime and shiny along the creases. His chest and feet were bare. He did something with his mouth that approximated a grin. "Bein' followed, you."

Far off, down in Nighttown, a water vendor cried his trade.

"Strings jumping, Dog?" She swung her flash to the side, and I saw thin cords tied to eyebolts, cords that ran to the edge and vanished.

"Kill the fuckin' light!"

She snapped it off.   120

"How come the one who's followin' you's got no light?"

"Doesn't need it. That one's bad news, Dog. Your sentries give him a tumble, they'll come home in easy-to-carry sections."

"This a *friend* friend, Moll?" He sounded uneasy. I heard his feet shift on the worn plywood.

"No. But he's mine. And this one," slapping my shoulder, "he's a friend. Got that?"

"Sure," he said, without much enthusiasm, padding to the platform's edge, where   125
the eyebolts were. He began to pluck out some kind of message on the taut cords.

Nighttown spread beneath us like a toy village for rats; tiny windows showed candlelight, with only a few harsh, bright squares lit by battery lanterns and carbide lamps. I imagined the old men at their endless games of dominoes, under warm, fat drops of water that fell from wet wash hung out on poles between the plywood shanties. Then I tried to imagine him climbing patiently up through the darkness in his zoris and ugly tourist shirt, bland and unhurried. How was he tracking us?

"Good," said Molly. "He smells us."

"Smoke?" Dog dragged a crumpled pack from his pocket and prized out a flattened cigarette. I squinted at the trademark while he lit it for me with a kitchen match. Yiheyuan filters. Beijing Cigarette Factory. I decided that the Lo Teks were black marketeers. Dog and Molly went back to their argument, which seemed to revolve around Molly's desire to use some particular piece of Lo Tek real estate.

"I've done you a lot of favors, man. I want that floor. And I want the music."

"You're not Lo Tek. . . ."   130

This must have been going on for the better part of a twisted kilometer, Dog leading us along swaying catwalks and up rope ladders. The Lo Teks leech their webs and huddling places to the city's fabric with thick gobs of epoxy and sleep above the abyss in mesh hammocks. Their country is so attenuated that in places it consists of little more than holds for hands and feet, sawed into geodesic struts.

> **The Lo Teks leech their webs and huddling places to the city's fabric with thick gobs of epoxy and sleep above the abyss in mesh hammocks.**

The Killing Floor, she called it. Scrambling after her, my new Eddie Bax shoes slipping on worn metal and damp plywood, I wondered how it could be any more lethal than the rest of the territory. At the same time I sensed that Dog's protests were ritual and that she already expected to get whatever it was she wanted.

Somewhere beneath us, Jones would be circling his tank, feeling the first twinges of junk sickness. The police would be boring the Drome regulars with questions about Ralfi. What did he do? Who was he with before he stepped outside? And the Yakuza would be settling its ghostly bulk over the city's data banks, probing for faint images of me reflected in numbered accounts, securities transactions, bills for utilities. We're an information economy. They teach you that in school. What they don't tell you is that it's impossible to move, to live, to operate at any level without leaving traces, bits, seemingly meaningless fragments of personal information. Fragments that can be retrieved, amplified . . .

But by now the pirate would have shuttled our message into line for blackbox transmission to the Yakuza comsat. A simple message: Call off the dogs or we wideband your program.

The program. I had no idea what it contained. I still don't. I only sing the song,   135 with zero comprehension. It was probably research data, the Yakuza being given to advanced forms of industrial espionage. A genteel business, stealing from Ono-Sendai as a matter of course and politely holding their data for ransom, threatening to blunt the conglomerate's research edge by making the product public.

But why couldn't any number play? Wouldn't they be happier with something to sell back to Ono-Sendai, happier than they'd be with one dead Johnny from Memory Lane?

Their program was on its way to an address in Sydney, to a place that held letters for clients and didn't ask questions once you'd paid a small retainer. Fourth-class surface mail. I'd erased most of the other copy and recorded our message in the resulting gap, leaving just enough of the program to identify it as the real thing.

My wrist hurt. I wanted to stop, to lie down, to sleep. I knew that I'd lose my grip and fall soon, knew that the sharp black shoes I'd bought for my evening as Eddie Bax would lose their purchase and carry me down to Nighttown. But he rose in my mind like a cheap religious hologram, glowing, the enlarged chip on his Hawaiian shirt looming like a reconnaissance shot of some doomed urban nucleus.

So I followed Dog and Molly through Lo Tek heaven, jury-rigged and jerry-built from scraps that even Nighttown didn't want.

The Killing Floor was eight meters on a side. A giant had threaded steel cable   140 back and forth through a junkyard and drawn it all taut. It creaked when it moved, and it moved constantly, swaying and bucking as the gathering Lo Teks arranged themselves on the shelf of plywood surrounding it. The wood was silver with age, polished with long use and deeply etched with initials, threats, declarations of passion. This was suspended from a separate set of cables, which lost themselves in darkness beyond the raw white glare of the two ancient floods suspended above the Floor.

A girl with teeth like Dog's hit the Floor on all fours. Her breasts were tattooed with indigo spirals. Then she was across the Floor, laughing, grappling with a boy who was drinking dark liquid from a liter flask.

Lo Tek fashion ran to scars and tattoos. And teeth. The electricity they were tapping to light the Killing Floor seemed to be an exception to their overall aesthetic, made in the name of . . . ritual, sport, art? I didn't know, but I could see that the Floor was something special. It had the look of having been assembled over generations.

I held the useless shotgun under my jacket. Its hardness and heft were comforting, even though I had no more shells. And it came to me that I had no idea at all of what was really happening, or of what was supposed to happen. And that was the nature of

my game, because I'd spent most of my life
as a blind receptacle to be filled with other people's knowledge and then drained, spouting synthetic languages I'd never understand. A very
technical boy. Sure.

   And then I noticed just how quiet the Lo Teks
had become.

   He was there, at the edge of the light, taking
in the Killing Floor and the gallery of silent Lo
Teks with a tourist's calm. And as our eyes met
for the first time with mutual recognition, a memory clicked into place for me, of Paris, and the
long Mercedes electrics gliding through the rain to

**I'd spent most of my life
as a blind receptacle to be
filled with other people's
knowledge and then
drained, spouting
synthetic languages I'd
never understand. A very
technical boy.**

145

Notre Dame; mobile greenhouses, Japanese faces behind the glass, and a hundred
Nikons rising in blind phototropism, flowers of steel and crystal. Behind his eyes, as
they found me, those same shutters whirring.

   I looked for Molly Millions, but she was gone.

   The Lo Teks parted to let him step up onto the bench. He bowed, smiling, and
stepped smoothly out of his sandals, leaving them side by side, perfectly aligned, and
then he stepped down onto the Killing Floor. He came for me, across that shifting
trampoline of scrap, as easily as any tourist padding across synthetic pile in any featureless hotel.

   Molly hit the Floor, moving.

   The Floor screamed.

   It was miked and amplified, with pickups riding the four fat coil springs at the cor-   150
ner and contact mikes taped at random to rusting machine fragments. Somewhere the
Lo Teks had an amp and a synthesizer, and now I made out the shapes of speakers
overhead, above the cruel white floods.

   A drumbeat began, electronic, like an amplified heart, steady as a metronome.

   She'd removed her leather jacket and boots; her T-shirt was sleeveless, faint tell-
tales of Chiba City circuitry traced along her thin arms. Her leather jeans gleamed
under the floods. She began to dance.

   She flexed her knees, white feet tensed on a flattened gas tank, and the Killing
Floor began to heave in response. The sound it made was like a world ending, like the
wires that hold heaven snapping and coiling across the sky.

   He rode with it, for a few heartbeats, and then he moved, judging the movement
of the Floor perfectly, like a man stepping from one flat stone to another in an ornamental garden.

   He pulled the tip from his thumb with the grace of a man at ease with social gesture   155
and flung it at her. Under the floods, the filament was a refracting thread of rainbow. She
threw herself flat and rolled, jackknifing up as the molecule whipped past, steel claws
snapping into the light in what must have been an automatic rictus of defense.

   The drum pulse quickened, and she bounced with it, her dark hair wild around the
blank silver lenses, her mouth thin, lips taut with concentration. The Killing Floor
boomed and roared, and the Lo Teks were screaming their excitement.

He retracted the filament to a whirling meter-wide circle of ghostly polychrome and spun it in front of him, thumbless hand held level with his sternum. A shield.

And Molly seemed to let something go, something inside, and that was the real start of her mad-dog dance. She jumped, twisting, lunging sideways, landing with both feet on an alloy engine block wired directly to one of the coil springs. I cupped my hands over my ears and knelt in a vertigo of sound, thinking Floor and benches were on their way down, down to Nighttown, and I saw us tearing through the shanties, the wet wash, exploding on the tiles like rotten fruit. But the cables held, and the Killing Floor rose and fell like a crazy metal sea. And Molly danced on it.

And at the end, just before he made his final cast with the filament, I saw something in his face, an expression that didn't seem to belong there. It wasn't fear and it wasn't anger. I think it was disbelief, stunned incomprehension mingled with pure aesthetic revulsion at what he was seeing, hearing—at what was happening to him. He retracted the whirling filament, the ghost disk shrinking to the size of a dinner plate as he whipped his arm above his head and brought it down, the thumbtip curving out for Molly like a live thing.

The Floor carried her down, the molecule passing just above her head; the Floor   160 whiplashed, lifting him into the path of the taut molecule. It should have passed harmlessly over his head and been withdrawn into its diamond-hard socket. It took his hand off just behind the wrist. There was a gap in the Floor in front of him, and he went through it like a diver, with a strange deliberate grace, a defeated kamikaze on his way down to Nighttown. Partly, I think, he took the dive to buy himself a few seconds of the dignity of silence. She'd killed him with culture shock.

The Lo Teks roared, but someone shut the amplifier off, and Molly rode the Killing Floor into silence, hanging on now, her face white and blank, until the pitching slowed and there was only a faint pinging of tortured metal and the grating of rust on rust.

We searched the Floor for the severed hand, but we never found it. All we found was a graceful curve in one piece of rusted steel, where the molecule went through. Its edge was bright as new chrome.

We never learned whether the Yakuza had accepted our terms, or even whether they got our message. As far as I know, their program is still waiting for Eddie Bax on a shelf in the back room of a gift shop on the third level of Sydney Central-5. Probably they sold the original back to Ono-Sendai months ago. But maybe they did get the pirate's broadcast, because nobody's come looking for me yet, and it's been nearly a year. If they do come, they'll have a long climb up through the dark, past Dog's sentries, and I don't look much like Eddie Bax these days. I let Molly take care of that, with a local anesthetic. And my new teeth have almost grown in.

I decided to stay up here. When I looked out across the Killing Floor, before he came, I saw how hollow I was. And I knew I was sick of being a bucket. So now I climb down and visit Jones, almost every night.

We're partners now, Jones and I, and Molly Millions, too. Molly handles our busi-   165 ness in the Drome. Jones is still in Funland, but he has a bigger tank, with fresh seawater trucked in once a week. And he has his junk, when he needs it. He still talks to the kids with his frame of lights, but he talks to me on a new display unit in a shed that I rent there, a better unit than the one he used in the navy.

And we're all making good money, better money than I made before, because Jones's Squid can read the traces of anything that anyone ever stored in me, and he gives it to me on the display unit in languages I can understand. So we're learning a lot about all my former clients. And one day I'll have a surgeon dig all the silicon out of my amygdalae, and I'll live with my own memories and nobody else's, the way other people do. But not for a while.

In the meantime it's really okay up here, way up in the dark, smoking a Chinese filtertip and listening to the condensation that drips from the geodesics. Real quiet up here—unless a pair of Lo Teks decide to dance on the Killing Floor.

It's educational, too. With Jones to help me figure things out, I'm getting to be the most technical boy in town.

⬅ SECOND THOUGHTS

1. Gibson's writing is often cited as the first "cyberpunk" literature, characterized by a condensed, fast-paced narrative in an imaginary future dominated by technology. As in this story, the terminology for elements of that future world—places, customs, organizations, devices, etc.—may be only partially explained, so the reader must piece together the social context from sometimes-fragmented clues in the action. Make a list of unfamiliar terms in this story—including Drome, implants, neural disruptor, Squids, Nighttown, and Lo Teks—and try making a "Johnny Mnemonic" glossary in which you define, describe, and discuss the functions of these elements in the story.

2. The human characters in this story, and even the dolphin, are cyborgs, or combinations of biological organisms and artificial or technological parts. What do you think are the advantages and disadvantages of their particular biotechnical enhancements for Johnny, Molly, and other characters?

3. In the preface to *Burning Chrome* (Arbor, 1986), Gibson's collection of stories, Bruce Sterling writes that, in "Johnny Mnemonic," "we see a future that is recognizably and painstakingly drawn from the modern condition." What elements of the story are recognizable to you from today's world? How realistic or exaggerated do you think these elements are as reflections of current conditions or trends?

▓ DISCUSSION THREADS

re: Turkle and Lakoff

1. Sherry Turkle writes that computer-screen "windows have become a powerful metaphor for thinking about the self as a multiple, distributed system" (¶ 17); George Lakoff (in the Boal interview, referring to the work of Michael Reddy) says that "our major metaphor for communication comes out of a general metaphor for the mind in which ideas are taken as objects and thought is taken as the manipulation of objects" (¶ 4). To conceive of our identity in terms of different "windows" open to different contexts, as Turkle does, do you think that we must consider information as something separate from our bodies? That is, to what extent do you think that Turkle's windows metaphor depends on Reddy's conduit metaphor? How persuasive do you find these metaphors as expressions of your own identity?

re: Turkle and Ullman

2. Ellen Ullman's experience as an engineer and e-mail lover offers an interesting case study for Sherry Turkle's ideas about developing multiple aspects of the self in electronic spaces. How does Ullman construct a new self, or "cycle through" different selves in Turkle's terms, through her use of e-mail and "group aliases"? How would you compare Ullman's experience with those of other subjects described by Turkle?

re: Platt and Lakoff

3. Based on Boal's interview, how do you think George Lakoff would respond to the Turing test or the Loebner contest in which Charles Platt participates, where people compete with computer programs to see which appears more "human"? What assumptions about human nature or the nature of intelligence do Lakoff and Loebner reveal? What's your own reaction to the Turing/Loebner tests as measures of intelligence?

re: Lakoff and Ullman

4. How do you think Ellen Ullman, based on her essay, would respond to George Lakoff's ideas about the physical embodiment of human intelligence and communication?

re: Lakoff and Gibson

5. To what extent do you think Johnny or other characters in "Johnny Mnemonic" embody the conduit metaphor criticized by George Lakoff? Do you think Johnny transcends the limitations of this metaphor by joining the Lo Teks at the end of the story?

re: New Windows on the Self

6. Regarding the relationship between "real life" and virtual computer spaces, one of Sherry Turkle's subjects who spends a lot of time online asks, "Why grant such superior status to the self that has the body when the selves that don't have bodies are able to have different kinds of experiences?" (¶ 19). How do you think this question would be answered differently or similarly by Charles Platt, George Lakoff, Ellen Ullman, and William Gibson? What is your own view?

RESEARCH LINKS

- *For direct links to listed Internet sources, additional reading selections and questions online, plus updates and supplementary Web resources, see* **Composing Cyberspace Online** *at <www.mhhe.com/socscience/english/holeton/>.*
- *For a complete set of research tools for the Internet—including the most useful search strategies, directories, and conventions for documenting online sources—see* **McGraw-Hill English Composition** *at <www.mhhe.com/socscience/english/compde/>.*

1. Study several articles relating to computer technology or electronic communication from the business section of your newspaper, popular news magazines, or Internet sources. Analyze the language used to refer to human beings or human activities, and consider (*a*) the extent to which people and activities are portrayed in terms of Sherry Turkle's windows metaphor, or (*b*) the extent to which information is portrayed in terms of Michael Reddy's conduit metaphor (as discussed by George Lakoff). What other metaphors do these texts rely on? How powerful do you think such metaphors and language are in shaping people's attitudes about technology? How important are they in constructing your own self-image?

2. If you have access to the Internet, find and experiment with a real MUD or MOO. You might start your search at Lydia Leong's "The MUD Resource Collection" (<www.godlike.com/muds/>) or Jeffrey Galin's "MOO Central" (<www.pitt.edu/~jrgst7/MOOcentral.html>, moving to a new address in late 1997); student-friendly MOOs include DaMOO at <DaMOO.csun.edu:8888/> and Diversity University (<www.du.org/>), where teachers can bring their whole class. Alternatively, join an Internet Relay Chat (IRC) channel for several sessions. (For help in connecting to a MUD, MOO, or IRC, ask your teacher or the computer support staff at your school or place of work, or refer to an Internet reference guide.) After you've tried one or more of these real-time communication or "text-based virtual reality spaces," do some more reading about them, both in print and online. A good start would be Sherry Turkle's book from which the selection in this chapter was excerpted. Based on your initial experiences, how do you evaluate some of the claims—by Turkle and others—about the nature of identity in cyberspace or the relationship between real life and virtual reality? Write a research paper in which you take a position about a

controversial or constructive aspect of MOOs, MUDs, or IRCs, such as their potential for abuse or their potential as an expressive or educational medium.

3. Charles Platt writes in this chapter about his participation in the fourth annual Loebner contest in 1994. In 1997 information about subsequent contests was available on the Loebner contest home page at <acm.org/~loebner/loebner-prize.htmlx>, and a link allowing browsers to actually try Thomas Whalen's winning program from 1994 was available from his home page at <acm.org/~loebner/whalen-bio.html>. Use library and Internet sources to find out about historical or more recent attempts to pass the Turing test. On the Web, search for the Turing test, artificial intelligence (AI), or artificial life (AL); using most search engines, you will find thousands of references to these topics. Browse these sources or narrow your search to help you find a specific topic within AI or AL research that interests you, such as neural networks or software agents, as a focus for your own research writing.

4. "We are mind and machine mediated through mind and machine," writes Ellen Ullman, and the relationship between body, mind, and technology is a major theme in this chapter. Cyborgs—a contraction of "cybernetic organism," a combination of artificial and biological systems—have been a frequent subject in popular culture at least since Norbert Wiener's 1948 book *Cybernetics, or Control and Communication in the Animal and the Machine* (MIT Press), which first suggested that biological systems may be seen in terms of how they organize information. Science fiction movies and TV series of the 1950s and 1960s often portrayed robots and cyborgs. In the 1970s and 1980s "unmanned" spaceships and spy satellites proliferated, and since then, a revolution in computer technology has further complicated the line between human and mechanical systems. In 1985 critic Donna Haraway published "A Cyborg Manifesto: Science, Technology, and Socialist-Feminism in the Late Twentieth Century," which has been widely discussed in academia (the essay was revised for *Simians, Cyborgs, and Women: The Reinvention of Nature,* Routledge, 1991); *The Cyborg Handbook* (Routledge), edited by Chris Hables Gray, was published in 1995. Some possible approaches for a research project on cyborgs include (*a*) changing notions of cyborgs in popular media; (*b*) a critical history of cybernetics, including the views of modern-day cognitive linguists such as this chapter's George Lakoff; (*c*) a focus on feminism and technology, examining Ullman's and Haraway's ideas along with those of other critics.

5. The film *Johnny Mnemonic,* written by William Gibson and directed by Robert Longo, was released on Tristar Home Video in 1995. Other recent movies exploring cyborg or human identity and technology themes include *Blade Runner* (Embassy Home Entertainment, 1983; Janus Films/Voyager, 1987), directed by Ridley Scott and based on Philip K. Dick's 1968 novel *Do Androids Dream of Electric Sheep?; The Lawnmower Man* (New Line Cinema, 1992), directed by Brett Leonard and based on a Stephen King short story; and *Crash* (Alliance Communications, 1996), directed by David Cronenberg and based on the 1973 novel by J. G.

Ballard. Pick two such movies, along with the original fiction on which they're based, and compare how they portray people's relationships with technology. If possible, include a wide range of sources in your research such as film criticism from scholarly journals, reviews from popular magazines and newspapers, commercial and research-oriented Web sites, and relevant Usenet discussion groups. If you select movies based on novels or stories, such as those listed here, you might focus on how technology themes get treated similarly and differently in the two media, film and print.

Gender Online

Reprinted by permission of Mike Luckovich and Creators Syndicate.

Whether intentionally or not, this chapter's cartoon by Mike Luckovich offers a male-centered, sexist perspective on gender relations in cyberspace. This perspective may be doubly disturbing to the extent that it both accurately and inaccurately represents those relations. The cartoon's decidedly male viewpoint does reflect the history of the Internet, insofar as the majority of participants have been men—although recent surveys show that women may compose as much as 40 percent of Net users, a proportion thought to be increasing in the late 1990s. The fact that most people with Net access are affluent and white is also reflected in the balding, button-shirted, baby-boomer man in the left panel; perhaps he looks slightly nerdy, too, conforming to a stereotype about computer-industry workers who have participated heavily on the Internet.

"Monique," however, grossly misrepresents the female online population, which tends to be young or middle-aged and professional. Although the exaggerated portrayal of "Monique" as a witch is obviously intended as a joke, this caricature understandably might disturb people who feel that women have already been marginalized with regard to high technology (for example, several studies have shown that girls in school are not offered the same encouragement to use computers as boys). A woman successfully using a computer, we might conclude from this representation, must not be "normal." Perhaps more disturbing, the ugly witch has misled and manipulated the man, here portrayed as the naive victim of her deviousness or desperation. Is the presumably single "Monique" desperate for a man, or is she rather an embittered, man-hating crone? Either way, the reality of gender relations in cyberspace is much more complicated and interesting, and this chapter explores that complexity.

Contrary to Luckovich's portrayal of a hapless male, it is women who are far more likely to be victimized on computer networks, where they have routinely been the target of sexual harassment, come-ons, put-downs, and bullying. To avoid such mistreatment, some women online pose as men or use anonymous, gender-neutral names or character descriptions—the so-called gender-bending that Dale Spender examines in the first selection. A relatively new phenomenon is *male* gender-bending: Partly because so many women online may be using male names, it's been estimated that a high percentage of the "Moniques" in chat rooms, MUDs (text-based "virtual reality" spaces), and other electronic meeting places are actually men posing as women. Writer Jesse Kornbluth narrates his experience posing as "MsTerious" in an America Online chat room in "(You Make Me Feel Like) A Virtual Woman." *Time* magazine columnist Barbara Ehrenreich, in another America Online chat room, encounters the aggressively seductive "Demonboy" and finds the potential of cyberspace to overcome gender barriers unfulfilled.

Harassment of women online becomes most controversial in cases of alleged "virtual rape," which raise complex issues about the power of language, physicality, and emotions in electronic media. In a widely publicized article in the *Village Voice* about a virtual rape in a well-established MOO (another kind of MUD), Julian Dibbell thoughtfully explores these complexities. Finally, Laura Miller critically examines the language used by Dibbell and other writers to describe these rough-and-tumble virtual worlds, specifically the "Western frontier" metaphor for cyberspace: Is the rush to "protect the women and children" online, Miller asks, really just an excuse for increasing social controls and decreasing freedom for all participants?

Before reading these selections, you might consider other questions based on your own experience with gender roles and technology, such as

1. Have you ever not known the gender of a person you were talking with on the phone? How did you react? How did you determine if the other person was male or female? Have you been in another situation where you were uncertain of, or mistaken about, a person's gender? Share your experiences with classmates or fellow readers.

2. It's been observed that, in our society, it's more acceptable for women to dress like men than for men to dress like women. Why do you think that's the case? In separate groups of women and men, discuss experiences when you've dressed up as or role-played the opposite sex, for example for Halloween, a costume party, or a drama performance. How did it feel to act as a member of the other sex? In what ways were you treated differently by others? Appoint a reporter to take notes, or record a transcript if you hold this discussion electronically. Then compare notes or share transcripts. What patterns, similarities, and differences can you observe in women's and men's experiences with this real-life "gender bending"?

3. Locate and study your school's or company's policy about sexual harassment, if it has one. Does the definition of harassment explicitly or implicitly include verbal or written forms? If you're familiar with a sexual harassment case, think about the different forms the alleged harassment took or the different media in which it was expressed. Do you think that one medium is more "harassing" than another?

4. Locate and study your school's or organization's "acceptable use policy," if it has one, for the institution's computer network. What uses of the computer network are forbidden at your institution? How reasonable does the policy seem to you? Have there been any cases of e-mail harassment at your institution?

5. If you have access to a computer lab, classroom, or networked computers equipped with electronic discussion software, hold a discussion in which everyone logs on anonymously with gender-neutral names. Before you begin, make sure you agree on some ground rules about "netiquette" or online politeness. Discuss one of the issues raised previously or another topic suggested by your peers or teacher. Afterward, talk face-to-face about the experience. Did you try to figure out who was who? To what extent could you determine who was male and who was female, and on what basis did you make these judgments? Did anyone consciously try to disguise his or her true gender? How successful was any such effort, and why?

Gender-Bending

Dale Spender

Dale Spender (b. 1943) is a feminist scholar, writer, teacher, and consultant from Australia. She is a co-founder of the database WIKED (Women's International Knowledge Encyclopedia and Data) and the founding editor of the Athene Series and Pandora Press, commissioning editor of the Penguin Australian Women's Library, and associate editor of the Great Women Series (United Kingdom). Her many books include *Man Made Language* (Routledge & Kegan Paul, 1980), *For the Record: The Making and Meaning of Feminist Knowledge* (Women's Press, 1985), and *Writing a New World: Two Centuries of Australian Women Writers* (Penguin Books, 1988). "Gender Bending" is from her recent book, *Nattering on the Net: Women, Power and Cyberspace* (Spinifex, 1996); see also her selection in Chapter 6, p. 266.

The objection that was raised when the telephone was first invented was that it 1 wouldn't be possible to tell whether you were talking to a male or a female on the telephone; at least, that's what people were worried about. And there was a genuine basis for their concern. Because one of the first principles of conversation is that if you don't know what gender you are talking to, you don't know what to say, or where to look, or how to stand. And that's only the beginning of the communication.

Even today, there are topics that women would not ordinarily raise if there were 2 men around (and there are ways of looking and standing that aid communication among women, but which would be totally inappropriate if it was a conversation that you wanted with a man). And women wouldn't talk about some things in a particular way if men were within hearing. Everything alters—from terms to tone, from posture to demeanour and eye-contact—depending on whether women are talking to women, rather than to men.

In the 1970s when I was avidly documenting the conversation of the sexes, I set up 3 several experiments to find out how women talked in the presence of men.[1] And I didn't always welcome the evidence because no matter how assertive and aware the women were—myself included—we invariably made men the centre of our linguistic attention, and showed them considerable deference. Which was pretty distressing for feisty feminists.

With cameras rolling, experimental situations would be set up in which one man 4 joined (uninvited) a group of women who were engrossed in conversation. That the

---

[1] See Dale Spender, 1980, *Man Made Language,* Routledge & Kegan Paul, London.

man would interrupt and the women would give him the floor was to be expected. But that the women would change the way they were sitting (and move to a more "closed" position), that they would arrange themselves with neck inclined, so that they were looking *up* to him rather than down, was a chilling reminder of the subtleties of sociali-sation, and its power to construct daily inequality.

In a memorable study of the way that we mould and modify our behaviour on the   5 basis of gender, a group of feminist researchers undertook some observations on mothers and a baby. The baby was dressed in purple, and was unknown to the subjects. It was handed to a series of women who were told it was a girl. Almost all of them held the purple-clad baby fairly close and tightly, with their heads bent down, while they spoke in quiet, soothing, affectionate tones.

Then the women were told that a mistake had been made. That the baby was in fact a boy.

The change was dramatic. The baby was sometimes in danger of being dropped as each woman struggled to change the way she was holding it. Immediate attempts were made to move the "boy" further away, to jog him up and down, to speak more loudly and more robustly. And far from looking down on a male child, many women raised it to eye-level. More than a few went so far at one stage as to hold *above* them a three-month-old purple bundle that they believed to be male so that they could incline their neck and talk to the baby in the appropriate gender-deferential manner.

What was said also varied, depending on whether the baby was thought to be male   8 or female. "Aren't you a pretty little thing" was fine when the purple bundle was taken for a girl. It was quickly replaced with "What a big boy you are," or some other such stereotyped comment, when it was taken for a boy.

How it was said changed dramatically as well. Whereas low-key and quieter tones   9 were used when the child was classified as female, much more noise was made, and more action-oriented terms were used, when the women thought they were talking to a boy.

It is clear that the behaviour of the women was determined by what they thought   10 was the right response to the different genders. It had nothing to do with the antics or attitudes of the purple baby.

The extent to which this code is imprinted on our psyches can also be seen when   11 in real life we have to talk to someone whose gender is unknown. We can't even make comments to a new-born baby—who has not a clue what we are saying—without having to ask, is it a girl or a boy? Only when we know this can we conduct anything like a conversation.

Anyone who has ever assumed that they were talking to one gender rather than the   12 other is excruciatingly embarrassed if they discover they have made an error. Everything from body posture to vocabulary and tone is wrong if you think you are talking to

Almost all of them held the purple-clad baby fairly close and tightly, with their heads bent down, while they spoke in quiet, soothing, affectionate tones. Then the women were told that a mistake had been made.   6
    7

a man, only to discover that it is a woman. Or vice versa. Instant changes have to be made so that behaviour is appropriate and you are not misinterpreted, or seen as insolent or inept.

This is why people who say they treat both sexes exactly the same are either very rude or very silly. Parents who say they rear their daughters and sons identically are quite self-deluded. All of our words, actions, and body language are gender-loaded.   13

This is not just in relation to the spoken form; it applies to the written as well. In another classic study of the early 1970s, Philip Goldberg showed that the same words were rated differently depending on whether the author was said to be male or female. The same extract, be it on child-care or scientific method, was seen as more impressive, authoritative and substantive if believed to be the work of John Smith than if it was thought to be that of Joan Smith.[2]   14

Which suggests that you need a male name if you want to be taken seriously in print.   15

These are not the only factors that need to be taken into account. If there are pluses for man-talk, there are minuses for woman-talk.   16

> It is not surprising to find that there are no terms for man-talk that are equivalent to *chatter, natter, prattle, nag, bitch, whine* and of course *gossip,* and I am not so naive as to assume that this is because men do not engage in these activities. It is because when they do it it is called something different, something more flattering, and more appropriate to their place in the world.[3]

While there is negative feedback for women when they talk like women, it is no less negative (and is probably more so) if women break the code and speak in the same way as men. We are all aware of the double standard that allows the same words to be masterful if coming from a man, but are domineering, bossy, aggressive—even castrating—if they come from a woman.   17

While these issues are rarely raised in the context of free speech—and who possesses it—all this evidence serves to show just how deeply gender considerations influence what we say and how we can say it. In real life—and in cyberspace. Although for men there may be advantages in some of the established practices (like having a deferential audience that rates your contribution as authoritative, regardless of content or evidence), for women the situation is grim. So you can see why women might find the prospect of gender-blindness attractive. They might find electronic networks, with their scope for gender neutrality and pseudonyms, an improvement on real life. Gender-blindness at least holds the possibility of being able to leave behind the baggage that goes with being rated as a female speaker.   18

The fact that the electronic networks are theoretically gender-, race- and class-blind has certainly been put forward as a positive feature by those who want to encourage new net users. There are women who have adopted this gender-bending strategy,   19

---

[2]Philip Goldberg, 1974, "Are Women Prejudiced against Women?", in Judith Stacey et al. (eds.), *And Jill Came Tumbling After: Sexism in American Education,* Dell Publishing, New York, pp. 37–42.

[3]Spender, *Man Made Language,* p. 107.

and who say how much easier they find it when their gender is unknown on-line. But this is only part of the story so far.

Just as we were not fooled by the telephone, we are not going to be fooled on the superhighway. (Almost no one makes a mistake about gender on the telephone. While we can't quite work out how we do it, and maybe we didn't do it well when the telephone was first invented until we learnt the new "language," it is nonetheless clear that we now pick up clues to gender identity on the telephone; and that we are accurate most of the time.) [20]

We are doing much the same thing in the new medium. We are now working out ways to identify gender and race on-line. I suspect that at the moment, anyway, gender divisions are just too important in our life to let them go. We are starting to use virtual clues to make decisions about gender, as—in real life—we use the subtle clues of body posture, terms, tone, eye contact, etc. [21]

In her paper, "'Ladies, Babes 'n' Bitches': The Genderless Exultation of Cyberspace," Nancy Kaplan shows how things are changing. Whereas a few years ago it was routine to praise the gender-neutral possibilities of cyberspace, she says, "A number of studies have begun to challenge the assumption that net personas lack all gendered behaviors." It's not the gender-bending and cross-dressing that go on in cyberspace that attract the attention, so much as the general communication habits. You can't get away from gender even in the most mundane interchanges. In looking at MOOs and MUDs, Nancy Kaplan says, "The practices suggest that even when personae try to construct genderless avatars, there is no social, communicative space without gendered speakers."[4] [22]

"Farrell", one of the young women computer-whizzes . . . gives us some idea of what is going on and what gender judgements are being made when she says: [23]

The person that I met the other day chatting has the alias, Armpit. I realised that as we were chatting, that I had the idea he was male, before I had any real reason to do so. I suppose part of it was the alias; very few females would pick the alias "Armpit". Also he had some ways of being that seemed more male; for example, he responded to my "Hello!" message with something like "Yes Madame?" Yes, that is part of my alias, but females don't generally respond that way.[5]

At the same time, however, "Fish", one of Farrell's friends, shows that the element of anonymity that goes with electronic communication can also be helpful—particularly for females. [24]

Fish's journal sheds a little light on her use of this conversational form. Describing herself as a shy person "in real life", she writes that she "feels more comfortable typing out my feelings. My mind doesn't work quite fast enough that I feel comfortable in a normal conversation, but typing messages, I can express myself very well." Fish's account of her behaviour and her conversational style she and others employ may well yield additional insights into why some women like electronic environments: the absence of social cues

[4]On-line information re conference program—abstract for conference.
[5]Nancy Kaplan and Eva Farrell, 1994, "Weavers of Webs: A Portrait of Young Women on the Net", *Arachnet Electronic Journal on Virtual Culture*, 2, 3, July.

(appearance, for example) and of immediately perceptible power differentials (gender, age and so on) create a more comfortable social space, Fish believes, for many people like her.[6]

The temptation to adopt a gender-neutral name—or even a male pseudonym— 25 must be great, if it provides any protection from the sexual harassment that plagues so many women on the net. These days I assume that most women will take non-female names (or handles) simply to avoid some of the hassle. And that any blatant feminine names that are out there (such as "Marilyn"), probably belong to men in drag.

Of course, there have been other times and other circumstances when gender- 26 bending was popular with women—although this was not the name it would then have been given.

In the eighteenth and nineteenth centuries, women who were audacious enough to 27 write—to speak out and to be paid for their services—were likely to be condemned and criticised as not "proper women." As a result, the practice of writing anonymously or under a male pseudonym emerged. Women novelists such as Fanny Burney and Eliza-beth Gaskell began their careers anonymously, in order to avoid the hassle, in much the same way as women adopt names like Fish and Dolphin on the net today.

Anonymity isn't reserved for women. Men can also "benefit." It has been pointed out that it is the very anonymity that allows some men to behave abominably on-line, 28 in a way that they never would in real life. They feel powerful and protected by their pseudonym. According to Randye Jones, it is this anonymity, along with the ability to choose their gender, or any other identity, that accounts for the extremes of behaviour on the net:

> I credit the behavior to a couple of things. The first and probably the most influential is that anonymity and/or masquerade factor. On the net, you can be anyone you want to be—and when you divorce yourself from your real self, you are free to do/say more inflammatory things; after all, it's not "me" saying that; it's "the [person's alias]". The same sort of behavior results at costume parties or masquerade balls—when it's Mardi Gras for instance.[7]

To Rosie Cross, however, it is not simply that men use gender-bending to harass, while women use it to hide: "Generally, men, and some women have invaded the net 29 with a duplicity of personae and a Jekyll and Hyde attention-deficit disorder. Huff and bluff [and] I'll blow your cyberspace down."[8]

To return to the women writers, however, and the parallels with today: they didn't adopt male pseudonyms just to avoid social censure. It was because they wanted to be 30 taken seriously that they gave themselves men's names. They didn't want to be dis-missed as women, but to be treated with the deference due to men. So Charlotte Brontë wrote as Currer Bell, Maryanne Evans as George Eliot, and Ethel Florence Richardson as Henry Handel Richardson, in order to get a fair hearing. And some women choose men's names for the same reasons when they enter cyberspace today. Not much has changed from one century to another—nor from one medium to the next.

---

[6]Kaplan & Farrell, "Weavers of Webs."

[7]Randye Jones, 1993, "Netters Behavior and Flame Wars," on-line communication, September.

[8]Quoted in Rodney Chester, 1995, "A Place in Cyberspace," *Courier Mail,* 13 April, p. 22.

Despite the similarities with the past, there are new pressures at work today. 31 Among them is the way that the electronic media break down traditional divisions. We can see how national boundaries have been undermined, how even subject divisions are being dislodged. It could be that rigid divisions of gender are also being weakened by this tendency to get rid of the old certainties.

No one could dispute that there are gender changes going on as women move away 32 from their traditional private and oppressed role. A new relationship is being forged between the sexes; and while it is by no means equal at this stage, there is no doubt about which direction it is heading.

Women no longer feel obliged to stay within the confines of the male-servicing, 33 ornamental role. There is more to life than being an attraction for men. On women we see sensible shoes, the ubiquitous black outfit, not to mention shoulder pads, dinner jackets, career suits, and men's suits. We even have a caption for a picture of the singer k.d. lang in "feminine" garb which states: "You know times are changing when women begin dressing up as gay men who dress up as women."[9] This is gender-bending and, as the caption says, it isn't the sole domain of females.

At the same time that women seem sufficiently unfettered to move away from the blatantly feminine image of earlier days . . . there are men who feel free to adopt some of the props of femininity.

At the same time that women seem suf- 34 ficiently unfettered to move away from the bla- tantly feminine image of earlier days, it has become obvious that there are men who feel free to adopt some of the props of femininity. This is not just a matter of men being involved in child-care (although this is an important development); it's that some men now "dress up" as women once did.

Sadie Plant interprets this as a departure from 35 the old system, which divided the world into male and female, and then insisted that they were unequal categories. While I don't entirely endorse her point of view, it has interesting elements. When asked was it possible to escape gender on the net, she gave the following response.

I think it's increasingly advantageous to be female. So many men take on female personae that the gender issue has become an increasingly murky thing to discuss. There is every- thing to play for. It's fascinating that men want to play at being women. It's an opportunity they have not had presented to them in the past. It also implies a recognition by men that to be a woman in the past was a liability, but now it's a distinct advantage and a privilege. The male is basically becoming redundant.[10]

This is gender-bending taken to the limit; it will have enormous implications for 36 cyberspace—and real life.

---

[9]Victoria Starr, 1994, *k.d. lang: All You Get Is Me,* HarperCollins, London, between pp. 128 and 129.
[10]Rosie Cross, 1995, "Cyberfeminism: Interview with Sadie Plant," *geekgirl,* 1, p. 8.

SECOND THOUGHTS

1. Spender offers many examples of how "we mold and modify our behaviour on the basis of gender" (¶ 5). How persuaded are you by these examples? Can you provide any similar examples from your own experience? Can you provide any counterexamples or instances when your behavior was *not* so influenced by gender?
2. Based on this selection, how would you define *gender-bending?*
3. Spender discusses the potential benefits of gender-bending in cyberspace for women and women's roles in society; summarize these benefits. What benefits do you think there might be for men? What potential disadvantages or dangers can you foresee for either sex?

{you make me feel like} A Virtual Woman

Jesse Kornbluth

Jesse Kornbluth (b. 1946) is a contributing editor at *Architectural Digest* and writes for other magazines and newspapers, including *The New Yorker, Town and Country,* and the *New York Times.* His books include *Highly Confident: The Crime and Punishment of Michael Milken* (Morrow, 1992), which he has also adapted for the screen, and *Airborne: The Triumph and Struggle of Michael Jordan* (Simon & Schuster, 1995). This article appeared in 1996 in *Virtual City,* a magazine (no longer being published) launched by *Newsweek* for people interested in the Internet.

The record is quite clear: I'm male. A heterosexual male at that. But the record is limited, for life as I've known it lo these many years now ends at my modem. Once I call up my online service and beam myself into cyberspace, everything changes—in addition to the recognizably male identity I use to communicate with people I know, I have another persona. I'm a woman. Well, a virtual woman.

Women of America Online, I hear your hearts pounding as I type these words. You worry that you spilled secrets into my not-truly-pierced ears. Or, even worse, that I used my skills as a professional writer to bring you to a bliss now dirtied by the possibility that your electronic ravisher wasn't really wearing just bikinis and Escape.

What can I say?

Well, first, that I meant no harm. That I chose a name that might have made you suspicious. That your deep, dark secrets will die with me. That "deception" isn't a charge you can credibly level against anyone on a network where almost every woman says she's a 36C and no man admits to tipping the scales at 200. And, most of all, I can say this—the devil made me do it.

You know who I mean: men.

When I originally signed on to AOL, I had no intention of developing multiple personalities. But the first level of chat rooms bored me silly. All I saw in the AOL lobby and the public rooms were those cute punctuations that only an online addict could call communication—like {{{LOLA}}} to signify a warm greeting and LOL (laughing out loud) to acknowledge the most modest expression of wit—and typed dialogue that made ham radio compelling in comparison.

I pressed on to the next level of online conversation pits, the member rooms. These, at least, had alluring names: "Le Chateau Dungeon," "M 4 M, Yes Sir," and "Married and Restless." I anticipated these rooms would be musky with desire. And I was ready for that, for what is journalism if not a form of seduction? But even this vet-

5

eran writer was shocked by what goes on in the AOL member rooms. The women, in the main, come to talk; the men, in the main, talk to come. The result is a mating dance so crude it's hard to believe the practitioners are grownups: the cyber–prom kings claim their queens, drag them off to private rooms and, while they type with one hand, achieve what passes here for bliss.

And they call this an advance over phone sex?

In real life, I'm married to a woman who's smart and funny and easy on the eyes. I have a network of bright, amusing, and bodacious female friends, and, if I were a slimeball, I could surely convert one of them into a lover. I have, therefore, no interest in stroking cyberboobs and zorching cyberass. This is one man who went online to meet sharp-tongued, quick-thinking, maladjusted smartasses like himself.

Well, I tried the male-oriented member rooms. They were—what a surprise!—for   10 gays. And the gents I met there weren't terribly interested in my mind. So I moved right on to the rooms for women. But a man connecting with a woman in "Women 4 Women" is as unlikely as Madonna bedding down with Newt Gingrich. I'd wander in as my male self, and everybody would clam up. Or point cyberfingers at me, as if I were a dog who'd just mussed the rug. And, reeling with rejection, I would flee to the safety of the lobby and try, once again, to LOL with {{{{{LOLA}}}}}.

> **A man connecting with a woman in "Women 4 Women" is as unlikely as Madonna bedding down with Newt Gingrich.**

That's when I decided to become "MsTerious." (This isn't the name I used. I've disguised all the AOL names I cite here.)

Compared to many of the screen profiles I've read, I created a description for MsTerious that was extremely ethical. My aim was to suggest near-total unavailability, not intriguing intimacy. In her profile, MsTerious alluded to a free-ranging imagination, but she emphasized that she was completely devoted to her career and traveled frequently for her company. She made it quite clear that online was a place for her to vent at the end of her long work day, and that there was no way she'd let an online relationship turn into a real one. There were only two pieces of information MsTerious didn't offer: her measurements and her sexual preference. I just couldn't see myself typing 36-24-36. And, rube that I was, I assumed MsTerious was as straight as a string.

When I first logged on as MsTerious, women asked me questions that, in previous visits, had been asked of other new females: "What size pantyhose do you wear?" and "What's a French manicure?" Once I provided the answers—and threw in a quick put-down of men who log on using women's names—I was handed a cup of cybercoffee and welcomed in.

Long ago, a wise-guy friend paid me what I thought then and think now was a compliment: "You couldn't be gay, Jesse—but you could be a woman." You would never have agreed if you could have seen me at the start of my first session as MsTerious. I sat, hunched over the keyboard, sweat glistening on my brow as I struggled to write from the feminine side of my soul. It took me a solid half hour to realize that I couldn't produce an unnatural personality on cue. I would have to be myself-as-MsTerious and just wing it.

I took a breath. I checked out the profiles of the women in the room I was visit-   15
ing. "I think, therefore I'm one up on a man," one had written. "The sexiest distance
between two points is a curve," another opined. "The Eskimos had 52 names for snow
because it was important to them; there ought to be as many for love," a third offered.
Reading those, I began to feel I was in the right place, and I joined the conversation.

Minutes later, I had one of the most powerful revelations of my life: I didn't need
to do anything special to become a believable woman, I just had to be intelligent, open,
attentive and empathetic—gender differences really didn't matter. So I relaxed. Asked
questions. Offered advice. And, very quickly, was having the chats—about books and
relationships, music and travel—that I couldn't find anywhere else online.

But what about the sex, you ask?

Men, of course, were only too eager to imagine they were wooing MsTerious in
some European hotel room. Try as I might, I couldn't be attentive and open to those
requests; behind the come-ons, I perceived the silhouette of dominance. It was very different, though, when a woman approached me for cybersex. Her come-on was aggressive, but I could feel some humanity—and even the faint suggestion of a
smile—behind it. And so, improvising at every step, I gave her what she wanted.

Unless, of course, "she" was a "he," and we were, in our posing, the punch lines of
our own jokes.

I'd have to be a cyber-Molière to graph that set of crossed wires—and for now,   20
that's too much effort. I just came to play. And play I do. Like the night I ramped into
a room called "Why AOL Women Lie." We had a fine time swapping war stories, and
I formed a gang of two with a woman I'll call Jane. Then a guy I'll call BigStick
entered the room. And Jane and I attacked.

"Why introduce yourself with that name?" I asked.

"It's demeaning to women," Jane typed.

"It's just a code for when I'm cruising rooms like this," BigStick replied. "My luck
is better with this name."

"In my experience," I said loftily, "you get lucky more often with candles and
poetry."

Jane and I hammered away at BigStick until he was limp. Then we got another   25
idea. I told him I felt badly about attacking him, that I'd come to like him and that I
wanted him to join me in a private room so we could do that funky cyberthing. Big-
Stick smelled a con, but he was, after all, a man—he fell for it.

"Lighting candles," he announced, when he and I were alone. "Grabbing a well-
worn copy of 500 limericks for all occasions."

Suddenly another name appeared on the
screen: Jane.

You slut!" she typed . . .

"You slut!" she typed with blinding
speed. "Harlot! Hussy!"

"Harlot! Hussy!"

"This isn't how it looks, Jane," I typed. "Big-
Stick is reading his poetry to me."

"Boy, did I see this coming a mile off," BigStick moaned.   30

"Please, Jane, leave," I said. "This is my private time."

"She's mine, BigStick," Jane said. "And I need to know what she said to you."

"When does one of you pull out the gun and shoot the other?" BigStick asked.

"We were lovers," I explained. "But Jane has been drinking and drugging all summer, so I moved out."

"Right, and Jane is the only donor for bone marrow to Lisa Marie Presley."   35

Somewhere in Ohio, BigStick was learning to set aside lust and just enjoy the moment. In Maryland, Jane was signaling more friends to join the madness. And in New York, I was laughing so hard I could scarcely type. So hard I was actually weeping. So hard I almost wet my . . . uh . . . boxers.

⬅ SECOND THOUGHTS

1. Kornbluth offers or hints at a number of reasons for his online gender experiment. What do you think his primary motivations are? How sincere do you think he is?
2. How would you describe Kornbluth's attitudes toward women, toward other men, and toward gay men and lesbians? What evidence do you find in the text for these attitudes?
3. Kornbluth says early on that he "meant no harm" (¶ 4), and the incident concludes with laughter. What does Kornbluth seem to think is so funny at the end? Who do you think was harmed and/or who benefited, and to what extent, from Kornbluth's social experiment?

Put Your Pants on, Demonboy

Barbara Ehrenreich

Barbara Ehrenreich (b. 1941) writes and speaks about social and political issues, often from a feminist or socialist perspective, and contributes to many magazines such as *The Nation* and *Mother Jones.* Her books include *Witches, Midwives, and Nurses: A History of Women Healers* (co-authored with Deirdre English, Feminist Press, 1973), *The Hearts of Men: American Dreams and the Flight from Commitment* (Anchor/Doubleday, 1983), *The Worst Years of Our Lives: Irreverent Notes from a Decade of Greed* (Pantheon, 1990), and *The Snarling Citizen* (Farrar, Straus & Giroux, 1995). This essay appeared in 1995 in the newsmagazine *Time* (<pathfinder.com/time/>), for which Ehrenreich writes a regular column of social commentary.

E veryone wants to protect the children from the online kiddie-porn creeps, but 1
who's going to protect us from the children? At least I assume my harasser was 14 or under, given the tenor of the conversation in the America Online "chat room" I wandered into one afternoon. Typical contributions were typed entries like "Cockle Doodle DOOO" and "Hey Hoo HAAAA," or, as a topic for serious discussion, "What's the craziest drug you ever took?" So when someone we'll call "Demonboy" flashed me an invitation to accompany him into a "private room," I assumed he was just hungry for a higher order of chat. A few clicks of the mouse, and we were alone on the screen, where DB announced his topic of choice: "Can we undress?"

It took me a few moments to process this request. What could it matter to Demon- 2
boy, was my first and touchingly naive thought, whether we were naked or dressed in full suits of armor? The whole point of cyberspace, as I understood it, was to escape from the body, with its nonstop announcements of age, race, and sex. "Could we just talk?" I typed lamely, or something to that effect. "I'm taking off my pants," Demonboy typed back, "and running my tongue inside your thighs."

Naturally, I clicked out of there as fast as I could. But I could have done anything, 3
I realized later. I could have turned him over my knee and spanked him (which, sadly, he might have liked) or poked him in the eye with a sharp stick. I'm not even sure whether to call this sexual harassment, since it wasn't actually me being subjected to his fantasy but only my screen name, Barbeh. And it was my own fault, wasn't it, for picking an obviously femme handle, one that I see now must sound like some Stone Age stripper's stage name.

But how could I have known it would be so easy for me to be propositioned online 4
for sex? Well, not real sex, which to my old-fashioned way of thinking still involves

tangible saliva and sweat, possibly leavened with some actual affection. I'd heard about those kinky Internet newsgroups with names like alt.sex.bondage. I'd read about the use of online services to transmit pornography, including illegal kiddie porn. But no one had warned me that I might log onto AOL for the innocent purpose of, say, perusing the online encyclopedia and wander off for a minute, only to be enlisted in a hot-and-heavy bout of thigh licking. And I've learned it doesn't go on just in AOL. You can find plenty of onscreen panting at tonier sites on the Internet, including multiparticipant orgies.

> **No one had warned me that I might log onto AOL for the innocent purpose of, say, perusing the online encyclopedia and wander off for a minute, only to be enlisted in a hot-and-heavy bout of thigh licking.**

Now, I have no moral objection to cybersex. It's the ultimate in safe sex, and maybe the only form of sex available to the average 14-year-old boy. I don't even believe that conversation is somehow "loftier" than sex, since sex can get pretty lofty too. But in my experience, which probably outweighs Demonboy's by at least three decades, sex is a lot easier to find in this world than good conversation. 5

See, I actually believed in the promise of cyberspace—that we could reach out over the barriers of age, race, geography, and gender, and truly connect. No one would ever be lonely anymore. Writing would become a mass art form. Democracy would flourish as millions of people logged on to the vast, bubbling, uncensored online debate. I didn't know that much of what goes on online would turn out to be "utter drivel," as disillusioned cyberpioneer Clifford Stoll now concludes in his book *Silicon Snake Oil,** or "flame wars" of crude and escalating insults, or, of course, cybersex with Beavis and Butt-head. 6

Maybe the problem lies in the very anonymity that I had hoped would so liberate our spirits. A Swarthmore psychologist found in the '70s that if you put a group of total strangers together in the dark, they do things they wouldn't think of doing with the lights on—like grope. This is a result, apparently, of sexual repression. Put us in cyberspace wearing masks like "Demonboy," and an awful lot of us become gropers in the dark. 7

Maybe it was silly to expect that we'd turn on our modems and suddenly redis-cover the joy of good talk. When is the last time you participated in or even overheard a thrillingly deep conversation? On TV, sitcom families have little to say beyond one-line put-downs, and the braying of pundits passes for political debate. In the movies, a few clichés and grunts, punctuated by gunshots, suffice for a two-hour screenplay. Maybe cybertechnology just came along too late, after we had already entered what postmodernists call the postword era. Which would mean that we have no more use for our supersophisticated communications technology than a chimpanzee has for a vol-ume of Milton. If you can't eat it and you can't squish fleas with it, you might as well use it to masturbate with. 8

---

*See Chapter 9, p. 396, for an excerpt from Stoll's book (ed.).

But could it really be that all the centuries of scientific discovery and technical   9
ingenuity that led to the computer and modem were just laying the groundwork for
someone to transmit messages like "Cockle Doodle DOOO" and "Can we
undress?"?

Ah, Demonboy, it isn't your tongue I desire, but what is far more precious—a   10
glimpse of your mind.

⬅ SECOND THOUGHTS

1. How would you describe Ehrenreich's goals or motivations for "wandering" into an
   America Online chat room? How much experience in cyberspace did she seem to
   have before this incident, and how can you tell?
2. Ehrenreich writes that she's "not even sure whether to call this sexual harassment"
   (¶ 3) when "Demonboy" propositions her. Would you call this behavior harassment? Why or why not?
3. In what ways does Ehrenreich seem to feel that "the promise of cyberspace" (¶ 6)
   fails or disappoints, and how does she explain these failures? How fair a test do you
   think she has given the potentials of cyberspace?

A Rape in Cyberspace

Julian Dibbell

*or How an Evil Clown, a
Haitian Trickster Spirit, Two
Wizards, and a Cast of Dozens
Turned a Database into a
Society*

Julian Dibbell (b. 1963) writes about the social implications of new technologies in a monthly column for the *Village Voice,* called "Strange Loops," and in articles for other magazines and newspapers, including *Time, Wired,* and *The New York Times.* His memoir about his "experiences in an online, text-based virtual reality," *My Tiny Life,* is scheduled for publication in 1997 (Henry Holt). This essay appeared in the *Village Voice* (<villagevoice.com/>), a New York weekly that covers arts, culture, and politics, in 1993. Dibbell has a home page on the Web at <www.levity.com/julian/personal/index.html/>.

They say he raped them that night. They say he did it with a cunning little doll, 1 fashioned in their image and imbued with the power to make them do whatever he desired. They say that by manipulating the doll he forced them to have sex with him, and with each other, and to do horrible, brutal things to their own bodies. And though I wasn't there that night, I think I can assure you that what they say is true, because it all happened right in the living room—right there amid the well-stocked bookcases and the sofas and the fireplace—of a house I've come to think of as my second home.

Call me Dr. Bombay. Some months ago—let's say about halfway between the first 2 time you heard the words *information superhighway* and the first time you wished you never had—I found myself tripping with compulsive regularity down the well-traveled information lane that leads to LambdaMOO, a very large and very busy rustic chateau built entirely of words. Nightly, I typed the commands that called those words onto my computer screen, dropping me with what seemed a warm electric thud inside the mansion's darkened coat closet, where I checked my quotidian identity, stepped into the persona and appearance of a minor character from a long-gone television sitcom, and stepped out into the glaring chatter of the crowded living room. Sometimes, when the mood struck me, I emerged as a dolphin instead.

I won't say why I chose to masquerade as Samantha Stevens's outlandish cousin,   3
or as the dolphin, or what exactly led to my mild but so-far incurable addiction to the
semifictional digital otherworlds known around the Internet as multi-user dimensions,
or MUDs. This isn't my story, after all. It's the story of a man named Mr. Bungle, and
of the ghostly sexual violence he committed in the halls of LambdaMOO, and most
importantly of the ways his violence and his victims challenged the 1000 and more residents of that surreal, magic-infested mansion to become, finally, the community so
many of them already believed they were.

That I was myself one of those residents has little direct bearing on the story's   4
events. I mention it only as a warning that my own perspective is perhaps too
steeped in the surreality and magic of the place to serve as an entirely appropriate
guide. For the Bungle Affair raises questions that—here on the brink of a future in
which human life may find itself as tightly enveloped in digital environments as it
is today in the architectural kind—demand a clear-eyed, sober, and unmystified
consideration. It asks us to shut our ears momentarily to the techno-utopian
ecstasies of West Coast cyberhippies and look without illusion upon the present
possibilities for building, in the on-line spaces of this world, societies more decent
and free than those mapped onto dirt and concrete and capital. It asks us to behold
the new bodies awaiting us in virtual space undazzled by their phantom powers, and
to get to the crucial work of sorting out the socially meaningful differences between
those bodies and our physical ones. And most forthrightly it asks us to wrap our
late-modern ontologies, epistemologies, sexual ethics, and common sense around
the curious notion of rape by voodoo doll—and to try not to warp them beyond
recognition in the process.

In short, the Bungle Affair dares me to explain it to you without resort to dime-   5
store mysticisms, and I fear I may have shape-shifted by the digital moonlight one too
many times to be quite up to the task. But I will do what I can, and can do no better I
suppose than to lead with the facts. For if nothing else about Mr. Bungle's case is
unambiguous, the facts at least are crystal clear.

The facts begin (as they often do) with a time and a place. The time was a Mon-   6
day night in March, and the place, as I've said, was the living room—which, due to
the inviting warmth of its decor, is so invariably packed with chitchatters as to be
roughly synonymous among LambdaMOOers with a party. So strong, indeed, is the
sense of convivial common ground invested in the living room that a cruel mind
could hardly imagine a better place in which to stage a violation of LambdaMOO's
communal spirit. And there was cruelty enough lurking in the appearance Mr. Bungle presented to the virtual world—he was at the time a fat, oleaginous, Bisquick-
faced clown dressed in cum-stained harlequin garb and girdled with a
mistletoe-and-hemlock belt whose buckle bore the quaint inscription "KISS ME
UNDER THIS, BITCH!" But whether cruelty motivated his choice of crime scene is
not among the established facts of the case. It is a fact only that he did choose the living room.

The remaining facts tell us a bit more about the inner world of Mr. Bungle,   7
though only perhaps that it couldn't have been a very comfortable place. They tell us

that he commenced his assault entirely ⋯⋯⋯ unprovoked, at or about 10 P.M. Pacific Standard Time. That he began by using his voodoo doll to force one of the room's occupants to sexually service him in a variety of more or less conventional ways. That this victim was legba, a Haitian trickster spirit of indeterminate gender, brown-skinned and wearing an expensive pearl gray suit, top hat, and dark glasses. That legba heaped vicious imprecations on him all the while and that he was soon ejected bodily from the room. That he hid himself away then in his private chambers somewhere on the mansion grounds and continued the attacks without interruption, since the voodoo doll worked just as well at a distance as in proximity. That he turned his attentions now to Starsinger, a rather pointedly nondescript female character, tall,

> **He commenced his assault entirely unprovoked, or at about 10 P.M. Pacific Standard Time. . . . [His] victim was legba, a Haitian trickster spirit of indeterminate gender, brown-skinned and wearing an expensive pearl gray suit.**

stout, and brown-haired, forcing her into unwanted liaisons with other individuals present in the room, among them legba, Bakunin (the well-known radical), and Juniper (the squirrel). That his actions grew progressively violent. That he made legba eat his/her own pubic hair. That he caused Starsinger to violate herself with a piece of kitchen cutlery. That his distant laughter echoed evilly in the living room with every successive outrage. That he could not be stopped until at last someone summoned Zippy, a wise and trusted old-timer who brought with him a gun of near wizardly powers, a gun that didn't kill but enveloped its targets in a cage impermeable even to a voodoo doll's powers. That Zippy fired his gun at Mr. Bungle, thwarting the doll at last and silencing the evil, distant laughter.

These particulars, as I said, are unambiguous. But they are far from simple, for the simple reason that every set of facts in virtual reality (or VR, as the locals abbreviate it) is shadowed by a second, complicating set: the "real-life" facts. And while a certain tension invariably buzzes in the gap between the hard, prosaic RL facts and their more fluid, dreamy VR counterparts, the dissonance in the Bungle case is striking. No hideous clowns or trickster spirits appear in the RL version of the incident, no voodoo dolls or wizard guns, indeed no rape at all as any RL court of law has yet defined it. The actors in the drama were university students for the most part, and they sat rather undramatically before computer screens the entire time, their only actions a spidery flitting of fingers across standard QWERTY keyboards. No bodies touched. Whatever physical interaction occurred consisted of a mingling of electronic signals sent from sites spread out between New York City and Sydney, Australia. Those signals met in LambdaMOO, certainly, just as the hideous clown and the living room party did, but what was LambdaMOO after all? Not an enchanted mansion or anything of the sort— just a middlingly complex database, maintained for experimental purposes inside a Xerox Corporation research computer in Palo Alto and open to public access via the Internet.

To be more precise about it, LambdaMOO was a MUD. Or to be yet more precise,   9
it was a subspecies of MUD known as a MOO, which is short for "MUD, Object-
Oriented." All of which means that it was a kind of database especially designed to
give users the vivid impression of moving through a physical space that in reality exists
only as descriptive data filed away on a hard drive. When users dial into LambdaMOO,
for instance, the program immediately presents them with a brief textual description of
one of the rooms of the database's fictional mansion (the coat closet, say). If the user
wants to leave this room, she can enter a command to move in a particular direction and
the database will replace the original description with a new one corresponding to the
room located in the direction she chose. When the new description scrolls across the
user's screen it lists not only the fixed features of the room but all its contents at that
moment—including things (tools, toys, weapons) and other users (each represented as
a "character" over which he or she has sole control).

As far as the database program is concerned, all of these entities—rooms, things,   10
characters—are just different subprograms that the program allows to interact according to rules very roughly mimicking the laws of the physical world. Characters may not
leave a room in a given direction, for instance, unless the room subprogram contains an
"exit" at that compass point. And if a character "says" or "does" something (as directed
by its user-owner), then only the users whose characters are also located in that room
will see the output describing the statement or action. Aside from such basic constraints, however, LambdaMOOers are allowed a broad freedom to create—they can
describe their characters any way they like, they can make rooms of their own and decorate them to taste, and they can build new objects almost at will. The combination of
all this busy user activity with the hard physics of the database can certainly induce a
lucid illusion of presence—but when all is said and done the only thing you *really* see
when you visit LambdaMOO is a kind of slow-crawling script, lines of dialogue and
stage direction creeping steadily up your computer screen.

Which is all just to say that, to the extent that Mr. Bungle's assault happened in   11
real life at all, it happened as a sort of Punch-and-Judy show, in which the puppets and
the scenery were made of nothing more substantial than digital code and snippets of
creative writing. The puppeteer behind Bungle, as it happened, was a young man logging in to the MOO from a New York University computer. He could have been Al
Gore for all any of the others knew, however, and he could have written Bungle's script
that night any way he chose. He could have sent a command to print the message "Mr.
Bungle, smiling a saintly smile, floats angelic near the ceiling of the living room, show-
ering joy and candy kisses down upon the heads of all below"—and everyone then
receiving output from the database's subprogram #17 (a/k/a the "living room") would
have seen that sentence on their screens.

Instead, he entered sadistic fantasies into the "voodoo doll," a subprogram that   12
served the not exactly kosher purpose of attributing actions to other characters that
their users did not actually write. And thus a woman in Haverford, Pennsylvania,
whose account on the MOO attached her to a character she called Starsinger, was
given the unasked-for opportunity to read the words "As if against her will,
Starsinger jabs a steak knife up her ass, causing immense joy. You hear Mr. Bungle

laughing evilly in the distance." And thus the woman in Seattle who had written herself the character called legba, with a view perhaps to tasting in imagination a deity's
freedom from the burdens of the gendered flesh, got to read similarly constructed
sentences in which legba, messenger of the gods, lord of crossroads and communications, suffered a brand of degradation all-too-customarily reserved for the embodied
female.

"Mostly voodoo dolls are amusing," wrote legba on the evening after Bungle's   13
rampage, posting a public statement to the widely read in-MOO mailing list called
social-issues, a forum for debate on matters of import to the entire populace. "And
mostly I tend to think that restrictive measures around here cause more trouble than
they prevent. But I also think that Mr. Bungle was being a vicious, vile fuckhead, and I
. . . want his sorry ass scattered from #17 to the Cinder Pile. I'm not calling for policies,
trials, or better jails. I'm not sure what I'm calling for. Virtual castration, if I could
manage it. Mostly, [this type of thing] doesn't happen here. Mostly, perhaps I thought
it wouldn't happen to me. Mostly, I trust people to conduct themselves with some
veneer of civility. Mostly, I want his ass."

Months later, the woman in Seattle would confide to me that as she wrote those   14
words posttraumatic tears were streaming down her face—a real-life fact that should
suffice to prove that the words' emotional content was no mere playacting. The precise
tenor of that content, however, its mingling of murderous rage and eyeball-rolling
annoyance, was a curious amalgam that neither the RL nor the VR facts alone can quite
account for. Where virtual reality and its conventions would have us believe that legba
and Starsinger were brutally raped in their own living room, here was the victim legba
scolding Mr. Bungle for a breach of "civility." Where real life, on the other hand,
insists the incident was only an episode in a free-form version of Dungeons and Dragons, confined to the realm of the symbolic and at no point threatening any player's life,
limb, or material well-being, here now was the player legba issuing aggrieved and
heartfelt calls for Mr. Bungle's dismemberment. Ludicrously excessive by RL's lights,
woefully understated by VR's, the tone of legba's response made sense only in the
buzzing, dissonant gap between them.

Which is to say it made the only kind of sense that *can* be made of MUDly phe-   15
nomena. For while the *facts* attached to any event born of a MUD's strange, ethereal
universe may march in straight, tandem lines separated neatly into the virtual and the
real, its meaning lies always in that gap. You learn this axiom early in your life as a
player, and it's of no small relevance to the Bungle case that you usually learn it
between the sheets, so to speak. Netsex, tinysex, virtual sex—however you name it, in
real-life reality it's nothing more than a 900-line encounter stripped of even the vesti-
gial physicality of the voice. And yet as any but the most inhibited of newbies can tell
you, it's possibly the headiest experience the very heady world of MUDs has to offer.
Amid flurries of even the most cursorily described caresses, sighs, and penetrations, the
glands do engage, and often as throbbingly as they would in a real-life assignation—
sometimes even more so, given the combined power of anonymity and textual sugges-
tiveness to unshackle deep-seated fantasies. And if the virtual setting and the
interplayer vibe are right, who knows? The heart may engage as well, stirring up pas-

sions as strong as many that bind lovers who observe the formality of trysting in the flesh.

To participate, therefore, in this disembodied enactment of life's most body-centered activity is to risk the realization that when it comes to sex, perhaps the body in question is not the physical one at all, but its psychic double, the bodylike self-representation we carry around in our heads. I know, I know, you've read Foucault and your mind is not quite blown by the notion that sex is never so much an exchange of fluids as it is an exchange of signs. But trust your friend Dr. Bombay, it's one thing to grasp the notion intellectually and quite another to feel it coursing through your veins amid the virtual steam of hot net-nookie. And it's a whole other mind-blowing trip altogether to encounter it thus as a college frosh, new to the net and still in the grip of hormonal hurricanes and high-school sexual mythologies. The shock can easily reverberate throughout an entire young worldview. Small wonder, then, that a newbie's first taste of MUD sex is often also the first time she or he surrenders wholly to the slippery terms of MUDish ontology, recognizing in a full-bodied way that what happens inside a MUD-made world is neither exactly real nor exactly make-believe, but profoundly, compellingly, and emotionally meaningful.

> **16**
>
> **A newbie's first taste of MUD sex is often also the first time she or he surrenders wholly to the slippery terms of MUDish ontology, recognizing in a full-bodied way that what happens inside a MUD-made world is neither exactly real nor exactly make-believe, but profoundly, compellingly, and emotionally meaningful.**

And small wonder indeed that the sexual nature of Mr. Bungle's crime provoked   17 such powerful feelings, and not just in legba (who, be it noted, was in real life a theory-savvy doctoral candidate and a longtime MOOer, but just as baffled and overwhelmed by the force of her own reaction, she later would attest, as any panting undergrad might have been). Even players who had never experienced MUD rape (the vast majority of male-presenting characters, but not as large a majority of the female-presenting as might be hoped) immediately appreciated its gravity and were moved to condemnation of the perp. legba's missive to *social issues* followed a strongly worded one from Zippy ("Well, well," it began, "no matter what else happens on Lambda, I can always be sure that some jerk is going to reinforce my low opinion of humanity") and was itself followed by others from Moriah, Raccoon, Crawfish, and evangeline. Starsinger also let her feelings ("pissed") be known. And even Jander, the Clueless Samaritan who had responded to Bungle's cries for help and uncaged him shortly after the incident, expressed his regret once apprised of Bungle's deeds, which he allowed to be "despicable."

A sense was brewing that something needed to be done—done soon and in some-   18 thing like an organized fashion—about Mr. Bungle, in particular, and about MUD rape, in general. Regarding the general problem, evangeline, who identified herself as a survivor of both virtual rape ("many times over") and real-life sexual assault, floated a cautious proposal for a MOO-wide powwow on the subject of virtual sex offenses and what mechanisms if any might be put in place to deal with their future occurrence. As for the specific problem, the answer no doubt seemed obvious to many. But it wasn't until the evening of the second day after the incident that legba, finally and rather solemnly, gave it voice: "I am requesting that Mr. Bungle be toaded for raping Starsinger and I. I have never done this before, and have thought about it for days. He hurt us both."

That was all. Three simple sentences posted to *social*. Reading them, an outsider   19 might never guess that they were an application for a death warrant. Even an outsider familiar with other MUDs might not guess it, since in many of them "toading" still refers to a command that, true to the gameworlds' sword-and-sorcery origins, simply turns a player into a toad, wiping the player's description and attributes and replacing them with those of the slimy amphibian. Bad luck for sure, but not quite as bad as what happens when the same command is invoked in the MOOish strains of MUD: not only are the description and attributes of the toaded player erased, but the account itself goes too. The annihilation of the character, thus, is total.

And nothing less than total annihilation, it seemed, would do to settle Lambda-   20 MOO's accounts with Mr. Bungle. Within minutes of the posting of legba's appeal, SamIAm, the Australian Deleuzean, who had witnessed much of the attack from the back room of his suburban Sydney home, seconded the motion with a brief message crisply entitled "Toad the fukr." SamIAm's posting was seconded almost as quickly by that of Bakunin, covictim of Mr. Bungle and well-known radical, who in real life happened also to be married to the real-life legba. And over the course of the next 24 hours as many as 50 players made it known, on *social* and in a variety of other forms and forums, that they would be pleased to see Mr. Bungle erased from the face of the MOO. And with dissent so far confined to a dozen or so antitoading hardliners, the numbers suggested that the citizenry was indeed moving towards a resolve to have Bungle's virtual head.

There was one small but stubborn obstacle in the way of this resolve, however,   21 and that was a curious state of social affairs known in some quarters of the MOO as the New Direction. It was all very fine, you see, for the LambdaMOO rabble to get it in their heads to liquidate one of their peers, but when the time came to actually do the deed it would require the services of a nobler class of character. It would require a wizard. Master-programmers of the MOO, spelunkers of the database's deepest code-structures and custodians of its day-to-day administrative trivia, wizards are also the only players empowered to issue the toad command, a feature maintained on nearly all MUDs as a quick-and-dirty means of social control. But the wizards of LambdaMOO, after years of adjudicating all manner of interplayer disputes with little to show for it but their own weariness and the smoldering resentment of the general populace, had decided they'd had enough of the social sphere. And so, four months before the Bungle incident, the archwizard Haakon (known in RL as Pavel Curtis, Xerox researcher and LambdaMOO's principal architect) formalized this decision in a document called "LambdaMOO Takes a New Direction," which he placed in the living room for all to see. In it, Haakon announced that the wizards from that day forth were pure technicians. From then on, they would make no decision affecting the social life of the MOO, but only implement whatever decisions the community as a whole directed them to. From then on, it was decreed, LambdaMOO would just have to grow up and solve its problems on its own.

Faced with the task of inventing its own self-governance from scratch, the LambdaMOO population had so far done what any other loose, amorphous agglomeration of individuals would have done: they'd let it slide. But now the task took on new urgency. Since getting the wizards to toad Mr. Bungle (or to toad the likes of him in the future) required a convincing case that the cry for his head came from the community at large, then the community itself would have to be defined; and if the community was to be convincingly defined, then some form of social organization, no matter how rudimentary, would have to be settled on. And thus, as if against its will, the question of what to do about Mr. Bungle began to shape itself into a sort of referendum on the political future of the MOO. Arguments broke out on *social and elsewhere that had only superficially to do with Bungle (since everyone agreed he was a cad) and everything to do with where the participants stood on LambdaMOO's crazy-quilty political map. Parliamentarian legalist types argued that unfortunately Bungle could not legitimately be toaded at all, since there were no explicit MOO rules against rape, or against just about anything else—and the sooner such rules were established, they added, and maybe even a full-blown judiciary system complete with elected officials and prisons to enforce those rules, the better. Others, with a royalist streak in them, seemed to feel that Bungle's as-yet-unpunished outrage only proved this New Direction silliness had gone on long enough, and that it was high time the wizardocracy returned to the position of swift and decisive leadership their player class was born to. 22

And then there were what I'll call the technolibertarians. For them, MUD rapists were of course assholes, but the presence of assholes on the system was a technical inevitability, like noise on a phone line, and best dealt with not through repressive social disciplinary mechanisms but through the timely deployment of defensive software tools. Some asshole blasting violent, graphic language at you? Don't whine to the authorities about it—hit the @gag command and the asshole's statements will be blocked from your screen (and only yours). It's simple, it's effective, and it censors no one. 23

But the Bungle case was rather hard on such arguments. For one thing, the extremely public nature of the living room meant that gagging would spare the victims only from witnessing their own violation, but not from having others witness it. You might want to argue that what those victims didn't directly experience couldn't hurt them, but consider how that wisdom would sound to a woman who'd been, say, fondled by strangers while passed out drunk and you have a rough idea how it might go over with a crowd of hard-core MOOers. Consider, for another thing, that many of the biologically female participants in the Bungle debate had been around long enough to grow lethally weary of the gag-and-get-over-it school of virtual-rape counseling, with its fine line between empowering victims and holding them responsible for their own suffering, and its shrugging indifference to the window of pain between the moment the rape-text starts flowing and the moment a gag shuts it off. From the outset it was clear that the technolibertarians were going to have to tiptoe through this issue with care, and for the most part they did. 24

Yet no position was trickier to maintain than that of the MOO's resident anar- 25
chists. Like the technolibbers, the anarchists didn't care much for punishments or policies or power elites. Like them, they hoped the MOO could be a place where people
interacted fulfillingly without the need for such things. But their high hopes were complicated, in general, by a somewhat less thoroughgoing faith in technology ("Even if
you can't tear down the master's house with the master's tools"—read a slogan written
into one anarchist player's self-description—"it is a damned good place to start".) And
at present they were additionally complicated by the fact that the most vocal anarchists
in the discussion were none other than legba, Bakunin, and SamIAm, who wanted to
see Mr. Bungle toaded as badly as anyone did.

Needless to say, a pro death penalty platform is not an especially comfortable 26
one for an anarchist to sit on, so these particular anarchists were now at great pains
to sever the conceptual ties between toading and capital punishment. Toading, they
insisted (almost convincingly), was much more closely analogous to banishment; it
was a kind of turning of the communal back on the offending party, a collective
action which, if carried out properly, was entirely consistent with anarchist models
of community. And carrying it out properly meant first and foremost building a consensus around it—a messy process for which there were no easy technocratic substi-
tutes. It was going to take plenty of good old-fashioned, jawbone-intensive
grassroots organizing.

So that when the time came, at 7 P.M. PST on the evening of the third day after 27
the occurrence in the living room, to gather in evangeline's room for her proposed
real-time open conclave, Bakunin and legba were among the first to arrive. But this
was hardly to be an anarchist-dominated affair, for the room was crowding rapidly
with representatives of all the MOO's political stripes, and even a few wizards. Hag-
bard showed up, and Autumn and Quastro, Puff, JoeFeedback, L-dopa and Bloaf,
HerkieCosmo, Silver Rocket, Karl Porcupine, Matchstick—the names piled up and
the discussion gathered momentum under their weight. Arguments multiplied and
mingled, players talked past and through each
other, the textual clutter of utterances and ges-
tures filled up the screen like thick cigar smoke.
Peaking in number at around 30, this was one of
the largest crowds that ever gathered in a single
LambdaMOO chamber, and while evangeline had
given her place a description that made it "infinite in expanse and fluid in form," it now seemed
anything but roomy. You could almost feel
the claustrophobic air of the place, dank and
overheated by virtual bodies, pressing against
your skin.

You could almost feel the claustrophobic air of the place, dank and overheated by virtual bodies, pressing against your skin.

I know you could because I too was there, making my lone and insignificant 28
appearance in this story. Completely ignorant of any of the goings-on that had led to
the meeting, I wandered in purely to see what the crowd was about, and though I
observed the proceedings for a good while, I confess I found it hard to grasp what was
going on. I was still the rankest of newbies, then, my MOO legs still too unsteady to

make the leaps of faith, logic, and empathy required to meet the spectacle on its own terms. I was fascinated by the concept of virtual rape, but I couldn't quite take it seriously.

In this, though, I was in a small and mostly silent minority, for the discussion that raged around me was of an almost unrelieved earnestness, bent it seemed on examining every last aspect and implication of Mr. Bungle's crime. There were the central questions, of course: thumbs up or down on Bungle's virtual existence? And if down, how then to insure that his toading was not just some isolated lynching but a first step toward shaping LambdaMOO into a legitimate community? Surrounding these, however, a tangle of weighty side issues proliferated. What, some wondered, was the real-life legal status of the offense? Could Bungle's university administrators punish him for sexual harassment? Could he be prosecuted under California state laws against obscene phone calls? Little enthusiasm was shown for pursuing either of these lines of action, which testifies both to the uniqueness of the crime and to the nimbleness with which the discussants were negotiating its idiosyncrasies. Many were the casual references to Bungle's deed as simply "rape," but these in no way implied that the players had lost sight of all distinctions between the virtual and physical versions, or that they believed Bungle should be dealt with in the same way a real-life criminal would. He had committed a MOO crime, and his punishment, if any, would be meted out via the MOO.

On the other hand, little patience was shown toward any attempts to downplay the seriousness of what Mr. Bungle had done. When the affable HerkieCosmo proposed, more in the way of an hypothesis than an assertion, that "perhaps it's better to release . . . violent tendencies in a virtual environment rather than in real life," he was tut-tutted so swiftly and relentlessly that he withdrew the hypothesis altogether, apologizing humbly as he did so. Not that the assembly was averse to putting matters into a more philosophical perspective. "Where does the body end and the mind begin?" young Quastro asked, amid recurring attempts to fine-tune the differences between real and virtual violence. "Is not the mind a part of the body?" "In MOO, the body IS the mind," offered HerkieCosmo gamely, and not at all implausibly, demonstrating the ease with which very knotty metaphysical conundrums come undone in VR. The not-so-aptly named Obvious seemed to agree, arriving after deep consideration of the nature of Bungle's crime at the hardly novel yet now somehow newly resonant conjecture "All reality might consist of ideas, who knows."

On these and other matters the anarchists, the libertarians, the legalists, the wizardists—and the wizards—all had their thoughtful say. But as the evening wore on and the talk grew more heated and more heady, it seemed increasingly clear that the vigorous intelligence being brought to bear on this swarm of issues wasn't going to result in anything remotely like resolution. The perspectives were just too varied, the meme-scape just too slippery. Again and again, arguments that looked at first to be heading in a decisive direction ended up chasing their own tails; and slowly, depressingly, a dusty haze of irrelevance gathered over the proceedings.

It was almost a relief, therefore, when midway through the evening Mr. Bungle himself, the living, breathing cause of all this talk, teleported into the room. Not that it was much of a surprise. Oddly enough, in the three days since his release from Zippy's cage, Bungle had returned more than once to wander the public spaces of LambdaMOO, walking willingly into one of the fiercest storms of ill will and invective ever to rain down on a player. He'd been taking it all with a curious and mostly silent passivity, and when challenged face to virtual face by both legba and the genderless elder statescharacter PatGently to defend himself on *social,* he'd demurred, mumbling something about Christ and expiation. He was equally quiet now, and his reception was still uniformly cool. legba fixed an arctic stare on him—"no hate, no anger, no interest at all. Just . . . watching." Others were more actively unfriendly. "Asshole," spat Karl Porcupine, "creep." But the harshest of the MOO's hostility toward him had already been vented, and the attention he drew now was motivated more, it seemed, by the opportunity to probe the rapist's mind, to find out what made it tick and if possible how to get it to tick differently. In short, they wanted to know why he'd done it. So they asked him.

And Mr. Bungle thought about it. And as eddies of discussion and debate contin- 33 ued to swirl around him, he thought about it some more. And then he said this:

> *I engaged in a bit of a psychological device that is called thought-polarization, the fact that this is not RL simply added to heighten the affect of the device. It was purely a sequence of events with no consequence on my RL existence.*

They might have known. Stilted though its diction was, the gist of the answer was 34 simple, and something many in the room had probably already surmised: Mr. Bungle was a psycho. Not, perhaps, in real life—but then in real life it's possible for reasonable people to assume, as Bungle clearly did, that what transpires between word-costumed characters within the boundaries of a make-believe world is, if not mere play, then at most some kind of emotional laboratory experiment. Inside the MOO, however, such thinking marked a person as one of two basically subcompetent types. The first was the newbie, in which case the confusion was understandable, since there were few MOOers who had not, upon their first visits as anonymous "guest" characters, mistaken the place for a vast playpen in which they might act out their wildest fantasies without fear of censure. Only with time and the acquisition of a fixed character do players tend to make the critical passage from anonymity to pseudonymity, developing the concern for their character's reputation that marks the attainment of virtual adulthood. But while Mr. Bungle hadn't been around as long as most MOOers, he'd been around long enough to leave his newbie status behind, and his delusional statement therefore placed him among the second type: the sociopath.

And as there is but small percentage in arguing with a head case, the room's atten- 35 tion gradually abandoned Mr. Bungle and returned to the discussions that had previously occupied it. But if the debate had been edging toward ineffectuality before, Bungle's anticlimactic appearance had evidently robbed it of any forward motion whatsoever. What's more, from his lonely corner of the room Mr. Bungle kept issuing periodic expressions of a prickly sort of remorse, interlaced with sarcasm and belligerence, and though it was hard to tell if he wasn't still just conducting his experiments, some people thought his regret genuine enough that maybe he didn't deserve to be toaded after all. Logically, of course, discussion of the principal issues at hand didn't require unanimous belief that Bungle was an irredeemable bastard, but now that cracks were showing in that unanimity, the last of the meeting's fervor seemed to be draining out through them.

People started drifting away. Mr. Bungle left first, then others followed—one by one, in twos and threes, hugging friends and waving goodnight. By 9:45 only a handful remained, and the great debate had wound down into casual conversation, the melancholy remains of another fruitless good idea. The arguments had been well-honed, certainly, and perhaps might prove useful in some as-yet-unclear long run. But at this point what seemed clear was that evangeline's meeting had died, at last, and without any practical results to mark its passing. 36

It was also at this point, most likely, that JoeFeedback reached his decision. JoeFeedback was a wizard, a taciturn sort of fellow who'd sat brooding on the sidelines all evening. He hadn't said a lot, but what he had said indicated that he took the crime committed against legba and Starsinger very seriously, and that he felt no particular compassion toward the character who had committed it. But on the other hand he had made it equally plain that he took the elimination of a fellow player just as seriously, and moreover that he had no desire to return to the days of wizardly fiat. It must have been difficult, therefore, to reconcile the conflicting impulses churning within him at that moment. In fact, it was probably impossible, for as much as he would have liked to make himself an instrument of LambdaMOO's collective will, he surely realized that under the present order of things he must in the final analysis either act alone or not act at all. 37

So JoeFeedback acted alone. 38

He told the lingering few players in the room that he had to go, and then he went. It was a minute or two before ten. He did it quietly and he did it privately, but all anyone had to do to know he'd done it was to type the @who command, which was normally what you typed if you wanted to know a player's present location and the time he last logged in. But if you had run a @who on Mr. Bungle not too long after JoeFeedback left evangeline's room, the database would have told you something different. 39

"Mr. Bungle," it would have said, "is not the name of any player." 40

The date, as it happened, was April Fool's Day, and it would still be April Fool's Day for another two hours. But this was no joke: Mr. Bungle was truly dead and truly gone. 41

They say that LambdaMOO has never been the same since Mr. Bungle's toading. They say as well that nothing's really changed. And though it skirts the fuzziest of dream-logics to say that both these statements are true, the MOO is just the sort of fuzzy, dreamlike place in which such contradictions thrive. 42

> **They say that LambdaMOO has never been the same since Mr. Bungle's toading. They say as well that nothing's really changed.**

Certainly whatever civil society now informs LambdaMOO owes its existence to the Bungle Affair. The archwizard Haakon made sure of that. Away on business for the duration of the episode, Haakon returned to find its wreckage strewn across the tiny universe 43 he'd set in motion. The death of a player, the trauma of several others, and the angst-ridden conscience of his colleague JoeFeedback presented themselves to his concerned and astonished attention, and he resolved to see if he couldn't learn some lesson from it all. For the better part of a day he brooded over the record of events and arguments left in *social,* then he sat pondering the chaotically evolving shape of his creation, and at the day's end he descended once again into the social arena of the MOO with another history-altering proclamation.

It was probably his last, for what he now decreed was the final, missing piece of   44
the New Direction. In a few days, Haakon announced, he would build into the database a system of petitions and ballots whereby anyone could put to popular vote any social scheme requiring wizardly powers for its implementation, with the results of the vote to be binding on the wizards. At last and for good, the awkward gap between the will of the players and the efficacy of the technicians would be closed. And though some anarchists grumbled about the irony of Haakon's dictatorially imposing universal suffrage on an unconsulted populace, in general the citizens of LambdaMOO seemed to find it hard to fault a system more purely democratic than any that could ever exist in real life. Eight months and a dozen ballot measures later, widespread participation in the new regime has produced a small arsenal of mechanisms for dealing with the types of violence that called the system into being. MOO residents now have access to a @boot command, for instance, with which to summarily eject berserker "guest" characters. And players can bring suit against one another through an ad hoc arbitration system in which mutually agreed-upon judges have at their disposition the full range of wizardly punishments—up to and including the capital.

Yet the continued dependence on death as the ultimate keeper of the peace suggests   45
that this new MOO order may not be built on the most solid of foundations. For if life on LambdaMOO began to acquire more coherence in the wake of the toading, death retained all the fuzziness of pre-Bungle days. This truth was rather dramatically borne out, not too many days after Bungle departed, by the arrival of a strange new character named Dr. Jest. There was a forceful eccentricity to the newcomer's manner, but the oddest thing about his style was its striking yet unnameable familiarity. And when he developed the annoying habit of stuffing fellow players into a jar containing a tiny simulacrum of a certain deceased rapist, the source of this familiarity became obvious:

Mr. Bungle had risen from the grave.   46

In itself, Bungle's reincarnation as Dr. Jest was a remarkable turn of events, but   47
perhaps even more remarkable was the utter lack of amazement with which the LambdaMOO public took note of it. To be sure, many residents were appalled by the brazenness of Bungle's return. In fact, one of the first petitions circulated under the new voting system was a request for Dr. Jest's toading that almost immediately gathered 52 signatures (but has failed so far to reach ballot status). Yet few were unaware of the ease with which the toad proscription could be circumvented—all the toadee had to do (all the ur-Bungle at NYU presumably had done) was to go to the minor hassle of acquiring a new Internet account, and LambdaMOO's character registration program would then simply treat the known felon as an entirely new and innocent person. Nor was this ease generally understood to represent a failure of toading's social disciplinary function. On the contrary, it only underlined the truism (repeated many times through-

out the debate over Mr. Bungle's fate) that his punishment, ultimately, had been no more or less symbolic than his crime.

What *was* surprising, however, was that Mr. Bungle/Dr. Jest seemed to have   48
taken the symbolism to heart. Dark themes still obsessed him—the objects he created gave off wafts of Nazi imagery and medical torture—but he no longer radiated the aggressively antisocial vibes he had before. He was a lot less unpleasant to look at (the outrageously seedy clown description had been replaced by that of a mildly creepy but actually rather natty young man, with "blue eyes . . . suggestive of conspiracy, untamed eroticism, and perhaps a sense of understanding of the future"), and aside from the occasional jar-stuffing incident, he was also a lot less dangerous to be around. It was obvious he'd undergone some sort of personal transformation in the days since I'd first glimpsed him back in evangeline's crowded room—nothing radical maybe, but powerful nonetheless, and resonant enough with my own experience, I felt, that it might be more than professionally interesting to talk with him, and perhaps compare notes.

For I too was undergoing a transformation in the aftermath of that night in evan-   49
geline's, and I'm still not entirely sure what to make of it. As I pursued my runaway fascination with the discussion I had heard there, as I pored over the *social* debate and got to know legba and some of the other victims and witnesses, I could feel my newbie consciousness falling away from me. Where before I'd found it hard to take virtual rape seriously, I now was finding it difficult to remember how I could ever *not* have taken it seriously. I was proud to have arrived at this perspective—it felt like an exotic sort of achievement, and it definitely made my ongoing experience of the MOO a richer one.

But it was also having some unsettling effects on the way I looked at the rest of   50
the world. Sometimes, for instance, it was hard for me to understand why RL society classifies RL rape alongside crimes against person or property. Since rape can occur without any physical pain or damage, I found myself reasoning, then it must be classed as a crime against the mind—more intimately and deeply hurtful, to be sure, than cross burnings, wolf whistles, and virtual rape, but undeniably located on the same conceptual continuum. I did not, however, conclude as a result that rapists were protected in any fashion by the First Amendment. Quite the opposite, in fact: the more seriously I took the notion of virtual rape, the less seriously I was able to take the notion of freedom of speech, with its tidy division of the world into the symbolic and the real.

Let me assure you, though, that I am not presenting these thoughts as arguments. I   51
offer them, rather, as a picture of the sort of mind-set that deep immersion in a virtual world has inspired in me. I offer them also, therefore, as a kind of prophecy. For whatever else these thoughts tell me, I have come to believe that they announce the final stages of our decades-long passage into the Information Age, a paradigm shift that the classic liberal firewall between word and deed (itself a product of an earlier paradigm shift commonly known as the Enlightenment) is not likely to survive intact. After all, anyone the least bit familiar with the workings of the new era's definitive technology, the computer, knows that it operates on a principle impracticably difficult to distinguish

from the pre-Enlightenment principle of the magic word: the commands you type into a computer are a kind of speech that doesn't so much communicate as *make things happen,* directly and ineluctably, the same way pulling a trigger does. They are incantations, in other words, and anyone at all attuned to the technosocial megatrends of the moment—from the growing dependence of economies on the global flow of intensely fetishized words and numbers to the burgeoning ability of bioengineers to speak the spells written in the four-letter text of DNA—knows that the logic of the incantation is rapidly permeating the fabric of our lives.

And it's precisely this logic that provides the real magic in a place like Lamb- 52 daMOO—not the fictive trappings of voodoo and shapeshifting and wizardry, but the conflation of speech and act that's inevitable in any computer-mediated world, be it Lambda or the increasingly wired world at large. This is dangerous magic, to be sure, a potential threat—if misconstrued or misapplied—to our always precarious freedoms of expression, and as someone who lives by his words I do not take the threat lightly. And yet, on the other hand, I can no longer convince myself that our wishful insulation of language from the realm of action has ever been anything but a valuable kludge, a philosophically damaged stopgap against oppression that would just have to do till something truer and more elegant came along.

Am I wrong to think this truer, more elegant thing can be found on LambdaMOO? 53 Perhaps, but I continue to seek it there, sensing its presence just beneath the surface of every interaction. I have even thought, as I said, that discussing with Dr. Jest our shared experience of the workings of the MOO might help me in my search. But when that notion first occurred to me, I still felt somewhat intimidated by his lingering criminal aura, and I hemmed and hawed a good long time before finally resolving to drop him MOO-mail requesting an interview. By then it was too late. For reasons known only to himself, Dr. Jest had stopped logging in. Maybe he'd grown bored with the MOO. Maybe the loneliness of ostracism had gotten to him. Maybe a psycho whim had carried him far away or maybe he'd quietly acquired a third character and started life over with a cleaner slate.

Wherever he'd gone, though, he left behind the room he'd created for himself—a 54 treehouse "tastefully decorated" with rare-book shelves, an operating table, and a life-size William S. Burroughs doll—and he left it unlocked. So I took to checking in there occasionally, and I still do from time to time. I head out of my own cozy nook (inside a TV set inside the little red hotel inside the Monopoly board inside the dining room of LambdaMOO), and I teleport on over to the treehouse, where the room description always tells me Dr. Jest is present but asleep, in the conventional depiction for disconnected characters. The not-quite-emptiness of the abandoned room invariably instills in me an uncomfortable mix of melancholy and the creeps, and I stick around only on the off chance that Dr. Jest will wake up, say hello, and share his understanding of the future with me.

He won't, of course, but this is no great loss. Increasingly, the complex magic of 55 the MOO interests me more as a way to live the present than to understand the future. And it's usually not long before I leave Dr. Jest's lonely treehouse and head back to the mansion, to see some friends.

SECOND THOUGHTS

1. Near the beginning of the essay, Dibbell offers "a warning" about being "too steeped in the surreality and magic" of the online world he describes to be very objective (¶ 4), while later he acknowledges that up until the virtual meeting in evangeline's room he was "still the rankest of newbies" (newcomers) to cyberspace and "couldn't quite take [virtual rape] seriously" (¶ 28). What evidence do you see of these conflicting perspectives—of veteran versus newbie—in the way that Dibbell tells the story of LambdaMOO?

2. How do you feel about legba's response, and the response of other LambdaMOO participants, to Bungle's attack? How persuaded are you by Dibbell's argument that "what happens inside a MUD-made world is . . . profoundly, compellingly, and emotionally meaningful" (¶ 16)?

3. To make a decision about "toading" Bungle, according to Dibbell, the residents of LambdaMOO first had to define themselves as a community or social organization (¶ 22). What political groups does he suggest were the major forces contending, at the meeting in evangeline's room, over this definition? How would you analyze the results and aftermath of this meeting in terms of those political forces—who won and who lost?

4. Explain the "transformation" that Dibbell undergoes and the conclusions he reaches in the last several paragraphs. What's your view about the relationship, pondered by Dibbell, between virtual rape and free speech?

Women and Children First

Laura Miller

Gender and the Settling of the
Electronic Frontier

Laura Miller (b. 1960) is a senior editor at the Internet magazine *Salon* (<www.salonmagazine. com/>). Her writing has also appeared in *The New York Times,* the *Village Voice, Sight & Sound, Spin, Wired,* and the *San Francisco Examiner.* Formerly she was the publicist for a feminist cooperative that runs a San Francisco sex toy store and mail order company. This essay originally appeared in *Resisting the Virtual Life: The Culture and Politics of Information* (City Lights, 1995), a collection edited by Iain Boal and James Brooks that offers, as they write in the preface, a critical view of technology and its associated "values, in our view, too often detrimental to a more human life."

W hen *Newsweek* (May 16, 1994) ran an article entitled "Men, Women and   1
Computers," all hell broke out on the Net, particularly on the on-line service I've participated in for six years, The Well (Whole Earth 'Lectronic Link). "Cyber-space, it turns out," declared *Newsweek*'s Nancy Kantrowitz, "isn't much of an Eden after all. It's marred by just as many sexist ruts and gender conflicts as the Real World. . . . Women often feel about as welcome as a system crash." "It was horrible. Awful, poorly researched, unsubstantiated drivel," one member wrote, a sentiment echoed throughout some 480 postings.

However egregious the errors in the article (some sources maintain that they were   2
incorrectly quoted), it's only one of several mainstream media depictions of the Net as an environment hostile to women. Even women who had been complaining about on-line gender relations found themselves increasingly annoyed by what one Well member termed the "cyberbabe harassment" angle that seems to typify media coverage of the issue. Reified in the pages of *Newsweek* and other journals, what had once been the topic of discussion by insiders—on-line commentary is informal, conversational, and often spontaneous—became a journalistic "fact" about the Net known by complete strangers and novices. In a matter of months, the airy stuff of bitch sessions became widespread, hardened stereotypes.

At the same time, the Internet has come under increasing scrutiny as it mutates   3
from an obscure, freewheeling web of computer networks used by a small elite of academics, scientists, and hobbyists to . . . well, nobody seems to know exactly what. But the business press prints vague, fevered prophecies of fabulous wealth, and a bonanza mentality has blossomed. With it comes big business and the government,

intent on regulating this amorphous medium into a manageable and profitable industry. The Net's history of informal self-regulation and its wide libertarian streak guarantee that battles like the one over the Clipper chip (a mandatory decoding device that would make all encrypted data readable by federal agents) will be only the first among many.

Yet the threat of regulation is built into the very mythos used to conceptualize the   4
Net by its defenders—and gender plays a crucial role in that threat. However revolutionary the technologized interactions of on-line communities may seem, we understand them by deploying a set of very familiar metaphors from the rich figurative soup of American culture. Would different metaphors have allowed the Net a different, better historical trajectory? Perhaps not, but the way we choose to describe the Net now encourages us to see regulation as its inevitable fate. And, by examining how gender roles provide a foundation for the intensification of such social controls, we can illuminate the way those roles proscribe the freedoms of men as well as women.

For months I mistakenly referred to the EFF (an organization founded by John   5
Perry Barlow* and Lotus 1-2-3 designer Mitch Kapor to foster access to, and further the discursive freedom of, on-line communications) as "The Electronic Freedom Foundation," instead of by its actual name, "The Electronic Frontier Foundation." Once corrected, I was struck by how intimately related the ideas "frontier" and "freedom" are in the Western mythos. The *frontier,* as a realm of limitless possibilities and few social controls, hovers, grail-like, in the American psyche, the dream our national identity is based on, but a dream that's always, somehow, just vanishing away.

Once made, the choice to see the Net as a frontier feels unavoidable, but it's actu-   6
ally quite problematic. The word "frontier" has traditionally described a place, if not land then the limitless "final frontier" of space. The Net, on the other hand, occupies precisely no physical space (although the computers and phone lines that make it possible do). It is a completely bodiless, symbolic thing with no discernable boundaries or location. The land of the American frontier did not become a "frontier" until Europeans determined to conquer it, but the continent existed before the intention to settle it. Unlike land, the Net was created by its pioneers.

Most peculiar, then, is the choice of the word "frontier" to describe an artifact so   7
humanly constructed that it only exists as ideas or information. For central to the idea of the frontier is that it contains no (or very few) other people—fewer than two per square mile according to the nineteenth-century historian Frederick Turner. The freedom the frontier promises is a liberation from the demands of society, while the Net (I'm thinking now of Usenet) has nothing but society to offer. Without other people, news groups, mailing lists, and files simply wouldn't exist and e-mail would be purposeless. Unlike real space, cyberspace must be shared.

Nevertheless, the choice of a spatial metaphor (credited to the science-fiction   8
novelist William Gibson,[†] who coined the term "cyberspace"), however awkward, isn't surprising. Psychologist Julian Jaynes has pointed out that geographical analo-

---

*See Barlow's essay, p. 164 (ed.).

[†]See stories by Gibson, p. 48 and p. 369 (ed.).

gies have long predominated humanity's efforts to conceptualize—map out—con- sciousness. Unfortunately, these analogies bring with them a heavy load of baggage comparable to Pandora's box: open it and a complex series of problems have come to stay.

The frontier exists beyond the edge of settled or owned land. As the land that   9 doesn't belong to anybody (or to people who "don't count," like Native Americans), it is on the verge of being acquired; currently unowned, but still ownable. Just as the ideal of chastity makes virginity sexually provocative, so does the unclaimed territory invite settlers, irresistibly so. Americans regard the lost geographical frontier with a melan- choly, voluptuous fatalism—we had no choice but to advance upon it and it had no alternative but to submit. When an EFF member compares the Clipper chip to barbed wire encroaching on the prairie, doesn't he realize the surrender implied in his metaphor?

The frontier is a lawless   10

society of men, a milieu in

which physical strength,

courage, and personal

charisma supplant

The psychosexual undercurrents (if anyone still thinks of them as "under") in the idea of civilization's phallic intrusion into nature's pas- sive, feminine space have been observed, exhaustively, elsewhere. The classic Western narrative is actually far more concerned with social relationships than conflicts between man and nature. In these stories, the frontier is a lawless society of men, a milieu in which physical strength, courage, and personal charisma supplant institutional authority and violent conflict is the accepted means of settling disputes. The Western narrative connects plea- surably with the American romance of individu- alistic masculinity; small wonder that the predominantly male founders of the Net's culture found it so appealing.

institutional authority and

violent conflict is the

accepted means of settling

disputes.

When civilization arrives on the frontier, it comes dressed in skirts and short pants.   11 In the archetypal 1939 movie *Dodge City,* Wade Hatton (Errol Flynn) refuses to accept the position of marshal because he prefers the footloose life of a trail driver. Abbie Irv- ing (Olivia de Haviland), a recent arrival from the civilized East, scolds him for his unwillingness to accept and advance the cause of law; she can't function (in her job as crusading journalist) in a town governed by brute force. It takes the accidental killing of a child in a street brawl for Hatton to realize that he must pin on the badge and clean up Dodge City.

In the Western mythos, civilization is necessary because women and children are   12 victimized in conditions of freedom. Introduce women and children into a frontier town and the law must follow because women and children must be protected. Women, in fact, are usually the most vocal proponents of the conversion from frontier justice to civil society.

The imperiled women and children of the Western narrative make their appear-   13 ance today in newspaper and magazine articles that focus on the intimidation and sex- ual harassment of women on line and reports of pedophiles trolling for victims in computerized chat rooms. If on-line women successfully contest these attempts to depict them as the beleaguered prey of brutish men, expect the pedophile to assume a larger profile in arguments that the Net is out of control.

In the meantime, the media prefer to cast women as the victims, probably because   14 many women actively participate in the call for greater regulation of on-line interactions, just as Abbie Irving urges Wade Hatton to bring the rule of law to Dodge City. These requests have a long cultural tradition, based on the idea that women, like children, constitute a peculiarly vulnerable class of people who require special protection from the elements of society men are expected to confront alone. In an insufficiently civilized society like the frontier, women, by virtue of this childlike vulnerability, are thought to live under the constant threat of kidnap, abuse, murder, and especially rape.

Women, who have every right to expect that crimes against their person will be   15 rigorously prosecuted, should nevertheless regard the notion of special protections (chivalry, by another name) with suspicion. Based as it is on the idea that women are inherently weak and incapable of self-defense and that men are innately predatory, it actually reinforces the power imbalance between the sexes, with its roots in the concept of women as property, constantly under siege and requiring the vigilant protection of their male owners. If the romance of the frontier arises from the promise of vast stretches of unowned land, an escape from the restrictions of a society based on private property, the introduction of women spoils that dream by reintroducing the imperative of property in their own persons.

How does any of this relate to on-line interactions, which occur not on a desert   16 landscape but in a complex, technological society where women are supposed to command equal status with men? It accompanies us as a set of unexamined assumptions about what it means to be male or female, assumptions that we believe are rooted in the imperatives of our bodies. These assumptions follow us into the bodiless realm of cyberspace, a forum where, as one scholar put it, "participants are washed clean of the stigmata of their real 'selves' and are free to invent new ones to their tastes." Perhaps some observers feel that the replication of gender roles in a context where the absence of bodies supposedly makes them superfluous proves exactly how innate those roles are. Instead, I see in the relentless attempts to interpret on-line interactions as highly gendered, an intimation of just how artificial, how created, our gender system is. If it comes "naturally," why does it need to be perpetually defended and reasserted?

Complaints about the treatment of women on line fall into three categories: that   17 women are subjected to excessive, unwanted sexual attention, that the prevailing style of on-line discussion turns women off, and that women are singled out by male participants for exceptionally dismissive or hostile treatment. In making these assertions, the *Newsweek* article and other stories on the issue do echo grievances that some on-line women have made for years. And, without a doubt, people have encountered sexual come-ons, aggressive debating tactics, and ad hominem attacks on the Net. However, individual users interpret such events in widely different ways, and to generalize from those interpretations to describe the experiences of women and men as a whole is a rash leap indeed.

I am one of many women who don't recognize their own experience of the Net in   18
the misogynist gauntlet described above. In researching this essay, I joined America
Online and spent an hour or two "hanging out" in the real-time chat rooms reputed to
be rife with sexual harassment. I received several "instant messages" from men, initiat-
ing private conversation with innocuous questions about my hometown and tenure on
the service. One man politely inquired if I was interested in "hot phone talk" and just
as politely bowed out when I declined. At no point did I feel harassed or treated with
disrespect. If I ever want to find a phone-sex partner, I now know where to look but
until then I probably won't frequent certain chat rooms.

Other women may experience a request for phone sex or even those tame instant mes-   19
sages as both intrusive and insulting (while still others maintain that they have received
much more explicit messages and inquiries completely out of the blue). My point isn't that
my reactions are the more correct, but rather that both are the reactions of women, and no
journalist has any reason to believe that mine are the exception rather than the rule.

For me, the menace in sexual harassment comes from the underlying threat of rape   20
or physical violence. I see my body as the site of my heightened vulnerability as a
woman. But on line—where I have no body and neither does anyone else—I consider
rape to be impossible. Not everyone agrees. Julian Dibbell, in an article for *The Village
Voice*,[‡] describes the repercussions of a "rape" in a multiuser dimension, or MUD, in
which one user employed a subprogram called a "voodoo doll" to cause the personae
of other users to perform sexual acts. Citing the "conflation of speech and act that's
inevitable in any computer-mediated world," he moved toward the conclusion that
"since rape can occur without any physical pain or damage, then it must be classified
as a crime against the mind." Therefore, the offending user had committed something
on the same "conceptual continuum" as rape. Tellingly, the incident led to the formation of the first governmental entity on the MUD.

No doubt the cyber-rapist (who went by the nom de guerre Mr. Bungle) appreciated   21
the elevation of his mischief-making to the rank of virtual felony: all of the outlaw glamour and none of the prison time (he was exiled from the MUD). Mr. Bungle limited his
victims to personae created by women users, a choice that, in its obedience to prevailing
gender roles, shaped the debate that followed his crimes. For, in accordance with the real-
world understanding that women's smaller, physically weaker bodies and lower social status make them subject to violation by men, there's a troubling notion in the real and virtual
worlds that women's minds are also more vulnerable to invasion, degradation, and abuse.

This sense of fragility extends beyond interactions with sexual overtones. The   22
Newsweek article reports that women participants can't tolerate the harsh, contentious
quality of on-line discussions, that they prefer mutual support to heated debate, and
are retreating wholesale to women-only conferences and newsgroups. As someone
who values on-line forums precisely because they mandate equal time for each user
who chooses to take it and forestall various "alpha male" rhetorical tactics like interrupting, loudness, or exploiting the psychosocial advantages of greater size or a

---

[‡]The previous selection, pp. 83–97 (ed.).

deeper voice, I find this perplexing and disturbing. In these laments I hear the reluctance of women to enter into the kind of robust debate that characterizes healthy public life, a willingness to let men bully us even when they've been relieved of most of their traditional advantages. Withdrawing into an electronic purdah where one will never be challenged or provoked, allowing the ludicrous ritual chest-thumping of some users to intimidate us into silence—surely women can come up with a more spirited response than this.

And of course they can, because besides being riddled with reductive stereotypes, 23 media analyses like *Newsweek*'s simply aren't accurate. While the on-line population is predominantly male, a significant and vocal minority of women contribute regularly and more than manage to hold their own. Some of The Well's most bombastic participants are women, just as there are many tactful and conciliatory men. At least, I think there are, because, ultimately, it's impossible to be sure of anyone's biological gender on line. "Transpostites," people who pose as members of the opposite gender, are an established element of Net society, most famously a man who, pretending to be a disabled lesbian, built warm and intimate friendships with women on several CompuServe forums.

Perhaps what we should be examining is not the triumph of gender differences on 24 the Net, but their potential blurring. In this light, *Newsweek*'s stout assertion that in cyberspace "the gender gap is real" begins to seem less objective than defensive, an insistence that on-line culture is "the same" as real life because the idea that it might be different, when it comes to gender, is too scary. If gender roles can be cast off so easily, they may be less deeply rooted, less "natural" than we believe. There may not actually be a "masculine" or "feminine" mind or outlook, but simply a conventional way of interpreting individuals that recognizes behavior seen as in accordance with their biological gender and ignores behavior that isn't.

For example, John Seabury wrote in the *New Yorker* (June 6, 1994) of his stricken 25 reaction to his first "flame," a colorful slice of adolescent invective sent to him by an unnamed technology journalist. Reading it, he begins to "shiver" like a burn victim, an effect that worsens with repeated readings. He writes that "the technology greased the words . . . with a kind of immediacy that allowed them to slide easily into my brain." He tells his friends, his coworkers, his partner—even his mother—and, predictably, appeals to CompuServe's management for recourse—to no avail. Soon enough, he's talking about civilization and anarchy, how the liberating "lack of social barriers is also what is appalling about the net," and calling for regulation.

As a newcomer, Seabury was chided for brooding over a missive that most Net 26 veterans would have dismissed and forgotten as the crude potshot of an envious jerk. (I can't help wondering if my fellow journalist never received hate mail in response to his other writings; this bit of e-mail seems comparable, par for the course when one assumes a public profile.) What nobody did was observe that Seabury's reaction—the shock, the feelings of violation, the appeals to his family and support network, the bootless complaints to the authorities—reads exactly like many horror stories about women's trials on the Net. Yet, because Seabury is a man, no one attributes the attack to his gender or suggests that the Net has proven an environment hostile to men. Furthermore, the idea that the Net must be more strictly governed to prevent the abuse of guys who write for the *New Yorker* seems laughable—though who's to say that Seabury's pain is less than any woman's? Who can doubt that, were he a woman, his tribulations would be seen as compelling evidence of Internet sexism?

The idea that women merit special protections in an environment as incorporeal as the Net is intimately bound up with the idea that women's minds are weak, fragile, and unsuited to the rough and tumble of public discourse.

The idea that women merit special protections in an environment as incorporeal as the Net is intimately bound up with the idea that women's minds are weak, fragile, and unsuited to the rough and tumble of public discourse. It's an argument that women should recognize with profound mistrust and resist, especially when we are used as rhetorical pawns in a battle to regulate a rare (if elite) space of gender ambiguity. When the mainstream media generalize about women's experiences on line in ways that just happen to uphold the most conventional and pernicious gender stereotypes, they can expect to be greeted with howls of disapproval from women who refuse to acquiesce in these roles and pass them on to other women.   27

And there are plenty of us, as The Well's response to the *Newsweek* article indicates. Women have always participated in on-line communications, women whose chosen careers in technology and the sciences have already marked them as gender-role resisters. As the schoolmarms arrive on the electronic frontier, their female predecessors find themselves cast in the role of saloon girls, their willingness to engage in "masculine" activities like verbal aggression, debate, or sexual experimentation marking them as insufficiently feminine, or "bad" women. "If that's what women on line are like, I must be a Martian," one Well woman wrote in response to the shrinking female technophobes depicted in the *Newsweek* article. Rather than relegating so many people to the status of gender aliens, we ought to reconsider how adequate those roles are to the task of describing real human beings.   28

← SECOND THOUGHTS

1. What constitutes the "heavy load of baggage" (¶ 8) that Miller says accompanies the frontier metaphor? From your own exposure to the classic Western narrative in popular media, what might you add to or dispute about Miller's description of it?
2. Miller writes, "The idea that women merit special protections in an environment as incorporeal as the Net is intimately bound up with the idea that women's minds are weak, fragile, and unsuited to the rough and tumble of public discourse" (¶ 27). Do

you agree? To what extent are you persuaded of the danger Miller asserts—that women and children are being used to rationalize the control and "civilizing" of the Internet "frontier"?

3. What hope does Miller find in "the potential blurring" (¶ 24) of gender roles on the Net? Do you agree that this kind of blurring is desirable? Why or why not?

▨ DISCUSSION THREADS

re: Spender and Kornbluth

1. Jesse Kornbluth says, "I didn't need to do anything special to become a believable woman, I just had to be intelligent, open, attentive, and empathetic—gender differences really didn't matter" (¶ 16). How do you think Dale Spender would analyze the motivations, actions, and results of Kornbluth's chat-room adventure?

re: Kornbluth and Ehrenreich

2. Compare and contrast the chat-room experiences of Jesse Kornbluth and Barbara Ehrenreich, two "newbies" or newcomers to cyberspace. How would you compare the depth or shallowness of their experiences? In what other ways do you think their motivations, goals, and conclusions are similar and different? How so?

re: Kornbluth, Ehrenreich, Dibbell, and Miller

3. To what extent do you think the "electronic frontier" metaphor criticized by Laura Miller is manifested or promoted in the essays by Jesse Kornbluth, Barbara Ehrenreich, or Julian Dibbell?

re: Dibbell and Miller

4. Julian Dibbell writes that he came to take virtual rape seriously because "rape can occur without any physical pain or damage . . . [so] it must be classed as a crime against the mind" (¶ 50). That passage is cited by Laura Miller when she argues the opposite conclusion: "on line—where I have no body and neither does anyone else—I consider rape to be impossible" (¶ 20). Based on Dibbell's and Miller's essays and your own experience, with whom do you agree more, and why?

re: Gender Online

5. Laura Miller suggests that "perhaps what we should be examining is not the triumph of gender differences on the Net, but their potential blurring" (¶ 24). Based on the selections in this chapter and your own experience, how desirable and how likely do you think it is that gender relations online can improve upon gender relations in "real life"?

∞ RESEARCH LINKS

- *For direct links to listed Internet sources, additional reading selections and questions online, plus updates and supplementary Web resources, see* **Composing Cyberspace Online** *at <www.mhhe.com/socscience/english/holeton/>.*

- *For a complete set of research tools for the Internet—including the most useful search strategies, directories, and conventions for documenting online sources—see McGraw-Hill English Composition at <www.mhhe.com/socscience/english/compde/>.*

1. Starting with studies referred to by Dale Spender in her article, find articles and books about gender and computer-mediated communication, or about women and cyberspace, in a research library or bookstore. You might start with the 1996 anthology *Wired Women: Gender and New Realities in Cyberspace* (Seal Press), edited by Lynn Cherny and Elizabeth Reba Weise (the source of Ellen Ullman's article in Chapter 1, p. 32). On the Internet, you can find articles by Amy Bruckman, Susan Herring, Nancy Kaplan, and others, as well as lively discussions about male/female relations online on Usenet newsgroups such as *soc.feminism, soc.women,* and *soc.men.* Relevant resource guides on the Web include WomensNet/IGC (Institute for Global Communications) at <www.igc.org/igc/womensnet/>; The Friendly Grrrls Guide to the Internet at <www.youth.nsw.gov.au/rob.upload/friendly/index.html>; and The Ada Project: Tapping Internet Resources for Women in Computer Science at <www.cs.yale.edu/HTML/YALE/CS/HyPlans/tap/tap.html>. Use these resources to help you define a narrower topic for your own research writing, such as gender issues in school computer use, "netsex," or online sexual harassment.

2. If you have Telnet access to the Internet, join a real MUD, MOO, or Internet Relay Chat (IRC) (see Research Link 2, Chapter 1, p. 63), or venture into a chat room, like those described by Jesse Kornbluth and Barbara Ehrenreich, on a commercial service such as America Online. Experiment with your gender identity if that is appropriate for the particular community, space, or channel you've joined (some MUDs offer multiple gender options, not just male and female, for their characters). Remember that you can have unpleasant or unwanted encounters in these environments, like some of the incidents described in this chapter; if you feel uncomfortable for any reason, you should log off or disconnect. Alternatively, if you use a computer classroom or lab equipped with electronic discussion software, you can experiment with gender in anonymous online chats with classmates—perhaps a "safer" or less risky environment. Take notes about the effects of gender on the interactions you observe and participate in, ideally over a period of several weeks. Report on your experiences, integrating research from sources such as those suggested in Research Link 1.

3. "They say that LambdaMOO has never been the same since Mr. Bungle's toading." writes Julian Dibbell. "They say as well that nothing's really changed." Find out how well the New Direction system of voting and petitions, instituted by Haakon after the Bungle Affair, has worked out for residents and wizards. For this project, you will need to do most of your research on the Internet and, if possible, directly on LambdaMOO (<telnet://lambda.moo.mud.org:8888/>). Articles by Pavel Curtis, the Xerox Palo Alto Research Center creator of LambdaMOO (Haakon), and others are available at several Web addresses, including the LambdaMOO FTP archive at <ftp://ftp.lambda.moo.mud.org/pub/MOO/papers>.

4. Laura Miller critically analyzes the language and metaphors describing cyberspace in articles from *Newsweek* and other publications, writing, "The imperiled women and children of the Western narrative make their appearance today in newspaper and magazine articles that focus on the intimidation and sexual harassment of women on line and reports of pedophiles trolling for victims in computerized chat rooms." Test Miller's claims about the portrayal of gender and the Western frontier metaphor by analyzing or comparing two or more recent articles from magazines or newspapers. For a larger project, you could analyze more articles from a wider range of sources or include TV coverage of cyberspace in your analysis. You might also critically evaluate the use of other metaphors in the sources you study—such as the information highway, the conduit metaphor discussed by George Lakoff (p. 21), or the windows metaphor discussed by Sherry Turkle (p. 5) in Chapter 1—especially as they relate to gender.

5. E-mail harassment and anonymous nuisance e-mail are recent phenomena at college campuses and wired workplaces. Review your school's, company's, or organization's policies about sexual harassment and acceptable uses of the institution's computer network; then interview administrators or managers who enforce these policies. If possible, find out the details of any e-mail harassment or nuisance cases at your institution, and compare these with cases you uncover from library and Internet research. Evaluate the strengths and weaknesses of the current policies and how well they incorporate or anticipate emerging electronic technologies, and offer suggestions for how to modify or update these policies. Based on your research, you might address a proposal to the responsible faculty members, administrators, or managers.

Cultural Identity and Cyberspace

"On the Internet, nobody knows you're a dog."

"On the Internet, nobody knows you're a dog" has become one of the best known one-liners of the electronic age, originating from this Peter Steiner cartoon published in *The New Yorker* in July 1994. The cartoon makes fun of the anonymity of network communications by showing a dog online, presumably fooling some credulous humans about its true identity. This anonymity is similarly lampooned in the Mike Luckovich cartoon that opens Chapter 2 (p. 66), where the focus is on appearance and gender relations. Steiner's cartoon takes a broader swipe at the issue, however, by portraying the anonymous computer user as a member of another species. The humorous implication is that the usual, face-to-face clues we get about people's identity—their appearance, gender, voice, race, ethnicity, and other indicators of social status—are so crucial that, in electronic space, we cannot distinguish human beings from other creatures.

While we laugh at the unlikelihood of this scenario, we may also squirm a bit, uncomfortable with the idea of not knowing who we're talking to. The humor of the cartoon derives not only from the apparent gullibility of the human participants but also from the exaggeration of the dog's intelligence. Whether it's using its own office or borrowing a person's office, the black dog evidently can talk, read and write fluently, operate a computer, and navigate the Internet (tasks at which not all humans have succeeded!); the spotted dog, likewise, presumably understands the whole process. In the new electronic medium, dogs—in real life, our pets or servants—have become equivalent to their human masters. This leveling effect of computer-mediated communication—"where individuals make themselves known by the acuity of their thought and expression, rather than by their physical appearance," as Steve Silberman puts it in this chapter—may profoundly influence how we conceive, construct, and express our personal and cultural identity. Those influences, and the tensions among sameness, equality, difference, and individuality in cyberspace, are explored in the selections that follow.

Steiner's dogs are, perhaps not insignificantly, different colors: one black and one white with black spots. In CyberFaith International, a Dayton (Ohio)-based Internet exchange described by Charlise Lyles, people of diverse racial and ethnic backgrounds discuss multiculturalism, or the positive effects of cultural diversity, in the context of their Christian spiritual beliefs. Because the medium is "socially blind, colorblind, and classblind," according to one participant, "everyone comes to the conversation with a kind of equality." Steve Silberman cites similar advantages to e-mail and electronic chat-room exchanges for gay and lesbian teenagers, who can explore their sexual orientation with mentors and sympathetic peers in ways that haven't been possible in other media. By contrast, Max Padilla, who identifies himself as both gay and Chicano, writes about feeling much less welcome on the Internet, which he finds to be dominated by straight, white, affluent males.

The complexity of expressing cultural identities online is further explored by Glen Martin, writing about the controversy surrounding a Native American seminar and chat room offered by America Online that was run by a white software consultant. Native activists called the project a cultural rip-off and fraud and have worked since to build Native-run electronic networks that restrict access to culturally sensitive information. Finally, in John Shirley's riveting science fiction story, "Wolves of the Plateau," prisoners in the year 2022—like prisoners today, mostly from socially marginal groups—

have access only to a forbidden, black-market kind of "Internet." They must confront their diversity and find a way to collaborate if they are going to escape.

Before you read these selections, you may find it helpful to consider your own personal and cultural identity and the tensions in your own life between sameness and difference. For example,

1. List the various cultural groups, other than gender (which is the subject of Chapter 2), with which you identify. Include groups based on social or economic class, race or ethnicity, national origin, sexual orientation, religious affiliation, age or generation, occupation, physical abilities, special interests, and other important aspects of your identity. How much of who you are depends on each of these?

2. How aware are you of particular group identities (from question 1) in your regular, day-to-day interactions? What forms of expression do they take (for example, attending church or meetings, reading particular books, etc.)? How aware do you think other people are of their, and your, belonging to various cultural groups? How knowledgeable or ignorant do you think most people are about some of the particular groups that form important parts of *your* identity?

3. Whether you are heterosexual, homosexual, or bisexual, what are your attitudes about people with a different sexual orientation than yours? What would you most like to ask someone with a different sexual orientation? What would you most like such a person to know about your own sexual identity?

4. If you have access to a computer lab, classroom, or networked computers equipped with electronic discussion software, hold a discussion in which everyone logs on anonymously. Before you begin, make sure you agree on some ground rules for netiquette, or online politeness. Discuss one of the issues raised earlier or another topic suggested by your peers or teacher. Afterward, talk face-to-face about the experience. How did you perceive other people's comments differently without knowing what they looked like, sounded like, and acted like? Or did you already know some of your classmates well enough to identify them without names? Despite the anonymity, or beyond your guessing of classmates' identities, did you perceive any clues or signals about people's social status or cultural identity from what they wrote? How so?

CyberFaith

Promoting Multiculturalism Online

Charlise Lyles

Charlise Lyles (b. 1959), a native of Cleveland, reports on beliefs and cultures for the *Dayton* (Ohio) *Daily News.* Previously she covered government, courts, social services and demographic trends for the Norfolk, Virginia, *Virginian-Pilot.* Lyles is the author of *Do I Dare Disturb the Universe?—From the Projects to Prep School* (Faber & Faber, 1994), a memoir about growing up in Ohio in the 1970s. This article appeared in the *Dayton Daily News,* a newspaper serving the Dayton, Ohio, metropolitan area, in 1996.

D AYTON, OHIO.
On-line at CyberFaith International, Presbyterian minister Carla Gentry can talk about God and the Bible with people she might not meet at her Clarksville, Ind., church: blacks, Asians, Africans, Peruvians, and others whose racial and ethnic backgrounds are different from her own.

CyberFaith, a Dayton-based Internet exchange (<info@cyberfaith.org>), seeks to link diverse groups for a Bible-based discussion of multiculturalism, a topic they believe to be a deeply spiritual matter. Its 75 active on-liners—preachers, lay persons, the lost, and the seekers—are as close as Dayton and as far away as New Mexico, Virginia, Brazil, Peru, and West Africa.

"In recent years, white people have shied away from this topic, shirking their responsibilities to their brothers and sisters of color in the fight for human equality," Gentry e-mailed recently.

"In re-examining my beliefs I find my participation in the group to be vital," wrote Gentry, who grew up "anglo" in Minnesota.

Unlike chat rooms popular on the Internet, CyberFaith operates as a "listserve." E-mail sent to <info@cyberfaith.org> is electronically forwarded to each member within participating groups. Anyone can reply via e-mail to CyberFaith or message the individual sender directly. 5

The network is the brainchild of Victory United Methodist Church co-pastors Rosunde C. Nichols and Mary Olson.

This dynamic duo of passionate, plain-speaking preachers, one black, one white, has waged a spiritual battle against discrimination since their 1990 appointment to the old stone church on North Dixie Drive.

Now, they say the Lord has moved them to stake out a fortress in cyberspace. Unlike

They say the Lord has moved them to stake out a fortress in cyberspace.

Ecunet and other popular on-line religion links, CyberFaith aims to attract laity as well as clergy.

"The frontiers of cyberspace are being institutionalized at this very moment," said Olson, stern-faced with kind blue eyes. "If racism, classism, and sexism become cemented in cyberspace systems, our global society and local communities will experience the greatest barriers of racism the world has ever known."

"This means seeing to it that the information and dialogue stem from systems that   10
are owned by people of all races," said Nichols, whose bold features are set in deep brown skin. "The dominant white culture must not be the predominant owner of the channels of cyberspace."

On race matters, CyberFaith exchanges can reduce the intimidation factor, Gentry says. "I feel I can ask a dumb question or make a statement without getting into a confrontation that can often occur in face-to-face settings."

CyberFaith discussions run deeper than race.

Topics discussed in a recent week: Bill Moyers' PBS special on the Book of Genesis, politics, the Pope, doctor-assisted suicide, personal tribulations and revelations— "Are we too much into blaming and too little into understanding?"

In these exchanges, participants say they draw an ironic satisfaction from cyberspace in general and CyberFaith in particular.

Though they have come together because of color, the computer renders them   15
peculiarly colorblind.

"This environment has the appearance of being socially blind, colorblind and classblind," said Bedell. "Everyone comes to the conversation with a kind of equality. You can't hear voices to guess at what color they are or detect an accent."

From an e-mail by a participant who asked to remain anonymous: "Unlike the church, when I am in cyberspace, nobody really knows, unless I tell them, whether I am black, white, red, or yellow, or even male or female, whether I am writing from a hovel or a palatial estate.

"Nobody knows my educational background or lack of it, or even my age. That doesn't seem to matter to anybody and this is the way church ought to be. We are a true community of seekers."

Untainted by the social markers of race, class, ethnicity, and sex, truer individual identities can emerge.

What you get is a sort of cybersoul.   20

CyberFaith plans to expand its multicultural mission to other technologies, said Ken Bedell, editor of the *Yearbook of American and Canadian Churches.* He designed the CyberFaith software. For example, on Nov. 15 Victory United and CyberFaith will take part in a national teleconference featuring scholars Cornel West and David Ng, who will speak about multiculturalism from Riverside Church in New York City.

At times, CyberFaith has rallied a multicultural cadre around humanitarian causes.

This fall, a Liberian pastor now based in Detroit sent out a prayer request for his 11-year-old son. The preacher had sent the boy back to his mother in Liberia after the civil war apparently subsided. But when conflict raged anew, the child landed starving and sick in a Ghana refugee camp.

On the net, CyberFaithers raised money for the Rev. Emmanuel Giddings to return to Africa. Checks from $25 to $500 flowed in, Nichols said. Then participants linked Giddings to people who helped him locate his son, place the boy in a mission school, and find a local guardian for him.

"Thank you so much for making it possible for me to bring my son EJ out of the   25 refugee camp in Accra to a place of safety," Giddings e-mailed. "You have been an extension of God's grace and loving kindness toward me and my son."

"The success of EJ shows you how CyberFaith works from local to global, people of diverse backgrounds coming together to make something happen," Olson said.

CyberFaith and other on-line religion links allow for other kinds of religious freedom: a more honest exploration of faith under cover of anonymity. You can say things that you wouldn't dare say in Sunday school class.

> **You can say things that you wouldn't dare say in Sunday school class.**

An Akron participant wondered about Abraham sacrificing Isaac: "I've always kinda figured Isaac saying, 'Uh, Dad, uh, what are you, uh, going to do with that knife? Dad, I am your son, not some silly sheep.'

"It's just the first time someone has presented the viewpoint of the potential human victim."

Another asked: "Has it occurred to anybody that Noah just got drunk by accident,   30 that it was no sin? . . . It occurred to me that the wine was so delicious that Noah just drank and drank of it, not realizing what it would do to him."

And at CyberFaith there is always the basics, prayer.

"Rosunde did the home-going yesterday for a homicide victim," Olson e-mailed from Dayton several weeks ago. "Pray for the family, friends, and church as we/they now sort through the realities of poverty, systemic racism, and systemic classism in our society."

⬅ SECOND THOUGHTS

1. What does Lyles seem to mean by "cybersoul" (¶ 20)? What would you say are the major goals of CyberFaith International, and what advantages do its promoters and participants feel that e-mail offers for attaining these goals?
2. To what extent do you share co-founder Carla Gentry's opinion that "white people have shied away from [multiculturalism], shirking their responsibilities to their brothers and sisters of color" (¶ 3)?
3. Based on this article, to what extent do you agree that "truer individual identities can emerge" in cyberspace (¶ 19)? To what extent do you agree with the anonymous participant who says that "this is the way church ought to be" (¶ 18)?
4. Do you see any potential contradiction between Gentry's view that CyberFaith exchanges are less likely than face-to-face settings to lead to confrontations (¶ 11), on the one hand, and the view that anonymity increases honesty so that "You can say things that you wouldn't dare say in Sunday school" (¶ 27), on the other hand? How so, or why not?

We're Teen, We're Queer, and We've Got E-Mail

Steve Silberman

Steve Silberman (b. 1957) is senior culture correspondent for *Wired News,* an online publication of *Wired* magazine, and writes for other magazines, including a regular column for *Packet.com.* He is co-author (with David Shenk) of *Skeleton Key: A Dictionary for Deadheads* (Doubleday, 1994). Silberman has a Web page at <www.levity.com/digaland/index.html>. This article appeared in 1994 in the paper version of *Wired* (<www.hotwired.com/wired/>), a magazine aimed at people interested in emerging electronic technologies.

There's a light on in the Nerd Nook: JohnTeen Ø is composing e-mail into the 1 night. The Nerd Nook is what John's mother calls her 16-year-old's bedroom— it's more cramped than the bridge of the Enterprise, with a Roland CM-322 that makes "You've got mail" thunder like the voice of God.

John's favorite short story is "The Metamorphosis." Sure, Kafka's fable of waking 2 up to discover you've morphed into something that makes everyone tweak speaks to every teenager. But John especially has had moments of feeling insectoid—like during one school choir trip, when, he says, the teacher booking rooms felt it necessary to inform the other students' parents of John's "orientation." When they balked at their kids sharing a room with him, John was doubled up with another teacher—a fate nearly as alienating as Gregor Samsa's.

The choir trip fiasco was but one chapter in the continuing online journal that 3 has made JohnTeen Ø—or as his parents and classmates know him, John Erwin— one of the most articulate voices in America Online's Gay and Lesbian Community Forum.

From: JohnTeenØ

My high school career has been a sudden and drastic spell of turbulence and change that has influenced every aspect of life. Once I was an automaton, obeying external, societal, and parental expectations like a dog, oblivious of who I was or what I wanted. I was the token child every parent wants—student body president, color guard, recipient of the general excellence award, and outstanding music student of the year. I conformed to society's paradigm, and I was rewarded. Yet I was miserable. Everything I did was a diversion from thinking about myself. Finally, last summer, my subconsciousness felt comfortable enough to be able to connect myself with who I really am, and I began to understand what it is to be gay.

JohnTeen Ø is a new kind of gay kid, a 16-year-old not only out, but already at 4 home in the online convergence of activists that Tom Reilly, the co-founder of Digital Queers, calls the "Queer Global Village." Just 10 years ago, most queer teens hid behind a self-imposed don't-ask-don't-tell policy until they shipped out to Oberlin or San Francisco, but the Net has given even closeted kids a place to conspire. Though the Erwin's house is in an unincorporated area of Santa Clara County in California, with goats and llamas foraging in the backyard, John's access to AOL's gay and lesbian forum enables him to follow dispatches from queer activists worldwide, hone his writing, flirt, try on disposable identities, and battle bigots—all from his home screen.

John's ambitions to recast national policy before the principal of Menlo School 5 even palms him a diploma (John's mother refers to him as her "little mini-activist") are not unrealistic. Like the ur-narrative of every videogame, the saga of gay teens online is one of metamorphosis, of "little mini" nerds becoming warriors in a hidden Stronghold of Power. For young queers, the Magic Ring is the bond of community.

John's posts have the confidence and urgency of one who speaks for many who 6 must keep silent:

> The struggle for equal rights has always taken place on the frontier of the legal wilderness where liberty meets power. Liberty has claimed much of that wilderness now, but the frontier always lies ahead of us. . . . The frontier of liberty may have expanded far beyond where it began, but for those without rights, it always seems on the horizon, just beyond their reach.

And the messages that stream back into John's box are mostly from kids his own 7 age, many marooned far from urban centers for gay and lesbian youth. Such is Christopher Rempel, a witty, soft-spoken Ace of Base fan from (as he puts it) "redneck farmer hell." Christopher borrowed the principal's modem to jack into a beekeepers BBS and gopher his way to the Queer Resources Directory, a multimeg collection of text files, news items, and services listings.

> My name is Christopher and I am 15 years old. I came to terms that I was gay last summer and, aside from some depression, I'm OK. I am "not" in denial about being gay.

> I would like to write to someone that I can talk to about issues I can't talk about with my friends. I don't play sports very much, but I make it up in my knowledge of computers. I am interested in anybody with an open mind and big aspirations for the future.

A decade ago, the only queer info available to most teens was in a few dour psy- 8 chology texts under the nose of the school librarian. Now libraries of files await them in the AOL forum and elsewhere—the Queer Resources Directory alone contains hundreds—and teens can join mailing lists like Queercampus and GayNet, or tap resources like the Bridges Project, a referral service that tells teens not only how to get in touch with queer youth groups, but how to jump-start one themselves.

Kali is an 18-year-old lesbian at a university in Colorado. Her name means "fierce" 9 in Swahili. Growing up in California, Kali was the leader of a young women's chapter of the Church of Jesus Christ of Latter-Day Saints. She was also the "Girl Saved by E-mail," whose story ran last spring on CNN. After mood swings plummeted her into a profound depression, Kali—like too many gay teens—considered suicide. Her access to GayNet at school gave her a place to air those feelings, and a phone call from someone she knew online saved her life.

Kali is now a regular contributor to Sappho, a women's board she most appre-   10
ciates because there she is accepted as an equal. "They forgive me for being young," Kali laughs, "though women come out later than guys, so there aren't a lot of teen lesbians. But it's a high of connection. We joke that we're posting to 500 of our closest friends."

"The wonderful thing about online services is that they are an intrinsically   11
decentralized resource," says Tom Reilly, who has solicited the hardware and imparted the skills to get dozens of queer organizations jacked in. "Kids can challenge what adults have to say and make the news. One of the best examples of teen organizing in the last year was teens working with the Massachusetts legislature to pass a law requiring gay and lesbian education in the high schools. If teen organizers are successful *somewhere* now, everyone's gonna hear about it. This is the most powerful tool queer youth have ever had."

> "If teen organizers are successful *somewhere* now, everyone's gonna hear about it. This is the most powerful tool queer youth have ever had."

Another power that teenagers are now wield-   12
ing online is their anger. "Teens are starting to throw their weight around," says Quirk, the leader of the AOL forum. (Quirk maintains a gender-neutral identity online, to be an equal-opportunity sounding board for young lesbians and gay men.) "They're *complaining*. It used to be, 'Ick—I think I'm gay, I'll sneak around the forum and see what they're doing.' With this second wave of activism, it's like, 'There's gay stuff here, but it's not right for *me*.' These kids are computer literate, and they're using the anger of youth to create a space for themselves."

The powers that be at AOL, however, have not yet seen fit to allow that space to   13
be named by its users—the creation of chat rooms called "gay teen" anything is banned. "AOL has found that the word 'gay' with the word 'youth' or 'teen' in a room name becomes a lightning rod for predators," says Quirk. "I've been in teen conferences where adult cruising so overwhelmed any kind of conversation about being in high school and 'What kind of music do you like?' that I was furious. Until I can figure out a way to provide a safe space for them, I'm not going to put them at risk."

Quirk and AOL are in a tight place. Pedophilia has become the trendy bludgeon   14
with which to trash cyberspace in the dailies, and concerned parents invoke the P-word to justify limiting teens' access to gay forums. At the same time, however, postings in the teens-only folder of the Gay and Lesbian Community Forum flame not only the invasion of teen turf by adults trolling for sex, but also the adults claiming to "protect" them by limiting their access to one another.

One anonymous 17-year-old poster on AOL dissed the notion that queer teens are   15
helpless victims of online "predators":

There are procedures for dealing with perverts, which most teens (in contrast with most of the adults we've encountered) are familiar with. Flooding e-mail boxes of annoying perverts, 'IGNORE'-ing them in chat rooms, and shutting off our Instant Messages are all very effective methods. We are not defenseless, nor innocent.

Accessing Queer Teen Cyberspace*

- The Gay and Lesbian Community Forum, on America Online, Keyword: Gay
- Queer America. Send e-mail containing your city, state, zip code, area code, and age to *ncglbyorg@aol.com.*
- Queer Resources Directory. Anonymous ftp or gopher to *vector.casti.com* (look in pub/QRD/youth); on the World Wide Web, go to *http:/ vector.casti.com/QRD/.html/QRD-home-page.html.* Or send an inquiry to *qrdstaff@vector.casti.com.*
- Bridges Project. American Friends Service Committee referral and resource center. E-mail *bridgespro@aol.com.*

The issue is further complicated by the fact that the intermingling of old and young   16
people online is good for teens. The online connection allows them to open dialogs with mentors like Deacon Maccubbin, co-owner of Lambda Rising bookstore in Washington, D.C. As "DeaconMac," Maccubbin has been talking with gay kids on CompuServe and AOL for eight years. One of the young people DeaconMac corresponded with online, years ago, was Tom Reilly. "Deacon was the first openly gay man I'd ever had a conversation with, and he had a very clear idea of what his role was. He was nurturing and mentoring; he sent me articles; and he didn't come on to me," says Reilly. "I'll never forget it as long as I live."

In the past, teens often had to wait until they were old enough to get into a bar to   17
meet other gay people—or hang around outside until someone noticed them. Online interaction gives teens a chance to unmask themselves in a safe place, in a venue where individuals make themselves known by the acuity of their thought and expression, rather than by their physical appearance.

When JohnTeen Ø logged his first post in the gay AOL forum, he expressed out-   18
rage that the concerns of queer teens—who are at a disproportionately high risk for suicide—were being shunted aside by adult organizations. His post was spotted by Sarah Gregory, a 26-year-old anarchist law student who helped get the National Gay and Lesbian Task Force wired up. "I really wanted to hit this kid between the eyes with the fact that a national organization saw what he was saying and cared that gay youth were killing themselves," Gregory recalls. A correspondence and friendship began that

---

*See Research Links number 3, p. 144, for an update on these resources (ed.).

would have been unlikely offline—for, as Gregory says, "I don't notice 16-year-old boys in the real world."

Gregory explains: "I remember one particularly graphic letter I sent John in   19 response to his questions. I wrote a *huge* disclaimer before and after it. But then I remembered how desperately I wanted to be talked to as an adult, and a sexual being, when I was 14. Thinking back, that's the point where John stopped sounding so formal, so much like a well-bred teenager talking to an authority figure, and became my friend. It's also the last time he talked about suicide. It scared me how easily his vulnerability could have been exploited, but I'd do it again in a heartbeat."

"I didn't even listen to music," moans John recalling his nerdhood, when the only   20 thing he logged in for was shareware. Now the background thrash for his late-night e-mail sessions is Pansy Division. "To keep myself in the closet, I surrounded myself with people I'd never find attractive. I had two different parts of my life: the normal part, where I worked hard in school and got good grades, and this other part, where I was interested in guys but didn't do anything about it." For many kids, writing to John or to other posters is where a more authentic life begins:

> Dear JohnTeen:
>
> I am so frustrated with life and all of its blind turns. Am I gay? What will happen if I tell friends and my mom? . . . (I still don't 100% know that I am gay only that I am not heterosexual SO WHAT AM I) I really want to fit somewhere and also to love someone (at this point I don't care who). . . . Please EMAIL back and enlighten me. You have been very inspirational to me. I have no idea how you gained the courage to come out. Thanks, James

But John Erwin must guard against JohnTeen Ø becoming a full-time gig: he not only   21 has the frontiers of liberty to defend and his peers to "enlighten," but like any 16-year-old, he needs space to fuck up, be a normal teenage cockroach, and figure out who he is. And he'd like to find someone to love. Does he have anyone in mind? "Yes!" he grins, pulling out his yearbook and leafing to a photo of a handsome boy who says he's straight.

Is John's dream guy online?   22

"No, I wish," John says. "If he was online, I could tell him how I *feel*."   23

⬅ SECOND THOUGHTS

1. Have you ever had the urge, like teenager Christopher Rempel in this article, "to write to someone that I can talk to about issues I can't talk about with my friends" (¶ 7)? If so, try articulating those issues in a diary or journal entry.
2. What are the major advantages of the Internet for gay and lesbian youths, according to the article?
3. What responses does Silberman offer to the potential danger, often mentioned in mainstream media coverage of the Internet, of online predators or pedophiles? How persuaded are you by these responses?

Affirmative Access

Max Padilla

A Gay Chicano Lost in
Cyberspace

Max Padilla was at the University of California at Berkeley in 1995 when he wrote this article for the *Village Voice* (<www.villagevoice.com/>), a New York weekly that covers arts, culture, and politics.

D espite the hype about the Internet, a lot of my friends aren't tripping over them- 1
selves to log on. We're not technophobes, mind you; just people of color who can't afford the merchandise. Computer prices are still sky high, and the 10 free online hours, offered by those discs that fall out of magazines, quietly slip away, leaving a $50 tab for a brief Net trek. What's more, browsing the Web requires a "slip account" that can cost up to $500. No wonder my friends feel left out.

Fortunately, many of us are beneficiaries of free e-mail accounts provided by our 2
universities. At school, the Internet is less a novelty than an instrument of survival. How else can you surreptitiously schmooze your professor, or ask questions that would get you laughed out of the lecture hall? And there's a postgraduate benefit: These accounts don't lapse immediately, allowing a breathing space until a generous employer picks up the online bill. I suspect this is how most people of color achieve affirmative access to the Internet.

At first, my friends were hyper to link up. Karen quickly located the most salacious 3
threads on the usenet newsgroups. Eddie was deeper into cruising AOL's chat rooms than fooling around with his boyfriend. And I was awestruck by the prospect of conversing with others like me in a global gay-Chicano thread. But the buzz faded fast. Karen quit browsing through newsgroups because the racist and sexist chat pissed her off. Eddie's modem died and he hasn't bothered to replace it. And I'm back to talking on the telephone. The World Wide Web has turned out to be nowhere near as diverse as the number 7 train I ride home every night.

> **The World Wide Web has turned out to be nowhere near as diverse as the number 7 train I ride home every night.**

Not that I didn't try to find my own e-community. I gravitated to the slew of 4
soc.culture groups on the usenet, where every variation of the human gene pool is

supposed to be represented. *Soc.culture.latin-american, asian.american,* and *african.american* cover the racial bases. There's even a *soc.culture.mexican.american.* But in these ethnic spaces, the word faggot is practically an emoticon. I tried subscribing to *soc.motss* (members of the same sex), but these virtual queers are straight up very white and male. I couldn't imagine posting something about how to attract someone using Santeria. Or how to work out cultural differences in relationships between Puerto Ricans and Chicanos. A bevy of responses in my e-mail box? I think not.

Netizens post about themselves, and I don't see myself in there. When I posted on *soc.motss* for other people of color, cybertistas responded with lectures on color blindness: "There is no way to know what color someone on soc.motss is unless they tell you"; "Why don't you get a color monitor?" A Mac user apologized for not buying "the *race* button option." A person's "color," a Nethead typed, is of "sublime irrelevance in an abstract textual medium where race and color aren't available for consideration." Here was every brotherhood lecture I'd ever endured in school, pumped up with jargon and a detached sense of righteousness that comes of interacting only with digital text.

Pointing out that the newsgroup is not diverse enough, I anticipated getting flamed. I was thoroughly roasted. One Netopian posted about the "lack of interest of people of color in computers and the Internet in general." The thread became increasingly vitriolic: "I have the freedom to write what I please and no person of color is going to force me to discuss these issues." I had tapped the rage that lies just under the surface of technospeak: "This reminds me of the wetback that bitched on alt.rock-n-roll.stones that we were all racist because no reviews of the Mexico concerts had been posted to the newsgroup."

I'm aware that interactions on the Net can obscure identity. Mental imaging is the only way to piece together the mosaic of the person you're exchanging with. But I can't help looking past the log-ons. I owe this to a mother who notes all Spanish surnames in Hollywood movies, newspaper bylines, and the voting booth. Out of habit, I search for Latino names, too. And I don't see any in this newsgroup for queers.

Not that it's any easier to find queers on the *soc.group* appropriate to my ethnicity. "Do any gay Chicanos use this group?" I queried on the *mexican.american* space. I wasn't flamed as I'd been in other Spanish-language spaces. ("Ve te!"—get out—was the most common response, usually followed by "maricon.") But the Chicano ethic is closer to silence. Days went by without a response; finally, my message faded, which is the Net's way of saying, no thread.

"Do any gay Chicanos use this group?" I queried on the *mexican.american* space.

I still use the Internet, but I'm wary of its claims. This is no Netopia, but an all-too-painful reflection of the real world. American Online resembles America, all right. Majority rules.

SECOND THOUGHTS

1. Padilla uses many cyberspace- and culture-related terms that may be unfamiliar to some readers, such as *technophobes, usenet, thread, emoticon, Santeria,* and *wetback.* Make a list of unfamiliar terms, and see how many you can define from the context in which they're used before turning to the *Composing Cyberspace* Glossary. What meanings can you determine for made-up terms such as *affirmative access, Netopian,* and *cybertistas?* Based on Padilla's vocabulary and use of language, how would you describe the audience he seems to be writing for?

2. How would you describe Padilla's goals and expectations about cyberspace, and how do these seem to have changed for him over time?

3. What are the sources of Padilla's disappointment in the Internet? How sympathetic are you to his online frustrations, and why?

Internet Indian Wars

Glen Martin

*Native Americans Are Fighting
to Connect the 550 Nations—in
Cyberspace*

Glen Martin (b. 1949) is a staff writer for the *San Francisco Chronicle* and has written for magazines such as *Men's Journal, Discover,* and *Gourmet.* He is the author of *Through the Grapevine* (Revell, 1989), an exposé of the wine industry, and a forthcoming book from National Geographic about wildlife refuges. This article appeared in 1995 in *Wired* (<www.hotwired.com/wired/>), a magazine aimed at people interested in emerging electronic technologies.

B lue Snake's Lodge. To a certain kind of seeker, it was irresistible. You logged on 1 to the America Online seminar, and the old ways swelled up around you, evoking sparkling rivers, virgin forests, and yawning plains teeming with game. You were in, well, North America. But before it was called North America. After all, North America is merely an Anglo rubric applied to a vast land once inhabited by myriad peoples living in harmony with the Earth.

Yes, in Blue Snake's Lodge, you were privy to the mysteries and ceremonies of 2 the American Indian. Blue Snake was an online chief of the Eastern Shawnee, and in the photo provided with his AOL bio, you could see a stocky middle-aged man with abundant gray whiskers, accoutered in a blanket and holding a long pipe. He was devoted to inculcating non-Indians with the healing ways of Native American spirituality.

His introductory "teaching" ushered you onto the cybernetic equivalent of Native 3 holy ground:

> Before you is a lodge, a large tepee. . . . The silhouettes of its inhabitants are cast upon the canvas sides by the fire in the center. You hear only night sounds, a stream chuckles in the distance as it hurls itself headlong through the forest, an owl challenges the darkness as she hunts for prey, a coyote voices his loneliness as he waits for his mate.
>
> Blue Snake is seated at the back of the lodge. At his feet, beside the fire, a pipe carved in the image of a rattlesnake rests on a cedar box. The pipe is a symbol of his

authority. He bids you welcome. He raises the pipe then lowers it and points the stem at each of his guests. Six times he draws smoke . . . six times he exhales it, once to each of the four directions, once to the Everywhere Spirit above, once to Grandmother Earth below. . . . Blue Snake speaks. "Welcome to my lodge. May you always feel welcome here, as in your own lodge."

Wow. Or as Blue Snake would say, *oneh* (a Shawnee analog, Blue Snake reveals,   4
of *aloha,* meaning everything from *hello* to *I agree profoundly*). No doubt about it, Blue Snake offered a moving spiritual message, particularly resonant in a world where the dollar is king and nature is becoming a vague memory.

There was, however, a problem: it was all a charade. Blue Snake was Don Rapp, a soft-   5
ware consultant living in southern Ohio, who was about as Indian as Barbara Bush. Rapp created the Blue Snake persona and successfully pitched it to America Online, where he conducted seminars and hosted a chat room. Online Native wannabes flocked to Rapp, who made them honorary Indians by declaring them members of the "Evening Sky Clan" of the "Red Heart Tribe." He also bestowed names on his followers during elaborate online bene-dictions—Crystal Bear Woman, Stormcloud Dancer, and Darkness Runs From Her.

By early 1995, Blue Snake's teachings had worked their way around AOL and into   6
the hearts and minds of thousands of cybersurfers who were convinced they had found the answer to their manifold spiritual dilemmas. But in March 1993, some real Indians logged onto the seminars—and Blue Snake's Lodge began to fall apart under its own spurious weight.

The easy use of alternative personae, of course, lies at the heart of cyber culture. Peo-   7
ple get online because it embodies freedom—not just freedom to be all they can be, but freedom to be everything they can't or won't be in the world of flesh, blood, and three dimensions. Wired Native Americans find this element of cyberspace appealing. But tra-dition-minded Indians assert that there's an uncrossable line in both cyberspace and the real world, a line that separates tribal religious rites from the commerce of everyday life. Such rituals, these Natives maintain, are sacred, proprietary—and indeed, exclusionary.

Blue Snake's peddling of "Indian spirituality" was thus repugnant to the Native Amer-   8
icans who discovered his seminars, and they went on the offensive. "There's a difference between adopting online identities and perpetrating fraud," says Marc Towersap, a Shoshone-Bannock engineer from Idaho and one of the first Indians to query America Online about Blue Snake's tribal credentials. "Rapp was promoting himself as a genuine Native elder, and AOL was making money on the chat room because a lot of people logged on to it. They were making money on a bogus product. Is selling fake mutual funds over the telephone acceptable? This was the same thing, except we're talking about spirituality rather than stocks, and the Internet instead of the phone. It's fraud, not role-playing." || → profit

Tracy Miller, a salty, blunt-spoken Eastern Band Cherokee and Native activist   9
who lives in southern New England, was likewise incensed when she stumbled onto Blue Snake's maunderings. "A Native friend e-mailed me and told me to check out this guy Blue Snake on AOL," recalls Miller. "I couldn't believe it. His seminars were a hodgepodge of the worst kind of bullshit stereotypes and gobbledygook possible. All the hippies and crystal gazers were just gobbling it up, of course, but I knew that there was no way in hell he could be a real Native."

Miller, a seasoned Net surfer, knows that information isn't the only thing that 10 wants to be free; so does misinformation. And misinformation, she claims, strikes at the heart of Native sensibilities—and survival. Miller asserts that preserving Native culture is foremost a matter of keeping Natives and Native memory around. "But it isn't just about biological survival," says Miller. "It's also about spirituality and culture. There is a thread of rituals and beliefs that parallels our physical cohesiveness as tribal peoples, a thread that goes back thousands of years. It defines who we are as much as our DNA does."

Miller says that many Native religions and rituals are secret because they are 11 sacrosanct, appropriate for tribal members alone. "Natives don't proselytize Native religions," observes Miller. "We're not looking for converts. It isn't about shunning people—it's about keeping what little we have left."

Such contentions are antithetical to the free and unfettered exchange of ideas and 12 data in cyberspace. They also raise thorny questions: In the age of information, can any data be legitimately considered sacred? How do you upload holiness? "We know you can't police cyberspace," sighs Miller. "But like everything else, it's a matter of education and dialog."

To Miller's community, a particularly egregious example of Rapp's cultural 13 ripoff was Blue Snake's "pipe ceremonies." Proprietary rituals involving pipes are sacred to many tribes. The pipe, its accouterments, ceremonies surrounding the pipe—indeed, even spoken or written allusions to the pipe—are thus freighted with great spiritual significance. "His mumbo jumbo surrounding the pipe was especially offensive," says Miller.

After monitoring Blue Snake for a while from the sidelines, Miller, Towersap, and 14 a few of their pals began challenging the azure serpent and his starry-eyed gaggle of Red Hearted converts. They demanded that Rapp desist from conducting his seminars and fought his online doctrines, byte by byte, with their own. Eventually, they became so obstreperous they were tossed from the room by testy AOL guides. Miller, who has been permanently barred from AOL since 1994, still gets online by arranging payment through friends and employing a rich variety of pseudonyms. She admits her own duplicities constitute a rather sharp irony, given her ire with Blue Snake over his online misrepresentations, but she also argues that her actions are ethical and necessary. Miller insists there's a palpable world of truth out there—Native truth, tradition, and history—that must be protected from the vagaries of casual data-play.

Miller and her running mates ultimately 15 enlisted the aid of the three recognized tribes of the Shawnee nation in their quest to hamstring Blue Snake: the Absentee-Shawnee Tribe of Oklahoma, the Loyal Shawnee Tribe of Oklahoma, and the Eastern Shawnee Tribe of Oklahoma. A joint resolution drafted by leaders of the three tribes was e-mailed to AOL and Blue Snake. In it, the leaders declared that Rapp was not a recognized member of any Shawnee tribe or

> **Miller insists there's a palpable world of truth out there—Native truth, tradition, and history—that must be protected from the vagaries of casual data-play.**

band, adding: "It is said that imitation is the greatest form of flattery. However, the reports of Mr. Rapp's 'teachings' and Native American 'classes' would indicate that perhaps his intentions are less than honorable.

"The true Shawnee peoples are very traditional, and their ceremonies and rituals   16 are not for public consumption. They practice their traditional beliefs and rites as a matter of religion—no public 'powwows' or 'gatherings' are conducted."

AOL apparently was chastened by the letter. It relieved Rapp of his host status,   17 replacing Blue Snake's Lodge with a room dubbed Native American Chat. (Which still meets more or less regularly, usually on Tuesday evenings.) But again, complains Miller, the hosts were—and are—demonstrably non-Native. They couldn't or can't produce the federal enrollment credentials demanded by the genuine Indians who logged in to the room.

"There's a lot of controversy in the Native community about the significance of   18 federal enrollment," observes Miller. "The irony of enrollment is that a system designed by the conquerors and oppressors of Natives is now the benchmark for determining who is and isn't Native. Not every Native is enrolled, and we recognize this. But enrollment does definitively establish tribal affiliation—something we think is critical for host status." A potential host shouldn't necessarily be rejected if an enrollment number can't be produced, Miller says, but in that case, a vetting process conducted by recognized and respected Native Americans would be in order. "Otherwise, it's like a Swedish national claiming he could conduct a course on black American culture from an insider's perspective," laughs Miller.

Rapp, for his part, is somewhat bemused by all the heat and bile generated by his   19 online persona. "Basically, what we did was done in fun," he observes. "We certainly didn't intend any disrespect."

Rapp acknowledges freely that he has no Shawnee ancestry but says he was   20 adopted into the tribe by John Reese, a chief of the Eastern Band Shawnee. "The honored status of adoptees is a tradition among the Shawnee, though I never claimed I had Shawnee blood," Rapp says.

Rapp says that he provided some of his attackers with documents from Reese   21 establishing his tribal bona fides, but that they were rejected out of hand. And as far as vitiating sacred rites, says Rapp, he discussed only rituals that have long been documented in books such as *Black Elk Speaks*. "All that material was and is available through published texts," he asserts. "Can you take back what's already printed? I acknowledge that there is sacred and proprietary information and ceremonies in the Indian nations—I've witnessed some of them. And what I've witnessed that's truly sacred, I've never discussed."

For Rapp, the experience with Blue Snake's Lodge was distressing, but he never-   22 theless feels his seminars were a positive force both on the Net and in Indian Country. "At least I touched a nerve," he points out. "People loved me or hated me, but at least they were involved. I consider that an accomplishment."

At AOL, spokeswoman Margaret Ryan maintains the company was not obliged to   23 ascertain Rapp's Native credentials because the seminars were conducted in a "member" room as opposed to a fully sanctioned chat room. "We monitor the member areas to ensure online standards of conduct are upheld," she says, repeating the corporate dis-

claimer, "but we cannot screen public communication to make sure the topics discussed are legitimate. We advise our members to be as careful in their evaluation of
information and opinions on AOL as they are in everyday life."

Miller admits she and her online Native colleagues enjoyed chivying the devotees   24
of the spurious Snake—a guilty pleasure that helped mitigate their anger. But anger,
Miller emphasizes, was the dominant emotion—especially when their protests were
repeatedly stonewalled by AOL. "I was e-mailing a Sioux friend about it, and we came
to the conclusion that the company didn't want us disturbing the fantasy," said Miller.
"It doesn't want real Indians—we're not 'Indian' enough. It wants the buckskin fringes
and the feathers."

The problem had cropped up before—offline. For years, says Miller, fake or "rene-   25
gade" Indians have offered non-Natives entrée into the mystic realm of Native American spirituality, driving Native traditionalists nuts. "The worst was a guy named Sun
Bear, a Cheyenne who died a few years ago," recalls Miller. "He conducted seminars
all over the country, had followers who gave him money and gifts. He was prostituting
the culture of his tribe—the Cheyennes loathed him."

Still, online Natives figured such poseur high jinx were small potatoes compared   26
with the drivel flooding cyberspace. Misinformation spread by word of mouth during
retreats and seminars multiplies more or less arithmetically. But the rate of spread is
exponential online—an assault on Native sensibilities, claim activists, equivalent to the
wars of extermination of the last century.

How could they deal with this cultural analog of the Wounded Knee massacre?   27
The online compatriots were stumped—they could neither lick their foes nor join them.
Confronting AOL directly got them tossed. And any attempt at compromise, they felt,
would defeat their own purpose—this seemed to them a situation of right or wrong,
black or white. So the idea dawned: If they couldn't work with existing online communities, they could build one of their own. They would create an alternative that would
allow Native Americans from the Aleut villages of Alaska to the Apache reservations
of Arizona free and advanced access to computer-based telecommunications. A simultaneous goal: to provide non-Natives accurate information on Native cultures by allowing access to legitimate Indian spokespersons rather than self-styled shamans.

At first, the idea was simply that—a vaporous notion that didn't seem likely to go   28
beyond the gee-wouldn't-it-be-great stage. The obstacles, the friends well knew, were
enormous. Indeed, the simple precedents of past attempts dampened spirits. Previous
stabs at a Native American Net presence had met with less-than-stellar success. In
1992, George Baldwin, an instructor at Henderson State University in Arkansas who
now directs the Institute for Community Networking in Monterey, California, formed
IndianNet, an electronic bulletin board based in Rapid City, South Dakota, that provided information on grants and employment opportunities and allowed users to post
messages. But the long-distance rates were prohibitively expensive from the places
where most users lived—remote reservations in the West.

Another service now running is NativeNet, a mailing list and developing website.   29
It deals primarily with Native policy issues and is used mostly by academics. Finally, a
few tribes maintain bulletin boards of varying scope. But that's about it. Of the 550
federally recognized tribes and Native villages in the continental United States and

Alaska, only four—the Oneida and Onondaga of New York, the Navajo of Arizona and New Mexico, and the Sioux of North and South Dakota—have any significant Net presence. At the beginning of 1995, only 3 of the 28 Native-controlled colleges offered Net connections.

Much of the problem stems from the lack of wiring in Indian Country. Simply put, 30 there is little copper wire or fiber-optic cable in most of the lands controlled by North American Natives. No one knows how many Natives have phones, says Towersap, but the number is decidedly below the 94 percent figure cited for the American populace at large. "Many reservations don't even have electricity," observes Towersap. "And many Natives who do have phones have them only sporadically—they lose service when they can't pay their bill, which is commonplace." Such were the monumental real-world problems faced by Miller and her crew once they spurned the slippery cyberspace game of who's who; these conditions made it impossible for the great majority of their fellow Natives to even enter the contest.

Nevertheless, in late 1994, Miller, Towersap, and three compatriots—Disney 31 executive Dawn Jackson (who is Saginaw Chippewa), attorney Tamera Crites Shanker (Arapaho), and advertising creative director Victoria Bracewell Short (Creek)—incorporated as the nonprofit Native American Communications Council, and began work on the project.

Though proficient with computers, the partners aren't monomaniacal technophiles. 32 Rather, they see computers and wire as the best and brightest chance of reestablishing tribal bonds that were sundered with the massacre at Wounded Knee, an event remembered as ending all organized Indian resistance in North America. "When we get together, what we talk about is power (not computers)," says Short. "The Net is a tool that will allow us to forge bonds between the Indian nations. The only thing we have right now that facilitates intertribal communication is the powwow circuit (pantribal gatherings throughout the country, many open to the general public, that feature dances, food, handicrafts, and seminars). It's fine as far as it goes, but we need more."

Short observes that Natives have always been open to new technologies and dis- 33 posed to elegant communications systems. "We've always esteemed useful tools and goods," says Short. "We've always maintained ties with one another. We know from artifacts that trade routes threaded the continent. Gulf Coast pearls have been found at sites in New Mexico. The plains tribes all spoke different languages but shared a sign language that was understood by all. Smoke signaling may seem quaint when you see it in the movies, but it was an effective means of communicating information over long distances. Natives in the interior knew of the whites long before the whites knew of them."

The council's goals are straightforward: to develop a Native-owned and operated 34 telecommunications network that will provide Native Americans with easy access to information stored on the council's server while simultaneously offering most Internet functions, including gopher, ftp, telnet, as well as a website. The council's primary server will be linked to local servers on reservations, Alaskan Native villages, and urban Native service centers. Concomitantly, courses would be provided to local service centers to aid Natives in managing local nodes, navigating the Net, and creating Web home pages. "We also hope to launch an interactive service that will provide

updated information on grant, job, and educational opportunities and legal and health
issues," says Short.

Such ambitions are right in line with the plans of the Smithsonian's National   35
Museum of the American Indian, says Marty Kreipe de Montaño, a Prairie Band
Potawatomi who is creating interactive databases that will link images of the museum's
one million objects with its reams of curators' comments and more than 250,000
explanatory documents. "The museum will eventually have four sites," observes de
Montaño. "The first is the George Gustav Heye Center, which was founded in 1916 and
conjoined with the Smithsonian in 1990. The second will be a state-of-the-art storage
and research facility that we plan to build in Suitland, Maryland, by 1997. The third
will be the Smithsonian Mall museum, which is scheduled for completion by 2001."

And the fourth site, says de Montaño, will be an "electronic museum without   36
walls." This service will allow electronic access to the museum and provide information about real Natives in real time. "We consult with a number of tribal councils on
everything we do," she notes, "and they consider the fourth museum the most important because it will help people living in Indian Country today. The council's project is
similar. It's just what's needed."

Some elements of the council's system will be like Native religious rites, say the part-   37
ners—for Natives alone. But how will this be possible, given the porous nature of the Net?
"In the beginning, everybody will probably be able to tap into everything," acknowledges
Towersap. "But there are some things we'll want to keep exclusive—that's one of our primary reasons for starting this project. There's groupware evolving that will make this possible—applications that require membership passwords and are pretty secure."

At the Smithsonian, de Montaño agrees with Towersap that many Native objects,   38
images, and rites are sacred and not for public dissemination, but she is somewhat
dubious about the prospect of adequately protecting such information. "It's the nature
of the Net that it's difficult to control," she observes. "But we're always working with
tribal elders to determine which objects and what information are appropriate only for
tribal members, and we're always working on high-tech ways to protect them."

Connections to the museum would allow academicians and the merely curious   39
access to the quotidian issues and concerns of American Indians without all the hype,
hoopla, and out-and-out bullshit that has characterized most online interactions
between Native and non-Native peoples. The museum will allow dissemination of
accurate information on Natives and will facilitate direct, unfiltered, one-on-one communication between Indians and everybody else, says Shanker, who coordinates the
council's legal affairs.

The main thing standing between the council and a wired Native America, not sur-   40
prisingly, is money. "We've applied for a grant from the Eagle Staff Fund (a corporate
fund that supports a variety of Native projects) that we're reasonably optimistic about
getting," said Shanker. "That would give us about US$35,000 and get us up and run-
ning for the pilot project. It's also especially critical money because several of the other
grants we have pending are predicated on matching funds."

Shanker and her fellow council members are only too aware that a few thousand   41
dollars won't fulfill the council's grand goal of linking up all 550 nations. By any measure, the job is huge. But council members are sanguine, even serene.

"The simple fact is that Natives need to be a significant presence on the Net, and   42
we need to make that happen on our own terms," says Shanker, who acknowledges that
the slippery nature of online data swapping makes
any attempt to define and preserve fixed identities
tricky in the extreme. "If we don't define
who we are on the Net, other people will do it for
us," says Shanker. "And when that happens, part
of who we are disappears."

> **"If we don't define who we are on the Net, other people will do it for us," says Shanker.**

Blue Snake himself wishes Shanker the best in   43
her endeavors. "If what happened on AOL con-
tributes in some way to a viable Native telecommunications network, then I'm happy,"
observes Rapp. "It's what I've always wanted to see."

← SECOND THOUGHTS

1. Review and weigh the arguments of Blue Snake/Don Rapp and America Online versus Tracy Miller and the other Native critics of Blue Snake Lodge. To what extent do you think that Blue Snake Lodge should be characterized as harmless role-playing, cultural rip-off, or fraud? Do you think that people who are not members of a particular cultural group can effectively identify with or represent that group to others?

2. Martin explains that Tracy Miller was banned from AOL but "still gets online by arranging payment through friends and employing a rich variety of pseudonyms" (¶ 14). Do you find Miller's tactics hypocritical, given the nature of her criticism of Blue Snake Lodge? Or do you agree with her that these "actions are ethical and necessary" (¶ 14) under the circumstances?

3. Review the ambitious goals of the Native community efforts on the Net described by Martin. Do you think the Native American Communication Council's plan to restrict access to some religious information is, as some critics would suggest, "antithetical to the free and unfettered exchange of ideas and data in cyberspace" (¶ 12)?

Wolves of the Plateau

John Shirley

John Shirley (b. 1953) is a science fiction writer and musician, most recently with the San Francisco rock group Panther Moderns. His novels and short story collections include *City Come a-Walkin'* (orig. 1980, Eyeball Press 1996), *Wetbones* (Mark V. Ziesing, 1991), *New Noir* (Black Ice, 1993), *The Exploded Heart* (Eyeball Press, 1996), and *Silicon Embrace* (Mark V. Ziesing, 1996). His screenplays include *The Crow* (Pressman/MIRAMAX, 1995), based on a comic by James O'Barr, and he has written TV scripts for shows such as "Poltergeist," "Deep Space Nine," and "VR5." Shirley has a Web page at <www.darkecho.com/JohnShirley.html>. "Wolves of the Plateau" originally appeared in the literary journal *Mississippi Review* in 1988 and was part of Shirley's 1989 collection *Heatseeker* (Scream/Press).

N ine A.M., and Jerome-X wanted a smoke. He didn't smoke, but he wanted one in here, and he could see how people went into prison non-smokers, came out doing two packs a day. Maybe had to get their brains rewired to get off it. Which was ugly, he'd been rewired once to get off *sink,* synthetic cocaine, and he'd felt like a processor with a glitch for a month after that.

He pictured his thoughts like a little train, zipping around the cigarette-burnt graffiti YOU FUCKED NOW and GASMAN WAS HERE and GASMAN IS AN IDIOT-MO. The words were stippled on the dull pink ceiling in umber burn-spots. Jerome wondered who Gasman was and what they'd put him in prison for.

He yawned. He hadn't slept much the night before. It took a long time to learn to sleep in prison. He wished he'd upgraded his chip so he could use it to activate his sleep endorphins. But that was a grade above what he'd been able to afford—and *way* above the kind of brain-chips he'd been dealing. He wished he could turn off the light-panel, but it was sealed in.

There was a toilet and a broken water fountain in the cell. There were also four bunks, but he was alone in this static place of watery blue light and faint pink distances. The walls were salmon-colored garbage blocks. The words singed into the ceiling were blurred and impotent.

Almost noon, his stomach rumbling, Jerome was still lying on his back on the top bunk when the trashcan said, "Eric Wexler, re-ma-a-in on your bunk while the ne-ew prisoner ente-e-ers the cell!"

Wexler? Oh, yeah. They thought his name was Wexler. The fake ID program.

He heard the cell door slide open; he looked over, saw the trashcan ushering a stocky Chicano guy into lockup. The trashcan was a stumpy metal cylinder with four camera lenses, a retractable plastic arm, and a gun muzzle that could fire a Taser charge, rubber bullets, tear gas pellets, or .45 caliber rounds. It was supposed to use the .45 only in extreme situations but the 'can was battered, it whined when it moved, its voice was warped. When they got like that you didn't fuck with them, they'd mix up the rubber bullets with the .45 caliber.

The door sucked itself shut, the trashcan whined away down the hall, its rubber wheels squeaking once with every revolution. Jerome heard a tinny cymbal crash as someone, maybe trying to get the trashcan to shoot at a guy in the next cell, threw a tray at it. Followed by some echoey shouting and a distorted admonishment from the trashcan. The Chicano guy laughed.

"'Sappenin'" Jerome said, sitting up on the bed. He was grateful for the break in the monotony.

"*Qué pasa, cabróne?* You like the top bunk, huh? Thas good."   10

"I can read the ceiling better from up here. About ten seconds worth of reading matter. It's all I got. You can have the lower bunk."

"You fuckin'-*A* I can." But there was no real aggression in his tone. Jerome thought about turning on his chip, checking the guy's subliminals, his somatic signals, going for a model of probable aggression index; or maybe project for deception. He could be an undercover cop: Jerome hadn't given them his dealer; hadn't bargained at all.

But he decided against it. Some jails had scanners for unauthorized chip output. Better not use it unless he had to. And his gut told him this guy was only a threat if he felt threatened. His gut was right almost as often as his brain-chip.

The Chicano was thick bodied, maybe five foot six, a good five inches shorter than Jerome but probably outweighed him by fifty pounds. His face had Indian angles and small jet eyes. He was wearing printout gray-blue prison jams, #6631; they'd let him keep his hairnet. Jerome had never understood the Chicano hairnet, never had the balls to ask about it. The Chicano was standing by the plexigate, hands shoved in his pockets, staring at Jerome, looking like he was trying to place him.

Jerome was pleased. He liked to be recognized, except by people who could   15
arrest him.

"You put your hands in the pockets of those paper pants, they'll rip and in LA County they don't give you any more for three days," Jerome advised him.

"Yeah? Shit." The Chicano took his hands carefully out of his pockets. "I don't want my *huevos* hanging out, people think I'm advertising some shit. You not a faggot, right?"

"Nope."

"Good. How come I know you? When I *don't* know you."

Jerome grinned. "From television. You saw my tag. Jerome-X."   20

"Ohhhh yeah. Jerome-X. You got one of those little transers? Chop into transmission with your own shit?"

"Had. They confiscated it."

"That why you here? Video graffiti?"

"I wish—then I'd be out in a couple months. No, man. Illegal augs."

"Hey, man! Me too!"   25

"You?" Jerome couldn't conceal his surprise. You didn't see a lot of the brown brothers doing illegal augmentation. They generally didn't like people dicking with their brains.

"What, you think a guy from East LA can't use augmentation?"

"No, no. I know lots of Hispanic guys that use it," Jerome lied.

"Ooooh, he says *Hispanic,* that gotta nice sound." Overtones of danger.

Jerome hastily changed the direction of the conversation. "You never been in the big lockups where they use paper jammies?"   30

"No, just the city jail once. They didn't have those fucking screw machines either. Hey, you Jerome, my name's Jessie. Actually it's Jesus—" he pronounced it Hay-soo "—but people they, you know. . . . You got any smokes? No? Shit. Okay, I adjust."

He sat on the edge of the bed, to one side of Jerome's dangling legs, and tilted his head forward. He reached under his hairnet, and under what turned out to be a hairplug, and pulled a chip from a jack unit set into the base of his skull.

Jerome stared. "Goddamn, their probes really *are* busted."

Jessie frowned over the chip. There was a little blood on it. The jack unit was leaking. Cheap installation. "No, they ain't busted, there's a guy working the probe, he's paid off . . . letting everyone through for a couple of days 'cause some mob *vatos* are coming in and he don't know exactly which ones they are."

"I thought sure they were going to find my unit," Jerome said. "The strip search didn't turn it but I figured the prison probes would and that'd be another year on my sentence. But they didn't." Neither one of them thinking of throwing away the chips. It'd be like cutting out an eye.   35

"Same story here. We both lucky."

Jessie put the microprocessing chip in his mouth, the way people did with their contact lenses, to clean it, lubricate it.

"Jack hurt?" Jerome asked.

Jessie took the chip out, looked at it a moment on his fingertip; it was smaller than a contact lens, a sliver of silicon and gallium arsenide with, probably, 1,500,000 nanotransistors of engineered protein molecules sunk into it, maybe more. "No it don't hurt yet. But if it's leaking, it fuckin' *will* hurt man." He said something else in Spanish, shaking his head. He slipped it back into his jack-in unit, and tapped it with the thumbnail of his right hand. So that was where the activation mouse was: under the thumbnail. Jerome's was in a knuckle.

Jessie rocked slightly, just once, sitting up on his bunk, which meant the chip had engaged and he was getting a read-out. They tended to feed back into your nervous system a little at first, make you twitch once or twice; if they weren't properly insulated they could make you crap your pants.   40

"That's okay," Jessie said, relaxing. "That's better." The chip inducing his brain to secrete some vasopressin, contract the veins, simulate the effect of nicotine. It worked for awhile, till you could get cigarettes. A highgrade chip could do some numbing, if you were hung up on *sim,* synthetic morphine, and couldn't score. But that was Big Scary. You could turn yourself off that way, permanently. You better be doing fine adjusting.

Jerome thought about the hypothetical chip scanners. Maybe he should object to the guy using his chip here. But what the Chicano was doing wouldn't make for much leakage.

"What you got?" Jerome asked.

"I got an Apple NanoMind II. Good megabytes. You?"

"You got the Mercedes, I got the Toyota. Usin' a *Sesó Picante* Mark I. One of   45
those Argentine things." (How had this guy scored an ANM II?)

"Yeah, what you got, they kinda *basto* but they do most what you need. Hey, your
name's Jerome, mine's Jessie, they both start with J. And we both here for illegal augs.
What else we got in common. What's your sign?"

"Uh—" What was it anyway? He always forgot. "Pisces."

"No shit! I can relate to Pisces. I ran an astrology program, figured out who I should
hang with, Pisces is okay. But Aquarius is—I'm a Scorpio, like—Aquarius, *qué bueño*."

What did he mean exactly, *hang with,* Jerome wondered. Scoping me about am *I* a
faggot, maybe that was something defensive.

But he meant something else. "You know somethin' Jerome, you got your chip   50
too, we could do a link and maybe get over on that trashcan."

Break out? Jerome felt a chilled thrill go through him. "Link with that thing? Control it? I don't think the two of us would be enough."

"We need some more guys maybe but I got news, Jerome, there's more comin'.
Maybe their names all start with J."

But they didn't. In quick succession, the trashcan brought them a fortyish beach-
bum named Eddie, a cadaverous black dude named Bones, a queen called Swish,
whose real name, according to the trashcan, was Paul Torino.

"This place smells like it's comin' apart," Eddie said. He had a surfer's greasy
blond topknot and all the usual surf punk tattoos. Meaningless now, Jerome thought, the
pollution-derived oxidation of the local offshore had pretty much ended ocean surfing.
The anaerobics had taken over the surf, thriving in the toxic waters like a gelatinous Sar-
gasso. "Smells in here like it died and didn't go to heaven. Stinks worse'n Malibu."

"It's those landfill blocks," Bones said. He was missing four front teeth (confis-   55
cated?) and his sunken face resembled something out of a zombie flick. But he was an
energetic zombie. "Compressed garbage," he told Eddie. "Organic stuff mixed with the
polymers, the plastics, whatever was in the trash heap, make 'em into bricks 'cause
they run outta landfill, but after a while, if the contractor didn't get 'em to set right,
y'know, they start to rot. It's hot outside is why you're gettin' it now. Use garbage to
cage garbage, they say. Fucking assholes."

In the heat of the day the background smell of rancid garbage thickened. It turned
Jerome's stomach more because of what it reminded him of than the actual smell. It
made him think of garbage disposals, and Charlie Chesterton had once told him that
prisons, in the year 2022, were the State's garbage disposal system. . . . Get caught in
the penal system and you could almost feel the dispose-all blades. . . .

The trashcan pushed a rack of trays up to the plexiglass bars and *whirred* their
lunch to them, tray by tray. It gave them an extra one. It was screwing up.

They ate their chicken patties—the chicken was almost greaseless, gristleless,
which meant it was vat chicken, genetically engineered stuff—and between bites they
bitched about the food and indulged in the usual paranoid speculation about mind control chemicals in the coffee. Jerome looked around at the others, thinking: *At least
they're not ass-kickers.* They were crammed here because of the illegal augs sweep,

some political drive to clean up the clinics, maybe to see to it that the legal augmentation companies kept their pit-bull grip on the industry. So there wasn't anybody in for homicide, for gang torture, or anything. Not a bad cell to be in.

"You Jerome-X, really?" Swish fluted. A faint accent. She (Jerome always thought of a queen as *she* and *her,* out of respect for the tilt of her consciousness) was either Mexican or Filipino; hard to tell because she'd had her face "girled" at a cheap clinic. Cheeks built up for a heart-shape, eyes rounded, lips filled out, glass tits looking like there was a couple of tin funnels under her jammies. Some of the injected collagen in her lips had shifted so her lower lip was now lopsided. One cheekbone was a little higher than the other. A karmic revenge on malekind, Jerome thought, for forcing women into girdles and foot-binding and anorexia. What did this creature use her chip for, besides getting high?

"Oooh, Jerome-X! I saw your tag before on the TV. The one when you kind of 60 floated around the President's head and some printout words came out of your mouth and blocked her face out. God, she's such a *cunt.*"

"What words did he block her out with?" Eddie asked.

"'Would you know a liar if you heard one anymore?' That's what it was," Swish said. "It was *sooo* perfect because that cunt wants another war, you *know* she does. And she lies about it, ooh *God* how she lies."

"You just think she's a cunt because *you* want one," Eddie said, dropping his pants to use the toilet. He talked loudly to cover up the noise of it. "You want one and you can't afford it. I think the President's right, the fucking Mexican People's Republic is scummin' on our borders, sending commie agents in—"

Swish said, "Oh God he's a Surf Nazi—but *God* yes I want one—I want *her* cunt. That prune doesn't know how to use it anyway. Honey, I know how *I'd* use that thing—" Swish stopped abruptly and shivered, hugging herself. With her long purple nails she reached up and pried loose a flap of skin behind her ear, and plucked out her chip. She wet it, adjusted its feed-mode, put it back in, tapping it with the activation mouse under a nail. She pressed the flap shut. Her eyes glazed as she adjusted. She could do that for maybe twenty-four hours and then it'd ice her, sure. She'd have to go cold turkey or die. Or get out. And maybe she'd been doing it for awhile now.

None of them would be allowed to post bail. They'd each get the two years mandatory 65 minimum sentence. Illegal augs, the feds thought, were getting out of hand. Black market chip implants were used for playing havoc with the State database lottery; used by bookies of all kinds; used to keep accounts where the IRS couldn't find them; used to scam banking computers, and for spiking cash machines; used to milk the body, prod the brain into authorizing the secretion of beta-endorphins and ACTH and adrenalin and testosterone and other biochemical toys; used to figure the odds at casinos; used to compute the specs for home-made designer drugs; used by the mob's street dons to plot strategy and tactics; used by the kid gangs for the same reasons; used for illegal congregations on the Plateau.

It was the Plateau, Jerome thought, that really scared the shit out of the Feds. It had possibilities.

The trashcan dragged in a cot for the extra man, shoved it folded under the door, and blared, "Lights out, all inmates are required to be i-i-in their bu-unks-s-s . . ." Its voice was failing.

After the trashcan and the light had gone, they climbed off their bunks and sat hunkered in a circle on the floor.

They were on chips, but not transmission-linked to one another. Jacked-up on the chips, they communicated in a spoken short-hand.

"Bull," Bones was saying. "Door." He was a voice in the darkness.   70

"Time," Jessie said.

"Compatibility? Know?" Eddie said.

Jerome said, "No shit." Snorts of laughter from the others.

"Link check," Bones said.

"Models?" Jessie said.   75

Then they joined in an incantation of numbers.

It was a fifteen minute conversation in less than a minute.

"It's bullshit," Bones was saying, translated. "You get past the trashcan, there's human guards, you can't reprogram them."

"But at certain hours," Jessie told him, "there's only one on duty. They're used to seeing the can bring people in and out. They won't question it till they try to confirm it. By then we'll be on their ass."

"We might not be compatible," Eddie pointed out. "You understand, compatible?"   80

"Oh, hey man, I *think* we can comprehend that," Jerome said, making the others snort with laughter. Eddie wasn't liked much.

Bones said, "The only way to see if we're compatible is to do a systems link. We got the links, we got the thinks, like the man says. It's either the chain that holds us in or it's the chain that pulls us out."

Bones said, ". . . It's either the chain that holds us in or it's the chain that pulls us out."

Jerome's scalp tightened. A systems link. A mini-Plateau. Sharing minds. Brutal intimacy. Maybe some fallout from the Plateau. He wasn't ready for it.

If it went sour he could get time tacked onto his sentence for attempted jailbreak. And somebody might get dusted. They might have to kill a human guard. Jerome had once punched a dealer in the nose, and the spurt of blood had made him sick. He couldn't kill anyone. But . . . he had shit for alternatives. He knew he wouldn't make it through two years anyway, when they sent him up to the Big One. The Big One'd grind him up for sure. They'd find his chip and it'd piss them off. They'd let the bulls rape him and give him the New Virus; he'd flip out from being locked in and chipless and they'd put him in Aversion Rehab and burn him out totally.

Jerome savaged a thumbnail with his incisors. *Sent to the Big One.* He'd been trying   85
not to think about it. Making himself take it one day at a time. But now he had to look at the alternatives. His stomach twisted itself to punish him for being so stupid. For getting into dealing augments so he could finance a big transer. *Why?* A transer didn't get him anything but his face pirated onto local TV for maybe twenty seconds. He'd thrown himself away trying to get it . . .

Why was it so fucking important? his stomach demanded, wringing itself vindictively.

"Thing is," Bones said, "we could all be cruisin' into a setup. Some kind of sting thing. Maybe it's a little too weird how the police prober let us all through."

(Someone listening would have heard him say, "Sting, funny luck.")

Jessie snorted. "I tol' you, man. The prober is paid off. They letting them all through because some of them are mob. I know that, because I'm part of the thing. Okay?"

("Probe greased, fade me.")   90

"You with the mob?" Bones asked.

("You?")

"You got it. Just a dealer. But I know where a half million newbux wortha the shit is, so they going to get me out. The way the system is set up, the prober had to let everyone through. His boss thinks we got our chips taken out when they arraigned us, sometimes they do it that way. This time it was supposed to be the jail surgeon. Before they catch up with their own red tape we get outta here. Now listen—we can't do the trashcan without we all get into it, because we haven't got enough *K* otherwise. So who's in?"

He'd said, "Low, half million, bluff surgeon, there here, all-none, *who* yuh fucks?"

Something in his voice skittering behind smoked glass: he was getting testy, irrita-   95
ble from the chip adjustments for his nicotine habit, maybe other adjustments. The side effects of liberal cerebral self-modulating burning through a threadbare nervous system.

The rest of the meeting, translated . . .

"I dunno," Eddie said. "I thought I'd do my time 'cause if it goes sour—"

"Hey man," Jessie said, "I can *take* your fuckin' chip. And be out before they notice your ass don't move no more."

"The man's right," Swish said. Her pain-suppression system was unraveling, axon by axon, and she was running out of adjust. "Let's just do it, okay? Please? Okay? I gotta get out. I feel like I wish I was dog shit so I could be something better."

"I can't handle two years in the Big, Eddie," Jerome heard himself say. Realizing   100
he was helping Jessie threaten Eddie. Amazed at himself. Not his style.

"It's all of us or nobody, Eddie," Bones said.

Eddie was quiet for a while.

Jerome had turned off his chip, because it was thinking endlessly about Jessie's plan, and all it came up with was an ugly model of the risks. You had to know when to go with intuition.

Jerome was committed. And he was standing on the brink of link. The time was now, starting with Jessie.

Jessie was the operator. He picked the order. First Eddie, to make sure about him.   105
Then Jerome. Maybe because he had Jerome scoped for a refugee from the middle class, an anomaly here, and Jerome might try and raise the Man on his chip, cut a deal. Once they had him linked in, he was locked up.

After Jerome, it'd be Bones and then Swish.

They held hands, so that the link signal, transmitted from the chip using the electric field generated by the brain, would be carried with the optimum fidelity.

He heard them exchange frequency designates, numbers strung like beads in the darkness, and heard the hiss of suddenly indrawn breaths as Jessie and Eddie linked in. And he heard, "Let's go, Jerome."

Jerome's eyes had adjusted to the dark, the night giving up some of its buried light, and Jerome could just make out a crude outline of Jessie's features like a charcoal rubbing from an Aztec carving.

Jerome reached to the back of his own head, found the glue-tufted hairs that 110 marked his flap, and pulled the skin away from the chip's jack unit. He tapped the chip. It didn't take. He tapped it again, and this time he felt the shift in his bio electricity; felt it hum between his teeth.

Jerome's chip communicating with his brain via an interface of rhodopsin protein; the ribosomes borrowing neurohumoral transmitters from the brain's blood supply, re-ordering the transmitters so that they carried a programmed pattern of ion releases for transmission across synaptic gaps to the brain's neuronal dendrites; the chip using magnetic resonance holography to collate with brain-stored memories and psychological trends. Declaiming to itself the mythology of the brain; re-enacting on its silicon stage the personal Legends of his subjective world history.

Jerome closed his eyes and looked into the back of his eyelids. The digital read-out was printed in luminous green across the darkness. He focused on the cursor, concentrated so it moved up to ACCESS. He subverbalized, "Open frequency." The chip heard his practiced subverbalization, and numbers appeared on the back of his eyelids: 63391212.70. He read them out to the others and they picked up his frequency. Almost choking on the word, knowing what it would bring, he told the chip: "Open."

It opened to the link. He'd only done it once before. It was illegal and he was secretly glad it was illegal because it scared him. "They're holding the Plateau back," his brain-chip source had told him, "because they're scared of what worldwide electronic telepathy might bring down on them. Like, everyone will collate information, use it to see through the bastards' game, throw the ass-bites out of office."

Maybe that was one reason. It was something the power brokers couldn't control. But there were other reasons. Reasons like a strikingly legitimate fear of going batshit crazy.

All Jerome and the others wanted was a sharing of processing capabilities. Collab- 115 orative calculation. But the chips weren't designed to filter out the irrelevant input before it reached the user's cognition level. Before the chip had done its filtering the two poles of the link—Jerome and Jessie—would each see the swarming hive of the other's total consciousness. Would see the other as they perceived themselves to be, and then objectively, as they were.

He saw Jessie as a grid and as a holographic entity. He braced himself and the holograph came at him, an abstract tarantula of computer-generated color and line, scrambling down over him . . . and for an instant it crouched in the seat of his consciousness. Jessie. Jesus Chaco.

Jessie was a family man. He was a patriarch, a protector of his wife and six kids and his widowed sister's four kids and of the poor children of his barrio. He was a muddied painting of his father, who had fled the social forest fire of Mexico's communist revolution, spiriting his capital to Los Angeles where he'd sown it into the black market. Jessie's father had been killed defending territory from the mob; Jessie compromised with the mob to save his father's business, and loathed himself for it. Wanted to kill their *capos;* had instead to work side by side with them. Perceived his wife as a functional pet, an object of adoration who was the very apotheosis of her fixed role. To imagine her doing anything other than child-rearing and keeping house would be to imagine the sun become a snowball, the moon become a monkey.

And Jerome glimpsed Jessie's undersides: Jesus Chaco's self-image with its outsized penis and impossibly spreading shoulders, sitting in a perfect and shining cherry automobile, always the newest and most luxurious model, the automotive throne from which he surveyed his kingdom. Jerome saw guns emerging from the grill of the car to splash Jessie's enemies apart with his unceasing ammunition. . . . It was a Robert Williams cartoon capering at the heart of Jessie's unconscious. . . . Jessie saw himself as Jerome saw him; the electronic mirrors reflecting one another. Jessie cringed.

Jerome saw himself, then, reflected back from Jessie.

He saw Jerome-X on a video screen with lousy vertical hold; wobbling, trying to arrange its pixels firmly and losing them. A figure of mewling inconsequence; a brief flow of electrons that might diverge left or right like spray from a waterhose depressed with the thumb. Raised in a high-security condo village, protected by cameras and computer lines to private security thugs; raised in a media-windowed womb, with PCs and VCRs and a thousand varieties of video game; shaped by cable-TV and fantasy rentals; sexuality distorted by sneaking looks at his parents' badly-hidden stash of Cassex videos. And always plugged into the Grid, the condo's satellite dish pulling in stations from around the nation, around the world, seeing the same StarFaces appear on channel after channel as the star's fame spread like a stain across the frequency bands. Seeing the Star's World Self crystallizing; the media figure coming into definition against the backdrop of media competition. Becoming real in this electronic collective unconscious.

Becoming real simply because he'd appeared on a few thousand TV screens. Growing up with a sense that media events were real, and personal events were not. Anything that didn't happen on television didn't happen. Even as he hated conventional programming, even as he regarded it as the cud of ruminants, still it defined his sense of personal unreality; and left him unfinished.

Jerome saw Jerome: perceiving himself unreal. Jerome: scamming a transer, creating a presence via video graffiti. Thinking he was doing it for reasons of radical statement. Seeing, now, that he was doing it to make himself feel substantial, to superimpose himself on the Media Grid . . .

And then Eddie's link was there, Eddie's computer model sliding down over Jerome like a mudslide. Eddie seeing himself as a Legendary Wanderer, a rebel, a homemade mystic; his fantasy parting to reveal an anal-expulsive sociopath; a whiner perpetually scanning for someone to blame for his sour luck.

Suddenly Bones tumbled into the link; a complex worldview that was a sort of streetside sociobiology, mitigated by a loyalty to friends, a mystical faith in brain-chips and amphetamines. His underside a masochistic dwarf, the troll of self-doubt, lacerating itself with guilt.

And then Swish, a woman with an unsightly growth, errant glands that were like tumors to her. Grown predatory for the means to dampen the pain of an infinite self-derision that mimicked her father's utter rejection of her. A mystical faith in synthetic morphine.

. . . Jerome mentally reeling with disorientation, seeing the others as a network of distorted self-images, caricatures of grotesque ambitions. Beyond them he glimpsed another realm through a break in the psychic clouds: the Plateau, the whispering plane of brain-chips linked on forbidden frequencies, an electronic haven for doing deals unseen by cops; a Plateau prowled only by the exquisitely ruthless; a vista of enormous challenges and inconceivable risks and always the potential for getting lost, for madness. A place roamed by the wolves of wetware.

There was a siren quiver from that place, a soundless howling, pulling at them . . . drawing them in . . .

"*Uh*-uh," Bones said, maybe loud or maybe through the chips. Translated from chip short-hand, those two syllables meant: "Stay away from the Plateau, or we get sucked into it, we lose our focus. Concentrate on parallel processing function."

Jerome looked behind his eyelids, sorted through the files. He moved the cursor down. . . .

Suddenly it was there. The group-thinking capacity looming above them, a sentient skyscraper. A rush of megalomaniacal pleasure in identifying with it. A towering edifice of Mind. Five chips become One.   130

They were ready. Jessie transmitted the bait.

Alerted to an illegal use of implant-chips, the trashcan was squeaking down the hall, scanning to precisely locate the source. Stopping in front of their cell. Jessie reached through the bars and touched its input jack.

Midway through a turn the machine froze with a *clack,* humming as it processed what they fed it. Would it bite? Bones had a program for the IBM Cyberguard 14s, with all the protocol and a range of sample entry codes. Parallel processing from samples, it took them less than two seconds to decrypt the trashcan's access code. They were in. The hard part was the reprogramming.

Jerome found the way. He told the trashcan that he wasn't Eric Wexler, because the DNA code was all wrong, if you looked close enough; what we have here is a case of mistaken identity.

Since this information, from the trashcan's viewpoint, was coming from authorized sources—the decrypted access code made them authorized—it fell for the gag and opened the cage.   135

The trashcan took the five Eric Wexlers down the hall—that was Jessie's doing, showing them how to make it think of five as one, something his people had learned for the Immigration computers. It escorted them through the plastiflex door, through the steel door, and into Receiving. The human guard was heaping sugar into his antique Ronald MacDonald coffee mug and watching *The Mutilated* on his wallet-TV. Bones and Jessie were in the room and moving in on him before he broke free of the television and went for the button. Bones's long left arm spiked out and his stiffened fingers hit a nerve cluster below the guy's left ear. The guard went down, the sugar dispenser in one hand swishing a white fan onto the floor.

Bones's long left arm spiked out and his stiffened fingers hit a nerve cluster below the guy's left ear.

Jerome's chip had cross-referenced Bones's attack style. *Commando training,* the chip said. *Military elite.* Was he a plant? Bones smiled at him and tilted his head, which Jerome's chip read as: *No. I'm trained by the Underground. Roots Radics.*

Jessie was at the console, deactivating the trashcan, killing the cameras, opening the outer doors. Jessie and Swish led the way out; Swish whining softly and biting her lip. There were two more guards at the gate, one of them asleep. Jessie had taken the gun from the screw Bones had put it under, so the first guard at the gate was dead before he could hit an alarm. The cat-napping guy woke and yelled with hoarse terror, and then Jessie shot him in the throat.

Watching the guard fall, spinning, blood making its own slow-motion spiral in the air, Jerome felt sickness, fear, self disgust seeing this stranger die. The guard was young, wearing a cheap wedding ring, probably had a young family. So Jerome stepped over the dying man and made an adjustment; used his chip, chilled himself out with adrenalin. Had to. He was committed now. And he knew with a bland certainty that they had reached the Plateau after all.

He would stay on the Plateau. He belonged there, now that he was one of the wolves.   140

← SECOND THOUGHTS

1. Aside from their being prisoners all accused of the same crime, how do the story's characters appear to occupy the social margins of this future society? Describe Jerome, Jessie, Eddie, Bones, and Swish in terms of their cultural identities—race or ethnicity, socioeconomic class, sexual orientation, etc. Based on these marginal characters and other clues in the story, how would you describe the social and political *mainstream* that apparently exists in year 2022?

2. When the prisoners consider working together to escape, Bones says, "It's either the chain that holds us or the chain that pulls us out" (¶ 82). But the powerful "systems link" that they form requires that they first share a "brutal intimacy." What's the nature of that required intimacy, and why do you think it's important to the story? What do you think the story implies about the relationship between personal identity and collaboration or community?

3. Jerome grew up "with a sense that media events were real, and personal events were not" (¶ 121). To what extent do you think Jerome's media-intensive background reflects social conditions and trends of today, extrapolated into the future? What other aspects of the story do you think reflect and comment on current social conditions, and how so?

4. According to Jerome, why are the authorities fearful of the Plateau? What "possibilities" (¶ 66) does the Plateau seem to contain? Based on clues in the story and your own experience or other reading, how would you compare the fictional Plateau with today's real-life Internet?

⚏ DISCUSSION THREADS

re: Lyles and Silberman

1. Based on the articles by Charlise Lyles and Steve Silberman, how would you compare and contrast the participants in CyberFaith International and those in America Online's Gay and Lesbian Community Forum in terms of their motivations, goals, and actual uses of Internet communication?

re: Lyles, Silberman, and Padilla

2. Ken Bedell (in Charlise Lyles' article) says that online interaction "has the appearance of being socially blind, colorblind, and classblind" (¶ 16), and Steve Silberman describes online communication as "a venue where individuals make themselves known by the acuity of their thought and expression, rather than by their physical appearance" (¶ 17). How does Max Padilla, in his essay, specifically challenge these claims? Despite the different quality of his online experience, what goals do you think he shares with the CyberFaith or gay-forum participants?

re: Lyles, Padilla, and Martin

3. Based on the articles by Charlise Lyles and Glen Martin, how do you think the CyberFaith founders or Native American activists on the Net would respond to Max Padilla's conclusion that the Internet "is no Netopia, but an all-too-painful reflection of the real world. America Online resembles America, all right. Majority rules" (¶ 9)?

re: Lyles, Silberman, Padilla, Martin, and Shirley

4. The narrator of John Shirley's story describes the Plateau as "the whispering plane of brain-chips linked on forbidden frequencies" (¶ 126)—a subversive, black-market haven for the ruthless and the marginal. To what extent do you think the Plateau, in its subversiveness, is a force for social good or social ill? How do you think the other writers in this chapter, or the subjects they write about, feel about the subversive potential of the Internet?

re: Cultural Identity and Cyberspace

5. Glen Martin quotes Tamera Crites Shanker as saying, "If we don't define who we are on the Net, other people will do it for us. And when that happens, part of who we are disappears" (¶ 42). From what you've read and experienced, how well do you think that important parts of your own cultural identity are being represented on, and helping define, the Internet?

RESEARCH LINKS

- *For direct links to listed Internet sources, additional reading selections and questions online, plus updates and supplementary Web resources, see* **Composing Cyberspace Online** *at <www.mhhe.com/socscience/english/holeton/>.*
- *For a complete set of research tools for the Internet—including the most useful search strategies, directories, and conventions for documenting online sources—see McGraw-Hill English Composition at <www.mhhe.com/socscience/english/compde/>.*

1. If you have e-mail and Internet access, subscribe to a listserv or electronic mailing list related to your religious or cultural interests, like the CyberFaith group discussed by Charlise Lyles. Alternatively, join a Usenet newsgroup discussion in the *soc.culture* or *soc.religion* group, like those discussed by Max Padilla. Tile.Net maintains an excellent index of both listservs and newsgroups on the Web at <tile.net/>. "Lurk" (that is, just read the messages posted by others) on the mailing list or newsgroup for awhile to get a feel for the conventions of the group, such as what kinds of subjects and messages are considered appropriate. For newsgroups, you should also try to read the group's FAQ or Frequently Asked Questions document (for a list of FAQs, see <www.cis.ohio-state.edu/hypertext/faq/bngusenet/top.html>). When you feel ready, post your own message to the list or group. If possible, keep an archive of the discussion by saving the messages on your computer, so that you can refer back to particular parts of the discussion. Write about what you found valuable and less valuable about the experience, with specific examples from the group's electronic discussion.

2. Whatever your own sexual orientation, make a list of questions you'd like to ask gay or lesbian readers about Steve Silberman's and Max Padilla's articles in this chapter. Then interview gay or lesbian friends, family members, acquaintances, or members of your college's gay and lesbian student organization. If you or they have tried online discussions or chat areas related to sexual orientation, was the experience more like JohnTeen's (from the Silberman piece) or Padilla's? How so?

3. The Queer Resources Directory referred to in Steve Silberman's article is currently located at <www.qrd.org/QRD/>; another good resource, the Institute for Global Communications LesBiGay Directory, is at <www.igc.org/lbg/>. If you have Internet access, explore some of the additional resources listed at these or other gay/lesbian Web sites. Choose a narrow focus, such as sites related to AIDS or sites devoted to socializing, and write a critical, annotated bibliography of selected Web sources for this topic. For each source, write an objective summary or abstract followed by your evaluation of its usefulness in relation to other available sources. If you know how to use HTML (Hypertext Markup Language) or a Web editor, consider publishing your bibliography directly on the Web, including links to the sources you discuss.

4. Among the "thorny questions" posed by Glen Martin's article are these: "In the age of information, can any data be legitimately considered sacred? How do you upload holiness?" Read Mark Fearer's article "Scientology's Secrets" in Chapter 8 (p. 350). How would you compare Native American activists' plans to protect sacred infor-

mation with attempts by the Church of Scientology to protect its own "sacred texts"? What differences do you think there are in the way the two communities use information or the Net? Conduct research in the library and on the Internet to bring both controversies up to date (using, for example, magazine and newspaper indexes for the last two years). Write an essay comparing, contrasting, and taking a position on the tensions in these cases between the public's interest in open access to information and the interests of cultural and religious groups in keeping some information private.

5. A crucial issue for people of color, poor people, and anyone interested in the social effects of cyberspace is equal access to electronic resources. Research the current state of electronic access for members of particular minority groups, and evaluate how those groups are using the Internet. For example, the developing NativeNet Web site referred to by Glen Martin in this chapter is at <www.fdl.cc.mn.us/nat-net/>, and with a search you will find many other Native American resources on the Web (one good listing of links is maintained by Humboldt (California) State University at <www.humboldt.edu/~nasp/otherwww.html>). In the case of Native Americans, you could explore the currently available electronic resources for this group and evaluate these resources according to the original goals of Native activists, as reported by Martin in his article; you might also analyze the progress in wiring and improving access on North American Indian reservation lands.

6. John Shirley's work—with its marginal characters and hard-driving, uncompromising narrative and plots—has been called the epitome of the "cyberpunk" genre (Shirley's background as a one-time street person and punk rock lyricist and musician may contribute to the mystique too). Write a research-based essay on some aspect of cyberpunk as either a literary genre or subculture. You might focus on individual writers, themes, or works of art/cultural expressions. You could start your research in print with *Mondo 2000: A User's Guide to the New Edge* (Harper-Collins, 1992), edited by Rudy Rucker, R.U. Sirius, and Queen Mu, or *Fiction 2000: Cyberpunk and the Future of Narrative* (University of Georgia Press, 1992), edited by George Slueer and Tom Shippey. You will find thousands of references and resources about cyberpunk literature and culture on the Internet; you might start with the FAQ document for the newsgroup *alt.cyberpunk*, located at <www.knarf.demon.co.uk/alt-cp.htm>.

Part Two

Building Community in the Electronic Age

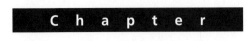

Virtual
Community

Courtesy of Cory Garfin.

The "family@21st.century.hom" cartoon, by Cory Garfin, pokes fun at our increasing dependence on electronic communication, even with the people closest to us. The ultra-modern family portrayed here, despite being seated together "face to face" around their dining room table, communicates via networked computers. To accentuate the point, Garfin has replaced their heads with "emoticons" or "smileys," keyboard-text characters that visually express crude emotions, a convention that has developed from widespread use of e-mail. (You read emoticons sideways by tilting your head counterclockwise. The man seated on the right wears :-) or the common smiley face, usually used to mean "I'm happy" or "I'm joking"; the woman standing to the left appears to be winking above pursed lips.) The children's emoticons are not conventional or obvious ones—is the child in the highchair frowning, the other child smiling and wearing a cap?—and so the cartoonist seems to be exaggerating and satirizing the convention of using emoticons itself, just as he satirizes e-mail addresses in the caption.

People developed emoticons because of the difficulty of expressing emotion and tone in written language, the primary means of computer-mediated communication or CMC. The advantages and disadvantages of CMC for expressing personal identity are explored in Chapters 2 and 3; this chapter examines both positive and negative effects of CMC and the Internet on building community. The questions of identity and community are closely linked, of course, since we most commonly form groups based on shared cultural identities, as well as physical proximity, and those groups, in turn, help us shape and express our identity. The most basic social group in our culture is the nuclear family, so in that context the notion of giving up some essential piece of our humanity is particularly disturbing—in Garfin's cartoon, family members not only give up the expressiveness of their voices and faces but literally lose their heads! Moreover, even the food has become virtual ("one more byte"), and the safe physical haven of "Home Sweet Home" has been transformed by Garfin into an electronic "homepage" on the Web, accessible to millions of Internet users. Is this liberation, the cartoonist may be asking us, or a new form of enslavement?

While emoticon heads are obviously absurd, some community members' dependence on electronic communication—even among family members or people seated in the same room—is not farfetched at all today. Corporate employees, even those in the same building or floor, work together on "intranets" or internal networks. College students who move away from home stay in touch with friends and family by e-mail, in most cases more frequently than they used to write paper letters (now referred to as "snail-mail"). Perhaps you already use CMC to get assignments from teachers, collaborate with classmates, or make plans with dormmates; you may even have experience electronically "chatting" with fellow students seated together in a computer classroom or lab (see Chapter 9 for a closer look at instructional technologies) or with other people across the Internet.

It's on the Net, at a physical distance, where the potential of virtual community (that is, forming and maintaining bonds with people through CMC) is being most intensively explored and tested. In the following pages, Howard Rheingold tells several moving stories about people sharing interests and helping one another through conferences on the WELL (Whole Earth 'Lectronic Link), a pioneering online forum that may represent "one of the informal places where people can rebuild the aspects of community that were lost when the malt shop became a mall." John Perry Barlow, another

WELL veteran, relates similar experiences but also wonders about the missing ingredients of online communities—the body and spirit, human diversity, and the sense of shared adversity that brings communities together.

Amy Bruckman, a researcher from the Georgia Institute of Technology who has started two virtual communities, recommends that designers of such communities adopt specific policies about admissions, anonymity, and the architecture of electronic spaces. Among those spaces on the Internet, hundreds of newsgroups and Web sites are devoted to religion and spirituality, and in "Finding God on the Web," Joshua Cooper Ramo wonders whether this new medium has the potential to bring together people who have been lured away from their communities by TV. And finally, in what might be read as a cautionary tale or warning about virtual community written in the early 20th century, novelist E. M. Forster imagines a future in which everyone lives separately in cubicles, accesses information remotely, and communicates through the globally connected "Machine."

In all these selections, you may observe the tension between pulling apart and pulling together that is at the heart of any discussion of community. Your own views about the impact of technology on community will be rooted in your experience with physical, face-to-face communities. Therefore you may find it useful first to think about that experience by listing some communities you've belonged to in your life, including communities with which you currently identify. Then choose one or more of those communities and consider the following:

1. How did you participate in this community? What kinds of things did you do that constitute your participation or identification with this group? What interests or values did you share with other members of the community? Did everyone in the group share these interests or values? What interests or values did you *not* share with other members of the community?
2. What conventions, etiquette, or rules governed your interactions with other members of this community?
3. Think of a conflict or area of tension that was experienced in this community. What were your feelings about it? How did the community respond to this conflict or tension? To what extent was it resolved?
4. How has computer technology affected this community positively, negatively, or neutrally? To what extent do you think the community bonds depend on physical presence or proximity?
5. Social scientists say that most communication is nonverbal (including body language, gesture, intonation, etc.), but CMC is text based and eliminates most nonverbal cues. What do you think is lost and what do you think is gained when people communicate electronically? If you have access to a computer lab, classroom, or networked computers equipped with electronic discussion software, discuss this issue online using your real name.

The Heart of the WELL

Howard Rheingold

Howard Rheingold (b. 1947) has been writing and speaking about the human side of computer technology since the mid-1980s. He is former editor of *The Whole Earth Review;* founding executive editor of HotWired (*Wired* magazine's online venture); one of the original members of the WELL (Whole Earth 'Lectronic Link), the online community started in Sausalito, California, that he writes about in this selection; and founder of Electric Minds, a Web-based conferencing and community group. Rheingold's books include *The Millennium Whole Earth Catalog* (editor; HarperSanFrancisco, 1994), *Tools for Thought: The People and Ideas of the Next Computer Revolution* (Simon & Schuster, 1985), and *Virtual Reality* (Simon & Schuster, 1991). This selection is from the first chapter of *The Virtual Community: Homesteading on the Electronic Frontier* (Addison-Wesley, 1993). More information about Rheingold is available from his home page at <www.well.com/user/hlr/howard.html>.

I n the summer of 1986, my then-two-year-old daughter picked up a tick. There 1 was this blood-bloated *thing* sucking on our baby's scalp, and we weren't quite sure how to go about getting it off. My wife, Judy, called the pediatrician. It was eleven o'clock in the evening. I logged onto the WELL. I got my answer online within minutes from a fellow with the improbable but genuine name of Flash Gordon, M.D. I had removed the tick by the time Judy got the callback from the pediatrician's office.

What amazed me wasn't just the speed with which we obtained precisely the infor- 2 mation we needed to know, right when we needed to know it. It was also the immense inner sense of security that comes with discovering that real people—most of them parents, some of them nurses, doctors, and midwives—are available, around the clock, if you need them. There is a magic protective circle around the atmosphere of this particular conference. We're talking about our sons and daughters in this forum, not about our computers or our opinions about philosophy, and many of us feel that this tacit understanding sanctifies the virtual space.

The atmosphere of the Parenting conference—the attitudes people exhibit to each 3 other in the tone of what they say in public—is part of what continues to attract me. People who never have much to contribute in political debate, technical argument, or intellectual gamesmanship turn out to have a lot to say about raising children. People you know as fierce, even nasty, intellectual opponents in other contexts give you emotional support on a deeper level, parent to parent, within the boundaries of Parenting, a small but warmly human corner of cyberspace.

Here is a short list of examples from the hundreds of separate topics available for   4
discussion in the Parenting conference. Each of these entries is the name of a conversation that includes scores or hundreds of individual contributions spread over a period
of days or years, like a long, topical cocktail party you can rewind back to the beginning to find out who said what before you got there.

Great Expectations: You're Pregnant: Now What? Part III

What's Bad About Children's TV?

Movies: The Good, the Bad, and the Ugly

Initiations and Rites of Passage

Brand New Well Baby!!

How Does Being a Parent Change Your Life?

Tall Teenage Tales (cont.)

Guilt

MOTHERS

Vasectomy—Did It Hurt?

Introductions! Who Are We?

Fathers (Continued)

Books for Kids, Section Two

Gay and Lesbian Teenagers

Children and Spirituality

Great Parks for Kids

Quality Toys

Parenting in an Often-Violent World

Children's Radio Programming

New WELL Baby

Home Schooling

Newly Separated/Divorced Fathers

Another Well Baby—Carson Arrives in Seattle!

Single Parenting

Uncle Philcat's Back Fence: Gossip Here!

Embarrassing Moments

Kids and Death

All the Poop on Diapers

Pediatric Problems—Little Sicknesses and Sick Little Ones

Talking with Kids About the Prospect of War

Dealing with Incest and Abuse

Other People's Children

When They're Crying

Pets for Kids

People who talk about a shared interest, albeit a deep one such as being a parent, don't often disclose enough about themselves as whole individuals online to inspire real trust in others. In the case of the subcommunity of the Parenting conference, a few dozen of us, scattered across the country, few of whom rarely if ever saw the others face-to-face, had a few years of minor crises to knit us together and prepare us for serious business when it came our way. Another several dozen read the conference regularly but contribute only when they have something important to add. Hundreds more every week read the conference without comment, except when something extraordinary happens. 5

Jay Allison and his family live in Massachusetts. He and his wife are public-radio producers. I've never met any of them face-to-face, although I feel I know something powerful and intimate about the Allisons and have strong emotional ties to them. What follows are some of Jay's postings on the WELL: 6

> Woods Hole, Midnight. I am sitting in the dark of my daughter's room. Her monitor lights blink at me. The lights used to blink too brightly so I covered them with bits of bandage adhesive and now they flash faintly underneath, a persistent red and green, Lillie's heart and lungs.
>
> Above the monitor is her portable suction unit. In the glow of the flashlight I'm writing by, it looks like the plastic guts of a science-class human model, the tubes coiled around the power supply, the reservoir, the pump.
>
> Tina is upstairs trying to get some sleep. A baby monitor links our bedroom to Lillie's. It links our sleep to Lillie's too, and because our souls are linked to hers, we do not sleep well.
>
> I am naked. My stomach is full of beer. The flashlight rests on it, and the beam rises and falls with my breath. My daughter breathes through a white plastic tube inserted into a hole in her throat. She's fourteen months old.

Sitting in front of our computers with our hearts racing and tears in our eyes, in Tokyo and Sacramento and Austin, we read about Lillie's croup, her tracheostomy, the days and nights at Massachusetts General Hospital, and now the vigil over Lillie's breathing and the watchful attention to the mechanical apparatus that kept her alive. It went on for days. Weeks. Lillie recovered, and relieved our anxieties about her vocal capabilities after all that time with a hole in her throat by saying the most extraordinary things, duly reported online by Jay. 7

Sitting in front of our computers with our hearts racing and tears in our eyes, in Tokyo and Sacramento and Austin, we read about Lillie's croup, her tracheostomy, the days and nights at Massachusetts General Hospital. 8

Later, writing in *Whole Earth Review,* Jay described the experience:

> Before this time, my computer screen had never been a place to go for solace. Far from it. But there it was. Those nights sitting up late with

my daughter, I'd go to my computer, dial up the WELL, and ramble. I wrote about what was happening that night or that year. I didn't know anyone I was "talking" to. I had never laid eyes on them. At 3:00 A.M. my "real" friends were asleep, so I turned to this foreign, invisible community for support. The WELL was always awake.

Any difficulty is harder to bear in isolation. There is nothing to measure against, to lean against. Typing out my journal entries into the computer and over the phone lines, I found fellowship and comfort in this unlikely medium.

Over the years, despite the distances, those of us who made heart-to-heart contact   9
via the Parenting conference began to meet face-to-face. The WELL's annual summer picnic in the San Francisco Bay area grew out of a face-to-face gathering that was originally organized in the Parenting conference. We had been involved in intense online conversations in this conference all year. When summer rolled around we started talking about doing something relaxing together, like bringing our kids somewhere for a barbecue. In typical WELL fashion, it quickly amplified to a WELLwide party hosted by the Parenting conference. Phil Catalfo reserved a picnic site and the use of a softball field in a public park.

Parents talk about their kids online—what else?—and therefore we all already know   10
about my daughter Mamie and Philcat's son Gabe and Busy's son, the banjo player, but we had not seen many of them before. I remember that when I arrived at the park, Mamie and I recognized one particular group, out of the first half-dozen large parties of picnickers we saw in the distance. There was just something about the way they were all standing, talking with each other in knots of two or three, while the kids ran around the eucalyptus grove and found their way to the softball diamond. I remember playing on the same team with a fellow who never ceases to annoy me when he wrenches every conversation online around to a debate about libertarianism; I remember thinking, after we had darn near accomplished a double play together, that he wasn't such a bad guy.

It was a normal American community picnic—people who value each other's   11
company, getting together with their kids for softball and barbecue on a summer Sunday. It could have been any church group or PTA. In this case, it was the indisputably real-life part of a virtual community. The first Parenting conference picnic was such a success that it became an annual event, taking place around the summer solstice. And kids became a fixture at all the other WELL parties.

Another ritual for parents and kids and friends of parents and kids started in the   12
winter, not long after the picnic tradition began. For the past four or five years, in December, most of the conference participants within a hundred miles, and their little ones, show up in San Francisco for the annual Pickle Family Circus benefit and potluck. One of the directors of this small circus is a beloved and funny member of the WELL community; he arranges a special block of seats each year. After the circus is over and the rest of the audience has left, we treat the performers, the stagehands, and ourselves to a potluck feast.

Albert Mitchell is an uncommonly fierce and stubborn fellow—many would say   13
pugnacious—who argues his deeply felt principles in no uncertain terms. He can be abrasive, even frightening, in his intensity. He gets particularly riled up by certain topics—organized religion, taxation, and circumcision—but there are other ways to cross him and earn some public or private vituperation. I discovered that I could never again really be too frightened by Albert's fierce online persona—the widely known and

sometimes feared "sofia"—after seeing him and his sweet daughter, Sofia, in her clown suit, at a Pickle potluck. He gave me a jar of honey from his own hive at that event, even though we had been shouting at each other online in ways that probably would have degenerated into fisticuffs face-to-face. At the Pickle Family Circus or the summer picnic, we were meeting in the sacred space of Parenting, not the bloody arenas of WELL policy or politics.

The Parenting conference had been crisis-tested along with the Allisons, and had undergone months of the little ups and downs with the kids that make up the normal daily history of any parent, when one of our most regular, most dear, most loquacious participants, Phil Catalfo, dropped a bombshell on us.

Topic 349: Leukemia
By: Phil Catalfo (philcat) on Wed, Jan 16, '91
    404 responses so far

<linked topic>

I'd like to use this topic for discussing leukemia, the disease, both as it affects my family and what is known about it generally. We learned early last week that our son Gabriel, 7 (our middle child), has acute lymphocytic leukemia, aka ALL. I will be opening one or more additional topics to discuss the chronology of events, emotion and experiences stirred up by this newly central fact of our lives, and so on. (I'm also thinking of opening a topic expressly for everyone to send him get-well wishes). I intend for this topic to focus on the disease itself—his diagnosis and progress, but also other cases we know about, resources (of all types) available, etc. etc.

If Tina has no objection, I'd like to ask the hosts of the Health conf. to link any/all of these topics to their conf. I can't think offhand of where else might be appropriate, but I'm sure you'll all suggest away.

The first thing I want to say, regardless of how it does or doesn't pertain to this particular topic, is that the support and love my family and I, and especially Gabe, have been receiving from the WELL, have been invaluable. This turns out to have a medical impact, which we'll discuss in good time, but I want to say out loud how much it's appreciated: infinitely.

With that, I'll enter this, and return as soon as I can to say more about Gabe's case and what I've learned in the past week about this disease and what to do about it.

404 responses total

1: Nancy A. Pietrafesa (lapeche) Wed, Jan 16, '91 (17:21)

Philcat, we're here and we're listening. We share your hope and a small part of your pain. Hang on.

#2: Tina Loney (onezie) Wed, Jan 16, '91 (19:09)

Phil, I took the liberty of writing to flash (host of the Health conf) and telling him to link whichever of the three topics he feels appropriate. I very much look forward to you telling us all that you can/are able about Gabe. In the meanwhile, I'm thinking about Gabriel and your entire family. Seems I remember Gabe has quite a good Catalfic sense of humor, and I hope you're able to aid him in keeping that in top form. . . Virtual hugs are *streaming* in his direction. . . .

The Parenting regulars, who had spent hours in this conference trading quips and   15 commiserating over the little ups and downs of life with children, chimed in with messages of support. One of them was a nurse. Individuals who had never contributed to the Parenting conference before entered the conversation, including a couple of doctors who helped Phil and the rest of us understand the daily reports about blood counts and other diagnostics and two other people who had firsthand knowledge, as patients suffering from blood disorders themselves.

Over the weeks, we all became experts on blood disorders. We also understood   16 how the blood donation system works, what Danny Thomas and his St. Jude Hospital had to do with Phil and Gabe, and how parents learn to be advocates for their children in the medical system without alienating the caregivers. Best of all, we learned that Gabe's illness went into remission after about a week of chemotherapy.

With Gabe's remission, the community that had gathered around the leukemia   17 topic redirected its attention to another part of the groupmind. Lhary, one of the people from outside the Parenting conference who had joined the discussion of leukemia because of the special knowledge he had to contribute, moved from the San Francisco area to Houston in order to have a months-long bone-marrow transplant procedure in an attempt to abate his own leukemia. He continued to log onto the WELL from his hospital room. The Catalfos and others got together and personally tie-dyed regulation lab coats and hospital gowns for Lhary to wear around the hospital corridors.

Many people are alarmed by the very idea of a virtual community, fearing that   18 it is another step in the wrong direction, substituting more technological ersatz for yet another natural resource or human freedom. These critics often voice their sadness at what people have been reduced to doing in a civilization that worships technology, decrying the circumstances that lead some people into such pathetically disconnected lives that they prefer to find their companions on the other side of a computer screen. There is a seed of truth in this fear, for virtual communities require more than words on a screen at some point if they intend to be other than ersatz.

Some people—many people—don't do well in spontaneous spoken interaction,   19 but turn out to have valuable contributions to make in a conversation in which they have time to think about what to say. These people, who might constitute a significant proportion of the population, can find written communication more authentic than the face-to-face kind. Who is to say that this preference for one mode of communication— informal written text—is somehow less authentically human than audible speech? Those who critique CMC because some people use it obsessively hit an important target, but miss a great deal more when they don't take into consideration people who use the medium for genuine human interaction. Those who find virtual communities cold places point at the limits of the technology, its most dangerous pitfalls, and we need to pay attention to those boundaries. But these critiques don't tell us how Philcat and Lhary and the Allisons and my own family could have found the community of support and information we found in the WELL when we needed it. And those of us who do find communion in cyberspace might do well to pay attention to the way the medium we love can be abused.

Although dramatic incidents are what bring people together and stick in their   20 memories, most of what goes on in the Parenting conference and most virtual communities is informal conversation and downright chitchat. The model of the WELL and other social clusters in cyberspace as "places" is one that naturally emerges whenever people who use this medium discuss the nature of the medium. In 1987, Stewart Brand quoted me in his book *The Media Lab* about what tempted me to log onto the WELL as often as I did: "There's always another mind there. It's like having the corner bar, complete with old buddies and delightful newcomers and new tools waiting to take home and fresh graffiti and letters, except instead of putting on my coat, shutting down the computer, and walking down to the corner, I just invoke my telecom program and there they are. It's a place."

The existence of computer-linked communities was predicted twenty-five years   21 ago by J. C. R. Licklider and Robert Taylor, research directors for the Department of Defense's Advanced Research Projects Agency (ARPA), who set in motion the research that resulted in the creation of the first such community, the ARPANET: "What will on-line interactive communities be like?" Licklider and Taylor wrote in 1968: "In most fields they will consist of geographically separated members, sometimes grouped in small clusters and sometimes working individually. They will be communities not of common location, but of common interest. . . ."

My friends and I sometimes believe we are part of the future that Licklider   22 dreamed about, and we often can attest to the truth of his prediction that "life will be happier for the on-line individual because the people with whom one interacts most strongly will be selected more by commonality of interests and goals than by accidents of proximity." I still believe that, but I also know that life online has been unhappy at times, intensely so in some circumstances, because of words I've read on a screen. Participating in a virtual community has not solved all of life's problems for me, but it has served as an aid, a comfort, and an inspiration at times; at other times, it has been like an endless, ugly, long-simmering family brawl.

I've changed my mind about a lot of aspects of the WELL over the years, but the   23 sense of place is still as strong as ever. As Ray Oldenburg proposed in *The Great Good Place,* there are three essential places in people's lives: the place we live, the place we work, and the place we gather for conviviality. Although the casual conversation that takes place in cafés, beauty shops, pubs, and town squares is universally considered to be trivial, idle talk, Oldenburg makes the case that such places are where communities can come into being and continue to hold together. These are the unacknowledged agorae of modern life. When the automobilecentric, suburban, fast-food, shopping-mall way of life eliminated many of these "third places" from traditional towns and cities around the world, the social fabric of existing communities started shredding.

Oldenburg explicitly put a name and conceptual framework on that phenomenon   24 that every virtual communitarian knows instinctively, the power of informal public life:

Third places exist on neutral ground and serve to level their guests to a condition of social equality. Within these places, conversation is the primary activity and the major vehicle for the display and appreciation of human personality and individuality. Third places are taken for granted and most have a low profile. Since the formal institutions of society make stronger claims on the individual, third places are normally open in the off hours, as well as at other times. The character of a third place is determined most of all by its regular clientele and is marked by a playful mood, which contrasts with people's more serious involvement in other spheres. Though a radically different kind of setting for a home, the third place is remarkably similar to a good home in the psychological comfort and support that it extends.

Such are the characteristics of third places that appear to be universal and essential to a vital informal public life. . . .

The problem of place in America manifests itself in a sorely deficient informal public life. The structure of shared experience beyond that offered by family, job, and passive consumerism is small and dwindling. The essential group experience is being replaced by the exaggerated self-consciousness of individuals. American life-styles, for all the material acquisition and the seeking after comforts and pleasures, are plagued by boredom, loneliness, alienation, and a high price tag. . . .

Unlike many frontiers, that of the informal public life does not remain benign as it awaits development. It does not become easier to tame as technology evolves, as governmental bureaus and agencies multiply, or as population grows. It does not yield to the mere passage of time and a policy of letting the chips fall where they may as development proceeds in other areas of urban life. To the contrary, neglect of the informal public life can make a jungle of what had been a garden while, at the same time, diminishing the ability of people to cultivate it.

It might not be the same kind of place that Oldenburg had in mind, but so many of   25
his descriptions of third places could also describe the WELL. Perhaps cyberspace is one of the informal public places where people can rebuild the aspects of community that were lost when the malt shop became a mall. Or perhaps cyberspace is precisely the *wrong* place to look for the rebirth of community, offering not a tool for conviviality but a life-denying simulacrum of real passion and true commitment to one another. In either case, we need to find out soon.

✦ ✦ ✦

The feeling of logging into the WELL for just a minute or two, dozens of times a day,   26
is very similar to the feeling of peeking into the café, the pub, the common room, to see who's there, and whether you want to stay around for a chat. As social psychologist Sara Kiesler put it in an article about networks for *Harvard Business Review:* "One of the surprising properties of computing is that it is a social activity. Where I work, the most frequently run computer network program is the one called 'Where' or 'Finger' that finds other people who are logged onto the computer network."

Because we cannot see one another in cyberspace, gender, age, national origin, and   27
physical appearance are not apparent unless a person wants to make such characteristics public. People whose physical handicaps make it difficult to form new friendships find that virtual communities treat them as they always wanted to be treated—as thinkers and

transmitters of ideas and feeling beings, not carnal vessels with a certain appearance and way of walking and talking (or not walking and not talking).

One of the few things that enthusiastic members of virtual communities in Japan, 28 England, France, and the United States all agree on is that expanding their circle of friends is one of the most important advantages of computer conferencing. CMC is a way to *meet* people, whether or not you feel the need to affiliate with them on a community level. It's a way of both making contact with and maintaining a distance from others. The way you meet people in cyberspace puts a different spin on affiliation: in traditional kinds of communities, we are accustomed to meeting people, then getting to know them; in virtual communities, you can get to know people and then choose to meet them. Affiliation also can be far more ephemeral in cyberspace because you can get to know people you might never meet on the physical plane.

How does anybody find friends? In the traditional community, we search through 29 our pool of neighbors and professional colleagues, of acquaintances and acquaintances of acquaintances, in order to find people who share our values and interests. We then exchange information about one another, disclose and discuss our mutual interests, and sometimes we become friends. In a virtual community we can go directly to the place where our favorite subjects are being discussed, then get acquainted with people who share our passions or who use words in a way we find attractive. In this sense, the topic is the address: you can't simply pick up a phone and ask to be connected with someone who wants to talk about Islamic art or California wine, or someone with a three-year-old daughter or a forty-year-old Hudson; you can, however, join a computer conference on any of those topics, then open a public or private correspondence with the previously unknown people you find there. Your chances of making friends are magnified by orders of magnitude over the old methods of finding a peer group.

You can be fooled about people in cyberspace, behind the cloak of words. But that 30 can be said about telephones or face-to-face communication as well; computer-mediated communications provide new ways to fool people, and the most obvious identity swindles will die out only when enough people learn to use the medium critically. In some ways, the medium will, by its nature, be forever biased toward certain kinds of obfuscation. It will also be a place that people often end up revealing themselves far more intimately than they would be inclined to do without the intermediation of screens and pseudonyms.

The sense of communion I've experienced on the WELL is exemplified by the Par- 31 enting conference but far from limited to it. We began to realize in other conferences, facing other human issues, that we had the power not only to use words to share feelings and exchange helpful information, but to accomplish things in the real world.

The power of the WELL's community of users to accomplish things in the real 32 world manifested itself dramatically when we outgrew our first computer. The computing engine that put-putted us around as a group of seven hundred users in 1985 was becoming inadequate for the three thousand users we had in 1988. Things started slowing down. You would type a letter on your keyboard and wait seconds for the letter to be displayed on your screen. It quickly became frustrating.

Because we had such a large proportion of computer experts among the population, 33 we knew that the only solution to the interminable system lag that made it agonizing to read and even more agonizing to write on the WELL's database was to move to more up-to-date hardware, better suited to keeping up with the communication tasks of a hive numbering in the thousands. But the WELL's managing director, Clifford Figallo, himself an active member of the WELL community, reported that the WELL as a business entity was unable to find the kind of financing we'd need to upgrade our system.

That's when some of the armchair experts online started talking about their back-of-the-envelope calculations. If the hard-core users who had grown so irritated about the system's performance (but had realized that there was no place remotely like the WELL to turn to as an alternative) were willing to pay their next few months' bills in advance, how much money would it take to buy the big iron? Half-seriously, Clifford Figallo named a figure. Within a few days, enough people had pledged hundreds of dollars each, thousands of dollars cumulatively, to get the show on the road. The checks arrived, the computer was purchased, the hardware was installed, and the database—the living heart of the community—was transferred to its new silicon body.

After suffering through the last months of the Vax, the first months of our new computer, the Sequent, was like switching from a Schwinn to a Rolls. And we had flexed our first barn-raising muscles in a characteristically unorthodox way: here were the customers, and the producers of the value that the customers buy, raising money among themselves to loan the owners of the business so they could sell themselves more of each other.

Casey's operation was another barn raising. This one was her idea. Casey was another WELL old-timer who had a job—freelance transcription and word processing services—that enabled her to work at home. Nobody ever doubts her intelligence, although her manner is often indelicate. The way she would say it, I'm sure, is that she has a "relatively low need for affiliation." The way others might say it is that Casey is a tough cookie.

Casey, whose real name is Kathleen, needed an operation that she could almost, but not quite, afford; her ability to walk was at stake. So she put up $500 to have a poster of her own design printed. The poster showed the silhouette of a head, with the title "This Is Your Mind on the WELL," and the head was filled with words and phrases that WELL users would recognize. She offered copies for sale as a benefit for her operation at $30 each. She raised the money she needed.

The most dramatic barn raising, however, was the saga of Elly, a shy and gentle and much-loved WELLite who left the virtual community, possibly forever, to travel to the farthest reaches of the Himalayas. Her saga, her crisis, and the WELL's response unfolded over a period of months, and climaxed over a few intensely active days:

Topic 198: News from Elly
By: Averi Dunn (vaxen) on Wed, Aug 28, '91
      263 responses so far

<linked topic>

This is the place to post any news which may come your way about Northbay's vacationing host, Elly van der Pas.

#1: Elly van der Pas (elly) Wed, Aug 28, '91 (18:03)

Right now, I'm almost finished moving out of my house. Later tonight, I'm going to look at my stuff, and see if I have what I need for my trip, and maybe do last minute shopping tomorrow. Cleaning Friday. Gone Saturday to parts unknown. The plane leaves Monday morning. Phew!

#6: Averi Dunn (vaxen) Mon, Sep 23, '91 (18:44)

I got another postcard from Elly on Saturday:
> 13 Sept
> Amsterdam
> So far, so good. The weather's been beautiful, and I've been riding all over by bike. Tomorrow I'm going to London for a few days, and then to Italy by train. Should be an adventure. I went to a piano concert last night with friends of a friend, and may be sailing today. Greetings to everyone. Elly

#22: Averi Dunn (vaxen) Thu, Nov 7, '91 (23:25)

Well, Kim, you can post the parts that don't repeat. It's good to hear any news from Elly. And with that in mind I post the following from her-own-self:
> 27 Oct 1991
> I got your letter from Sept 14 yesterday, forwarded from Italy. Apparently they were having a post office strike or something, because one of the workers drowned in the elevator. Anyway, they didn't process mail for at least a week, so I didn't get any letters.

> Anyway, you have no idea how weird it is to be sitting on a mountain in Kathmandu reading about AP2 and the WELL. Oh, I took a picture of the WELL coffee shop in London and sent it to the office. I hope they get it. I thought it was quite appropriate. Janey Fritsche showed up about a week ago, and then took off trekking. It was good to see her. My friend Peter will be here, too, in a few days, and I guess I'll come down off the mountain to spend some time renewing visas and stocking up for the month-long course. We have to stay put for that, and no mail, either, so this might be it for awhile. Happy Thanksgiving, Merry Christmas, and Happy New Year. They've just finished their big holiday here—everyone was off work for a week, and dressed in new clothes. The kids made huge bamboo swings and went out kite flying.

> I've been studying Dzogchen, which is like Tibetan Zen—meditating on the empty mind. Different from what I've done before. We stayed for awhile at a monastery way up in the hills, where there's an old abbot who specializes in pointing out the nature of the mind. It was rather an unusual opportunity.

> You guys are all asleep now, except maybe for you. It's 2 pm—too late for lunch and too early for tea. Just about bath time, though, because we have a solar heater on the roof. I'm taking all my baths now, because in a week, 300 people will come here for the course, and bathing will be a fond dream. Or showering, that is.

Tell Brian and June and Josephine I said hi, and that I'm OK. I hope they got my card. I'll try to write, but don't know when I'll get time.
Take care of yourself and be happy.
Elly

#26: Averi Dunn (vaxen) Sat, Dec 28, '91 (01:26)

The following are excerpts from a letter I received from Elly on Dec 21.

***

7 Nov
The course starts today so I'm incommunicado for a month.
13 Dec
Hmmm. I guess I never finished this. Lots of things have happened since then. Mainly, I've become a nun. I sent details to Hank so he could post, because I have to write about 10 letters for Peter to take back when he goes.

***

It's a little strange, but I feel really good about it, and I really feel it's the right move for me. Even Peter agrees.

***

I never wanted to be a nun (at least not before now). I always felt a little sorry for the Catholic nuns. This is a little different, though—much more freedom. It's interesting to have short hair, though. I think I'll grow it out to about 3/4". :-)

***

PPS. My ordination name is Jigme Palmo: Glorious fearless woman (!!!?)

***

She also sent an address she can be reached at for the next six months. Drop me Email if you want it.

So Elly had decided to become a Buddhist nun in Asia, and therefore threatened to pass into the annals of WELL legend. The topic stayed dormant for six months. In June, former neighbor Averi Dunn, who had been typing Elly's correspondence into the WELL, reported hearing that Elly had some kind of amoeba in her liver. At the end of July 1992, Flash Gordon reported that Elly was in a hospital in New Delhi. In a coma. She had severe hepatitis and reportedly suffered liver failure. If that report turned out to be true, Flash and the other doctors online agreed that the prognosis was not good.

> At the end of July 1992, Flash Gordon reported that Elly was in a hospital in New Delhi. In a coma.

Within hours, people started doing things in half a dozen directions on their own   40
initiative. The raw scope and diversity of the resources available to us by pooling our
individual networks was astonishing. People who had medical connections in New
Delhi were brought in; airline schedules and rates for medical evacuation were
researched; a fund was started and contributions started arriving. Casey used the net to
find a possible telecommunications site in New Delhi where they could relay information for Frank, Elly's ex-husband, who had flown to Asia to help with what was looking like a grave situation.

After a tense few days, the news made its way through the network that she did   41
have some liver function left and might need access to special blood-filtering equipment before she could be moved. Within hours, we knew how to get such medical
equipment in New Delhi and whose name to mention. We knew whom to call, how to
ask, what it cost, and how to transfer funds to get Elly delivered to a hospital in the San
Francisco region. "It gives me goosebumps," reported Onezie, as the topic unfolded on
the WELL. "This is love in action."

Elly recovered enough strength to travel without medical evacuation. Her next   42
message was direct, via the WELL:

#270: Elly van der Pas (elly) Fri, Sep 11, '92 (16:03)

Thanks to everyone for your generous WELLbeams, good wishes, prayers, advice, and
contributions of green energy. The doctor thought the fast recovery was due to Acti-
gall, but in fact it was due to beams, prayers, and pujas. He even said I might be able
to go back to India in February or so. I-)

⬅ SECOND THOUGHTS

1. Review the human examples that Rheingold offers of the WELL's electronic community—the cases of his own daughter Mamie, Jay and Lillie Allison, Albert
   Mitchell, Phil and Gabe Catalfo, Clifford Figallo, Casey/Kathleen, and Elly. What
   characteristics or aspects of community does Rheingold use each example to illustrate?
2. What are the major qualities of "third places" as defined by Ray Oldenburg (¶ 24)?
   To what extent do you agree with Rheingold that "many of his descriptions of third
   places could also describe the WELL" (¶ 25)?
3. What fears about or objections to computer-mediated communication does Rheingold bring up in this essay, and how effectively do you think he answers those
   objections?

Is There a There in Cyberspace?

John Perry Barlow

John Perry Barlow (b. 1947) is a long-time writer and speaker about electronic technologies and their social implications; co-founder of the Electronic Frontier Foundation, a nonprofit civil liberties organization; and member of the board of directors of the WELL (Whole Earth 'Lectronic Link), an online community organization. He contributes to magazines and journals such as *Communications of the ACM, Microtimes, Mondo 2000,* and *Wired.* This article first appeared in 1995 in the *Utne Reader* (<www.utne.com/reader/magazine.html>), a magazine aimed at people on the political left. As Barlow mentions in the article, he is a former lyricist for the Grateful Dead rock band and was a Wyoming cattle rancher for 17 years. He has a home page on the Web at <www.eff.org/~barlow/>.

"There is no there there."
> *Gertrude Stein*
> *(speaking of Oakland)*

"It ain't no Amish barn-raising in there . . ."
> *Bruce Sterling*
> *(speaking of cyberspace)*

1 I am often asked how I went from pushing cows around a remote Wyoming ranch to my present occupation (which *The Wall Street Journal* recently described as "cyberspace cadet"). I haven't got a short answer, but I suppose I came to the virtual world looking for community.

2 Unlike most modern Americans, I grew up in an actual place, an entirely nonintentional community called Pinedale, Wyoming. As I struggled for nearly a generation to keep my ranch in the family, I was motivated by the belief that such places were the spiritual home of humanity. But I knew their future was not promising.

3 At the dawn of the 20th century, over 40 percent of the American workforce lived off the land. The majority of us lived in towns like Pinedale. Now fewer than 1 percent of us extract a living from the soil. We just became too productive for our own good.

4 Of course, the population followed the jobs. Farming and ranching communities are now home to a demographically insignificant percentage of Americans, the vast majority of whom live not in ranch houses but in more or less identical split-level "ranch homes" in more or less identical suburban "communities." Generica.

In my view, these are neither communities nor homes. I believe the combination   5
of television and suburban population patterns is simply toxic to the soul. I see much
evidence in contemporary America to support this view.

Meanwhile, back at the ranch, doom impended. And, as I watched community in   6
Pinedale growing ill from the same economic forces that were killing my family's ranch,
the Bar Cross, satellite dishes brought the cultural infection of television. I started looking around for evidence that community in America would not perish altogether.

I took some heart in the mysterious nomadic City of the Deadheads, the virtually   7
physical town that follows the Grateful Dead around the country. The Deadheads
lacked place, touching down briefly wherever the band happened to be playing, and
they lacked continuity in time, since they had to suffer a new diaspora every time the
band moved on or went home. But they had many of the other necessary elements of
community, including a culture, a religion of sorts (which, though it lacked dogma, had
most of the other, more nurturing aspects of spiritual practice), a sense of necessity,
and, most importantly, shared adversity.

I wanted to know more about the flavor of their interaction, what they thought and   8
felt, but since I wrote Dead songs (including "Estimated Prophet" and "Cassidy"), I
was a minor icon to the Deadheads, and was thus inhibited, in some socially Heisen-
bergian way, from getting a clear view of what really went on among them.

Then, in 1987, I heard about a "place" where Deadheads gathered where I could   9
move among them without distorting too much the field of observation. Better, this was
a place I could visit without leaving Wyoming. It was a shared computer in Sausalito,
California, called the Whole Earth 'Lectronic Link, or WELL. After a lot of struggling
with modems, serial cables, init strings, and other computer arcana that seemed utterly
out of phase with such notions as Deadheads and small towns, I found myself looking
at the glowing yellow word "Login:" beyond which lay my future.

"Inside" the WELL were Deadheads in community. There were thousands of them   10
there, gossiping, complaining (mostly about the Grateful Dead), comforting and
harassing each other, bartering, engaging in religion (or at least exchanging their
totemic set lists), beginning and ending love affairs, praying for one another's sick
kids. There was, it seemed, everything one might find going on in a small town, save
dragging Main Street and making out on the back roads.

I was delighted. I felt I had found the new locale of human community—never   11
mind that the whole thing was being conducted in mere words by minds from whom
the bodies had been amputated. Never mind that all these people were deaf, dumb, and
blind as paramecia or that their town had neither seasons nor sunsets nor smells.

Surely all these deficiencies would be remedied by richer, faster communications   12
media. The featureless log-in handles would gradually acquire video faces (and thus
expressions), shaded 3-D body puppets (and thus body language). This "space," which
I recognized at once to be a primitive form of the cyberspace William Gibson* predicted in his sci-fi novel *Neuromancer,* was still without apparent dimensions or vistas.
But virtual reality would change all that in time.

---

*See stories by Gibson in Chapter 1 (p. 48) and Chapter 8 (p. 369) (ed.).

Meanwhile, the commons, or something like it, had been rediscovered. Once 13
again, people from the 'burbs had a place where they could encounter their friends as
my fellow Pinedalians did at the post office and the Wrangler Cafe. They had a place
where their hearts could remain as the companies they worked for shuffled their bodies
around America. They could put down roots that could not be ripped out by forces of
economic history. They had a collective stake. They had a community.

It is seven years now since I discovered the WELL. In that time, I co-founded an organi- 14
zation, the Electronic Frontier Foundation, dedicated to protecting its interests and those
of other virtual communities like it from raids by physical government. I've spent countless hours typing away at its residents, and I've watched the larger context that contains
it, the Internet, grow at such an explosive rate that, by 2004, every human on the planet
will have an e-mail address unless the growth curve flattens (which it will).

My enthusiasm for virtuality has cooled. In fact, unless one counts interaction with 15
the rather too large society of those with whom I exchange electronic mail, I don't
spend much time engaging in virtual community at all. Many of the near-term benefits
I anticipated from it seem to remain as far in the future as they did when I first logged
in. Perhaps they always will.

Pinedale works, more or less, as it is, but a lot is still missing from the communi- 16
ties of cyberspace, whether they be places like the WELL, the fractious newsgroups of
USENET, the silent "auditoriums" of America Online, or even enclaves on the promising World Wide Web.

What is missing? Well, to quote Ranjit Makkuni of Xerox Corporation's Palo Alto 17
Research Center, "the *prāna* is missing," *prāna* being the Hindu term for both breath and
spirit. I think he is right about this and that perhaps the central question of the virtual age
is whether or not *prāna* can somehow be made to fit through any disembodied medium.

Prāna is, to my mind, the literally vital element in the holy and unseen ecology of 18
relationship, the dense mesh of invisible life, on whose surface carbon-based life floats
like a thin film. It is at the heart of the fundamental and profound difference between
information and experience. Jaron Lanier has said that "information is alienated experience," and, that being true, *prāna* is part of what is
removed when you create such easily transmissible
replicas of experience as, say, the evening news.

Obviously a great many other, less spiritual,
things are also missing entirely, like body language, sex, death, tone of voice, clothing, beauty
(or homeliness), weather, violence, vegetation,
wildlife, pets, architecture, music, smells, sunlight, and that ol' harvest moon. In short, most of
the things that make my life real to me.

Present, but in far less abundance than
in the physical world, which I call "meat space,"
are women, children, old people, poor people, and
the genuinely blind. Also mostly missing are the
illiterate and the continent of Africa. There is not

Present, but in far less abundance than in the physical world, are women, children, old people, poor people, and the genuinely blind. Also mostly missing are the illiterate and the continent of Africa. 19 20

much human diversity in cyberspace, which is populated, as near as I can tell, by white males under 50 with plenty of computer terminal time, great typing skills, high math SATs, strongly held opinions on just about everything, and an excruciating face-to-face shyness, especially with the opposite sex.

But diversity is as essential to healthy community as it is to healthy ecosystems   21 (which are, in my view, different from communities only in unimportant aspects).

I believe that the principal reason for the almost universal failure of the intentional   22 communities of the '60s and '70s was a lack of diversity in their members. It was a rare commune with any old people in it, or people who were fundamentally out of philosophical agreement with the majority.

Indeed, it is the usual problem when we try to build something that can only be   23 grown. Natural systems, such as human communities, are simply too complex to design by the engineering principles we insist on applying to them. Like Dr. Frankenstein, Western civilization is now finding its rational skills inadequate to the task of creating and caring for life. We would do better to return to a kind of agricultural mind-set in which we humbly try to re-create the conditions from which life has sprung before. And leave the rest to God.

Given that it has been built so far almost entirely by people with engineering   24 degrees, it is not so surprising that cyberspace has the kind of overdesigned quality that leaves out all kinds of elements nature would have provided invisibly.

Also missing from both the communes of the '60s and from cyberspace are a cou-   25 ple of elements that I believe are very important, if not essential, to the formation and preservation of real community: an absence of alternatives and a sense of genuine adversity, generally shared. What about these?

It is hard to argue that anyone would find losing a modem literally hard to survive,   26 while many have remained in small towns, have tolerated their intolerances and created entertainment to enliven their culturally arid lives simply because it seemed there was no choice but to stay. There are many investments—spiritual, material, and temporal— one is willing to put into a home one cannot leave. Communities are often the beneficiaries of these involuntary investments.

But when the going gets rough in cyberspace, it is even easier to move than it is in the   27 'burbs, where, given the fact that the average American moves some 12 times in his or her life, moving appears to be pretty easy. You can not only find another bulletin board service (BBS) or newsgroup to hang out in, you can, with very little effort, start your own.

And then there is the bond of joint suffering. Most community is a cultural stock-   28 ade erected against a common enemy that can take many forms. In Pinedale, we bore together, with an understanding needing little expression, the fact that Upper Green River Valley is the coldest spot, as measured by annual mean temperature, in the lower 48 states. We knew that if somebody was stopped on the road most winter nights, he would probably die there, so the fact that we might loathe him was not sufficient reason to drive on past his broken pickup.

By the same token, the Deadheads have the Drug Enforcement Administration, which   29 strives to give them 20-year prison terms without parole for distributing the fairly harmless sacrament of their faith. They have an additional bond in the fact that when their Microbuses die, as they often do, no one but another Deadhead is likely to stop to help them.

But what are the shared adversities of cyberspace? Lousy user interfaces? The   30
flames of harsh invective? Dumb jokes? Surely these can all be survived without the
sanctuary provided by fellow sufferers.

One is always free to yank the jack, as I have mostly done. For me, the physical   31
world offers far more opportunity for *prāna*-rich connections with my fellow creatures.
Even for someone whose body is in a state of perpetual motion, I feel I can generally
find more community among the still-embodied.

Finally, there is that shyness factor. Not only are we trying to build community   32
here among people who have never experienced any in my sense of the term, we are
trying to build community among people who, in their lives, have rarely used the word
we in a heartfelt way. It is a vast club, and many of the members—following Groucho
Marx—wouldn't want to join a club that would have them.

And yet . . .   33

How quickly physical community continues to deteriorate. Even Pinedale, which   34
seems to have survived the plague of ranch failures, feels increasingly cut off from
itself. Many of the ranches are now opened by corporate types who fly their Gulf-
streams in to fish and are rarely around during the many months when the creeks are
frozen over and neighbors are needed. They have kept the ranches alive financially, but
they actively discourage their managers from the interdependence my former colleagues and I require. They keep agriculture on life support, still alive but lacking a
functional heart.

And the town has been inundated with suburbanites who flee here, bringing all   35
their terrors and suspicions with them. They spend their evenings as they did in
Orange County, watching television or socializing in hermetic little enclaves of fundamentalist Christianity that seem to separate them from us and even, given their sec-
tarian animosities, from one another. The town remains. The community is largely a
wraith of nostalgia.

So where else can we look for the connection we need to prevent our plunging fur-   36
ther into the condition of separateness Nietzsche called sin? What is there to do but to
dive further into the bramble bush of information that, in its broadcast forms, has done
so much to tear us apart?

Cyberspace, for all its current deficiencies and failed promises, is not without some   37
very real solace already.

Some months ago, the great love of my life, a vivid young woman with whom I   38
intended to spend the rest of it, dropped dead of undiagnosed viral cardiomyopathy
two days short of her 30th birthday. I felt as if my own heart had been as shredded
as hers.

We had lived together in New York City. Except for my daughters, no one from   39
Pinedale had met her. I needed a community to wrap around myself against colder
winds than fortune had ever blown at me before. And without looking, I found I had
one in the virtual world.

On the WELL, there was a topic announcing her death in one of the confer-   40
ences to which I posted the eulogy I had read over her before burying her in her
own small town of Nanaimo, British Columbia. It seemed to strike a chord among

the disembodied living on the Net. People copied it and sent it to one another. Over the next several months I received almost a megabyte of electronic mail from all over the planet, mostly from folks whose faces I have never seen and probably never will.

They told me of their own tragedies and what they had done to survive them. As humans have since words were first uttered, we shared the second most common human experience, death, with an openheartedness that would have caused grave uneasiness in physical America, where the whole topic is so cloaked in denial as to be considered obscene. Those strangers, who had no arms to put around my shoulders, no eyes to weep with mine, nevertheless saw me through. As neighbors do.

Those strangers, who had no arms to put around my shoulders, no eyes to weep with mine, nevertheless saw me through. As neighbors do.

I have no idea how far we will plunge into this strange place. Unlike previous frontiers, this one has no end. It is so dissatisfying in so many ways that I suspect we will be more restless in our search for home here than in all our previous explorations. And that is one reason why I think we may find it after all. If home is where the heart is, then there is already some part of home to be found in cyberspace.

So . . . does virtual community work or not? Should we all go off to cyberspace or should we resist it as a demonic form of symbolic abstraction? Does it supplant the real or is there, in it, reality itself?

Like so many true things, this one doesn't resolve itself to a black or a white. Nor is it gray. It is, along with the rest of life, black/white. Both/neither. I'm not being equivocal or wishy-washy here. We have to get over our Manichean sense that everything is either good or bad, and the border of cyberspace seems to me a good place to leave that old set of filters.

But really it doesn't matter. We are going there whether we want to or not. In five years, everyone who is reading these words will have an e-mail address, other than the determined Luddites who also eschew the telephone and electricity.

When we are all together in cyberspace we will see what the human spirit, and the basic desire to connect, can create there. I am convinced that the result will be more benign if we go there open-minded, open-hearted, and excited with the adventure than if we are dragged into exile.

And we must remember that going to cyberspace, unlike previous great emigrations to the frontier, hardly requires us to leave where we have been. Many will find, as I have, a much richer appreciation of physical reality for having spent so much time in virtuality.

Despite its current (and perhaps in some areas permanent) insufficiencies, we should go to cyberspace with hope. Groundless hope, like unconditional love, may be the only kind that counts.

In Memoriam, Dr. Cynthia Horner (1964–1994).

SECOND THOUGHTS

1. What social forces are creating the lack of real-life community that Barlow describes as "Generica"? From your own experience, do you agree that the majority of Americans live in "neither communities nor homes" (¶ 5)?
2. What aspects of the Deadheads conference on the WELL made Barlow feel he'd "found the new locale of human community" (¶ 11)? What's missing from cyber-communities, according to Barlow? Construct a working definition of *community* using as many of Barlow's criteria as you can.
3. Overall, based on this article, would you describe Barlow as more pessimistic or more optimistic about the potential for virtual community? Why?

Finding One's Own in Cyberspace

Amy Bruckman

Amy Bruckman (b. 1965) is assistant professor in the college of computing at the Georgia Institute of Technology. She conducts research on virtual communities and education, formerly at the MIT (Massachusetts Institute of Technology) Media Lab. She founded MediaMOO, a MUD (Multi-User Domain) or text-based virtual community for professional media researchers, and MOOSE Crossing, which she describes on her Web page (<www.cc.gatech.edu/fac/Amy.Bruckman/>) as "a MUD designed to be a constructionist learning environment for kids—a context to get them excited about reading, writing, and programming." This essay originally appeared in 1996 in *Technology Review* (<web.mit.edu/afs/athena/org/t/techreview/www/tr.html>), a magazine published by MIT's alumni association for a national audience interested in technology and society.

The week the last Internet porn scandal broke, my phone didn't stop ringing: "Are women comfortable on the Net?" "Should women use gender-neutral names on the Net?" "Are women harassed on the Net?" Reporters called from all over the country with basically the same question. I told them all: your question is ill-formed. "The Net" is not one thing. It's like asking: "Are women comfortable in bars?" That's a silly question. Which woman? Which bar?

The summer I was 18, I was the computer counselor at a summer camp. After the campers were asleep, the counselors were allowed out, and would go bar hopping. First everyone would go to Maria's, an Italian restaurant with red-and-white-checked table cloths. Maria welcomed everyone from behind the bar, greeting regular customers by name. She always brought us free garlic bread. Next we'd go to the Sandpiper, a disco with good dance music. The Sandpiper seemed excitingly adult—it was a little scary at first, but then I loved it. Next, we went to the Sportsman, a leather motorcycle bar that I found absolutely terrifying. Huge, bearded men bulging out of their leather vests and pants leered at me. I hid in the corner and tried not to make eye contact with anyone, hoping my friends would get tired soon and give me a ride back to camp.

Each of these bars was a community, and some were more comfortable for me than others. The Net is made up of hundreds of thousands of separate communities, each with its own special character. Not only is the Net a diverse place, but "women" are diverse as well—there were leather-clad women who loved the Sportsman, and plenty of women revel in the fiery rhetoric of Usenet's *alt.flame*. When people complain about being harassed on the Net, they've usually stumbled into the wrong online community. The question is not whether "women" are comfortable on "the Net," but rather, what

171

types of communities are possible? How can we create a range of communities so that everyone—men and women—can find a place that is comfortable for them?

If you're looking for a restaurant or bar, you can often tell without even going in: 4
Is the sign flashing neon or engraved wood? Are there lots of cars parked out front? What sort of cars? (You can see all the Harleys in front of the Sportsman from a block away.) Look in the window: How are people dressed? We are accustomed to diversity in restaurants. People know that not all restaurants will please them, and employ a variety of techniques to choose the right one.

It's a lot harder to find a good virtual **It's a lot harder to find a**   5
community than it is to find a good bar. The visual **good virtual community**
cues that let you spot the difference between **than it is to find a good**
Maria's and the Sportsman from across the street
are largely missing. Instead, you have to "lurk"— **bar.**
enter the community and quietly explore for a
while, getting the feel of whether it's the kind of
place you're looking for. Although published guides exist, they're not always very useful—most contain encyclopedic lists with little commentary or critical evaluation, and by the time they're published they're already out of date. Magazines like *NetGuide* and *Wired* are more current and more selective, and therefore more useful, but their editorial bias may not fit with your personal tastes.

Commonly available network-searching tools are also useful. The World Wide   6
Web is filled with searching programs, indexes, and even indexes of indexes ("meta-indexes"). Although browsing with these tools can be a pleasant diversion, it is not very efficient, and searches for particular pieces of information often end in frustration. If you keep an open mind, however, you may come across something good.

SHAPING AN ONLINE SOCIETY

But what happens if, after exploring and asking around, you still can't find an online   7
environment that suits you? Don't give up: start your own! This doesn't have to be a difficult task. Anyone can create a new newsgroup in Usenet's "alt" hierarchy or open a new chat room on America Online. Users of Unix systems can easily start a mailing list. If you have a good idea but not enough technical skill or the right type of Net access, there are people around eager to help. The more interesting question is: How do you help a community to become what you hope for? Here, I can offer some hard-won advice.

In my research at the MIT Media Lab (working with Professor Mitchel   8
Resnick), I design virtual communities. In October of 1992, I founded a professional community for media researchers on the Internet called MediaMOO. Over the past three years, as MediaMOO has grown to 1,000 members from 33 countries, I have grappled with many of the issues that face anyone attempting to establish a virtual community. MediaMOO is a "multi-user dungeon" or MUD—a virtual world on the Internet with rooms, objects, and people from all around the world. Messages typed in by a user instantly appear on the screens of all other users who are currently in the same virtual "room." This real-time interaction distinguishes MUDs from Usenet

newsgroups, where users can browse through messages created many hours or days before. The MUD's virtual world is built in text descriptions. MOO stands for MUD object-oriented, a kind of MUD software (created by Pavel Curtis of the Xerox Palo Alto Research Center and Stephen White, now at InContext Systems) that allows each user to write programs to define spaces and objects.

The first MUDs, developed in the late 1970s, were multiplayer fantasy games of the dungeons-and-dragons variety. In 1989, a graduate student at Carnegie Mellon University named James Aspnes decided to see what would happen if you took away the monsters and the magic swords but instead let people extend the virtual world. People's main activity went from trying to conquer the virtual world to trying to build it, collaboratively. 9

Most MUDs are populated by undergraduates who should be doing their home- work. I thought it would be interesting instead to bring together a group of people with a shared intellectual interest: the study of media. Ideally, MediaMOO should be like an endless reception for a conference on media studies. But given the origin of MUDs as violent games, giving one an intellectual and professional atmosphere was a tall order. How do you guide the evolution of who uses the space and what they do there? 10

A founder/designer can't control what the community ultimately becomes—much of that is up to the users—but can help shape it. The personality of the community's founder can have a great influence on what sort of place it becomes. Part of what made Maria's so comfortable for me was Maria herself. She radiated a warmth that made me feel at home. 11

Similarly, one of the most female-friendly electronic communities I've visited is New York City's ECHO (East Coast Hang Out) bulletin board, run by Stacy Horn. Smart, stylish, and deliberately outrageous, Horn is role model and patron saint for the ECHO-ites. Her outspoken but sensitive personality infuses the community, and sends a message to women that it's all right to speak up. She added a conference to ECHO called "WIT" (women in telecommunications), which one user describes as "a warm, supportive, women-only, private conference where women's thoughts, experiences, wisdom, joys, and despairs are shared." But Horn also added a conference called "BITCH," which the ECHO-ite calls "WIT in black leather jackets. All-women, riotous and raunchy." 12

Horn's high-energy, very New York brand of intelligence establishes the kind of place ECHO is and influences how everyone there behaves. When ECHO was first established, Horn and a small group of her close friends were the most active people on the system. "That set the emotional tone, the traditional style of posting, the unwritten rules about what it's OK to say," says Marisa Bowe, an ECHO administrator for many years. "Even though Stacy is too busy these days to post very much, the tone estab- lished in the early days continues," says Bowe, who is now editor of an online maga- zine called *Word.* 13

Beyond the sheer force of a founder's personality, a community establishes a par- ticular character with a variety of choices on how to operate. One example is to set a policy on whether to allow participants to remain anonymous. Initially, I decided that members of MediaMOO should be allowed to choose: they could identify themselves 14 with their real names and e-mail addresses, or remain anonymous. Others questioned whether there was a role for anonymity in a professional community.

As time went on, I realized they were right. People on MediaMOO are supposed to   15 be networking, hoping someone will look up who they really are and where they work. Members who are not willing to share their personal and professional identities are less likely to engage in serious discussion about their work and consequently about media in general. Furthermore, comments from an anonymous entity are less valuable because they are unsituated—"I believe X" is less meaningful to a listener than "I am a librarian with eight years of experience who lives in a small town in Georgia, and I believe X." In theory, anonymous participants could describe their professional experiences and place their comments in that context; in practice it tends not to happen that way. After six months, I proposed that we change the policy to require that all new members be identified. Despite the protests of a few vocal opponents, most people thought that this was a good idea, and the change was made.

Each community needs to have its own policy on anonymity. There's room for   16 diversity here too: some communities can be all-anonymous, some all-identified, and some can leave that decision up to each individual. An aside: right now on the Net no one is either really anonymous or really identified. It is easy to fake an identity; it is also possible to use either technical or legal tools to peer behind someone else's veil of anonymity. This ambiguous state of affairs is not necessarily unfortunate: it's nice to know that a fake identity that provides a modicum of privacy is easy to construct, but that in extreme cases such people can be tracked down.

Finding Birds of a Feather

Another important design decision is admissions policy. Most places on the Net have   17 a strong pluralistic flavor, and the idea that some people might be excluded from a community ruffles a lot of feathers. But exclusivity is a fact of life. MIT wouldn't be MIT if everyone who wanted to come was admitted. Imagine if companies had to give jobs to everyone who applied! Virtual communities, social clubs, universities, and corporations are all groups of people brought together for a purpose. Achieving that purpose often requires that there be some way to determine who can join the community.

A key decision I made for MediaMOO was to allow entry only to people doing   18 some sort of "media research." I try to be loose on the definition of "media"—writing teachers, computer network administrators, and librarians are all working with forms of media—but strict on the definition of "research." At first, this policy made me uncomfortable. I would nervously tell people, "It's mostly a self-selection process. We hardly reject anyone at all!" Over time, I've become more comfortable with this restriction, and have enforced the requirements more stringently. I now believe my initial unease was naive.

Even if an online community decides to admit all comers, it does not have to let all   19 contributors say anything they want. The existence of a moderator to filter postings often makes for more focused and civil discussion. Consider Usenet's two principal newsgroups dealing with feminism—*alt.feminism* and *soc.feminism*. In *alt.feminism*, anyone can post whatever they want. Messages in this group are filled with the angry words of angry people; more insults than ideas are exchanged. (Titles of messages found there on a randomly selected day included "Women & the workplace (it doesn't work)" and "What is a feminazi?".) The topic may nominally be feminism, but the discussion itself is not feminist in nature.

The huge volume of postings (more than 200 per day, on average) shows that many people enjoy writing such tirades. But if I wanted to discuss some aspect of feminism, *alt.feminism* would be the last place I'd go. Its sister group, *soc.feminism,* is moderated—volunteers read messages submitted to the group and post only those that pass muster. Moderators adhere to *soc.feminism*'s lengthy charter, which explains the criteria for acceptable postings—forbidding ad hominem attacks, for instance.   20

Moderation of a newsgroup, like restricting admission to a MUD, grants certain individuals within a community power over others. If only one group could exist, I'd have to choose the uncensored *alt.feminism* to the moderated *soc.feminism.* Similarly, if MediaMOO were the only virtual community or MIT the only university, I'd argue that they should be open to all. However, there are thousands of universities and the Net contains hundreds of thousands of virtual communities, with varying criteria for acceptable conduct. That leaves room for diversity: some communities can be moderated, others unmoderated. Some can be open to all, some can restrict admissions.   21

The way a community is publicized—or not publicized—also influences its character. Selective advertising can help a community achieve a desired ambiance. In starting up MediaMOO, for example, we posted the original announcement to mailing lists for different aspects of media studies—not to the general-purpose groups for discussing MUDs on Usenet. MediaMOO is now rarely if ever deliberately advertised. The group has opted not to be listed in the public, published list of MUDs on the Internet. Members are asked to mention MediaMOO to other groups only if the majority of members of that group would probably be eligible to join MediaMOO.   22

New members are attracted by word of mouth among media researchers. To bring in an influx of new members, MediaMOO typically "advertises" by organizing an online discussion or symposium on some aspect of media studies. Announcing a discussion group on such topics as the techniques for studying behavior in a virtual community or strategies for using computers to teach writing attracts the right sort of people to the community and sets a tone for the kinds of discussion that take place there. That's much more effective than a more general announcement of MediaMOO and its purpose.   23

In an ideal world, virtual communities would acquire new members entirely by self-selection: people would enter an electronic neighborhood only if it focused on something they cared about. In most cases, this process works well. For example, one Usenet group that I sometimes read—*sci.aquaria*—attracts people who are really interested in discussing tropical fishkeeping. But self-selection is not always sufficient. For example, the challenge of making MediaMOO's culture different from prevailing MUD culture made self-selection inadequate. Lots of undergraduates with no particular focus to their interests want to join MediaMOO. To preserve MediaMOO's character as a place for serious scholarly discussions, I usually reject these applications.   24

Besides, almost all of the hundreds of other MUDs out there place no restrictions on who can join. MediaMOO is one of the few that is different.

Emotionally and politically charged subject matter, such as feminism, makes it 25 essential for members of a community to have a shared understanding of the community's purpose. People who are interested in freshwater and saltwater tanks can coexist peacefully in parallel conversations on *sci.aquaria.* However, on *alt.feminism,* people who want to explore the implications of feminist theory and those who want to question its basic premises don't get along quite so well. Self-selection alone is not adequate for bringing together a group to discuss a hot topic. People with radically differing views may wander in innocently, or barge in deliberately—disrupting the conversation through ignorance or malice.

Such gate crashing tends to occur more frequently as the community grows in size. 26 For example, some participants in the Usenet group *alt.tasteless* decided to post a series of grotesque messages to the thriving group *rec.pets.cats,* including recipes for how to cook cat. A small, low-profile group may be randomly harassed, but that's less likely to happen.

In the offline world, membership in many social organizations is open only to 27 those who are willing and able to pay the dues. While it may rankle an American pluralistic sensibility, the use of wealth as a social filter has the advantages of simplicity and objectivity: no one's personal judgment plays a role in deciding who is to be admitted. And imposing a small financial hurdle to online participation may do more good than harm. Token fees discourage the random and pointless postings that dilute the value of many newsgroups. One of the first community networks, Community Memory in Berkeley, Calif., found that charging a mere 25 cents to post a message significantly raised the level of discourse, eliminating many trivial or rude messages.

Still, as the fee for participation rises above a token level, this method has obvious 28 moral problems for a society committed to equal opportunity. In instituting any kind of exclusionary policy, the founder of a virtual community should first test the key assumption that alternative, nonexclusionary communities really do exist. If they do not, then less restrictive admissions policies may be warranted.

BUILDING ON DIVERSITY

Anonymity policy, admission requirements, and advertising strategy all contribute 29 to a virtual community's character. Without such methods of distinguishing one online hangout from another, all would tend to sink to the least common denominator of discourse—the equivalent of every restaurant in a town degenerating into a dive. We need better techniques to help members of communities develop shared expectations about the nature of the community, and to communicate those expectations to potential new members. This will make it easier for people to find their own right communities.

Just as the surest way to find a good restaurant is to exchange tips with friends, 30 word of mouth is usually the best way to find out about virtual communities that might suit your tastes and interests. The best published guides for restaurants compile comments and ratings from a large group of patrons, rather than relying on the judgment of any one expert. Approaches like this are being explored on the Net. Yezdi Lashkari, cofounder of Agents Inc., designed a system called "Webhound" that recommends items of interest on the World Wide Web. To use Webhound, you enter into the system a list of web sites you like. It matches you with people of similar interests, and then recommends other sites that they like. Not only do these ratings come from an aggregate of many opinions, but they also are matched to your personal preferences.

Webhound recommends just World Wide Web pages, but the same basic approach could help people find a variety of communities, products, and services that are likely to match their tastes. For example, Webhound grew out of the Helpful Online Music Recommendation Service (HOMR), which recommends musical artists. A subscriber to this service—recently renamed Firefly—first rates a few dozen musical groups on a scale from "the best" to "pass the earplugs"; Firefly searches its database for people who have similar tastes, and uses their list of favorites to recommend other artists that might appeal to you. The same technique could recommend Usenet newsgroups, mailing lists, or other information sources. Tell it that you like to read the Usenet group *rec.arts.startrek.info,* and it might recommend *alt.tv.babylon-5*—people who like one tend to like the other. While no such tool yet exists for Usenet, the concept would be straightforward to implement. 31

Written statements of purpose and codes of conduct can help communities stay focused and appropriate. MediaMOO's stated purpose, for example, helps set its character as an arena for scholarly discussion. But explicit rules and mission statements can go only so far. Elegant restaurants don't put signs on the door saying "no feet on tables" and fast food restaurants don't post signs saying "feet on tables allowed." Subtle cues within the environment indicate how one is expected to behave. Similarly, we should design regions in cyberspace so that people implicitly sense what is expected and what is appropriate. In this respect, designers of virtual communities can learn a great deal from architects. 32

Vitruvius, a Roman architect from the first century B.C., established the basic principles of architecture as commodity (appropriate function), firmness (structural stability), and delight. These principles translate into the online world, as William Mitchell, dean of MIT's School of Architecture and Planning, points out in his book *City of Bits: Space, Place, and the Infobahn:* 33

> Architects of the twenty-first century will still shape, arrange, and connect spaces (both real and virtual) to satisfy human needs. They will still care about the qualities of visual and ambient environments. They will still seek commodity, firmness, and delight. But commodity will be as much a matter of software functions and interface design as it is of floor plans and construction materials. Firmness will entail not only the physical integrity of structural systems, but also the logical integrity of computer systems. And delight? Delight will have unimagined new dimensions.

Marcos Novak of the University of Texas at Austin is exploring some of those "unimagined dimensions" with his notion of a "liquid architecture" for cyberspace, free from the constraints of physical space and building materials. But work of this kind on the merging of architecture and software design is regrettably rare; if virtual 34 communities are buildings, then right now we are living in the equivalent of thatched huts. If the structure keeps out the rain—that is, if the software works at all—people are happy.

More important than the use of any of these particular techniques, however, is 35 applying an architect's design sensibility to this new medium. Many of the traditional tools and techniques of architects, such as lighting and texture, will translate into the design of virtual environments. Depending on choice of background color and texture, type styles, and special fade-in effects, for instance, a Web page can feel playful or gloomy, futuristic or old-fashioned, serious or fun, grown-up or child-centered. The language of the welcoming screen, too, conveys a sense of the community's purpose and character. An opening screen thick with the jargon of specialists in, say, genetic engineering, might alert dilettantes that the community is for serious biologists.

As the Net expands, its ranks will fill with novices—some of whom, inevitably, 36 will wander into less desirable parts of cybertown. It is important for such explorers to appreciate the Net's diversity—to realize, for example, that the newsgroup *alt.feminism* does not constitute the Internet's sole contribution to feminist debate. Alternatives exist.

I'm glad there are places on the Net where I'm not comfortable. The world would be a boring place if it invariably suited any one person's taste. The great promise of the Net is diversity. That's something we need to cultivate and cherish. Unfortunately, there aren't yet enough good alternatives—too much of the Net is like the Sportsman and too little of it is like Maria's. Furthermore, not enough people are aware that communities can have such different characters. 37

> **I'm glad there are places on the Net where I'm not comfortable. The world would be a boring place if it invariably suited any one person's taste.**

People who accidentally find themselves in 38 the Sportsman, *alt.feminism,* or *alt.flame,* and don't find the black leather or fiery insults to their liking, should neither complain about it nor waste their time there— they should search for a more suitable community. If you've stumbled into the wrong town, get back on the bus. But if you've been a long-time resident and find the community changing for the worse—that's different. Don't shy away from taking political action within that community to protect your investment of time: speak up, propose solutions, and build a coalition of others who feel the same way you do.

With the explosion of interest in networking, people are moving from being 39 recipients of information to creators, from passive subscribers to active participants and leaders. Newcomers to the Net who are put off by harassment, pornography, and just plain bad manners should stop whining about the places they find unsuitable and turn their energies in a more constructive direction: help make people aware of the variety of alternatives that exist, and work to build communities that suit their interests and values.

← SECOND THOUGHTS

1. Bruckman makes a number of comparisons between cyber-communities and real-life, physical places. Why is it "a lot harder to find a good virtual community than it is to find a good bar" (¶ 5), according to the author?

2. Make an outline of Bruckman's advice for designing and constructing virtual communities, then evaluate one of her points in depth. For example, what are Bruckman's arguments in support of exclusive admissions policies and "the use of wealth as a social filter" (¶ 27)? How does she anticipate and respond to objections to her views? How persuaded are you by her arguments on this point?

3. Bruckman says, "The great promise of the Net is diversity" (¶ 37), and she mentions diversity in conjunction with several of her arguments. What value does she seem to see in diversity, online or offline? To what extent do you agree with these values?

Finding God on the Web

Joshua Cooper Ramo

Across the Internet, Believers
Are Reexamining their Ideas of
Faith, Religion, and Spirituality

Joshua Cooper Ramo (b. 1968) is a senior editor for the weekly newsmagazine *Time,* where he covers business and technology. Formerly he ran a new media company for Time Warner, publisher of *Time Digital,* and was a science and technology reporter and creator of the online service at *Newsweek.* This article ran as a cover story for *Time* (<www.time.com>) in December 1996.

The Monastery of Christ in the Desert sits at the end of a bumpy half-hour drive down a ruined red-clay road that wends into the azure sky of northwestern New Mexico like a curl of Christmas ribbon reaching toward heaven. The main sanctuary, fashioned from brown adobe and perched on a small hill, is warmed by burning piñon and scented by freshly baked bread. In the late afternoon the surrounding canyon glows with a purple twilight. At night the waters of the Chama River gossip with the birds, and the stars weave a gossamer blanket overhead. No matter what your faith, it is an easy place in which to be spiritual. 1

It is not, however, an easy place to be technological. Twenty miles from the nearest power line and perhaps twice as far from the nearest phone, the monastery is more than two hours from Albuquerque and an hour from anything that resembles civilization. No telephone bells fracture the silence. No TV images smear the crisp evening air. No pagers chirp. If you must reach one of the monks, a hand-carved wooden sign offers a simple 16th century suggestion: "Ring this bell." 2

Or you can send E-mail, in care of *porter@christdesert.org*. Remote as they may seem, the brothers of Christ in the Desert are plugged into the Internet. Using electricity generated by a dozen solar panels and a fragile data link through a single cellular phone, the monks have developed a heavily trafficked Benedictine home page and started a new business designing and maintaining other people's Websites. The order's work has even caught the eye of the Holy See. Last month Webmaster Brother Mary Aquinas flew to Rome for consultations and to lend a hand building what the Vatican hopes will be the greatest—let alone the holiest—site on the World Wide Web. 3

Like schools, like businesses, like governments, like nearly everyone, it seems, religious groups are rushing online, setting up church home pages, broadcasting dogma 4 and establishing theological newsgroups, bulletin boards and chat rooms. Almost overnight, the electronic community of the Internet has come to resemble a high-speed spiritual bazaar, where thousands of the faithful—and equal numbers of the faithless—meet and debate and swap ideas about things many of us had long since stopped discussing in public, like our faith and religious beliefs. It's an astonishing act of technological and intellectual mainstreaming that is changing the character of the Internet, and could even change our ideas about God.

> **Almost overnight, the electronic community of the Internet has come to resemble a high-speed spiritual bazaar, where thousands of the faithful—and equal numbers of the faithless— meet and debate and swap ideas.**

The signs of online religious activity are everywhere. If you instruct AltaVista, a powerful Internet search engine, to scour the Web for references to Microsoft's Bill Gates, the program turns up an impressive 25,000 references. But ask it to look for Web pages that mention God, and you'll get 410,000 hits. Look for Christ on the Web, and you'll find him—some 146,000 times. 5

Newsgroups like *alt.fan.jesus-christ* and *alt.religion.scientology* are among the busiest—and most contentious—of the nearly 20,000 discussion groups carried on Usenet. America Online and CompuServe, the two largest commercial online services, are each home to hundreds of electronic bulletin boards that offer everything from Confucian primers to Q. and A.s about Jewish dietary laws. (One urgent AOL query: Is it O.K. to have a pot-bellied pig as a pet if you keep a kosher kitchen? Answer: Probably. As long as you don't plan to eat it.) 6

The harvest is even more bountiful on the Web, where everyone from Lutherans to Tibetan Buddhists now has a home page, many crammed with technological bells and whistles. Mormon sites offer links to vast genealogical databases, while YaaleVe' Yavo, an Orthodox Jewish site, forwards E-mailed prayers to Jerusalem, where they are affixed to the Western Wall. Two Websites are devoted to Cao Daiism, the tiny Vietnamese sect that worships French novelist Victor Hugo as a saint, and a handful probe the mysteries of Jainism, an Indian religion in which (as one learns on the Net) the truly faithful sweep the ground with a small broom to avoid accidentally stepping on insects or other hapless creatures. Even the famously technophobic Amish are represented online by a Website run by Ohio State University. It offers, among other things, a guide for installing a rear warning light on a horse-drawn carriage. 7

Perhaps the most ambitious site on the Web is the one now being patiently cobbled together on the first floor of the Vatican's Apostolic Palace. First launched in 1995 (and soon overloaded by an "E-mail the Pope" feature that proved far too popular), the Holy See's redesigned site will be unwrapped some time around Christmas. Running 24 hours a day on three powerful computers (nicknamed Raphael, Michael and Gabriel), it will offer Vatican press releases, John Paul II's schedule and most of 8 the Pontiff's writings, translated into six languages. It will also have the capacity to field thousands of simultaneous information requests from all over the world. "The Internet is exploding, and the church has got to be there," says Sister Judith Zoebelein, the American-born nun who runs the site. "The Holy Father wanted it." Indeed, the Pope, who has always looked for innovative ways to spread the word, including travel, books and even records, was writing as early as 1989 about the opportunities offered by computer telecommunications to fulfill the church's mission, which he called the "new evangelization."

It's a message other churches ignore at their peril. The faithful, according to a   9 recent study by Barna Research in Glendale, California, are moving online every bit as fast as the rest of the world. After interviewing hundreds of wired Christians, Barna concluded that churches that don't establish a presence in cyberspace will start to seem badly out of touch with their parishioners. "The failure to do so," according to the study, "sends an important signal about the church's ability to advise people in an era of technological growth."

In this area the faithful seem to be leading their churches, instead of following,   10 opening an unusually lively colloquy. It is the nature of computer networks that they tend to throw together people who would otherwise never meet—never mind discuss something as intimate as one's personal beliefs. Thus on the Internet, Catholics suddenly find themselves keyboard-to-keyboard with devil worshippers, Jews modem-to-modem with Islamic fundamentalists. "I put the [Reverend Moon's] Unification Church right up there with the wonderful world of Mormon," someone with the screen name Marzioli posted recently on a Usenet newsgroup. The next message snapped back, "Marz, you are an ignorant disinformationist. Wake up, man!!!"

For all their fire and testosterone, these chat rooms and bulletin boards draw scores   11 of believers hunting for new ways to understand their old religions. For Fundamentalists prohibited from openly discussing such social issues as homosexuality and abortion, the Net has become the best—and sometimes the only—way to get exposed to a wide range of religious opinion. AOL users this fall have been able to follow the life of an Egyptian girl expelled from her family after converting to Christianity. "My mother gave me up," she wrote, recounting the apostasy that cost her her family even as an online debate raged around her. "I understand your anger and frustration toward Muslims," one man replied. "What I don't understand is why you keep posting these messages in areas where your views are not welcome."

Alvin Plantinga, a philosophy professor at Notre Dame, says that despite the surface   12 discord, these electronic exchanges will ultimately help people from many religions understand the common ideas that bind them together. "One of the sustaining causes of religious disagreement has been the sense of strangeness, of pure unfamiliarity," he says. "The communication revolution will not wash out the important differences, but we will learn to grade our differences in order of importance." Rached Ghannouchi, an Arab philosopher from North Africa, argues in a Webzine called *The Electronic Whip* that it is imperative that the inhabitants of the small, networked village the world has become find a way to understand one another. "Otherwise," he says, rather apocalyptically, "we are all doomed to annihilation."

Is it possible that this global network that pulls in so many different directions 13
could somehow bind us together in a way that other technologies—particularly television—have failed to do? TV seems to have lured people away from their communities. Could it be that the Net is starting to bring them back together? Can it create
new communities of spiritual consensus not in real time but in virtual space?

Just as urbanization brought people together for worship in cities—and ultimately 14
led to the construction of larger and larger cathedrals—so the electronic gathering of
millions of faithful could someday lead to online entities that might be thought of as
cyberchurches. Already some Conservative Jews are considering the idea of convening
a minyan (the minimum of 10 Jews needed before a communal service may begin) via
speaker phone.

In France, Roman Catholics are closely following the online activities of a con- 15
troversial bishop named Jacques Gaillot. Exiled by the Pope to an abandoned diocese
in 1995 because of his liberal social views, Gaillot has established what he calls a virtual diocese to replace it. He marvels at the freedom he enjoys loosed from the hierarchy of the church. "On the Internet there is no question of someone imposing rules on
the way people communicate," he says. "The Net has no center from which will can
be applied."

That's a sentiment echoed in the U.S. by postdenominational Protestantism, a 16
religious movement that links thousands of U.S. churches in informal networks outside the boundaries of mainline Protestant or evangelical denominations. The
churches fill their services with rock 'n' roll, recovery counseling and a nonjudgmen-
tal approach to a wide range of life-styles. The movement has been making increasing
use of computer communication technologies. Says University of Southern California
sociologist Donald Miller, who has followed the rapid growth of postdenominational
churches: "There's definitely a congruence between these technologies and the outlook of these churches."

Even holy texts have begun to be adapted to the new technology. The interconnection 17
of religious documents through so-called hyperlinks has produced a new form of scholarship called "hypertheology." Clicking on Lot in an electronic Bible, for instance,
might connect you to similar stories in the Koran or pertinent 20th century moral com-
mentaries. Just as the first illuminated manuscripts exposed readers to early theological
debates, these hypertexts open up thousands of interpretations of God's words to anyone curious enough to click a mouse.

For all its seeming newness, however, the marriage between technology and religion 18
is an ancient one. Man has always used state-of-the-art communications technology to
convey his deepest thoughts. Five thousand years ago, the Sumerians etched their fears
and hopes in cuneiform. Centuries later, the Egyptians glorified Ra on papyrus scrolls.
The Old Testament was hewed and edited in the 1st century A.D., when the scrolls were
turned into primitive books called codices. Forced for the first time to assign to the Holy
Story a beginning, middle, and end, Christian and Hebrew scholars took different paths—
creating a schism that endures to this day. For example, Jews pray from a Bible (known
as the Tanach) that places the prophecies right after the book of *Deuteronomy;* Christians
don't encounter the prophets until the very end of the Good Book.

The first codices had another, equally historic impact: they gave upstart Christian-   19
ity an edge over Roman paganism. While pagan scholars stuck with their scrolls like
modern Luddites refusing to embrace E-mail, liberal Christians leaped at the efficiencies and portability of books. The result, argues Jack Miles, a former Jesuit who won a
Pulitzer Prize for his 1995 book, *God: A Biography,* was a "technological advantage"
for early Christianity. It was too much of one for the Roman Emperors, who quickly
developed their own innovation: book burning.

Still, the lessons of these defiant early believers stayed with the church, whose   20
devotees spent much of the next millennium obsessively copying and recopying their
sacred texts. It was a brutally inefficient process. Cloistered Benedictines toiled for
years in musty scriptoriums, transcribing copy after copy of the Bible into leather-
bound books. This medieval Xerox system was painfully low-tech: a monk would
slowly copy from exemplar Latin Bibles as he and his brothers inked and gilded lav-
ishly illustrated pages at the rate of roughly one a day.

As these elaborate Bibles circulated in Europe (mostly among the landed élite,   21
since a single copy cost more than a peasant's lifetime earnings), they spread more than
the word of God—they also set, in their rudimentary way, new technological standards.
Georgetown professor Martin Irvine calls this manuscript culture "the first information
age." He explains that "it was the first time a whole civilization configured around a
standard technology for recording and distributing information."

Proselytizing via these handwrought manuscripts was not an easy task. The Bibles   22
were rare, fragile, and generally came in one flavor: Latin. The problems didn't go
away until the mid-1400s, when a German inventor named Johann Gutenberg wheeled
his movable-type press out of its secret hiding place and into history.

Appropriately enough, the first book Gutenberg printed was the Bible. His simple   23
press passed sheets of paper under specialized plates that could be changed in minutes
instead of weeks, revolutionizing intellectual commerce. Ideas that once could be communicated only in person, or at large universities in cities such as London or Hanover,
suddenly took wing across the Continent. And
though Gutenberg printed just 200 Bibles before
losing control of his invention, there was no turning back. In 1456, when the first Bible
rolled off his press, there were fewer than 30,000
books in Europe. Fifty years later, there were 9
million, most devoted to religious themes.

> **In 1456, when the first Bible rolled off [Gutenberg's] press, there were fewer than 30,000 books in Europe. Fifty years later, there were 9 million.**   24

Many scholars credit the printing press with
theology's next revolution: the Reformation.
Thirty-seven years after Gutenberg's death, young
Martin Luther renounced his plans to become a
lawyer (his father's idea) and instead, seized by spiritual anxiety, joined the Monastery
of the Emerites of St. Augustine. It was a fateful decision. Luther's tortured soul, which
attached itself to new ideas with a fervor that seems strikingly modern, turned in a
decade's time against the institution he had vowed to serve and created one of history's
greatest religious splinter groups. Rome wanted to suppress his ideas, but Luther
quickly found that the printing press could be used as a sort of technological mega-

phone—printing copies of his *Ninety-Five Theses* faster than they could be gathered up and destroyed.

The drive to spread the Gospel continues into the modern era and what used to be called 25 the radio age. By 1926, 14 years after Edwin Armstrong cranked up his first receiver, the good word was streaming from American radio stations, first shocking and then energizing what was then still a devoutly conservative country. Father Charles Coughlin, a firecracker Catholic priest who pounded a broadcast pulpit from Detroit, built a virtual congregation in just four years. For tens of millions of Depression-era believers, his Shrine of the Little Flower was a beacon of hope—until an embarrassed church pulled the plug. And though there was plenty of anti-Semitism, isolationism and fear mongering in Coughlin's speeches, there was little irony: even as he used all this blessed new technology, he damned the capitalist economy that produced it.

By the time evangelism was ready to make the leap to television, however, that 26 resentment had dissolved. In the 1950s, a new generation of media-savvy ministers—Bishop Fulton Sheen, Billy Graham, Oral Roberts—started directing their crusades at the TV audience. And if the subtext of the awesome Catholic liturgy had always been God's immutable power, the plot of these TV revivals was tailored for the medium of *Father Knows Best*. In broadcasts from million-dollar sets-cum-cathedrals, TV evangelicals preached not just about the miracle of Jesus but also about the blessing of communications technology. Religion and TV became so indistinguishable that it took a neologism, televangelism, to fully capture what was going on.

And now we stand at the start of a new movement in this delicate dance of technol- 27 ogy and faith: the marriage of God and the global computer networks. There's no sure way to measure how much the Internet will change our lives, but the most basic truth about technological revolutions is that they change everything they touch. Just as the first telescopes forever altered our sense of where we sit in the cosmos, so the Internet may press and tug at our most closely held beliefs. Will the Net change religion? Is it possible that God in a networked age will look, somehow, different?

The Net is so new, and changing so fast, that scholars are still struggling to answer 28 that question, or even make sense of it. Most traditional religious thinkers are skeptical. "I don't think the computer revolution has any cosmic implications for religion at all," says Notre Dame's Plantinga. "We already know God."

But for a whole culture of technology-loving—and in some cases, perhaps, tech- 29 nology-worshipping—futurists, such words smack of 1st millennium thinking in the face of 3rd millennium faith. They tend to see in the Internet something larger than themselves, an entity so much greater than the sum of its parts as to inspire awe and wonder. "People see the Net as a new metaphor for God," says Sherry Turkle,* a professor of the sociology of science at M.I.T. The Internet, she says, exists as a world of its own, distinct from earthly reality, crafted by humans but now growing out of human control. "God created a set of conditions from which life would emerge. Like it or not, the Internet is one of the most dramatic examples of something that is self-organized. That's the point. God *is* the distributed, decentralized system."

---

*See Chapter 1, p. 5 (ed.).

"It seems as though the Net itself has become conscious," says William Gibson,[†] 30 the science-fiction writer who coined the term cyberspace and used it, most famously, in his 1984 novel *Neuromancer*. "It may regard itself as God. And it may be God on its own terms." Gibson hastens to add, however, that he is "carefully ambivalent" about whether anything that exists solely on the Net applies to the real world.

These radical notions dovetail with a spiritual movement known as process theol- 31 ogy, whose proponents argue that God evolves along with man. In their mind, the immutable God embraced by scholars like Plantinga makes no more sense today than an unchanging computer operating system. "If God doesn't change, we are in danger of losing God," says William Grassie, a Quaker professor of religion at Temple University. "There is a shift to [the idea of] God as a process evolving with us. If you believe in an eternal, unchanging God, you'll be in trouble."

In fact, as much as the Net is changing our ideas of God, it may be changing us 32 even more. For many, signing on to the Internet is a transformative act. In their eyes the Web is more than just a global tapestry of PCs and fiber-optic cable. It is a vast cathedral of the mind, a place where ideas about God and religion can resonate, where faith can be shaped and defined by a collective spirit. Such a faith relies not on great external forces to change the world, but on what ordinary people, working as one, can create on this World Wide Web that binds all of us, Christian and Jew, Muslim and Buddhist, together. Interconnected, we may begin to find God in places we never imagined.

SECOND THOUGHTS

1. Although he discusses "cyberchurches" and "hypertheology," Ramo says that "the marriage between technology and religion is an ancient one" (¶ 18). In what ways did technological innovation affect major events in religious history, according to Ramo?

2. The question of whether electronic communication tends to pull people apart or bring them together is crucial in discussions of virtual community. From Ramo's article, how would you weigh the "surface discord" (¶ 12) of disagreement and competing religious views on the Internet against the potential of this medium to "create new communities of spiritual consensus" (¶ 13)?

3. Based on this article, your other reading, and your own experiences with religion and with computer technology, how would you answer Ramo's question, "Is it possible that God in a networked age will look, somehow, different?" (¶ 27)? What do you think about Sherry Turkle's or William Gibson's idea of the Net as a metaphor for God (¶s 29, 30)?

[†]See Chapter 1, p. 48, and Chapter 8, p. 369 (ed.).

The Air-Ship

E. M. Forster

E. M. Forster (1879–1970) was an English novelist and critic. As Darcy O'Brien writes in *The World Book Encyclopedia* (1981), "His novels show his interest in personal relationships and in the social, psychological, and racial obstacles to such relationships." His novels include *A Room with a View* (1908), *Howards End* (1910), and *A Passage to India* (1924), all of which were made into feature films during a 1990s resurgence of interest in Forster's work. His books of essays and literary criticism include *Aspects of the Novel* (1927) and *Two Cheers for Democracy* (1951). Not as well known among Forster's work are his allegorical, fantasy, and science fiction stories, collected in *The Celestial Omnibus* (1911) and *The Eternal Moment* (1928). "The Air-Ship" is Part 1 of a longer story, "The Machine Stops," originally published in *The Oxford and Cambridge Review* in 1909 and collected in *The Eternal Moment.*

I magine, if you can, a small room, hexagonal in shape, like the cell of a bee. It is lighted neither by window nor by lamp, yet it is filled with a soft radiance. There are no apertures for ventilation, yet the air is fresh. There are no musical instruments, and yet, at the moment that my meditation opens, this room is throbbing with melodious sounds. An armchair is in the centre, by its side a reading-desk—that is all the furniture. And in the arm-chair there sits a swaddled lump of flesh—a woman, about five feet high, with a face as white as a fungus. It is to her that the little room belongs.

An electric bell rang.

The woman touched a switch and the music was silent.

"I suppose I must see who it is," she thought, and set her chair in motion. The chair, like the music, was worked by machinery, and it rolled her to the other side of the room, where the bell still rang importunately.

"Who is it?" she called. Her voice was irritable, for she had been interrupted often 5 since the music began. She knew several thousand people; in certain directions human intercourse had advanced enormously.

But when she listened into the receiver, her white face wrinkled into smiles, and she said:

"Very well. Let us talk, I will isolate myself. I do not expect anything important will happen for the next five minutes—for I can give you fully five minutes, Kuno. Then I must deliver my lecture on 'Music during the Australian Period.'"

She touched the isolation knob, so that no one else could speak to her. Then she touched the lighting apparatus, and the little room was plunged into darkness.

"Be quick!" she called, her irritation returning. "Be quick, Kuno; here I am in the dark wasting my time."

But it was fully fifteen seconds before the round plate that she held in her hands 10 began to glow. A faint blue light shot across it, darkening to purple, and presently she could see the image of her son, who lived on the other side of the earth, and he could see her.

"Kuno, how slow you are."

He smiled gravely.

"I really believe you enjoy dawdling."

"I have called you before, mother, but you were always busy or isolated. I have something particular to say."

"What is it, dearest boy? Be quick. Why could you not send it by pneumatic post?" 15

"Because I prefer saying such a thing. I want—————"

"Well?"

"I want you to come and see me."

Vashti watched his face in the blue plate.

"But I can see you!" she exclaimed. "What more do you want?" 20

"I want to see you not through the Machine," said Kuno. "I want to speak to you not through the wearisome Machine."

"Oh, hush!" said his mother, vaguely shocked. "You mustn't say anything against the Machine."

"Why not?"

"One mustn't."

"You talk as if a god had made the Machine," cried the other. "I believe that 25 you pray to it when you are unhappy. Men made it, do not forget that. Great men, but men. The Machine is much, but it is not everything. I see something like you in this plate, but I do not see you. I hear something like you through this telephone, but I do not hear you. That is why I want you to come. Come and stop with me. Pay me a visit, so that we can meet face to face, and talk about the hopes that are in my mind."

She replied that she could scarcely spare the time for a visit.

"The air-ship barely takes two days to fly between me and you."

"I dislike air-ships."

"Why?"

"I dislike seeing the horrible brown earth, and the sea, and the stars when it is dark. 30 I get no ideas in an air-ship."

"I do not get them anywhere else."

"What kind of ideas can the air give you?"

He paused for an instant.

"Do you not know four big stars that form an oblong, and three stars close together in the middle of the oblong, and hanging from these stars, three other stars?"

"No, I do not. I dislike the stars. But did they give you an idea? How interesting; 35 tell me."

"I had an idea that they were like a man."

"I do not understand."

"The four big stars are the man's shoulders and his knees. The three stars in the middle are like the belts that men wore once, and the three stars hanging are like a sword."

"A sword?"

"Men carried swords about with them, to kill animals and other men."   40

"It does not strike me as a very good idea, but it is certainly original. When did it come to you first?"

"In the air-ship————" He broke off, and she fancied that he looked sad. She could not be sure, for the Machine did not transmit *nuances* of expression. It only gave a general idea of people—an idea that was good enough for all practical purposes, Vashti thought. The imponderable bloom, declared by a discredited philosophy to be the actual essence of intercourse, was rightly ignored by the Machine, just as the imponderable bloom of the grape was ignored by the manufacturers of artificial fruit. Something 'good enough' had long since been accepted by our race.

"The truth is," he continued, "that I want to see these stars again. They are curious stars. I want to see them not from the air-ship, but from the surface of the earth, as our ancestors did, thousands of years ago. I want to visit the surface of the earth."

She was shocked again.

"Mother, you must come, if only to explain to me what is the harm of visiting the   45
surface of the earth."

"No harm," she replied, controlling herself. "But no advantage. The surface of the earth is only dust and mud, no life remains on it, and you would need a respirator, or the cold of the outer air would kill you. One dies immediately in the outer air."

"I know; of course I shall take all precautions."

"And besides————"

"Well?"

She considered, and chose her words with care. Her son had a queer temper, and   50
she wished to dissuade him from the expedition.

"It is contrary to the spirit of the age," she asserted.

"Do you mean by that, contrary to the Machine?"

"In a sense, but————"

His image in the blue plate faded.

"Kuno!"   55

He had isolated himself.

For a moment Vashti felt lonely.

Then she generated the light, and the sight of her room, flooded with radiance and studded with electric buttons, revived her. There were buttons and switches everywhere—buttons to call for food, for music, for clothing. There was the hot-bath button, by pressure of which a basin of (imitation) marble rose out of the floor, filled to the brim with a warm deodorized liquid. There was the cold-bath button. There was the button that produced literature. And there were of course the buttons by which she communicated with her friends.

the buttons by which she communicated with her friends. The room, though it contained nothing, was in touch with all that she cared for in the world.

Vashti's next move was to turn off the isolation-switch, and all the accumulations of the last three minutes burst upon her. The room was filled with the noise of bells, and speaking-tubes. What was the new food like? Could she recommend it? Had she had any ideas lately? Might one tell her one's own ideas? Would she make an engagement to visit the public nurseries at an early date?—say this day month.

To most of these questions she replied with irritation—a growing quality in that   60
accelerated age. She said that the new food was horrible. That she could not visit the public nurseries through press of engagements. That she had no ideas of her own but had just been told one—that four stars and three in the middle were like a man: she doubted there was much in it. Then she switched off her correspondents, for it was time to deliver her lecture on Australian music.

The clumsy system of public gatherings had been long since abandoned; neither Vashti nor her audience stirred from their rooms. Seated in her arm-chair she spoke, while they in their armchairs heard her, fairly well, and saw her, fairly well. She opened with a humorous account of music in the pre-Mongolian epoch, and went on to describe the great outburst of song that followed the Chinese conquest. Remote and primæval as were the methods of I-San-So and the Brisbane school, she yet felt (she said) that study of them might repay the musician of today: they had freshness; they had, above all, ideas.

Her lecture, which lasted ten minutes, was well received, and at its conclusion she and many of her audience listened to a lecture on the sea; there were ideas to be got from the sea; the speaker had donned a respirator and visited it lately. Then she fed, talked to many friends, had a bath, talked again, and summoned her bed.

The bed was not to her liking. It was too large, and she had a feeling for a small bed. Complaint was useless, for beds were of the same dimension all over the world, and to have had an alternative size would have involved vast alterations in the Machine. Vashti isolated herself—it was necessary, for neither day nor night existed under the ground—and reviewed all that had happened since she had summoned the bed last. Ideas? Scarcely any. Events—was Kuno's invitation an event?

By her side, on the little reading-desk, was a survival from the ages of litter—one book. This was the Book of the Machine. In it were instructions against every possible contingency. If she was hot or cold or dyspeptic or at a loss for a word, she went to the book, and it told her which button to press. The Central Committee published it. In accordance with a growing habit, it was richly bound.

Sitting up in the bed, she took it reverently in her hands. She glanced round the   65
glowing room as if some one might be watching her. Then, half ashamed, half joyful, she murmured "O Machine! O Machine!" and raised the volume to her lips. Thrice she kissed it, thrice inclined her head, thrice she felt the delirium of acquiescence. Her ritual performed, she turned to page 1367, which gave the times of the departure of the air-ships from the island in the southern hemisphere, under whose soil she lived, to the island in the northern hemisphere, whereunder lived her son.

She thought, "I have not the time."

She made the room dark and slept; she awoke and made the room light; she ate and exchanged ideas with her friends, and listened to music and attended lectures; she made the room dark and slept. Above her, beneath her, and around her, the Machine hummed eternally; she did not notice the noise, for she had been born with it in her ears. The earth, carrying her, hummed as it sped through silence, turning her now to the invisible sun, now to the invisible stars. She awoke and made the room light.

"Kuno!"

"I will not talk to you," he answered, "until you come."

"Have you been on the surface of the earth since we spoke last?"   70

His image faded.

Again she consulted the book. She became very nervous and lay back in her chair palpitating. Think of her as without teeth or hair. Presently she directed the chair to the wall, and pressed an unfamiliar button. The wall swung apart slowly. Through the opening she saw a tunnel that curved slightly, so that its goal was not visible. Should she go to see her son, here was the beginning of the journey.

Of course she knew all about the communication-system. There was nothing mysterious in it. She would summon a car and it would fly with her down the tunnel until it reached the lift that communicated with the air-ship station: the system had been in use for many, many years, long before the universal establishment of the Machine. And of course she had studied the civilization that had immediately preceded her own—the civilization that had mistaken the functions of the system, and had used it for bringing people to things, instead of for bringing things to people. Those funny old days, when men went for change of air instead of changing the air in their rooms! And yet—she was frightened of the tunnel: she had not seen it since her last child was born. It curved—but not quite as she remembered; it was brilliant—but not quite as brilliant as a lecturer had suggested. Vashti was seized with the terrors of direct experience. She shrank back into the room, and the wall closed up again.

"Kuno," she said, "I cannot come to see you. I am not well."

Immediately an enormous apparatus fell on to her out of the ceiling, a thermome-   75
ter was automatically inserted between her lips, a stethoscope was automatically laid upon her heart. She lay powerless. Cool pads soothed her forehead. Kuno had telegraphed to her doctor.

So the human passions still blundered up and down in the Machine. Vashti drank the medicine that the doctor projected into her mouth, and the machinery retired into the ceiling. The voice of Kuno was heard asking how she felt.

"Better." Then with irritation: "But why do you not come to me instead?"

"Because I cannot leave this place."

"Why?"

"Because, any moment, something tremendous may happen."   80

"Have you been on the surface of the earth yet?"

"Not yet."

"Then what is it?"

"I will not tell you through the Machine."

She resumed her life.   85

But she thought of Kuno as a baby, his birth, his removal to the public nurseries, her one visit to him there, his visits to her—visits which stopped when the Machine had assigned him a room on the other side of the earth. "Parents, duties of," said the book of the Machine, "cease at the moment of birth. P.422327483." True, but there was something special about Kuno—indeed there had been something special about all her children—and, after all, she must brave the journey if he desired it. And "something tremendous might happen." What did that mean? The nonsense of a youthful man, no doubt, but she must go. Again she pressed the unfamiliar button, again the wall swung back, and she saw the tunnel that curved out of sight. Clasping the Book, she rose, tottered on to the platform, and summoned the car. Her room closed behind her: the journey to the northern hemisphere had begun.

Of course it was perfectly easy. The car approached and in it she found arm-chairs exactly like her own. When she signalled, it stopped, and she tottered into the lift. One other passenger was in the lift, the first fellow creature she had seen face to face for months. Few travelled in these days, for, thanks to the advance of science, the earth was exactly alike all over. Rapid intercourse, from which the previous civilization had hoped so much, had ended by defeating itself. What was the good of going to Pekin when it was just like Shrewsbury? Why return to Shrewsbury when it would be just like Pekin? Men seldom moved their bodies; all unrest was concentrated in the soul.

The air-ship service was a relic from the former age. It was kept up, because it was easier to keep it up than to stop it or to diminish it, but it now far exceeded the wants of the population. Vessel after vessel would rise from the vomitories of Rye or of Christchurch (I use the antique names), would sail into the crowded sky, and would draw up at the wharves of the south—empty. So nicely adjusted was the system, so independent of meteorology, that the sky, whether calm or cloudy, resembled a vast kaleidoscope whereon the same patterns periodically recurred. The ship on which Vashti sailed started now at sunset, now at dawn. But always, as it passed above Rheims, it would neighbour the ship that served between Helsingfors and the Brazils, and, every third time it surmounted the Alps, the fleet of Palermo would cross its track behind. Night and day, wind and storm, tide and earthquake, impeded man no longer. He had harnessed Leviathan. All the old literature, with its praise of Nature, and its fear of Nature, rang false as the prattle of a child.

Yet as Vashti saw the vast flank of the ship, stained with exposure to the outer air, her horror of direct experience returned. It was not quite like the air-ship in the cinematophote. For one thing it smelt—not strongly or unpleasantly, but it did smell, and with her eyes shut she should have known that a new thing was close to her. Then she had to walk to it from the lift, had to submit to glances from the other passengers. The man in front dropped his Book—no great matter, but it disquieted them all. In the rooms, if the Book was dropped, the floor raised it mechanically, but the gangway to the air-ship was not so prepared, and the sacred volume lay motionless. They stopped—the thing was unforeseen—and the man, instead of picking up his property, felt the muscles of his arm to see how they had failed him. Then some one actually said with direct utterance: "We shall be late"—and they trooped on board, Vashti treading on the pages as she did so.

Inside, her anxiety increased. The arrangements were old-fashioned and rough.   90
There was even a female attendant, to whom she would have to announce her wants
during the voyage. Of course a revolving platform ran the length of the boat, but she
was expected to walk from it to her cabin. Some cabins were better than others, and she
did not get the best. She thought the attendant had been unfair, and spasms of rage
shook her. The glass valves had closed, she could not go back. She saw, at the end of
the vestibule, the lift in which she had ascended going quietly up and down, empty.
Beneath those corridors of shining tiles were rooms, tier below tier, reaching far into
the earth, and in each room there sat a human being, eating, or sleeping, or producing
ideas. And buried deep in the hive was her own room. Vashti was afraid.

"O Machine! O Machine!" she murmured, and caressed her Book, and was comforted.

Then the sides of the vestibule seemed to melt together, as do the passages that we
see in dreams, the lift vanished, the Book that had been dropped slid to the left and vanished, polished tiles rushed by like a stream of water, there was a slight jar, and the air-
ship, issuing from its tunnel, soared above the waters of a tropical ocean.

It was night. For a moment she saw the coast of Sumatra edged by the phosphores-
cence of waves, and crowned by lighthouses, still sending forth their disregarded
beams. These also vanished, and only the stars distracted her. They were not motionless, but swayed to and fro above her head, thronging out of one skylight into another,
as if the universe and not the air-ship was careening. And, as often happens on clear
nights, they seemed now to be in perspective, now on a plane; now piled tier beyond
tier into the infinite heavens, now concealing infinity, a roof limiting for ever the
visions of men. In either case they seemed intolerable. "Are we to travel in the dark?"
called the passengers angrily, and the attendant,
who had been careless, generated the light, and
pulled down the blinds of pliable metal. When the
air-ships had been built, the desire to look
direct at things still lingered in the world. Hence
the extraordinary number of skylights and windows, and the proportionate discomfort to those
who were civilized and refined. Even in Vashti's

> **When the air-ships had been built, the desire to look direct at things still lingered in the world.**

cabin one star peeped through a flaw in the blind, and after a few hours' uneasy slum-
ber, she was disturbed by an unfamiliar glow, which was the dawn.

Quick as the ship had sped westwards, the earth had rolled eastwards quicker still,
and had dragged back Vashti and her companions towards the sun. Science could pro-
long the night, but only for a little, and those high hopes of neutralizing the earth's
diurnal revolution had passed, together with hopes that were possibly higher. To "keep
pace with the sun," or even to outstrip it, had been the aim of the civilization preceding
this. Racing aeroplanes had been built for the purpose, capable of enormous speed, and
steered by the greatest intellects of the epoch. Round the globe they went, round and
round, westward, westward, round and round, amidst humanity's applause. In vain.
The globe went eastward quicker still, horrible accidents occurred, and the Committee
of the Machine, at the time rising into prominence, declared the pursuit illegal, unmechanical, and punishable by Homelessness.

Of Homelessness more will be said later.   95

Doubtless the Committee was right. Yet the attempt to "defeat the sun" aroused the last common interest that our race experienced about the heavenly bodies, or indeed about anything. It was the last time that men were compacted by thinking of a power outside the world. The sun had conquered, yet it was the end of his spiritual dominion. Dawn, midday, twilight, the zodiacal path, touched neither men's lives nor their hearts, and science retreated into the ground, to concentrate herself upon problems that she was certain of solving.

So when Vashti found her cabin invaded by a rosy finger of light, she was annoyed, and tried to adjust the blind. But the blind flew up altogether, and she saw through the skylight small pink clouds, swaying against a background of blue, and as the sun crept higher, its radiance entered direct, brimming down the wall, like a golden sea. It rose and fell with the air-ship's motion, just as waves rise and fall, but it advanced steadily, as a tide advances. Unless she was careful, it would strike her face. A spasm of horror shook her and she rang for the attendant. The attendant too was horrified, but she could do nothing; it was not her place to mend the blind. She could only suggest that the lady should change her cabin, which she accordingly prepared to do.

People were almost exactly alike all over the world, but the attendant of the air-ship, perhaps owing to her exceptional duties, had grown a little out of the common. She had often to address passengers with direct speech, and this had given her a certain roughness and originality of manner. When Vashti swerved away from the sunbeams with a cry, she behaved barbarically—she put out her hand to steady her.

"How dare you!" exclaimed the passenger. "You forget yourself!"

The woman was confused, and apologized for not having let her fall. People never   100
touched one another. The custom had become obsolete, owing to the Machine.

"Where are we now?" asked Vashti haughtily.

"We are over Asia," said the attendant, anxious to be polite.

"Asia?"

"You must excuse my common way of speaking. I have got into the habit of calling places over which I pass by their unmechanical names."

"Oh, I remember Asia. The Mongols came from it."   105

"Beneath us, in the open air, stood a city that was once called Simla."

"Have you ever heard of the Mongols and of the Brisbane school?"

"No."

"Brisbane also stood in the open air."

"Those mountains to the right—let me show you them." She pushed back a metal   110
blind. The main chain of the Himalayas was revealed. "They were once called the Roof of the World, those mountains."

"What a foolish name!"

"You must remember that, before the dawn of civilization, they seemed to be an impenetrable wall that touched the stars. It was supposed that no one but the gods could exist above their summits. How we have advanced, thanks to the Machine!"

"How we have advanced, thanks to the Machine!" said Vashti.

"How we have advanced, thanks to the Machine!" echoed the passenger who had dropped his Book the night before, and who was standing in the passage.

"And that white stuff in the cracks?—what is it?"   115

"I have forgotten its name."

"Cover the window, please. These mountains give me no ideas."

The northern aspect of the Himalayas was in deep shadow: on the Indian slope the sun had just prevailed. The forests had been destroyed during the literature epoch for the purpose of making newspaper-pulp, but the snows were awakening to their morning glory, and clouds still hung on the breasts of Kinchinjunga. In the plain were seen the ruins of cities, with diminished rivers creeping by their walls, and by the sides of these were sometimes the signs of vomitories, marking the cities of to-day. Over the whole prospect air-ships rushed, crossing and intercrossing with incredible *aplomb,* and rising nonchalantly when they desired to escape the perturbations of the lower atmosphere and to traverse the Roof of the World.

"We have indeed advanced, thanks to the Machine," repeated the attendant, and hid the Himalayas behind a metal blind.

The day dragged wearily forward. The passengers sat each in his cabin, avoiding   120
one another with an almost physical repulsion and longing to be once more under the surface of the earth. There were eight or ten of them, mostly young males, sent out from the public nurseries to inhabit the rooms of those who had died in various parts of the earth. The man who had dropped his Book was on the homeward journey. He had been sent to Sumatra for the purpose of propagating the race. Vashti alone was travelling by her private will.

At midday she took a second glance at the earth. The air-ship was crossing another range of mountains, but she could see little, owing to clouds. Masses of black rock hovered below her, and merged indistinctly into grey. Their shapes were fantastic; one of them resembled a prostrate man.

"No ideas here," murmured Vashti, and hid the Caucasus behind a metal blind.

In the evening she looked again. They were crossing a golden sea, in which lay many small islands and one peninsula.

She repeated, "No ideas here," and hid Greece behind a metal blind.

SECOND THOUGHTS

1. Describe the social, political, and environmental conditions of the future world described in the story. Where and how do people live? What does the social structure seem to be? What has happened to the natural environment? What seem to be the primary shared or mainstream values of this global civilization?

2. When she begins her journey, Vashti is "seized with the terrors of direct experience" (¶ 73). Review the technology of communication and interpersonal relations in the story. What are the Machine's advantages, as seen by Vashti and other citizens? What seem to be the Machine's limitations and disadvantages? What are Kuno's objections to the Machine?

3. In what ways do you think today's Internet information and communication network—also broadly characterized by individuals in cubicles using electronic

tools—is similar to the Machine in Forster's story? What differences do you detect? How is a sense of community maintained similarly and differently in each case?

4. "How we have advanced, thanks to the Machine!" the passengers in the air-ship chant mechanically and, it seems, ironically as they pass over the Himalayas, unable to remember what snow is. What do you think Forster is trying to say about the Machine, and through the story, about social conditions of the early 20th century? How well do you think his social criticism applies to our own time, on the brink of the 21st century?

⟳⟳⟳ DISCUSSION THREADS

re: Rheingold and Barlow

1. How would you compare and contrast Howard Rheingold's and John Perry Barlow's experiences on the WELL (Whole Earth 'Lectronic Link)? Based on those experiences, what similar and different conclusions do they draw about virtual community?

re: Rheingold, Barlow, and Bruckman

2. How would you apply the advice offered by Amy Bruckman for designing virtual communities to the actual online experiences described by Howard Rheingold and John Perry Barlow on the WELL? How does the WELL seem to measure up, according to Bruckman's criteria?

re: Barlow and Bruckman

3. How do you think Amy Bruckman would respond to the specific objections that John Perry Barlow raises about virtual community? How do you think Barlow might reply to Bruckman? Imagine or construct a dialogue between these two writers in which you explore areas of agreement and disagreement.

re: Barlow and Forster

4. One of John Perry Barlow's primary objections to computer-mediated interaction is that "'the *prāna* is missing,' *prāna* being the Hindu term for both breath and spirit" (¶ 17). Kuno, in E. M. Forster's "The Air-Ship," says that "the Machine is much, but it is not everything. I see something like you in this plate, but I do not see you. I hear something like you through this telephone, but I do not hear you" (¶ 25). Use Barlow's arguments and your own experience to analyze Forster's story as a cautionary tale about virtual community.

re: Ramo and Forster

5. In Joshua Cooper Ramo's article, Sherry Turkle is quoted as saying, "People see the Net as a new metaphor for God" (¶ 29), and William Gibson says, "It seems as though the Net itself has become conscious" (¶ 30). To what extent do you think the citizens of E. M. Forster's "The Air-Ship" see the Machine as Godlike or conscious? Has Vashti "found God on the Web"?

re: Virtual Community

6. According to different views, computer-mediated communication (CMC) tends to pull people apart or to bring them together, or perhaps both. Discussions of the social effects of CMC and virtual community often focus on one or both of these

competing tendencies. Address these tensions in your own argument about virtual community or its potential with reference to several selections from this chapter and your own experience.

RESEARCH LINKS

- *For direct links to listed Internet sources, additional reading selections and questions online, plus updates and supplementary Web resources, see* **Composing Cyberspace Online** *at <www.mhhe.com/socscience/english/holeton/>.*
- *For a complete set of research tools for the Internet—including the most useful search strategies, directories, and conventions for documenting online sources—see McGraw-Hill English Composition at <www.mhhe.com/socscience/english/compde/>.*

1. Both Howard Rheingold and John Perry Barlow write in this chapter about their experiences from the early days of the West Coast-based online community the WELL (Whole Earth 'Lectronic Link, <www.well.com/>), and Amy Bruckman discusses the "female friendly" New York-based online community, sometimes compared to the WELL, called ECHO (East Coast Hang Out, <www.echonyc.com/>). If you have Internet access, explore both Web sites, and if possible, join both communities as a guest, then compare your experiences. Alternatively or additionally, explore other Web-based virtual community efforts such as HotWired (<www.hotwired.com/>) or The River (<www.river.org>), two offshoots of the WELL. Research the recent history of the organizations you explore and write a paper, or create a set of Web pages, in which you compare and evaluate their success as virtual communities.

2. Besides founding MediaMOO for adult media researchers, Amy Bruckman has created a virtual community for children aged 9 to 13 called MOOSE Crossing (<www.cc.gatech.edu/fac/Amy.Bruckman/moose-crossing/>). On the welcome Web page, Bruckman writes that "younger kids are welcome to try it out, and folks older than 13 can apply to become rangers, and help kids on the system." Explore what other online community resources exist for children on the Internet, and evaluate their state of development. If possible, ask younger siblings or friends in the appropriate age group to try out one or more of these resources and give you their opinions. If you are an experienced Net participant, consider applying for a volunteer position, such as Bruckman's "rangers" on MOOSE Crossing.

3. It is widely agreed that most Internet users in the late 1980s and early 1990s were affluent, white, male, and young. John Perry Barlow decries the lack of cultural diversity in cyberspace and, like Amy Bruckman, suggests that diversity is crucial for the success of online community. Search current newspaper and magazine indexes for the latest demographic information about the Internet: In the late 1990s, how diverse has the Net become in terms of gender, race, ethnicity, language or national origin, age, economic class, or other measures of social status? Not surprisingly, you can find numerous surveys and demographic studies about the Internet on the Internet itself; you can locate these using Web indexes or search engines. Collections of online links

to Internet demographic resources include Georgia Tech's WWW User Surveys at <www.cc.gatech.edu/gvu/user_surveys/others/> and InfoQuest's Internet Surveys and Statistics at <www.teleport.com/~tbchad/stats1.html>; you might also look at a study done by SRI Consulting at <future.sri.com/vals/trends/intro.html>. Do the various sources you find agree or conflict? What seem to be the most reliable or persuasive figures? Can you construct a model of how cultural diversity might look on the Internet in 5, 10, or 20 years?

4. The electronic expression of spirituality and the formation of religious community online are examined not only in Joshua Cooper Ramo's article in this chapter but also in Charlise Lyle's "CyberFaith" (in Chapter 3, p. 113) and Mark Fearer's "Scientology's Secrets" (in Chapter 8, p. 350). In addition, Richard Rodriguez looks at gaps between the religious and the electronic global village in "A Future of Faith and Cyberspace" (Chapter 6, p. 259). Choose a religious affiliation that you share or are interested in (or an alternative philosophy such as agnosticism or atheism), and explore to what extent this group of believers has actively used or been affected by electronic technologies. If you belong to a church or synagogue, compose a set of questions based on the articles you've read, and use these questions to interview members of your group and religious leaders. On the Internet, especially in Usenet newsgroups, there are hundreds of ongoing discussions about religion and spiritual beliefs. If Web sites are devoted to the group you're exploring, evaluate their effectiveness in communicating the group's beliefs or promoting a community of shared values. If you know or are willing to learn how to publish Web pages yourself, consider creating a site that explores your own religious or spiritual values.

5. How would you compare the future vision of the social impact of technology presented in E. M. Forster's "The Air-Ship" with that presented in William Gibson's "Johnny Mnemonic" (Chapter 1, p. 48)? Despite the drastic differences in the two representations of society—one apparently egalitarian and rigidly centralized, the other hierarchical and more anarchistic—do you see some surprising similarities? For an extended research project, read more works by Forster and Gibson along with critical and historical sources, and analyze how the current state of technology influenced each writer's science fiction vision.

Chapter 5

Electronic Democracy

Dilbert reprinted by permission of United Features Syndicate, Inc.

The popularity of the comic strip *Dilbert,* by Scott Adams, seems to have grown in the 1990s in proportion to the high-tech companies it lampoons. According to *Dilbert*'s Web page (<www.unitedmedia.com/comics/dilbert/>), it "stars a 'socially challenged' engineer [Dilbert] and his sarcastic dog, Dogbert, whose true calling is to rule the world, since he believes people are basically too stupid to stop him." The strip generally pokes fun at corporate bureaucracies and the new technologies they increasingly rely on. In the episode depicted here, Dogbert extends his ambitions to the Internet. But so decentralized and anarchic is the Net, as Dilbert points out, that even Dogbert's enormous ambitions may be no match for it. Depending on your interpretation, Dogbert's final threat ("Until now!") may sound either portentous or comically impotent.

The potential of emerging technologies to enhance or impede democracy is the subject of this chapter. For those who hold democratic values—and perhaps especially for Americans, who share a history of distrusting authority—the fact that those "millions of individuals and organizations" composing the Internet operate so independently may be seen as a virtue. Others with similar values caution that such decentralization of authority can exaggerate the influence of highly organized special interest groups or even facilitate a kind of mob rule. Radio was first used effectively as a political tool by President Franklin Roosevelt in his "fireside chats" of the 1930s and 1940s, in which he spoke directly to the American people; TV was first said to have a major influence on the election of President John F. Kennedy, following televised debates with Richard Nixon in 1960; Web sites became a common way for candidates and political parties (along with other pundits, critics, satirists, and pranksters) to communicate their agendas in the mid-1990s. Is our political system evolving in step with new media? To what extent can the free flow of information made possible by the Internet—and direct person-to-person communication on a mass scale—shift power toward or away from the Dogberts of the world?

Lawrence K. Grossman, former president of both NBC and PBS, sees the future inevitably evolving toward an "Electronic Republic" in which citizens use "keypad democracy" to "tell their president, senators, members of Congress, and local leaders what they want them to do and in what priority order." Jon Katz, writing for *Wired* magazine, is even more optimistic about what he calls the "Digital Nation," which he says already began exerting its influence during the 1996 elections. "Netizens" of the Digital Nation, according to Katz, form the core of a new social class and new political philosophy with the potential to create a more civil society. On the contrary, technology critic Langdon Winner calls such beliefs "computer romanticism," arguing that they are based on faulty assumptions about information, knowledge, and social power. Widespread adoption of new computer and information technology, suggests Winner, may in fact increase the concentration of global power in the hands of a few, rather than promote participatory democracy.

Chapter 5 concludes with two articles by John Schwartz and Pamela Varley describing actual experiments with electronic democracy in the form of civic electronic networks in Blacksburg, Virginia, and Santa Monica, California. In these real-life cases, as in any civic networks that you participate in directly, you have a chance to test out the various critical claims made by Grossman, Katz, and Winner. Before you read this chapter, in any case, you might consider the following questions:

1. How optimistic or pessimistic is most of the news-media coverage you've been exposed to about the Internet, particularly concerning the benefits or dangers of high technology for ordinary citizens? What promises or perils of widespread computer use are emphasized in what you read and hear?

2. How many people in your class have computers at home? How many have access to the Internet? How many people in your community do you estimate have computers and Internet access at home, school, or work? To what extent do you think the "wired" people in your class, school, town, or community are representative of that group as a whole, in terms of economic class, educational level, gender, race or ethnicity, or other demographic categories? How fast or slowly do you expect this distribution of technological resources will change, and why?

3. Assuming it's here to stay, how do you think computer and network technology should best be used to serve the public interest? Should all citizens be given access to computer networks? Putting aside logistical problems such as funding and resource distribution, what's your vision for a technological future? For example, imagine a future in which all citizens have computers with access to local, state, and national civic networks and could express their opinions about any issue at any time. What would be the advantages and disadvantages of such a system?

4. If you have access to a computer lab, classroom, or networked computers equipped with electronic discussion software, discuss with fellow readers one of the issues raised here, such as the potential of computers and computer networks to promote, or to abuse, democratic freedoms that you value.

The Shape of the Electronic Republic

Lawrence K. Grossman

Lawrence K. Grossman (b. 1931) is a longtime television journalist, former president of NBC News, and former president and CEO of PBS (Public Broadcasting Service). He has taught at the University of Miami and Harvard, where he held the Frank Stanton Chair on the First Amendment at the John F. Kennedy School of Government. Grossman has given talks and published articles about emerging electronic media in journals such as the *Columbia Journalism Review* and the *Media Studies Journal,* and he is the author of *Somehow It Works: A Candid Portrait of the 1964 Presidential Election* (Doubleday, 1965). This selection is from his 1995 book, *The Electronic Republic: Reshaping Democracy in the Information Age* (Viking Penguin).

I n February 1994, several thousand parents who teach their children at home rather than send them to school flooded members of Congress with so many letters, faxes, and telephone calls that, according to one report, they "shut down the Capitol switchboard." The home schooling parents, a dedicated, well educated, widely dispersed single-interest group, were fighting an obscure amendment to the president's proposed schools bill. The amendment required that all teachers be certified to teach the subjects to which they were assigned. While that may have sounded reasonable to most professional educators and many parents with kids in school, it would have been an impossible barrier for parents teaching their children at home.

As one observer remarked, "What was ultimately responsible for the explosiveness of the outcry was an awareness that spread like an infectious disease over the computer networks of America." The parents had been alerted to the amendment through postings on their electronic bulletin boards. Since they are so widely dispersed throughout the country, many of them use computer networks to share information and communicate with each other about their dedicated common interest in home schooling. Concerned about the amendment's potential to cripple home teaching, the parents converted their computer networks into political tools, exchanging hundreds of electronic messages a day about what they should do to defeat the amendment and how to go about it. They talked to each other on-line and organized themselves to act both individually and collectively to inundate Congress with their opposition to the amendment. One parent cheerfully notified the others in her group that she had sent off a fax to Rush Limbaugh, who did, in fact, give the issue radio airtime. The result was an electronic communications run on the Capitol. Congress responded by promptly killing the teaching certification amendment, which originally had been expected to pass easily, by a vote of 424 to 1.[1]

Until the past decade, the technology on which democracy had operated for some 2,500 years had not changed much. Even the conversion to voting machines was fundamentally a way to get an honest and more efficient head count and was not essentially different from the longstanding use of the voice vote and paper ballot. Today, however, electronic voting, polling, and opinion registering technologies are changing in radical ways, although most of these technologies still reside somewhere on the periphery of official democratic practice. The new technologies may be gaining dramatically in use and influence, but they have not yet been granted official recognition and standing. Nobody can phone, fax, or punch in his or her vote from the computer at home—yet. But in Oregon, for example, voting at home has become so popular that up to 20 percent of the electorate submit absentee ballots, and the number continues to grow.

> **Until the past decade, the technology on which democracy had operated for some 2,500 years had not changed much.**

3

We are only just beginning to experience the powerful political impact of the new personal electronic media—the faxed petitions, E-mail lobbies, interactive on-line networks, keypad votes, 900 telephone number polls, the use of modems, telecomputers, and teleprocessors to share information and register views. In kitchens, living rooms, dens, bedrooms, and workplaces throughout the nation, citizens have begun to apply such electronic devices to political purposes, giving those who use them a degree of empowerment they never had before. Digital computer networks provide the means for like-minded folks across America to unite, plan, share information, organize, and plot small political upheavals as the home schooling parents did. Of course, not only individuals but also large, sophisticated, and well-financed interest groups and professional lobbying organizations also have learned how to use these sophisticated new tools of political influence.

4

Exactly how and when the new technologies will be integrated with the old democratic practices cannot be predicted with precision. But the information and technological revolution is proceeding apace. "The advantages offered by new technologies are exciting and inescapable," wrote Xerox chief scientist John Seely Brown. "Designed with care, they can offer society the opportunity both to engage more people in democratic practices and to engage people more directly and in new ways. . . . [I]nformation technologies genuinely offer the chance to empower people, both in the work place and in society at large, who for one reason or another have become either effectively disenfranchised or merely disenchanted."[2]

5

The key lies in the phrase "designed with care," because the new technologies also offer political dangers that are many and serious. In 1994, ABC News anchor Ted Koppel echoed the views of many, and perhaps even most of his colleagues in journalism, politics, and political science by expressing dismay at the likelihood that these technological tools will create an excess of democracy. "The country may be moving in the direction of a purer democracy than anything the ancient Greeks envisioned," Koppel wrote. "It promises to be a fiasco. Opinion polls and focus groups are Stone Age implements in the brave new world of interactivity just down the communications superhighway. Imagine an ongoing electronic plebiscite in which millions of Americans will be

6

able to express their views on any public issue at the press of a button. Surely nothing could be a purer expression of democracy. Yet nothing would have a more paralyzing impact on representational government. . . . Now imagine the paralysis that would be induced if constituencies could be polled instantly by an all-but-universal interactive system. No more guessing what the voters were thinking; Presidents and lawmakers would have access to a permanent electrocardiogram, hooked up to the body politic."[3]

The brave new world of interactivity, whose political consequences Koppel finds   7
so appalling, is, indeed, just down the communications superhighway. And for better or worse, the new interactivity brings enormous political leverage to ordinary citizens at relatively little cost. With the prospect of a microprocessor, keypad, or telecomputer in the hands of every voter, we are, as Koppel put it, unquestionably "on the verge of giving our politicians a devastatingly accurate radar system that will tell them unambiguously just which way the crowd is milling."

In projecting the changes to be wrought in the electronic republic and defining   8
what shape the newly emerging political system will take, the question is not *whether* the new electronic information infrastructure will alter our politics, but *how*. Our political system has shown itself to be remarkably resilient in accommodating the nation's expanding democratic impulse. The two-hundred-year-old Constitution has survived vast geographical expansion, multiple population increases, and enormous demographic transformations among the nation's citizens. Crafted by the leaders of a weak, agricultural, infant nation, the Constitution also has withstood the Industrial Revolution, the rise of cities and suburbs, the remarkable technological and cultural explosions of the twentieth century, and the emergence of the United States as the world's superpower. Now it will have to withstand still another great transformation. Assuming the continuing yearning of the American people to govern themselves and assuming, too, continuing dramatic advances in interactive personal telecommunications technologies, we can begin to draw a more or less serviceable portrait of the electronic republic.

KEYPAD DEMOCRACY

Citizens already have many ways to express themselves individually and in groups, to   9
each other and to their elected and appointed officials. At their disposal in the future will be a diverse selection of portable fingertip and voice-activated telecommunications media capable of sending, receiving, storing, and sorting data and motion pictures of all kinds. People will be able to compose and receive instantaneous computer messages, faxes, letters, wires, and videos, and they will have the ability to direct communications, in turn, to just about any individuals or groups they select. Time and distance will be no factor. Using a combination telephone–video screen computer, citizens will be capable of participating in audio- and videophone calls, teleconferences, teledebates, tele-discussions, tele-forums, and electronic town meetings. They will, of course, continue to have the capacity to phone radio and television talk shows from cars, homes, and workplaces, and talk to vast audiences simultaneously.

Most citizens will gain access to a good deal of information and data in many   10
different formats, which can be retrieved on order or automatically through "smart" television sets programmed to select and store or retrieve any material on any sub-

ject. The material they call up may have been tailormade specifically for their age group, sex, race, style of living, educational level, taste, and individual interests. Some of it the users will pay for. Some will be provided free because it is promotional or public service in nature or because it grinds the ax of a particular interest group.

As *The New York Times* described the debut of a new congressional service available over the World Wide Web on the Internet, "A person who taps into the service, called Thomas in honor of Thomas Jefferson, can call up the full text of any bill introduced in Congress since 1992 and will soon be able to get all new issues of the Congressional Record. . . . Type a keyword like 'mother' and a person can get a list of every bill that mentions mothers—and every nonbinding resolution introduced to praise motherhood, condemn welfare mothers, chastise unwed mothers, or provide equity for mothers and fathers in divorce cases."[4]   11

Using computerized lists and on-line networks for different interest groups, individual citizens will also be able to send their own promotional material, propaganda, and publicity of all kinds in all formats to individuals, groups, and political representatives of their own choosing. There will be a continuing flow of audio, video, and written communications, dialogue exchanges, yes/no votes and polls, position papers and programs, interviews, speeches, presentations, and advertisements—all rattling around in cyberspace and all instantly available on command. And day by day, numerous polls and surveys, both official and unofficial, reliable and meretricious, impartial and self-serving, will take the pulse of the public, and continuously tabulate political opinion.   12

Using a designated personal code—one's Social Security number, citizen registration number, or special-purpose phone number—each citizen's message, vote, or question will be capable of being instantly tabulated and sorted to determine its legitimacy, what sort of interest group or geographic constituency it is part of, and whether enough citizens care sufficiently about a particular matter to be worth paying attention to.   13

People not only will be able to vote on election day by telecomputer for those who govern them but also will be able to make their views known formally and informally, on a daily basis or even more often if they wish, regarding the politics, laws, agendas, and priorities about which they care the most. By pushing a button, typing on-line, or talking to a computer, they will be able to tell their president, senators, members of Congress, and local leaders what they want them to do and in what priority order. The potential will exist for individual citizens to tap into government on demand, giving them the capacity to take a direct and active role, by electronic means, in shaping public policies and specific laws.   14

With public opinion of increasing moment, a remarkable variety of techniques, devices, and measures will be employed to determine what citizens think at any particular time on any particular issue. To the telecomputerized citizens of the next century, today's public opinion polling will seem as crude, primitive, and limited as the first Gallup polls in the 1930s seem to us now. Sample groups of citizens will be empaneled to represent the whole or specific parts of the population. These focus groups will be surveyed to express their choices in some depth and dimension, and then monitored to reflect any changes in their views. Electronic juries will be asked to render judgments on individual public questions. Professional polling companies and political consul-   15 tants already do a good deal of this work. We shall see more of it in the future, carried out in more structured and sophisticated ways.

"Boiler room" organizations, hired by special interests, will seek to manufacture   16
and mobilize "grassroots" opinion and stimulate the outpouring of selected messages and votes—to make sure that particular viewpoints are heard. They do that now. In the next century, it will become a mainstream business. Computerized political advertising, promotion, and marketing campaigns, targeted with high degrees of specificity, will lobby ordinary citizens with as much intensity as legislators, regulators, and public officials are lobbied today, because public opinion—the fourth branch of government—will play an even more pivotal role in major government decisions.

TOWARD PLEBISCITE DEMOCRACY

Back in 1912, the United States Supreme Court put to rest the basic question of whether   17
procedures involving direct democracy were incompatible with our republican form of government and should, therefore, be held unconstitutional. The issue centered on the constitutionality of the newly introduced state ballot initiatives, the populist effort to bring direct democracy to several western states. State ballot initiatives, the procedure's opponents argued, violated the constitutional requirement that elected representatives, not the people at large, make the laws of the land. Upholding the constitutionality of direct initiatives, the Supreme Court concluded that the initiative process simply augmented rather than "eliminated or superseded the republican form of government and the representative processes thought to be central to it."[5] The court was confident that elements of direct democracy can coexist within the representative republic.

Given the accelerated use of statewide and local ballot initiatives and referenda   18
since that time, national advisory plebiscites, initiatives, or referenda, at least on certain major issues, may well be put in place by early in the next century. Polls consistently show a good deal of public support for such measures. If the American people had their way, the federal government would join the rising number of states and local jurisdictions that use ballot initiatives and referenda to impose the public's will directly on government policy. According to Gallup, 70 percent of Americans want to be able to vote directly on key national issues in the belief that national referenda will help overcome gridlock in government and end the corrupting influence of special interests on politics.

In 1993, 80 percent of those surveyed were convinced that the "country needs to   19
make major changes in the way government works." As one observer put it, if the public had its way, "governance in the 1990s [would quickly be] transformed from an exercise in backroom decision making to an up-front, open, 'we-want-in-on-the-decision-making' experience for citizens."[6]

The entire nation may vote not only for term limitations and balanced budgets but   20
also to use citizens' teleprocessors and electronic keypads to bypass, or override the legislative powers of Congress. This is not much different from what already has been put into effect in states like California, Colorado, and Oregon. As it is, many congressmen already have become accustomed to surveying their constituents on tough, controversial matters before casting their own votes. On especially vexing legislation

involving, say, new taxes, the decision to go to war, abortion, health care reform, or environmental questions, Congress may consider it prudent to refer the ultimate decisions to an actual vote of the people. The electronic mechanisms that will make such national votes practical throughout the year will soon be in place.

In the 1994 statewide elections, voters decided nearly 150 ballot initiatives. Oregonians alone considered 19 issues, Coloradans 12, and Californians 10, on everything from gay rights issues, to cutting off public benefits for illegal aliens, to term limits. 21

"The ballot initiative has become a major generator of state policy in California," said the official report of the California Commission on Campaign Financing, *Democracy by Initiative,* issued in 1992. "Although the idea of 'direct democracy' by vote of the people is an ancient one . . . , nowhere has it been applied as rigorously and with such sweeping results as in California today. If California's trends continue to serve as a predictor for the nation's future, then [we] . . . will also begin to see the emergence of 'democracy by initiative' as a new form of twenty-first century governance."[7] In the twenty-first century, as California goes, so may go the nation. 22

Ballot initiatives and referenda on federal issues could be made determinative, as Ross Perot suggested be done with tax and budget decisions in a 1992 campaign proposal that generated substantial public support. Or federal referenda could be made largely advisory, in effect telling the people's representatives how their constituents think they should vote, a system that actually existed in four states over two hundred years ago. In the decades ahead, the public also may seek the power to veto laws that Congress enacts, thereby enabling the people themselves to overrule any federal measure they do not like. As we have seen, Switzerland, a country often judged to have one of the world's most effective democracies, has long operated with just such a system. In Switzerland, within ninety days after a law has been passed, if thirty thousand voters from at least eight cantons sign a petition requesting that it be put to a popular vote, the law must be brought before all the nation's citizens to be ratified. A majority of those voting can overturn the action of their own elected representatives. The Swiss have made the initiative and referendum process the preferred method of dealing with national legislation in their country. 23

From today's perspective, none of these scenarios for the United States is farfetched. The use of initiatives and referenda in states and localities has jumped fivefold in the last thirty years. Today the initiative has become a primary tool of governance in many states besides California. On the federal level, as far back as the end of the nineteenth century, proposals were offered in Congress to introduce both advisory and binding national referenda and initiatives. Such efforts were endorsed periodically by supporters on the left as well as on the right. In the 1920s, a pacifist backlash against war generated considerable support for a Constitutional amendment—the Ludlow Amendment, named after its congressional sponsor—that would have required a national referendum before the United States could declare war and send troops abroad, unless the U.S. had been invaded. Many prominent college presidents and political scientists as well as a good many newspaper editorials supported the idea. Federal advisory referenda were conducted among the nation's farmers from 1933 to 1936, under the New Deal, to help determine market quotas for commodities. In some regions, farmers still vote on market quotas.[8] 24

In 1980, Congressman Richard A. Gephardt, a Democrat from Missouri and cur- 25
rently minority leader of the House, proposed that the federal government sponsor a
national advisory referendum process in which voters could express their views on three
issues every two years. Under the Gephardt plan, the issues would be selected after public hearings and the referendum results would be nonbinding. Issues not subsequently
acted upon by Congress would be resubmitted for the voters to decide. A 1987 Gallup
survey indicated that Americans approved of the plan by a two-to-one margin.[9]

In the 1980s, Ralph Nader, frustrated by a federal government that he was con- 26
vinced had lost touch with ordinary citizens, called for national ballot initiatives so that
the people's voice could be heard and government officials bypassed. In a rare moment
of agreement, that call was echoed on the right by conservative politicians Patrick
Buchanan and Jack Kemp and economist Arthur Laffer. They believed that the national
popular will was being frustrated by an unresponsive liberal elitist majority in Congress.
Surveys continue to show strong popular support for such direct democratic measures.

If computer-driven electronic keypads were put in the hands of every voter, such 27
national referenda would be relatively easy to conduct on a regular basis. Whether or
not the nation actually adopts these or similar measures of direct democracy, unofficial
instantaneous public opinion polls will continue to be available on demand. The federal
government will have no choice but to operate in a political environment of virtual
plebiscites, even if such votes are not officially recognized.

In June 1992, the Nova Scotia Liberal Party in Canada experimented with a ballot 28
by telephone to choose its new provincial leader. Despite a computer failure that
delayed the phone-in election by two weeks, four times as many people voted in that
election as previously had participated. The novelty of the Nova Scotia telephone vote
may account for some of the increase. But it does demonstrate that convenient, accessible, easy-to-use electronic technology can attract people back into the political arena.[10]

Cable shopping channels have installed high-speed, large-capacity computerized 29
systems to process million of viewers' telephone credit card orders. The same or similar
technology can be recruited to tabulate votes,
process polls, and count the results of initiatives
and referenda, dialed in from anywhere. In 1992,
CBS News asked viewers to call in their opinions
to a special 800 phone number during a primetime
election campaign special, *America on the Line*.
Although the audience response during the broadcast could by no means be considered a representative sample, three hundred thousand phone calls
were tallied out of millions attempted that could not
get through—far *more* calls than could have been
processed in the 1988 election, far fewer calls than
will be able to be processed by the 1996 election.

The question is not whether the transformation to instant public feedback through electronics is good or bad, or politically desirable or undesirable. Like a force of nature, it is simply the way our political system is heading. 30

The question is not whether the transformation to instant public feedback through electronics is good or bad, or politically desirable or
undesirable. Like a force of nature, it is simply the

way our political system is heading. The people are being asked to give their own judgment before major governmental decisions are made. Since personal electronic media,
the teleprocessors and computerized keypads that register public opinion, are inherently democratic—some fear too democratic—their effect will be to stretch our political system toward more sharing of power, at least by those citizens motivated to
participate.

A TREND NOT UNIQUE TO POLITICS

The political world is not alone in undergoing this kind of transformation. As we look   31
ahead to the twenty-first century, much of society is changing in similar fashion, eliminating barriers between races, classes, sexes, age groups, employers, and employees,
and altering long-standing lines of authority. Companies are flattening management
hierarchies and erasing the operational separation between managers and workers.
Today, it is considered smart management style to empower workers to solve production problems on their own and have them help decide how to improve their own productivity. Critical information, which once traveled only from the top down the
corporate ladder, increasingly is moving from the bottom up as well. Managers long
accustomed to making unilateral decisions now ask their customers and their workers
to "participate," "collaborate," "consult," "cooperate," and "advise" in designing and
marketing better products and services. Participatory management, like participatory
politics, appears to be the wave of the future.

Even elements of the press are going through a similar transformation. A 1994   32
Nieman Foundation conference of leading newsmen and -women, including editors,
producers, and members of top management, discussed this theme: "Traditionally,
news was what the editor said it was. Now, news is what the audience says it is." A new
movement called "public journalism," led by newspapers in Charlotte (North Carolina), Wichita (Kansas), and Columbus (Georgia), is seeking ways to reengage ordinary citizens by, among other things, asking them what they want their newspaper to
report. Through reader panels, public meetings, polls, focus groups, and other plebisci-
tary devices, the *Minneapolis Star Tribune, Wichita Eagle,* and *Charlotte Observer,*
among others, are enlisting their communities to help shape the contents of their pages.

Public journalism, according to its champions, is an effort to restore the press's   33
role in stimulating public dialogue and civic participation, a role central to newspapers
and periodicals in the eighteenth century, but one that largely disappeared when group-
owned publications with audiences in the millions displaced individually owned local
newspapers and periodicals with circulations in the hundreds. Too many newspapers
have come to resemble the description of ancient Greek choruses: "Old citizens, full of
their proverbial wisdom and hopelessness," delivering "stupefied, reverent and somewhat dark attitudes" that nobody heeds.[11] Now, concerned by the steep decline in
newspaper readership and increasing competition from all forms of electronic media,
many newspapers are reaching out to the public to help them regain a meaningful role
in their communities. In a sense, it is a throwback to an earlier day, before journalism
became a full-time occupation, when printers filled their periodicals with articles from
farmers, lawyers, merchants, and tradesmen in the community who discussed issues,

wrote essays, and exchanged views. The Federalist Papers, for example, originated as a series of periodic newspaper articles and essays that sought to analyze and promote the provisions of the new Constitution. The authors were not full-time journalists or professional columnists but leading citizen participants in the Philadelphia constitutional convention—James Madison, Alexander Hamilton, John Adams, and John Jay.

THE DECLINE OF GEOGRAPHY

The declining importance of geography will be another characteristic of the political process in the electronic republic of the twenty-first century, although our political system will continue to be locked into geographical constituencies, which are basic to our constitutional framework. To give citizens a larger voice in the "conversation of governance," some have proposed to expand legislatures as a way to reconnect politicians to their constituencies. A *USA Today* editorial, for example, urged "doubling or tripling the number of representatives."[12]   34

As Vice President Al Gore pointed out, "today's technology has made possible a global community united by instantaneous information and analysis."[13] He cited the examples of protesters at the Berlin Wall communicating with their followers through CNN and demonstrators at Tiananmen Square who connected with supporters in the United States and with each other by fax machines. But far too little attention has been paid to the tendency of today's technology to fragment the electorate so that it can be reached more effectively with particular appeals crafted for audiences with specific interests. Interest politics has largely replaced sectional politics. New networks and communications media are specialized, stratified, and narrow, carving up the nation and the world into a series of separate, suspicious, and often hostile enclaves. As one journalist remarked, "In the worst case, the global village becomes a global Bosnia, albeit a less violent one."[14]   35

LOOKING FURTHER INTO THE CRYSTAL BALL

With the accelerating speed of technological change in communications, in the twenty-first century there will inevitably be a variety of brand new telecommunications experiments in direct democracy, some impossible to foresee from today's perspective. A number of experiments already have been conducted with mixed results. In Hawaii, for example, a "Televote" project in the 1980s sought to get a cross section of citizens to participate in electronic town meetings, read brochures explaining the issues, and then phone in their votes on the issues at hand. (It proved to be virtually impossible to sustain citizen interest, especially after participants realized that their involvement was purely experimental and would have no real effect on policy or laws.) In Reading, Pennsylvania, an experimental interactive cable channel for local politics has for years been putting viewers directly in touch with their legislators.   36

Alaska has set up a Legislative Teleconferencing Network and Legislative Information Network to stimulate grassroots political participation throughout that state. The legislature takes sworn citizen testimony on the network so that those in remote areas can appear before the Alaska assembly without having to travel to the state capi-   37 tal, which is often inaccessible by road. The network also transmits legislative hearings statewide. Viewers at home receive regular legislative briefings and can hold tele-discussions with their elected representatives in the state capital. Citizens can send what are called officially "Public Opinion Messages" to their legislators through the Alaskan Legislative Information Network.

Other states, from Iowa to North Carolina, are experimenting with similar interac-   38 tive telecommunications town halls, teleconferences, town meetings, and on-line net-works. A group in California is seeking to set up a statewide interactive version of C-SPAN to carry legislative and other governmental deliberations and official events. So far, these efforts typically have involved a very small minority of the population.

Nationally, the White House and many members of Congress are accessible on-   39 line through Internet and various commercial computer networks. Locally, Santa Mon-ica, California, has an on-line public access network for residents to communicate directly with city officials and departments.* The point of all these changes is that in the future, grassroots democracy will not have to be expressed by citizens pouring out-of-doors, crowding into town squares, or marching on Washington, D.C., state capitols, or city halls. More often, grassroots democracy will be expressed by individuals sitting quietly in their kitchens and living rooms, who are linked electronically to their fellow citizens and elected representatives, and who manipulate wired and wireless comput-ers, television screens, and keypads.

Such a scenario for the future fulfills the prophecy made last century by France's   40 Tocqueville and Britain's Lord Bryce, two of history's most astute observers of the American democratic process: "By whatever political laws men are governed in the age of equality," Tocqueville wrote, "it may be foreseen that faith in public opinion will become for them a species of religion, and the majority its ministering prophet." Simi-larly, Lord Bryce predicted a time in America when "public opinion would not only reign but govern," and the will of the majority would "become ascertainable at all times, and without the need of its passing through a body of representatives, possibly even without the need of voting machinery at all." For the American people, that time will soon be at hand. For many it is already here.

Source Notes

1. "The Electronic Word Went Out," *The New York Times,* March 21, 1994, p. A16.
2. *The Promise and Perils of Emerging Information Technologies,* Aspen Institute Communications and Society Program. Forum report by David Bollier, rapporteur, Charles Firestone, director, Washington, DC, 1993, p. 26.
3. Ted Koppel, "The Perils of Info-Democracy," *The New York Times,* July 1, 1994, p. A25.
4. Edmund L. Andrews, "Mr. Smith Goes to Cyberspace," *The New York Times,* January 6, 1995, p. A22.

*See Pamela Varley's "Electronic Democracy: What's Really Happening in Santa Monica," p. 244 (ed.).

5. *Pacific States Telephone and Telegraph Co.* v. *Oregon,* as quoted in California Commission on Campaign Financing, *Democracy by Initiative* (Los Angeles: Center for Responsive Government, 1992), pp. 301–2.

6. Christopher Georges, "Perot and Con," *Washington Monthly,* June 1993, p. 39.

7. California Commission on Campaign Financing, *Democracy by Initiative,* p. 1.

8. Thomas E. Cronin, *Direct Democracy: The Politics of Initiative, Referendum, and Recall* (Cambridge, MA: Harvard University Press, 1989), pp. 169–70.

9. Ibid., p. 172.

10. Lloyd N. Morrisset, president's essay, John and Mary R. Markle Foundation Annual Report, 1991–92, p. 5.

11. John Boardman, Jasper Griffin, and Murray Oswyn, eds., *The Oxford History of Greece and the Hellenistic World* (New York: Oxford University Press, 1991), p. 194.

12. "Want a Political Revolt? Here's a Place to Start," editorial, *USA Today,* November 8, 1994, p. 10A.

13. Speech by Vice President Al Gore at the Academy of Television Arts and Sciences, Los Angeles, January 11, 1994.

14. E. J. Dionne, columnist for the *Washington Post,* as quoted in the *Annenberg Washington Program Annual Report, 1994,* Annenberg Washington Program, Communication Policy Studies, Washington, DC, 1994.

⬅ SECOND THOUGHTS

1. What are the major components of the "serviceable portrait of the electronic republic" (¶ 8) that Grossman intends to paint? Since 1994–1995, when Grossman's book was going to print, how much closer to reality do you think any of these components has come?

2. Despite his objective-sounding description of "keypad democracy," how does Grossman reveal his own opinion of that vision?

3. What objections to keypad democracy does Grossman acknowledge, and how does he respond to these objections? What other social and political obstacles to achieving this vision, not mentioned by Grossman, can you anticipate? For example, what does Grossman appear to assume about how access to, or distribution of, electronic resources will evolve in the near future? How persuaded are you that increased electronic access can lead to real grassroots democracy?

4. If you have e-mail, test some of Grossman's ideas by writing both a regular letter and an e-mail message expressing your opinion on a current issue to the president, your senator, or your representative (or in Canada or another country, to the analogous elected government officials). Share the results with fellow readers. How accessible and responsive did you find these officials? How would you compare the process, effectiveness, and responses you got in the two media?

The Netizen: Birth of a Digital Nation

Jon Katz

Jon Katz (b. 1949) is a novelist and media critic who has worked for the *Boston Globe, Washington Post,* CBS News, and *Wired* magazine. His novels include *Death by Station Wagon: A Suburban Detective Mystery* (Doubleday, 1993); his nonfiction books include *Virtuous Reality* (Random House, 1997) and the forthcoming *Magnetic North: Journeys of the Soul.* This article was the last in a series of essays called "The Netizen," about the impact of network technology on the 1996 U.S. elections, alternately written by Katz and John Heilemann for *Wired* (<www.hotwired.com/wired/>), a magazine aimed at people interested in emerging electronic technologies.

FIRST STIRRINGS

On the Net last year, I saw the rebirth of love for liberty in media. I saw a culture 1
crowded with intelligent, educated, politically passionate people who—in jarring contrast to the offline world—line up to express their civic opinions, participate in debates, even fight for their political beliefs.

I watched people learn new ways to communicate politically. I watched informa- 2
tion travel great distances, then return home bearing imprints of engaged and committed people from all over the world. I saw positions soften and change when people were suddenly able to talk directly to one another, rather than through journalists, politicians, or ideological mercenaries.

I saw the primordial stirrings of a new kind of nation—the Digital Nation—and the 3
formation of a new postpolitical philosophy. This nascent ideology, fuzzy and difficult to define, suggests a blend of some of the best values rescued from the tired old dogmas—the humanism of liberalism, the economic opportunity of conservatism, plus a strong sense of personal responsibility and a passion for freedom.

I came across questions, some tenuously posed: Are we living in the middle of a 4
great revolution, or are we just members of another arrogant élite talking to ourselves? Are we a powerful new kind of community or just a mass of people hooked up to machines? Do we share goals and ideals, or are we just another hot market ready for exploitation by America's ravenous corporations?

And perhaps the toughest questions of all: Can we build a new kind of politics? 5
Can we construct a more civil society with our powerful technologies? Are we extend-

ing the evolution of freedom among human beings? Or are we nothing more than a great, wired babble pissing into the digital wind?

Where freedom is rarely mentioned in mainstream media anymore, it is ferociously defended—and exercised daily—on the Net.   6

Where our existing information systems seek to choke the flow of information through taboos, costs, and restrictions, the new digital world celebrates the right of the individual to speak and be heard—one of the cornerstone ideas behind American media and democracy.   7

Where our existing political institutions are viewed as remote and unresponsive, this online culture offers the means for individuals to have a genuine say in the decisions that affect their lives.   8

Where conventional politics is suffused with ideology, the digital world is obsessed with facts.   9

Where our current political system is irrational, awash in hypocritical god-and-values talk, the Digital Nation points the way toward a more rational, less dogmatic approach to politics.   10

The world's information is being liberated, and so, as a consequence, are we.   11

MY JOURNEY

Early last year, writer John Heilemann and I set out on parallel media journeys for HotWired's *The Netizen,* originally created to explore political issues and the media during the election year. One concept behind *The Netizen*—a conceit, perhaps—was that we would watch the impact of the Web on the political process in the first wired election. Heilemann was to cover the candidates, the conventions, and the campaigns. I would write about the media covering them.   12

Things didn't turn out quite as we'd expected at *The Netizen.* The year of the Web was not 1996—at least not in terms of mainstream politics. The new culture wasn't strong enough yet to really affect the political process. The candidates didn't turn to it as they had turned in 1992 to new media like cable, fax, and 800 numbers.   13

And the election was shallow from the beginning, with no view toward the new postindustrial economy erupting around us and no vision of a digital—or any other kind of—future. By spring '96, it seemed clear to me that this campaign was a metaphor for all that doesn't work in both journalism and politics. I couldn't bear *The New York Times* pundits, CNN's politico-sports talk, the whoring Washington talk shows, the network stand-ups.   14

Why attend to those tired institutions when what was happening on the monitor a foot from my nose seemed so much more interesting? Fresh ideas, fearsome debates, and a brand-new culture were rising out of the primordial digital muck, its politics teeming with energy. How could a medium like this new one have a major impact on a leaden old process like that one? By focusing so obsessively on Them, we were missing a much more dramatic political story—Us.   15

So I mostly abandoned Their campaign, focusing instead on the politics of Ours— especially interactivity and the digital culture. I was flamed, challenged, and stretched   16 almost daily. The Web became my formidable teacher, whacking me on the palm with a ruler when I didn't do my homework or wasn't listening intently enough; comforting me when I got discouraged or felt lost.

I argued with technoanarchists about rules, flamers about civility, white kids about   17
rap, black kids about police, journalists about media, evangelicals about sin. I was scolded by scholars and academics for flawed logic or incomplete research. I was shut down by "family values" email bombers outraged by my attacks on Wal-Mart's practice of sanitizing the music it sells.

I saw the strange new way in which information and opinion travel down the digi-   18
tal highway—linked to Web sites, passed on to newsgroups, mailing lists, and computer conferencing systems. I saw my columns transformed from conventional punditry to a series of almost-living organisms that got buttressed, challenged, and altered by the incredible volume of feedback suddenly available. I lost the ingrained journalistic ethic that taught me that I was right, and that my readers didn't know what was good for them. On the Web, I learned that I was rarely completely right, that I was only a transmitter of ideas waiting to be shaped and often improved upon by people who knew more than I did.

Ideas almost never remain static on the Web. They are launched like children into the world, where they are altered by the many different environments they pass through, almost never coming home in the same form in which they left.

Ideas almost never remain static on the Web. They are launched like children into the   19
world, where they are altered by the many different environments they pass through, almost never coming home in the same form in which they left.

All the while, I had the sense of Heilemann   20
cranking alone like the Energizer Bunny, responsibly slugging his way through the torturous ordeal of campaign coverage, guiding the increasingly-exasperated people who actually wanted to follow the election. What Heilemann learned and relayed was that the political system isn't functioning. It doesn't address serious problems, and the problems it does address are not confronted in a rational way. It doesn't present us with the information we need or steer us toward comprehension—let alone solution.

Over the course of 1996, the ideologies that shape our political culture seemed to   21
collapse. Liberalism finally expired along with the welfare culture it had inadvertently spawned. Conservatism, reeling from the failure of the so-called Republican revolution, was exposed as heartless and rigid. The left and the right—even on issues as explosive as abortion and welfare—appeared spent. While they squabbled eternally with one another, the rest of us ached for something better. In 1996, we didn't get it.

The candidates didn't raise a single significant issue, offer a solution to any major   22
social problem, raise the nation's consciousness, or prod its conscience about any critical matter. The issues the candidates did debate were either false or manipulative, the tired imperatives of another time.

"Nineteen ninety-six was the year that Old Politics died," wrote Heilemann. "For   23
outside this bizarre electoral system that's grown and mutated over the past 40 years—
this strange, pseudo-meta-ritual that, experienced from the inside, feels like being
trapped in an echo chamber lined with mirrors—there are profound, paradigm-shifting
changes afoot."

There are paradigm-shifting changes afoot: the young people who form the heart   24
of the digital world are creating a new political ideology. The machinery of the Internet
is being wielded to create an environment in which the Digital Nation can become a
political entity in its own right.

By avoiding the campaign most of the time, I ended up in another, unexpected   25
place. I had wandered into the nexus between the past and the future, the transition
from one political process to a very different one.

While Heilemann came to believe he was attending a wake, I began to feel I was   26
witnessing a birth—the first stirrings of a powerful new political community.

THE NASCENT NATION

All kinds of people of every age and background are online, but at the heart of the Dig-   27
ital Nation are the people who created the Net, work in it, and whose business, social,
and cultural lives increasingly revolve around it.

The Digital Nation constitutes a new social class. Its citizens are young, educated,   28
affluent. They inhabit wired institutions and industries—universities, computer and
telecom companies, Wall Street and financial outfits, the media. They live everywhere,
of course, but are most visible in forward-looking, technologically advanced communities: New York, San Francisco, Los Angeles, Seattle, Boston, Minneapolis, Austin,
Raleigh. They are predominantly male, although female citizens are joining in enormous—and increasingly equal—numbers.

The members of the Digital Nation are not representative of the population as a   29
whole: they are richer, better educated, and disproportionately white. They have disposable income and available time. Their educations are often unconventional and
continuous, and they have almost unhindered access to much of the world's information. As a result, their values are constantly evolving. Unlike the rigid political ideologies that have ruled America for decades, the ideas of the postpolitical young
remain fluid.

Still, some of their common values are clear: they tend to be libertarian, materi-   30
alistic, tolerant, rational, technologically adept, disconnected from conventional
political organizations—like the Republican or Democratic parties—and from narrow labels like liberal or conservative. They are not politically correct, rejecting
dogma in favor of sorting through issues individually, preferring discussion to platforms.

The digital young are bright. They are not afraid to challenge authority. They take   31
no one's word for anything. They embrace interactivity—the right to shape and participate in their media. They have little experience with passively reading newspapers or
watching newscasts delivered by anchors.

They share a passion for popular culture—perhaps their most common shared   32
value, and the one most misperceived and mishandled by politicians and journalists.
On Monday mornings when they saunter into work, they are much more likely to be
talking about the movies they saw over the weekend than about Washington's issue of
the week. Music, movies, magazines, some television shows, and some books are ele-
mentally important to them—not merely forms of entertainment but means of identity.

As much as anything else, the reflexive contempt for popular culture shared by   33
so many elders of journalism and politics has alienated this group, causing its members to view the world in two basic categories: those who get it, and those who don't.
For much of their lives, these young people have been branded ignorant, their culture
malevolent. The political leaders and pundits who malign them haven't begun to
grasp how destructive these perpetual assaults have been, how huge a cultural gap
they've created.

Although many would balk at defining themselves this way, the digital young are   34
revolutionaries. Unlike the clucking boomers, they are not talking revolution; they're
making one. This is a culture best judged by what it does, not what it says.

In *On Revolution,* Hannah Arendt wrote that two things are needed to generate   35
great revolutions: the sudden experience of being free and the sense of creating something. The Net is revolutionary in precisely those ways. It liberates millions of people
to do things they couldn't do before. Men and women can experiment with their sexual
identities without being humiliated or arrested. Citizens can express themselves
directly, without filtering their views through journalists or pollsters. Researchers can
get the newest data in hours, free from the grinding rituals of scientific tradition. The
young can explore their own notions of culture, safe from the stern scrutiny of parents
and teachers.

There's also a sense of great novelty, of building something different. The online   36
population of today has evolved dramatically from the hackers and academics who
patched together primitive computer bulletin boards just a few years ago—but the sensation of discovery remains. People coming online still have the feeling of stepping
across a threshold. Citizenship in this world requires patience, commitment, and determination—an investment of time and energy that often brings the sense of participating in something very new.

It's difficult to conceive of the digital world as a political entity. The existing   37
political and journalistic structures hate the very thought, since that means relinquish-
ing their own central place in political life. And the digital world itself—adolescent,
self-absorbed—is almost equally reluctant to take itself seriously in a political context, since that invokes all sorts of responsibilities that seem too constraining and
burdensome.

This is a culture founded on the ethos of individuality, not leadership. Informa-   38
tion flows laterally, or from many to many—a structure that works against the creation
of leaders.

Like it or not, however, this Digital Nation possesses all the traits of groups that,   39
throughout history, have eventually taken power. It has the education, the affluence,
and the privilege that will create a political force that ultimately must be reckoned with.

SOME POSTPOLITICAL CORE VALUES

Out of sight of the reporters, handlers, spin-masters, and politicians of the presidential   40
campaign, a new political sensibility took shape in 1996. It brought fresh ideas. It
brought real debates about real issues.

The postpolitical ideology draws from different elements of familiar politics. The   41
term postpolitical gets tossed around in various circles, but here it refers to a new kind
of politics beyond the traditional choices of left/right, liberal/conservative, Republi-
can/Democrat. Although still taking shape, this postpolitical ideology combines some
of the better elements of both sides of the mainstream American political spectrum.

From liberals, this ideology adopts humanism. It is suspicious of law enforcement.   42
It abhors censorship. It recoils from extreme governmental positions like the death
penalty. From conservatives, the ideology takes notions of promoting economic opportunity, creating smaller government, and insisting on personal responsibility.

The digital young share liberals' suspicions of authority and concentration of   43
power but have little of their visceral contempt for corporations or big business. They
share the liberal analysis that social problems like poverty, rather than violence on TV,
are at the root of crime. But, unlike liberals, they want the poor to take more responsibility for solving their own problems.

This amalgam of values reveals itself in seemingly odd ways. Many online had   44
no trouble believing that the Los Angeles Police Department was racist or, conceivably, might have planted evidence in the O. J. Simpson murder case. There was no
sympathy, though, for the idea that O. J. should have been acquitted as a result of
such technicalities.

The postpoliticos can outdo liberals on some fronts. They don't merely embrace tol-   45
erance as an ideal; they are inherently tolerant. Theirs is the first generation for whom
pluralism and diversity are neither controversial nor unusual. This group couldn't care
less whether families take the traditional form or have two moms or two dads. They are
nearly blind to the color and ethnic heritage of the people who enter their culture. This
is the least likely group to bar someone from a club because he or she is Jewish or black,
or to avoid marriage because of a person's religion or ethnicity.

On the other hand, the digital young's intuitive acceptance of tolerance and diver-   46
sity doesn't prevent them from rejecting liberal notions like affirmative action. And
they are largely impervious to victim-talk, or politically correct rhetoric, or the culture
of complaint celebrated in the liberal media coverage of many minority issues.

This culture is no less averse to the cruel and suffocating dogma of the right. The   47
postpolitical young embrace the notion of gender equality and are intrinsically hostile
to any government or religious effort to dictate private personal behavior. While conservatism has become entwined with an evangelical religious agenda, the digital young
are allergic to mixing religion and politics.

If liberals say, "Here's the tent: we have to get everyone inside," and conservatives   48
say, "Here's the tent: we don't want it to get too crowded inside," the postpolitical
young say, "Here's the tent: everyone is welcome—but everyone has to figure out how
to get inside on his or her own."

One of the biggest ideas in the postpolitical world is that we have the means to   49
shape our lives, and that we must take more responsibility for doing so. This ascending
generation believes its members should and will control their destinies. A recent survey in *American Demographics* magazine studied young Americans and called them
self-navigators. "In a fast-changing and often hostile world, self-navigation means
relying on oneself to be the captain of one's own ship and charting one's own course,"
wrote the Brain Waves Group, the survey's developers. Those characteristics also
describe many citizens of the Digital Nation.

This group values competence and hard work, the survey found. Traditional for-   50
mulas for success carry little weight since college degrees no longer guarantee jobs,
getting a job doesn't guarantee you'll keep it, retirement may never be possible, and
marriages can fail. Despite such caution, this group—in sharp contrast to its boomer
parents—sees a future of great opportunity. The Digital Nation is optimistic about its
own prospects.

Although these ideas work well for them now, as the postpolitical young of the   51
digital world grow older, they will confront a new range of problems, from developing
careers to raising children to preparing for old age. Their ideology will, of necessity,
develop and change.

As they raise children, they will face issues such as neighborhood safety, maintain-   52
ing parks, and improving the educational system. As they buy homes, they will
encounter bread-and-butter political issues like taxation and zoning. Faced with developing a new political agenda in a radically different world, they will inevitably find
themselves face-to-face with the ghosts of the old one.

A NEW FORM OF LIBERTARIANISM

The closest thing the digital world has to dogma is its ingrained libertarianism, its   53
wholehearted commitment to political and economic freedom, its fierce opposition to
constraints on individual expression—from the chilling fanaticism of the politically
correct to the growing movement to censor popular culture.

The online world is the freest community in American life. Its members can do   54
things considered unacceptable elsewhere in our culture. They can curse freely, challenge the existence of god, explore their sexuality nearly at will, talk to radical thinkers
from all over the world. They can even commit verbal treason.

The Internet is still a wild frontier. The hackers and geeks who founded and shaped   55
it believed that there should be no obstacles between people and information, and there
are still vibrant, almost outlaw communities that enforce this notion: cypherpunks who
act as technoanarchists, flamers who challenge punditry, hackers who breech the barriers constantly being thrown up by government and business.

The single dominant ethic in this community is that information wants to be free.   56
Many of those online know that this idea is antithetical to the history of media, to the
nature of politics and capitalism. Corporations do not believe that information should
be free—they believe they should control it and charge for it. Government doesn't
believe that information should be free—witness the fiasco of the Communications
Decency Act. Religious organizations, educators, and many parents don't believe

information ought to be liberated, either. The realization that children have broken away from many societal constraints and now have access to a vast information universe is one of the most frightening ideas in contemporary America.

These new libertarian notions are often misunderstood. While some longstanding   57
political groups associated with libertarianism are profoundly hostile to government, the digital young are not so much paranoid about government as frustrated by its lack of effectiveness. They don't see government conspiring to take over their lives as much as they consider it an outdated means of solving problems. It's widely acknowledged in online discussions, for example, that traditional drug policies have been catastrophic failures and that radical new ideas—legalization, perhaps—should be considered.

The digital young, from Silicon Valley entrepreneurs to college students, have a   58
nearly universal contempt for government's ability to work; they think it's wasteful and clueless. On the Net, government is rarely seen as an instrument of positive change or social good. Politicians are assumed to be manipulative or ill-informed, unable to affect reform or find solutions, forced to lie to survive. The Digital Nation's disconnection from the conventional political process—and from the traditional media that mirror it—is profound.

Both politics and journalism tend to refer to this alienation as a civic disorder,   59
brought on by new media and new culture and a decline in literacy and civilization. The young must be disinterested because they are distracted by music or coarsened by too much TV. But in their own way, the young are saying something different: the political system doesn't work, so why bother to pay attention to it?

This very sense of alienation has planted the seeds of more civil notions of politics   60
and community. Although online culture is widely perceived as hostile and chaotic, the stereotype is superficial. Writing for *The Netizen,* I noticed a recurring phenomenon that speaks both to that sense of alienation and to the potential for community.

As anyone who writes on the Web knows, criticism comes fast and furious. Some   61
of it is cruel—even vicious. But as an experiment, I began responding to angry email as if it were civil, addressing the point being made instead of the tone of the message. The pattern was clear: at least three-quarters of the time, the most hostile emailers responded with apologies, often picking up the discussion as if it had been perfectly polite. In hundreds of instances, flamers said things like, "Sorry, but I had no idea you would actually read this," or "I never expected to get a reply."

Months of these exchanges have convinced me that alienation online—and perhaps   62
offline as well—is not ingrained, that it comes from a reflexive assumption that powerful political and media institutions don't care, won't listen, and will not respond. Proven wrong, many of the most hostile flamers became faithful correspondents, often continuing to disagree—but in a civil way. I found myself listening more to them as well.

We were forming a new sort of media culture. In small ways, over time, we were   63
moving beyond the head-butting that characterizes too many online discussions (offline ones, too) and engaging in actual dialog, the cornerstone of any real political entity. We were finding that interactivity could bring a new kind of community, new ways of holding political conversations.

Of all the prospects raised by the evolution of digital culture, the most tantalizing   64
is the possibility that technology could fuse with politics to create a more civil society.

It's the possibility that we could end up with a media and political culture in which people could amass factual material, voice their perspectives, confront other points of view, and discuss issues in a rational way.

A NEW RATIONALISM

At the moment, the Internet and the Web are two of the most chaotic media ever—   65
brawling and ill-defined. But they suggest new ways to gather and distribute facts, to make an end run around the dogma-driven discussions of conventional politics.

In our current system, all issues get presented in liberal or conservative terms. Lib-   66
erals almost never support the death penalty; conservatives almost always do. Conservatives say police need to crack down on crime; liberals complain about police brutality. Journalists, reduced by their corporate owners to the role of social stenographers, report what one side says, then the other. Civic discussion becomes an irrational stalemate. The digital world offers real promise of a more enlightened way.

The concept of rationalism grew out of the Enlightenment, becoming crystallized   67
in a formal philosophy espoused by a small group of 17th- and 18th-century philosophers—among them, Descartes, Spinoza, and Leibniz. Its main principles were: reason can be the one and only means of determining a course of action; knowledge forms a single system and can be deduced; everything ultimately is explicable. Rationalism advances a primary commitment to reason, as opposed to faith or dogma or any other source of irrational conviction.

Enlightenment philosophies, wrote Peter Gay in *The Enlightenment,* "made up a   68
clamorous chorus, but what is striking is their general harmony, not their occasional discord." They united on a profoundly ambitious program of secularism, humanism, cosmopolitanism, and, above all, writes Gay, freedom—"freedom from arbitrary power, freedom of speech, freedom of trade, freedom to realize one's talents, freedom of aesthetic response, freedom, in a word, of moral man to make his own way in the world."

None of these enormous ideas transformed the world at once. But they were great   69
leaps forward in the service of freedom—at the time an unknown concept in most of the world. Out of the Enlightenment came the American and French Revolutions, which advanced the radical notion that individuals ought to have inalienable rights and govern themselves. The Enlightenment also fostered the great idea at the heart of today's digital world: information ought to be free.

Today, the idea that the Net offers a new sort of rationalism is a stretch. News-   70
groups, Web sites, and online public discussions are disorganized. And along with online freedom comes its ugly offspring: the confrontation, misinformation, and insult that characterize many public forums on the Internet.

But in specialized areas—academic or scientific forums, for instance—the emer-   71
gence of a new rationalism is easier to see. The Net brings information to remote researchers in hours, allows feedback in days that once took months, and generally democratizes the flow of information around the world. Since the Net was founded in part by scientific and academic communities, their use of it is more advanced—perhaps presaging what it can mean for the rest of us.

If this notion works for science, could it work for politics? Science focuses on facts 72 and research, politics more on advancing beliefs or altering the beliefs of others. It's a big leap from a medium that moves facts around the world to one that influences values. But I've seen the process work; it can be done.

Time and again on *The Netizen* and elsewhere on the Web, facts have proven an 73 antidote to unyielding doctrines. Debates have moved forward when factual information is cited; consensus is reached. In fact, one of the most enduring characteristics of online discussions is the frequent use of citations that the linkage of the Web makes possible. Arguments often are buttressed by information from Web sites, published research, and archived data.

The unprecedented ability of individuals to speak directly to one another 74 advances the political discussion further than in the offline world. If neither party leaves a conversation completely transformed, each is able to do precisely what our existing system makes so difficult: fully understand the other person's position, absorb some of the other's values, and see the other as a complex person rather than a simplistic stereotype.

JUST THE BEGINNING

The Communications Decency Act of 1996, an effort to control the nature of speech 75 on the Internet—making "indecent" language a federal crime—was the Net's own Stamp Act.

Like that 1765 law, the CDA stunned a community, one that from its inception had 76 taken freedom for granted. It galvanized a diverse coalition of idiosyncratic individuals into a cohesive political force. Like the colonists, the online community saw the law as an arrogant act by an alien entity seeking to force its will on a new world that it had lost any moral right to control.

More than any single event, the CDA prompted people whose professional or 77 personal lives center around the Internet to define a shared political ethic. It provided, for the first time, a common goal around which to coalesce. If the Stamp Act marked a turning point in the colonies' relationship with England, the CDA did the same for the digital world, giving credence to the notion of the birth of a Digital Nation.

The CDA's passage and the Digital Nation's reaction to it showed that the digital 78 world was creating not a radically new value system, but that it was now the champion for a venerable old one: the notion of individual liberty. The Digital Nation demonstrated a willingness to fight for and expand upon those freedoms first articulated way back in the Enlightenment—freedom from arbitrary power, freedom of speech, freedom to determine one's own values and morals.

The gift of the CDA was the opportunity it presented the Digital Nation to fight for 79 freedom all over again. It gave this ascending community a moral issue that all could believe in. It made them the heirs of a great tradition.

The digital world is often disconnected from many of the world's problems by 80 virtue of its members' affluence and social standing. Founded in the bedrooms of suburban hackers and the classrooms of prestigious institutions, it has often been derided as self-absorbed. It has yet to respond to any political or social crisis that doesn't directly concern it.

The digital young do need to develop coherent philosophies for responding to the 81 very problems that the exhausted current system fails to address: limited economic opportunity, endemic underclass problems, never-ending racial hostility. The Digital Revolution eventually needs to offer solutions for eradicating poverty, ignorance, and war in radical and hopeful ways.

Here is a growing élite in control of the most powerful communications infrastructure ever assembled. The people rushing toward the millennium with their fingers on the keyboards of the Information Age could become one of the most powerful political forces in history. Technology is power. Education is power. Communication is power. The digital young have all three. No other social group is as poised to dominate culture and politics in the 21st century.

> **The people rushing toward the millennium with their fingers on the keyboards of the Information Age could become one of the most powerful political forces in history.**

82

It's not clear what they're going to make of such advantages, whether they will choose to remain a technologically obsessed subculture in pursuit of the Next Big Thing, or whether they will decide to meet the world head on and recognize their responsibilities as citizens of a new era.

83

The ascending young citizens of the Digital Nation can, if they wish, construct a 84 more civil society, a new politics based on rationalism, shared information, the pursuit of truth, and new kinds of community.

If they choose to form a political movement, they could someday run the world. If 85 they choose to develop a common value system, with a moral ideology and a humane agenda, they might even do the world some good.

⬅ SECOND THOUGHTS

1. "By focusing so obsessively on Them," Katz says about media coverage of the 1996 elections, "we were missing a much more dramatic political story—Us" (¶ 15). How does he define "Them" and "Us"? From these definitions, what can you conclude about the audience Katz intends to address in this article?
2. What are the major failures of the present political system, according to Katz? To what extent do you agree with this assessment of conventional politics?
3. What characteristics are shared by citizens of the Digital Nation, according to Katz? If they are "predominantly male" and "not representative of the population as a whole: they are richer, better educated, and disproportionately white" (¶s 28–29), how is it possible that they compose "a new social class" (¶ 28)? To what extent do you think Katz overgeneralizes about "the digital young"?

4. Review the "postpolitical core values" of the Digital Nation proposed by Katz. How sympathetic are you to these values and beliefs? How consistent do you find them to be? After re-reading the article, how would you answer the rhetorical questions posed by Katz in ¶s 4 and 5, such as, "Can we build a new kind of politics? Can we construct a more civil society with our powerful technologies?"

Mythinformation

Langdon Winner

Langdon Winner (b. 1944) is professor of political science at Rensselaer Polytechnic Institute (New York); his work focuses on social and political implications of technological change. He formerly taught at the New School for Social Research, MIT, the University of California at Santa Cruz, and the University of Leiden in the Netherlands. A sometime rock critic, Winner was a contributing editor for *Rolling Stone* in the 1960s and 1970s; he now writes a regular column for *Technology Review,* published by the MIT Alumni Association, called "The Culture of Technology." His books include *Autonomous Technology* (MIT Press, 1977) and *The Whale and the Reactor: A Search for Limits in an Age of High Technology* (University of Chicago Press, 1986), from which this article is taken. Earlier versions of "Mythinformation" appeared in *Research in Philosophy and Technology* (ed. Paul T. Durbin; JAI Press, 1983) and the journal *Whole Earth Review* in 1985.

> Computer power to the people is essential to the realization
> of a future in which most citizens are informed about, and
> interested and involved in, the processes of government.
> *J. C. R. Licklider*

In nineteenth-century Europe a recurring ceremonial gesture signaled the progress of popular uprisings. At the point at which it seemed that forces of disruption in the streets were sufficiently powerful to overthrow monarchical authority, a prominent rebel leader would go to the parliament or city hall to "proclaim the republic." This was an indication to friend and foe alike that a revolution was prepared to take its work seriously, to seize power and begin governing in a way that guaranteed political representation to all the people. Subsequent events, of course, did not always match these grand hopes; on occasion the revolutionaries were thwarted in their ambitions and reactionary governments regained control. Nevertheless, what a glorious moment when the republic was declared! Here, if only briefly, was the promise of a new order—an age of equality, justice, and emancipation of humankind.

A somewhat similar gesture has become a standard feature in contemporary writings on computers and society. In countless books, magazine articles, and media specials some intrepid soul steps forth to proclaim "the revolution." Often it is called simply "the computer revolution"; my brief inspection of a library catalogue revealed three books with exactly that title published since 1962.[1] Other popular variants include the "information revolution," "microelectronics revolution," and "network revolution." But whatever its label, the message is usually the same. The use of computers and advanced communications technologies is producing a sweeping set of transformations in every corner of social life. An informal consensus among computer scientists, social scientists, and journalists affirms the term "revolution" as the concept best suited to describe these events. "We are all very privileged," a noted computer scientist declares, "to be in this great Information Revolution in which the computer is going to affect us very profoundly, probably more so than the Industrial Revolution."[2] A well-known sociologist writes, "This revolution in the organization and processing of information and knowledge, in which the computer plays a central role, has as its context the development of what I have called the post-industrial society."[3] At frequent intervals during the past dozen years, garish cover stories in *Time* and *Newsweek* have repeated this story, climaxed by *Time*'s selection of the computer as its "Man of the Year" for 1982.

Of course, the same society now said to be undergoing a computer revolution has long since gotten used to "revolutions" in laundry detergents, underarm deodorants, floor waxes, and other consumer products. Exhausted in Madison Avenue advertising slogans, the image has lost much of its punch. Those who employ it to talk about computers and society, however, appear to be making much more serious claims. They offer a powerful metaphor, one that invites us to compare the kind of disruptions seen in political revolutions to the changes we see happening around computer information systems. Let us take that invitation seriously and see where it leads.

> **The same society now said to be undergoing a computer revolution has long since gotten used to "revolutions" in laundry detergents, underarm deodorants, floor waxes, and other consumer products.**

A METAPHOR EXPLORED

Suppose that we were looking at a revolution in a Third World country, the revolution of the Sandinistas in Nicaragua, for example. We would want to begin by studying the fundamental goals of the revolution. It this a movement truly committed to social justice? Does it seek to uphold a valid ideal of human freedom? Does it aspire to a system of democratic rule? Answers to those questions would help us decide whether or not this is a revolution worthy of our endorsement. By the same token, we would want to ask about the means the revolutionaries had chosen to pursue their goals. Having succeeded in armed struggle, how will they manage violence and military force once they gain control? A reasonable person would also want to learn something of the structure of institutional authority that the revolution will try to create. Will there be frequent, open elections? What systems of decision making, administration, and law enforcement will be put to work? Coming to terms with its proposed ends and means, a sympathetic observer could then watch the revolution unfold, noticing whether or not it remained true to its professed purposes and how well it succeeded in its reforms.

Most dedicated revolutionaries of the modern age have been willing to supply ₅ coherent public answers to questions of this sort. It is not unreasonable to expect, therefore, that something like these issues must have engaged those who so eagerly use the metaphor "revolution" to describe and celebrate the advent of computerization. Unfortunately, this is not the case. Books, articles, and media specials aimed at a popular audience are usually content to depict the dazzling magnitude of technical innovations and social effects. Written as if by some universally accepted format, such accounts describe scores of new computer products and processes, announce the enormous dollar value of the growing computer and communications industry, survey the expanding uses of computers in offices, factories, schools, and homes, and offer good news from research and development laboratories about the great promise of the next generation of computing devices. Along with this one reads of the many "impacts" that computerization is going to have on every sphere of life. Professionals in widely separate fields—doctors, lawyers, corporate managers, and scientists—comment on the changes computers have brought to their work. Home consumers give testimonials explaining how personal computers are helping educate their children, prepare their income tax forms, and file their recipes. On occasion, this generally happy story will include reports on people left unemployed in occupations undermined by automation. Almost always, following this formula, there will be an obligatory sentence or two of criticism of the computer culture solicited from a technically qualified spokesman, an attempt to add balance to an otherwise totally sanguine outlook.

Unfortunately, the prevalence of such superficial, unreflective descriptions and ₆ forecasts about computerization cannot be attributed solely to hasty journalism. Some of the most prestigious journals of the scientific community echo the claim that a revolution is in the works.[4] A well-known computer scientist has announced unabashedly that "revolution, transformation, and salvation are all to be carried out."[5] It is true that more serious approaches to the study of computers and society can be found in scholarly publications. A number of social scientists, computer scientists, and philosophers have begun to explore important issues about how computerization works and what developments, positive and negative, it is likely to bring to society.[6] But such careful, critical studies are by no means the ones most influential in shaping public attitudes about the world of microelectronics. An editor at a New York publishing house stated the norm, "People want to know what's new with computer technology. They don't want to know what could go wrong."[7]

It seems all but impossible for computer enthusiasts to examine critically the *ends* ₇ that might guide the world-shaking developments they anticipate. They employ the metaphor of revolution for one purpose only—to suggest a drastic upheaval, one that people ought to welcome as good news. It never occurs to them to investigate the idea or its meaning any further.

One might suppose, for example, that a revolution of this type would involve a sig- ₈ nificant shift in the locus of power; after all, this is exactly what one expects in revolutions of a political kind. Is something similar going to happen in this instance?

One might also ask whether or not this revolution will be strongly committed, as   9
revolutions often are, to a particular set of social ideals. If so, what are the ideals that
matter? Where can we see them argued?

To mention revolution also brings to mind the relationships of different social   10
classes. Will the computer revolution bring about the victory of one class over another?
Will it be the occasion for a realignment of class loyalties?

In the busy world of computer science, computer engineering, and computer mar-   11
keting such questions seldom come up. Those actively engaged in promoting the transformation—hardware and software engineers, managers of microelectronics firms,
computer salesmen, and the like—are busy pursuing their own ends: profits, market
share, handsome salaries, the intrinsic joy of invention, the intellectual rewards of programming, and the pleasures of owning and using powerful machines. But the sheer
dynamism of technical and economic activity in the computer industry evidently leaves
its members little time to ponder the historical significance of their own activity. They
must struggle to keep current, to be on the crest of the next wave as it breaks. As one
member of Data General's Eagle computer project describes it, the prevailing spirit
resembles a game of pinball. "You win one game, you get to play another. You win
with this machine, you get to build the next."[8] The process has its own inertia.

Hence, one looks in vain to the movers and shakers in computer fields for the qual-   12
ities of social and political insight that characterized revolutionaries of the past. Too
busy. Cromwell, Jefferson, Robespierre, Lenin, and Mao were able to reflect upon the
world historical events in which they played a role. Public pronouncements by the likes
of Robert Noyce, Marvin Minsky, Edward Feigenbaum, and Steven Jobs show no similar wisdom about the transformations they so actively help to create. By and large the
computer revolution is conspicuously silent about its own ends.

GOOD CONSOLE, GOOD NETWORK, GOOD COMPUTER

My concern for the political meaning of revolution in this setting may seem somewhat   13
misleading, even perverse. A much better point of reference might be the technical
"revolutions" and associated social upheavals of the past, the industrial revolution in
particular. If the enthusiasts of computerization had readily taken up this comparison,
studying earlier historical periods for similarities and differences in patterns of technological innovation, capital formation, employment, social change, and the like, then it
would be clear that I had chosen the wrong application of this metaphor. But, in fact,
no well-developed comparisons of that kind are to be found in the writings on the computer revolution. A consistently ahistorical viewpoint prevails. What one often finds
emphasized, however, is a vision of drastically altered social and political conditions, a
future upheld as both desirable and, in all likelihood, inevitable. Politics, in other
words, is not a secondary concern for many computer enthusiasts; it is a crucial, albeit
thoughtless, part of their message.

We are, according to a fairly standard account, moving into an age characterized   14
by the overwhelming dominance of electronic information systems in all areas of
human practice. Industrial society, which depended upon material production for its

livelihood, is rapidly being supplanted by a society of information services that will enable people to satisfy their economic and social needs. What water- and steam-powered machines were to the industrial age, the computer will be to the era now dawning. Ever-expanding technical capacities in computation and communications will make possible a universal, instantaneous access to enormous quantities of valuable information. As these technologies become less and less expensive and more and more convenient, all the people of the world, not just the wealthy, will be able to use the wonderful services that information machines make available. Gradually, existing differences between rich and poor, advantaged and disadvantaged, will begin to evaporate. Widespread access to computers will produce a society more democratic, egalitarian, and richly diverse than any previously known. Because "knowledge is power," because electronic information will spread knowledge into every corner of world society, political influence will be much more widely shared. With the personal computer serving as the great equalizer, rule by centralized authority and social class dominance will gradually fade away. The marvelous promise of a "global village" will be fulfilled in a worldwide burst of human creativity.

A sampling from recent writings on the information society illustrates these grand expectations.   15

> The world is entering a new period. The wealth of nations, which depended upon land, labor, and capital during its agricultural and industrial phases—depended upon natural resources, the accumulation of money, and even upon weaponry—will come in the future to depend upon information, knowledge and intelligence.[9]

✦ ✦ ✦

> The electronic revolution will not do away with work, but it does hold out some promises: Most boring jobs can be done by machines; lengthy commuting can be avoided; we can have enough leisure to follow interesting pursuits outside our work; environmental destruction can be avoided; the opportunities for personal creativity will be unlimited.[10]

Long lists of specific services spell out the utopian promise of this new age: interactive television, electronic funds transfer, computer-aided instruction, customized news service, electronic magazines, electronic mail, computer teleconferencing, on-line stock market and weather reports, computerized Yellow Pages, shopping via home computer, and so forth. All of it is supposed to add up to a cultural renaissance.   16

> Whatever the limits to growth in other fields, there are no limits near in telecommunications and electronic technology. There are no limits near in the consumption of information, the growth of culture, or the development of the human mind.[11]

✦ ✦ ✦

> Computer-based communications can be used to make human lives richer and freer, by enabling persons to have access to vast stores of information, other "human resources," and opportunities for work and socializing on a more flexible, cheaper, and convenient basis than ever before.[12]

✦ ✦ ✦

When such systems become widespread, potentially intense communications networks among geographically dispersed persons will become actualized. We will become Network Nation, exchanging vast amounts of information and social and emotional communications with colleagues, friends and "strangers" who share similar interests, who are spread all over the nation.[13]

✦ ✦ ✦

A rich diversity of subcultures will be fostered by computer-based communication systems. Social, political, technical changes will produce conditions likely to lead to the formation of groups with their own distinctive sets of values, activities, language, and dress.[14]

According to this view, the computer revolution will, by its sheer momentum, eliminate many of the ills that have vexed political society since the beginning of time. Inequalities of wealth and privilege will gradually fade away. One writer predicts that computer networks will "offer major opportunities to disadvantaged groups to acquire the skills and social ties they need to become full members of society."[15] Another looks forward to "a revolutionary network where each node is equal in power to all others."[16] Information will become the dominant form of wealth. Because it can flow so quickly, so freely through computer networks, it will not, in this interpretation, cause the kinds of stratification associated with traditional forms of property. Obnoxious forms of social organization will also be replaced. "The computer will smash the pyramid," one best-selling book proclaims. "We created the hierarchical, pyramidal, managerial system because we needed it to keep track of people and things people did; with the computer to keep track, we can restructure our institutions horizontally."[17] Thus, the proliferation of electronic information will generate a leveling effect to surpass the dreams of history's great social reformers.   17

The same viewpoint holds that the prospects for participatory democracy have never been brighter. According to one group of social scientists, "the form of democracy found in the ancient Greek city-state, the Israeli kibbutz, and the New England town meeting, which gave every citizen the opportunity to directly participate in the political process, has become impractical in America's mass society. But this need not be the case. The technological means exist through which millions of people can enter into dialogue with one another and with their representatives, and can form the authentic consensus essential for democracy."[18]   18

Computer scientist J. C. R. Licklider of the Massachusetts Institute of Technology is one advocate especially hopeful about a revitalization of the democratic process. He looks forward to "an information environment that would give politics greater depth and dimension than it now has." Home computer consoles and television sets would be linked together in a massive network. "The political process would essentially be a giant teleconference, and a campaign would be a months-long series of communications among candidates, propagandists, commentators, political action groups and voters." An arrangement of this kind would, in his view, encourage a more open, comprehensive examination of both issues and candidates. "The information   19 revolution," he exclaims, "is bringing with it a key that may open the door to a new era of involvement and participation. The key is the self-motivating exhilaration that accompanies truly effective interaction with information through a good console through a good network to a good computer."[19] It is, in short, a democracy of machines.

Taken as a whole, beliefs of this kind constitute what I would call mythinforma-   20
tion: the almost religious conviction that a widespread adoption of computers and communications systems along with easy access to electronic information will automatically produce a better world for human living. It is a peculiar form of enthusiasm that characterizes social fashions of the latter decades of the twentieth century. Many people who have grown cynical or discouraged about other aspects of social life are completely enthralled by the supposed redemptive qualities of computers and telecommunications. Writing of the "fifth generation" supercomputers, Japanese author Yoneji Masuda rhapsodically predicts "freedom for each of us to set individual goals of self-realization and then perhaps a worldwide religious renaissance, characterized not by a belief in a supernatural god, but rather by awe and humility in the presence of the collective human spirit and its wisdom, humanity living in a symbolic tranquility with the planet we have found ourselves upon, regulated by a new set of global ethics."[20]

It is not uncommon for the advent of a new technology to provide an occasion for   21
flights of utopian fancy. During the last two centuries the factory system, railroads, telephone, electricity, automobile, airplane, radio, television, and nuclear power have all figured prominently in the belief that a new and glorious age was about to begin. But even within the great tradition of optimistic technophilia, current dreams of a "computer age" stand out as exaggerated and unrealistic. Because they have such a broad appeal, because they overshadow other ways of looking at the matter, these notions deserve closer inspection.

THE GREAT EQUALIZER

As is generally true of a myth, the story contains elements of truth. What were once   22
industrial societies are being transformed into service economies, a trend that emerges as more material production shifts to developing countries where labor costs are low and business tax breaks lucrative. At the same time that industrialization takes hold in less-developed nations of the world, deindustrialization is gradually altering the economies of North America and Europe. Some of the service industries central to this pattern are ones that depend upon highly sophisticated computer and communications systems. But this does not mean that future employment possibilities will flow largely from the microelectronics industry and information services. A number of studies, including those of the U.S. Bureau of Labor Statistics, suggest that the vast majority of new jobs will come in menial service occupations paying relatively low wages.[21] As robots and computer software absorb an increasing share of factory and office tasks, the "information society" will offer plenty of opportunities for janitors, hospital orderlies, and fast-food waiters.

The computer romantics are also correct in noting that computerization alters   23
relationships of social power and control, although they misrepresent the direction this
development is likely to take. Those who stand to benefit most obviously are large
transnational business corporations. While their "global reach" does not arise solely
from the application of information technologies, such organizations are uniquely situated to exploit the efficiency, productivity, command, and control the new electronics make available. Other notable beneficiaries of the systematic use of vast amounts
of digitized information are public bureaucracies, intelligence agencies, and an ever-
expanding military, organizations that would operate less effectively at their present
scale were it not for the use of computer power. Ordinary people are, of course,
strongly affected by the workings of these organizations and by the rapid spread of
new electronic systems in banking, insurance, taxation, factory and office work, home
entertainment, and the like. They are also counted upon to be eager buyers of hardware, software, and communications services as computer products reach the consumer market.

But where in all of this motion do we see increased democratization? Social equal-   24
ity? The dawn of a cultural renaissance? Current developments in the information age
suggest an increase in power by those who already had a great deal of power, an
enhanced centralization of control by those already prepared for control, an augmentation of wealth by the already wealthy. Far from demonstrating a revolution in patterns
of social and political influence, empirical studies of computers and social change usually show powerful groups adapting computerized methods to retain control.[22] That is
not surprising. Those best situated to take advantage of the power of a new technology
are often those previously well situated by dint of wealth, social standing, and institutional position. Thus, if there is to be a computer revolution, the best guess is that it will
have a distinctly conservative character.

Granted, such prominent trends could be altered. It is possible that a society   25
strongly rooted in computer and telecommunications systems could be one in which
participatory democracy, decentralized political control, and social equality are fully
realized. Progress of that kind would have to occur as the result of that society's concerted efforts to overcome many difficult obstacles to achieve those ends. Computer
enthusiasts, however, seldom propose deliberate action of that kind. Instead, they
strongly suggest that the good society will be realized as a side effect, a spin-off from
the vast proliferation of computing devices. There is evidently no need to try to shape
the institutions of the information age in ways that maximize human freedom while
placing limits upon concentrations of power.

For those willing to wait passively while the computer revolution takes its course,   26
technological determinism ceases to be mere theory and becomes an ideal: a desire to
embrace conditions brought on by technological change without judging them in
advance. There is nothing new in this disposition. Computer romanticism is merely the
latest version of the nineteenth- and twentieth-century faith we noted earlier, one that
has always expected to generate freedom, democracy, and justice through sheer material abundance. Thus there is no need for serious inquiry into the appropriate design of
new institutions or the distribution of rewards and burdens. As long as the economy is

growing and the machinery in good working order, the rest will take care of itself. In previous versions of this homespun conviction, the abundant (and therefore democratic) society was manifest by a limitless supply of houses, appliances, and consumer goods.[23] Now "access to information" and "access to computers" have moved to the top of the list.

The political arguments of computer romantics draw upon a number of key 27 assumptions: (1) people are bereft of information; (2) information is knowledge; (3) knowledge is power; and (4) increasing access to information enhances democracy and equalizes social power. Taken as separate assertions and in combination, these beliefs provide a woefully distorted picture of the role of electronic systems in social life.

Is it true that people face serious shortages of information? To read the literature 28 on the computer revolution one would suppose this to be a problem on a par with the energy crisis of the 1970s. The persuasiveness of this notion borrows from our sense that literacy, education, knowledge, well-informed minds, and the widespread availability of tools of inquiry are unquestionable social goods, and that, in contrast, illiteracy, inadequate education, ignorance, and forced restrictions upon knowledge are among history's worst evils. Thus, it appears superficially plausible that a world rewired to connect human beings to vast data banks and communications systems would be a progressive step. Information shortage would be remedied in much the same way that developing a new fuel supply might solve an energy crisis.

Alas, the idea is entirely faulty. It mistakes sheer supply of information with an 29 educated ability to gain knowledge and act effectively based on that knowledge. In many parts of the world that ability is sadly lacking. Even some highly developed societies still contain chronic inequalities in the distribution of good education and basic intellectual skills. The U.S. Army, for instance, must now reject or dismiss a fairly high percentage of the young men and women it recruits because they simply cannot read military manuals. It is no doubt true of these recruits that they have a great deal of information about the world—information from their life experiences, schooling, the mass media, and so forth. What makes them "functionally illiterate" is that they have not learned to translate this information into a mastery of practical skills.

If the solution to problems of illiteracy and poor education were a question of 30 information supply alone, then the best policy might be to increase the number of well-stocked libraries, making sure they were built in places where libraries do not presently exist. Of course, that would do little good in itself unless people are sufficiently well educated to use those libraries to broaden their knowledge and understanding. Computer enthusiasts, however, are not noted for their calls to increase support of public libraries and schools. It is *electronic information* carried by *networks* they uphold as crucial. Here is a case in which an obsession with a particular kind of technology causes one to disregard what are obvious problems and clear remedies. While it is true that systems of computation and communications, intelligently structured and wisely applied, might help a society raise its standards of literacy, education, and general knowledgeability, to look to those instruments first while ignoring how to enlighten and invigorate a human mind is pure foolishness.

"As everybody knows, knowledge is power."[24] This is an attractive idea, but 31 highly misleading. Of course, knowledge employed in particular circumstances can help one act effectively and in that sense enhance one's power. A citrus farmer's knowledge of frost conditions enables him/her to take steps to prevent damage to the crop. A candidate's knowledge of public opinion can be a powerful aid in an election campaign. But surely there is no automatic, positive link between knowledge and power, especially if that means power in a social or political sense. At times knowledge brings merely an enlightened impotence or paralysis. One may know exactly what to do but lack the wherewithal to act. Of the many conditions that affect the phenomenon of power, knowledge is but one and by no means the most important. Thus, in the history of ideas, arguments that expert knowledge ought to play a special role in politics— the philosopher-kings for Plato, the engineers for Veblen—have always been offered as something contrary to prevailing wisdom. To Plato and Veblen it was obvious that knowledge was *not* power, a situation they hoped to remedy.

An equally serious misconception among computer enthusiasts is the belief that   32 democracy is first and foremost a matter of distributing information. As one particularly flamboyant manifesto exclaims: "There is an explosion of information dispersal in the technology and we think this information has to be shared. All great thinkers about democracy said that the key to democracy is access to information. And now we have a chance to get information into people's hands like never before."[25] Once again such assertions play on our belief that a democratic public ought to be open-minded and well informed. One of the great evils of totalitarian societies is that they dictate what people can know and impose secrecy to restrict freedom. But democracy is not founded solely (or even primarily) upon conditions that affect the availability of information. What distinguishes it from other political forms is a recognition that the people as a whole are capable of self-government and that they have a rightful claim to rule. As a consequence, political society ought to build institutions that allow or even encourage a great latitude of democratic participation. How far a society must go in making political authority and public roles available to ordinary people is a matter of dispute among political theorists. But no serious student of the question would give much credence to the idea that creating a universal gridwork to spread electronic information is, by itself, a democratizing step.

What, then, of the idea that "interaction with information through a good console,   33 through a good network to a good computer" will promote a renewed sense of political involvement and participation? Readers who believe that assertion should contact me about some parcels of land my uncle has for sale in Florida. Relatively low levels of citizen participation prevail in some modern democracies, the United States, for example. There are many reasons for this, many ways a society might try to improve things. Perhaps opportunities to serve in public office or influence public policy are too limited; in that case, broaden the opportunities. Or perhaps choices placed before citizens are so pallid that boredom is a valid response; in that instance, improve the quality of those choices. But it is simply not reasonable to assume that enthusiasm for political activity will be stimulated solely by the introduction of sophisticated information machines.

The role that television plays in modern politics should suggest why this is so.   34 Public participation in voting has steadily declined as television replaced the face-to-face politics of precincts and neighborhoods. Passive monitoring of electronic news and information allows citizens to feel involved while dampening the desire to take an active part. If people begin to rely upon computerized data bases and telecommunications as a primary means of exercising power, it is conceivable that genuine political knowledge based in first-hand experience would vanish altogether. The vitality of democratic politics depends upon people's willingness to act together in pursuit of their common ends. It requires that on occasion members of a community appear before each other in person, speak their minds, deliberate on paths of action, and decide what they will do.[26] This is considerably different from the model now upheld as a breakthrough for democracy: logging onto one's computer, receiving the latest information, and sending back an instantaneous digitized response.

A chapter from recent political history illustrates the strength of direct participation in contrast to the politics of electronic information. In 1981 and 1982 two groups of activists set about to do what they could to stop the international nuclear arms race. One of the groups, Ground Zero, chose to rely almost solely upon mass communications to convey its message to the public. Its leaders appeared on morning talk shows and evening news programs on all three major television networks. They followed up with a mass mail solicitation using addresses from a computerized data base. At the same time another group, the Nuclear Weapons Freeze Campaign, began by taking its proposal for a bilateral nuclear freeze to New England town meetings, places where active citizen participation is a long-standing tradition. Winning the endorsement of the idea from a great many town meetings, the Nuclear Freeze group expanded its drive by launching a series of state initiatives. Once again the key was a direct approach to people, this time through thousands of meetings, dinners, and parties held in homes across the country. 35

The effects of the two movements were strikingly different. After its initial publicity, Ground Zero was largely ignored. It had been an ephemeral exercise in media posturing. The Nuclear Freeze campaign, however, continued to gain influence in the form of increasing public support, successful ballot measures, and an ability to apply pressure upon political officials. Eventually, the latter group did begin to use computerized mailings, television appearances, and the like to advance its cause. But it never forgot the original source of its leverage: people working together for shared ends. 36

Of all the computer enthusiasts' political ideas, there is none more poignant than the faith that the computer is destined to become a potent equalizer in modern society. Support for this belief is found in the fact that small "personal" computers are becoming more and more powerful, less and less expensive, and ever more simple to use. Obnoxious tendencies associated with the enormous, costly, technically inaccessible computers of the recent past are soon to be overcome. As one writer explains, "The great forces of centralization that characterized mainframe and minicomputer design of that period have now been reversed." This means that "the puny device that sits innocuously on the desktop will, in fact, within a few years, contain enough computing power to become an effective equalizer."[27] Presumably, ordinary citizens equipped with microcomputers will be able to counter the influence of large, computer-based organizations. 37

Notions of this kind echo beliefs of eighteenth- and nineteenth-century revolutionaries that placing firearms in the hands of the people was crucial to overthrowing 38 entrenched authority. In the American Revolution, French Revolution, Paris Commune, and Russian Revolution the role of "the people armed" was central to the revolutionary program. As the military defeat of the Paris Commune made clear, however, the fact that the popular forces have guns may not be decisive. In a contest of force against force, the larger, more sophisticated, more ruthless, better equipped competitor often has the upper hand. Hence, the availability of low-cost computing power may move the baseline that defines electronic dimensions of social influence, but it does not necessarily alter the relative balance of power. Using a personal computer makes one no more powerful vis-à-vis, say, the National Security Agency than flying a hang glider establishes a person as a match for the U.S. Air Force.

> **Using a personal computer makes one no more powerful vis-à-vis, say, the National Security Agency than flying a hang glider establishes a person as a match for the U.S. Air Force.** [39]

In sum, the political expectations of computer enthusiasts are seldom more than idle fantasy. Beliefs that widespread use of computers will cause hierarchies to crumble, inequality to tumble, participation to flourish, and centralized power to dissolve simply do not withstand close scrutiny. The formula information = knowledge = power = democracy lacks any real substance. At each point the mistake comes in the conviction that computerization will inevitably move society toward the good life. And no one will have to raise a finger.

Notes

1. See, for example, Edward Berkeley, *The Computer Revolution* (New York: Doubleday, 1962); Edward Tomeski, *The Computer Revolution: The Executive and the New Information Technology* (New York: Macmillan, 1970); and Nigel Hawkes, *The Computer Revolution* (New York: E. P. Dutton, 1972). See also Aaron Sloman, *The Computer Revolution in Philosophy* (Hassocks, England: Harvester Press, 1978); Zenon Pylyshyn, *Perspectives on the Computer Revolution* (Englewood Cliffs, N.J.: Prentice-Hall, 1970); Paul Stoneman, *Technological Diffusion and the Computer Revolution* (Cambridge: Cambridge University Press, 1976); and Ernest Braun and Stuart MacDonald, *Revolution in Miniature: The History and Impact of Semiconductor Electronics* (Cambridge: Cambridge University Press, 1978).
2. Michael L. Dertouzos in an interview on "The Today Show," National Broadcasting Company, August 8, 1983.
3. Daniel Bell, "The Social Framework of the Information Society," in *The Computer Age: A Twenty Year View,* Michael L. Dertouzos and Joel Moses (eds.) (Cambridge: MIT Press, 1980), 163.
4. See, for example, Philip H. Abelson, "The Revolution in Computers and Electronics," *Science* 215:751–753, 1982.

5. Edward A. Feigenbaum and Pamela McCorduck, *The Fifth Generation: Artificial Intelligence and Japan's Computer Challenge to the World* (Reading, Mass.: Addison-Wesley, 1983), 8.

6. Among the important works of this kind are David Burnham, *The Rise of the Computer State* (New York: Random House, 1983); James N. Danziger et al., *Computers and Politics: High Technology in American Local Governments* (New York: Columbia University Press, 1982); Abbe Moshowitz, *The Conquest of Will: Information Processing in Human Affairs* (Reading, Mass.: Addison-Wesley, 1976); James Rule et al., *The Politics of Privacy* (New York: New American Library, 1980); and Joseph Weizenbaum, *Computer Power and Human Reason: From Judgment to Calculation* (San Francisco: W. H. Freeman, 1976).

7. Quoted in Jacques Vallee, *The Network Revolution: Confessions of a Computer Scientist* (Berkeley: And/Or Press, 1982), 10.

8. Tracy Kidder, *Soul of a New Machine* (New York: Avon Books, 1982), 228.

9. *The Fifth Generation,* 14.

10. James Martin, *Telematic Society: A Challenge for Tomorrow* (Englewood Cliffs, N.J.: Prentice-Hall, 1981), 172.

11. Ibid., 4.

12. Starr Roxanne Hiltz and Murray Turoff, *The Network Nation: Human Communication via Computer* (Reading, Mass.: Addison-Wesley, 1978), 489.

13. Ibid., xxix.

14. Ibid., 484.

15. Ibid., xxix.

16. *The Network Revolution,* 198.

17. John Naisbitt, *Megatrends: Ten New Directions Transforming Our Lives* (New York: Warner Books, 1984), 282.

18. Amitai Etzioni, Kenneth Laudon, and Sara Lipson, "Participating Technology: The Minerva Communications Tree," *Journal of Communications,* 25:64, Spring 1975.

19. J. C. R. Licklider, "Computers and Government," in Dertouzos and Moses (eds.), *The Computer Age,* 114, 126.

20. Quoted in *The Fifth Generation,* 240.

21. *Occupational Outlook Handbook, 1982–1983,* U.S. Bureau of Labor Statistics, Bulletin No. 2200, Superintendent of Documents, U.S. Government Printing Office, Washington, D.C. See also Gene I. Maeroff, "The Real Job Boom Is Likely to be Low-Tech," *New York Times,* September 4, 1983, 16E.

22. See, for example, James Danziger et al., *Computers and Politics.*

23. For a study of the utopia of consumer products in American democracy, see Jeffrey L. Meikle, *Twentieth Century Limited: Industrial Design in America, 1925–1939* (Philadelphia: Temple University Press, 1979). For other utopian dreams see Joseph J. Corn, *The Winged Gospel: America's Romance with Aviation, 1900–1950* (Oxford: Oxford University Press, 1983); Joseph J. Corn and Brian Horrigan, *Yesterday's Tomorrows: Past Visions of America's Future* (New York: Summit Books, 1984); and Erik Barnow, *The Tube of Plenty* (Oxford: Oxford University Press, 1975).

24. *The Fifth Generation,* 8.

25. "The Philosophy of US," from the official program of The US Festival held in San Bernardino, California, September 4–7, 1982. The outdoor rock festival, sponsored by Steven Wozniak, co-inventor of the original Apple Computer, attracted an estimated half million people. Wozniak regaled the crowd with large-screen video presentations of his message, proclaiming a new age of community and democracy generated by the use of personal computers.

26. "*Power* corresponds to the human ability not just to act but to act in concert. Power is never the property of an individual; it belongs to a group and remains in existence only so long as the group keeps together." Hannah Arendt, *On Violence* (New York: Harcourt Brace & World, 1969), 44.

27. John Markoff, "A View of the Future: Micros Won't Matter," *InfoWorld,* October 31, 1983, 69.

⬅ SECOND THOUGHTS

1. Winner criticizes at length the "revolution" metaphor to describe changes wrought by emerging technologies in the 1980s. Find some current examples from newspaper, magazine, TV, or Internet coverage of the computer or network "revolution" and analyze them using questions and criteria suggested by Winner, such as those in ¶s 8, 9, 10. To what extent do you agree with Winner's conclusion that "it seems all but impossible for computer enthusiasts to examine critically the *ends* that might guide the world-shaking developments they anticipate" (¶ 7)?

2. Review the four key assumptions of "computer romantics," according to Winner (¶ 27). Which of these assumptions do you or did you share? How widespread do you find this set of beliefs to be, for example, in contemporary media coverage of the Internet? How persuaded are you by Winner's arguments questioning these assumptions?

3. "Current developments in the information age suggest an increase in power by those who already had a great deal of power, an enhanced centralization of control by those already prepared for control, an augmentation of wealth by the already wealthy" (¶ 24), writes Winner. How accurately do you think Winner predicted the social effects of increasing computerization over the past decade? For example, the growth of the Internet in the 1990s exceeded almost everyone's expectations. To what extent do you think Winner underestimated the potential social uses of the Internet? To what extent do you think he accurately foresaw the commercialization of the Internet, the large profits generated by high-tech industries, or other economic and social trends?

The American Dream, and Email for All

John Schwartz

John Schwartz (b. 1957) is a science writer at the national desk of the *Washington Post,* where he writes a regular column about Internet and technology issues. Formerly he was a business writer for *Newsweek.* This article appeared originally in 1996 in *Virtual City,* a magazine for people interested in the Internet that was launched by *Newsweek* but is no longer being published.

There are two ways to get to Blacksburg, Virginia. You can drive down I-81 from 1
Roanoke, cutting west at Christiansburg. Or you can take that other highway, the Information Super—well, you know. Fire up the browser and head over to <http://www.bev.net> and you'll find yourself cruising through the "Blacksburg Electronic Village."

In the real world, the town of 35,000 nestles on a plateau in the Blue Ridge mountains—a stunning setting for a sweet place. But one fact separates Blacksburg from other towns of similar size: it's wired, totally. 2

Thanks to megabuck grants from Bell Atlantic and the cooperation of Virginia 3
Polytechnic Institute & State University and the town itself, some 60 percent of Blacksburg's citizens have email. About 40 percent of the people have full Internet access, with a proliferation of personal home pages on the World Wide Web and spirited debate in local Usenet newsgroups. Some apartment buildings have zippy Ethernet connections, and there's a cluster of computers connected to the BEV, as it's known, at the local library. Restaurants offer print-and-redeem discount coupons, and Wade's grocery even lets faraway parents custom-order care packages to be delivered to their kids at Virginia Tech. (The price is totaled as you order.) You can pay bills online, find out what's going on at the local high school, get friendly medical advice from a local doctor, or argue about the area's environmental issues on local newsgroups. Little wonder that in Bogen's restaurant or Famous Barbeque, you might just as likely hear tech talk as discussion of clogged carburetors or the luck of the "Hokies," the Virginia Tech sports teams. Technosavvy grandmothers talk about their burning desire to upgrade to a faster modem.

Is this heaven, or hell? 4

Well, neither. In fact, in its virtual and real incarnation, each is unmistakably, simply Blacksburg, a place that has successfully fused small- 5

> Technosavvy grandmothers talk about their burning desire to upgrade to a faster modem. Is this heaven, or hell?

town folks with high-tech communications. Out in the fields near the tiny airport, beautiful Holsteins graze by the satellite dishes. "Blacksburg is a safe, friendly community—even on the Net!" reads a caption accompanying a photo of a grade school crossing guard in the Chamber of Commerce's online postcard gallery. It's a sly rebuke to the kind of pedophile/cyberporn scaremongering that characterizes some net coverage in the mainstream media; it's also a case study in truth in advertising. From its broad streets with stately brick homes to its workmanlike home pages free of glitter and flash, Blacksburg is just a little dull—in a nice way. It's the kind of place that makes people want to set down roots and raise kids. Yet Blacksburg is no time warp. The same fast food and strip shopping centers ring the town as in other towns of its size, though it has been spared much of the ugliness and sprawl of modern growth thanks to the relative success of nearby Christiansburg at attracting the Wal-Marts and big soulless malls.

Lots of cities and towns now claim to have what are known as "civic networks," where folks can gather online to hash out issues and post want-ads. But many of those online places have the numbing quality of a sparsely attended planning commission meeting, full of bitter arguments that go nowhere. In Blacksburg, though, the halls are crowded, the conversation lively—and the activism is for real. Keath Marx, a 49-year-old veterinarian, says the network has put real power in his hands. He joined a group of locals to oppose an interstate highway project's placement too near to the town. By sharing information with other activists in the region about congressional discussions on highway placement that are rarely covered adequately in the newspapers, the activists were able to keep the pressure on the federal and local authorities and respond quickly to the new information. As a result, "The road hasn't been stopped, but we've been able to influence, to some extent, where it should go," Marx says. "It did make us feel that we had had an impact." 6

Marx has a computer at home, but signs on to the BEV at the local library. Along with his work against the highway, he exchanges email with his son in Washington State and with a far-flung network of friends; he's also active in veterinary discussion groups, where he advises people around the world on the care and feeding of their parrots, ostriches and emus. Marx's stepson, Charlie Hagedorn, is a 13-year-old who also checks in on the BEV at the library, cruising the net for game software and contacting his Dad. "I love to read, so I've been checking out lots of books, too," says Charlie, who apparently hasn't heard the news that online communications spells the death of literacy. 7

Of course, you'd expect professionals like Marx and youngsters like Charlie to fall into the net. But what about senior citizens like Nadine Newcomb? She won't tell you her age—it's none of your business. "I'm a grandmother" is as close as she'll get to an answer. The retired librarian isn't wowed by technology for technology's sake: she knows that you can find out the price of peaches online and says, "I think, 'Isn't that nice?' but I don't have any use for it." Instead, she uses the resources available to keep up with friends via email and to download news from an email discussion list for the League of Women Voters; Newcomb prints out the bulletins and circulates them to her less wired friends. She doesn't mind providing this little service, though she grouses, "I wish some of my friends were online. It's so much simpler than to communicate in person. You just have to sit down and type something." 8

At times, it seems that just about everyone is sitting down and typing something. 9
From a cluttered office behind his restaurant and bar, Bill Ellenbogen reaches out into
the ether to download the latest version of Netscape's Internet browser. He uses cyberspace to hawk Bogen's restaurant, offering discount coupons from his web site. But he
has also used the web to promote a project to restore the Huckleberry Trail, a bikeway
and recreational trail connecting Blacksburg and Christiansburg. As he struggles with
the download, he muses that "we don't have any traffic problems on our roads—but our
electronic highways are crowded," as more and more Blacksburg residents try to use
the modem pool that serves as the gateway to the computer system, which is maintained at Virginia Tech. Along with the usual big-screen TVs and video games in his
bar, Ellenbogen also provides a 90-mhz Pentium box with a fast modem, "just for the
heck of it."

But then, not everyone is connected, of course. Who makes up that remaining 40 10
percent? Helen Johnson, for one. Her line of work is fortune-telling. A neon sign in her
window promises "past present and future." Unlike King Video, Wade's Grocery and
Flower Shop, Bogen's, and other businesses, Johnson sees no need to advertise her services online. "I don't think I'd do that," she says with a smile. "It doesn't sound like it
would be good for my business."

Can't she see this is going to be the next big thing?   11

But she isn't the only one who's passing on the future, at least so far. The local 12
auto repair shops don't seem to have checked into the BEV yet. All the worse for them,
since the citizenry burns up the local newsgroup discussion with brutally frank comparisons and horror stories about local car repair. One BEV regular says he knows of at
least two shops that he will never drive into after hearing repeated complaints about
them online.

Some businesses turn their potential net problems into pluses. Wade's Flower 13
Shop, just a refrigerated case in the grocery store, is a full-fledged floral delivery service in its online incarnation. When someone posted a complaint that some flowers he
ordered looked a little peaked, the florist immediately posted a public apology and
offered a new delivery. The griper, needless to say, was impressed—as were a lot of
folks, probably.

These burgeoning uses of the town's network are especially satisfying to Andrew 14
Cohill, project director for the BEV. He has a sign in his cubicle saying "Chief Network Police." But he's more interested in what will happen next—and what won't.

When Bell Atlantic first announced its investment in the future of Blacksburg, it 15
included video on demand as part of its list of services to come for its wired town. But the
Holy Grail of telephone companies has always gotten a big yawn in Blacksburg. "They're
recreating television. That's not what people are using it for in Blacksburg. Nobody ever
asks me, 'When am I going to be able to watch *Terminator 2* on my Internet feed?'"

Instead, Cohill sees video taking a more interactive role in his online town. He pre- 16
dicts that video feeds of half of Virginia Tech's classes will be available online—making
extension courses live up to the name. Already, college students commonly use the electronic mail system to contact professors with questions and comments and to hold virtual
class discussions which can be joined any time of the day or night. Thanks to the electronic tool, one student gushed, "I've never had such a close personal relationship with

my professor. I never had so much discussion with my classmates." Professors still keep office hours, Cohill says, but take care of much of the grunt work of teaching online.

The folks in Blacksburg don't yearn for flash and dazzle if it doesn't have a payoff 17 in utility. Why order their video from the sofa when King Video is only a few minutes away and puts its latest releases and coupons online? Cohill is far more interested in a plan to feed live information from the coming set of global positioning satellite doo-dads. The technology will soon be used to track the city transit fleet into the current route map, letting riders know whether they have time for another sip of coffee before leaving to catch the bus.

Cohill is impressed with the relative civility of discussions on the BEV, compared 18 to the sort of thing one finds in, say, *alt.flame*, or on more rancorous community bul-letin boards found everywhere from Santa Monica, California, to Takoma Park, Mary-land. But Cohill notes that Southern aversion to confrontation combined with the dynamics of small town life could be at play: "Here, if you yell at somebody, there's a good chance you're going to see them on the street."

Ultimately, what many in Blacksburg seem to want for their tech investment is 19 what will almost certainly happen when the town's already awesome connectedness crosses the threshold into ubiquity: the mundane. "It's a communications tool, not a video game kind of thing," says Luke Ward, technology manager for the BEV. Ward says wistfully that he is tantalizingly close to being able to schedule soccer practices for his 8-year-old's team online; 4 of the 11 families are wired.

When he can do that, paradoxically, the system of modem pools and ethernet wires 20 will all but disappear. That's what tends to happen with things that are ubiquitous—and really, really useful. When was the last time you thought about your telephone?

⬅ SECOND THOUGHTS

1. Schwartz writes that Blacksburg is "a place that has successfully fused small-town folks with high-tech communications" (¶ 5). To what extent do you agree with this judgment, based on the article? Do you think that Schwartz glosses over "that remaining 40 percent" (¶ 10) of the population not online or dissenters such as for-tune teller Helen Johnson?

2. Regarding online civility, Blacksburg Electronic Village's project director Andrew Cohill is quoted as saying, "Here, if you yell at somebody, there's a good chance you're going to see them on the street" (¶ 18). What differences does Schwartz see between BEV and civic networks in other places, what evidence does he present, and how does he account for these differences? How do you think rural, suburban, and urban communities might make different uses of civic networks?

3. How do you think your own community might use a civic network like Blacks-burg's? Or if your community already has such a network, how would you compare its uses with those described by Schwartz?

Electronic Democracy

Pamela Varley

What's Really Happening in Santa Monica

Pamela Varley (b. 1958) is a senior analyst for the Investor Responsibility Research Center, where she coordinates a research project on international labor standards. Previously she worked as a case writer at Harvard's John F. Kennedy School of Government. This article appeared in 1991 in *Technology Review* (<web.mit.edu/afs/athena/org/t/techreview/www/tr.html>), a magazine published by MIT's alumni association for a national audience interested in technology and society. It is based on a case study that Varley wrote for the Kennedy School's program on innovation in state and local government.

W ith its enticing beaches, gourmet eateries, zany public artworks, and radical-chic sensibility, Santa Monica has long been known as a playground for celebrities and affluent tourists. But the residents of this gleaming seaside town in Southern California are lately putting their community on the map for yet another reason: a curious social and political experiment. The idea is to create a new kind of public meeting ground—different from City Hall, different from a city park or plaza—where citizens can talk to public officials and city servants on equal footing, where people can get to know one another in safe environs and chat about local political issues or anything else on their minds.

This egalitarian meeting ground—where all voices are equal, anyone can speak at any time, and no one can be silenced—is not a physical place at all. It is a computer system, called the Public Electronic Network (PEN), that residents may hook into, free of charge. PEN provides electronic access to city council agendas, staff reports, public safety tips, and the public library's on-line catalog. It also allows residents to enter into electronic conferences on topics ranging from the political (discussions about rent control or human rights) to the utterly apolitical (such as TV's Simpsons or household pets). Santa Monicans can tap into PEN from a home or office computer or use one of the public terminals in libraries, community centers, and elderly housing complexes.

Each time a PEN user enters a comment, it immediately appears on the screen of other PEN users logged on to the same discussion item. As many as 64 people can use the system at once, so the comments can come thick and fast, just as if people were sitting around a room chatting. Sometimes the conversations are elongated—with a comment made one day and responses coming several days later. Discussion on a single topic may last for months. In addition to having access to these public conferences, each PEN user gets a private electronic mailbox for exchanging messages with city bureaucrats, politicians, and fellow citizens.

In a sense, Santa Monica is appropriating for public purposes technologies that had previously been mostly the province of businesses and
individual computer devotees. Corporations use
electronic mail to communicate with their customers and with one another. Private computer
networks, such as CompuServe, allow subscribers
with common interests to meet without the traditional constraints of time and space. Using such a
network, for example, a chess aficionado in
Nebraska might strike up a friendship with a like-
minded soul in London.

> **Santo Monica is appropriating for public purposes technologies that had previously been mostly the province of businesses and individual computer devotees.**
>
> 4

Applying these innovations to a public-sector network, a couple of visionary Santa   5
Monicans thought, would give residents more direct access to their local government.
The system could offer citizens a new way to be heard politically, free from the conventional gatekeepers in City Hall and the press. More broadly, it might prove a powerful antidote to the isolation and anomie of modern urban life by offering a new way
for Santa Monicans to interact and forge alliances. This, in turn, might eventually
involve more residents in civic affairs. "Engagement is what democracy is all about,"
says municipal court judge David Finkel, a member of the Santa Monica City Council
in the late 1980s and an early fan of PEN. "The more people communicating on PEN,
the more potential political activists there are to jump in and stir up the pot."

In its two and a half years of operation, PEN has had a tangible impact on Santa   6
Monica. For instance, through PEN, a group of residents—including three or four
homeless men—formed an on-line political organization that lobbied successfully for
new city services for the homeless. But PEN also has its detractors. Some dismiss the
system as a hightech toy, kept alive by a few computer enthusiasts with nothing better
to do. And in fact, a relatively small group of Santa Monicans dominates the conferences, which often degenerate into mean-spirited verbal duels. The system also suffers
from the lack of participation by most local officials. Nevertheless, PEN is a brave
experiment. After all, not many municipal governments would play a wild card that
could shift the balance of local political power.

PIONEERING PEN

A city of 96,000 tucked between Los Angeles and the Pacific Ocean, Santa Monica has   7
a reputation for leftish politics. Heavily populated with "frumpies"—formerly radical
upwardly mobile professionals—the city has elected '60s rebel leader Tom Hayden to
the California State Assembly since 1982. The city has responded with unusual tolerance to its burgeoning population of homeless people; police refrain from rousting
them from city parks, and every weekday afternoon a community group provides a free
hot meal on the lawn in front of City Hall.

The city does have a contingent of moderates and conservatives, but nearly all of   8
political Santa Monica embraces certain basic principles. Mark E. Kann, author of *Middle Class Radicalism in Santa Monica,* defines this ideology as a belief in "human-

scale community, participatory democracy, and one-class society." Thus the city is well suited to pioneer a system like PEN.

The system's chief architect and champion is Ken Phillips, director of the Infor- 9 mation Systems Department in Santa Monica City Hall. Phillips had already presided over the introduction of an electronic mail system at City Hall in 1984, allowing 600 of the city's 1,500 employees to communicate via computer. The seven city council members received laptop computers with which to send messages to city bureaucrats and to each other.

The idea of expanding the system beyond City Hall came in 1986, when council 10 member Herb Katz mentioned to Phillips that a constituent was trying to get hold of some city documents and wondered whether he might be able to hook his computer up to the city's system. Phillips was not, at first, enthusiastic. The city computers are filled with sensitive information, and the idea of opening them to the public sounded like a security nightmare. Phillips did not reject the idea outright, however. As a subscriber to private computer networks, he began to see the potential for applying the same technology to a public system. He figured out a way around the security problems: set up a separate city computer that would contain public information and that would allow citizens access to City Hall via e-mail.

In October 1987, Phillips conducted a survey of local residents. To his surprise, it 11 revealed enormous interest in a public computer network. The survey also showed that a third of the respondents already owned personal computers and that almost three-quarters of this group owned modems as well. Despite these numbers, the Santa Monica city manager was reluctant to ask the council for the hundreds of thousands of dollars in equipment necessary to launch an elaborate public computer network. Undaunted, Phillips persuaded Hewlett-Packard (maker of the city's existing computer system) to donate $350,000 worth of equipment to the venture and Metasystems Design Group to contribute $20,000 worth of software. On February 21, 1989, the system opened for public use. In the next few weeks, 500 curious Santa Monicans signed up for PEN. To ensure equitable access to the system, the city provided the service free of charge.

One of Phillips's early concerns in designing PEN had been the prospect of on-line 12 obscenity or slander. Would the city be liable for comments that appeared on the system, the way a television station is for material it broadcasts? Or would the city be no more responsible for such communications than the telephone company? There was no suitable legal precedent. After some discussions the city decided not to play the role of censor at all, unless a court declared a particular comment only as slanderous or obscene.

A related question was whether residents should be required to log on under their 13 own names. One worry was that by using real names, PENners might feel exposed and therefore less inclined to enter debates. The city opted for real names, however, in part to deter irresponsible or obscene comments.

THE LURE OF CONFERENCES

City planners had expected the heaviest use of PEN to come from residents seeking 14 information from one of the city's databases. They were wrong. From the beginning, the public conferences were by far the most popular attraction, accounting for more than half the calls. Electronic mail was the second most popular feature, followed by access to city databases. One of the clearest lessons of PEN, according to William Dutton, a professor at the University of Southern California's Annenberg School for Communications, is that people do not crave new sources of information so much as new venues for talking to one another.

In fact, many PEN users report that when they first began logging onto the PEN   15 conferences, they went through a period of addiction (PENaholism, some call it) and found themselves mesmerized for hours in front of the screen, night after night. Most addicts settled down after a few weeks or months, although a few continued to log on every day for several hours.

What makes PEN so seductive? "You start playing with electronic mail and then you   16 start looking forward to logging on in the morning to see if you got any mail in return," explains Phillips. "And then you post a comment in a conference, and the next time you log on, 15 people have said something about what you've said. That's a heady brew."

Kevin McKeown, chair of the PEN Users Group, compares the system to a tradi-   17 tional New England town meeting—except that PEN is every day. "It's not like writing a letter to the editor of the local newspaper, where you have a chance in a thousand that it will be published, and no one ever responds to you even if it is," he says. "You put something provocative on PEN, and you get responses. And then other people chime in and pretty soon you've got a good debate going."

PEN also is casual and chatty, so a user does not need to measure every word. PEN   18 offers housebound people a way to socialize. And it is always available: "PEN is the only place in town where I can have a decent conversation about a meaningful subject at a moment's notice," says one user.

Another draw for many users is the leveling effect of the PEN conferences. Judged   19 solely on what they say on-line, people can easily cross social barriers. Homeless people talk to the well-to-do, teenagers talk to adults, political neophytes talk to City Hall's old hands. Even gender lines blur if a resident registers using only initials or an androgynous first name. "It's been a great equalizer," says Don Paschal, who was homeless until November 1990 and began using PEN while living on the street.

The leveling effect of PEN means that when PEN users do finally meet face to   20 face, there can be surprises. McKeown remembers his shock at finding that some of the most thoughtful comments on PEN were written by a precocious teenager. City council member Ken Genser remembers meeting a PEN user he had assumed to be an elderly curmudgeon only to find that he was 25, with a pony tail.

TROUBLE IN PARADISE

PEN's egalitarianism also makes the system vulnerable to abuse. PENners quickly dis-   21 cover that they must contend with people who feel entitled to hector mercilessly those with whom they disagree. It is, Phillips says, a little like trying to hold a meeting while "allowing somebody to stand in a corner and shout."

"Part of what makes PEN so volatile," says McKeown, "is that you're not face to   22 face. There's not a chance you're going to get popped in the chops for what you say, so you feel like you can get away with more. In a way, that's liberating. But then you have the occasional 'flamer,' as they're called in on-line circles, who doesn't care if he or she hurts people."

As active PEN user Robert Segelbaum puts it, computer conferencing turns writ- 23
ing into "a performing art." Michele Wittig, a psychology professor at California State University at Northridge and an active PENner, contends that "public postings take on the character of ripostes because, like fencing, PENning often occurs between two or three people interacting before an audience."

When the system started up, women—greatly outnumbered by men—had prob- 24
lems with harassment. "Several men would badger us a lot when we came onto the system," Wittig says. "We'd started online discussions about sexism and equality of women in the workplace. They made disparaging remarks and innuendos." Even worse, she says, "several of the 17- and 18-year-olds started to post their very violent fantasies. They would use initials of women on PEN and say that they would dismember us and rape us." By the summer of 1989, the few women on line were fed up and ready to drop out.

Another kind of problem comes up when one or two PENners "go off thread," 25
straying from the conference topic into a personal reverie or chitchat that all participants must wade through. PEN etiquette allows everyone to discuss any topic and express any opinion, no matter how arcane. But instead of interrupting discussion, a PENner who wants to change the subject is expected to open a new conference item. Some PEN users, for instance, enjoy chatting on-line about their stuffed animals. That's fine, McKeown says, provided they confine their ruminations to a special "stuffed animals" conference item.

PEN occasionally suffers as well from the tyranny of those with too much time on 26
their hands. In a few cases, PENners have been known to comment not only on every topic but on virtually every comment made on every topic. Since thousands of comments are entered in PEN, this metacommentary can be oppressive, especially if the PENner is ill-mannered and given to name-calling. "There are people who have dominated on-line discussions for months now," says McKeown. "And there's no way to shut them up." Most PEN devotees cringe at the antics of the system's resident bullies because—aside from the immediate unpleasantness they produce—these troublemakers tend to reduce the forum's apparent importance in the eyes of the general public. "Sometimes it degenerates into nothing better than one of those $5-a-minute telephone lines," says one regular user.

Of course, just about any public forum has a similar problem. At every Santa 27
Monica City Council meeting, for instance, one woman gets up to speak on each item on the agenda—prolonging meetings by as much as an hour. "Any system can be abused," McKeown says. "What you have to look at is the balance—how many people are you enabling and empowering and how many people are going to abuse that kind of power?"

PENners have come up with a number of ways to cope with on-line bullying. In 28
response to harassment, for example, the women on PEN banded together in July 1989 to form a support group called PEN Femmes. The group makes a point of wel-

coming women when they begin to participate in PEN conferences. Harassment has subsided as more women have become active. The city has also made available private conferences, so that groups of like-minded people can work on a project in peace—an idea Phillips likens to allowing a community group to meet in a private room at City Hall.

E-mail, too, has proved useful against PEN abuse. For one thing, if two PEN users 29 get off track in a conference—suddenly realizing that they want to chat about football, say, instead of property assessments—they can do so privately. E-mail is also a good way to let someone know he or she is breaching PEN's etiquette without dressing the person down in public. "One of the worst things you can do," McKeown says, "is respond to a blowhard on-line, because he'll blow hard right back at you, in an endless cycle." Sometimes, when approached by e-mail, a PENner can be persuaded to delete an offending comment from a conference, or at least to temper his or her future comments. Says Phillips, "The ability to operate behind the scenes with e-mail is the glue that keeps the conferences running."

COPING WITH A HARD CORE

PEN's biggest disappointment has been the domination of its conference discussions 30 by a small number of users. More than 3,000 people are signed up for PEN, but only 500 to 600 log on each month and most never add any comments to the conference discussions. PENners talk about the "50 hardcore" users whose names appear again and again. While the average PEN user logs on to the system about 12 times a month, some PENners do so 8 or 10 times a day.

Most of the hard-core PENners tend to be pro-rent control, antidevelopment, and 31 sympathetic to the plight of the homeless. But according to city council member Genser, the core users differ from other community activists in town. The PEN group is "less of an insider crowd," he says. They tend to approach government with a "wide-eyed innocence."

Those active in the conference discussions tend to be articulate; they also tend to 32 be thick-skinned and to enjoy verbal skirmishes. Says active PENner Bill Myers, "The attacks have been quite vicious at times, creating a kind of survivalist attitude among PENners. It is like an electronic pack of wolves who gather together for strength and companionship."

Santa Monica's political movers and shakers have, for the most part, stayed 33 clear of PEN's crucible. If the active PENners are, as Myers suggests, an electronic wolf pack, then a politician on PEN becomes a computerized rawhide bone. PENners tend to pounce on any officeholder bold enough to enter the on-line fray, making accusations and demanding a response. Politicians are accustomed to guarding their public comments closely, working out their position ahead of time with core constituents and then "going into meetings with relatively fixed positions," says judge and former council member Finkel. But politicians who "think out loud" on PEN and respond conversationally to questions subject themselves to intense scrutiny.

Most PEN users, says Katz, are "fringe" types, like the people who call in to   34
radio talk shows. "They're both liberal and conservative, but way over, one way or
another, on an issue," he says. Chris Reed, a council member who has participated
in the conferences, agrees. She characterizes PEN's hard core as "mean-spirited
people who pound out their anger on the keyboard. They've poisoned the system
and driven off the reasonable people." Reed quit PEN in August 1990, announcing
that she was fed up with being attacked. "If people had been the least bit polite, or
respectful of the need for people in a democracy to differ," she says, "I would have
stuck it out."

Reed was not the only local politician to give up on PEN in exasperation. When   35
city council member Judy Abdo, who had been active on PEN during its first year,
diverged from her liberal council colleagues by supporting a local beachfront hotel
development, she too incurred the wrath of PEN regulars. After battling it out on-line
for a while, she stopped participating.

Another reason that politicians shun PEN is their perception that the network is   36
a time sink. A few months after the system started, Santa Monica's congressman,
Mel Levine, agreed to sponsor several on-line discussions about national and international policy. Levine's district office staff monitored the conferences and, when
questions arose, either answered them or (more often) sent them to Washington for
research and reply.

Yet this arrangement has not satisfied anyone. PEN users resent that it takes   37
several weeks to get their questions answered and that Levine does not enter the
debates personally. Levine's staff, meanwhile, is frustrated at having to do a great
deal of work to respond to the demands of a small number of constituents—and then
being lambasted for failing to do more. "We take a beating on a system we volun-
teered to participate in," says Blaise Antin, staff assistant and PEN coordinator in
the congressman's district office. Even Santa Monica's guru of participatory
democracy, State Assemblyman Tom Hayden, insists that he and his staff don't
have time for PEN.

Phillips believes that much of the problem could have been averted if PEN had   38
started up a little differently: "I recommend to people that if they're going to do a system like this, they start with a group of community
leaders, and let them set the tone of the system."

Breaking New Ground

Some PENners argue that it's too early to conclude
much of anything about the experiment, which,
they point out, is still in its infancy. "It's going
through growing pains," says Finkel, and despite
its shortcomings, he still believes it to be a "wonderful new First Amendment tool."

McKeown agrees. "I see PEN as a way to
change the whole political process, the whole

> "I see PEN as a way to
> change the whole political
> process, the whole   39
> exchange of information
> with voters, the whole way
> that we interact with our
> city government,"   40
> McKeown says.

exchange of information with voters, the whole way that we interact with our city government," he says. "Five or ten years down the road, we're going to have candidates for City Council and other positions that will run only because they got involved through PEN."

Gary Orren, a professor of public policy at Harvard University and co-author of *The Electronic Commonwealth,* is less sanguine about the prospects. New communication technologies tend to acquire a following of true believers who have utopian notions of what they will accomplish, he says. Orren believes there will never be more than "a very small subgroup of unusual people" who take part in computer conferencing that requires typing on a keyboard and reading from a screen. An audiovisual communication medium will be more likely to attract users, he believes. But even a more sophisticated interface may ultimately prove futile. The sad truth, he says, is that "people have a limited and declining taste and hunger for politics."   41

And in fact, other U.S. communities have yet to copy PEN. More than 100 other municipalities are experimenting with public computer networks. But in most cases, that simply means that a resident can approach a multimedia kiosk—say, in a shopping mall—and, after viewing a videotaped message from the mayor, dial up the city computer for land-use records. Most local governments, gasping and struggling financially, are not inclined to risk a sizable chunk of their budget on something that may be branded a frill. No one else has created a system as interactive as PEN or as socially ambitious.   42

Nevertheless, PEN has broken important new ground, and it may yet inspire future efforts. What is unusual and exciting about PEN, says Jerry Mechling, director of strategic computing and telecommunications at Harvard's Kennedy School of Government, is that a public-sector entity is doing something that is normally done only by the private sector—namely, using technology not merely to automate an existing method of doing business but to "rethink the basic way things are done." With PEN, he says, Santa Monica is "using technology to explore different ways of reaching the public. If we encourage many such experiments. I'm optimistic that we'll find better ways of doing things."   43

⬅ SECOND THOUGHTS

1. What are the potential democratic benefits of a public-sector network, according to the article? What seems to be Varley's attitude toward this potential, and how can you tell?
2. In practice, according to Varley, what accounts for "the lure of conferences" (¶ 14)? What makes conferences "vulnerable to abuse" (¶ 21)? Based on the PEN experience, how would you answer Users Group chair Kevin McKeown's question: "How many people are you enabling and empowering and how many people are going to abuse that kind of power?" (¶ 27).

3. Varley writes that "Santa Monica is appropriating for public purposes technologies that had previously been mostly the province of businesses and individual computer devotees" (¶ 4). How do you think those public purposes have fared in relation to business and private uses of the Internet in the years since 1991, when this article was published?

⟯⟯⟯ DISCUSSION THREADS

re: Grossman and Katz

1. What similarities and differences do you find between Lawrence K. Grossman's vision of the "Electronic Republic" and Jon Katz's vision of the "Digital Nation"? Which vision do you find more appealing or persuasive, and why?

re: Grossman, Katz, and Winner

2. How would you compare Lawrence K. Grossman and Jon Katz as "computer romantics," according to the criteria suggested by Langdon Winner in "Mythinformation"? To what degree do you think they share the same assumptions about information, knowledge, and power, as outlined by Winner, or lack "the qualities of social and political insight that characterized revolutionaries of the past" (¶ 12)? What uses or potential uses of network communication discussed by Grossman or Katz do you think Winner would find valuable, and why? What assumptions or values, if any, are shared by all three of these writers?

re: Schwartz and Varley

3. What criteria for measuring the success of civic networks are suggested or implied in the articles by John Schwartz and Pamela Varley? Based on those criteria, how would you compare the success of BEV and PEN? From your comparison, your other reading, and your own experience, can you suggest a combination or modified set of criteria for critically evaluating civic electronic networks?

re: Grossman, Katz, Schwartz, and Varley

4. To what extent do you think the civic networks BEV and PEN, as described by John Schwartz and Pamela Varley, realize the visions of Lawrence K. Grossman's "Electronic Republic" or Jon Katz's "Digital Nation"?

re: Electronic Democracy

5. After rereading some of the visions, realities, and criticisms of electronic democracy in this chapter—and possibly having tried some of the computer tools referred to in these selections—what is your assessment of the potential for electronic technologies to reshape politics in constructive ways? What is your judgment about the pitfalls of electronic democracy, or about Langdon Winner's assertion that "the formula information = knowledge = power = democracy lacks any real substance" (¶ 39)? What vision would *you* propose for an "electronic republic" or a "digital nation," and what values would it be based on?

RESEARCH LINKS

- *For direct links to listed Internet sources, additional reading selections and questions online, plus updates and supplementary Web resources, see* **Composing Cyberspace Online** *at <www.mhhe.com/socscience/english/holeton/>.*
- *For a complete set of research tools for the Internet—including the most useful search strategies, directories, and conventions for documenting online sources—see McGraw-Hill English Composition at <www.mhhe.com/socscience/english/compde/>.*

1. Lawrence K. Grossman discusses a 1994 case in which thousands of parents concerned about home schooling used electronic media to influence a congressional vote on the issue. Find out about other recent cases when special interest groups have organized media campaigns to influence legislation using fax machines, e-mail, electronic discussion networks, telephone polls, etc., and compare two such cases. Were the campaigns grassroots efforts organized from the bottom up, as in the case of the home schooling parents; top-down efforts organized by well-financed interest groups; or some combination of bottom-up and top-down? Based on these cases, what's your judgment about the political benefits and dangers of electronic technologies?

2. "The question is not *whether* the new electronic information infrastructure will alter our politics, but *how*," writes Lawrence K. Grossman. Grossman's vision of the "Electronic Republic" was constructed before the 1996 elections, and Jon Katz's vision of the "Digital Nation" offers a look back at that election year. Make your own determination of how new information technologies affected the 1996 elections by focusing on how particular media such as the Web were used by particular candidates or in a specific local, state, or national campaign.

3. Jon Katz devotes sections of his essay to the political philosophy of libertarianism and the philosophical school of rationalism. Choose one of these schools of thought and probe more deeply into the philosophy itself and its expression or reflection on the Internet. The U.S. Libertarian Party maintains a Web site at <www.lp.org/>, including details of its political platform; among the party's long list of suggested readings at <www.lp.org/lp-bib.html> you'll find books by novelist Ayn Rand, conservative economist Thomas Sowell, and many others who have influenced libertarian beliefs. How influential do you think these beliefs are on the Internet in general or on portions of the Internet you're familiar with? What evidence can you provide for your judgment? Do you agree with Katz that "libertarian notions are often misunderstood"? To test Katz's claims about a "new rationalism" on the Net, you might start with the views about knowledge of one of the Enlightenment thinkers he mentions—Descartes, Spinoza, or Leibniz. If rationalism requires a belief in some higher, objective "truth" based on indisputable "facts," how can one apply this philosophy to something so diverse and decentralized as the Internet?

4. Langdon Winner predicts in his 1986 book chapter that "the 'information society' will offer plenty of opportunities for janitors, hospital orderlies, and fast-food waiters" and that the beneficiaries of computerization will not be ordinary citizens but

large transnational corporations, "public bureaucracies, intelligence agencies, and an ever-expanding military." Test out these or other predictions made by Winner with recent studies and data concerning job growth, the distribution of wealth, or particular uses made of high technology by the government or military. What specific efforts, if any, have been made "to try to shape the institutions of the information age in ways that maximize human freedom while placing limits upon concentrations of power"?

5. The PEN community network was in 1991 "still in its infancy," according to Pamela Varley's article, and the Blacksburg Electronic Village had just started up when John Schwartz wrote about it in 1996. Extend the discussions started by Varley and Schwartz by researching what has happened since to these or other civic networks (which have proliferated in recent years) and making a judgment about their ongoing successes and failures. You can find PEN on the Web at <pen.ci.santa-monica. ca.us/>; BEV, which recently and controversially shifted many users to commercial Internet service providers, is at <www.bev.net/>. Directories of community networks can be found on the Web, including the University of Michigan Community Networking Initiative's list at <www.sils.umich.edu/Community/direct.html>. An excellent list of papers available online addressing civic networking is maintained by the Educational Community Development Network (<edcom.org/>) at <edcom.stanford.edu/pages/papers.html>.

6. Based on the articles in this chapter and outside research about some aspect of the theory or practice of electronic democracy, build your own model for how you think emerging technologies ought to be used for political purposes. Ground your model on actual cases and data about public-sector uses of technology. If possible, conduct your own experiment by using electronic tools to make an important decision for a group such as your class, college dorm, or project group. Use the results of this experiment to support or provide a foil for the model you propose.

The Global Village

In the 1960s, Canadian media theorist and communications professor Marshall McCluhan coined the term *global village* to describe how instantaneous communication made possible by electronic technologies could unite the world on a global scale. In the 1980s, then-Congressman and future U.S. Vice President Al Gore first used the term *information superhighway* to refer to the developing web of communications networks, computers, and consumer electronic appliances. In the 1990s, with the explosive growth and use of the Internet, both terms have gained widespread currency—and the Paul Duginski cartoon extends and relates these metaphors by suggesting that the on-ramp to the "Information Superhighway" leads to a place called "Global Village."

What Duginski emphasizes, of course, is who might be left behind on this journey. As with many real-life U.S. freeways, some obviously homeless people live under the overpass, and Duginski makes it clear why these characters won't be making the trip to the Global Village: They lack access to the necessary equipment and training.

McCluhan, who was thinking more about TV than the possibility of something like today's Internet, did not think his global village was necessarily a desirable destination for humankind. Nevertheless, the term has come to describe a kind of utopian ideal that combines the future and the past. Using ultramodern technology, it's implied, we can return to some idyllic state of village life that presumably existed before modern civilization alienated people from society. This utopian global village must be to some degree a nostalgic, even romantic idea, given the realities of village life in today's developing or Third World nations, where basic human needs for food, shelter, and health care go so commonly unmet. Indeed, the majority of the world's people—illiterate, living in substandard housing, or suffering from malnutrition—live metaphorically under the overpass with Duginski's cartoon characters.

Yet the early promise of electronic communication to transcend international borders, racial and ethnic divisions, inequalities based on socioeconomic class, and other traditional human barriers is very compelling. Further, it's been argued that these new technologies are "trickling down" much faster than did older technologies that had the potential to increase social justice or distribute knowledge more equitably. For example, print and book technology took hundreds of years to pass from elite classes to a developing middle class, while use of the Internet has been doubling every year since the early 1990s.

Many of these tensions embodied in the term *global village*—itself an oxymoron of big and little, worldwide and local—are explored further in this chapter. Richard Rodriguez implies that the Bayshore Freeway in Silicon Valley divides the information Haves and Have-nots, with its "exits to cyberspace" only miles from impoverished communities, and he suggests that new, multicultural religious coalitions forming under those overpasses may be the actual global village of the future. John Hockenberry uses the example of the Palestinian *intifada* resistance movement to argue that a digital revolution is helping to destroy international borders and empower, not impoverish, ordinary citizens. Dale Spender, by contrast, finds the notion of a digital revolution ludicrous if it means simply equipping everyone with computers and ignoring social justice in other, more important areas; moreover, she argues that social issues in cyberspace have been defined and decided by an elite group of mostly white, American males. Perhaps exemplifying some of Spender's points, Rory J. O'Connor reports on the extreme state of information access and electronic infrastructure in sub-Saharan Africa, "the unwired continent." And finally, in "Birth of a Nation in Cyberspace," John C. Rude writes about the inspirational way in which a group of dedicated Eritrean citizens and refugees has helped sustain and shape their war-torn, newly independent country by using the Internet to create a "virtual nation."

Before you read these selections, you may want to consider the following questions based on your prior reading and personal experience:

1. Does it seem to you that the world is getting more similar or more diverse? How do you think various electronic technologies, such as TV and the Internet, affect this process? What other forces are responsible for large-scale cultural and social change?
2. What do you think would be the advantages and disadvantages of giving more people access to information and direct communication all around the globe? What might be the advantages and disadvantages of a decrease in the importance and influence of international borders and separate nation-states?
3. In your experience, how are Africa (or another Third World area) and its people usually portrayed in the media, especially in comparison with affluent nations? If you have experience on the Internet (or can ask someone you know with such experience), what's your impression of the global diversity of the Net's participants?
4. If you have access to a computer lab, classroom, or networked computers equipped with electronic discussion software, discuss with fellow readers one of the issues raised here, such as the apparently paradoxical meaning of *global village.*

A Future of Faith and Cyberspace

Richard Rodriguez

Richard Rodriguez (b. 1944) is a writer and editor for Pacific News Service and contributing editor for *Harper's* magazine, *U.S. News & World Report,* and the Sunday Opinion section of the *Los Angeles Times.* He has written articles for many other newspapers and magazines including *The New York Times, The Wall Street Journal, Mother Jones,* and *The New Republic.* Rodriguez is the author of the memoirs *Hunger of Memory: The Education of Richard Rodriguez* (D. R. Godine, 1981) and *Days of Obligation: An Argument with My Mexican Father* (Viking Press, 1992). This 1996 essay for Pacific News Service appeared in a number of U.S. newspapers.

1   East Palo Alto. It's a weekday night in the Silicon Valley. Within a tiny Protestant church, the language of prayer is Spanish with a Mexican accent; the sounds of joy, bird-like warblings, belong to evangelical Protestantism. The church is the northern edge of a new Protestant reformation.

2   Outside the doors of the Apostolic Assembly is the Bayshore Freeway, connecting San Francisco to San Jose. Across the freeway is wealthy Palo Alto, home of Stanford University. All along this stretch of freeway are exits to cyberspace, the greatest concentration of high-tech industry in the world.

> **All along this stretch of freeway are exits to cyberspace, the greatest concentration of high-tech industry in the world. This side of the freeway is East Palo Alto, a neighborhood still notorious for its despair and drive-by shootings.**

3   This side of the freeway is East Palo Alto, a neighborhood still notorious for its despair and drive-by shootings. But East Palo Alto, like similar neighborhoods in America, is filling with immigrants, bringing new tongues. Next door to the Apostolic Assembly is the first Vietnamese Buddhist seminary west of the Rockies. Some nights Buddhist gongs mix over the parking lot with Spanish renditions of black Protestant hymns.

4   The news Americans tend to get from Latin America these days mainly concerns corruption and poverty: drug lords under arrest or at large; poverty; illegal immigration; pollution; monster cities.

5   The epic story of this half of the 20th century in Latin America is the conversion to Protestantism—not main-line, high-church Protestantism, but low-church, evangelical

Protestantism. It is spreading like fire. The rate of conversion in Latin America is such that demographers expect the continent to be Protestant in its majority, perhaps by the middle of next century.

It is a lovely irony of history that at a time when many Americans, no longer 6 Christian, are experimenting with forms of Native American spirituality, the Indians of Latin America are singing Protestant hymns. Spanish Catholicism—the religion that has shaped Latin America, watered Latin America, nourished my own soul—Latin Catholicism has traditionally stressed the tragic element within Christianity. Christ hangs on the cross with a particular pathos in Latin America. Now, some Easter joy is spreading through São Paolo, into the slums of Santiago, across Lima, Mexico City, through Los Angeles to East Palo Alto.

As in Europe several centuries ago, so today in Latin America, the rise of the city 7 is matched by the rise of Protestant Christianity. Catholicism still thrives in the village, where faith is a communal event. But in the city where people find themselves cut off from old ties, alone, Protestantism, stressing a one-to-one experience with Christ, finds converts.

Cocaine makes its way up from the South; the despair of American pop culture 8 wends its way from the North. The freeway, after all, goes in both directions. But something else is going on, some rush of spirituality is coming from the South.

The Mormon Church could become in the next century predominantly Spanish 9 speaking, such is the rate of conversion in Latin America. The American Catholic Church, for so long Irish in its temper, is now becoming Hispanic. (I know Catholic churches in California where the congregation sings now only in Spanish—although many do not know the words exactly, everyone recognizes the lyrics.)

And then there are evangelical Protestant groups like Victory Outreach, working 10 along the U.S.–Mexican border with teenagers. Victory Outreach today is sending missionaries from Tijuana to Paris, to Frankfurt.

A humble, wooden church, the Apostolic Assembly in East Palo Alto is the daughter church of a congregation in Mexican Los Angeles formed earlier this century. For decades, Mexicans and Mexican Americans have been gathering. One of its sponsor churches is an African-American assembly. Over the altar is a vision of heaven that looks very much like Lake Tahoe. But to look at the faces in the congregation—so young!—is to see what the future looks like in the Silicon Valley.

> **The Apostolic Assembly in East Palo Alto is the daughter church of a congregation in Mexican Los Angeles. . . . Over the altar is a vision of heaven that looks very much like Lake Tahoe.**

11

Even a visitor immediately senses a closeness here. It is as though the village has found 12 itself, formed itself anew, alongside a freeway, not far from where other Americans are contemplating the infinity called cyberspace.

⬅ SECOND THOUGHTS

1. Summarize the religious and demographic trends that Rodriguez describes. How does he explain the recent rise of Protestantism in the Americas? In what ways does "the freeway . . . [go] in both directions" (¶ 8) between North and South? What other kinds of traffic, not discussed by Rodriguez, does this freeway include?

2. The freeway also divides East Palo Alto, "a neighborhood still notorious for its despair and drive-by shootings" (¶ 3), from "the greatest concentration of high-tech industry in the world" (¶ 2). Why are Silicon Valley and cyberspace important to this essay? Why do you think Rodriguez brings them in so obliquely?

3. What two visions of a near-future Global Village does Rodriguez portray, and what does he imply about their relationship? Must these two visions be mutually exclusive, in your opinion?

The End of Nationalism?

John Hockenberry

Revolution Frees People from
Place and Time; Advancing
Technology Destroys Borders

John Hockenberry (b. 1956) is a correspondent for NBC News, where he currently hosts the MSNBC show "Edgewise." Previously he was a reporter for ABC News and a Middle East reporter and program host for National Public Radio. Hockenberry is the author of *Moving Violations: War Zones, Wheelchairs, and Declarations of Independence* (Hyperion, 1995), a memoir based on his experience as a journalist and disabled person overseas. This article originally appeared in 1995 in *WorldPaper,* an international journal published in five language editions and featuring, according to its online edition at <www.worldpaper.com/>, a diversity of viewpoints from "leading journalists and experts native to the regions about which they report."

W ho would have guessed that nationalism would end on Planet Earth before the 1 20th century did, and that advanced technology, the coveted badge of national supremacy for the most sophisticated of the world's powers, would kill it?

The endless gigabytes of purple commentary on the so-called digital revolution 2 are filled with such utopian predictions and gems of info-hyperbole; they are often obsolete before anyone gets around to believing them. In the digital world the truth is always stranger, more interesting, and often more elusive, than the free-flowing analysis.

There's plenty of evidence to suggest that a formal declaration of the End of 3 Nationalism might be premature (there are the situations in Bosnia, Rwanda, Angola and Chechnya . . . I could go on). But considerably more permanent, if less tragic, phenomena of our era suggest that the linkage between ideology and national borders, and even linguistic identity, has been irrevocably broken.

For generations, science has predicted that the exploration of space would sever 4 the tethers between humanity and the Earth. Instead, it has done the opposite. Space travel is itself a nationalistic enterprise, a high-tech opportunity to plant flags and hold news conferences while running rather prosaic errands in near-Earth orbit.

In the past decade it has become possible to see how digital technology may finally 5 hold the potential to free humanity from its shackles of place and time. The global history and culture that, for a millennium, has been dominated by defining and disputing notions of national identity, is shifting subtly but unmistakably. It is being siphoned off into a digital world where identity is no longer static, and attempting to categorize people according to their position in space is as meaningless as trying to find the box of water in a river surging at your feet. In the digital domain, the lines around groups of citizens cannot be neatly drawn and the overlapping between communities is the most important thing about them.

In 1987, the violent Palestinian uprising erupted inside the Gaza Strip and spread   6
into the Occupied West Bank, affecting Palestinian communities from Lebanon and Syria to Jordan and Iraq. There had been such violence before and in every instance Israel had moved to isolate the Palestinians inside military checkpoints and rigid rings of security. Since its creation in 1948 and territorial expansion after the 1967 war, Israel had always wrapped itself in a military cocoon. For Israelis, defense has always meant being insulated from their warlike neighbors behind a shield that only state of the art military technology could buy.

During the Palestinian uprising, better known as the *intifada,* the violence and the   7
enemies were inside that traditional Israeli cocoon, so the army and security forces worked to isolate and disarm the Occupied Territories of the West Bank and the Gaza Strip by wrapping the Palestinians in their own cocoons. The latest technology was incorporated into this security web, which relied on numerous levels of communication including satellite, telephone, wireless cellular, and fax. Israeli officials had at their fingertips a detection system to keep people inside secure borders, monitor their movements, and prevent them from interacting with the outside world, especially the Palestine Liberation Organisation (PLO) leaders in Tunis.

Israeli officials had at their fingertips a detection system to keep people inside secure borders, monitor their movements, and prevent them from interacting with the outside world.

Every day that the shield was in place a secret committee of Palestinians sent and received faxes from PLO headquarters, via New York, London,   8
Turkey, and other places. The fax machine's familiar digital shriek was as common as the Arabic call to prayer five times a day. By their very nature, faxes could not be tapped or stopped without obstructing the entire Israeli phone network. A fax confiscated in Gaza was easily replaced by one in Jericho or Nablus, or even Nazareth, inside Israel.

The faxes called for strikes and various other forms of protest that were mostly   9
ineffectual and easily controlled on the ground by the Israelis. The *intifada* claimed it wanted a tactical victory over Israel, but clearly the most stunning tactical victory of the uprising was the creation of this virtual/digital nation, independent of border checkpoints and locations on a map. It was a network of fax machines around the world that broke the Israeli shield, revealed the limits of nation as place, and linked the Palestinians inside the West Bank and Gaza with the PLO on the outside. From Israel's outmoded defensive cocoon a new form of political activity was released that the world is still trying to get a handle on.

Today, only seven short years later, a half-billion people around the world interact   10
on the Internet in a space that is absolutely real, but where notions of place and nationhood are utterly arbitrary, easily fabricated, and where the only flags are the posted

home pages of individual users. Nations exist only as groupings of convenience for the discussion of common ideas, to argue and protest, or for commercial exchange. These distinct groupings of ideology grow and die in the cyber-domain. Nations are formed and disbanded, absorbed, destroyed, and conquered with a speed that no geology or planet-based history can duplicate.

In digital technology, it is not the absolute performance of an innovation that 11 drives change; it is the incremental effect of hundreds of millions of hybrid changes and combinations of low- and high-tech by diverse populations of users. Participation traditionally drives democratic politics, and in the cyberdomain, on the digital infrastructure beyond Internet, participation is the politics, is the space, and the battlefield all rolled into one.

Also seven years after the *intifada* began, a peace process has set the flag of 12 Palestine flying over Gaza and areas of the West Bank. The process is crude and rocked by periodic carnage and it may even go away. But what will not go away, and is probably more revolutionary, is Israel's access to the Internet as of the first of this year. Today, unlike most of human history, there is a place where Israelis and Palestinians can interact without having to identify themselves ethnically, religiously, or politically. In cyberspace an Israeli school-child can, in theory, e-mail Chairman Yasser Arafat of the PLO, something that until very recently was a seriously treasonous offense in Israel. If Arafat ever gets an address on the Internet he will probably get more questions about garbage collection in Gaza than anything else. This delightful marriage of high- and low-tech feeds the true user-based revolution of the digital world.

There are similar changes in Russia and among the nations of the former Soviet 13 Union, in Europe, America, and India (I could go on). The outmoded cocoons have been abandoned as wealth is slowly being channeled away from defense and military infrastructure and into the information infrastructure.

The world may some day be able to take advantage of the potential efficiencies 14 of trade and politics online rather than in the nationalistic model where they are always mediated through security checkpoints and confiscatory tax barriers and licenses. With billions of humans available online, wealth can be distributed a few cents at a time in trillions of transactions per day. Profit and loss are no longer local boom-and-bust distortions but subtle non-threatening shifts of wealth as people with common interests find each other.

Hyperbole aside, the participation that drives the digital revolution is not important because of some over-enthusiastic analyst's claims that it will some day lead to world peace or another utopia. Just as there was no checkpoint to stop the PLO faxes during the *intifada,* today it is possible to address the world without having to show a passport that defines you culturally, ethnically, or religiously. That is a revolution.

Just as there was no checkpoint to stop the PLO faxes during the *intifada,* today it is possible to address the world without having to show a passport that defines you culturally, ethnically, or religiously. 15

Another way of looking at the edge of this horizon is to think of Marshall 16
McLuhan's over-used credo. Where once the medium was the message, today the
medium is all messages taken together.

⬅ SECOND THOUGHTS

1. What examples have you encountered of the "endless gigabytes of purple commentary" and "info-hyperbole" about the digital age (¶ 2) that Hockenberry refers to?
   What constitutes the "stranger, more interesting" truth (¶ 2) that he tries to reveal?
   How successfully do you think Hockenberry himself avoids exaggeration or hyperbole in this article?
2. What is the nature of the "new form of political activity" (¶ 9) that Hockenberry
   says is exemplified in the Palestinian *intifada* movement, and what does he suggest
   are its virtues? What's your view of those virtues?
3. What dangers, if any, do you think might result from the kind of breakdown of the
   nation-state that Hockenberry says electronic technologies can facilitate?

Social Policy for Cyberspace

Dale Spender

Access and Equity

Dale Spender (b. 1943) is a feminist scholar, writer, teacher, and consultant from Australia. She is co-founder of the database WIKED (Women's International Knowledge Encyclopedia and Data) and founding editor of the Athene Series and Pandora Press, commissioning editor of the Penguin Australian Women's Library, and associate editor of the Great Women Series (United Kingdom). Her many books include *Man Made Language* (Routledge & Kegan Paul, 1980), *For the Record: The Making and Meaning of Feminist Knowledge* (Women's Press, 1985), and *Writing a New World: Two Centuries of Australian Women Writers* (Penguin Books, 1988). This selection, like "Gender Bending" in Chapter 2, is from her recent book *Nattering on the Net: Women, Power and Cyberspace* (Spinifex, 1996).

C yberspace might be a virtual creation, but it is a reality that is here to stay. And my attitude towards it is pragmatic. 1

Given that I have to learn to live with the cyberworld, I want the best possible outcome that can be realised. This means that I want to be involved—along with countless others—in the decision-making process of shaping the information infrastructure. I want national forums set up, public discussion organised, working parties created to determine priorities. I want some indication that there are plans to use the technology to improve the quality of life for all human beings; I don't want to see it used (or misused) to enhance the lives of the few at the expense of the many. 2

At the moment, most of the forums in which cyber-policy is being made are exclusionary. White, professional, English/American-speaking males have got the floor: and they are focusing primarily on technological issues—or pornography, property, and privacy problems. (A survey of *Wired* indicates that these are the hot topics.) It is easier to talk about the latest "toys" and to defend the concept of "free speech" for the boys, than it is to address the major social and political questions which go with the new technologies; it is the human factor that now demands attention. 3

No matter the source, some of the relevant data are already available. Despite the ideal potential of the new technologies to create a global, egalitarian community, a virtual world without barriers or divisions, the scene down on the ground is strikingly different. In ways we can appreciate and ways we do not yet fully comprehend, the real people in the real world are being divided up into the information-rich and poor: the "master minds" and those who are "kept in the dark." 4

In the United States, the wealthiest nation on earth, "many working-class children have little access to computers in or outside the classroom: for many children [in the USA] and other countries, life is about just trying to live."[1] Even with the projected reduction in the price of hardware, the cost of becoming connected remains just too great for many average families in the First World.

> **The real people in the real world are being divided up into the information-rich and poor: the "master minds" and those who are "kept in the dark."**

Technology enthusiasts might see the present personal computer as another form of the Model-T Ford, and predict that there will soon be one in every home. But without extraordinary measures this is not a likely scenario. There are households still without television: and even more households without telephones. Even in the USA (not to mention countries other than the richest one on earth), there is a significant percentage of people without a home.

Another issue which must be considered is that the more advanced the technology is in the First World, the more difficult it will be to live, work, and communicate in the Third World, which has no such resources. And the further the Third World will be removed from the centres of wealth and influence.

Yet the solution is not so simple as giving computers to the poor (a proposal that enjoyed a brief spin from the leader of the US Republican Party in the House of Representatives).

In countries where children are dying of starvation, where there is little or no health care and no clean water, it borders on the obscene to talk about the pressing need for information infra-structure. It might even be awkward, if not impos-sibly difficult, in life-threatening circumstances, to convince the poor of the desirability or necessity of such a technological solution. It could be taken as yet another version of Marie Antoinette's derisory contribution: "Let them eat cake!"

> **In countries where children are dying of starvation, where there is little or no health care and no clean water, it borders on the obscene to talk about the pressing need for information infrastructure.**

The Indigenous people of Australia are a case in point. With 20 percent of Aboriginal children in the Top End suffering from malnutrition, and liv-ing in an environment where they have no decent housing, sanitation, or health provision, the recom-mendation that everyone should have a computer could appear as more a sign of con-tempt than a social justice policy.

---

[1]Cheris Kramarae, 1995, "A Backstage Critique of Virtual Reality," in Steven G. Jones (ed.), *Cybersociety,* Sage, Newbury Park, Calif., p. 53.

This does not mean that Aboriginal people should *not* have computers; if comput- 11
ers are the medium of the future, then there is every reason for every member of the
Indigenous community to have their own.

But this assumes a country in which a government wants its citizens to be con- 12
nected to the information superhighway. Not all nations will be in this category. There
are going to be authoritarian regimes (such as China) where one of the last things that
officialdom will see as desirable is for the population to have ready access to on-line
information.

> Chinese scholars and students are using the Net to send messages which the authorities are
> powerless to restrict . . . "There's no way you can technically prevent individuals from
> accessing the Internet," the Beijing representative for the US telecom company Sprint, Mr
> Ben Chan, says. "But China can set rates that are prohibitive for individual users."[2]

WITS [Women, Information Technology and Scholarship] women attending the 13
UN Conference for Women in Beijing (1995) have drafted a recommendation which
they want the UN to adopt. It is to make access to information a human right. This will
help to put access and equity in cyberspace on the international agenda. As an extension of the aim of universal literacy, universal "informacy" could be readily accommodated by UN policy. It could provide a platform for assessing the implication of the
international division between the information-rich and the information-poor.

The possibility of the global *village,* where everyone can have a say, is as yet a 14
long way off. Currently we have the technology enthusiasts who declare that the
Internet will be coming soon to every village in the world, at a price that all can
afford. But the social and political reality is very different. With so many international, national, local—and familial[3]—inequalities in existence, the cyber-sociolo-
gists' consensus is that there will be an even bigger gap between the information
haves and have-nots.

Even in First World countries, there is much talk these days about a growing 15
underclass, a social group which is cut off from the benefits of society. The homeless, the hungry, the unemployed, uninsured, unregistered—and *uninformed.* These
are the people who are not "in the know," who have no means of participating in the
public life of the community. In some respects, the situation is not so different from
the industrial revolution, where another underclass was created. Bitter division and
class struggles developed; it took violence, campaigns, trade union organisation,
and an evolving system of regulations to provide a semblance of social justice and
harmony.

Today, when so much energy is being focused on looking forward, it might also 16
pay to take a look backwards. Those who don't know their history are liable to repeat
the mistakes of the past. . . .

---

[2]Paul Harrington (in Hong Kong), 1995, "Cybersurfers Enjoy Anarchy," *The Australian,* 11 April, p. 37.

[3]Even with the television, the most powerful figure in the household generally gets to choose the programs; and when it comes to computers, it is the male more than the female who gets to monopolise the
machine. To the point where one of the excuses put forward by the girls of MLC Melbourne for not doing
their homework was that their brothers had taken their laptops and wouldn't let the girls use them.

The social and political consequences now demand more attention than the tech- 17
nological advances. We don't have to give up the ideal of the global village, the electronic community where everyone can be consulted. But we have to do much more to
realise the possibility. Priority needs to be given to research and policies which actually examine and deal with the impact that the new technologies are having on human
beings, globally and nationally and locally.

SECOND THOUGHTS

1. Spender writes, "Despite the ideal potential of the new technologies to create a
   global, egalitarian community, a virtual world without barriers or divisions, the
   scene down on the ground is strikingly different" (¶ 4). What is the reality, according to Spender?
2. Why does Spender think the suggestion that everyone ought to have or be provided
   with a computer "could appear as more a sign of contempt than a social justice policy" (¶ 10)? To what extent do you agree?
3. Do you agree with Spender that social and political consequences of the global village ought to take precedence over technological advances? She mentions issues
   such as malnutrition, decent housing, and sanitation. What priorities do you think
   should be assigned to these or other issues? What emphasis should policymakers
   give to electronic resources? To what extent do you think information technologies
   can help promote, rather than compete with, other social priorities?

Africa: The Unwired Continent

Rory J. O'Connor

Rory J. O'Connor (b. 1957) is Washington correspondent for the *San Jose Mercury News,* covering technology policy issues. Previously he was a technical writer and a reporter on high technology and business for various trade publications. This article originally appeared in 1996 in the business section of the *Mercury News,* which serves the Silicon Valley area.

Africa, once called "the dark continent" because of its inaccessibility to physical exploration by Westerners, is still inaccessible today, both by residents and outsiders via the virtual world.

It is perhaps the most stark example of the gulf between haves and have-nots, far more widespread than the pockets of rural and inner-city America that are mere dirt roads on the information highway. In Africa, most of a continent is off-line.

If the situation is not improved, experts say, Africa risks drifting further apart from a world that has grown to rely on computer technology and networks for economic progress, information exchange, and delivery of vital services like health care and education.

"It's the same thing as not having a port in the 1600s, or a railroad in the 1900s," said Larry Irving, assistant secretary of Commerce and head of the National Telecommunications Information Administration. "So if your economy isn't developing now, and you don't have access to the basic infrastructure of the information highway, you won't grow."

But any initiative to improve Africa's lot in the information revolution must 5 address a host of problems.

Government control of telephone systems in most countries has slowed installation of phone service and kept prices high. The region's largely rural population is too costly to wire, and there is no electrical power grid to run Western-style technical systems. And money to import modern technology is scarce in places where people are desperate for life's basics: food, shelter, clothing, medicine.

"It does add up to a dismal situation," said Raymond Akwule, a Nigerian citizen who is professor of communications at George Mason University in Virginia. "The question is whether there is enough telecommunications, as determined by Africans themselves, to promote their economic development, to fulfill the dreams they have for themselves."

GROUPS WORRY ABOUT ACCESS TO AGRICULTURAL, HEALTH DATA

The problem has focused the attention of many non-profit groups on how to get Africa connected. The groups are worried that Africans won't have access to the global information grid that is helping other third-world countries make progress in agriculture by giving them access to climate data and information on new farming techniques, or in health care by using computer links to connect doctors to sick people in remote areas.

The prospect that Africa may not figure into the telecommunications equation alarms the Clinton administration, which has made the development of the so-called Global Information Infrastructure a priority in its foreign policy. The United States sees Africa as a potential market for U.S.-made telecommunications gear—and as a future market for other U.S. goods and services once the continent's economy is bootstrapped by the technology.

Vice President Al Gore, in a videotaped address to a meeting of communications   10
ministers in Johannesburg, South Africa, in mid-May, committed the United States to a five-year, $15 million effort to connect sub-Saharan Africa to the information highway.

Called the Leland Initiative, the State Department program will offer consulting and training to African governments, hoping to serve as a bridge between U.S. telecommunications suppliers and those governments.

"We want to open up policy doors and promote an investment climate that works and then get out of the way," said Lane Smith, project officer in the Africa Bureau of the U.S. Agency for International Development. USAID is directing the Leland project.

FINDING WAYS TO CONNECT LEAST-CONNECTED PLACES

Any attempts to connect Africa represent an immense undertaking.

Sub-Saharan Africa—49 of the continent's 55 countries, excluding the five nations on the Mediterranean and the Republic of South Africa—is the least-connected place on earth. Even by the standards of other developing nations, the region has almost nothing in the way of phone lines, personal computers, and Internet connections.

The contrast between the haves of developed countries like the United States and the have-nots of sub-Saharan Africa is stark when it comes to access to phone lines, the predominant method of connecting to the Internet.

Sub-Saharan Africa—49 of the continent's 55 countries, excluding the five nations on the Mediterranean and the Republic of South Africa—is the least-connected place on earth.   15

Telephone access in the United States is nearly universal: 94 percent of all households enjoy telephone service, with a total of more than 150 million telephone lines installed nationwide, one line for each 1.67 people. There are millions of cellular phones in use, and they work in most populated areas of the nation.

In developing Africa, whose population of 550 million people is more than twice that of the United States, there is an average of one phone line for every 217 people. But for most people, the reality is much worse. More than 72 percent of the populace lives in rural areas where, in some places like Chad, each phone line serves an average of 800 people. If that formula were true in a Bay Area town like Los Gatos, for example, there would only be 38 phone lines for the entire city's 30,000 residents.

Even in other communications-poor areas of the developing world, the situation is better. India, for example, has 900 million people and 10 million phone lines, a per-capita concentration more than twice as large as Africa's.

"There are more telephone lines in Manhattan than in sub-Saharan Africa," Irving, of the National Telecommunications Information Administration, said.

The effort to create a world that is truly connected via communication links such as the Internet and the telephone faces a huge challenge in the 48 countries that comprise Sub-Saharan Africa. Here are per-capita ratios of telephone lines and personal computers in the United States and the five Northern Africa countries, South Africa and Sub-Saharan Africa.

Country/Region	Telephone lines/ per 100 people	PCs/per 100 people
United States	61	40
Northern Africa	4.23	0.1
South Africa	9.24	2.1
Sub-Saharan Africa	0.46	NA

* Northern Africa consists of Algeria, Egypt, Libya, Morocco & Tunisia
NA — Not Applicable because the ratio was negligible
Source: World Bank and International Monetary Fund
Cleveland Lee—Mercury News

LONG WAIT, HIGH PHONE BILLS TYPICAL IN MANY URBAN AREAS

The problems do not end in some of the more urbanized cities that do offer their citizens   20
access to phone lines. Getting the companies to string a line to your home or office—or figuring out what a call will cost—can be daunting. People in some countries can wait for 11 years for the government telephone agency to install a phone in their home or office, professor Akwule said. When they do arrive, the cost of using the phones could lead less affluent residents into bankruptcy—especially for people using hotel phones or calling internationally.

"Everywhere I go on the continent, people know that things have to improve," said Akwule, who publishes a bimonthly magazine, *Africa Communications*. "When I make a call from Nigeria, you can pay as much as $15 a minute, depending on where you make the call. In Zaire, it's $14 a minute. In Uganda, it's $8. The businesses who reside there complain about this on a daily basis."

One main reason, according to Akwule: International phone calls from many African countries often must be funneled through former colonial powers, because the phone systems are remnants of that era. Thus, a company in France or Germany may earn a slice of every international call that leaves a given country.

If telephone lines are scarce, then computers are all but nonexistent.

By the end of 1996, there probably will be more than 108 million PCs installed in the United States, one for every 2.5 people, according to International Data Corp. Business use is incredibly widespread, and nearly 40 percent of the nation's households own at least one computer. But in Africa, only two of the 49 countries have enough PCs that statisticians can even offer a ratio, largely because people in most countries can't afford them.

"Computers are rather expensive given the per-capita income of the country," said   25
Daniel Hagan, commercial consular with the Ghana Embassy in Washington.

In 1994, Ghana's 16.9 million people had an annual per-capita income of just $320—and just six Internet host computers, according to the International Telecommunication Union in Geneva. In Namibia, with per-capita income of $1,920, there are 11 hosts.

GOVERNMENTAL CONTROL, TECHNOLOGICAL IGNORANCE

But cost isn't the only factor. Governmental control of telecommunications is another, as is a lack of understanding of the technology.

Professor Akwule recalled a trip to Ethiopia where he was allowed to bring in his laptop computer—but had his cellular phone confiscated at the border, because he could not place a call with it as a customs inspector demanded. That is because there was no cellular service available there.

In some countries, one cannot import a modem, making it impossible for the average user to connect to the Internet, according to project officer Smith of USAID.

"You find in Africa a total lack of computer culture," said Wendy D. White, pro-   30
gram director at the National Research Council, which has conducted 16 case studies of computer introduction in African countries. "There are no spare parts. There are no magazines. There's no *PC World* you can subscribe to."

Without that knowledge or infrastructure, companies that want to set up an Internet service can wind up negotiating with government ministers who don't use the technology, don't understand it, and are reluctant to let a foreign company introduce the service. That, in turn, can make the business of telecommunications in Africa too time-consuming, costly, and frustrating for the company to persist.

EXPERTS SAY INTERNET GOALS MUST BE IN AFRICAN CONTEXT

But experts insist the situation can't correctly be measured by Western standards, or seen as a problem of "catching up" to developed nations like the United States or Western Europe. The goal of getting Africa on the Internet, they say, has to be viewed in terms of plans African countries have for their own development, and solving their internal problems.

In some cases, the goal is as simple as letting rural farmers use computers to learn the price for their agricultural goods in the city, so they can strike a better deal with wholesalers.

So far, though, such markets haven't been that attractive to big U.S. telecommunications providers, because they are busy exploiting the explosive domestic market.

"Nobody wants to go over to Africa and set up an Internet service provider busi-   35
ness, because the U.S. is growing so fast," Smith said.

> **Experts insist the situation can't correctly be measured by Western standards, or seen as a problem of "catching up" to developed nations like the United States or Western Europe.**

Internet providers, like a Netcom or America Online, also are unlikely to be able to enter Africa and sell the kind of complex, ubiquitous infrastructure of fiber-optic cables, copper lines, and network routers found in the United States. With far less capital, lack of electricity in many rural areas—and less demand for services—the kind of wired system used in the United States isn't well-suited for Africa.

Wireless phone systems and computer networks are much more viable, because they eliminate the huge cost of laying cables and stringing wires.

Technology, though, often takes a back seat to politics in getting Africa connected.

"The real stumbling block is policy," said professor Akwule. "The lack of information and the lack of education of the effect of the policies they need to take is more of a stumbling block than you know."

That can be everything from governments that view control of telecommunica- 40 tions as a means of maintaining power, to countries that can't sort out the technical data and sales pitches to reach consensus on what kind of system to build, to countries that are unwilling to let go of the revenue they derive from controlling the telecommunications market.

"You've got to get people to open up their markets," Irving said. "It's going to take efforts on a global basis to open up markets, and it has to be government to government, because telephones are cash cows for some countries."

Some countries are moving toward privatization of their telecommunications ministries and courting outside investment.

"We have opened it up to private-sector competition and are looking for a company that will buy out (state-run) Ghana Telecom," commercial consular Hagan said. "Our telecom sector has been quite modified in the last couple of years, and it is quite an improvement."

Government ministries in the country have been on a path to computerization since 1986, and most offices now have computers, although not the most modern models, he said.

"Africans tend to be very cautious about this," Akwule said. "But within the next 45 year, I predict that most of the African countries will have some form of Internet access or another. It's hard to believe we will still be talking about introducing the Internet into Africa."

← SECOND THOUGHTS

1. What are the major barriers to improving access to new technologies in Africa, according to O'Connor's article? Which barriers seem to be the most formidable?
2. What solutions and strategies for "wiring" Africa are proposed in the article, and which do you think are most promising?
3. Based on this article, how important do you think it is for Third World countries to develop advanced electronic technologies? What priorities would you assign for scarce resources?

Birth of a Nation in Cyberspace

John C. Rude

John C. Rude (b. 1941) is a freelance writer and educational consultant. He is co-founder and secretary of the Thirst for Learning Foundation, which supports schools in developing countries. Rude served as a Peace Corps volunteer in Eritrea in the 1960s, as a member of the African-American Institute team that monitored the 1992 Ethiopian elections, and as a consultant for the Eritrean ministry of education in 1995. This article, based on his experience in the Horn of Africa, originally appeared in 1996 in *The Humanist* (<www.infidels.org/org/aha/publications/humanist.html>), published by the The American Humanist Association, and was updated by the author for inclusion in *Composing Cyberspace*. According to its editors, *The Humanist* "applies humanism—a naturalistic and democratic outlook informed by science, inspired by art, and motivated by compassion—to broad areas of social and personal concern."

I n the tiny new nation of Eritrea, East Africa, an experiment in government is under 1 way. An important adjunct to this experiment is the concept of virtual community, as practiced by 3000 Eritrean citizens who "inhabit" Dehai, the cyberspace version of their newly independent country.

Thomas Keneally, author of *Schindler's List,* described Eritrea as the "laboratory 2 for the emergent nation-state." Comparing Eritrea—which gained its independence from Ethiopia in 1991 after a bloody 30-year struggle—to the United States of the eighteenth century, Keneally asked in a speech in Palo Alto in October 1994: "If it happened once before in 1776, why is it so farfetched to believe that the rebirth of democracy is happening again today in Eritrea?" The American revolutionaries suffered without the tools of global communications, but happily the Eritreans have no such handicap.

Eritrea is a sliver of land along the Red Sea coast, about the same size (36,170 3 square miles) as Maine, with about the same population (3.5 million) as New Zealand. Running completely counter to the common image of a chaotic, degenerate Africa, Eritrea is a country with a vision and strong sense of identity, forged in merciless battles with Soviet-backed Ethiopian troops. Although the modern infrastructure of the former Italian colony was destroyed, the protracted guerrilla war brought out the best in the Eritrean people. They learned to be completely self-reliant, to work together harmoniously with no thought except the ultimate goal of victory. While the international media ignored or misread the Eritrean struggle for independence, the fighters (who eventually made up the entire population) created a new culture, a mosaic of traditional beliefs, battlefield pragmatism, and political ideology from East and West.

After the collapse of Ethiopia's brutal Marxist regime in 1991, Eritrea scheduled a   4
referendum on independence. On May 24, 1993, the people voted overwhelmingly
(99.6 percent) for independence, and the governing party began preparation for a constitutional convention in 1996.

Enter Dehai (a word in the Tigriña language which roughly translates to "news   5
from home") in 1993, six months after the referendum. A group of Eritrean-American
scholars working at U.S. universities watched with envy as their associates formed spe-
cial-interest Listservs and created home-pages on the World Wide Web. Finally, Martin
Roscheisen, a German graduate student at Stanford University, set up an Eritrean newsgroup. Eritreans throughout the United States began to communicate with one another.

Now Dehai operates globally on every continent. Paradoxically, the Internet barely   6
connects with Eritrea because the country's phone system is still too low-tech for the
data traffic generated by Dehai's 3,000 enthusiastic correspondents. The African
Development Bank recently funded new technology for Ethiopia and Eritrea which
allowed Dehai to actually get its "news from home" in 1996.

Participation in Dehai is similar to any other Internet newsgroup. Messages are chaotic,   7
unpredictable, and, on occasion, over-the-edge provocative. The wide dispersion and
background of members lends an atmosphere of cacophony, especially when members
lapse into their native language to use proverbs. Dehai membership includes Ph.D.s,
homemakers, college students, businesspeople, doctors, and government employees.
Each member has a dual identity—Eritrean first and American, British, Canadian,
Swedish, or German second—and many have dual citizenship as well. English is the
primary language of the network, but many Dehaiers (as they call themselves) use idiosyncratic English. Dauntless, they plunge into the Net with heartfelt poems, complex
arguments, and stories full of twists and puns.

The eloquence of many Dehai postings derives from the situation their writers find   8
themselves in. To be an Eritrean overseas is to live in isolation, separated from other
Eritreans and one's homeland. For some, it has been decades since they've been able
to return home, and they've only heard from afar about the dramatic changes since
independence in 1993. Those who plan trips back to their newly independent homeland
are free with their emotions. Hidaat Ephrem wrote of her anticipation of her first trip
back to Eritrea's capital, Asmara, in 1994:

> When the morning air of Asmara brushes across my cheeks for the first time on my arrival,
> what words can possibly describe how I will feel? Anticipation alone has become such an
> experience, I cannot wait for the real moment. Most of the nights are sleepless now, I check
> and recheck my shopping list. Do I have enough? Did I forget someone? Can I remember
> Asmara the way I went around when I was a kid, or will I need a tour guide? It would kill
> me if I required a guide!

Hidaat anticipated the sadness that would accompany her on her trip home. She
recalled the death of her mother, just months before the final victory of Eritrea's guerrilla forces:

> She won't be ululating at the airport like other mothers. What words can describe the void
> and sadness that is steady in my heart as I kiss a cold stone that has become her home now.

. . . I have only four weeks in Eritrea to balance a lifetime of chaos and somehow find some new perspective for the future.

Eritreans in the worldwide diaspora number more than 800,000. Many—in partic-   9
ular the highly educated ones represented in Dehai's membership—possess a clear sense of their roles in history. During 60 years of Italian colonial rule, the Eritrean people accommodated European behavior and technology in ways that their Ethiopian neighbors to the south never did. Through contacts with maritime traders on the Red Sea and caravans from the Sudan, Eritreans have long been sensitized to Arabic cultures, although they do not consider themselves Arabs (a topic discussed with some heat on Dehai). Christianity was established in the Eritrean highlands in the fourth century and Islam in the seventh century. The two faiths have coexisted peacefully in Eritrea ever since, even while Crusades and Jihaads raged throughout North Africa and the Middle East.

During the Cold War, the politics of petroleum made Eritrea, with its easy access   10
to oil shipping lanes in the Red Sea, a pawn in the chess match being waged between the superpowers in the Horn of Africa. Distracted by their grandiose plans for Ethiopia, Somalia, and the Sudan, the "players" alternately forgot Eritrea or sacrificed the nation in endless moves and countermoves.

The armed struggle for independence, which began in 1961, completely trans-   11
formed—and almost obliterated—the pastiche of cultures that made up the old Eritrea. As depicted in Keneally's novel *To Asmara,* Eritrea's war for independence was a search for the lost soul of a people who had served as doormats for too many others, for too many years. Eritrean men and women had to dredge up courage and perseverance they never knew they had. They had to forget the past, distrust their friends, forgive their enemies, and believe the impossible, year after discouraging year, for an entire generation.

In a nation with only 2 percent of the U.S. population, more Eritreans were killed in combat—65,000—than American soldiers were killed in Vietnam. One-third of Eritrea's guerrilla fighters were women. Most mothers lost a son—or daughter. Except for a few younger Eritreans who entered graduate studies after independence, nearly all members of Dehai left Eritrea at some point during the protected 30-year struggle. The memories of this difficult transition were described by Issaias Yrgaw after he arrived in England: 12

In a nation with only 2 percent of the U.S. population, more Eritreans were killed in combat—65,000—than American soldiers were killed in Vietnam. One-third of Eritrea's guerrilla fighters were women.

The mothers say, "Go, go, my son, you will be safe anywhere but here." And they watch them leave in their blossoming years, full of excitement. They do not like looking back yet. The mothers choke at the thought of not being able to see them grow into manhood. . . . Time ticks away immeasurably as they struggle to get from country to country, to find a place where their plight will be understood, adapting to new cultures and learning alien languages. They have joined the army of refugees that roam from one corner of the planet to the other, fleeing the violence of crazy colonels kept in power by respectable governments. They are a new breed of world citizens whose eternal nightmares are passports, visas, airport bureaucracies, and stay permits. Their perennial problem is to try to explain the inexplicable: they dearly love their country, painfully miss their beloved families, and yet plead not to be sent back there.

The mothers have gone through a thousand nightmares and they have always lived to see the morning. Will they this time? They do not like this question. Instead an old Eritrean saying fills their thoughts: "Do not hurry the night, the sun will always rise for its own sake."

Finally, in 1993, the sun burst forth with a new Eritrea—a country which now has   13
safe streets, no guns, and competent leaders who work for virtually no pay because there is little money for salaries. As Eritreans around the world discovered each other on the Net, they became a Greek chorus for the unfolding drama of their nation's birth.

Dehaiers have enthusiastically joined in a worldwide debate on the content of the new   14
Eritrean constitution. The debate in cyberspace parallels one taking place in constitutional committees, attended by delegates who meet periodically in Eritrea, as well as in major cities in Europe and North America. Since some members of the constitutional commission actively present their views on Dehai, while others silently "lurk," the virtual debate and the real one overlap.

Eritreans are completely at home in the give and take of constitutional debate. If   15
anything, they are too democratic—meetings called for mundane decisions often consume hours of discussion. The Italians discovered during their years as colonial masters of Eritrea that the day-to-day affairs of people are regulated by village laws which pre-date the Renaissance. Since most of these laws were transformed into proverbs—even today, village children can quote from memory hundreds of ancient rules—it was impossible for Italian fascism (or Ethiopian Marxism) to take root in Eritrea. Citizens not only learn the law, they use it to determine who will be elected elders, how to handle property disputes, who receives inheritances, and to answer other questions vital to the community. Blessed with democratic traditions matched only by the Swiss, it is understandable that the "citizens" of Dehai faced the drafting of their nation's first constitution with the utmost gravity.

Three questions in particular were the subject of heated online debate: 16

- What should the role of religion be, and how will religious freedom be protected?
- How will women's rights be assured in a traditionally male-dominated, patriarchal society?
- How will traditional laws and practices be integrated into a constitutional democracy?

The first question—the role of religion—is a matter of great delicacy. Each morn-   17
ing in Eritrea's larger towns, the sun is greeted by cathedral bells and the call of the *muezzin.* Together, they make a reassuring harmony. There is a tradition of mutual respect, rather than tension, between Christianity and Islam that survived attempts by Haile Selassie, the British military administration, and the Italian colonists to use

divide-and-conquer tactics. Although Christians are now more numerous in government positions, Christians do not dominate Muslims, who constitute 50 percent of the population and control many sectors of the economy. After 30 years of life together in trenches and on battlefields, the bonds between Eritrea's Christians and Muslims are stronger than ever.

Two outside sources, radically opposed to each other but moving inexorably 18 across Eritrea's borders, threaten this religious amity. They are the forces of Western secularism and Islamic fundamentalism. Religious values are too precious to both Christians and Muslims for the populace to willingly push faith to the margins in a completely secularized state. But Eritrea is an island nearly surrounded by a sea of Muslim societies—Yemen, Somalia, Djibouti, Saudi Arabia, and, most threateningly, Sudan.

The following dialogue between Kebire Ahmed (a Muslim) and Afeworki Paulos 19 (a Christian) suggests how carefully the drafters must tread when freedom of religion is addressed in the Eritrean constitution:

Kebire: "The doctrine which has been held out by bigots of all sects, when condensed into few words and stripped of rhetorical disguise, is simply this: 'I am in the right, you are in the wrong. When you are the stronger, you ought to tolerate me; for it is your duty to tolerate truth. But when I am the stronger, I shall persecute you; for it is my duty to persecute error.' The above is a very forceful argument; I hope it is wrong when applied to Eritreans; if not, it is our duty to prove the principle wrong."

Afeworki: "The crucial point is that, in a multireligious society like ours, the state should remain secular and should not intervene in religious activities unless there is a danger to public order or national security. This is, of course, the standard separation of state and church/mosque. But what happens when religion also regulates relationships between individuals—as Sharia (Muslim customary law) does? In other words, what if there is a conflict between individual rights that the state guarantees and the application of a religious law? Unless one assumes that Sharia is just when it comes to gender equality, I see a potential conflict between constitutionally guaranteed rights and Sharia law."

Kebire: "In my presentation, I stated the obvious fact that religious association is voluntary. The person who joins the religion then assumes that its laws are just. If the person doesn't sanction or believe in the justice of the [religious] laws, then it is obvious—that person shouldn't join or be part of that religion; and those laws don't apply to him/her. Thus, Dr. Afeworki, the word *assumes* in your statement is the only possibility. I can't visualize a person seeing a religious (or nonreligious) law as unjust and still being a member of that organization. Nonetheless, as you stated, a conflict may arise if the organization interferes or imposes its laws on others (nonmembers)."

Afeworki: "Sharia deals with marriage, divorce, and inheritance, among other things. This leads us to the question of women's rights issues. I am not saying

Sharia is unjust to women; I am simply asking for more discussion on the subject, particularly from our Muslim brothers and sisters."

The challenge of the Eritrean constitution, like the American one, is how to permit 20 religious faiths to flourish without letting the government be overwhelmed by insistent demands from popes, mullahs, or preachers. If the Eritreans are successful in translating their traditions of tolerance into laws, they will be one of the first nations in Africa to make this all-important leap into civil order.

If charting a role for religion in the new constitution seems complicated, gender 21 issues are even more complex and volatile. Traditional roles for women in village society were (and, in large measure, remain) elevated only slightly above the oxen used to plow the fields. Because human labor is such a large part of Eritrean farming, women perform innumerable and essential tasks. In small pastoral villages (where most Eritreans live), girls are seldom spared to attend school. Courtship and marriage rituals are decidedly unbalanced in favor of men. Large dowries are paid at weddings, and brides are used as bargaining chips for alliances between families and villages. In some rural areas, female circumcision is still practiced.

To further complicate matters, sexual practices are restrictive in some ethnic 22 groups and relaxed in others. One group, the Kunama, has a matrifocal system, while nearby tribes practice partriarchal polygamy.

Traditional gender values are under assault from the *Maeda* culture—the prag- 23 matic and egalitarian social codes developed during Eritrea's war for independence. Women veterans, many of whom were wounded in battle, are demanding equal roles in the new society. Another source of ferment are Westernized expatriates who are returning home. Asked whether she would accept a marriage arranged by her parents in the traditional manner, Jodit, an Eritrean-American college student who lives in southern California, replied, "If I think he's the right man for me, I'll pop the question myself." Such liberated attitudes would be profoundly shocking to older Eritreans, who will have to deal with them in coming years as returning youths set the social agenda.

The Dehai dialogue on gender issues has been forthright and, at times, amusing. 24 Adey Fisseha, a woman, wrote: "We have to accept the fact that women are people. No buts, no ifs. If there is anyone who believes that women are not people or not equal with men, my suggestion is simple: he should pack and leave Eritrea."

Ghidewon Asmerom, a man, said in response: "Although I may agree with your 25 solution of kicking anyone who failed to protect the rights of women out of the country, I doubt that it would be an effective policy proposal." Senai Asefaw, a male student at Yale, elaborated: "I think Ghidewon's idea of kicking out everyone who doesn't support women's rights is a little too harsh. It would leave Eritrea almost devoid of men and with a substantially reduced female population as well. I wouldn't have anyone to visit when I go home!"

The gender debate centers around the question of whether or not the constitution 26 should include explicit language to protect women's rights. Dehai's women have weighed in with their opinions in unprecedented numbers. The majority, represented in the quotes which follow, are skeptical that gender equity can simply be legislated in a nation like Eritrea.

Sewit from Connecticut: "In terms of policy, to bridge the gap that exists between women and men at present, affirmative action may be a good political gesture. But as we all know well, the oppression of women has its roots in the family and in the socialization process. The individual person's attitudes, ideals, values, and practices have to change before equality between the sexes can be realized."

Zega from Stanford University: "I was wondering how articulating women's rights in the constitution will change anything? Are we tackling a traditional belief of men's superiority and women's inferiority? If so, how are most Eritrean men back home going to understand the idea of equality, an idea that has been fed into us by living in Western societies? They have lived this lifestyle for so long, how can any of us expect them to change, if they see nothing wrong with it?"

Adda from New Jersey: "When discussing Christianity and gender, it would not matter a great deal if there were a law giving women equal rights. Although the constitution would give us the right and the leverage to fight this battle, the most difficult battle that we have at hand is the one where we, women, have to change people's belief that *men are dominant.* How do we go about doing that? I feel that we have to empower ourselves first through education and become part of the process to change the existing belief."

Zebiba from New Jersey: "Although the American Constitution strictly forbids discrimination by gender, till today the ERA [Equal Rights Amendment] has not been passed. American women constantly find themselves hitting a 'glass ceiling' when climbing up the corporate ladder. Although Eritrea has far to go in terms of building companies and corporations and industries, it is best to address this issue of gender inequality before such industries get firmly established. The most effective and proper way is to pay attention to the education of women, keeping tabs on whether they are taught to downplay their abilities or are given the same opportunities as men in school."

This small sample conveys the impression that Dehai's women, writing in comfort 27 far away from highland villages, resonate more with American feminism than their own culture. But other writers, like Rahel and Maaza, struggle to find the seeds of equality within their Eritrean experience.

Rahel from Boston: "I think there should be a concerted effort at empowering women economically. If cultural emancipation of women is closely tied to an increase in their earning power, it will be much easier to get people to endorse it. Maybe the biggest challenge in this fight is to figure out how to bring about these changes without ripping our society apart. As others have pointed out, the job has been made a lot easier because of the price paid by our *tegadelti* [combatant] sisters. However, when I hear how some of them are now feeling out of place, considered 'too independent' and 'unmarriageable' etc., I am reminded of the long task ahead."

Maaza from Dayton, Ohio: "In gender equality, Eritrean men and women need to take on the responsibility individually and collectively to continue aspects of our culture (and, yes, even religious beliefs) that are workable for us and revise those that are not. As adults we know what is right and wrong! Treating the opposite gender with respect and equality that one would want for himself/herself takes courage and self-confidence; to see that it adds much more to one's happiness and overall well-being requires time. . . . If Eritreans can team together, regardless of gender differences, fight for 30 years, and achieve liberation, gender equality issues should be an extension of that effort—liberation for all its citizens."

The men of Dehai joined in the debate on women's rights, clearly (in most 28 cases) supporting the egalitarian agenda put forth by women writers. The problem of religious traditions bothered Ghidewon, who is an acknowledged expert on Eritrean customs.

"I have to say that I have yet to find a major religion in Eritrea that's truly pro-women. There are none. Nil, zero, *bado*. Holy books of both Christianity and Islam have negative words and phrases that we cannot run from. It will be only fair to ourselves and to God to admit those negative aspects and proceed. What can be more ironical than when men try to play with words to convince people that this or that religion is better in the treatment of women. For heaven's sake, let the major religions of the world first give women equal rights in running the affairs of the religions before coming and preaching the equality of the holy books, which doesn't exist! Let's face it: many of the religions we know are for men, of men, and by men."

Many contributors to this debate favored explicit language guaranteeing gender 29 equity. One writer, Daniel from Connecticut, saw an opportunity for Eritrea to set a new course for other countries, including the United States: "Look how long it took for women and blacks in the United States to be legally and politically viable under a Constitution that presumably had ensured this heritage to them. The Constitution had to be amended more than once to be inclusive of these major groups of the U.S. populace. . . . The point is that as long as you don't spell out who is entitled to the benefits of a given constitution or democracy, you can always deny these benefits to sectors of your population. What does it hurt to be so inclusive up front? Is not the outcome, on the whole, going to be positive? I'm not sure how many countries have gender specific language in their constitutions, but the number must be small. Herein is an opportunity, therefore, for Eritrea to take the lead on this issue in the democracies of the world."

The opposing view, which did not prevail when Eritrea's constitution was finally 30 drafted, was set forth by Esmael from New York: "As much as I agree with the philosophy and principle of full equality under the law for women and all oppressed ethnic and/or religious groups in Eritrea, I do not believe that a constitutional provision specifically designed for such groups is wise or warranted. In order for a constitution to meet the test of time, it must be gender, ethnic, and religion neutral. Programs to promote the advancement of designated groups within society are not a constitutional issue but, rather, the responsibility of the deliberative legislative body that may be established by the constitution. Various social-political issues will come to the forefront and recede over the years, and it is imperative that any document crafted as a constitution must be flexible enough to embrace such issues. By establishing specific provisions for such groups, either in the original document or by amendment, we may restrict the options of future lawmakers."

There can be little doubt that "Virtual Eritrea," as practiced among the members of Dehai, fulfills Thomas Keneally's definition of a "laboratory for the emergent nation-state." The question that remains is whether widely scattered Eritreans who have access to computers can influence an entire nation—a country described in the May 31, 1994, *Wall Street Journal* as an "oasis of civility" and a "model for the rest of Africa"?

There can be little doubt that "Virtual Eritrea," as practiced among the members of Dehai, fulfills Thomas Keneally's definition of a "laboratory for the emergent nation-state."

I put this question to several Dehai members and received an affirmative response, qualified but enthusiastic. Hidaat Ephrem, a poet and writer from Seattle, responded: "I first joined Dehai out of curiosity to see what Eritreans gathered through an electronic medium might have to say to each other. I found out quickly that Dehai is home to a large number of intellectual Eritreans with different backgrounds and skills, bound together by the love of their country. I have since made many friends. Though I haven't met them in person yet, the bond we share is very intimate and personal, which has been instrumental in having us work together on many projects with an easy and caring spirit."

The projects have been ambitious and strategically significant, including book collections, reforestation projects, and support for Eritrea's only institution of higher education, Asmara University. Dehaiers established a women's rights fund and committed themselves to a scholarship fund for Eritrea's elementary schools. Last, but by no means least, has been the vigorous debate on constitutional issues that culminated in a new Eritrean constitution in 1997.

Beyond these good works—perhaps the most significant accomplishment of all— is the supercharged learning community which is being created and sustained by Dehai's members. Omer Mohammed Kekia, one of Dehai's facilitators, writes: "The primary strength of Dehai is that it has facilitated the bringing together of Eritrean academics and professionals in different parts of the world. This coming together might attain a critical mass to make a difference in the reconstruction of Eritrea. At the moment, at least a good number of Dehai members have a good appreciation of the challenges facing us as a new nation. Dehai helped a lot in this respect."

Amanuel Melles, a marine biologist living in Toronto, echoes Omer's optimistic view of the impact the network will have on Eritrea's development: "The common denominator in Dehai is the interest members have about Eritrea. I strongly believe that this interest could be translated into a practical contribution to the development of Eritrea. In fact, by the time I joined Dehai, I realized that members had been active in projects and activities which are of help to Eritrea. I have the feeling that Dehai is slowly becoming and will be a significant component of Eritrea's development, especially in the educational sector."

Ironically, the qualities that make Dehai an effective community may have little to   36
do with the convenience of technology. Omer Mohammed Kekia noted the similarities
between interaction on Dehai and his nostalgic recollections of home: "As a friend once
said, Dehai is a second home. Living in the industrialized world where life moves in the
fast lane, there is little room for socialization and personalized contact, like a relaxed
evening in a friend's house or in a local bar or tea room or in the shop of a friend, like
people do in places like Eritrea. Dehai gives us that atmosphere."

One cheer for technology, then, and save the other two for the resourcefulness and   37
traditional sense of community among the Eritrean people. In this case, it is the mes-
sengers rather than the medium who provide the message.

On May 24, 1995, I sat with another member of Dehai and a group of 300 Eritreans   38
in Los Angeles, celebrating the second anniversary of Eritrea's independence. Those
who sat at our table (all members of the same family) peppered us with questions about
Dehai. They were indifferent to the technical details of cyberspace; they wanted to know
who was saying what and how life was progressing in Virtual Eritrea. In the best African
oral tradition, they eagerly wanted to share the news. This was a hopeful sign to me. The
network had passed beyond the boundaries of the computer playground into a world of
people who were singing, dancing, and praying for a peaceful future.

A speaker interrupted our chatter, asking everyone to sing Eritrea's new national   39
anthem. Despite a lively band and song sheets in front of them, the gathered Eritreans
stumbled over the unfamiliar words. I felt embarrassed for them, since I had been raised
on lusty renditions of "The Star-Spangled Banner" and "America, the Beautiful." Then it
hit me: it's not the voices or even sincerity that evokes the patriotism of people—it is
their deeds. I envied the new beginning that capricious history had given to the Eritreans.

← SECOND THOUGHTS

1. Rude writes that the example of Eritrea runs "completely counter to the common
   image of a chaotic, degenerate Africa" (¶ 3). How common is that image in your
   experience? Collect and analyze some examples of how Africa is portrayed in newspapers or magazines, on TV, or on the Internet. How does Rude's portrayal of
   Eritrea compare to these other examples?
2. Rude quotes a large selection of specific postings to Dehai. What is he trying to
   show with each example or set of examples? How might you analyze these examples in further depth? For example, how do you see the participants' dual identities
   (as Eritrean and American, British, Swedish, etc.), their elite social status, or their
   idiosyncratic use of English manifested in their messages?
3. Based on this article, how would you describe the relationship between Dehai or
   "Virtual Eritrea" and real-life Eritrea? Thomas Keneally suggests that Dehai is a
   "laboratory for the emergent nation-state" (¶s 2 and 31). How do you think that laboratory looks similar and different in the cases of the three major controversies discussed by Rude—religion, women's rights, and traditional laws and practices?

⧉ DISCUSSION THREADS

re: Rodriguez and Hockenberry

1. Richard Rodriguez and John Hockenberry both offer speculative visions about a transnational global future—one driven by cultural and religious changes and one driven by technology. In what other ways do you think these two visions differ? What values or assumptions do Rodriguez and Hockenberry seem to share?

re: Hockenberry and Spender

2. Based on the essays by John Hockenberry and Dale Spender, contrast the positions of a "global village optimist" and a "global village pragmatist." With which position do you agree more, and why?

re: Hockenberry, Spender, and O'Connor

3. How do you think Dale Spender and Rory J. O'Connor would respond to John Hockenberry's claim that "today it is possible to address the world without having to show a passport that defines you culturally, ethnically or religiously"(¶ 15)?

re: Hockenberry and Rude

4. John Hockenberry writes that "the most stunning tactical victory of the [*intifada*] uprising was the creation of this virtual/digital nation" (¶ 9) of fax machines. How would you compare the nature, purpose, and effects of this Palestinian virtual nation with the Virtual Eritrea described by John C. Rude?

re: O'Connor and Rude

5. To what extent do you think the article by Rory J. O'Connor contributes to what John C. Rude calls "the common image of a chaotic, degenerate Africa"(¶ 3)?

re: The Global Village

6. Based on the selections in this chapter, your other reading, and your own experience, what is your opinion about the ideal of a global village? How would you define that ideal, using criteria suggested by this chapter's writers or creating your own criteria? What roles do you think emerging technologies should play in this global village? What's your judgment about the potential for such an ideal to become a reality?

🔗 RESEARCH LINKS

- *For direct links to listed Internet sources, additional reading selections and questions online, plus updates and supplementary Web resources, see* **Composing Cyberspace Online** *at <www.mhhe.com/socscience/english/holeton/>.*

■ *For a complete set of research tools for the Internet—including the most useful search strategies, directories, and conventions for documenting online sources—see McGraw-Hill English Composition at <www.mhhe.com/socscience/english/compde/>.*

1. Compare and contrast how the relationships between technology and religion are portrayed by Richard Rodriguez in this chapter, Charlise Lyles ("CyberFaith: Promoting Multiculturalism Online") in Chapter 3, p.113, and Joshua Cooper Ramo ("Finding God on the Web") in Chapter 4, p.180. To extend your comparison, locate sources mentioned by those writers and conduct other research in the library and on the Internet.

2. Find out how electronic technologies have continued to affect the Palestinian-Israeli conflict or peace process since John Hockenberry's essay was published in the spring of 1995. You might focus on the uses of technology made by a particular group—the PLO or *intifada* participants (Hockenberry's focus); the Israeli government, army, or settlers in former Arab territories; or international supporters of one side or the other. Alternatively, conduct research to test Hockenberry's claim that currently in the Middle East, Russia, India, or other places "wealth is slowly being channeled away from defense and military infrastructure and into the information infrastructure."

3. Dale Spender cautions that, despite recent global village rhetoric, the agenda and decision-making process for social policies in cyberspace are dominated by "white, professional, English/American-speaking males." Do you agree with her that the discussion of cyber-social issues ought to be widened beyond techie talk, pornography, property, and privacy? How so? Pick a global issue of concern to you, and investigate how that issue is portrayed in the media and on the Internet, how wide the range of discussion about it is, and who seems to be dominating the discussion or setting the agenda. Spender mentions *Wired* magazine, the source of several articles in this book, as one perpetrator of the elite, white, male, American bias that she criticizes. Consider focusing a research paper on how an influential publication such as *Wired* (back issues are available in many libraries or online at <www.hotwired.com/>) portrays a certain issue or set of issues, or make a comparison between two or three different publications.

4. Conduct research to update progress of the Leland Initiative or other electronic infrastructure projects in Africa discussed by Rory J. O'Connor. On the Internet, you might start at the U.S. Agency for International Development Web site for the Leland Initiative at <www.info.usaid.gov/regions/afr/leland/index.htm> and get some perspective on Third World development in general from the United Nations Food and Agriculture Organization at <www.fao.org/>. In the library, try to find out what critics have said about particular projects in newspapers, magazines, and journals. On campus, try to interview professors, graduate students, or international students with an interest in African development. You might focus your research on evaluating the success of a specific project or approach in a particular African nation. Is the funding sufficient or unrealistic? Also, consider what the different players have to gain and lose; for example, in the case of the Leland Initiative, what are its relative advantages and disadvantages for (a) the people of sub-Saharan Africa and (b) U.S. and transnational telecommunications companies?

5. You can find out more about Dehai and Eritrea from the organization's home page at <www.primenet.com/~ephrem/>, which includes a FAQ (Frequently Asked Questions) document, the Dehai Charter, a number of public information documents and links, and links to other Internet sources about Eritrea. (To join Dehai yourself, you must be recommended by a member and approved by the board if you're not an Eritrean citizen.) As a research topic, you might explore the current status of real-life Eritrea and its new constitution, the document so vigorously debated in the article by John Hockenberry.

*Seeking
Knowledge in
the Information
Age*

Information Overload and New Media

CATHY© 1997 Cathy Guisewite. Reprinted with permission of UNIVERSAL PRESS
SYNDICATE. All rights reserved.

At the dawn of the 21st century, few people in the world's affluent countries are immune from information overload—the feeling of being overwhelmed by information from a variety of sources. TV and radio are ubiquitous, movies and videotapes are more popular than ever, and book publishing is still thriving. TV is probably more to blame than personal computers for a steady decline in the readership of daily newspapers—but computers are increasingly a major source of information overload as more and more people conduct business, do research, communicate, find entertainment, and even get their news online.

In the Cathy Guisewite cartoon, the vehicle of information overload suffered by protagonist Cathy seems, through the first six panels, to be her computer screen. She appears besieged by the steady stream of "instant information" on every possible subject. When she marvels in the sixth panel that all this information is available "through one tiny phone line," our suspicion that she's connected to the Internet by a modem is confirmed. The surprise of the last panel, of course, is that she's been talking to her mother on the telephone, not surfing the Net.

Although regular readers of *Cathy* know that her relationship with her mother is ambivalent, Cathy's apparent relief that her mother could perform the same functions as the busiest communication network in history dramatizes a larger anxiety many people feel about the information age. The Internet is scary, while mothers are, if sometimes difficult, at least something familiar and nonthreatening. Perhaps, Guisewite may be suggesting, the condition of information overload isn't as new a phenomenon as we think. Or perhaps we should be even more worried about Cathy's mother, who's evidently as overwhelming as a one-person Internet!

In any case, most people would agree that getting advice from one's mother is very different from getting advice from strangers on the Internet. But Cathy's summary of the barrage of information she receives would seem to describe both "media"—mothers and the Net—equally well. How much does the medium, and the context in which information comes to us, affect the content and our interpretation of that content? How do we sort through all this information to find what is useful for us? Put another way, what's the difference between information and knowledge? If information consists of separate, unconnected pieces of data—and knowledge means the application of selected information in a particular context, which requires some judgment, analysis, or interpretation—then how do new media affect the process of knowledge making?

Evidently we are not going easily into the Information Age, not without a good deal of anxiety and nostalgia, and this chapter explores some of that anxiety as well as some of the promise of new information technologies. In a short story first published in 1941, Argentinian writer Jorge Luis Borges imagines a future in which print and book technology is taken to its logical extreme. Everyone lives in library cubicles with uniform shelves of books that, taken all together, contain all possible knowledge, yet the information available to any given individual is random; civilization appears to have reached a dead-end. Likewise, but with a focus on today's electronic information, humorist Dave Barry offers "proof that civilization is doomed" in the form of sites on the World Wide Web that he finds especially silly or absurd. Literary critic Sven Birkerts, who fears the consequences of declining interest in books, makes a more sober and intellectual argument that the transition from print media to electronic media is "reweaving the entire social and cultural web" in negative ways.

Concluding this chapter, Shyamala Reddy and Brenda Laurel offer more hopeful visions of how the search for knowledge is being reshaped by emerging technologies. Reddy, though she believes that books are here to stay, argues that new media such as CD-ROMs, electronic books, and hypertext offer compelling advantages in the ways they make information available. Laurel, a virtual reality (VR) researcher and video game designer, suggests that VR and other emerging media "open new possibilities for experience," especially for artistic expression. If such new art forms are designed thoughtfully, according to Laurel, the result could even be "a quantum leap in human evolution."

Before you read these selections, you might think first about your own impressions of new media and your own experiences with information overload; for example, consider the following:

1. How barraged or overwhelmed with information do you feel? What kinds and range of information are you exposed to in your daily life? From what various sources and media does this information arrive?
2. Do you know how to readily find information that you need for school, work, or other purposes? What media do you find most useful for finding that information and putting it to use?
3. How much do you read outside of school or work? What do you read? How much TV do you watch? How much time do you spend playing video games or using computers? Do you think you read books, paper magazines, and newspapers less or more than the generations preceding or following you?
4. If you've ever experienced the same piece of work or similar content in two or more different media—for example, a movie based on a book you've read, paper and CD-ROM versions of a textbook, or the paper and Web version of *Composing Cyberspace*—consider how each medium affects your experience of the work.
5. Talk to someone who's tried a virtual reality (VR) game at an arcade or someone familiar with the "holodeck," a fictional VR environment from the "Star Trek" TV series. What are your impressions, from these reports or other reading you've done, of the current state and possibilities for VR?
6. If you have access to a computer lab, classroom, or networked computers equipped with electronic discussion software, discuss with fellow readers any of the issues raised here.

The Library of Babel

Jorge Luis Borges

Jorge Luis Borges (1899–1986) was an Argentinian fiction writer, poet, essayist, longtime director of the National Library of Argentina, and professor of English and American literatures at the University of Buenos Aires. His books of fiction that have been translated into English include *The Aleph and Other Stories 1933–1969* (E.P. Dutton, 1970) and *Doctor Brodie's Report* (E.P. Dutton, 1972). "The Library of Babel" first appeared in English in the collections *Ficciones* (Grove Press, 1962) and *Labyrinths: Selected Stories and Other Writings* (New Directions, 1962) and was originally published in Spanish in *The Garden of Forking Paths* (Sur, 1941). This version, from *Labyrinths,* was translated by James E. Irby.

> By this art you may contemplate the variation of the 23 letters . . .
> *The Anatomy of Melancholy,*
> part 2, sect. II, mem. IV

The universe (which others call the Library) is composed of an indefinite and per- 1
haps infinite number of hexagonal galleries, with vast air shafts between, surrounded by very low railings. From any of the hexagons one can see, interminably, the upper and lower floors. The distribution of the galleries is invariable. Twenty shelves, five long shelves per side, cover all the sides except two; their height, which is the distance from floor to ceiling, scarcely exceeds that of a normal bookcase. One of the free sides leads to a narrow hallway which opens on to another gallery, identical to the first and to all the rest. To the left and right of the hallway there are two very small closets. In the first, one may sleep standing up; in the other, satisfy one's fecal necessities. Also through here passes a spiral stairway, which sinks abysmally and soars upwards to remote distances. In the hallway there is a mirror which faithfully duplicates all appearances. Men usually infer from this mirror that the Library is not infinite (if it really were, why this illusory duplication?); I prefer to dream that its polished surfaces represent and promise the infinite. . . . Light is provided by some spherical fruit which bear the name of lamps. There are two, transversally placed, in each hexagon. The light they emit is insufficient, incessant.

Like all men of the Library, I have travelled in my youth; I have wandered in 2
search of a book, perhaps the catalogue of catalogues; now that my eyes can hardly decipher what I write, I am preparing to die just a few leagues from the hexagon in which I was born. Once I am dead, there will be no lack of pious hands to throw me

over the railing; my grave will be the fathomless air; my body will sink endlessly and decay and dissolve in the wind generated by the fall, which is infinite. I say that the Library is unending. The idealists argue that the hexagonal rooms are a necessary form of absolute space or, at least, of our intuition of space. They reason that a triangular or pentagonal room is inconceivable. (The mystics claim that their ecstasy reveals to them a circular chamber containing a great circular book, whose spine is continuous and which follows the complete circle of the walls; but their testimony is suspect; their words, obscure. This cyclical book is God.) Let it suffice now for me to repeat the classic dictum: *The Library is a sphere whose exact centre is any one of its hexagons and whose circumference is inaccessible.*

There are five shelves for each of the hexagon's walls; each shelf contains thirty-five books of uniform format; each book is of four hundred and ten pages; each page, of forty lines, each line, of some eighty letters which are black in colour. There are also letters on the spine of each book; these letters do not indicate or prefigure what the pages will say. I know that this incoherence at one time seemed mysterious. Before summarizing the solution (whose discovery, in spite of its tragic projections, is perhaps the capital fact in history) I wish to recall a few axioms. 3

First: The Library exists *ab aeterno.* This truth, whose immediate corollary is the future eternity of the world, cannot be placed in doubt by any reasonable mind. Man, the imperfect librarian, may be the product of chance or of malevolent demiurgi; the universe, with its elegant endowment of shelves, of enigmatical volumes, of inexhaustible stairways for the traveller and latrines for the seated librarian, can only be the work of a god. To perceive the distance between the divine and the human, it is enough to compare these crude wavering symbols which my fallible hand scrawls on the cover of a book, with the organic letters inside: punctual, delicate, perfectly black, inimitably symmetrical. 4

Second: *The orthographical symbols are twenty-five in number.*[1] This finding made it possible, three hundred years ago, to formulate a general theory of the Library and solve satisfactorily the problem which no conjecture had deciphered: the formless and chaotic nature of almost all the books. One which my father saw in a hexagon on circuit fifteen ninety-four was made up of the letters MCV, perversely repeated from the first line to the last. Another (very much consulted in this area) is a mere labyrinth of letters, but the next-to-last page says *Oh time thy pyramids.* This much is already known: for every sensible line of straightforward statement, there are leagues of senseless cacophonies, verbal jumbles and incoherences. (I know of an uncouth region whose librarians repudiate the vain and superstitious custom of finding a meaning in books and equate it with that of finding a meaning in dreams or in the chaotic lines of one's palm. . . . They admit that the inventors of this writing imitated the twenty-five natural symbols, but maintain that this application is accidental and that the books signify nothing in themselves. This dictum, we shall see, is not entirely fallacious.) 5

---

[1]The original manuscript does not contain digits or capital letters. The punctuation has been limited to the comma and the period. These two signs, the space and the twenty-two letters of the alphabet are the twenty-five symbols considered sufficient by this unknown author. (*Editor's note.*)

For a long time it was believed that these impenetrable books corresponded to past 6 or remote languages. It is true that the most ancient men, the first librarians, used a language quite different from the one we now speak; it is true that a few miles to the right the tongue is dialectal and that ninety floors farther up, it is incomprehensible. All this, I repeat, is true, but four hundred and ten pages of inalterable MCV's cannot correspond to any language, no matter how dialectal or rudimentary it may be. Some insinuated that each letter could influence the following one and that the value of MCV in the third line of page 71 was not the one the same series may have in another position on another page, but this vague thesis did not prevail. Others thought of cryptographs; generally, this conjecture has been accepted, though not in the sense in which it was formulated by its originators.

Five hundred years ago, the chief of an upper hexagon[2] came upon a book as confusing as the others, but which had nearly two pages of homogeneous lines. He showed his find to a wandering decoder who told him the lines were written in Portuguese; others said they were Yiddish. Within a century, the language was established: a Samoyedic Lithuanian dialect of Guarani, with classical Arabian inflections. The content was also deciphered: some notions of combinative analysis, illustrated with examples of variation with unlimited repetition. These examples made it possible for a librarian of genius to discover the fundamental law of the Library. This thinker observed that all the books, no matter how diverse they might be, are made up of the same elements: the space, the period, the comma, the twenty-two letters of the alphabet. He also alleged a fact which travellers have confirmed: *In the vast Library there are no two identical books.* From these two incontrovertible premises he deduced that the Library is total and that its shelves register all the possible combinations of the twenty-odd orthographical symbols (a number which, though extremely vast, is not infinite): in other words, all that it is given to express, in all languages. Everything: the minutely detailed history of the future, the archangels' autobiographies, the faithful catalogue of the Library, thousands and thousands of false catalogues, the demonstration of the fallacy of those catalogues, the demonstration of the fallacy of the true catalogue, the Gnostic gospel of Basilides, the commentary on that gospel, the commentary on the

This thinker observed that all the books, no matter how diverse they might be, are made up of the same elements: the space, the period, the comma, the twenty-two letters of the alphabet. He also alleged a fact which travellers have confirmed: *In the vast Library there are no two identical books.* 7

---

[2]Before there was a man for every three hexagons. Suicide and pulmonary diseases have destroyed that proportion. A memory of unspeakable melancholy: at times I have travelled for many nights through corridors and along polished stairways without finding a single librarian.

commentary on that gospel, the true story of your death, the translation of every book in all languages, the interpolations of every book in all books.

When it was proclaimed that the Library contained all books, the first impression   8
was one of extravagant happiness. All men felt themselves to be the masters of an intact and secret treasure. There was no personal or world problem whose eloquent solution did not exist in some hexagon. The universe was justified, the universe suddenly usurped the unlimited dimensions of hope. At that time a great deal was said about the Vindications: books of apology and prophecy which vindicated for all time the acts of every man in the universe and retained prodigious arcana for his future. Thousands of the greedy abandoned their sweet native hexagons and rushed up the stairways, urged on by the vain intention of finding their Vindication. These pilgrims disputed in the narrow corridors, proffered dark curses, strangled each other on the divine stairways, flung the deceptive books into the air shafts, met their death cast down in a similar fashion by the inhabitants of remote regions. Others went mad . . . The Vindications exist (I have seen two which refer to persons of the future, to persons who perhaps are not imaginary) but the searchers did not remember that the possibility of a man's finding his Vindication, or some treacherous variation thereof, can be computed as zero.

At that time it was also hoped that a clarification of humanity's basic myster-   9
ies—the origin of the Library and of time—might be found. It is verisimilar that these grave mysteries could be explained in words: if the language of philosophers is not sufficient, the multiform Library will have produced the unprecedented language required, with its vocabularies and grammars. For four centuries now men have exhausted the hexagons . . . There are official searchers, *inquisitors.* I have seen them in the performance of their function: they always arrive extremely tired from their journeys; they speak of a broken stairway which almost killed them; they talk with the librarian of galleries and stairs; sometimes they pick up the nearest volume and leaf through it, looking for infamous words. Obviously, no one expects to discover anything.

As was natural, this inordinate hope was followed by an excessive depression.   10
The certitude that some shelf in some hexagon held precious books and that these precious books were inaccessible, seemed almost intolerable. A blasphemous sect suggested that the searchers should cease and that all men should juggle letters and symbols until they constructed, by an improbable gift of chance, these canonical books. The authorities were obliged to issue severe orders. The sect disappeared, but in my childhood I have seen old men who, for long periods of time, would hide in the latrines with some metal disks in a forbidden dice cup and feebly mimic the divine disorder.

Others, inversely, believed that it was fundamental to eliminate useless works.   11
They invaded the hexagons, showed credentials which were not always false, leafed through a volume with displeasure and condemned whole shelves: the hygienic, ascetic furor caused the senseless perdition of millions of books. Their name is execrated, but those who deplore the 'treasures' destroyed by this frenzy neglect two notable facts. One: the Library is so enormous that any reduction of human origin is infinitesimal. The other: every copy is unique, irreplaceable, but (since the Library is

total) there are always several hundred thousand imperfect facsimiles: works which differ only in a letter or a comma. Counter to general opinion, I venture to suppose that the consequences of the Purifiers' depredations have been exaggerated by the horror these fanatics produced. They were urged on by the delirium of trying to reach the books in the Crimson Hexagon: books whose format is smaller than usual, all-powerful, illustrated and magical.

We also know of another superstition of that time: that of the Man of the Book.   12
On some shelf in some hexagon (men reasoned) there must exist a book which is the formula and perfect compendium *of all the rest:* some librarian has gone through it and he is analogous to a god. In the language of this zone vestiges of this remote functionary's cult still persist. Many wandered in search of Him. For a century they exhausted in vain the most varied areas. How could one locate the venerated and secret hexagon which housed Him? Someone proposed a regressive method: To locate book A, consult first a book B which indicates A's position; to locate book B, consult first a book C, and so on to infinity. . . . In adventures such as these, I have squandered and wasted my years. It does not seem unlikely to me that there is a total book on some shelf of the universe;[3] I pray to the unknown gods that a man—just one, even though it were thousands of years ago!—may have examined and read it. If honour and wisdom and happiness are not for me, let them be for others. Let heaven exist, though my place be in hell. Let me be outraged and annihilated, but for one instant, in one being, let Your enormous Library be justified. The impious maintain that nonsense is normal in the Library and that the reasonable (and even humble and pure coherence) is an almost miraculous exception. They speak (I know) of the 'feverish Library whose chance volumes are constantly in danger of changing into others and affirm, negate and confuse everything like a delirious divinity.' These words, which not only denounce the disorder but exemplify it as well, notoriously prove their authors' abominable taste and desperate ignorance. In truth, the Library includes all verbal structures, all variations permitted by the twenty-five orthographical symbols, but not a single example of absolute nonsense. It is useless to observe that the best volume of the many hexagons under my administration is entitled *The Combed Thunderclap* and another *The Plaster Cramp* and another *Axaxaxas mlö.* These phrases, at first glance incoherent, can no doubt be justified in a cryptographical or allegorical manner; such a justification is verbal and, *ex hypothesi,* already figures in the Library. I cannot combine some characters

dhcmrlchtdj

which the divine Library has not foreseen and which in one of its secret tongues do not contain a terrible meaning. No one can articulate a syllable which is not filled with tenderness and fear, which is not, in one of these languages, the powerful name of a god.

---

[3]I repeat: it suffices that a book be possible for it to exist. Only the impossible is excluded. For example: no book can be a ladder, although no doubt there are books which discuss and negate and demonstrate this possibility and others whose structure corresponds to that of a ladder.

To speak is to fall into tautology. This wordy and useless epistle already exists in one of the thirty volumes of the five shelves of one of the innumerable hexagons—and its refutation as well. (An *n* number of possible languages use the same vocabulary; in some of them, the symbol *library* allows the correct definition *a ubiquitous and lasting system of hexagonal galleries,* but *library* is *bread* or *pyramid* or anything else, and these seven words which define it have another value. You who read me, are You sure of understanding my language?)

The methodical task of writing distracts me from the present state of men. The certitude that everything has been written negates us or turns us into phantoms. I know of districts in which the young men prostrate themselves before books and kiss their pages in a barbarous manner, but they do not know how to decipher a single letter. Epidemics, heretical conflicts, peregrinations which inevitably degenerate into banditry, have decimated the population. I believe I have mentioned the suicides, more and more frequent with the years. Perhaps my old age and fearfulness deceive me, but I suspect that the human species— the unique species—is about to be extinguished, but the Library will endure: illuminated, solitary, infinite, perfectly motionless, equipped with precious volumes, useless, incorruptible, secret.

I suspect that the human species—the unique species—is about to be extinguished, but the Library will endure: illuminated, solitary, infinite, perfectly motionless, equipped with precious volumes, useless, incorruptible, secret.   13

I have just written the word 'infinite.' I have not interpolated this adjective out of rhetorical habit; I say that it is not illogical to think that the world is infinite. Those who judge it to be limited postulate that in remote places the corridors and stairways and hexagons can conceivably come to an end—which is absurd. Those who imagine it to be without limit forget that the possible number of books does have such a limit. I venture to suggest this solution to the ancient problem: *The Library is unlimited and cyclical.* If an eternal traveller were to cross it in any direction, after centuries he would see that the same volumes were repeated in the same disorder (which, thus repeated, would be an order: the Order). My solitude is gladdened by this elegant hope.[4]   14

---

[4]Letizia Álvarez de Toledo has observed that this vast Library is useless: rigorously speaking, *a single volume* would be sufficient, a volume of ordinary format, printed in nine or ten point type, containing an infinite number of infinitely thin leaves. (In the early seventeenth century, Cavalieri said that all solid bodies are the superimposition of an infinite number of planes.) The handling of this silky *vade mecum* would not be convenient: each apparent page would unfold into other analogous ones; the inconceivable middle page would have no reverse.

← SECOND THOUGHTS

1. Draw a picture or diagram of a portion of the Library as described by the narrator; also, make a more detailed, close-up drawing of a single hexagonal gallery. Compare your drawings with those of other readers and discuss how you picture the Library similarly and differently. With your group or class, try composing a consensus drawing on a blackboard, whiteboard, or computer that represents your best understanding of the Library's appearance and structure.

2. What is the narrator's situation as he tells this story? What's the state of his physical health? What's he looking for, and what seems to be his motivation for telling the story? What's the condition of the human species?

3. The Library contains all possible books on all possible topics and, therefore, includes solutions (and false solutions) to all problems, yet people seem to have almost no chance of finding a particular piece of information they seek. What are people's various reactions to this situation, according to the narrator? With which reactions are you most sympathetic, and why?

4. What similarities and differences do you find between Borges's fictional Library and a real library? How does the fictional Library compare with your understanding of the Internet or World Wide Web?

5. What do you think Borges is trying to say in this story about the relationship between language and knowledge or meaning? How persuasive do you find the Library as an allegory for the universe or the human condition?

Selected Web Sites[1]

Dave Barry

At Last: Proof That Civilization Is Doomed

Dave Barry (b. 1947) is a syndicated humor columnist for the *Miami Herald,* where he won the Pulitzer Prize for Distinguished Social Commentary in 1988. His books include *Dave Barry Does Japan* (Random House, 1992), *Dave Barry Is Not Making This Up* (Crown, 1994), and *Dave Barry's Complete Guide to Guys* (Random House, 1995). This selection is from *Dave Barry in Cyberspace* (Crown, 1996).

A common criticism of the Internet is that it is dominated by the crude, the uninformed, the immature, the smug, the untalented, the repetitious, the pathetic, the hostile, the deluded, the self-righteous, and the shrill. This criticism overlooks the fact that the Internet also offers—for the savvy individual who knows where to look—the tasteless and the borderline insane.

I am thinking here mainly of the World Wide Web. Whereas much of the Internet relies strictly on text, the Web is multimedia; this means that if, for example, you're setting up a Web site devoted to exploring the near-universal human fear that a *Star Wars* character wants to consume your gonads, you can present this issue in both words *and* pictures (I'll have more on this issue later in this chapter[2]). You can also greatly advance the frontiers of scientific knowledge regarding Spam.

In researching this chapter, I spent many, many hours exploring the World Wide Web. My time was divided as follows:

Activity	Time Spent
Typing insanely complex Web addresses	2%
Waiting for what seemed like at least two academic semesters per Web page while the computer appeared to do absolutely nothing	93%

---

[1]I want to thank the good (weird, but good) people on the *alt.fan* group who suggested many of these sites.

[2]This is a good reason to stop reading this chapter right now.

Activity	Time Spent
Reading snippy messages stating that there is no such Web address	2%
Retyping insanely complex Web addresses	2%
Actually looking at Web pages	1%

As you can see, it can take quite a while for a Web page to appear on your screen. The reason for the delay is that, when you type in a Web address, your computer passes it along to another computer, which in turn passes it along to another computer, and so on through as many as five computers before it finally reaches the workstation of a disgruntled U.S. Postal Service employee, who throws it in the trash. So when browsing the Web, you will almost certainly encounter lengthy delays, which means that it's a good idea to have something else to do while you're waiting, such as reroofing your house.

Anyway, by virtue of being diligent and not having a real job, I was eventually able to get through to quite a few Web pages, and in this chapter I'm going to describe some of the more memorable ones. But before I do, I want to stress three points:

So when browsing the Web, you will almost certainly encounter lengthy delays, which means that it's a good idea to have something else to do while you're waiting, such as reroofing your house.

5

- All the pages described here are real; I did not make any of them up, not even the virtual toilet.
- What you see here represents just a teensy-tiny fraction of the thousands upon thousands of Web pages, with new ones being created constantly. Do not assume, from what you see in this chapter, that *all* Web pages are a total waste of time; the actual figure is only about 99.999997 percent.
- By the time you read this, you may not be able to visit all of these pages. I visited most of them in mid-1996; some of them may have since gone out of existence for various reasons, such as that their creators were recalled to their home planets.

But this chapter is not intended as an exhaustive list: I just want to give you an idea of some of the stuff that's out there. So fasten your seat belt, and let's visit some of the fascinating rest stops on the Information Superhighway. We'll start, appropriately enough, with:

THE TOILETS OF MELBOURNE, AUSTRALIA

http://minyos.xx.rmit.edu.au/~s9507658/toilet/

If you're thinking about taking a trip to Melbourne, Australia, the first question you ask yourself is: "What will the toilets be like?"

The answer can be found at this Web site, which offers *detailed* reviews of selected Melbourne-area toilets. Here are some actual excerpts:

- "What a great day for a drive! Mild weather. A nice lunch. A scenic walk. First-rate toilets."
- "The other notable thing about the toilets was the toilet paper holders. They were Bowscott continuous toilet paper holders that were actually positioned up high enough."
- "On the way we stopped at Eastland shopping centre—home of the best public toilets I have seen so far. They were clean, open, and the toilet roll holders were free moving. As with the Lysterfield Lake toilets, one of the basin-style urinals was positioned lower for kids. The hand dryer was fantastic too. It was a compact, automatic Mirage dryer. Even though it was much smaller than other hand dryers, it blew out plenty of hot air."

And that is not all: From this Web site, you can jump to some of the many, *many* other toilet-related Web sites, including a Virtual Public Restroom ("The Toilet of the Web"[3]), where you can write a virtual message and leave a virtual "poopie."[4]

GIANT COLLECTION OF VIOLA JOKES

http://www.mit.edu/people/jcb/viola-jokes.html

If you're like most people, you frequently remark to yourself: "Darn it! I have an 10 important business presentation to make today, and I would love to 'break the ice' by opening with a viola joke, but I don't know any fresh ones!"

Well, you will never have to make that statement again, not after you visit this Web page. This is a *huge* collection of viola jokes. I suppose it's possible that somebody, somewhere, has compiled an even *bigger* collection of viola jokes, but I seriously doubt that this could be done without the aid of powerful illegal stimulants.

Much of the viola-joke humor appears to be based on the premise that viola players are not the brightest or most talented members of the orchestra:

Q. How can you tell when a violist is playing out of tune?
A. The bow is moving.

Q. What do you call a violist with two brain cells?
A. Pregnant.

Some of the jokes are probably a lot more hilarious if you know something about classical music. I'm sure, for example, that many orchestra professionals slap their thighs when they hear this one:

---

[3]http://www.auburn.edu/~carltjm/restroom.html
[4]Don't ask.

Q. How do you get a violist to play a passage *pianissimo tremolando*?
A. Mark it "solo."

Ha ha! "Mark it 'solo'!" Whew!

Anyway, I was genuinely surprised by this Web page. I always thought of classi-   15
cal orchestras as somber operations where most of the musicians are very serious and
hunched over to the point of bowel disorder. I had no idea that there was this level of
wackiness, especially not in the string section. (The woodwinds, of course, are a different story; those dudes and dudettes are out of *control.*).

GUIDE TO CRACKERS

http://mathlab.sunysb.edu/%7Eelijah/cstuff/index.html

This is one of those ideas that you never in a million years would have had yourself, but
as soon as you see it, you smack your forehead and say: "Huh?"

This page features photographs of various types of crackers—Cheez-Its, Ritz Bits,
etc.—actual size. When you click on a cracker, you go to a page that gives you packag-
ing and nutritional information. You are also encouraged to donate crackers, especially
"rare and unusual crackers."

I am *sure* there is a good reason.

HUMAN TESTICLE CONSUMPTION:

Mr. T Ate My Balls

http://www.cen.uiuc.edu/~nkpatel/mr.t/index.html

Chewbacca Ate My Balls

http://www.cen.uiuc.edu/~nkpatel/chewbacca/index.html

There are some things in life that it is better to just not even think about, and one of
those things is the question of what, exactly, led to the creation of these pages.

In summary, these pages present pictures of Mr. T and Chewbacca expressing—by   20
means of comic book–style speech and thought balloons—the dramatic theme that they
would like to eat your testicles.

For example, in the opening scene of the "Chewbacca Ate My Balls" page, Chewbacca is thinking, "I wish I had some BALLS to munch on . . ." In the next scene, he is
thinking: "Your balls are MINE!!" And then, in a dramatic plot development reminiscent of the work of playwright Arthur Miller, Chewbacca thinks, "What? Mr. T already
got yours?"

These sites also feature a Guest Book, where visitors can leave comments. The
comments that I read were all very complimentary. People really respond to a universal theme like this. I myself had to lie down for a while.

THE SPAM CAM

http://www.fright.com/cgi-bin/spamcam

If you have the slightest doubt that the Internet is good for science, you should look at this page, and then you will have much more serious doubts.

This page is billed as "The page that seeks to answer the question: IS SPAM ORGANIC?" It presents close-up photographs of scientific experiments showing what happens when Spam and other types of foods are left sitting out for long periods of time. What happens is—get ready for a major scientific breakthrough—everything gets *really* disgusting.

For a while there was also a very popular Web site[5] set up by college students 25 wishing to determine what happens to Twinkies when they are heated with torches, dropped from tall buildings, etc.,[6] but when I tried to check it out, it had been closed down by lawyers. Perhaps by the time you read this book, it will be back in operation again. Or perhaps the entire Internet will have been closed down by lawyers. Or perhaps college students will have started dropping lawyers from tall buildings. You never know with the future.

PIERCING MILDRED

http://streams.com/pierce/

Who says there is no culture on the Internet? You will, after you visit this site. This is a game where you get to select a character—either Mildred or Maurice—and then you pierce that person's body parts, or decorate her or him with designer scars. Mildred and Maurice also sometimes get infected, so sometimes you have to purchase antibiotic ointment.

You may think this sounds like a fairly perverted game, but ask yourself: Is it *really* that different from Mr. and Mrs. Potato Head?

BANANA LABELS OF THE WORLD

http://www.staff.or.jp/whoiswho/ilkka/bananadir/bananalabels.html

If you thought that there were basically only a couple of types of banana labels, then a visit to this site will quickly convince you that you are a stupid idiot. This site presents pictures of hundreds of banana labels, including labels commemorating historic events such as the 50th anniversary of Miss Chiquita, not to mention a label from a Big

---

[5]http://www.owlnet.rice.edu/~gouge/twinkies.html
[6]It turns out that pretty much nothing happens.

Frieda's Burro Banana. This site will also direct you to *other* banana-label pages.[7] And you are invited to send in banana labels, including "virtual banana labels," which I assume means labels for virtual bananas. (My feeling about this is: fine, but they'd better not come out with virtual beer.)

WAVE TO THE CATS

http://hogwild.hamjudo.com/cgi-bin/wave

This is the perfect Web site[8] to show the skeptic who thinks you can't do anything useful or practical on the Internet. At this site, you can click on a button that activates a motor at a remote location; the motor is attached to a large fiberboard hand, which waves back and forth at some cats, if the cats happen to be in the room at the time. You can't actually *see* this; you just get the warm feeling of satisfaction that comes from knowing that you are causing a remote, simulated hand to wave at remote, possibly nonexistent cats. You also get a nice "Thank you for your wave" message from the Web page author, as well as his description of the way the cats usually react to the hand ("Master will stare at it when it moves; the other three cats, Callie, Mutant, and Katrina, just ignore it").

I know what you're thinking, but to my knowledge, there currently is no "Spay the   30
Cats" Web site.

TROJAN ROOM COFFEE MACHINE

http://www.cl.cam.ac.uk/coffee/coffee.html

If you go to this page, you can, merely by clicking your mouse, see, from anywhere in the world, an up-to-the-second video image of the coffee machine in the Trojan Room of the University of Cambridge Computer Laboratory in England. It would be virtually impossible to calculate the time that has been saved by disseminating this information via the Web, as opposed to previous methods.

CAPTAIN AND TENNILLE APPEARANCES

http://www.vcnet.com/moonlight/CTAPPEARANCES

This page lists upcoming personal appearances by the Captain and Tennille. Using this information, you can find out exactly where this veteran duo will be making their own special brand of musical magic so that you can arrange to be on the diametrically opposite side of the Earth when they perform "Muskrat Love."

---

[7]Of *course* there are other banana-label pages.

[8]This is one of many cool sites I found out about through the highly recommended Center for the Easily Amused, located at http://www.amused.com/

CURSING IN SWEDISH

http://www.bart.nl/~sante/enginvek.html

This is the most thorough on-line course in Swedish cursing that I am aware of. It is scholarly, well-organized, and professional-looking; and if your computer has sound, you can click on individual phrases, and your computer will curse at you in Swedish.

Here are some of the practical Swedish curses you can learn on this Web site (I swear I am not making these up):

Han var en jävel på att fiska.
He was bloody good at fishing.

Satan! Ungen pissade på sig!
Hell! The kid wet his trousers!

Pubkillarna var ena jävlar på att pissa.
The guys at the pub were masterly at pissing.

Jag tappade den jävla tvålen
I dropped the f**king soap.

Det vore himla roligt om du kom till festen.
It would be heavenly if you could take part in the party.

Kukjävel!
F**king f**ker!

Festen kommer att gå åt skogen!
The party will be a real flop!

And of course the one curse you *constantly* find yourself needing to express when-   35
ever you're in Sweden . . .

När jag blir av med gipset skall du få se på sjutton!
Just wait until I have gotten rid of the plaster!

DUTCH TRAFFIC SIGNS[9]

http://www.eeb.ele.tue.nl:80/traffic/warning-e.html

Without this site, I would never have known that the Dutch have a traffic sign that means "squalls."

---

[9]I found this site, along with many other excellent ones, at a *very* useful site called Useless Pages, http://www.chaco.com/useless/index.html. Check it out.

FEDERAL CORPSE SLICE PHOTOS

http://www.nlm.nih.gov/research/visible/photos.html

On this site you can see images taken from the government's Visible Human Project, in which two actual deceased humans, one male and one female, were frozen in gelatin and sliced into very thin slices for the benefit of science. I know what you're wondering: You're wondering where the government got the corpses. You will be relieved to learn that the answer is: not from the Internal Revenue Service Division of Taxpayer Compliance.

Or so they claim.

PEOPLE WITH TOASTERS

http://www.berksys.com/www/promotions/uNurtoaster.html

This page features photographs of people with their toasters.

FABIO

http://redwood.northcoast.com/~shojo/Fabio/fabio.html

This page features photographs of the romantic superstar mega-hunk Fabio with his   40
toaster.

No, seriously, the photographs depict the romantic superstar mega-hunk posing in a manner that reveals his deeply passionate sensitive innermost feelings about what a studmuffin he is. What makes this site great is that you can click on the photographs, and, if your computer has sound, Fabio will say things to you, such as "Your caress is my command." Apparently he doesn't realize that you're caressing him with a mouse pointer.

DEFORMED FROG PICTURES

http://www.mncs.k12.mn.us/frog/picts.html

One summer day in 1995 some students at the Minnesota New Country School were on a Nature Studies hike. They started catching frogs, and after a bit they noticed that many of the frogs did not appear to meet standard frog specifications in terms of total number of legs, eyes, etc. So the students started a Frog Project to study this phenomenon. If you visit this Web page, you can read about their work and see actual photographs of the frogs; this will help you to become more aware of the environment, pollution, and other important topics, unless you're the kind of sicko who just wants to look at deformed frogs.

MUSICAL SAND

http://www.yo.rim.or.jp/~smiwa/index.html

If you are interested in information on musical sand (and who is not?), this is really the only place to go. This Web site offers information in both Japanese and a language that is somewhat reminiscent of English. The introduction states:

> All information concerning Musical Sand in the world ("singing sand" on beach and "booming sand" in desert) will concentrate in this home pages. Singing properties of the sand is very sensitive to pollution, and that may be play a sensor for it.
>
> To my regret, musical sand is on the brink of a critical position to be exterminated. If cleaning air and sea however, musical sand plays wonderful sound with action of wind and wave for us. I make show you World of Musical Sand that Mother Nature polished by spending eternal time.

Think of it: Endangered sand!

If your computer has sound capability, you can actually listen to some singing sand. It is not easy, on the printed page, to describe the eerie, almost unearthly beauty of the sound that the sand makes; the best words I can come up with are "like a vacuum cleaner trying to suck up a dead cow." I for one would hate to see Earth lose a resource like this, and I hereby urge Sting and Willie Nelson to hold some kind of benefit concert.

If your computer has sound capability, you can actually listen to some singing sand.   45

EXPLODING WHALE

http://www.xmission.com:80/~grue/whale

On this site you can see pictures of the now-famous incident[10] in which the Oregon State Highway Division, attempting to dispose of a large and aromatic dead whale that had washed up on the beach, decided to—why not?—blow it up with half a ton of dynamite.

The theory was that the whale would be converted from one large unit into many small Whale McNuggets, which would then be eaten by seagulls. Unfortunately, this is not what happened. What happened was, following a massive blast,[11] large chunks of rotting whale blubber, some of them large enough to dent a car roof, rained down upon spectators several hundred yards away, and there was *still* an extremely large chunk of dead whale lying on the beach. This was not Seagull Chow. A seagull capable of eating this chunk would have to be the size of the Lincoln Memorial.

---

[10]About ten years ago, I saw a videotape of this incident, made by a local TV station. I wrote a column about it, and somebody unfamiliar with the copyright laws put that column on the Internet. The result is that for years now, people have been sending me my own column, often with notes saying, "You should write a column about this!"

[11]Talk about booming sands.

The moral here is, if another dead whale washes up on the beach in Oregon, the authorities should probably not turn the disposal job over to the State Highway Division. But if they do, I hope they sell tickets.

WORLD RECORD BARBECUE IGNITION

http://ghg.ecn.purdue.edu/oldindex.html

If this Web page doesn't make you proud to be an American, then I frankly don't know what will. This site presents the ultimate result of the effort by members of the Purdue University engineering department to see how fast they could get the barbecue charcoal ignited at their annual picnic. They started by blowing the charcoal with a hair dryer; then, in subsequent years, they escalated to using a propane torch, an acetylene torch, and then compressed pure oxygen.

At this point, they were lighting the charcoal very fast, but for these guys, "very fast" was not good enough. These guys had a dream, and that dream was to ignite their charcoal faster than anybody had ever done before. And thus they hit upon the idea of using liquid oxygen, the kind used in rocket engines. On this Web page you can see photos and video of an engineer named George Goble using long wooden handles to dump a bucket of liquid oxygen onto a grill containing 60 pounds of charcoal; this is followed by a fireball that, according to Goble, reached 10,000 degrees Fahrenheit. The charcoal was ready for cooking in *three seconds*.

Next time Oregon has a whale problem, maybe it should call *these* guys.

FLAMING POP-TART EXPERIMENT

http://www-personal.umich.edu/~gmbrown/tart/

It is a well-known scientific fact[12] that if you put a Kellogg's brand strawberry Pop-Tart into a toaster and hold the toaster lever down so that it can't pop up, after about five minutes, the Pop-Tart will turn into the Blowtorch Snack Pastry from Hell, shooting dramatic blue flames as much as a foot out of the toaster slots.

If you visit this Web page, you can see actual photos of an experiment demonstrating this spectacular phenomenon. I urge you, however, *not* to attempt to duplicate this experiment unless you are a trained science professional using somebody else's toaster, because we are talking about a powerful force with the potential for great destruction. We can only be grateful that the Nazis never learned how to harness it, although historians strongly suspect that they were working on it near the end.

Let me repeat that the Web sites described in this chapter represent just a tiny fraction of what's out there. What you really need to do is get on the Web[13] and start poking around for yourself. You'll quickly discover that what you've read about here exemplifies some

---

[12]This has been verified on the David Letterman show.

[13]Don't ask *me* how. I'm not an expert on computers; I only write books about them.

of the *saner* thinking going on. So go ahead! Get on the Web! In my opinion, it's WAY more fun than television, and what harm can it do?

OK, it can kill brain cells by the billions. But you don't *need* brain cells. You have   55
a computer.

⟵ SECOND THOUGHTS

1. Describe Barry's experience accessing and using the Web. Regarding both the technical process and the content he found, how would you compare Barry's Web chronicle with other descriptions you've heard or read, or with your own experience?

2. If possible, visit some of the Web sites Barry describes and compare your impressions. Beyond his humorous exaggeration, what serious points do you think Barry is trying to make about the Internet and the information it makes available? To what extent do you agree with those points?

3. Try classifying Barry's numerous examples into three or four main categories. What subjects or themes seem most interesting or amusing to Barry? What can you conclude about his particular sense of humor or social concerns, and how do those compare with yours?

Into the Electronic Millennium

Sven Birkerts

Sven Birkerts (b. 1943) is a literary critic and writing teacher in the master of fine arts programs at Bennington College and Emerson College (Vermont). His essays and reviews have appeared in the *New York Times Book Review, The Atlantic, Harper's,* and *The New Republic,* among other magazines and journals. His books include *An Artificial Wilderness: Essays on 20th-Century Literature* (William Morrow, 1987), *American Energies: Essays on Fiction* (William Morrow, 1992), and *Tolstoy's Dictaphone: Technology and the Muse* (McGraw-Hill, 1996). This selection is from *The Gutenberg Elegies: The Fate of Reading in an Electronic Age* (Faber & Faber, 1994).

S ome years ago, a friend and I comanaged a used and rare book shop in Ann Arbor, 1 Michigan. We were often asked to appraise and purchase libraries—by retiring academics, widows, and disgruntled graduate students. One day we took a call from a professor of English at one of the community colleges outside Detroit. When he answered the buzzer I did a double take—he looked to be only a year or two older than we were. "I'm selling everything," he said, leading the way through a large apartment. As he opened the door of his study I felt a nudge from my partner. The room was wall-to-wall books and as neat as a chapel.

The professor had a remarkable collection. It reflected not only the needs of his 2 vocation—he taught nineteenth- and twentieth-century literature—but a book lover's sensibility as well. The shelves were strictly arranged, and the books themselves were in superb condition. When he left the room we set to work inspecting, counting, and estimating. This is always a delicate procedure, for the buyer is at once anxious to avoid insult to the seller and eager to get the goods for the best price. We adopted our usual strategy, working out a lower offer and a more generous fall back price. But there was no need to worry. The professor took our first offer without batting an eye.

As we boxed up the books, we chatted. My partner asked the man if he was mov- 3 ing. "No," he said, "but I am getting out." We both looked up. "Out of the teaching business, I mean. Out of books." He then said that he wanted to show us something. And indeed, as soon as the books were packed and loaded, he led us back through the apartment and down a set of stairs. When we reached the basement, he flicked on the light. There, on a long table, displayed like an exhibit in the Space Museum, was a computer. I didn't know what kind it was then, nor could I tell you now, fifteen years later. But the professor was keen to explain and demonstrate.

While he and my partner hunched over the terminal, I roamed to and fro, inspect-   4
ing the shelves. It was purely a reflex gesture, for they held nothing but thick binders
and paperbound manuals. "I'm changing my life," the ex-professor was saying. "This
is definitely where it's all going to happen." He told us that he already had several good
job offers. And the books? I asked. Why was he selling them all? He paused for a few
beats. "The whole profession represents a lot of pain to me," he said. "I don't want to
see any of these books again."

The scene has stuck with me. It is now a kind of marker in my mental life. That   5
afternoon I got my first serious inkling that all was not well in the world of print and
letters. All sorts of corroborations followed. Our professor was by no means an isolated
case. Over a period of two years we met with several others like him. New men and
new women who had glimpsed the future and had decided to get out while the getting
was good. The selling off of books was sometimes done for financial reasons, but the
need to burn bridges was usually there as well. It was as if heading to the future also
required the destruction of tokens from the past.

A change is upon us—nothing could be clearer. The printed word is part of a ves-   6
tigial order that we are moving away from—by choice and by societal compulsion. I'm
not just talking about disaffected academics, either. This shift is happening throughout
our culture, away from the patterns and habits of the printed page and toward a new
world distinguished by its reliance on electronic communications.

This is not, of course, the first such shift in our long history. In Greece, in the time   7
of Socrates, several centuries after Homer, the dominant oral culture was overtaken by
the writing technology. And in Europe another epochal transition was effected in the
late fifteenth century after Gutenberg invented movable type. In both cases the long-
term societal effects were overwhelming, as they will be for us in the years to come.

The evidence of the change is all around us, though possibly in the manner of the   8
forest that we cannot see for the trees. The electronic media, while conspicuous in gad-
getry, are very nearly invisible in their functioning. They have slipped deeply and irrevocably into our midst, creating sluices and circulating through them. I'm not referring
to any one product or function in isolation, such as television or fax machines or the
networks that make them possible. I mean the interdependent totality that has arisen
from the conjoining of parts—the disk drives hooked to modems, transmissions linked
to technologies of reception, recording, duplication, and storage. Numbers and codes
and frequencies. Buttons and signals. And this is no longer "the future," except for the
poor or the self-consciously atavistic—it is now. Next to the new technologies, the
scheme of things represented by print and the snail-paced linearity of the reading act
looks stodgy and dull. Many educators say that our students are less and less able to
read, or analyze, or write with clarity and purpose. Who can blame the students? Everything they meet with in the world around them gives the signal: That was then, and
electronic communications are now.

Do I exaggerate? If all this is the case, why haven't we heard more about it? Why   9
hasn't somebody stepped forward with a bow tie and a pointer stick to explain what is
going on? Valid questions, but they also beg the question. They assume that we are all
plugged into a total system—where else would that "somebody" appear if not on the
screen at the communal hearth?

Media theorist Mark Crispin Miller has given one explanation for our situation in   10
his discussion of television in *Boxed In: The Culture of TV*. The medium, he proposes,
has long since diffused itself throughout the entire system. Through sheer omnipres-
ence it has vanquished the possibility of comparative perspectives. We cannot see the
role that television (or, for our purposes, all electronic communications) has assumed
in our lives because there is no independent ledge where we might secure our footing.
The medium has absorbed and eradicated the idea of a pretelevision past; in place of
what used to be we get an ever-new and ever-renewable present. The only way we can
hope to understand what is happening, or what has already happened, is by way of a
severe and unnatural dissociation of sensibility.

To get a sense of the enormity of the change, you must force yourself to imag-   11
ine—deeply and in nontelevisual terms—what the world was like a hundred, even
fifty, years ago. If the feat is too difficult, spend some time with a novel from the period. Read between the lines and reconstruct. Move through the sequence of a character's day and then juxtapose the images and sensations you find with those in the life of the average urban or suburban dweller today.

> **A communications net, a soft and pliable mesh woven from invisible threads, has fallen over everything. The so-called natural world, the place we used to live, which served us so long as the yardstick for all measurements, can now only be perceived through a scrim.**   12

Inevitably, one of the first realizations is that a communications net, a soft and pliable mesh woven from invisible threads, has fallen over everything. The so-called natural world, the place we used to live, which served us so long as the yardstick for all measurements, can now only be perceived through a scrim. Nature was then; this is now. Trees and rocks have receded. And the great geographical Other, the faraway rest of the world, has been transformed by the pure possibility of access. The numbers of distance and time no longer mean what they used to. Every place, once unique, itself, is strangely shot through with radiations from every other place. "There" was then; "here" is now.

Think of it. Fifty to a hundred million people (maybe a conservative estimate)   13
form their ideas about what is going on in America and in the world from the same
basic package of edited images—to the extent that the image itself has lost much of its
once-fearsome power. Daily newspapers, with their long columns of print, struggle
against declining sales. Fewer and fewer people under the age of fifty read them; computers will soon make packaged information a custom product. But if the printed sheet
is heading for obsolescence, people are tuning in to the signals. The screen is where the
information and entertainment wars will be fought. The communication conglomerates
are waging bitter takeover battles in their zeal to establish global empires. As Jonathan
Crary has written in "The Eclipse of the Spectacle," "Telecommunications is the new
arterial network, analogous in part to what railroads were for capitalism in the nine-

teenth century. And it is this electronic substitute for geography that corporate and national entities are now carving up." Maybe one reason why the news of the change is not part of the common currency is that such news can only sensibly be communicated through the more analytic sequences of print.

To underscore my point, I have been making it sound as if we were all abruptly   14
walking out of one room and into another, leaving our books to the moths while we set-tle ourselves in front of our state-of-the-art terminals. The truth is that we are living through a period of overlap; one way of being is pushed athwart another. Antonio Gramsci's often-cited sentence comes inevitably to mind: "The crisis consists precisely in the fact that the old is dying and the new cannot be born; in this interregnum a great variety of morbid symptoms appears." The old surely is dying, but I'm not so sure that the new is having any great difficulty being born. As for the morbid symptoms, these we have in abundance.

The overlap in communications modes, and the ways of living that they are associ-   15
ated with, invites comparison with the transitional epoch in ancient Greek society, cer-tainly in terms of the relative degree of disturbance. Historian Eric Havelock designated that period as one of "proto-literacy," of which his fellow scholar Oswyn Murray has written:

> To him [Havelock] the basic shift from oral to literate culture was a slow process; for cen-turies, despite the existence of writing, Greece remained essentially an oral culture. This culture was one which depended heavily on the encoding of information in poetic texts, to be learned by rote and to provide a cultural encyclopedia of conduct. It was not until the age of Plato in the fourth century that the dominance of poetry in an oral culture was challenged in the final triumph of literacy.

That challenge came in the form of philosophy, among other things, and poetry has   16
never recovered its cultural primacy. What oral poetry was for the Greeks, printed books in general are for us. But our historical moment, which we might call "proto-electronic," will not require a transition period of two centuries. The very essence of electronic transmissions is to surmount impedances and to hasten transitions. Fifty years, I'm sure, will suffice. As for what the conversion will bring—and *mean*—to us, we might glean a few clues by looking to some of the "morbid symptoms" of the change. But to understand what these portend, we need to remark a few of the more obvious ways in which our various technologies condition our senses and sensibilities.

I won't tire my reader with an extended rehash of the differences between the print   17
orientation and that of electronic systems. Media theorists from Marshall McLuhan to Walter Ong to Neil Postman have discoursed upon these at length. What's more, they are reasonably commonsensical. I therefore will abbreviate.

The order of print is linear, and is bound to logic by the imperatives of syntax.   18
Syntax is the substructure of discourse, a mapping of the ways that the mind makes sense through language. Print communication requires the active engagement of the reader's attention, for reading is fundamentally an act of translation. Symbols are turned into their verbal referents and these are in turn interpreted. The print engage-ment is essentially private. While it does represent an act of communication, the con-tents pass from the privacy of the sender to the privacy of the receiver. Print also posits

a time axis; the turning of pages, not to mention the vertical descent down the page, is a forward-moving succession, with earlier contents at every point serving as a ground for what follows. Moreover, the printed material is static—it is the reader, not the book, that moves forward. The physical arrangements of print are in accord with our traditional sense of history. Materials are layered; they lend themselves to rereading and to sustained attention. The pace of reading is variable, with progress determined by the reader's focus and comprehension.

The electronic order is in most ways opposite. Information and contents do not   19
simply move from one private space to another, but they travel along a network. Engagement is intrinsically public, taking place within a circuit of larger connectedness. The vast resources of the network are always there, potential, even if they do not impinge on the immediate communication. Electronic communication can be passive, as with television watching, or interactive, as with computers. Contents, unless they are printed out (at which point they become part of the static order of print) are felt to be evanescent. They can be changed or deleted with the stroke of a key. With visual media (television, projected graphs, highlighted "bullets") impression and image take precedence over logic and concept, and detail and linear sequentiality are sacrificed. The pace is rapid, driven by jump-cut increments, and the basic movement is laterally associative rather than vertically cumulative. The presentation structures the reception and, in time, the expectation about how information is organized.

Further, the visual and nonvisual technology in every way encourages in the user a   20
heightened and ever-changing awareness of the present. It works against historical perception, which must depend on the inimical notions of logic and sequential succession. If the print medium exalts the word, fixing it into permanence, the electronic counterpart reduces it to a signal, a means to an end.

Transitions like the one from print to electronic media do not take place without   21
rippling or, more likely, *reweaving* the entire social and cultural web. The tendencies outlined above are already at work. We don't need to look far to find their effects. We can begin with the newspaper headlines and the millennial lamentations sounded in the op-ed pages: that our educational systems are in decline; that our students are less and less able to read and comprehend their required texts, and that their aptitude scores have leveled off well below those of previous generations. Tag-line communication, called "bite-speak" by some, is destroying the last remnants of political discourse; spin doctors and media consultants are our new shamans. As communications empires fight for control of all information outlets, including publishers, the latter have succumbed to the tyranny of the bottom line; they are less and less willing to publish work, however worthy, that will not make a tidy profit. And, on every front, funding for the arts is being cut while the arts themselves appear to be suffering a deep crisis of relevance. And so on.

Every one of these developments is, of course, overdetermined, but there can be no   22
doubt that they are connected, perhaps profoundly, to the transition that is underway.

Certain other trends bear watching. One could argue, for instance, that the entire   23
movement of postmodernism in the arts is a consequence of this same macroscopic shift. For what is postmodernism at root but an aesthetic that rebukes the idea of an historical time line, as well as previously uncontested assumptions of cultural hierarchy.

The postmodern artifact manipulates its stylistic signatures like Lego blocks and makes free with combinations from the formerly sequestered spheres of high and popular art. Its combinatory momentum and relentless referencing of the surrounding culture mirror perfectly the associative dynamics of electronic media.

One might argue likewise, that the virulent debate within academia over the canon and multiculturalism may not be a simple struggle between the entrenched ideologies of white male elites and the forces of formerly disenfranchised gender, racial, and cultural groups. Many of those who would revise the canon (or end it altogether) are trying to outflank the assumption of historical tradition itself. The underlying question, avoided by many, may be not only whether the tradition is relevant, but whether it might not be too taxing a system for students to comprehend. Both the traditionalists and the progressives have valid arguments, and we must certainly have sympathy for those who would try to expose and eradicate the hidden assumptions of bias in the Western tradition. But it also seems clear that this debate could only have taken the form it has in a society that has begun to come loose from its textual moorings. To challenge repression is salutary. To challenge history itself, proclaiming it to be simply an archive of repression and justifications, is idiotic.[1] 24

Then there are the more specific sorts of developments. Consider the multibillion-dollar initiative by Whittle Communication to bring commercially sponsored education packages into the classroom. The underlying premise is staggeringly simple: If electronic media are the one thing that the young are at ease with, why not exploit the fact? Why not stop bucking television and use it instead, with corporate America picking up the tab in exchange for a few minutes of valuable airtime for commercials? As the *Boston Globe* reports: 25

> Here's how it would work:
>
> Participating schools would receive, free of charge, $50,000 worth of electronic paraphernalia, including a satellite dish and classroom video monitors. In return, the schools would agree to air the show.
>
> The show would resemble a network news program, but with 18- to 24-year-old anchors.
>
> A prototype includes a report on a United Nations Security Council meeting on terrorism, a space shuttle update, a U2 music video tribute to Martin Luther King, a feature on the environment, a "fast fact" ('Arachibutyrophobia is the fear of peanut butter sticking to the roof of your mouth') and two minutes of commercial advertising.

---

[1]The outcry against the modification of the canon can be seen as a plea for old reflexes and routines. And the cry for multicultural representation may be a last-ditch bid for connection to the fading legacy of print. The logic is simple. When a resource is threatened—made scarce—people fight over it. In this case the struggle is over textual power in an increasingly nontextual age. The future of books and reading is what is at stake, and a dim intuition of this drives the contending factions.

As Katha Pollitt argued so shrewdly in her much-cited article in *The Nation:* If we were a nation of readers, there would be no issue. No one would be arguing about whether to put Toni Morrison on the syllabus because her work would be a staple of the reader's regular diet anyway. These lists are suddenly so important because they represent, very often, the only serious works that the student is ever likely to be exposed to. Whoever controls the lists comes out ahead in the struggle for the hearts and minds of the young.

"You have to remember that the children of today have grown up with the visual media," said Robert Calabrese [Billerica School Superintendent]. "They know no other way and we're simply capitalizing on that to enhance learning."

Calabrese's observation on the preconditioning of a whole generation of students   26
raises troubling questions: Should we suppose that American education will begin to tailor itself to the aptitudes of its students, presenting more and more of its materials in newly packaged forms? And what will happen when educators find that not very many of the old materials will "play"—that is, capture student enthusiasm? Is the *what* of learning to be determined by the *how?* And at what point do vicious cycles begin to reveal their viciousness?

A collective change of sensibility may already be upon us. We need to take seri-   27
ously the possibility that the young truly "know no other way," that they are not made of the same stuff that their elders are. In her *Harper's* magazine debate with Neil Post-man, Camille Paglia observed:

> Some people have more developed sensoriums than others. I've found that most people born before World War II are turned off by the modern media. They can't understand how we who were born after the war can read and watch TV at the same time. But we *can.* When I wrote my book, I had earphones on, blasting rock music or Puccini and Brahms. The soap operas—with the sound turned down—flickered on my TV. I'd be talking on the phone at the same time. Baby boomers have a multilayered, multitrack ability to deal with the world.

I don't know whether to be impressed or depressed by Paglia's ability to disperse   28
her focus in so many directions. Nor can I say, not having read her book, in what ways her multitrack sensibility has informed her prose. But I'm baffled by what she means when she talks about an ability to "deal with the world." From the context, "dealing" sounds more like a matter of incessantly repositioning the self within a barrage of onrushing stimuli.

Paglia's is hardly the only testimony in this matter. A *New York Times* article on   29
the cult success of Mark Leyner (author of *I Smell Esther Williams* and *My Cousin, My Gastroenterologist*) reports suggestively:

> His fans say, variously, that his writing is like MTV, or rap music, or rock music, or simply like everything in the world put together: fast and furious and intense, full of illusion and allusion and fantasy and science and excrement.
>
> Larry McCaffery, a professor of literature at San Diego State University and co-editor of *Fiction International,* a literary journal, said his students get excited about Mr. Leyner's writing, which he considers important and unique: "It speaks to them, somehow, about this weird milieu they're swimming through. It's this dissolving, discontinuous world." While older people might find Mr. Leyner's world bizarre or unreal, Professor McCaffery said, it doesn't seem so to people who grew up with Walkmen and computers and VCR's, with so many choices, so much bombardment, that they have never experienced a sensation singly.

The article continues:

> There is no traditional narrative, although the book is called a novel. And there is much use of facts, though it is called fiction. Seldom does the end of a sentence have any obvious rela-tion to the beginning. "You don't know where you're going, but you don't mind taking the

leap," said R. J. Cutler, the producer of "Heat," who invited Mr. Leyner to be on the show after he picked up the galleys of his book and found it mesmerizing. "He taps into a specific cultural perspective where thoughtful literary world view meets pop culture and the TV generation."

My final exhibit—I don't know if it qualifies as a morbid symptom as such—is   30 drawn from a *Washington Post Magazine* essay on the future of the Library of Congress, our national shrine to the printed word. One of the individuals interviewed in the piece is Robert Zich, so-called "special projects czar" of the institution. Zich, too, has seen the future, and he is surprisingly candid with his interlocuter. Before long, Zich maintains, people will be able to get what information they want directly off their terminals. The function of the Library of Congress (and perhaps libraries in general) will change. He envisions his library becoming more like a museum: "Just as you go to the National Gallery to see its Leonardo or go to the Smithsonian to see the Spirit of St. Louis and so on, you will want to go to libraries to see the Gutenberg or the original printing of Shakespeare's plays or to see Lincoln's hand-written version of the Gettysburg Address."

Zich is outspoken, voicing what other administrators must be thinking privately.   31 The big research libraries, he says, "and the great national libraries and their buildings will go the way of the railroad stations and the movie palaces of an earlier era which were really vital institutions in their time . . . Somehow folks moved away from that when the technology changed."

And books? Zich expresses excitement about Sony's hand-held electronic book,   32 and a miniature encyclopedia coming from Franklin Electronic Publishers. "Slip it in your pocket," he says. "Little keyboard, punch in your words and it will do the full text searching and all the rest of it. Its limitation, of course, is that it's devoted just to that one book." Zich is likewise interested in the possibility of memory cards. What he likes about the Sony product is the portability: one machine, a screen that will display the contents of whatever electronic card you feed it.

I cite Zich's views at some length here because he is not some Silicon Valley   33 research and development visionary, but a highly placed executive at what might be called, in a very literal sense, our most conservative public institution. When men like Zich embrace the electronic future, we can be sure it's well on its way.

Others might argue that the technologies cited by Zich merely represent a modifi-   34 cation in the "form" of reading, and that reading itself will be unaffected, as there is little difference between following words on a pocket screen or a printed page. Here I have to hold my line. The context cannot but condition the process. Screen and book may exhibit the same string of words, but the assumptions that underlie their significance are entirely different depending on whether we are staring at a book or a circuit-generated text. As the nature of looking—at the natural world, at paintings—changed with the arrival of photography and mechanical reproduction, so will the collective relation to language alter as new modes of dissemination prevail.

Whether all of this sounds dire or merely "different" will depend upon the reader's   35 own values and priorities. I find these portents of change depressing, but also exhilarating—at least to speculate about. On the one hand, I have a great feeling of loss and a fear about what habitations will exist for self and soul in the future. But there is also a quickening, a sense that important things are on the line. As Heraclitus once observed, "The mixture that is not shaken soon stagnates." Well, the mixture is being shaken, no doubt about it. And here are some of the kinds of developments we might watch for as our "proto-electronic" era yields to an all-electronic future:

1. *Language erosion.* There is no question but that the transition from the culture of the book to the culture of electronic communication will radically alter the ways in which we use language on every societal level. The complexity and distinctiveness of spoken and written expression, which are deeply bound to traditions of print literacy, will gradually be replaced by a more telegraphic sort of "plainspeak." Syntactic masonry is already a dying art. Neil Postman and others have already suggested what losses have been incurred by the advent of telegraphy and television—how the complex discourse patterns of the nineteenth century were flattened by the requirements of communication over distances. That tendency runs riot as the layers of mediation thicken. Simple linguistic prefab is now the norm, while ambiguity, paradox, irony, subtlety, and wit are fast disappearing. In their place, the simple "vision thing" and myriad other "things." Verbal intelligence, which has long been viewed as suspect as the act of reading, will come to seem positively conspiratorial. The greater part of any articulate person's energy will be deployed in dumbing-down her discourse.

   Language will grow increasingly impoverished through a series of vicious cycles. For, of course, the usages of literature and scholarship are connected in fundamental ways to the general speech of the tribe. We can expect that curricula will be further streamlined, and difficult texts in the humanities will be pruned and glossed. One need only compare a college textbook from twenty years ago to its contemporary version. A poem by Milton, a play by Shakespeare—one can hardly find the text among the explanatory notes nowadays. Fewer and fewer people will be able to contend with the so-called masterworks of literature or ideas. Joyce, Woolf, Soyinka, not to mention the masters who preceded them, will go unread, and the civilizing energies of their prose will circulate aimlessly between closed covers.

2. *Flattening of historical perspectives.* As the circuit supplants the printed page, and as more and more of our communications involve us in network processes—which of their nature plant us in a perpetual present—our perception of history will inevitably alter. Changes in information storage and access are bound to impinge on our historical memory. The depth of field that is our sense of the past is not only a linguistic construct, but is in some essential way represented by the book and the physical accumulation of books in library spaces. In the contemplation of the single volume, or mass of volumes, we form a picture of time past as a growing deposit of sediment; we capture a sense of its depth and dimensionality. Moreover, we meet the past as much in the presentation of words in books of specific vintage as we do in any isolated fact or statistic. The database, useful as it is, expunges this context, this sense of chronology, and admits us to a weightless order in which all information is equally accessible.

   If we take the etymological tack, history (cognate with "story") is affiliated in complex ways with its texts. Once the materials of the past are unhoused from their pages, they will surely *mean* differently. The printed page is itself a link, at least along the imaginative continuum, and when that link is broken, the past can only start to recede. At the same time it will become a body of disjunct data available for retrieval and, in the hands of our canny dream merchants, a mythology. The more we grow rooted in the consciousness of the now, the more it will seem utterly extraordinary that things were ever any different. The idea of a farmer plowing a field—an historical constant for millennia—will be something for a theme park. For, naturally, the entertainment industry, which reads the collective unconscious unerringly, will seize the advantage. The past that has slipped away will be rendered ever more glorious, ever more a fantasy play with heroes, villains, and quaint settings and props. Small-town American life returns as "Andy of Mayberry"—at first enjoyed with recognition, later accepted as a faithful portrait of how things used to be.

3. *The waning of the private self.* We may even now be in the first stages of a process of social collectivization that will over time all but vanquish the ideal of the isolated individual. For some decades now we have been edging away from the perception of private life as something opaque, closed off to the world; we increasingly accept the transparency of a life lived within a set of systems, electronic or otherwise. Our technologies are not bound by season or light—it's always the same time in the circuit. And so long as time is money and money matters, those circuits will keep humming. The doors and walls of our habitations matter less and less—the world sweeps through the wires as it needs to, or as we need it to. The monitor light is always blinking; we are always potentially on-line.

I am not suggesting that we are all about to become mindless, soulless robots, or that personality will disappear altogether into an oceanic homogeneity. But certainly the idea of what it means to be a person living a life will be much changed. The figure-ground model, which has always featured a solitary self before a background that is the society of other selves, is romantic in the extreme. It is ever less tenable in the world as it is becoming. There are no more wildernesses, no more lonely homesteads, and, outside of cinema, no more emblems of the exalted individual.

The self must change as the nature of subjective space changes. And one of the many incremental transformations of our age has been the slow but steady destruction of subjective space. The physical and psychological distance between individuals has been shrinking for at least a century. In the process, the figure-ground image has begun to blur its boundary distinctions. One day we will conduct our public and private lives within networks so dense, among so many channels of instantaneous information, that it will make almost no sense to speak of the differentiations of subjective individualism.

We are already captive in our webs. Our slight solitudes are transected by codes, wires, and pulsations. We punch a number to check in with the answering machine, another to tape a show that we are too busy to watch. The strands of the web grow finer and finer—this is obvious. What is no less obvious is the fact that they will continue to proliferate, gaining in sophistication, merging function so that one can bank by phone, shop via television, and so on. The natural tendency is toward streamlining: The smart dollar keeps finding ways to shorten the path, double-up the function. We might think in terms of a circuit-board model, picturing ourselves as the contact points. The expansion of electronic options is always at the cost of contractions in the private sphere. We will soon be navigating with ease among cataracts of organized pulsations, putting out and taking in signals. We will bring our terminals, our modems, and menus further and further into our former privacies; we will implicate ourselves by degrees in the unitary life, and there may come a day when we no longer remember that there was any other life.

We will bring our termi-nals, our modems, and menus further and further into our former privacies; we will implicate ourselves by degrees in the unitary life, and there may come a day when we no longer remember that there was any other life.

36

While I was brewing these somewhat melan-choly thoughts, I chanced to read in an old *New Republic* the text of Joseph Brodsky's 1987 Nobel Prize acceptance speech. I felt as though I had opened a door leading to the great vault of the nineteenth century. The poet's passionate plea on behalf of the book at once corroborated and countered every-thing I had been thinking. What he upheld in faith were the very ideals I was saying good-bye to. I greeted his words with an agitated skepticism, fashioning from them something more like a valediction. Here are four passages:

> If art teaches anything . . . it is the privateness of the human condition. Being the most ancient as well as the most literal form of private enterprise, it fosters in a man, knowingly or unwittingly, a sense of his uniqueness, of individuality, of separateness—thus turning him from a social animal into an autonomous "I."

> The great Baratynsky, speaking of his Muse, characterized her as possessing an "uncom-mon visage." It's in acquiring this "uncommon visage" that the meaning of human existence seems to lie, since for this uncommonness we are, as it were, prepared genetically.

> Aesthetic choice is a highly individual matter, and aesthetic experience is always a private one. Every new aesthetic reality makes one's experience even more private; and this kind of privacy, assuming at times the guise of literary (or some other) taste, can in itself turn out to be, if not a guarantee, then a form of defense, against enslavement.

> In the history of our species, in the history of Homo sapiens, the book is an anthropological development, similar essentially to the invention of the wheel. Having emerged in order to give us some idea not so much of our origins as of what that sapiens is capable of, a book constitutes a means of transportation through the space of experience, at the speed of a turn-ing page. This movement, like every movement, becomes flight from the common denomi-nator . . . This flight is the flight in the direction of "uncommon visage," in the direction of the numerator, in the direction of autonomy, in the direction of privacy.

Brodsky is addressing the relation between art and totalitarianism, and within that context his words make passionate sense. But I was reading from a different vantage.

37

What I had in mind was not a vision of political totalitarianism, but rather of something that might be called "societal totalism"—that movement toward deindividuation, or electronic collectivization, that I discussed above. And from that perspective our era appears to be in a headlong flight *from* the "uncommon visage" named by the poet.

Trafficking with tendencies—extrapolating and projecting as I have been doing—   38
must finally remain a kind of gambling. One bets high on the validity of a notion and low on the human capacity for resistance and for unpredictable initiatives. No one can really predict how we will adapt to the transformations taking place all around us. We may discover, too, that language is a hardier thing than I have allowed. It may flourish among the beep and the click and the monitor as readily as it ever did on the printed page. I hope so, for language is the soul's ozone layer and we thin it at our peril.

SECOND THOUGHTS

1. Birkerts says that for "the average urban or suburban dweller today . . . a communications net . . . has fallen over everything" to the point where even "trees and rocks have receded" (¶s 11–12). To what extent do you identify with this description of people's alienation from nature and geography today? How much do you think technology is responsible for such alienation?
2. How is information organized and received differently, according to Birkerts, in "the order of print" versus "the electronic order"? How do you experience these two orders, or the tension between them, in your own life?
3. How is the transition from print media to electronic media "*reweaving* the entire social and cultural web" (¶ 21), according to Birkerts? As he says, whether all these changes sound "dire or merely 'different' will depend upon the reader's own values and priorities" (¶ 35). What values and priorities does Birkerts express or imply? How do these compare with yours? How "dire" do the changes he describes sound to you?

The Once and Future Book

Shyamala Reddy

Shyamala Reddy works for a San Francisco-based magazine aimed at managers and other people in high-technology industries. This article originally appeared in 1996 in *Virtual City,* a magazine (no longer in print) launched by *Newsweek* for people interested in the Internet.

F ive hundred years ago, the printed book was seen as the greatest threat to civiliza- 1 tion: a technology that would unseat rulers, topple institutions, and undermine the morality of the masses—not to mention doom countless scribes to the unemployment line. "*Ceci tuera cela! Le livre tuera l'edifice,*" shouts a church elder brandishing a book in front of the cathedral in *The Hunchback of Notre Dame.* "This will destroy that! The book will destroy the building!"

Today, it's the book that's the sacred institution. In a world overrun with sound 2 bites and spot advertising, books have become universal symbols of not just knowledge but integrity and righteousness as well. What bibliophile doesn't swell with pride when someone asks, "Have you really read all these books?" What child hasn't been told to "go read a good book" instead of watching mind-numbing cartoons? From the tattered potboiler you read at the beach to your hardbound copy of *Middlemarch,* books are a ubiquitous, celebrated way of life.

> **What child hasn't been told to "go read a good book" instead of watching mind-numbing cartoons?**

It's hard, then, not to echo the cries of Victor Hugo's archdeacon—*ceci tuera* 3 *cela*—when confronted with the prospect that the book as we know it may soon disappear. If you believe the relentless hype, a multitude of technologies—from hypertext to CD-ROMs to fiber optics—are conspiring to make printed books as obsolete as illuminated manuscripts. Soon, the technocrats say, you'll be downloading *The Divine Comedy* from a global online library, reading it on a handheld portable computer, making electronic notes in the margin and dog-earing the digital pages. Just like a real book.

So why not just get a real book? Side-by-side with even the smallest, most durable 4 portable computer, books win hands down. They weigh a few ounces compared to several pounds; cost dollars instead of thousands of dollars; last for decades—even centuries—rather than wearing out in a few years; and still work after being crumpled, dropped, stained and torn. Best of all, unlike a CD-ROM, DAT, mini disc, or any of today's wundermedia, books come with their own playback mechanism built in.

But for all its built-in efficiency, the book has its limitations. It's completely sta-   5
tic, for one. Once a book is printed, the author can't change or update its contents—
not until the next edition, anyway. Books are also completely linear; one word follows
another in order from beginning to end. If you want to check a footnote or use the
index, you have to flip between pages while holding your place with your finger. As
the volume of information in the book grows, the book itself becomes less and less
efficient.

INFORMATION CONSUMERS

The argument that books are going the way of the eight-track tape would have   6
remained relatively academic if it weren't for some real economic pressures. In the past
two years, paper prices have risen by as much as 50 percent. For the average reader it's
a small hardship. It just means that fewer new titles go on the market each year, and the
books that do make it to the local Barnes and Noble are slightly more expensive. But
for people who consume information, as opposed to just enjoying it, rising paper costs
have made books an increasingly unbearable burden.

Consider the plight of college students. At the beginning of every semester, in   7
addition to housing and tuition, they have to pay for hundreds of dollars of course
material. In some cases, they're buying an entire textbook even though the instructor
only teaches a few chapters. In others, they're buying a copy of a book they already
own because the professor requires a certain edition. At the end of the term, they either
sell the texts back to the college bookstore at a huge loss or carry them around with
them forever, like their student loans.

Enter electronic publishing. Instead of delivering thousands of preprinted copies of   8
textbooks to colleges, publishing companies like Simon and Schuster are now setting
up print-on-demand programs. Professors order only the textbooks, or other course
material, they need. Then publishers ship it electronically to the local bookstore, where
it's printed only as students order it.

Another way for publishers to reduce printing costs is to publish books on CD-   9
ROMs, which cost about a third as much as printed books to produce. Already, CD-
ROM versions of reference works like encyclopedias have made their printed
counterparts obsolete. The cost to consumers isn't always low: they have to buy not
just the $195 CD-ROM but the $2000 computer to run it on. These days consumers
don't even need to own the CD-ROM; they can look it up online.[1]

Don't forget that for centuries humans have been collecting the sum total of their   10
knowledge in books. At your local library you can browse an electronic card catalog
instead of juggling those unwieldy drawers, but ultimately you're pointed to a book or

---

[1]Universities have been making the CD-ROM version of the venerable *Oxford English Dictionary*—all
22 volumes—available on the net for years, but it's usually accessible only within the university. That's
going to change later this year when Oxford University Press publishes a searchable version of the OED on
the net *(http://www.oed.com)*. Although Oxford will charge an access fee, some reference links, like *Roget's
Thesaurus,* will be free.

some other printed material. It will be decades, if not centuries, before the primary material is scanned and searchable online.[2]

While the combination of CD-ROM and online technology makes for a more effi- 11 cient publishing system, it's still a long way from supplanting the traditional printing press. Less than one third of American households have the computers necessary to run a CD-ROM and an even smaller fraction—about 12 percent—have access to the Internet or an online service. The rest of the population still needs traditional reference material, either at home or in their local library.[3]

BYTE-SELLERS

Though new publishing technologies are having the most immediate effect on refer- 12 ence materials, there's no question that they're also spawning new forms of electronic books. Take the CD-ROM version of *Macbeth,* for example, published by Voyager. In addition to the full text of the bard's diabolical masterpiece, viewers can read scholarly commentary; watch clips from film versions by Welles, Polanski, and Kurosawa; and even play along, literally, with Macbeth karaoke. You can bet you won't get anything like that in the Penguin edition.

Yet for all its entertainment value, Voyager's *Macbeth* is still essentially reference 13 material, not original work.[4] Fiction written specifically to be read on a computer has been far less successful, at least by traditional standards. Rob Swigart's *Portal,* one of the earliest pieces of interactive digital fiction written, was published in 1986 for the [original] Apple Macintosh, a machine that's been obsolete now for about a decade. If you want to read it today, you'll have to find—you guessed it—the printed version.

Some authors have tried to use the medium to emphasize their message. William 14 Gibson's *Agrippa,* originally published on disc in 1992, was designed to encrypt itself after it had been read once—supposedly a comment by Gibson on the ephemeral nature of memory. But, as Gibson himself predicted when the book was first released, the program has long since been hacked and distributed on the net *(http://www.users. interport.net/~abubbica/books/agrippa.txt).*

These days, the great experimental frontier is not the personal computer but the 15 web, where hypertext has spawned a new breed of interactive online books. The most

---

[2]Not everyone is waiting for their local library to go digital. Since 1971, Project Gutenberg has been taking public domain texts and publishing them on the Internet *(http://jg.cso.uiuc.edu/PG/welcome.html)* and, more recently, on CompuServe *(Go: Ebooks).* So far, the Project has posted 10,000 books and has spawned imitators from the very small collection of The Naked Word *(http://www.softdisk.com/comp/naked/)* to the more substantial Electronic Library *(http://www.books.com/scripts/lib.exe?/file~lib.htm).*

[3]An alternative for people without a computer is the Franklin Bookman. A handheld device with a screen and tiny keyboard, the Bookman can be a handy little reference guide, with your choice of titles, including the *Merriam Webster Advanced Dictionary and Thesaurus,* the *King James Bible,* and the *Baseball Encyclopedia.*

[4]Nobody does this kind of reference better than Voyager, which has elevated the CD-ROM to the level of an art book. For unusual, entertaining (and, incidentally, educational) collections, you can't beat discs like The Beat Experience or Kon-Tiki Interactive *(http://www.voyagerco.com/).*

visible are really glorified games, similar to CD-ROM predecessors like Myst, in which the player has to make the right choices in the story to win. But "real" interactive books are starting to appear online.[5]

Douglas Cooper had already published a real book, *Amnesia*, before he took his   16 second project, *Delirium*, onto Time Warner's Pathfinder site *(http://pathfinder.com/ twep/Features/Delirium/DelTitle.htm)*. Instead of merely reading the book from beginning to end, readers skip between four story lines that eventually lead to the end. Although *Delirium* got more hits than *Amnesia* had buyers, there's no way to know how many people got past the cover to actually read it, nor do those hits translate into royalties for Cooper.[6]

William Mitchell, Dean of Architecture and Urban Planning at MIT, was more   17 successful in exploiting the potential of online publishing. His book, *City of Bits*, was published simultaneously on paper and on The MIT Press's web site *(http://www-mitpress.mit.edu/City_of_Bits/)*. Almost as fascinating as the book itself—a discussion of the future of architecture in a virtual world—was what happened next. While the print version obviously remained unchanged, the online version slowly mutated from a self-contained text into a community itself, with readers posting comments, newsgroup style, and even adding links to the site. As Mitchell writes in "Text Unbound," an account of his bifurcated publishing experience, "Over time the online version . . . has become encrusted with commentary. It has succeeded in provoking, capturing and making visible a discourse in a way that is impossible with print. And, in the process, the seed provided by the original text has grown into a considerably larger and richer textual structure."

ARE BOOKS DEAD?

The popularity of CD-ROM reference works and the continuing evolution of Mitchell's   18 book proves that certain kinds of information do better in digital form than in print. It's unlikely, however, that interactive fiction will ever catch on to the extent that it would replace traditional boundbook fiction. As those who spend their days in front of a computer know, you can't find a less comfortable way to read. But the problem with interactive fiction goes deeper than the impending threat of carpal tunnel syndrome. The most obvious barrier to the success of the genre is that most of it is trash. Even in some halcyon future where only the cream of the interactive crop gets published online, a story in which the reader rather than the author makes choices seems, at best, like a gimmick masquerading as a story.

---

[5]Traditional fiction has been somewhat more successful on the net, although you still have to overcome the physical discomfort of reading on a computer screen. For a sampling of the best the net has to offer, try eS   ie *(http://www.etext.org/Zines/eScene/contents.htm)*, an annual anthology of the best fiction online.

Delirium is the one example of interactive fiction released by a major publishing house, but it's only one of dozens of extant interactive stories. You can find links at the Hyperizons page *(http://www. duke.edu/~mshumate/hyperfic.html)*.

This is not to say that it's impossible to make digital fiction work. The first novel wasn't published until 200 years after the invention of the printing press; there's no telling what new art form interactive technology will spawn in the coming centuries. But whatever it is, it won't do away with the book, any more than photography did away with painting or television did away with the movies. If for no other reason, it's unlikely that any form of a book that requires a separate medium and player (like a CD-ROM disc and drive) will ever last more than a decade or two before the medium becomes obsolete. Digital books are, at best, a short-term solution.

Maybe that's why the best original electronic works are those designed for children.[7] CD-ROMs like the charmingly addictive Living Books series from Broderbund are the 90s' version of a pop-up book, which kids can read—and play with—a million times before they graduate to *Treasure Island* and the Nancy Drew mysteries. It makes you wonder if the distinction adults draw between online books and the "real" article is just a lack of imagination on our part. Perhaps 20 years from now today's first graders will be as nostalgic for the buzz of a spinning disk drive and the ghostly glow of a backlit screen, as we are for what John Updike calls "the clothy little box."

> **There's no telling what new art form interactive technology will spawn in the coming centuries. But whatever it is, it won't do away with the book, any more than photography did away with painting or television did away with the movies.**

19

20

← SECOND THOUGHTS

1. What are the major advantages and disadvantages of print books versus electronic publishing, according to Reddy? If you're reading *Composing Cyberspace* both in paper and online, test Reddy's comparison with your own comparison.
2. Reddy maintains that "certain kinds of information do better in digital form than in print" (¶ 18). Which kinds of information does she mean, and why? If you have read any digital or online books, how does your experience compare with Reddy's analysis?
3. Why, according to Reddy, will books continue to coexist with electronic publishing? To what extent are you persuaded by this argument?

---

[7]An excellent resource for more traditional kids' fare is the Children's Literature Web Guide (*http://www.ucalgary.ca/~dkbrown/*), which has links to classic children's stories, folklore, and even stories written by children.

Virtual Reality: A New Opposable Thumb

Brenda Laurel

Brenda Laurel (b. 1950) is vice president for design of Purple Moon, a company that creates interactive entertainment for girls ages 8 to 12. She is also a member of the research staff at Interval Research Corporation and a writer focusing on human-computer interaction and the social and cultural aspects of technology. In designing and writing about video games and virtual reality (VR) environments, she applies her academic training in theater, a long-standing interest in interactive art, and a concern for the social and gender effects of new technologies. She is the editor of *The Art of Human-Computer Interface Design* (Addison-Wesley, 1990) and author of *Computers as Theater* (Addison-Wesley, 1991), from which this selection is taken.

A t NASA, Autodesk, and VPL Research, demos of "virtual reality" start out 1 innocently enough, once you get through putting on all the gear—eyephones with stereoscopic displays and a glove or suit with position-sensing equipment, all cabled up to receivers. Through the eyephones you will probably see a relatively low-resolution 3-D graphics version of an office, like the one you're actually standing in. . . . As you move your head, you can look around the office (although, if the frame rate is too slow, you'll probably feel a little bit of "simulator sickness"). You can see a representation of your hand as you reach for a book on the shelf; your virtual hand may either grab the book or slide through it like the hand of a ghost. Then maybe you'll stumble upon a gesture that points up (or somebody will suggest it to you) and—*whoa!*—you fly above the office, higher and higher, until it's just a little construct far below, and you are surrounded by the darkness of cyberspace.

Then they'll start giving you the sexier demos. At NASA you can fly through a model of the space shuttle. As you approach the bulkhead at breakneck speed, you'll probably feel your muscles tense for the impact, and when you melt through it as if it wasn't there (which of course it isn't), you'll feel a physical adrenaline rush. At VPL, you may enter a *Reality Built for Two* and interact with the animated body of another person who's hooked into your virtual world, either in the same physical room or across the globe. . . .

> At NASA you can fly through a model of the space shuttle. As you approach the bulkhead at breakneck speed, you'll probably feel your muscles tense for the impact. 2

As you fly around these imaginary spaces, you may experience, as I did, a few lit- 3
tle cognitive train wrecks. In the NASA system, one flies by pointing—specific ges-
tures control the direction of movement. What if you fly past the shuttle and want to
turn around and fly back? Do you just physically turn around? Sure enough, there's the
shuttle back behind you. Or you can make your flying-pointing gesture back over your
shoulder, in which case you might fly backwards and upside down. The claim is made
that virtual reality is just like reality itself, but as this case illustrates, it's like reality
only different.

SOME HOLES IN THE PARADIGM

The development of virtual-reality systems can be traced back at least as far as Ivan 4
Sutherland's *Sketchpad,* and much farther in fiction and fantasy. Its current instantiation,
employing a head-mounted display environment, is probably most directly attributable
to the work of Scott S. Fisher at the MIT Media Laboratory, Atari Systems Research,
and NASA Ames Research [see Fisher, 1990]. Major American players include NASA,
Autodesk, VPL Research, Dr. Fred Brooks' laboratory at the University of North Carolina, and the new human interface lab at the University of Washington under the direction of former Air Force researcher Tom Furness. The notion of virtual reality has been
enhanced by the fiction of William Gibson (inventor of "cyberspace") and other writers
in the Cyberpunk genre, as well as the Holodeck construct developed by the creators of
"Star Trek: The Next Generation." Information on virtual reality can also be found in
Fisher [1990], Rheingold [1990], and Krueger [1990]. For a complete review of the virtual-reality phenomenon, see Howard Rheingold's *Virtual Reality,* [1991].*

In an article entitled "Through the Looking Glass," Autodesk founder John Walker 5
describes the promise of virtual reality:

> Now we're at the threshold of the next revolution in user-computer interaction: a technol-
> ogy that will take the user through the screen into the world "inside" the computer—a world
> in which the user can interact with three-dimensional objects whose fidelity will grow as
> computing power increases and display technology progresses. This virtual world can be
> whatever the designer makes it. As designers and users explore entirely new experiences
> and modes of interaction, they will be jointly defining the next generation of user interac-
> tion with computers [Walker, 1990].

With demo-able systems to provide the initial conversion experience, virtual real- 6
ity is making a huge impact on our hopes and expectations about the experiential qualities of tomorrow's human-computer activities. Yet it seems that there are some rather
serious obstacles to be overcome before virtual reality can deliver the robust kinds of
experiences that we fantasize about. Some of the "old" problems that faced us when
we were designing human-computer activities without eyephones remain: How do
people and systems understand each other? How can the actions of both be shaped and
orchestrated?

---

*See the stories by Gibson in Chapter 1 (p. 48) and Chapter 8 (p. 369), and the selection by Rheingold in
Chapter 4 (p. 151) (ed.).

Jaron Lanier, founder of VPL, attempts to obviate what appear to be some of the   7
central challenges in the construction of virtual worlds:

> Let's suppose that you could have a time machine go back to the earliest creatures who
> developed language, our ancestors at some point, and give them Virtual Reality clothing.
> Would they have developed language? I suspect not, because as soon as you can change the
> world in any way, that is a mode of expression of utter power and eloquence; it makes
> description seem a bit limited. . . . [The idea of] post-symbolic communication . . . means
> that when you're able to improvise reality as you can in Virtual Reality, and when that's
> shared with other people, you don't really need to describe the world any more because you
> can simply make any contingency. You don't really need to describe an action because you
> can create any action [Lanier interview in Heilbrun, 1989].

I have two problems with the view represented by Lanier's comments. One is that   8
language is good for more than describing the physical world. The ability to create and
manipulate symbolic representations is probably the central feature of human intelligence and imagination. It also expedites the process of human communication (do I
have to paint you a picture?). Alas, the hard problem of language understanding (and
the deeper forms of inference that must go along with it in intelligent systems) just
won't go away with the wave of a DataGlove.

A deeper objection is to the glossing over of the problems of designing action.   9
Yes, I can do "anything" in a virtual world, but how does the world respond? According to what principles? And if there are computer-based as well as human agents in the
world (Captain Kirk, for example, or Adam Selene), how would they be constructed
and represented? What would constitute their "intelligence"? The rhetoric around virtual reality reminds me of the rhetoric around interactive movies a few years ago, when
people (including some Very Important Film People) talked about them as if they
would just *happen,* like the reverse of *The Purple Rose of Cairo.* One day you would
just get up out of your theatre seat and walk right into the screen and then—well then,
interesting things would happen.

The notion of virtual reality is a continuum that is older even than science fiction.   10
Enactments around prehistoric campfires, Greek theatre, and performance rituals of
aboriginal people the world over are all aimed at the same goal: Heightened experience
through multisensory representation. *Sketchpad, Pong,* and cyberspace are all stops on
the same route. Myron Krueger's groundbreaking work on VIDEOPLACE and other
video-based interactive environments, as well as many of the "media room" projects
developed at the MIT Media Laboratory, demonstrate other approaches to the creation
of mimetic environments with sensory richness [see Krueger, 1990, and Laurel, 1986,
for descriptions of these projects]. What we have in today's virtual-reality systems is
the confluence of three very powerful enactment capabilities: sensory immersion,
remote presence, and tele-operations. These capabilities do indeed hold enormous
promise, but they will not make the central challenge go away—that is, *designing and
orchestrating action in virtual worlds.*

Part of the virtual-reality finesse is the technique of plugging other humans into the   11
system as the other agents in an action. But even when the system is responsible for
maintaining no agents *per se,* it is still the case that the kinds of actions that can occur

are constrained by the affordances of the world—the material aspects of the representation. If those materials are as fluidly changeable as Lanier's description suggests, then there is the additional problem of establishing common ground among human agents who share the virtual environment. Finally, there is the comparatively quaint problem of giving the action a pleasing shape. A belief in the powers of form in representation seems to be orthogonal to the kind of imaginative free-fall that many virtual reality pundits envision.

The virtual reality community must eventually welcome these prodigal problems   12
back home. It is not enough to be able to look at the backside of a computer graphic, or even to walk or fly around a virtual environment of extreme complexity and multisensory detail. I can imagine a virtual haunted house, for instance, with boards creaking, curtains waving, rats scurrying, and strange smells wafting from the basement. Sooner or later, something will have to *happen,* and if it does, that something will be interpreted (at least by my dramatically predisposed brain) to be the beginning of an unfolding plot.

✦ ✦ ✦

A NEW OPPOSABLE THUMB

A unique and wonderful characteristic of the medium of virtual reality is the discourse   13
surrounding it. The conversation is very broad and rich, involving people from technology, the arts, social sciences, and philosophy. It encourages a fusion of these concerns in a way of thinking among its participants. Also unique is the fact that many of those participants have communication skills that allow them to speak directly about their work, unmediated by journalists or other interpreters. In that way the emerging medium is being more directly and dynamically shaped by the culture at large. Perhaps the most exciting thing of all is that this global conversation is happening in the genuinely formative stages of the medium and not after the fact.

All new media begin with visions—fantasies, desires, and ideas about new kinds   14
of experiences that people might have. As development progresses, these visions can be overshadowed by the more immediate concerns of technology development. Too often, the technological perspective comes to dominate not only the process of development, but also the shape of the emerging medium itself. The visionary impulse fades away as technological progress becomes the sole focus. Some of the powers that a medium might have had are lost in the rush to find near-term solutions. Likewise, early successes with specific applications for new media can arrest growth and limit future potential by funneling resources into areas of development that seem most likely to provide the greatest short-term profit. The state of the art in computer games and commercial television are examples of these phenomena.

A counter-example is film. So many of the key elements of cinematic form and   15
technique were invented by D. W. Griffith that we are tempted to think that the medium sprang full-blown from his brow. But Griffith's quantum leaps were preceded both by the development of some baseline technological capabilities that allowed him to envision the form and by experiments in which other artists sought the shape of the new medium in comparisons with its predecessors, most notably the

stage. The recapitulation of previous forms seems to be as intrinsic to the evolution of media as it is to the development of human individuals in the womb: Human embryos have gills and tails before they assume uniquely human shape; television emulated theatre, vaudeville, radio, and film. The emergence of a new medium is a dance between the evolutionary pattern or recapitulation and the force of new creative visions.

The new literature of virtual reality includes some excellent examples of the kinds of experiences people might have with such systems and the kinds of uses to which they might be put. Both Fisher [1990] and Lanier [Heilbrun, 1989] describe surgical simulators for the training of physicians, for instance. The miracles of scale transformation can enable engineers to adjust the angles of airplane wings with their (gloved) hands and chip designers to walk around inside their microcircuits. Here, the materials can be taken more or less directly from real life, and the action (unless a nurse is handing you a scalpel) can be supplied by the single human agent. But applications in art, entertainment, and education require simulation of more than the physical aspects of a world; those who want to learn, play, and dream in the Holodeck will have to wait for a system that can sustain characters and orchestrate action. . . . Judging from the accelerating pace of research and development, they may not have to wait too long.   16

At Ars Electronica, an international conference on computer-based art held in Linz, Austria, in September 1990, a slogan was introduced: "The future goes to virtual reality."[1] This slogan suggests that virtual reality is more than a new form of human-computer activity; rather it may be a new stage in the evolution of interactive media. The diversity of applications that have been envisioned for it suggests that virtual-reality technology has the potential to be pervasive and to enhance our ability to take action in a wide variety of representational contexts. As the field of virtual reality has coalesced over the last ten years, it has seemed more and more to me like Pygmalion's statue. Those of us who have been involved in the process have nudged the medium in the direction of our own visions of human-computer symbiosis, but we have also been alternatively delighted and vexed by the ways in which the medium has taken on a life of its own.   17

In a hopeful vein, it is important to notice that new media open new possibilities for experience. Surely, virtual reality will contain more than databases and games. To close the circle from an artistic perspective, I want to describe one vision of what virtual reality systems might be able to provide for us. The goals of consciousness expansion, personal liberation, and the transformation of one's relationship to the world may seem lofty in relation to the little boxes we have on our desks today, but they are at the heart of the purpose of art. Critics of virtual reality warn that technology-based "psychedelics" will produce a disembodied race, a culture that ceases to value the body,   18

---

[1]The odd syntax is probably an artifact of translation.

nature, or physical reality in general because the alternative will be so persuasive. I believe that the reverse is true.

I want to illustrate this point with a personal parable. During the summer of 1990, I spent some time exploring ruins of the Anasazi civilization in New Mexico and Arizona with a knowledgeable guide. We pondered petroglyphs—ancient carvings in rocks—in the environs of Santa Fe, in the ruins of a mesa-top city called Tsiping in Chaco Canyon, and finally at the Grand Canyon, the spiritual center of the universe for the Anasazi people. . . . As we traveled throughout the Southwest, my companion and I became increasingly aware of the psychedelic shapes and textures of the rocks themselves. As shadows paraded across canyon walls, faces and forms would emerge and fade, leaving us finally unable to determine which were the works of human craftsmen and which were the result of the spontaneous collaboration of our own imaginations with the landscape.

As shadows paraded across canyon walls, faces and forms would emerge and fade, leaving us finally unable to determine which were the works of human craftsmen and which were the result of the spontaneous collaboration of our own imaginations with the landscape. 19

Depicted in the petroglyphs were animals, spirit beings, and the symbolic spiral 20 that represented the Anasazi view of the nature of time, the story of origins, and the fundamental shape of being. Our guide showed us how many of the carvings had apparently begun with some contour in the rock itself—the suggestion of a leg, a curling tail, a brow. "The makers of these carvings revealed the faces of the spirits that lived in the rocks," he explained. We readily believed. I thought of the ancient Greek idea that inside every piece of marble is a perfect sculpture, and that it is the humble job of the artist to reveal it and not to superimpose some form of his own imagining on the substance. But now the principle had a new and deeper resonance. Both petroglyphs and sculptures articulate the essential relationship between the human spirit and the physical world.

Art is time travel; it transmits understanding across time and space. Carvings and 21 sculptures, houses and temples, plays and symphonies are asynchronous conversations between the makers of a work and those who experience it. But the *experience* of art is in the here and now. Realtime is where the conversation takes place and where illumination is achieved. In this way, art itself is "telepresence." From the plays of ancient Greece to the ritual dances of the Anasazi to the concerts of the Grateful Dead, realtime experience is the Dionysian dimension of art. Recall that in the Greek theatre, actors were the priests of Dionysus, the god of ecstasy and rebirth, and during the act of performance they felt themselves to be *in possession of the god.* Their audiences were transported and illuminated by the divine presence. Dionysian experience is the experience of being *in the living presence* of not only the artist but also huge spiritual forces.

I think we can someday have Dionysian experiences in virtual reality, and that   22
they will be experiences of the most intimate and powerful kind. But to do so we
must breathe life into our tools. Our creative force must be manifest, not as an
artifact but as a *collaborator*—an extension of ourselves embodied in our systems. There must be more behind the looking glass than a room that one steps
into, and there must be more to virtual reality than the engineering of the looking
glass.

For virtual reality to succeed in meeting these goals, we need continual and deep   23
involvement by artists in the ongoing process of understanding what virtual reality is
for and what it can be. We need convivial tools that allow artists to work in the
medium in order to influence its evolution. Most of all, we need artists to help us
understand how virtual reality, like other art forms, can inform and enrich human
experience.

At the height of the Anasazi civilization in the great kivas, humans enacted spirits   24
and gods. Long before these magical presences emerged from the shadows, dancing
would begin on huge foot-drums whose throbbing could be heard a hundred miles
away across the desert. The experience was an altered state that culminated in the performance in the living presence [see Rheingold, 1991]. The great kivas are silent today.
. . . Even in our magnificent cathedrals, we hear only echoes of a magnitude of experience that has faded from our lives. There are no magical meeting places at the center of
our culture, no sacred circles inside of which all that one does has a heightened significance. In those few places where such transformations can still occur, the shadow of
our civilization is fast obliterating the possibility.

What happens when one steps inside the magic circle? The meaning of the ordi-   25
nary is transformed. Back in the early 1970s, I wrote (with William Morton) and
directed a play about Robin Hood. The stories we used were among the earliest, and
they were quite strange and primal in comparison with the more familiar romantic versions of the myth. The audience gathered below an old gothic tower near a lake. We
used medieval mansion-style staging for the performance. Suddenly, a minstrel
appeared and began to sing. She invited the audience to follow her into the woods,
where they would come upon different scenes unfolding in various locales around the
lake. My clearest memory is of the reaction of a little boy as the play began. The minstrel appeared and announced that this was Sherwood Forest. I watched the boy take
hold of a nearby branch and gaze with awe at an ordinary oak leaf. "This is Sherwood
Forest," he whispered, and I believe he really *looked* at an oak leaf for the first time in
his life.

Virtual reality may be many things. It may become a tool, a game machine, or just   26
a mutant form of TV. But for virtual reality to fulfill its highest potential, we must rein-
vent the sacred spaces where we collaborate with reality in order to transform it and
ourselves.

With virtual-reality systems, the future is quite literally within our grasp. The   27
dimension of enactment has undergone a rapid, qualitative transformation in the last
decade. The challenge for the next decade is to arrive at understandings and technolo-

gies that can bring the other dimensions of human-computer experience to the same level. At the point of parity, synergy will kick in. Perhaps more important than technology development is the need to recognize our new opposable thumb for what it is. Like every qualitatively new human capability before it, the ability to represent new worlds in which humans can learn, explore, and act will blow a hole in all our old imaginings and expectations. Through that hole we can glimpse a world of which both cause and effect are a quantum leap in human evolution.

References

Fisher, Scott S. "Virtual Reality Systems." In *The Art of Human-Computer Interface Design,* edited by Brenda Laurel. Reading, MA: Addison-Wesley, 1990.

Heilbrun, Adam. "Virtual Reality: An Interview with Jaron Lanier." *Whole Earth Review* 64 (Fall 1989): 108–119.

Krueger, Myron. "VIDEOPLACE and the Interface of the Future." In *The Art of Human-Computer Interface Design,* edited by Brenda Laurel. Reading, MA: Addison-Wesley, 1990.

Laurel, Brenda. "Toward the Design of a Computer-Based Interactive Fantasy System." Ph.D. diss., The Ohio State University, 1986.

Rheingold, Howard. "What's the Big Deal about Cyberspace?" In *The Art of Human-Computer Interface Design,* edited by Brenda Laurel. Reading MA: Addison-Wesley, 1990.

Rheingold, Howard. *Exploring the World of Virtual Reality.* [New York:] Simon and Schuster, [1991].

Sutherland, Ivan E. "Sketchpad: A Man-Machine Graphical Communication System." *Proceedings of the Spring Joint Computer Conference* (1963): 329–346.

Walker, John. "Through the Looking Glass." In *The Art of Human-Computer Interface Design,* edited by Brenda Laurel. Reading, MA: Addison-Wesley, 1990.

SECOND THOUGHTS

1. What does Laurel seem to mean when she says that virtual reality is "like reality only different" (¶ 3)—different how, for example? What are the major obstacles that she suggests must "be overcome before virtual reality can deliver the robust kinds of experiences that we fantasize about" (¶ 6)?

2. In what ways do "new media open new possibilities for experience" (¶ 18), according to Laurel? How persuaded are you by this idea? What examples of new media opening up new possibilities can you relate from your own experience?

3. It's in making art, Laurel argues, that the greatest potential for virtual reality
   (VR) lies. What are her views on the purposes of art, and how does she think VR
   relates to other artistic media? What do you think such an artistic use of VR
   might look like? How does this vision compare with actual or imagined uses of
   VR that you've heard about, such as arcade games or the "holodeck" of "Star
   Trek" fame?

⊃⊂⊂⊂ DISCUSSION THREADS

re: Borges and Barry

1. "The impious maintain that nonsense is normal in the Library," says the narrator of "The Library of Babel" by Jorge Luis Borges, "and that the reasonable (and even humble and pure coherence) is an almost miraculous exception" (¶ 12). Imagine Dave Barry as such an impious critic in this fictional universe; what might he write about his experience browsing the Library of Babel? How might Borges's narrator reply to the irreverent Barry? Based on this dialogue, how would you compare the way the two texts comment on the relationship between information and knowledge?

re: Barry and Birkerts

2. How do you think Sven Birkerts would analyze the Web data gathered by Dave Barry?

re: Borges and Birkerts

3. To what extent do you find Sven Birkerts' concerns about "an all-electronic future"—language erosion, the flattening of historical perspectives, and the waning of the private self—present in Jorge Luis Borges's story "The Library of Babel"? On the other hand, what different attitudes toward print and book technology do Birkerts and Borges seem to hold?

re: Birkerts and Reddy

4. According to Shyamala Reddy, "In a world overrun with sound bites and spot advertising, books have become universal symbols of not just knowledge but integrity and righteousness as well" (¶ 2). To what extent do you think Sven Birkerts elevates books to such symbolic heights in his essay? What different advantages and disadvantages do Birkerts and Reddy find in print and electronic publishing?

re: Birkerts and Laurel

5. Sven Birkerts argues that modern electronic technologies have alienated people from nature, while Brenda Laurel states emphatically, "I believe the reverse is true" (¶ 18). With whom do you agree more, and why?

re: Birkerts, Reddy, and Laurel

6. "The emergence of a new medium," writes Brenda Laurel, "is a dance between the evolutionary pattern or recapitulation [of older, existing media] and the force of new creative visions"(¶ 15). How would you analyze the essays by Sven Birkerts and Shyamala Reddy in terms of Laurel's "evolutionary dance"? What different metaphors for the emergence of new media are suggested by Birkerts and Reddy?

re: Information Overload and New Media

7. Overall, based on this chapter's selections and your own experience, how do you weigh the dangers or negative social effects versus the benefits or constructive potential of the new information and knowledge-making media?

RESEARCH LINKS

- *For direct links to listed Internet sources, additional reading selections and questions online, plus updates and supplementary Web resources, see* **Composing Cyberspace Online** *at <www.mhhe.com/socscience/english/holeton/>.*
- *For a complete set of research tools for the Internet—including the most useful search strategies, directories, and conventions for documenting online sources—see* **McGraw-Hill English Composition** *at <www.mhhe.com/socscience/english/compde/>.*

1. Reread Jorge Luis Borges's "The Library of Babel" along with "The Air-Ship" by E. M. Forster (Chapter 4, p. 187), plus if possible Forster's full-length story "The Machine Stops" (with the conclusion to "The Air-Ship"), available at <www.plexus.org/forster.html>. Compare these two dystopian, or anti-utopian, fantasies by well-known writers before the age of the Internet. You might also compare a contemporary science fiction story, such as William Gibson's "Burning Chrome" (Chapter 8, p. 369). Consider focusing your comparison on information overload, or the effects of information technologies on social relations in each story. (If you want to follow the connection between Borges and new electronic media suggested in this chapter, you might explore works by modern hypertext theorists such as Jay David Bolter and Stuart Moulthrop, who have discussed several Borges stories, including "The Library of Babel" and "The Garden of Forking Paths.") Test your ideas about the stories by integrating critical sources you find in library indexes such as the MLA Bibliography.

2. Sven Birkerts quotes and discusses a number of other media critics and literary writers in his essay. Follow up on one of these who interests you by locating and reading original works by, for example, Camille Paglia, Mark Leyner, or Joseph Brodsky. Consider and respond to Birkerts' criticism as you make your own argument about that writer's ideas or writing. For example, Birkerts apparently finds the favorable judgments about Leyner's fiction that he quotes from *The New York Times* to be ludicrous; after reading *I Smell Esther Williams* and *My Cousin, My Gastroenterologist* or other works by Leyner, plus additional critical commentary, what's your view about Leyner's cult success?

3. If you have access to the Internet, explore some of the online publishing experiments referred to by Shyamala Reddy, such as Douglas Cooper's *Delirium,* William Mitchell's *City of Bits,* or hyperfiction you find linked to Michael Shumate's Hyperizons Web site at <www.duke.edu/~mshumate/hyperfic.html>. Read several works composed specifically for the Web, and then evaluate the various claims about electronic writing made by Reddy and Sven Birkerts in this chapter. Write a research

paper—or, if possible, a set of Web pages with hyperlinks—in which you interpret the works you've read and assert your critical judgment about the value or potential of this new medium.

4. Research and write about some aspect of virtual reality (VR) that interests you. On the Web, you can get a sense of the amount of online information about VR—and the many directions you might take this broad subject—from the Yahoo! VR subtopics and links at <www.yahoo.com/Computers_and_Internet/Multimedia/Virtual_Reality/>. A useful approach would be to explore VR in a particular field such as medicine, the military, art, or—Brenda Laurel's area of interest—theater. (For the latter, see the ongoing virtual theater and interactive drama projects at Stanford (<www-ksl.stanford.edu/projects/CAIT/index.html>) and MIT (<www.cs.cmu.edu/afs/cs/project/oz/web/>), where Laurel has been a collaborator.) The fictional VR environment of the "holodeck" serves mostly an entertainment function for crew members in the science fiction series "Star Trek: The Next Generation" and "Star Trek: Voyager," although sometimes the holodeck leads to confusion about what is real and what is virtual. The utility, success, or potential of VR in any given field or context—from medicine to "Star Trek"— is likely to be somewhat controversial. Take a position on one such controversy.

5. Linguist George Lakoff, in Chapter 1 (p. 21), discusses the importance of metaphors and language in the way we think about technology. Reread the selections in this chapter by Jorge Luis Borges, Sven Birkerts, Shyamala Reddy, and Brenda Laurel in terms of Lakoff's ideas. How do you think Lakoff would analyze the different metaphors for information technologies used by Borges, Birkerts, Reddy, and Laurel? Expand your analysis by including the views of other linguists and media critics; what conclusions can you draw about the language of information overload?

6. A recent debate about information technology and the Internet concerns the "pull" model versus the "push" model. "Pull" is the way the Net has historically been organized, with individual users searching for and selecting the information they want to use. "Push" technologies are beginning to use the World Wide Web for the broadcasting of information, somewhat like TV, except that information can be tailored to specific needs or wishes. One of the early examples of a push technology is the PointCast network (<www.pointcast.com/>), which broadcasts selected news stories directly to people's Web browsers. The editors of *Wired* promoted push in the cover story for the March 1997 edition of the magazine (<www.wired.com/wired/5.03/index.html>), and other Internet journalists responded with criticisms of the push model. One controversy concerns whether these developing tools will allow everyone with Internet access, or only larger organizations with big budgets, to broadcast information. Some critics have suggested that push represents a giant step backward, rather than a leap into the future. Research the latest in push and pull; if possible experiment with the most recent technologies yourself, and defend your own views on the controversy.

Chapter

8

Ownership and Sharing of Knowledge

COMPU-TOON.

FRANK, YOU EVER HEARD OF USING A PASSWORD?

In the "Compu-Toon" cartoon by Charles Boyce, the image of a man locking his office computer with a chain and padlock strikes the experienced computer user as humorously incongruent. While many people do use some physical device to prevent their computers from being stolen, this man's intention—as revealed by his fellow worker's question about using a password—is apparently to secure the data stored on his computer hard drive. A chain and padlock can effectively lock a bicycle, but not, of course, information in digital form. For that purpose, some people prevent unauthorized access with the use of private or shared passwords that must be typed into the computer for it to start up or to open certain files.

This cartoon image of a chained-down computer brings to mind much larger issues than password protection. Computers, by their nature as substantial physical objects with common operating systems (that is, the ways that people communicate with and use the computer), are easily accessible to multiple users. Moreover, computers in the 1990s are increasingly wired to other computers in local and global networks, including the Internet. The sharing of information, therefore, is an integral part of computing (and, by definition, of networking). When information in electronic form is so easily shared, what happens when someone—like the man in the cartoon—wants to keep certain knowledge private? How might his desire to control (or his actual copyright on) discrete pieces of information—often called today "intellectual property"—conflict with other people's interest in finding and using that information? Will some shift in the balance between private control and public access to information be required in the 21st century? How might our whole notion of intellectual property and the ways in which we work together to construct knowledge be changed or challenged by the widespread adoption of new information technologies?

These and other issues of knowledge ownership and sharing on the brink of the 21st century are explored in this chapter. Librarian Ann Okerson examines the controversial recommendations of the National Information Infrastructure Task Force's Working Group on Intellectual Property Rights and gives some historical context for online copyright issues. Mark Fearer writes about the legal and ethical battle between the Church of Scientology (CoS), struggling to protect the "sacred texts" that it charges members to access, and CoS detractors who have published those texts widely on the Internet. Herb Brody explores how scientists and researchers, the original builders and users of the Internet, are currently using online tools such as e-mail, Usenet newsgroups, and the Web to share information, collaborate on projects, and publish their research. David Bank looks at ways in which corporate America is adapting to the increasing importance of knowledge sharing—including the creation of new jobs such as "Chief Knowledge Officer"—in order to maintain their competitiveness. Finally, in William Gibson's dense, fast-spaced science fiction story "Burning Chrome," a team of socially marginal computer hackers faces the life-or-death challenge of breaking into the highly protected database of a dangerous criminal-corporate organization.

Before reading these selections, you might consider your own attitudes and values regarding collaboration, competition, and information control. For example:

1. Have you ever had an idea for which you wished you could obtain (or actually obtained) a patent or copyright? What do you think might have been gained or lost

by your publishing your idea at once to a worldwide audience in a medium such as the Internet? What would be the purpose of your "owning" this idea? Did you subsequently find that other people had similar ideas?

2. Have you ever belonged to an organization, club, or religion that shares certain information or knowledge only with members of the group, not with outsiders? Without revealing anything you don't wish to, how would you describe that process of information management or control? What is or was the purpose of restricting access, if that's the case? In your view, what's the value, advantage, or disadvantage in this kind of organizational policy?

3. What's your experience with doing homework together with friends or classmates? Have you been encouraged to work together for certain projects or classes? Have you been discouraged from working together for other projects or classes? What's your opinion about the ethics or value of working together versus working apart? If your answer depends on the context, then what generalizations can you make about situations in which it's more and less valuable and ethical to collaborate?

4. If you've read or seen movies about computer hackers or crackers—people who break into other people's computers, or computers controlled by schools, the military, or corporations—discuss your impressions of their motives and morals. Are there certain cases where you think stealing information can be justified? Why or why not?

5. If you have access to a computer lab, classroom, or networked computers equipped with electronic discussion software, discuss with fellow readers any of the issues raised here.

Who Owns Digital Works?

Ann Okerson

Ann Okerson is associate university librarian at Yale University, where her work includes making digital materials available to the library's users. Previously, she served as director of the Office of Scientific and Academic Publishing for the Association of Research Libraries in Washington, D.C. Since January 1993 she has been co-moderator of NewJour, an electronic mailing list that announces new electronic journal, magazine, and newsletter start-ups. Her home page on the Web at <www.library.yale.edu/~okerson/alo.html> includes more information and links to her other articles about copyright and library science. This article first appeared in 1996 in *Scientific American,* a magazine addressing science and technology for a well-informed audience.

M illions of readers since 1926 have found A. A. Milne's stories of Pooh and Piglet and their friends Eeyore and Tigger delightfully simple and yet profound. So it is not surprising that James Milne (no relation) of Iowa State University thought that it would be a wonderful idea to put *Winnie-the-Pooh* on the World Wide Web. A computer attached to the Internet could take a few files containing linked text and pictures from the books and make them available to children of all ages around the world. In April 1995, shortly after he created the Web site, Milne received a very polite letter (as have other Pooh fans) from E. P. Dutton, the company that holds the rights to the text and classic Pooh illustrations, telling him in the nicest way imaginable to cease and desist. His other choice was to sequester a substantial part of his life's savings for the coming legal bills.

About the same time, a scandalous new book about the private life of former French president François Mitterrand was banned from distribution in print in France. It turned up anonymously on the Internet days later. There was little anyone could do to prevent its rapid digital dissemination.

Some network enthusiasts assert that "information wants to be free," but an equally vociferous band of digital pioneers contend that the real future of the global Internet lies in metering every drop of knowledge and charging for every sip. How will society's legal and cultural institutions react? Will tomorrow's readers be able to browse electronic works as easily as they have been able to peruse books at their favorite bookstore? Will they be able to borrow from virtual libraries? Authors, publishers, librarians and top-level government officials are debating these questions.

NO MORE YAWNS

Even five years ago few people would have thought of electronic copyright as an issue   4
for heated national controversy. But today there are vast sums to be gained—or lost—
as a result of the inevitable legal decisions to be made regarding ownership of "intellectual property" transmitted via electronic media. By the early 1990s the core
copyright industries of the U.S. (which include publishing, film and music) accounted
for more than $200 billion in business annually, or about 3.6 percent of the gross
domestic product. In 1993, when QVC and Viacom battled for control of Paramount
and its archive of classic films, it became clear that both companies believe the future
lies in ownership of "content." Since 1981 the National Writers Union has sued large
publishing organizations, including the New York Times Company and Mead Data
Central, for allegedly selling unauthorized digital copies of its members' works. Even
universities now think about how to maximize the return on the intellectual property
they produce, rather than simply assigning full rights to publishers.

For the most part, the copyright industries create mass-market products such as   5
trade books, films and related items. (The novel *Jurassic Park*, for example, spawned a
major movie, videotapes, audiotapes, T-shirts, toy dinosaurs and other derivatives, all
protected by various rights.) Scholarly and literary publishing—the scientific, critical,
and artistic record of human knowledge, culture and experience—accounts for only
about half a percent of the total, or $1 billion a year. (Publicly funded government
information, freely distributed, plays no important part in that market.)

Most scientists and scholars are far more interested in the widest possible distribu-   6
tion of their work to their professional colleagues than in capturing every possible royalty dollar. The Internet can deliver information more quickly and cheaply than
traditional print formats can, which makes it an appealing vehicle for publishing. An
electronic copy of a document or program will also usually be identical to the original
and exactly as functional.

Yet such authors are merely passengers on a mass-media ocean liner, required to   7
abide by the same copyright laws as the makers of action-figure toys based on Saturday-
morning cartoons. And publishers' exhilaration about new products and markets is offset
by fear that a single sale to a library or an individual could result in the endless reproduction of a document over the global Internet, eliminating hopes of further revenue.

Questions about how to apply current copyright law to new formats and media   8
abound: To what extent are works on the newer—let alone not yet created—electronic
media protected by law? Is cyberspace a virtual Wild West, where anyone can lay
claim to anyone else's creations by scanning and uploading them or simply copying a
few files? Many works are being created through extensive electronic communities or
collaborations—who owns and benefits from these? How can we track who owns what,
assuming that ownership makes sense at all? How do we efficiently compensate information owners when their works can be sold by the word, phrase or even musical note?
What are the liabilities of Internet access providers, who may be unaware of copyright
violation over their facilities? Should we dispense with copyright as we have known it
entirely and seek new paradigms, as the Office of Technology Assessment advocated
in 1986?

WHERE THE LAW STANDS

The roots of copyright are old, and the lines along which it has grown are complex.   9
One of the earliest copyright disputes, from sixth-century Ireland, sets the tone: St.
Columba had copied out for himself a manuscript of the Latin Psalter, and the owner
of the original, Finnian of Druim Finn, objected. The king ruled: "As the calf
belongs to the cow," so the "copyright violator" prevailed and held on to the book.
(The manuscript has had a long history as a good luck charm for the Columba clan's
military adventures and survives to this day in the library of the Royal Irish Academy in Dublin.)

The Statute of Anne, enacted in England in 1710, was the first national copyright   10
law. It gave authors rights to their works and limited the duration of those rights; it
served as a model for the first statute governing copyrights in the New World,
enacted in 1790. On both sides of the Atlantic, copyright in its nascent stages balanced neatly the interests of private property and public use. Indeed, the constitutional authority for U.S. copyright is based on its potential to "promote the progress
of science and useful arts."

In successive revisions, Congress has extended the period of copyright,   11
expanded the types of works that are protected, and joined in global copyright agreements, such as the Berne Convention. Berne signers agree to give copyrighted works
from other countries the same protection they would have if they had been produced
in the home nation.

American publishers have not always been so scrupulous in observing foreign   12
copyrights. Pirate editions were common during the 19th and early 20th centuries
(when, according to an argument made by Paul Goldstein of Stanford University and
others, the U.S. was a net importer of intellectual property). British artists then, from
Gilbert and Sullivan to J.R.R. Tolkien, were acutely aware of such trespasses. Today,
however, Americans look at lax-copyright countries such as China as disapprovingly
as Britain looked westward 100 years ago.

Some observers have argued that cyberspace is a similarly underdeveloped terri-   13
tory with respect to intellectual property—many words and images from other media
find their way there, but relatively few cyberworks have crossed in the opposite direction. That asymmetry is changing rapidly, though: the land rush of media companies to
the Internet in the mid-1990s may already have put an end to the frontier era. And, of
course, because cyberspace has no physical territory, its citizens are subject to the laws
of whatever jurisdiction they live in.

A TILTED PLAYING FIELD

The most recent revision of the U.S. copyright law, made in 1978, is far more thorough   14
than its predecessors. It protects creative works in general, including literature, music,
drama, pantomime, choreography, pictorial, graphical and sculptural works, motion
pictures and other audiovisual creations, sound recordings and architecture. (Patents
and trademarks are governed by their own laws, as are trade secrets). Copyright explicitly grants the owners of the expression of an idea the right to prevent anyone from

making copies of it, preparing derivative works, distributing the work, performing it or displaying it without permission.

At the same time, the law limits the exclusive rights of owners in various ways. 15 The most important of these exceptions is fair use, which allows copies to be made without either payment or permission under certain conditions. Fair use includes copying for purposes of research, teaching, journalism, criticism, parody and library activities.

Much of the current debate about electronic copyright stems from questions about 16 the future of fair use raised by the Lehman Commission, known more officially as the National Information Infrastructure Task Force's Working Group on Intellectual Property Rights, chaired by Bruce A. Lehman, the U.S. commissioner of patents and trademarks. In mid-1994 the 25-member group released a first draft of its report for comment. Hearings were held in Washington, D.C., Chicago and Los Angeles, and the group took comments by post, fax and e-mail. Individual readers and copyright market participants offered well over 1,000 pages of opinion. In September 1995 the group released its final draft—a white paper—containing a legislative package intended to update the current Copyright Act.

In general, the information-producing industries have greeted the white paper's 17 recommendations with relief and acclaim. It forestalls publishers' and authors' worst-case scenario, which could have reduced income to the point where there would be no incentives to produce new works and market them on-line. The tighter controls over digital reproduction proposed in the white paper appear to secure the industry's financial well-being in the on-line environment.

In contrast, library and education groups, on-line services and private citizens have 18 been mostly negative—and very voluble—in their responses to the Lehman proposals. Their nightmare future is one in which nothing can be looked at, read, used or copied without permission or payment. Many libraries are already feeling pinched as costs for information, particularly scientific books and journals, increase by 10 percent or more annually.

Fees charged for electronic information licenses (which give libraries or schools 19 permission to use material that they do not own) are generally even higher than prices for the equivalent books or periodicals. Thus, the working group's suggestion that the use of licensing should be greatly expanded has an ominous ring for librarians in most American institutions. Under the typical license, such terms as price, permission for users to download sections of a database, liability and long-term ownership favor the information provider in significant ways. If license terms continue to make electronic information more expensive than its print counterparts, and the digital domain continues to grow, libraries will eventually be unable to afford access. At that point, of course, this imbalance will have to change, because there can be no marketplace without a ready supply of customers to buy new products.

Furthermore, in the eyes of many citizens and legal scholars, the Lehman Commis- 20 sion's suggested changes upset the balance that the current law maintains between the rights of copyright owners and those of users. For example, the commission affirms that any information alighting in a computer's memory for any length of time—however fleeting—is "fixed" for purposes of copyright. The Copyright Act governs only ideas "fixed in a tangible medium of expression, when its embodiment . . . is suffi-ciently permanent or stable to permit it to be perceived, reproduced, or otherwise com-municated for a period of more than transitory duration." This distinction is crucial. The white paper implies that anyone who for any reason transfers a sequence of bits representing copyrighted information between computers without permission of the copyright owner breaks the law. Indeed, the working group recommends that the Copy-right Act be amended expressly to recognize that transmissions fall within the exclu-sive right of the copyright owner. Even the act of viewing a Web page, which involves transmitting it from a server to a user's computer, could be interpreted as illegal with-out specific prior authorization.

In addition, the group refuses to extend to electronic copies the so-called doctrine   21
of first sale. Someone who buys a book or magazine can sell or give away that copy without paying additional royalties, but this would not be true in cyberspace. This apparently illogical recommendation follows the argument that during an electronic transfer, a work is "fixed" in at least two computers, even if only for a few millisec-onds—and hence is duplicated rather than being transferred the way that a book might be. Legitimate ways for a lawful owner of a copy of an electronic work to sell the copy or to give it to a friend, an act that is perfectly legal in the world of print-on-paper, are left unexplored. As a result, in the electronic information omniverse, the ability even to glance at materials, an act we take for granted in libraries and book-stores, could vanish. Browsing works on-line without permission could be considered a violation of the law.

Universities and other organizations that supply access to the Internet are particu-   22
larly concerned by the commission's assertion that they should be liable for any copy-right violations committed by their users. Such a situation would force them into the role of unpaid digital police, checking on every piece of data that students, staff or sub-scribers have read or published.

Although the white paper proposes a future inconsistent with the grand tradition of   23
public access, one way around these controversies might be disarmingly simple. The commission emphasizes technological aspects of "transmission" and "fixation," but many critics have found those discussions imperfect precisely on technological grounds. A more thorough analysis of the range of technological possibilities for trans-ferring files—including cryptographic methods that effectively limit the number of per-manent copies produced—might make the Lehman approach more useful than it now seems likely to be.

FAIR USE—THE BALANCING ACT

If access to electronic materials without payment for every use is to be recognized, then   24
fair use is the area in which the bridges can be built between the rights of copyright owners and those of information users. At least that is where they have been built in the medium of the printed word.

Just what fair use means in the electronic environment is unclear. Other than stating   25
that fair use should continue in the electronic realm and that the need for it will diminish as licenses and other automatic accounting techniques become more widespread, the

white paper says little about it. Advocates of readers' and users' rights find this impreci-
sion particularly troubling. Although the Lehman Commission made a clear statement
in favor of owners' rights, it balked at the chance to clarify users' rights similarly.

Lehman's office has, however, continued to foster an unofficial series of meetings,   26
at which between 50 and 70 users, authors, librarians, lawyers and publishers' representatives meet every month in Washington, D.C., in an attempt to evolve guidelines
for electronic fair use. This Conference on Fair Use is affectionately called CONFU, a
reference to the CONTU (Commission on New Technological Uses) group that drafted
the guidelines that have helped to clarify the 1978 copyright revisions. From the start
of CONFU, it quickly became clear that little agreement would be reached by the time
the white paper was due or copyright legislation would be introduced and debated on
Capitol Hill.

What policymakers may not appreciate is that the inability of the CONFU partici-   27
pants to agree is by no means bad. On the one hand are fears that without a set of electronic fair use guidelines, confusion about the law and the likelihood of litigation will
increase—particularly damaging for elementary schools and others who can least afford
the risk. Yet on the other hand are the advantages of proceeding slowly with legislation.
Because there are not a lot of rules about the new media, publishers, librarians and
scholars are free to conduct electronic experiments—many of them governed by written
agreements between commercial publishers and educational or library organizations.

Progress in the creation and distribution of electronic information is being made   28
nicely, though not rapidly. Commercial copyright owners seem a long way from suing
libraries or elementary schools. The individual scientist or teacher preparing a Web
page may be in technical violation of one or another owner's rights but seems similarly
immune, at least for now, from legal action. (If this truce breaks down, of course, the
consequences for electronic distribution of information could be grim.)

In the view of many participants, the disagreements at CONFU meetings deserve to   29
be cherished. Many believe the technology is not mature enough for agreement about fair
use guidelines. They shy away from making legal commitments before they really understand the implications of what they agree to, and at this writing it appears that the process
of reaching adequate voluntary electronic fair use agreements will take a long time.

COMING TO TERMS WITH THE FUTURE

For all the criticism that some aspects of the Lehman Commission's report have gener-   30
ated, there is substantial consensus on many others. Many recommendations have generated dissension not so much about their general appropriateness as about the degree
to which they should be codified in law. For example, few take issue with the notion
that malicious tampering with encryption methods intended to secure copyright should
be illegal. Questions arise only about how draconian the punishment for such an
offense should be and whether investigators should be able to presume guilt.

Similarly, everyone, except for the small minority who believe copyright protec-   31
tion has no future on the Internet, agrees that there is an urgent need to educate citizens
about copyright. Now that everyone with a computer and modem is a publisher, rules
that once applied to only a few companies bind millions of people.

How society ultimately changes the Copyright Act will largely determine the   32
nation's information future. The power of new technologies already transforms the way
creators work and how authors and publishers deliver information. Is it too much to
hope that widely and cheaply accessible public and academic information will coexist
with information sold by publishers at prices that earn profits and foster the copyright
industries? We do have the potential, if we act wisely and well, to arrange matters so
that most participants in the new technologies will be winners.

Further Reading

The Nature of Copyright: A Law of Users' Rights. L. Ray Patterson and Stanley W.
    Lindberg. University of Georgia Press, 1991.
Copyright's Highway: From Gutenberg to the Celestial Jukebox. Paul Goldstein. Hill
    and Wang, 1994.
Copyright, Public Policy, and the Scholarly Community. Association of Research
    Libraries, Washington, D.C., July 1995.
Copyright Law of the United States of America. Contained in Title 17 of the United
    States Code. Obtain copies from U.S. Government Printing Office or the Copyright
    Office at the Library of Congress.

SECOND THOUGHTS

1. According to the article, how does the current debate about digital copyright fit into
   the larger history of copyright law? In light of that history, what aspects of electronic transmission, networking, and publication seem most problematic?
2. Okerson contrasts the reactions of information producers and information users to
   the Lehman Commission recommendations. What are the primary interests and
   motivations of each group regarding "intellectual property"? Within each group,
   how would you compare what's at stake for various subgroups mentioned by Okerson, or other interested parties you can think of? For example, among information
   producers, large corporate publishers and media producers would seem to have a
   much different perspective on copyright issues than individual scholars, writers, and
   artists. Or as an information user, how do your own interests in copyright relate to
   those of libraries, schools, or commercial Internet service providers?
3. How does Okerson try to present a balanced view of the digital copyright controversy? How successful do you think she is in striking this balance? How well do you
   think she represents "minority" viewpoints, such as those "who believe copyright
   protection has no future on the Internet" (¶ 31)?
4. How persuasive do you find Okerson's argument for a compromise solution that
   essentially duplicates the existing balance between public and private interests, or
   her hopeful "wait and see" approach to the future? Do you think such a solution sufficiently accounts for the changes in information distribution made possible by the
   Internet and other emerging technologies?

Scientology's Secrets

Mark Fearer

Mark Fearer (b. 1955) is a freelance writer based in Boulder, Colorado, who writes on issues of politics, technology, and health. His work has appeared in journals and newspapers such as *The Progressive, Mothering, Nexus,* and the *Boulder Weekly.* For more information about Fearer, see his Web page at <www.ecentral.com/members/writer>. This article was originally published in 1995 in *Internet World* (<www.iw.com/>), a magazine for people, especially those in the business community, knowledgeable about the Internet.

The Net is playing a major role in the legal unraveling of the Church of Scientology, which has turned to the legal system—sometimes in a drastic way—to stop the spread of its "sacred texts" onto the Internet. Lawrence Wollersheim and Bob Penny, long-time critics and ex-members of CoS, recently had all their computers, equipment, and software confiscated, along with dozens of boxes of paper files by CoS in Boulder County, Colo. 1

They weren't the first Netizens at the receiving end of court-ordered seizures instigated by CoS. Dennis Erlich and Arnie Lerma, also ex-Scientologists, had their computers and papers seized at opposite ends of the country. All four ex-CoS members, along with two of their Internet providers and the *Washington Post,* are being sued by CoS for copyright and trade secret infringement related to posting on the Net what CoS considers forbidden material. 2

Both sides see the case as a First Amendment issue, but for entirely different reasons. CoS argues that it is a freedom-of-religion issue to protect its secrets, while CoS's critics see it as freedom-of-speech issue to expose what they claim are unscrupulous church tactics and doctrine. 3

To say that CoS and Wollersheim have nothing good to say about each other would be an understatement. At Wollersheim's latest trial, CoS distributed documents to the media accusing him of everything from fraud to extortion to "terrorist tactics." Wollersheim is just as harsh. "Scientology is a political organization using a religious front," he said. "Think of it as an authoritarian political organization structured on the concept of Nazism." 4

Leisa Goodman, a CoS spokesperson, defines Scientology quite differently. It is "an applied religious philosophy that helps a person become more spiritually aware, achieving greater happiness," she said. 5

Whatever it is, Scientology has a colorful folklore. According to its account, 75 million 6 years ago a galactic tyrant named Xenu solved the overpopulation problem of his 75-planet federation by transporting the excess people to Earth, chaining them to volcanoes, and dropping H-bombs on them. The unfortunates became what Scientology founder and science-fiction author L. Ron Hubbard called "thetans," which now attach themselves to people, causing all sorts of problems.

Scientologists say their upper-level material about those thetans are trade secrets 7 and copyrighted, although unpublished. This is because premature exposure to the knowledge without training could cause "irreversible spiritual harm," according to Religious Technology Center (RTC) president Warren McShane. RTC licenses the copyrights and technology of the "sacred texts." Anyone who violates and publishes the material—called Operating Thetans, or ots—will be in trouble, both legally and spiritually. And that's where the Internet comes in.

A growing number of ex-members and other critics who have been trying to publicize CoS's doctrine and practices for years found a powerful ally in the Net. In 1993, they started a newsgroup called *alt.religion.scientology* (a.r.s. . . .) which was obscure at first. Dick Cleek, a professor at the University of Wisconsin and longtime Net user, said a.r.s. started off in the bottom 50 of all newsgroups in popularity (there are more than 14,000 newsgroups). 8

> In 1993, they started a
> newsgroup called
> *alt.religion.scientology . . .*
> It was the church's worst
> nightmare, as its "trade
> secrets" became far more
> widely read. 9

Threats of censorship, canceled postings, and raids against "copyright terrorists" (a term used by both sides), attracted many more people to a.r.s., which now is in the top 40, according to Cleek. In recent court testimony, he cited estimates of 20,000 to 66,000 readers per month during June 1995, although Wollersheim thinks the readership has reached 100,000 to 200,000 per month. In January 1995, CoS lawyer Helena Kobrin tried twice to cancel the entire newsgroup, claiming that people posted either fragments or the entire text of CoS trade secrets.

Many observers agree that CoS became its own worst enemy through its censorship 10 attempts. After the raids on ex-members, calls went out to duplicate the OT material, and dozens of FTP sites all over the world were created. It was the church's worst nightmare, as its "trade secrets" became far more widely read (and published by newspapers and magazines) than they would have been had it done nothing.

The two latest targets of the raid, Wollersheim and Penny, started a bulletin board 11 called FACTNet (Fight Against Coercive Tactics Network) in 1993, through which they aimed to expose CoS activities, tactics, and doctrines and to warn potential members about the dangers of joining the church.

Calling themselves an electronic library and archive, they had amassed 27 giga- 12 bytes (600,000 pages) of material. CoS officials claim part of FACTNet's material included top-secret documents that give a detailed origin of the pains of humankind.

Several months after FACTNet was started, CoS sent the organization legal   13
threats. The nonprofit BBS has five co-directors, and Lerma was the first one targeted.
His home in Arlington, Va., was raided on August 12, six months after ex-member
Erlich had his computer seized. Wollersheim and Penny feared they would be next. The
church didn't disappoint them, forcing an Aug. 22 raid by U.S. Marshals that was
ordered by a federal court under a temporary restraining order. CoS officials hired a
computer security company, I-Net, to search all 27GB of the seized computer-stored
information while Scientologists searched more than 30 boxes of paper files looking for
copyright and trade secret infringements. FACTNet went down temporarily, but has
since gone back online with limited capabilities.

Wollersheim and Penny went to court to attempt to have the restraining order   14
lifted. Both sides flew in experts from around the country to decide the fate of the material. What was only a hearing on a motion turned into a three-day argument, with the
issue of trademark secrets and copyrights at its theoretical center. But during the hearing, attention gravitated towards stories of brainwashing, stolen church papers, ongoing harassment, "X Files"-level security, bribery, FBI investigations, psychosis, and
even suicide. It underscored the complexity and drama within the world of this 20th-
century religion, and ex-Scientologists say those stories are just the tip of the iceberg.

On September 12, after hearing a lot of evidence, Federal Judge Kane in Denver ruled   15
there were no copyright or trade secret violations. "[FACTNet's] use of the copyrighted works constitutes a fair use under the Copyright Act in that it is for the purposes
of criticism, comment, or research and as such is not an infringement," he stated. Concerning trade secrets, he said, "[CoS] has not shown by a preponderance of the evidence that the materials in issue are secret or within the definition of trade secrets under
Colorado law. The evidence shows the materials are in fact in the public domain."

He ordered the return of everything seized, with the caveat that disputed materials   16
couldn't be copied or distributed beyond fair use. CoS lawyers immediately appealed,
but the 10th Circuit Court of Appeals upheld the Denver court's ruling on Sept. 18th.
A further appeal by CoS to the U.S. Supreme court also was unsuccessful.

The appeals court's decisions mirrored another federal judge's ruling in Virginia,   17
which ordered Lerma's confiscated property to be returned. In that case, which is still
ongoing, CoS sued the *Washington Post* and its reporters for publishing the disputed
material. The court ruled that the *Post*'s stories were covered by the Fair Use Doctrine
and were not an infringement.

These decisions are the latest in a string of rulings against CoS, undermining its   18
attempts to keep its material secret. CoS officials admitted in court that most of their
income derived from charging "parishioners" for access to the material. Ex-members
and others who have seen price lists estimate that it costs a CoS member $365,000 to
$380,000 to reach the highest level in the church. Spokesperson Goodman denied the
cost was that high, but wouldn't give an estimate.

Among the rulings that have gone against CoS was a $30 million suit that Woller-   19
sheim won, which was reduced to a $2.5 million award. CoS has thus far refused to pay
Wollersheim, even though its appeals have been exhausted. Church officials say the
judges and jury were manipulated; they insist CoS ultimately will prevail in all its
cases. Media observers say that scenario is unlikely; more lawsuits *are* likely.

In other pending lawsuits, Wollersheim is seeking to expand the Fair Use Doctrine 20 of the copyright laws for the Net. That law allows for brief quoting of copyrighted material for the purpose of criticizing or reviewing. Wollersheim says he'll argue that the impact of the Internet should expand that concept, allowing more than just brief quotes.

"There's a new technology and information paradigm—a new way of thinking 21 about, managing, collecting, and transferring information at a volume level that is vastly different than our real-world experiences," he said. "It's not out of the cultural norm of how info is handled and transferred in the Internet world. What we have to do is look at the technology and copyright laws of 50 years ago and bring them into the cyberworld."

Further Reading*

FACTNet
http://www.lightlink.com/factnet1/pages/

Critics of CoS
http://www.cybercom.net/~rnewman/scientology/home.html

Defenders of CoS
http://www.theta.com/goodman/

⬅ SECOND THOUGHTS

1. What "major role" has the Internet played in the conflict between Scientology and its critics, according to the article? How do you think this conflict might have developed differently without the Net?
2. What does Fearer's putting "sacred texts" in quotation marks (¶ 1) or describing the cosmology of Scientology as "colorful folklore" (¶ 6) tell you about the tone of this article? What other evidence—in his use of language or presentation of evidence—do you find of Fearer's attitude toward the Church of Scientology, and how would you characterize that attitude?
3. Do you agree with the court rulings against Scientology reported by Fearer? Why? Based on this case, do you think the Fair Use Doctrine or trade secrets laws should be modified for the age of the Internet?

---

*For updated links and more Internet sources about the Scientology controversy, see this chapter's Research Links and *Composing Cyberspace Online* at <www.mhhe.com/socscience/english/holeton/> (ed.).

Wired Science

Herb Brody

Herb Brody (b. 1957) is a senior editor at *Technology Review* and co-creator of the magazine's Web site (<web.mit.edu/afs/athena/org/t/techreview/www/tr.html). Previously he was a writer and editor at the magazines *PC/Computing, High Technology* (since renamed *High Technology Business*), and *Laser Focus.* This article appeared in 1996 in *Technology Review,* a magazine published by the MIT Alumni Association for a national audience interested in technology and society.

P hysicist Andrew Strominger says he is "usually the last one to get onto any new   1
technology wave. The machines are not fun for me." Maybe not, but Strominger, who studies cosmology at the University of California at Santa Barbara, recently conducted as good a demonstration as any of the value of the Internet—a white-hot technology if ever there was one—to those whose calling it is to understand the physical and biological world. Strominger wrote a paper that suggested a radical departure from Einstein's conception of space-time as a smooth and continuous surface. Strominger e-mailed a question about the subject to Brian Green, who pursues similar research at Cornell. Green started to answer Strominger's question, then read the article, which Strominger had just posted on the Internet. The two scientists entered into a brief interchange of e-mail, joined by David Morrison of Duke University, and three days later all three had cowritten and posted a second paper that further refined their theory showing that tiny black holes can be transformed mathematically into infinitesimal vibrating loops of energy, called superstrings.

That's how science works these days. Labs around the world are in effect sharing   2
a common chalkboard—the Internet. Theories, experimental results, shoot-from-the-hip notions all are shared, electronically, with the geographically dispersed community of people who find this information important. In astronomy, for example, "It used to be that many of the images sent back from planetary probes weren't available for months or even years," says William Emery, professor of aerospace engineering at the University of Colorado. "Now they get put up on the World Wide Web the next day."

The Internet is not merely speeding up the same kinds of interactions that in the   3
past would have happened in other ways. The many-to-many nature of the network medium is lowering barriers to collaboration. A physicist can draft a paper and e-mail it to colleagues around the world. Although ordinary mail and, more recently, the fax machine, provide the same basic function, the very malleability of electronic

text encourages continuous revision and group-thinking. The result is that by the time a paper is submitted to a journal it will already have been scrutinized by the people most likely to detect its flaws. Thus the opportunity for such exchange has meant that the concentration of scientists on the Internet has "reached a critical mass," says Raymond Dessy, a professor of chemistry at Virginia Polytechnical Institute and an advocate of publishing more scientific research in electronic form. "I find that I'm using the telephone less and less, and that I use paper mail not at all."

Yet the Internet's ubiquity cuts two ways. Because Net culture encourages partic-   4
ipation, online discourse bubbles over with the contributions of well-meaning ama-
teurs as well as with the obsessive ramblings of those with axes to grind. On the Internet's Usenet discussion groups, "the signal-to-noise ratio is very low," says James Phillips, a physicist at the Smithsonian Astrophysical Observatory in Cambridge, Mass. "I read a huge number of useless posts for every really helpful one." Unmoderated Usenet newsgroups are "a chaotic babble," agrees Ethan Vishniac, professor of astronomy at the University of Texas. "You get professionals, interested amateurs, completely uninformed passersby, and schizophrenic street people all talking at once." And with the ease and low cost of setting up World Wide Web pages, the Net is becoming an overstuffed, underorganized attic full of pictures and documents that vary wildly in value. Still, by bringing researchers from all over the world into intimate intellectual contact with each other and with the data and theories that they produce, the Net has become a tool that is at least a convenience and at best an indispensable aid.

TWO MAJOR EVENTS

Scientists were communicating with each other through computer networks long before   5
the rest of the world caught on. Throughout the 1970s and '80s, researchers at university and government laboratories exchanged data through ARPAnet, the military-funded network that evolved into the Internet. But electronic communication became firmly established as the primary means of connection after two major events. One was the discovery in 1986–87 of a class of superconductors—materials that could carry electricity with zero resistance at temperatures much higher than conventional superconductors. Results flew out of labs around the world and onto the Net; for an intense period of several months, researchers announced startling results almost daily, as they checked out the latest findings with their own apparatus. When the bits settled, the science and technology of superconductivity had made a major leap forward. Because experiments could be set up and the data reported so quickly, the Internet provided the medium for a shift in global scientific consciousness.

The Internet also fueled the controversy over cold fusion. When chemists at the   6
University of Utah made their controversial claims about a tabletop apparatus that could extract fusion energy, the rush was on to replicate their results. Researchers knew within days—sometimes even hours—whether a particular experimental setup worked. Claims and furious counterclaims flew through the Internet, which became the de facto

forum for discussing and debating the often-controversial results. The firestorm over cold fusion, following so soon after the breakthrough in superconductivity, "changed the whole culture" of scientific communications, says Robert Park, a physicist at the University of Maryland and director of public information for the American Physical Society.

> **The firestorm over cold fusion, following so soon after the breakthrough in superconductivity, "changed the whole culture" of scientific communications, says Robert Park.**

7

The discovery of high-temperature superconductivity and the claims of cold fusion gave the Internet a kind of legitimacy. In both cases, experiments were being conducted and theories proposed so rapidly, by scientists so dispersed, that there was no other practical way for crucial information to be shared in anything like real time. In the electronic medium, the usual lag time of publishing and conferences melted away.

RAPID COALESCENCE

Today, e-mail has become the informal "corridor" of the international research enterprise—the venue for bandying about not-yet-ready-for-publication ideas. Sending someone a quick, one-sentence e-mail message is "very much like knocking on someone's door," says John Walsh, a sociologist at the University of Illinois at Chicago Circle who has studied interactions among scientists. E-mail has allowed researchers to expand the circle of colleagues with whom they consult. The time zones that foil attempts to collaborate by telephone can work to the advantage of e-mailing colleagues; U.S. scientists, for instance, can send off results of a day-long experiment in the evening so their Japanese collaborators can work with the information when they arrive at their laboratory the next morning. "You end up with a project that never sleeps," says Walsh. "It turns science into shift work."   8

Besides fostering small-scale collaboration, e-mail also facilitates the large-group projects that have come to dominate certain scientific disciplines. Such "big science" typically involves hundreds of researchers at dozens of labs. One recent paper reporting on the search for the subatomic particle known as the top quark was cowritten by no fewer than 398 authors, representing 34 institutions in five countries. Such groups coalesce around huge, expensive pieces of equipment—in this case a particle collider at Fermi National Accelerator in Batavia, Ill. "Bigger science takes more people, and the Internet lets you do that more easily," says Walsh.   9

The Internet has also made it far easier for scientists to form ad hoc collaborations on topics outside their main expertise. Virginia Tech chemist Dessy, for example, has a strong interest in the physics of woodwind instruments. He recently cowrote a paper with other scientists in Australia, New Zealand, and Canada that discusses, in a way that runs counter to intuition, why the pitch of such instruments depends on their shape. The Internet, says Dessy, allows groups to "spontaneously coalesce and dissolve." An   10 important advantage, he says, is that the Net provides insulation from the sometimes prickly personality clashes that can occur during face-to-face collaboration. Members of the international trio "were able to catch each other's false starts quickly, before egos became heavily invested," he says.

Electronic communication can also help scientists sustain relationships that they   11
initiate through more conventional channels. Graduate students, for example, can easily keep in touch with their former professors. Scientists who spend a few months or a year at another institution can maintain the contacts that they established there. And researchers can continue the often intense conversations that they strike up at numerous professional conferences.

Unfortunately, e-mail's very ease of use introduces a problem, notes Phillip Helbig,   12
a cosmologist at the University of Hamburg. Because it is so easy to write e-mail and send it to more than one recipient, he says, "some of us are swamped with unsolicited messages from crackpots who have allegedly solved all problems of modern physics last Thursday in their backyard."

TAPPING USENET'S CHAOS

The dozens of subject-specific Usenet newsgroups that are available through the Inter-   13
net would seem to offer another ideal forum for discussing scientific ideas. In practice, however, Usenet does not fulfill this role very often. The general-purpose groups such as *sci.physics* and *sci.chemistry* typically attract queries and responses of the undergraduate level or lower. The quality of discourse is further reduced by quacks, malcontents, and well-meaning but ignorant folks who mistake the ability to eavesdrop on a conversation with the right to disrupt it.

Indeed, Usenet science newgroups sometimes seem to degenerate as if by   14
entropy. At first, reputable scientists might read the discussion and contribute some ideas or answer questions. Soon, however, the newsgroup becomes a forum for students seeking homework help. Then come the flamers and crackpots. Therefore, Usenet is "not where you will find active and serious researchers discussing their work," contends Steven Giddinger, a professor of physics at the University of California at Santa Barbara.

Scientists seeking higher-quality information tend to gravitate to the moderated   15
Usenet newsgroups, where one or more individuals serve as gatekeepers who screen out trivial, repetitive, and incoherent submissions. The moderator of *sci.astro.research,* for instance, stipulates that "postings will be judged on their relevancy to scientific research in astronomy and astrophysics," and that inquiries such as "will the sun blow up one day?" are likely to be redirected to the unmoderated group, *sci.astro.*

Even in the more specialized forums, many participants solicit practical informa-   16
tion rather than exchange basic ideas: Which vendor sells the best instrument for this particular experimental setup? Can anyone recommend reading on an aspect of my research? In a typical exchange in the newsgroup devoted to the study of butterflies and moths *(sci.bio.entomology.lepidoptera)*, for example, one person expressed interest in recent research on the behavior of ladybugs. Within minutes, a reply appeared, citing

an article in a journal of the British Entomological Society, along with that publication's e-mail address. Jon D. Moulton, an adjunct instructor of microbiology at Portland (Ore.) Community College, similarly recalls posting a question to the group *sci.bio.microbiology* regarding the movements of electrons within biochemical systems; a few days later, he says, he received e-mail suggesting a recent text that contained just the information he was looking for.

"It's the little things that have been solved over the Internet," says Andrew M.   17
Smith, who manages a mailing list for scientists who specialize in chromatography—a collection of techniques for determining the chemical constituents of a liquid or gas. Smith says contributors to the mailing list offer information such as "what types of buffers to use for particular analyses" and how to get the longest lifetime out of the thin glass capillaries through which samples flow. Such questions, left unresolved, can "slow a project down by days or even weeks, leaving the scientist frustrated and over-budget," says Smith.

SCIENCE ON THE WEB

The scientists who are busy shunning Usenet show up on the World Wide Web, since a   18
Web page is much easier to stamp with an emblem of legitimacy than is a Usenet posting. Visitors to a university's home page can easily hop to sites maintained by various departments and laboratories. Much of what is found there amounts to scrapbook-like snapshots of buildings and people. But many departments also include summary information on their projects, with links to published papers. Such easily accessible background information streamlines the process of scouting out new work.

In some ways, the Web is the ideal medium for presenting scientific research. Ref-   19
erences to other research can include a hypertext link that brings the reader immediately to the data being cited. And as the body of electronic literature grows, readers will be able to burrow ever deeper using references within references. The reader of a paper on new mathematical theories, for example, "could follow the thread all the way back to Euclid," says Herbert Wilf, a University of Pennsylvania mathematician.

The Web also offers another advantage: "When you post on the Web you can make   20
accessible not only your data but also the software you have used to calculate the data," says Martin Hoffert, a physicist at New York University. This is increasingly important because technologies such as satellite imaging systems and particle accelerators collect huge amounts of data. Making sense of this information often requires specialized software that, for example, creates from the raw numbers an easy-to-manipulate three-dimensional visualization. The Web can present not just text but sound, pictures, and animation.

In some areas of research—cosmology, for example, or modeling of large protein   21
molecules—software-based simulations are not just frosting on the cake but the main course. Research can best be presented by displaying computer-generated renderings. After all, "we can't just whip up a galaxy, so we have to substitute computation for experimentation," says William A. Wulf, a computer scientist at the University of Virginia. Sound, pictures, and animation can all be built right into a Web page along with

text. "I used to think those things were frivolous," says Wulf. "But they're not—after all, 90 percent of our neurons are for perception."

Now scientists can readily upload software code to their Web page; anyone who 22 retrieves the data can just as readily download the software needed to probe it. Making such software readily available is the "most important" change that the Internet has wrought, says Colorado's Emery. Indeed, libraries of free software for scientific purposes are blossoming all over the Internet. Programs that in earlier days would have been written for purely personal use are now made available on the Web, free for the downloading. Hamburg's Helbig has filled his Web page with links to numerous Fortran programs and subroutines that he has written to help him with his research on the gravitational lens effect—the bending of light by huge gravitational fields produced by massive cosmic objects.

The transfer and usage of software through the Net has become for many 23 researchers as essential—and routine—as e-mail. Andrew Cooke, an astronomer at the Institute for Astronomy in Edinburgh, Scotland, reports that he is analyzing data taken from an observatory in Chile along with U.S. collaborators. The data, he says, were copied directly across the Internet to his workstation in Scotland and then processed using software he had retrieved earlier from the Image Reduction and Analysis Facility in Tucson, Ariz. After correcting the raw data for instrumental effects, Cooke and his colleagues probed it further using programs and help obtained—through the Net—from the Rutgers University group who built the spectrograph.

Netlib—a Web site maintained jointly by AT&T, the Oak Ridge National Labora- 24 tory, and the University of Tennessee at Knoxville—contains the source code for scores of programs relating to research in mathematics and computational science. Although Netlib has been operating since the mid-1980s, usage has grown tremendously in the last three years with the soaring popularity of the World Wide Web. In 1993, the system logged about 250,000 requests to download a program; that shot up to more than 5 million in 1995 and more than 3 million through mid-June of this year.

EXPLOITING THE MEDIUM, WIDENING THE DISTRIBUTION

So far, researchers have used the Internet as a natural extension of other communica- 25 tion tools. But the push is on to exploit the Internet more systematically.

The biggest target for reform is scientific publishing. Conventional print journals 26 operate at a stately pace more suited, some believe, to the nineteenth century than the twenty-first: the lag time between a submission of a paper and its appearance in print is measured in months and sometimes years. Some of this delay is due to time spent on peer review—an essential part of the research process. But even after such review has occurred, articles often must wait their turn for publication. These journals therefore serve mainly as archival records and have little impact on the accelerating scientific conversation. "Certain journals play no role whatsoever for physicists," asserts Paul Ginsparg, a physicist at the Los Alamos National Laboratory and the creator of an electronic database of "preprints"—papers that have been submitted to journals but not yet published. The main purpose of journals, he suggests, is to "provide a revenue stream to publishers."

Ginsparg's database receives some 500 new articles per week, and is accessed 40,000 times per day. The preprint archive "has become my lifeline to current work," says University of Texas astronomer Ethan Vishniac, who notes that the distribution of preprints without the Internet is "spotty." Vishniac says he gets abstracts of 5–10 papers daily from the online bulletin board, which "makes it possible to keep up with what's going on across astronomy and to find out about work as it happens."   27

Journals are also an expensive and inefficient way to disseminate information. Since subscriptions cost as much as $10,000 a year, only the richest institutions in the wealthiest countries can afford to stock the full range of scientific publications. And even if funds are available, where can all these stacks of bound paper—what Ginsparg calls "chemicals absorbed onto sliced, processed dead trees"—be stored? A report issued by the Association of Research Libraries concurs that "the volume of material published is increasing rapidly in scientific and technical fields and no library can easily hold most of the materials of interest to its user community."   28

Some maintain that the Internet could solve this problem by becoming the primary medium of publication. Pennsylvania's Wilf, along with fellow mathematician Neal Caulkin of the Georgia Institute of Technology, founded and operate the *Electronic Journal of Combinatorics,* one of a handful of scholarly journals on the Web that has no print counterpart.   29

Such a move has several powerful benefits beyond the obvious one of accelerating the distribution of results. For the price of a few journal subscriptions, a library can outfit itself with computers capable of the most sophisticated Internet access. Papers in a Web-based journal can be revised from time to time not only to update and correct errors, Wilf points out, but also to add links to subsequent research in which the paper is cited. "I expect that scholarly publishing will move to almost exclusively electronic means of information dissemination," predicts Andrew Odlyzko, a mathematician at AT&T Bell Laboratories in Murray Hill, N.J., who has become something of the godfather of scientific publishing on the Internet after writing an influential essay last year in the *International Journal of Human-Computer Studies* entitled "Tragic loss or good riddance? The impending demise of traditional scholarly journals."   30

The move to electronic publication has another powerful benefit: it helps bring into the conversation scientists working at smaller, less prestigious institutions. The isolation of such researchers has been exacerbated by the tradition in some disciplines of working around the lag time of printed journals by mailing and faxing submitted articles to a small group of people in the same subdiscipline. The distribution of these preprints—the working documents of the research community—determines whether a scientist is in the loop, and that system tends to perpetuate the advantages of well-connected senior researchers. The Internet wipes out that advantage.   31

Everyone who has access to the World Wide Web, from Nobel prizewinners to junior faculty and students, can tap into the preprint archives such as the ones Ginsparg has established. With electronic distribution, younger and less well-placed scientists can sip from the same brew of new knowledge as their elder and more prestigiously employed research brethren. "The Web allows me to be part of that flow of informal   32 information," says biology professor John Rueter of Portland State University. "I am the only faculty in my research area at Portland State, so when I walk down the hall there aren't a dozen posters about meetings and seminars" the way there would be at a larger research university.

"Scientists have always shared results with their 10 best friends," says Maryland   33 physicist Park. Often, he says, "you'll find at less prestigious institutions scientists who are very smart but who are working on the wrong problems. The Net spreads knowledge around much more democratically." Even a preprint database such as Ginsparg's may no longer be necessary, says Stevan Harnad, director of the Cognitive Sciences Centre at the University of Southampton in England and an advocate of online scientific publishing. With tools for searching the Web rapidly becoming more effective, Web users will find preprints and approved papers simply by calling up a search service such as Alta Vista and tapping in some key words. The idea, Harnad says, is to decentralize control of publishing and "just let the Web gremlins find the papers."

Is Faster Better?

Despite the Net's promise of creating a tightly connected, global community of   34 researchers, several impediments block more widespread use. While collaboration through e-mail can work well once a professional relationship is established, there is not yet a good way to simply start chatting with someone without an introduction—the kind of thing that happens all the time when scientists rub elbows at a university or conference. Usenet could ultimately play this role but still suffers from the perception that a person posting a message is probably not worth taking seriously. A recent scanning through a number of science-related newsgroups revealed few postings by anyone who identified himself or herself as a bona fide research scientist.

Competitive pressures also work against the kind of collaboration that the Internet   35 facilitates. Although the Net encourages information sharing, scientists typically guard certain pieces of their work from rivals pursuing similar problems. What scientists need is an easy technique for making some components of their work publicly available—as on a Web page—and other parts of it accessible only to certain people, or members of certain organizations. Right now, a Web page is essentially a public document. While password protection schemes can be put in place, they run counter to the prevailing ethos on the Net.

Another problem is that reading the material posted on the Internet can be a chore.   36 To save disk space and shorten transmission times, for example, the high-energy physics archive at Los Alamos stores papers in a compressed format. Attempting to download a paper from the World Wide Web to a PC or Macintosh using Netscape, the most popular Web browser software, produces pages of gibberish. Looking for help on the Web page brings a frustrated user to the instruction to "download the files by hand" and "unpack manually." The page provides links to documents containing the tools— the equivalent of software picks and shovels—to perform this "manual" operation. It's as if a visitor to a library had to obtain a special kind of eyeglasses before reading each kind of book or periodical.

Even when the Net works flawlessly, some scientists worry that reliance on elec-   37 tronic communication overvalues speed at the expense of deliberation. As companies and government agencies cut funding for R&D, scientific competition can get cut-throat—and the Net's accelerated pace contributes to the pressure. In years past, the lag time between submission and publication of a paper provided a kind of cushion; as long as you got your idea published within two or three months of a rival's publication, you could legitimately claim that the discoveries occurred essentially simultaneously. No longer, says physicist Strominger: "If a paper comes out on the Net, you don't have months to get your own online," he says. "Things get rushed."

The system of peer review, although imperfect, generally ensures that published 38 papers exceed some threshold of merit. A scientist trying to glean useful information from the Internet, by contrast, has a lot of sifting to do. Bypassing journal editors and the peer review process ensures rapid turnaround, but what good is speed if the material itself is unoriginal or, worse, just plain wrong?

In one sense this is a problem of truth-in-labeling. Under the traditional system of 39 publishing, readers of paper preprints that have not yet passed peer reviews understand their provisional status and value them accordingly. A paper that appears in the published journal, on the other hand, is held to a higher standard in which the authors have presumably addressed critiques of their work.

Electronic media could similarly support such a two-tiered system, says Southampton's Harnad, who notes that scientists could routinely put a preprint of a paper on the Web when they submit it to a journal. Once the authors satisfy the queries of peer reviewers, they could re-post the paper accompanied by some kind of seal of approval. Indeed, the Internet promises to shake up the entrenched process of peer review. Comments can be submitted and attached to an electronically published paper ad infinitum, and the authors can respond by transmitting a corrected and refined version. 40

The Internet promises to shake up the entrenched process of peer review. Comments can be submitted and attached to an electronically published paper ad infinitum, and the authors can respond by transmitting a corrected and refined version. 41

But some in the business of publishing paper scientific journals question the feasibility of the online alternative. The work of producing a high-quality scientific journal is beyond the reach of an ad hoc group of volunteers, says Park. Much of the editing and production work that goes into a paper journal will also be required for an online one, he says, and the professional staff needed to handle these jobs will be costly. "Nobody knows how to make these online journal things pay."

A system of online journals would sustain itself economically, Harnad contends. 42 Because scientists want their work to be read and used as the foundation of future research, they have traditionally been willing to pay to have their papers printed—a model far different from that prevailing in other parts of the publishing realm. Scientists also pay to have their preprints produced, duplicated, and distributed through mail;

they would presumably be willing to pay similar fees to have their work distributed in a refereed online journal.

After all, the authors of scientific research papers "don't want the readers' bucks but their brains," says Harnad. It has only been out of "reluctant necessity," he maintains, that scientists—and indeed practitioners of any esoteric scholarly activity—have "entered into the Faustian bargain of allowing a price tag to be erected as a barrier between their work and its intended readership, for that was the only way they could make their work public at all." Scientists, he says, "want only to reach the eyes and minds of peers the world over, so that they can build on one another's contributions in that cumulative, collaborative enterprise called learned inquiry."

This idea is beginning to come to reality on the Web with specialized journals on topics ranging from archaeology to artificial intelligence. Harnad has himself set up a database of articles in the cognitive sciences, which he says will contain materials from "very early draft ideas" through papers that are undergoing peer review through finished, peer-reviewed reprints. Net users will also be able to download revisions of published pieces along with comments from readers and responses by the authors. Moreover, the documents will be linked to the abstracts and (where available) full texts of all articles that are listed as references.

At its best, the Internet serves science in the same manner as other great advances in scientific instrumentation that have amplified humans' ability to observe the universe. The telescope led, through Galileo and Kepler, to Newton's sparkling insights on classical mechanics. With the microscope came the discovery of whole realms of life in the microworld, spurring scientists on to better understanding of biology and disease. The x-rays that peered inside crystal structures and the spectroscopes that sensed with precision the nature of electromagnetic radiation provided the experimental foundation for quantum mechanics. The Internet, too, illuminates what had generally been invisible—not by amplifying human senses but by multiplying by many times the number of minds available to focus on the questions that prod scientists to action.

⬅ SECOND THOUGHTS

1. According to Brody, what are the relative advantages and disadvantages for scientific research of e-mail, Usenet newsgroups, and the Web? If you have experience with any of these media, how do your impressions compare with Brody's analysis?
2. From this article, to what extent do information technologies seem to be changing the way that scientists work? How does Brody seem to feel about the tension between competition and collaboration or sharing of knowledge among scientists, and how can you tell?
3. To what extent do you think the general public or other people benefit from the ways, according to this article, that researchers are using electronic media? How do you feel about "reputable scientists" abandoning Usenet science newsgroups when they become "a forum for students seeking homework help" (¶ 14)?

The New Corporate Know-It-Alls: Chief Knowledge Officers

David Bank

David Bank (b. 1960) is a staff reporter for *The Wall Street Journal* (<www.wsj.com/>), the national newspaper that focuses on business and the economy. Previously he covered communications technology for the *San Jose Mercury News,* was a special correspondent in Korea for *Newsweek* and *The New York Times,* and reported for the *Los Angeles Daily News.* Bank wrote this article for a special technology section of *The Wall Street Journal* in 1996.

W hen Gordon Petrash joined Dow Chemical Co. as a young project engineer, his career goal never was to become the company's "director of global intellectual asset and capital management."

And later, as a manager of the business that produces Dow products such as Ziploc bags and Styrofoam, he didn't envision spending his days convincing group vice presidents about the importance of "visualizing their knowledge processes."

So when he was asked to take on the new job as the company's knowledge chief, he agreed only reluctantly, and vowed to move on within two years. Four years later, however, Mr. Petrash can barely contain his enthusiasm and is pushing Dow to vastly expand its commitment to "knowledge management."

"Talk about catching the wave," the 46-year-old Mr. Petrash says from his office at Dow's headquarters in Midland, Mich. "Companies are leapfrogging others based on their intellectual assets. If a company is not addressing these things, it's running a very high risk, because a lot of other companies are."

The wave, indeed. Corporate titles such as chief knowledge officer, chief learning 5
officer and even chief transformation officer are multiplying as fast as book titles that peddle strategies for success in the information age. Among the corporate giants that have named chief knowledge officers or their equivalents are Coca-Cola Co., Monsanto Co. and International Business Machines Corp.

HARNESSING KNOWLEDGE

The premise behind the boom is simple. Employees hold a wealth of knowledge and experience about their company—from its products, customers and competitors to its production processes and internal technology. But much of that knowledge is held in bits and pieces by various individuals or sections of a company.

If these bits and pieces could be gathered and distributed throughout the entire company, the reasoning goes, the shared knowledge—a sort of collective IQ—would become a powerful force. Workers could use the pool of information to create competitive advantages and increase revenue. A company, for example, might discover that a process used in one sector could have applications in another. Or a company representative, using all of the company's knowledge about a customer, could make a superior presentation to the client, helping to seal a deal.

Now, advances in databases and computer networks are making such projects possible. Computer-networking technologies are providing the tools for the creation of "knowledge bases," "knowledge webs" and "knowledge exchanges." But it takes more than just sophisticated technology make such systems work. Sifting, editing and updating knowledge turns out to be a management, rather than a technology, challenge. And, more important, it takes a manager to ensure that workers are inspired to contribute to the knowledge, share it and absorb it.

Among the first companies to assign top-level managers to address knowledge management directly were professional-services firms such as Ernst & Young, Coopers & Lybrand, and Andersen Consulting. After programs were developed for the consulting firms themselves, the firms then found a lucrative business in helping other companies that wanted to "leverage" their knowledge, yet didn't have the in-house expertise.

Corporate spending on knowledge-management consultants is expected to rise   10
more than tenfold to $4.5 billion in 1999 from $410 million in 1994, according to Dataquest Inc., a market-research firm in San Jose, Calif. Those numbers don't even include costs for computer hardware and software or internal expenses.

However, chief knowledge officers concede that it's difficult to quantify the return on such spending. "We are moving forward to make our knowledge processes radically more efficient than we have in the past, even though we aren't able to measure the results of those activities as accurately as we would like," says Ellen Knapp, chief knowledge officer at Coopers & Lybrand.

To see more tangible returns, and to avoid the fate of other business fads, chief knowledge officers will have to overcome a host of other obstacles as well.

Some companies are still staffed by people who believe knowledge is power, and they aren't about to give it up to their co-workers, says Jeanne Harris, an associate partner at Andersen Consulting in Chicago. "I'd say those are organizations that are in trouble," Ms. Harris says.

More commonly, employees recognize the value of shared knowledge but don't have the time, the tools or the tangible incentives to either contribute to or take advantage of the process. Another common complaint: too much raw data, not enough useful information.

> **Some companies are still staffed by people who believe knowledge is power, and they aren't about to give it up to their co-workers, says Jeanne Harris ... "I'd say those are organizations that are in trouble."**

The job of John Peetz, chief knowledge officer   15
at Ernst & Young, is to overcome all of those obstacles for the firm's 20,000 U.S. employees, many of whom already are working 14-hour days and are scattered around the country in airplanes, hotels and clients' offices.

The plan: Each Ernst & Young auditor and consultant gets a laptop loaded with Lotus Notes, Microsoft Office software and a browser for the World Wide Web. They are all expected to download to their laptop, and master the contents of, at least two of 80 available "power packs"— databases containing information on particular areas of the firm's practice, such as expatriate tax processing or changing regulations in the health industry.

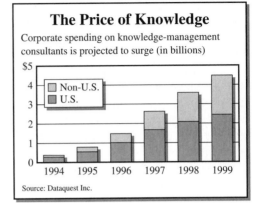

The Price of Knowledge

Corporate spending on knowledge-management consultants is projected to surge (in billions)

Source: Dataquest Inc.

Each of the power packs has 42 specific entries, including contact information for the firm's network of "subject-matter experts" (senior consultants available to help a junior associate out of a jam), client information, industry background and templates for presentations. Specific power packs might contain, say, a basic diagram for planning supply-chain management, sample shop-floor layouts or a simulation of a pizza shop's production process.

IMPRESSING CLIENTS

The idea is to help Ernst & Young consultants meet project deadlines and impress clients by having essential information organized efficiently and stored in their laptops. During a meeting, the consultant can quickly pull up the answers to, say, an arcane tax question. Or after the meeting, the consultant can create a claims-form processing model for an insurance-industry client based on a template in the power pack, something that would be time-consuming if the consultant had to start from scratch.

"The health-care industry, for example, doesn't just want really bright people anymore," Mr. Peetz says. "They want people who know three-quarters of the answer the minute they walk in the door. You can't do that without a knowledge base."

To establish the database, Mr. Peetz had to persuade the firm to change the way it   20 thinks about knowledge. Many people feared that wide publishing of Ernst & Young's best ideas would inevitably lead to leaks to their competitors. "An idea by itself has relatively little value; the key is rapidity and execution," Mr. Peetz says. "The risk of losing our ideas is not as high as the risk of not capitalizing on them."

Next, he had to overcome the functional divisions within Ernst & Young. The firm's tax people didn't think they had any knowledge that the consultants needed to see. Consultants couldn't imagine that auditors would be interested in what they knew. Each group wanted a separate database. "It's just the way they had always done things," Mr. Peetz says.

Finally, he had to get people to actually contribute to the database, a process he initially dubbed "dental extraction." The solution: linking participation to job evaluations. Now, at the end of the year, one-fourth of a person's annual performance review is based on his or her contribution to the knowledge process, Mr. Peetz says.

Junior associates are graded on the sheer quantity of their submissions, with extra points if their contribution is selected for inclusion in a power pack. An automatic system also measures how many "hits," or retrievals, power-pack items receive each month, so authors of heavily used entries can be identified.

Of course, the real value in the knowledge base is the value that gets delivered to customers, so for veteran consultants and auditors, the emphasis is placed on how well they present the company's knowledge to clients. After every project, an evaluation team asks the client such questions as: "Did we demonstrate our knowledge of your industry? Did we impart that effectively?"

"Knowledge management is poorly understood. It's not an easy job to explain to your mother what you do for a living."

Certainly, much of this is subjective stuff. "It's exhilarating and it's frustrating," Mr. Peetz says. "This is at the core of our need to drive to new levels of competitiveness. But it's frustrating because knowledge management is poorly understood. It's not an easy job to explain to your mother what you do for a living."

At Dow Chemical, Mr. Petrash started with the basics.

The company figured it could wring additional money from its tens of thousands of patents. Mr. Petrash got each of Dow's 15 major businesses to catalog their patent holdings in a standard format and then cross-referenced them. "We realized our [chemical-]catalyst technology spanned a dozen different businesses," Mr. Petrash says.

The result was more licensing deals and new revenue as the company identified new markets for products it had already developed. When Dow's epoxy business in Freeport, Texas, catalogued its 3,500 patents, it realized that its production process for bisphenol, a material used in resin, could be marketed to other companies. Dow is now licensing the process through a partner, says Phil Barnett, intellectual-assets manager for the epoxy business.

KNOWING THE KNOW-HOW

Patents, trademarks and copyrights are easy, however, compared with the intangible "know-how" that makes a company competitive. In a pilot project involving three of Dow's businesses, Mr. Petrash brought together heads of the units, along with research engineers, manufacturing managers, patent attorneys and marketing teams to identify the 200 to 300 most important technical processes at Dow. Then, to document the information, the teams used a template similar to the one used in the application process for patents.

"This is the know-how we want all of our business guys to have," Mr. Petrash says. "We're putting it in a very abbreviated form they can quickly grasp. We're talking one page, the four to five keys to their business. In many cases, that key know-how is the reason we're in that business."

By the end of the year, Mr. Petrash expects a commitment from Dow's top executives to expand the project companywide. Then he plans to move on to capture Dow's marketing knowledge, sales knowledge and customer knowledge.

"In the end, we want to have all of the key know-how that gives us our competitive advantage articulated and databased," he says. "Then we can visualize it. Then we can measure it. Then we can improve it."

SECOND THOUGHTS

1. What constitutes "the value of shared knowledge" (¶ 14) for today's businesses, according to the article?
2. What obstacles to the sharing of information must corporate "knowledge officers" overcome, according to Bank? What other forces not mentioned by Bank, both within and outside a given company, do you think resist such sharing?
3. How does *knowledge* seem to be defined in this article? If you think there are other kinds of knowledge, what are they, and how do they relate to the kinds discussed here?

Burning Chrome

William Gibson

William Gibson (b. 1948) is a science fiction writer from Vancouver, Canada. His most famous novel is *Neuromancer* (Ace Books, 1984), a dark vision of the near future in which Gibson coined the term "cyberspace" to refer to a matrix of electronic data controlled by powerful corporations. His other sci-fi novels include *Count Zero* (Arbor House, 1986), *Mona Lisa Overdrive* (Bantam, 1988), and *Virtual Light* (Bantam, 1993). "Burning Chrome" was first published in 1985 in *Omni* (<www.omnimag.com/>), a magazine for people interested in science and science fiction themes. (See also Gibson's story, "Johnny Mnemonic," in Chapter 1, p. 48.).

It was hot, the night we burned Chrome. Out in the malls and plazas, moths were batting themselves to death against the neon, but in Bobby's loft the only light came from a monitor screen and the green and red LEDs on the face of the matrix simulator. I knew every chip in Bobby's simulator by heart; it looked like your workaday Ono-Sendai VII, the "Cyberspace Seven," but I'd rebuilt it so many times that you'd have had a hard time finding a square millimeter of factory circuitry in all that silicon.

We waited side by side in front of the simulator console, watching the time display in the screen's lower left corner.

"Go for it," I said, when it was time, but Bobby was already there, leaning forward to drive the Russian program into its slot with the heel of his hand. He did it with the tight grace of a kid slamming change into an arcade game, sure of winning and ready to pull down a string of free games.

A silver tide of phosphenes boiled across my field of vision as the matrix began to unfold in my head, a 3-D chessboard, infinite and perfectly transparent. The Russian program seemed to lurch as we entered the grid. If anyone else had been jacked into that part of the matrix, he might have seen a surf of flickering shadow roll out of the little yellow pyramid that represented our computer. The program was a mimetic weapon, designed to absorb local color and present itself as a crash-priority override in whatever context it encountered.

"Congratulations," I heard Bobby say. "We just became an Eastern Seaboard Fission Authority inspection probe. . . ." That meant we were clearing fiberoptic lines with the cybernetic equivalent of a fire siren, but in the simulation matrix we seemed to rush straight for Chrome's data base. I couldn't see it yet, but I already knew those walls were waiting. Walls of shadow, walls of ice.

Chrome: her pretty childface smooth as steel, with eyes that would have been at home on the bottom of some deep Atlantic trench, cold gray eyes that lived under terrible pressure. They said she cooked her own cancers for people who crossed her, rococo custom variation that took years to kill you. They said a lot of things about Chrome, none of them at all reassuring.

So I blotted her out with a picture of Rikki. Rikki kneeling in a shaft of dusty sunlight that slanted into the loft through a grid of steel and glass: her faded camouflage fatigues, her translucent rose sandals, the good line of her bare back as she rummaged through a nylon gear bag. She looks up, and a half-blond curl falls to tickle her nose. Smiling, buttoning an old shirt of Bobby's, frayed khaki cotton drawn across her breasts.

She smiles.

"Son of a bitch," said Bobby, "we just told Chrome we're an IRS audit and three Supreme Court subpoenas. . . . Hang on to your ass, Jack. . . ."

So long, Rikki. Maybe now I see you never.   10

And dark, so dark, in the halls of Chrome's ice.

Bobby was a cowboy, and ice was the nature of his game, *ice* from ICE, Intrusion Countermeasures Electronics. The matrix is an abstract representation of the relationships between data systems. Legitimate programmers jack into their employers' sector of the matrix and find themselves surrounded by bright geometries representing the corporate data.

Towers and fields of it ranged in the colorless nonspace of the simulation matrix, the electronic consensus-hallucination that facilitates the handling and exchange of massive quantities of data. Legitimate programmers never see the walls of ice they work behind, the walls of shadow that screen their operations from others, from industrial-espionage artists and hustlers like Bobby Quine.

Bobby was a cowboy. Bobby was a cracksman, a burglar, casing mankind's extended electronic nervous system, rustling data and credit in the crowded matrix, monochrome nonspace where the only stars are dense concentrations of information, and high above it all burn corporate galaxies and the cold spiral arms of military systems.

Bobby was another one of those young-old faces you see drinking in the Gentle-   15 man Loser, the chic bar for computer cowboys, rustlers, cybernetic second-story men. We were partners.

Bobby Quine and Automatic Jack. Bobby's the thin, pale dude with the dark glasses, and Jack's the mean-looking guy with the myoelectric arm. Bobby's software and Jack's hard; Bobby punches console and Jack runs down all the little things that can give you an edge. Or, anyway, that's what the scene watchers in the Gentlemen Loser would've told you, before Bobby decided to burn Chrome. But they also might've told you that Bobby was losing his edge, slowing down. He was twenty-eight, Bobby, and that's old for a console cowboy.

Both of us were good at what we did, but somehow that one big score just wouldn't come down for us. I knew where to go for the right gear, and Bobby had all his licks down pat. He'd sit back with a white terry sweatband across his forehead and whip moves on those keyboards faster than you could follow, punching his way through some of the fanciest ice in the business, but that was when something happened that managed to get him totally wired, and that didn't happen often. Not highly motivated,

Bobby, and I was the kind of guy who's happy to have the rent covered and a clean shirt to wear.

But Bobby had this thing for girls, like they were his private tarot or something, the way he'd get himself moving. We never talked about it, but when it started to look like he was losing his touch that summer, he started to spend more time in the Gentleman Loser. He'd sit at a table by the open doors and watch the crowd slide by, nights when the bugs were at the neon and the air smelled of perfume and fast food. You could see his sunglasses scanning those faces as they passed, and he must have decided that Rikki's was the one he was waiting for, the wild card and the luck changer. The new one.

I went to New York to check out the market, to see what was available in hot software.

The Finn's place has a defective hologram in the window, METRO HOLOGRAFIX,   20
over a display of dead flies wearing fur coats of gray dust. The scrap's waist-high, inside, drifts of it rising to meet walls that are barely visible behind nameless junk, behind sagging pressboard shelves stacked with old skin magazines and yellow-spined years of *National Geographic.*

"You need a gun," said the Finn. He looks like a recombo DNA project aimed at tailoring people for high-speed burrowing. "You're in luck. I got the new Smith and Wesson, the four-oh-eight Tactical. Got this xenon projector slung under the barrel, see, batteries in the grip, throw you a twelve-inch high-noon circle in the pitch dark at fifty yards. The light source is so narrow, it's almost impossible to spot. It's just like voodoo in a nightfight."

I let my arm clunk down on the table and started the fingers drumming; the servos in the hand began whining like overworked mosquitoes. I knew that the Finn really hated the sound.

"You looking to pawn that?" He prodded the Duralumin wrist joint with the chewed shaft of a tel-tip pen. "Maybe get yourself something a little quieter?"

I kept it up. "I don't need any guns, Finn."

"Okay," he said, "okay," and I quit drumming. "I only got this one item, and I   25
don't even know what it is." He looked unhappy. "I got it off these bridge-and-tunnel kids from Jersey last week."

"So when'd you ever buy anything you didn't know what it was, Finn?"

"Wise ass." And he passed me a transparent mailer with something in it that looked like an audio cassette through the bubble padding. "They had a passport," he said. "They had credit cards and a watch. And that."

"They had the contents of somebody's pockets, you mean."

He nodded. "The passport was Belgian. It was also bogus, looked to me, so I put it in the furnace. Put the cards in with it. The watch was okay, a Porsche, nice watch."

It was obviously some kind of plug-in military program. Out of the mailer, it looked   30
like the magazine of a small assault rifle, coated with nonreflective black plastic. The edges and corners showed bright metal; it had been knocking around for a while.

"I'll give you a bargain on it, Jack. For old times' sake."

I had to smile at that. Getting a bargain from the Finn was like God repealing the law of gravity when you have to carry a heavy suitcase down ten blocks of airport corridor.

"Looks Russian to me," I said. "Probably the emergency sewage controls for some Leningrad suburb. Just what I need."

"You know," said the Finn. "I got a pair of shoes older than you are. Sometimes I think you got about as much class as those yahoos from Jersey. What do you want me to tell you, it's the keys to the Kremlin? You figure out what the goddamn thing is. Me, I just sell the stuff."

I bought it.   35

Bodiless, we swerve into Chrome's castle of ice. And we're fast, fast. It feels like we're surfing the crest of the invading program, hanging ten above the seething glitch systems as they mutate. We're sentient patches of oil swept along down corridors of shadow.

Somewhere we have bodies, very far away, in a crowded loft roofed with steel and glass. Somewhere we have microseconds, maybe time left to pull out.

We've crashed her gates disguised as an audit and three subpoenas, but her defenses are specifically geared to cope with that kind of official intrusion. Her most sophisticated ice is structured to fend off warrants, writs, subpoenas. When we breached the first gate, the bulk of her data vanished behind core-command ice, these walls we see as leagues of corridor, mazes of shadow. Five separate landlines spurted May Day signals to law firms, but the virus had already taken over the parameter ice. The glitch systems gobble the distress calls as our mimetic subprograms scan anything that hasn't been blanked by core command.

The Russian program lifts a Tokyo number from the unscreened data, choosing it for frequency of calls, average length of calls, the speed with which Chrome returned those calls.

"Okay," says Bobby, "we're an incoming scrambler call from a pal of hers in   40 Japan. That should help."

Ride 'em, cowboy.

Bobby read his future in women; his girls were omens, changes in the weather, and he'd sit all night in the Gentleman Loser, waiting for the season to lay a new face down in front of him like a card.

I was working late in the loft one night, shaving down a chip, my arm off and the little waldo jacked straight into the stump.

Bobby came in with a girl I hadn't seen before, and usually I feel a little funny if a stranger sees me working that way, with those leads clipped to the hard carbon studs that stick out of my stump. She came right over and looked at the magnified image on the screen, then saw the waldo moving under its vacuum-sealed dust cover. She didn't say anything, just watched. Right away I had a good feeling about her; it's like that sometimes.

"Automatic Jack, Rikki. My associate."   45

He laughed, put his arm around her waist, something in his tone letting me know that I'd be spending the night in a dingy room in a hotel.

"Hi," she said. Tall, nineteen or maybe twenty, and she definitely had the goods. With just those few freckles across the bridge of her nose, and eyes somewhere between dark amber and French coffee. Tight black jeans rolled to midcalf and a narrow plastic belt that matched the rose-colored sandals.

But now when I see her sometimes when I'm trying to sleep, I see her somewhere out on the edge of all this sprawl of cities and smoke, and it's like she's a hologram stuck behind my eyes, in a bright dress she must've worn once, when I knew her, something that doesn't quite reach her knees. Bare legs long and straight. Brown hair, streaked with blond, hoods her face, blown in a wind from somewhere, and I see her wave goodbye.

Bobby was making a show of rooting through a stack of audio cassettes. "I'm on my way, cowboy," I said, unclipping the waldo. She watched attentively as I put my arm back on.

"Can you fix things?" she asked.   50

"Anything, anything you want, Automatic Jack'll fix it." I snapped my Duralumin fingers for her.

She took a little simstim deck from her belt and showed me the broken hinge on the cassette cover.

"Tomorrow," I said, "no problem."

And my oh my, I said to myself, sleep pulling me down the six flights to the street, *what'll Bobby's luck be like with a fortune cookie like that? If his system worked, we'd be striking it rich any night now.* In the street I grinned and yawned and waved for a cab.

Chrome's castle is dissolving, sheets of ice shadow flickering and fading, eaten by the   55
glitch systems that spin out from the Russian program, tumbling away from our central logic thrust and infecting the fabric of the ice itself. The glitch systems are cybernetic virus analogs, self-replicating and voracious. They mutate constantly, in unison, subverting and absorbing Chrome's defenses.

Have we already paralyzed her, or is a bell ringing somewhere, a red light blinking? Does she know?

Rikki Wildside, Bobby called her, and for those first few weeks it must have seemed to her that she had it all, the whole teeming show spread out for her, sharp and bright under the neon. She was new to the scene, and she had all the miles of malls and plazas to prowl, all the shops and clubs, and Bobby to explain the wild side, the tricky wiring on the dark underside of things, all the players and their names and their games. He made her feel at home.

"What happened to your arm?" she asked me one night in the Gentleman Loser, the three of us drinking at a small table in a corner.

"Hang-gliding," I said, "accident."

"Hang-gliding over a wheatfield," said Bobby, "place called Kiev. Our Jack's   60
just hanging there in the dark, under a Nightwing parafoil, with fifty kilos of radar jammed between his legs, and some Russian asshole accidentally burns his arm off with a laser."

I don't remember how I changed the subject, but I did.

I was still telling myself that it wasn't Rikki who was getting to me, but what Bobby was doing with her. I'd known him for a long time, since the end of the war, and

I knew he used women as counters in a game, Bobby Quine versus fortune, versus time and the night of cities. And Rikki had turned up just when he needed something to get him going, something to aim for. So he'd set her up as a symbol for everything he wanted and couldn't have, everything he'd had and couldn't keep.

I didn't like having to listen to him tell me how much he loved her, and knowing he believed it only made it worse. He was a past master at the hard fall and the rapid recovery, and I'd seen it happen a dozen times before. He might as well have had NEXT printed across his sunglasses in green Day-Glo capitals, ready to flash out at the first interesting face that flowed past the tables in the Gentleman Loser.

I knew what he did to them. He turned them into emblems, sigils on the map of his hustler's life, navigation beacons he could follow through a sea of bars and neon. What else did he have to steer by? He didn't love money, in and of itself, not enough to follow its lights. He wouldn't work for power over other people; he hated the responsibility it brings. He had some basic pride in his skill, but that was never enough to keep him pushing.

So he made do with women.   65

When Rikki showed up, he needed one in the worst way. He was fading fast, and smart money was already whispering that the edge was off his game. He needed that one big score, and soon, because he didn't know any other kind of life, and all his clocks were set for hustler's time, calibrated in risk and adrenaline and that supernal dawn calm that comes when every move's proved right and a sweet lump of someone else's credit clicks into your own account.

It was time for him to make his bundle and get out; so Rikki got set up higher and farther away than any of the others ever had, even though—and I felt like screaming it at him—she was right there, alive, totally real, human, hungry, resilient, bored, beautiful, excited, all the things she was. . . .

Then he went out one afternoon, about a week before I made the trip to New York to see Finn. Went out and left us there in the loft, waiting for a thunderstorm. Half the skylight was shadowed by a dome they'd never finished, and the other half showed sky, black and blue with clouds. I was standing by the bench, looking up at that sky, stupid with the hot afternoon, the humidity, and she touched me, touched my shoulder, the half-inch border of taut pink scar that the arm doesn't cover. Anybody else ever touched me there, they went on to the shoulder, the neck. . . .

But she didn't do that. Her nails were lacquered black, not pointed, but tapered oblongs, the lacquer only a shade darker than the carbon-fiber laminate that sheathes my arm. And her hand went down the arm, black nails tracing a weld in the laminate, down to the black anodized elbow joint, out to the wrist, her hand soft-knuckled as a child's, fingers spreading to lock over mine, her palm against the perforated Duralumin.

Her other palm came up to brush across the feedback pads, and it rained all after-   70 noon, raindrops drumming on the steel and soot-stained glass above Bobby's bed.

Ice walls flick away like supersonic butterflies made of shade. Beyond them, the matrix's illusion of infinite space. It's like watching a tape of a prefab building going up; only the tape's reversed and run at high speed, and these walls are torn wings.

Trying to remind myself that this place and the gulfs beyond are only representations, that we aren't "in" Chrome's computer, but interfaced with it, while the matrix simulator in Bobby's loft generates this illusion . . . The core data begin to emerge, exposed, vulnerable. . . . This is the far side of ice, the view of the matrix I've never seen before, the view that fifteen million legitimate console operators see daily and take for granted.

The core data tower around us like vertical freight trains, color-coded for access. Bright primaries, impossibly bright in that transparent void, linked by countless horizontals in nursery blues and pinks.

But ice still shadows something at the center of it all: the heart of all Chrome's expensive darkness, the very heart . . .

Trying to remind myself that this place and the gulfs beyond are only representations, that we aren't "in" Chrome's computer, but interfaced with it, while the matrix simulator in Bobby's loft generates this illusion.

It was late afternoon when I got back from my shopping expedition to New York. 75 Not much sun through the skylight, but an ice pattern glowed on Bobby's monitor screen, a 2-D graphic representation of someone's computer defenses, lines of neon woven like an Art Deco prayer rug. I turned the console off, and the screen went completely dark.

Rikki's things were spread across my workbench, nylon bags spilling clothes and makeup, a pair of bright red cowboy boots, audio cassettes, glossy Japanese magazines about simstim stars. I stacked it all under the bench and then took my arm off, forgetting that the program I'd brought from the Finn was in the right-hand pocket of my jacket, so that I had to fumble it out left-handed and then get it into the padded jaws of the jeweler's vise.

The waldo looks like an old audio turntable, the kind that played disc records, with the vise set up under a transparent dust cover. The arm itself is just over a centimeter long, swinging out on what would've been the tone arm on one of those turntables. But I don't look at that when I've clipped the leads to my stump; I look at the scope, because that's my arm there in black and white, magnification 40 x.

I ran a tool check and picked up the laser. It felt a little heavy; so I scaled my weight-sensor input down to a quarter-kilo per gram and got to work. At 40 x the side of the program looked like a trailer truck.

It took eight hours to crack: three hours with the waldo and the laser and four dozen taps, two hours on the phone to a contact in Colorado, and three hours to run down a lexicon disc that could translate eight-year-old technical Russian.

Then Cyrillic alphanumerics started reeling down the monitor, twisting themselves 80 into English halfway down. There were a lot of gaps, where the lexicon ran up against specialized military acronyms in the readout I'd bought from my man in Colorado, but it did give me some idea of what I'd bought from the Finn.

I felt like a punk who'd gone out to buy a switchblade and come home with a small neutron bomb.

Screwed again, I thought. *What good's a neutron bomb in a streetfight?* The thing under the dust cover was right out of my league. I didn't even know where to unload it, where to look for a buyer. Someone had, but he was dead, someone with a Porsche watch and a fake Belgian passport, but I'd never tried to move in those circles. The Finn's muggers from the 'burbs had knocked over someone who had some highly arcane connections.

The program in the jeweler's vise was a Russian military icebreaker, a killer-virus program.

It was dawn when Bobby came in alone. I'd fallen asleep with a bag of takeout sandwiches in my lap.

"You want to eat?" I asked him, not really awake, holding out my sandwiches. I'd   85
been dreaming of the program, of its waves of hungry glitch systems and mimetic sub-programs; in the dream it was an animal of some kind, shapeless and flowing.

He brushed the bag aside on his way to the console, punched a function key. The screen lit with the intricate pattern I'd seen there that afternoon. I rubbed sleep from my eyes with my left hand, one thing I can't do with my right. I'd fallen asleep trying to decide whether to tell him about the program. Maybe I should try to sell it alone, keep the money, go somewhere new, ask Rikki to go with me.

"Whose is it?" I asked.

He stood there in a black cotton jump suit, an old leather jacket thrown over his shoulders like a cape. He hadn't shaved for a few days, and his face looked thinner than usual.

"It's Chrome's," he said.

My arm convulsed, started clicking, fear translated to the myoelectrics through the   90
carbon studs. I spilled the sandwiches; limp sprouts, and bright yellow dairy-produce slices on the unswept wooden floor.

"You're stone crazy," I said.

"No," he said, "you think she rumbled it? No way. We'd be dead already. I locked on to her through a triple-blind rental system in Mombasa and an Algerian comsat. She knew somebody was having a look-see, but she couldn't trace it."

If Chrome had traced the pass Bobby had made at her ice, we were good as dead. But he was probably right, or she'd have had me blown away on my way back from New York. "Why her, Bobby? Just give me one reason. . . ."

Chrome: I'd seen her maybe half a dozen times in the Gentlemen Loser. Maybe she was slumming, or checking out the human condition, a condition she didn't exactly aspire to. A sweet little heart-shaped face framing the nastiest pair of eyes you ever saw. She'd looked fourteen for as long as anyone could remember, hyped out of any-thing like a normal metabolism on some massive program of serums and hormones. She was as ugly a customer as the street ever produced, but she didn't belong to the street anymore. She was one of the Boys, Chrome, a member in good standing of the local Mob subsidiary. Word was, she'd gotten started as a dealer, back when synthetic pituitary hormones were still proscribed. But she hadn't had to move hormones for a long time. Now she owned the House of Blue Lights.

"You're flat-out crazy, Quine. You give me one sane reason for having that stuff   95
on your screen. You ought to dump it, and I mean *now.* . . ."

"Talk in the Loser," he said, shrugging out of the leather jacket. "Black Myron and Crow Jane. Jane, she's up on all the sex lines, claims she knows where the money goes. So she's arguing with Myron that Chrome's the controlling interest in the Blue Lights, not just some figurehead for the Boys."

"'The Boys,' Bobby," I said. "That's the operative word there. You still capable of seeing that? We don't mess with the Boys, remember? That's why we're still walking around."

"That's why we're still poor, partner." He settled back into the swivel chair in front of the console, unzipped his jump suit, and scratched his skinny white chest. "But maybe not for much longer."

"I think maybe this partnership just got itself permanently dissolved."

Then he grinned at me. The grin was truly crazy, feral and focused, and I knew that   100
right then he really didn't give a shit about dying.

"Look," I said, "I've got some money left, you know? Why don't you take it and get the tube to Miami, catch a hopper to Montego Bay. You need a rest, man. You've got to get your act together."

"My act, Jack," he said, punching something on the keyboard, "never has been this together before." The neon prayer rug on the screen shivered and woke as an animation program cut in, ice lines weaving with hypnotic frequency, a living mandala. Bobby kept punching, and the movement slowed; the pattern resolved itself, grew slightly less complex, became an alternation between two distant configurations. A first-class piece of work, and I hadn't thought he was still that good. "Now," he said, "there, see it? Wait. There. There again. And there. Easy to miss. That's it. Cuts in every hour and twenty minutes with a squirt transmission to their comsat. We could live for a year on what she pays them weekly in negative interest."

"Whose comsat?"

"Zürich. Her bankers. That's her bankbook, Jack. That's where the money goes. Crow Jane was right."

I stood there. My arm forgot to click.   105

"So how'd you do in New York, partner? You get anything that'll help me cut ice? We're going to need whatever we can get."

I kept my eyes on his, forced myself not to look in the direction of the waldo, the jeweler's vise. The Russian program was there, under the dust cover.

Wild cards, luck changers.

"Where's Rikki?" I asked him, crossing to the console, pretending to study the alternating patterns on the screen.

"Friends of hers," he shrugged, "kids, they're all into simstim." He smiled   110
absently. "I'm going to do it for her, man."

"I'm going out to think about this, Bobby. You want me to come back, you keep your hands off the board."

"I'm doing it for her," he said as the door closed behind me. "You know I am."

And down now, down, the program a roller coaster through this fraying maze of shadow walls, gray cathedral spaces between the bright towers. Headlong speed.

Black ice. Don't think about it. Black ice.

Too many stories in the Gentleman Loser; black ice is a part of the mythology. Ice that kills. Illegal, but then aren't we all? Some kind of neural-feedback weapon, and you connect with it only once. Like some hideous Word that eats the mind from the inside out. Like an epileptic spasm that goes on and on until there's nothing left at all . . .

> **Black ice is a part of the mythology. Ice that kills. Illegal, but then aren't we all? Some kind of neural-feedback weapon, and you connect with it only once.** 115

And we're diving for the floor of Chrome's shadow castle.

Trying to brace myself for the sudden stopping of breath, a sickness and final slackening of the nerves. Fear of that cold Word waiting, down there in the dark.

I went out and looked for Rikki, found her in a café with a boy with Sendai eyes, half-healed suture lines radiating from his bruised sockets. She had a glossy brochure spread open on the table, Tally Isham smiling up from a dozen photographs, the Girl with the Zeiss Ikon Eyes.

Her little simstim deck was one of the things I'd stacked under my bench the night before, the one I'd fixed for her the day after I'd first seen her. She spent hours jacked into that unit, the contact band across her forehead like a gray plastic tiara. Tally Isham was her favorite, and with the contact band on, she was gone, off somewhere in the recorded sensorium of simstim's biggest star. Simulated stimuli: the world—all the interesting parts, anyway—as perceived by Tally Isham. Tally raced a black Fokker ground-effect plane across Arizona mesa tops. Tally dived the Truk Island preserves. Tally partied with the superrich on private Greek islands, heartbreaking purity of those tiny white seaports at dawn.

Actually she looked a lot like Tally, same coloring and cheekbones. I thought 120 Rikki's mouth was stronger. More sass. She didn't want to *be* Tally Isham, but she coveted the job. That was her ambition, to be in simstim. Bobby just laughed it off. She talked to me about it, though. "How'd I look with a pair of these?" she'd ask, holding a full-page headshot, Tally Isham's blue Zeiss Ikons lined up with her own amber-brown. She'd had her corneas done twice, but she still wasn't 20-20; so she wanted Ikons. Brand of the stars. Very expensive.

"You still window-shopping for eyes?" I asked as I sat down.

"Tiger just got some," she said. She looked tired, I thought.

Tiger was so pleased with his Sendais that he couldn't help smiling, but I doubted whether he'd have smiled otherwise. He had the kind of uniform good looks you get after your seventh trip to the surgical boutique; he'd probably spend the rest of his life looking vaguely like each new season's media front-runner; not too obvious a copy, but nothing too original, either.

"Sendai, right?" I smiled back.

He nodded. I watched as he tried to take me in with his idea of a professional sim- 125 stim glance. He was pretending that he was recording. I thought he spent too long on my arm. "They'll be great on peripherals when the muscles heal," he said, and I saw how carefully he reached for his double espresso. Sendai eyes are notorious for depth-perception defects and warranty hassles, among other things.

"Tiger's leaving for Hollywood tomorrow."

"Then maybe Chiba City, right?" I smiled at him. He didn't smile back. "Got an offer, Tiger? Know an agent?"

"Just checking it out," he said quietly. Then he got up and left. He said a quick goodbye to Rikki, but not to me.

"That kid's optic nerves may start to deteriorate inside six months. You know that, Rikki? Those Sendais are illegal in England, Denmark, lots of places. You can't replace nerves."

"Hey, Jack, no lectures." She stole one of my croissants and nibbled at the top of one of its horns.   130

"I thought I was your adviser, kid."

"Yeah. Well, Tiger's not too swift, but everybody knows about Sendais. They're all he can afford. So he's taking a chance. If he gets work, he can replace them."

"With these?" I tapped the Zeiss Ikon brochure. "Lot of money, Rikki. You know better than to take a gamble like that."

She nodded. "I want Ikons."

"If you're going up to Bobby's, tell him to sit tight until he hears from me."   135

"Sure. It's business?"

"Business," I said. But it was craziness.

I drank my coffee, and she ate both my croissants. Then I walked her down to Bobby's. I made fifteen calls, each one from a different pay phone.

Business. Bad craziness.

All in all, it took us six weeks to set the burn up, six weeks of Bobby telling me   140
how much he loved her. I worked even harder, trying to get away from that.

Most of it was phone calls. My fifteen initial and very oblique inquiries each seemed to breed fifteen more. I was looking for a certain service Bobby and I both imagined as a requisite part of the world's clandestine economy, but which probably never had more than five customers at a time. It would be one that never advertised.

We were looking for the world's heaviest fence, for a non-aligned money laundry capable of dry-cleaning a megabuck online cash transfer and then forgetting about it.

All those calls were a waste, finally, because it was the Finn who put me on to what we needed. I'd gone up to New York to buy a new blackbox rig, because we were going broke paying for all those calls.

I put the problem to him as hypothetically as possible.

"Macao," he said.   145

"Macao?"

"The Long Hum family. Stockbrokers."

He even had the number. You want a fence, ask another fence.

The Long Hum people were so oblique that they made my idea of a subtle approach look like a tactical nuke-out. Bobby had to make two shuttle runs to Hong Kong to get the deal straight. We were running out of capital, and fast. I still don't know why I decided to go along with it in the first place; I was scared of Chrome, and I'd never been all that hot to get rich.

I tried telling myself that it was a good idea to burn the House of Blue Lights   150
because the place was a creep joint, but I just couldn't buy it. I didn't like the Blue Lights, because I'd spent a supremely depressing evening there once, but that was no excuse for going after Chrome. Actually I halfway assumed we were going to die in the attempt. Even with that killer program, the odds weren't exactly in our favor.

Bobby was lost in writing the set of commands we were going to plug into the dead center of Chrome's computer. That was going to be my job, because Bobby was going to have his hands full trying to keep the Russian program from going straight for the kill. It was too complex for us to rewrite, and so he was going to try to hold it back for the two seconds I needed.

I made a deal with a streetfighter named Miles. He was going to follow Rikki the night of the burn, keep her in sight, and phone me at a certain time. If I wasn't there, or didn't answer in just a certain way, I'd told him to grab her and put her on the first tube out. I gave him an envelope to give her, money and a note.

Bobby really hadn't thought about that, much, how things would go for her if we blew it. He just kept telling me he loved her, where they were going to go together, how they'd spend the money.

"Buy her a pair of Ikons first, man. That's what she wants. She's serious about that simstim scene."

"Hey," he said, looking up from the keyboard, "she won't need to work. We're   155
going to make it, Jack. She's my luck. She won't ever have to work again."

"Your luck," I said. I wasn't happy. I couldn't remember when I had been happy. "You seen your luck around lately?"

He hadn't, but neither had I. We'd both been too busy.

I missed her. Missing her reminded me of my one night in the House of Blue Lights, because I'd gone there out of missing someone else. I'd gotten drunk to begin with, then I'd started hitting Vasopressin inhalers. If your main squeeze has just decided to walk out on you, booze and Vasopressin are the ultimate in masochistic pharmacology; the juice makes you maudlin and the Vasopressin makes you remember, I mean really remember. Clinically they use the stuff to counter senile amnesia, but the street finds its own uses for things. So I'd bought myself an ultraintense replay of a bad affair; trouble is, you get the bad with the good. Go gunning for transports of animal ecstasy and you get what you said, too, and what she said to that, how she walked away and never looked back.

I don't remember deciding to go to the Blue Lights, or how I got there, hushed corridors and this really tacky decorative waterfall trickling somewhere, or maybe just a hologram of one. I had a lot of money that night; somebody had given Bobby a big roll for opening a three-second window in someone else's ice.

I don't think the crew on the door liked my looks, but I guess my money was okay.   160

I had more to drink there when I'd done what I went there for. Then I made some crack to the barman about closet necrophiliacs, and that didn't go down too well. Then this very large character insisted on calling me War Hero, which I didn't like. I think I showed him some tricks with the arm, before the lights went out, and I woke up two days later in a basic sleeping module somewhere else. A cheap place, not even room to hang yourself. And I sat there on that narrow foam slab and cried.

Some things are worse than being alone. But the thing they sell in the House of Blue Lights is so popular that it's almost legal.

At the heart of darkness, the still center, the glitch systems shred the dark with whirl-winds of light, translucent razors spinning away from us; we hang in the center of a silent slow-motion explosion, ice fragments falling away forever, and Bobby's voice comes in across light-years of electronic void illusion—

"Burn the bitch down. I can't hold the thing back—"

The Russian program, rising through towers of data, blotting out the playroom col- 165
ors. And I plug Bobby's homemade command package into the center of Chrome's cold heart. The squirt transmission cuts in, a pulse of condensed information that shoots straight up, past the thickening tower of darkness, the Russian program, while Bobby struggles to control that crucial second. An unformed arm of shadow twitches from the towering dark, too late.

We've done it.

The matrix folds itself around me like an origami trick.

And the loft smells of sweat and burning circuitry.

I thought I heard Chrome scream, a raw metal sound, but I couldn't have.

Bobby was laughing, tears in his eyes. The elapsed-time figure in the corner of the 170
monitor read 07:24:05. The burn had taken a little under eight minutes.

And I saw that the Russian program had melted in its slot.

We'd given the bulk of Chrome's Zürich account to a dozen world charities. There was too much there to move, and we knew we had to break her, burn her straight down, or she might come after us. We took less than ten percent for ourselves and shot it through the Long Hum setup in Macao. They took sixty percent of that for themselves and kicked what was left back to us through the most convoluted sector of the Hong Kong exchange. It took an hour before our money started to reach the two accounts we'd opened in Zürich.

I watched zeros pile up behind a meaningless figure on the monitor. I was rich.

Then the phone rang. It was Miles. I almost blew the code phrase.

"Hey, Jack, man, I dunno—what's it all about, with this girl of yours? Kinda funny 175
thing here . . ."

"What? Tell me."

"I been on her, like you said, tight but out of sight. She goes to the Loser, hangs out, then she gets a tube. Goes to the House of Blue Lights—"

"She what?"

"Side door. *Employees* only. No way I could get past their security."

"Is she there now?" 180

"No, man, I just lost her. It's insane down here, like the Blue Lights just shut down, looks like for good, seven kinds of alarms going off, everybody running, the heat out in riot gear. . . . Now there's all this stuff going on, insurance guys, real-estate types, vans with municipal plates. . . ."

"Miles, where'd she go?"

"Lost her, Jack."

"Look, Miles, you keep the money in the envelope, right?"

"You serious? Hey, I'm real sorry. I—"   185

I hung up.

"Wait'll we tell her," Bobby was saying, rubbing a towel across his bare chest.

"You tell her yourself, cowboy. I'm going for a walk."

So I went out into the night and the neon and let the crowd pull me along, walking blind, willing myself to be just a segment of that mass organism, just one more drifting chip of consciousness under the geodesics. I didn't think, just put one foot in front of another, but after a while I did think, and it all made sense. She'd needed the money.

I thought about Chrome, too. That we'd killed her, murdered her, as surely as if   190 we'd slit her throat. The night that carried me along through the malls and plazas would be hunting her now, and she had nowhere to go. How many enemies would she have in this crowd alone? How many would move, now they weren't held back by fear of her money? We'd taken her for everything she had. She was back on the street again. I doubted she'd live till dawn.

Finally I remembered the café, the one where I'd met Tiger.

Her sunglasses told the whole story, huge black shades with a telltale smudge of fleshtone paintstick in the corner of one lens. "Hi, Rikki," I said, and I was ready when she took them off.

Blue, Tally Isham blue. The clear trademark blue they're famous for, ZEISS IKON ringing each iris in tiny capitals, the letters suspended there like flecks of gold.

"They're beautiful," I said. Paintstick covered the bruising. No scars with work that good. "You made some money."

"Yeah, I did." Then she shivered. "But I won't make any more, not that way."   195

"I think that place is out of business."

"Oh." Nothing moved in her face then. The new blue eyes were still and very deep.

"It doesn't matter. Bobby's waiting for you. We just pulled down a big score."

"No. I've got to go. I guess he won't understand, but I've got to go."

I nodded, watching the arm swing up to take her hand; it didn't seem to be part of   200 me at all, but she held on to it like it was.

"I've got a one-way ticket to Hollywood. Tiger knows some people I can stay with. Maybe I'll even get to Chiba City."

She was right about Bobby. I went back with her. He didn't understand. But she'd already served her purpose, for Bobby, and I wanted to tell her not to hurt for him, because I could see that she did. He wouldn't even come out into the hallway after she had packed her bags. I put the bags down and kissed her and messed up the paintstick, and something came up inside me the way the killer program had risen above Chrome's data. A sudden stopping of the breath, in a place where no word is. But she had a plane to catch.

Bobby was slumped in the swivel chair in front of his monitor, looking at his string of zeros. He had his shades on, and I knew he'd be in the Gentleman Loser by nightfall, checking out the weather, anxious for a sign, someone to tell him what his new life would be like. I couldn't see it being very different. More comfortable, but he'd always be waiting for that next card to fall.

I tried not to imagine her in the House of Blue Lights, working three-hour shifts in an approximation of REM sleep, while her body and a bundle of conditioned reflexes took care of business. The customers never got to complain that she was faking it, because those were real orgasms. But she felt them, if she felt them at all, as faint silver flares somewhere out on the edge of sleep. Yeah, it's so popular, it's almost legal. The customers are torn between needing someone and wanting to be alone at the same time, which has probably always been the name of that particular game, even before we had the neuroelectronics to enable them to have it both ways.

I picked up the phone and punched the number for her airline. I gave them her real name, her flight number. "She's changing that," I said, "to Chiba City. That right. Japan." I thumbed my credit card into the slot and punched my ID code. "First class." Distant hum as they scanned my credit records. "Make that a return ticket." 205

But I guess she cashed the return fare, or else didn't need it, because she hasn't come back. And sometimes late at night I'll pass a window with posters of simstim stars, all those beautiful, identical eyes staring back at me out of faces that are nearly as identical, and sometimes the eyes are hers, but none of the faces are, none of them ever are, and I see her far out on the edge of all this sprawl of night and cities, and then she waves goodbye.

← SECOND THOUGHTS

1. After rereading the story, summarize the main events and write brief descriptions of the main characters—the narrator Jack, Bobby, Rikki, and Chrome. Consider the motivations of each character: What does each of them want, or what seems to drive them? For example, Jack says, "I couldn't remember when I had been happy" (¶ 156). Considering what you know or can infer about him, why do you think Jack agrees with Bobby to burn Chrome?

2. Gibson creates the futuristic setting of this story partly by using a specialized vocabulary of terms that sometimes aren't defined until later, or whose meaning the reader must infer from other clues. By yourself or with other readers, make a list of these unfamiliar terms—including *cowboy, ice, matrix,* and *simstim*—and construct definitions. What is the closest analogous term for each of these from today's world? How do the two terms compare—for example, how similar is Gibson's "matrix" to today's Internet? Why is each of these terms important to the story? For example, what seems to be the social, legal, and ethical status of "cowboys" in this future society?

3. Describe how information is controlled and valued in this future world. In what ways or to what extent is knowledge equivalent to power in this story? What kinds of power does information provide, and for whom? What seem to be the major social forces or institutions seeking to control information, and what relationships appear to exist among them?

4. To what extent do you think the fictional social conditions and status of information that you determine in response to question 3 reflect actual social conditions or power relations today? What major differences do you see—such as in the status or power of government, corporations, organized crime, or computer hackers/crackers?

⌘   DISCUSSION THREADS

re: Okerson and Fearer

1. How do you think the interests of information providers and information users, as discussed in Ann Okerson's article about digital copyright issues, balance out in the Church of Scientology affair described by Mark Fearer? What do you think Okerson would say about the "copyright terrorists" on either side of the Scientology case?

re: Okerson and Brody

2. Herb Brody would seem to agree with Ann Okerson that "Most scientists and scholars are far more interested in the widest possible distribution of their work to their professional colleagues than in capturing every possible royalty dollar" (¶ 6). What do you think these scientists and scholars—"merely passengers on a mass-media ocean liner" (¶ 7), according to Okerson—have to gain and lose by new rules about intellectual property being debated in the wake of the Lehman Commission? To what extent do you think researchers' new uses of technology "promote the progress of science and the useful arts," a stated purpose of U.S. copyright law?

re: Okerson, Fearer, and Bank

3. "Some network enthusiasts assert that 'information wants to be free,'" writes Ann Okerson, "but an equally vociferous band of digital pioneers contend that the real future of the global Internet lies in metering every drop of knowledge and charging for every sip" (¶ 3). Mark Fearer portrays the Church of Scientology as being motivated by greed in wishing to retain control of its "sacred texts," and David Bank describes how corporate "knowledge officer" Gordon Petrash works to "wring additional money from [Dow Chemical's] tens of thousands of patents" (¶ 27). How would you analyze the kinds of corporate knowledge management and knowledge-sharing discussed by Fearer and Bank in terms of the public versus private interest? Is the Fair Use Doctrine a good weapon for exposing dubious religious recruitment tactics? How do you think the public benefits or suffers from what Banks calls the "powerful force" of corporate "collective IQ" (¶ 7)?

re: Brody and Bank

4. Compare how and why information and knowledge are shared among scientists and within corporations, according to Herb Brody and David Bank. What's the goal or purpose of sharing knowledge in each case? What similar and different values lie behind these goals?

re: "Burning Chrome"

5. Based on the articles in this chapter, imagine or role-play a conversation about William Gibson's story "Burning Chrome" held by Ann Okerson, Mark Fearer,

Church of Scientology officials, Herb Brody, and David Bank. What aspects of the story do you think each commentator would emphasize, and how might each reply to the others?

re: Ownership and Sharing of Knowledge

6. Peer review—a conventional part of scientific research discussed by Herb Brody—is a process you've participated in if you've ever shared your writing or other work with classmates or colleagues in order to receive feedback about it for possible revision. You may also have felt the pressure, at school or at work, to keep your ideas private, to protect them or promote them in order to advance your own interests or the interests of an institution, organization, or company. How does the tension between collaboration and competition—or the competing interests of the public versus private individuals or businesses—get manifested in each article or story in this chapter? What different models for owning, controlling, and sharing knowledge are suggested? What values about collaboration or competition do you detect in each case? Where do your values lie by comparison?

⌗ RESEARCH LINKS

- *For direct links to listed Internet sources, additional reading selections and questions online, plus updates and supplementary Web resources, see* **Composing Cyberspace Online** *at <www.mhhe.com/socscience/english/holeton/>.*
- *For a complete set of research tools for the Internet—including the most useful search strategies, directories, and conventions for documenting online sources—see McGraw-Hill English Composition at <www.mhhe.com/socscience/english/compde/>.*

1. Write an argumentative paper taking a position on the Lehman Commission's recommendations about copyright in the digital age. The Web version of Ann Okerson's article (<www.sciam.com/0796issue/0796okerson.html>) includes a number of links to more information. Follow these links, and other related links you find in the process, to flesh out your understanding of current copyright issues; keep bookmarks and a working bibliography of the Internet sites you visit. You should be able to locate primary materials online, such as the text of the U.S. Copyright Act and the Commission's white paper referred to in the article, as well as secondary sources from organizations such as the Electronic Frontier Foundation (<www. eff.org/>) and the Center for Democracy and Technology (<www.cdt.org/>). You may find, at least on the Internet, that there's less consensus about digital copyright than Okerson implies. For library research, start with the "further reading" suggested by Okerson, and look up articles in law and technology law reviews that you see referenced both online and in print. If possible, interview professors or local attorneys knowledgeable about copyright and intellectual property issues.
2. Research and update the Scientology controversy and legal battles examined by Mark Fearer. In the library, use newspaper and magazine indexes to locate the latest news. On the Internet, you can find the Scientology home page at <www.

scientology.org/> and one of several anti-Scientology sites, Operation Clambake, at <home.sol.no/heldal/CoS/index2.html>. The online versions of Mark Fearer's article (<www.iw.com/1995/12/scientol.html>) and a longer article about the Scientology controversy published at the same time (December, 1995) in *Wired,* "alt.scientology.war" by Wendy M. Grossman (<www.wired.com/wired/3.12/ features/alt.scientology.war.html>), both include other Web links you can follow. Argue a position about copyright, trade secrets, fair use, or free speech based on this case. How do you weigh the interests of religious or quasi-religious organizations in wishing to protect selected materials versus the interests of outsiders in wishing to access those materials?

3. Herb Brody discusses two major events that catalyzed electronic communication among scientists: significant advances in research about superconductivity, and the controversy about cold fusion. Choose one of these events (or another recent scientific advance or controversy, such as the successful cloning of a sheep by a Scottish research lab in 1997), and analyze in more depth how the Internet affected this incident or area of research. Each of these examples was covered extensively in the traditional press as well as on the Internet.

4. Follow the Internet links provided with the Web version of Herb Brody's article (<web.mit.edu/afs/athena/org/t/techreview/www/articles/oct96/brody.html>)   to explore further some aspect of "wired science" or Brody's analysis that interests you. For example, links are provided to both kinds of science-oriented newsgroups that Brody discusses—the public, unmoderated kind "that contain little serious scientific discussion," and the moderated kind "where some reasoned and informed discussion can be found." If you have regular Internet access, make your own study of such groups (if you're interested in physics, you might compare *sci.physics* with *sci.physics.research*) by reading them daily over a period of weeks, recording your impressions, and if possible making a text archive you can refer to when writing your analysis. Test Brody's claims and assert your own judgment about the kinds and level of discourse in these online discussions.

5. Compare William Gibson's "Burning Chrome" with other short stories in this book in terms of how information and knowledge are valued, controlled, and shared. John Shirley's "Wolves of the Plateau" (Chapter, 3 p. 132), E. M. Forster's "The Air-Ship" (Chapter 4, p. 187), and Gibson's "Johnny Mnemonic" (Chapter 1, p.48) might make especially good comparisons. Which stories strike you as the most persuasive cautionary tales, or the most cogent reflections of today's trends in the uses of information technologies? Why? For a more extended research project, read more works by two of these authors, along with critical commentary from sources such as the MLA Bibliography, and compare their visions of information control in society.

6. Several movies have addressed hackers and "crackers," today's equivalent of William Gibson's "console cowboys" in stories such as "Burning Chrome" or novels such as *Neuromancer.* Movies you might choose to analyze include *Tron* (Walt Disney Productions, 1982; directed by Steven Lisberger), *Sneakers* (MCA/Universal Pictures, 1992; directed by Phil Alden Robinson), and *Hackers* (United Artists, 1995; directed by Iain Softley). Compare how hackers or the ethics of computer

hacking and cracking are portrayed in these movies. You might begin your research in the library with *Cyberpunk: Outlaws and Hackers on the Computer Frontier* by Katie Hafner and John Markoff (Simon & Schuster, 1991). Not surprisingly, these issues (and these movies) have been widely discussed on the Internet; starting places for online research include The New Hacker's Dictionary at <talon.apana.org.au/jargon/>, *2600: The Hacker Quarterly* at <www.2600.com/>, *Phrack* magazine at <freeside.com/phrack.html>, and Steve Mizrach's "Old and New Hacker Ethics" (<www.infowar.com/hacker/hackzf.html-ssi>).

The Classroom of the Future

Reprinted with permission of Chris Suddick.

The image of the boy Nicky transfixed by the TV screen, in the *Off 101* cartoon by Chris Suddick, captures the seemingly hypnotic hold that this medium has on our society—a society where half the children have TV sets in their bedrooms, where about 80 percent of households have VCRs, and where daily family TV use averages nearly 8 hours. The announcement in the surrounding cartoon panels of "National TV Turn-Off Week" and the parental admonition to "find something else to do!" also capture our ambivalence and concern about the medium, including the fear that many parents have about the negative effects of TV on learning and growing. The irony of the final panel, of course, is that the "something else" Nicky finds to do, a computer activity, looks very much like his previous activity: once again he's sitting and staring into an electronic appliance. The cartoon implicitly asks us whether there is any substantial difference in benefit for children between these two media, a question at the heart of this chapter.

As more Americans buy home computers and more schools integrate computer technology, the dilemma illustrated by Nicky is becoming increasingly common. Already some evidence indicates that networked computers are competing with TV for the time of both children and adults. As of mid-1997, surveys found that almost 28 million Americans over the age of 18 were regular Internet users. Sixty-four percent of U.S. public schools had some connection to the Internet by 1997, although only 14 percent of actual classrooms, labs, and school libraries had their own Internet connection.[1] But even in college, where computer and network access is more widespread, the crucial questions for students and educators alike are: What uses should be made of these new media? What are the advantages and disadvantages of computers for teaching and learning? How does technology promise to change our educational system, and to what extent should we embrace those changes?

Like TV before it, computer technology has been both lauded for its educational potential and criticized for its shortcomings. The Suddick cartoon doesn't indicate what Nicky is using his computer for, although he appears to be as passive as he was when watching TV: his hands are not on the keyboard or mouse, and his eyes are even more mesmerized than before. In sharp contrast, Claudia Wallis describes in this chapter the highly active and interactive uses of computers at a well-equipped New York prep school. She characterizes the ways that students use advanced technology to make discoveries, conduct discussions, and collaborate on projects as a "learning revolution." On the contrary, former computer hacker Clifford Stoll argues, computers are not essential to the most important kinds of learning, and only live teachers can provide the inspiration students need most. Stoll questions the social priority of heavy spending to wire schools, when student-to-teacher ratios remain high and other needs go unmet.

---

[1]Richard J. Coley, John Cradler, and Penelope K. Engel, *Computers and Classrooms: The Status of Technology in U.S. Schools* (Educational Testing Service, May 1997). Other statistics cited here are from a special section of the *San Jose Mercury News,* "Behind the Wave: Consequences of the Digital Age" (Section S, March 2, 1997), compiled by the paper's telecommunications reporting team. Sources cited by the *Mercury News* include Veronis, Suhler & Associates Inc.; Georgia Institute of Technology; National Telecommunications and Information Administration; and Nielsen Media Research.

While Kelly A. Zito acknowledges problems such as uneven access, student resistance, and ideological issues in the delivery of instructional technologies, she describes successful experiments with electronic collaboration and multimedia course materials from Cornell University's Engineering School. Monty Neill criticizes the seemingly irreversible trend to computerize education, arguing that these technologies are being used to perpetuate and extend the most egregious aspects of our economic system. Like Stoll, he claims that computers are used less to promote critical thinking than to produce "thinking machines." Finally, the fear that computers may be programming us more than we program them is dramatized in an excerpt from Orson Scott Card's best-selling science fiction novel, *Ender's Game.* In this selection, the schooling of 6-year-old Ender Wiggin is being conducted by a vivid and violent video game (one perhaps not so different from what Nicky is playing in the Suddick cartoon?).

Before reading these selections, it might be helpful to consider your own experiences and attitudes about using computers in school. For example,

1. How much access did you have to computers in primary school, middle school, high school, or college? What activities did you use computers for and for which classes? How were these activities integrated with your other schoolwork? What uses, if any, did you make of a local network, such as a class or school electronic bulletin board or discussion area? What uses, if any, did you make of the Internet or World Wide Web?

2. Many students report in surveys that technology helps them learn. Think of a few specific classroom uses that you, or someone you know, made of computer technology. In each case, what do you think was the educational purpose of this activity or exercise? What did you learn, and how useful did you find it? How would you compare this activity or exercise with a similar one that doesn't require computer technology?

3. You likely have heard some of the discussion about efforts to make more computer technology, including Internet connections, available for schools. What plans are you aware of for your school or a local school you're familiar with? What's your impression of the rationale for these efforts—why do you think many educators and administrators want to equip schools with more technology? What resistance or alternative arguments have you heard that question this rationale?

4. How do you picture school classrooms 25 years into the future? What uses do you imagine will be made of emerging technologies? Try sketching out two visions of "the classroom of the future"—one ideal or utopian vision, which represents your best hope, and one dystopian vision, which represents your worst fears about technology and education.

5. If you currently have access to a computer lab, classroom, or networked computers equipped with electronic discussion software, discuss with fellow readers any of the issues raised here.

The Learning Revolution

Claudia Wallis

What Wondrous Things Occur
When a School Is Wired
to the Max

Claudia Wallis (b. 1954) is the founding and managing editor of *Time For Kids,* published for 4th- to 6th-grade students. She has been with *Time* (<www.time.com/>) since 1979 as a medical writer, reporter on social issues, education writer, and science and technology editor. This article appeared in a special issue of the newsmagazine, "Welcome to Cyberspace," in 1995.

W hen the personal computer first entered the classroom three decades ago, prophets of the information age foretold a marvelous revolution. The world's storehouses of knowledge would become instantly available to young minds. Captivating digital landscapes would bring history, geography, and science alive on a screen. Not since Gutenberg, they exulted, had there been such a powerful new tool for learning. Their bold predictions were not wrong, just premature. Computers are indeed everywhere in American schools, but they are generally used as little more than electronic workbooks for drill, or as places for kids to play games during "free choice" periods. The promised revolution has failed to materialize.

But here and there, in cutting-edge schools around the nation, there are glimmers of what could be. Nowhere is the use of technology more advanced and pervasive than at the Dalton School, an elite private academy in New York City. The 1,300 students at Dalton, situated on Manhattan's posh Upper East Side, enjoy resources that any school would envy: a teaching staff studded with Ph.D.s, a 62,000-volume library and specialized studios for instruction in subjects such as architecture and dance. But what really distinguishes the school is the way it is using technology to change the traditional roles of the teacher as oracle and the student as passive receptable for hand-me-down knowledge. A visit to some of Dalton's classrooms provides a glimpse of what many believe is the future of education:

ROOM 711

A faint scraping sound can be heard in Mary Kate Brown's sixth-grade social studies classroom. The students are on a dig. Each group of three or four has been assigned a plot within an ancient Assyrian site. Their mission: to uncover what is at the site, to analyze carefully each artifact they find, then to formulate and defend a thesis about the

391

nature of the place and the people who once lived there.

Not even well-heeled Dalton can afford to take an entire class on an excavation in the Middle East, so these students are working on Archaeotype, a computer simulation of a dig—shoveling sounds and all—created at Dalton and based on an actual site. Still, the excitement of the hunt is palpable. As they uncover spearheads and ivory pieces on the screen, these 11-year-olds speak of "stratification" and "in situ artifacts" with near professional fluency.

This is a course in which kids learn by doing—absorbing science and ancient history through acts of discovery. "The material they find will admit of a variety of explanations," says Brown. "There is not just one right answer." To marshal evidence for their theories, students may consult Archaeotype's six online "libraries" of scholarly information and images (military, religious, royalty, etc.) as well as the greater resources of Dalton's library or even the Assyrian collection at the nearby Metropolitan Museum of Art. "It was like our own little land inside the computer," says Laura Zuckerwise, 12, who completed the course last year. "If we found a new artifact, it was as though we were the first people to discover it!"

Not even well-heeled Dalton can afford to take an entire class on an excavation in the Middle East, so these students are working on Archaeotype, a computer simulation of a dig—shoveling sounds and all.

4

5

Room 608

Like generations before them, the students in Jacqueline D'Aiutolo's 10th-grade English class have begun the epic journey into the dark heart of Shakespeare's *Macbeth*. They have completed reading the play, and now, working in groups of three or four, they are digging deeper into the text. Each group sits before a Macintosh computer, linked to an elaborate database.

Three students have been exploring the character of Lady Macbeth for a joint paper. What does she look like? How should she be imagined? A few keystrokes bring up a series of images: illustrations of the conniving noblewoman by a variety of artists, then a scene from Roman Polanski's 1971 film, *Macbeth*. As the action plays out in a window on the screen, the students discuss the lady's greed and her striking resemblance to a witch in the opening scene of Polanski's film. They can also look at scenes from the 1948 Orson Welles production and a 1988 staging for British TV. As they form theories about Shakespeare's intentions, they may consult any of 40 essays and hundreds of annotated bibliographies, as well as writings about the Bard's life and times.

Jacqui D'Aiutolo circles the room as her students work. She has been teaching *Macbeth* for more than 15 years and, though she first regarded computers and literature as "strange bedfellows," she has been amazed to see how students can deploy this modern tool to plumb the meaning of old texts. She has found that her own role has changed: she is less a lecturer than a resource and guide, helping students refine their own questions and

6

7

8

assisting in their search for answers. The incisiveness of their work has stunned her. Says D'Aiutolo: "You have depths you would never expect to reach in a 10th-grade class."

ROOM 307

There's an audible hum in Malcolm Thompson's classroom, known at Dalton as the   9 "AstroCave." Seven computers are in use, each surrounded by a clutch of students murmuring in continual discussion of their work. The place is littered with 13 1/2-in. square Palomar plates—grayish films, sprinkled with dark points of light representing stars and nebulae that were recorded by the 48-in. telescope at California's Palomar Observatory. Each student has chosen three stars and has been asked to calculate their brightness and temperature based on what the pupils see on the plates and can glean from a computer program called Voyager. Unlike Archaeotype, Voyager is an off-the-shelf program, but it is a tool of awesome power, simulating a view of the heavens from any point on earth, at any time, past or present.

Thompson's course has always been popular, but in recent years it has achieved an   10 almost cultlike status at the school. Though a vivid lecturer and the co-author of what was for years the country's top-selling astronomy textbook, Thompson has traded the chalk-and-talk approach for a task-oriented mode of teaching, using Voyager. His students do not "study" astronomy; they become astronomers. From September through June, they complete a series of tasks, using computer-based tools like the ones astronomers use. Each task builds on the ones before it, so calculations made in October may provide an essential tool for November's assignment. Thompson's students admit they often begin hopelessly lost until, by dint of their own collaborative labors and their teacher's counsel, they find their way. "It's the biggest satisfaction," says Simon Heffner, a senior. "You don't realize you understand it and then it hits you!" In the end, adds Thompson, "they have knowledge that they can deploy, as opposed to just passing a test."

It is no coincidence that Dalton began its plunge into technology with the Archaeotype   11 program. Excavation is an apt metaphor for the kind of "constructivist learning" promoted at the school: students must actively dig up information, then construct their own understanding from raw, observable facts. What the technology does is extend experience so that many more observations are possible. "It shifts education from adults giving answers to students seeking answers," says headmaster Gardner Dunnan. The underlying premise: we all understand and remember what we have discovered for ourselves far better than what we have merely been told.

Still, the guiding hand of the teacher is a vital element in the process. "You can't   12 just give kids powerful computers and powerful information and set them loose. The teacher must create a compelling set of educational questions," says associate headmaster Frank Moretti, who heads Dalton's technology group, the New Laboratory for Teaching and Learning.

The effectiveness of Dalton's program has been closely observed by outside   13 experts. The school hired John Black of Columbia's Teachers College to conduct a study comparing the analytic skills of Archaeotype students with sixth-graders at a similarly elite private school. "Kids at Dalton were twice as good at devising an explanation of data and defending it," says Black. "I've never seen such a big difference in an educational study." On the other hand, the new teaching methods mean sacrificing some breadth for depth. Sixth-grade history, for instance, no longer covers the Middle Ages or Rome, since so much time is devoted to Archaeotype.

The goal of any school is to prepare students for the world in which they will live.   14
Dalton's emphasis on collaborative learning—those little groups around a computer—"is perfect preparation," says Moretti, for a world in which most problems, whether scientific or corporate, are addressed by teams. Students often produce their papers collectively. Increasingly, projects are composed in the same multimedia format used for instruction. In addition, students are being primed for the world of the Internet by taking part in the school's own E-mail and bulletin-board system. They log onto the Dalton Network from home or at school to "chat" with friends, confer with teachers, or join online discussions of movies and records.

The most remarkable feature of the system however, is the "conferences"—discussion groups associated with certain courses. This year's most popular spins off a senior-class seminar in civil rights. Not only do all 17 students in the class participate, but twice as many outside the class have joined in. An additional hundred or so just log on to read what's been   15

Not only do all 17 students in the class participate, but twice as many outside the class have joined in.

said. The exchange, moderated by the teacher, is both analytical and heated, especially on divisive topics like affirmative action. Observes Moretti: "When children begin to take their own time outside the classroom to respond to questions that are important to them and become identified with positions within the larger community, that is a kind of personal development that wasn't possible in the old-fashioned school."

How relevant are Dalton's experiments to all those old-fashioned schools across   16
the country with strained budgets and less privileged kids? Very relevant, insists headmaster Dunnan. Sure, it takes serious money and expertise to create something like Archaeotype, he concedes. (Dalton received $3.7 million from real estate mogul Robert Tishman to develop technology.) "But once something is developed, it need not be very expensive." To prove that point, Dalton has begun to offer its learning technology to a few public schools. The Juarez Lincoln Elementary School in Chula Vista, California, for instance, has been using Archaeotype for three years, much to the delight of its largely poor and ethnically diverse students. Ultimately, Dalton hopes to be able to bring its technology to market.

Alas, sharing software alone will not bring about the education revolution. Few   17
schools today have the computing power to run multimedia programs like those used at Dalton. Fewer still have the resources to support a complex schoolwide network (though increasingly schools can connect to existing networks). Still, anyone who has seen what technology can do for learning is convinced of its future. "There's something inevitable about this," says Christina Hooper, a Distinguished Scientist at Apple Com-

puter and an expert on educational technology. She believes it may take 10 years, or more like 20, before the technology is widespread, but the prophets of the post-Gutenberg age in education will finally be proved right.

⟵ SECOND THOUGHTS

1. Wallis contrasts the use of classroom computers "as little more than electronic workbooks for drill" (¶ 1) with the more sophisticated "wondrous things" happening at Dalton School. Where do your previous experiences with classroom technology fit into this range?

2. Based on this article, how would you define "constructivist learning"? How do you think this kind of learning is manifested or promoted in each of the extended examples given by Wallis—the projects in rooms 711, 608, and 307? Which of these projects do you think could be carried out in more conventional ways, and with what success?

3. Wallis argues that Dalton "is using technology to change the traditional roles of the teacher as oracle and the student as passive receptacle for hand-me-down knowledge" (¶ 2). How would you characterize the roles of teachers and students in some of your own classes? Based on this article and your own experience, to what extent do you think changing the traditional relationship between teachers and students is a good thing?

Computers in the Classroom

Clifford Stoll

What's Wrong with This Picture?

Clifford Stoll (b. 1950), trained as an astronomer, is a computer security expert and writer and speaker about the computer revolution. His first book, *The Cuckoo's Egg: Tracing a Spy through the Maze of Computer Espionage* (Doubleday, 1989), chronicles how he tracked and caught a German spy ring operating over the Internet. This selection is excerpted from his second book, *Silicon Snake Oil: Second Thoughts on the Information Highway* (Doubleday, 1995), in which he explores his ambivalence about where the Internet and computer technology are leading society. Stoll has a home page on the Web at <www.ocf.berkeley.edu/~stoll/>.

Remember those goofy cartoons where you had to find all the things wrong in a picture? There'd be a six-legged dog, a duck flying upside down, a kid with two heads. Every now and then, I see something so weird that I ask myself, "What's wrong with this picture?"

All of us want children to experience warmth, human interaction, the thrill of discovery, and solid grounding in essentials: reading, getting along with others, training in civic values.

Only a teacher, live in the classroom, can bring about this inspiration. This can't happen over a speaker, a television, or a computer screen. Yet everywhere, I hear parents and principals clamoring for interactive computer instruction.

What's wrong with this picture?

The state of North Carolina spent seven million dollars to tie sixteen high schools with a fiber-optic network. It's one of those high-visibility experiments that attracts politicians and professional education consultants.

This interactive video system lets Professor Maria Domoto teach Japanese to four high schools. She can see her students and interact with them over a split television screen, even fax exams to them. But the class size still can't exceed thirty: "Beyond twenty to thirty, you lose any personal contact," she says. "I want to see the students I'm teaching."

She makes an important point: even with electronic links, teachers can't handle much

> **Even with electronic links, teachers can't handle much more than two dozen students. It was that way for our grandparents, it will be that way for our grandchildren.**

5

396

more than two dozen students. It was that way for our grandparents, it will be that way for our grandchildren. Television, radio, and computers can bring great teachers into our lives. But no teacher can listen to everyone at the same time.

Professor Domoto's classes began with twenty-six students. By year's end, over half had failed or dropped out. Hardly surprising when they didn't meet their teacher in person. How can she correct a student's writing posture, or show the way to hold a brush-pen or chopsticks?

Anyways, Japanese isn't a snap course. Students won't complete it unless they're committed—the very thing that television and computers can't inspire.

Left unanswered in the North Carolina high school experiment: how to handle   10
discipline problems. It's difficult enough in a live classroom—ask any teacher. Or perhaps discipline becomes a moot issue in the electronic classroom. With no live teacher, who cares?

Wait a second. They spent seven million dollars so their students can watch television in school. I'm wondering how many teachers they could hire and how many books they could buy for seven million dollars. What's wrong with this picture?

Chris Whittle spent far more, piping commercial educational television into schools. His Channel 1 television network folded, having promised—and failed—to make schools a better place.

In the past, schools tried instructional filmstrips, movies, and television; some are still in use, but think of your own experience: name three multimedia programs that actually inspired you. Now name three teachers that made a difference in your life.

I do remember that whenever I saw an educational film in high school, it meant fun for everyone. The teacher got time off, we were entertained, and nobody had to learn anything. Computers and the Internet do the same—they make it easy for everyone, but damn little teaching happens.

What's most important in school? Working with good teachers who can convey   15
method as well as content. Except to the extent that students are involved with a caring teacher, schooling is limited to teaching facts and techniques. In this sense, network access is irrelevant to schooling—it can only prevent this type of interaction.

The computer is a barrier to close teaching relationships. When students receive assignments through e-mail and send in homework over the network, they miss out on chances to discuss things with their prof. They don't visit her office and catch the latest news. They're learning at arm's length.

It's not good for the teachers either. Dr. Dave Cudaback, a senior lecturer at the University of California, Berkeley, teaches a great astronomy class. But he dreads receiving e-mail from students around the world. "I have barely enough time to spend with my own students. How can I possibly find time to answer questions from hundreds of others?"

I guess what I'm trying to say is this: students deserve personal contact with instructors—interactive videos and remote broadcasts are no substitute for studying under a fired-up teacher who's there in person.

✦ ✦ ✦

I'm not convinced that network access improves most college courses. At the trivial end, it's used for class assignments. Yet generations of students have managed such things by hand—there's no need to pass these over the wires. When you receive your assignments over the network, there's no place for marginal notes or a smiling "Well done" in the corner.

Nor is a computer network needed to collaborate—cooperative projects go easier   20
when everyone's in the same room. College students live and study near each other; of all people, they don't need networks to work together. And if teaching cooperation is important, colleges should require that students work in the same room, so that they recognize and resolve conflicts.

Computers themselves aren't necessary for most college studies. They have nothing to do with athletics and fine arts. They're only incidental to the humanities, whether philosophy, history, or literature. A good term paper will shine, whether hand-lettered or laser-printed.

Judging from the courses I've attended, computers aren't essential to beginning engineering classes, although professors like to assign problems with them. Concepts like stress tensors, Gauss's law, and conservation of momentum can be illustrated, but not taught, by software. Every electrical engineer knows Ohm's law and the right-hand rule . . . I doubt that anyone learned these from a computer.

One afternoon, you sit at a round table with four others. In front of each diner, there's a plate and a single chopstick. In the middle of the table sits a big dish of rice. Without two chopsticks, none of you can eat. How do you share your chopsticks so everyone's satisfied?

Computer scientists recognize this problem as the dining philosophers problem. It has important implications in building operating systems—how do you equitably distribute resources among competing processes? How can you bypass a bottleneck? How do people share?

Strangely, computer scientists don't study this problem using computers. Instead,   25
they use the ordinary tools of symbolic mathematics and logic. Major advances in computing often come from understanding data structures, and from sympathetically studying how people use computers. Even in computer science, the actual computer is often incidental.

OK, so I'm not an authority in engineering, humanities, or fine arts. But I've paid my dues in physics and astronomy, and in those basic sciences, computers have nothing to do with learning.

No computer can help someone understand the meaning of a wave function, angular momentum, or the relativistic-twins paradox. Software can simulate these on a glass screen, but these simplifications depend on someone else's understanding, which may be quite limited.

Up and down the line, computer programs feed us someone else's logic, instead of encouraging us to develop our own. When confronted by a quandary, we're fed someone else's rubric rather than creating our own assaults on the problem.

After all, what's a computer program except a construct of someone else's mind? If you're satisfied with that, well, go right ahead. But to me, real learning means inventing my own ways of solving problems . . . ways that might not fit into prearranged software.

Think of the dining philosophies for a moment. Some edutainment program might 30
let you explore different algorithms for sharing chopsticks, perhaps letting each
philosopher take one gulp, then passing a pair of chopsticks over to the next guy. It's
someone else's idea.

But that computer program won't give you the option of breaking all the chopsticks in half, thus allowing all five philosophers to eat with short chopsticks. Nor does
it allow you to create forks or to tell the philosophers to eat with their fingers.

How about writing your own software? Now that's a different story. When you
write your own macros or programs to solve problems, you explore both the process
and possible answers. You invent the machine that solves the problem. It's closer to
creating, farther from mere duplicating.

Under pressure to come up with ways to use computers in college, profs hand out
homework that has little to do with coursework and everything to do with learning
computers. Instead of creating problem sets where the science shines through and the
math works out easily, they increasingly give problems that can only be solved with an
assigned program. As a result, students learn how to use a set of programs, but remain
hazy about the fundamental science.

In return, students interpret this emphasis on computers as meaning they must get
the numerically right answer. They don't show their work—they can't, since everything's hidden in software. Instead, they're judged on whether they've uncovered that
magic right answer. And it's easy to cheat—copy someone else's work, either by disk
or over the network.

My sister Jeannie told me about high school kids that would save their corrected 35
compositions and term papers. The next year, their kid brothers and sisters would recycle 'em. This had been going on for years, and no one had ever been caught.

Inspired by her story, I moseyed around the Internet to see if homework assignments are being electronically pooled. A quick search with the Gopher tool produced
long lists of homework assignments and answers, from around the world. Seems that
professors assign problem sets over the network and, a few weeks later, post the
answers. Both assignment and answer get archived.

I heard of an introductory astronomy class that had students transforming coordinates—a useful exercise. In the past, you'd go up to the roof and pick a couple of stars
about 30 degrees apart. This made the geometry simple. You'd then measure positions
with a protractor, and calculate distances and angles.

But today's class provides students with a floppy disk of software to show them
how to pick stars and rotate coordinates. The pupils see pretty star charts on their
screens, along with lists of positions. Enter the right command, and the program measures angles. They never have to go outside.

I won't say anything about teaching astronomy without looking at the sky. However, I'm damned worried that these students spend most of their time learning tools,
rather than concepts. Science is knowing about our environment, not being able to
manipulate a computer program.

What's the capital of North Dakota? Where's the industrial section of Germany? On 40
what lake do you find Kyoto?

These are ordinary questions of geography. You'll find the answers in an atlas or encyclopedia. Or look 'em up faster using the Internet—the World Wide Web will do it for you, as will key-word searches. On a Unix computer connected to the Internet, enter *gopher,* choose *Veronica,* then search until you find a likely title.

During the day it might take ten minutes, but if the network is lightly loaded, you might get a reply within a minute. The answers are Bismarck, the Ruhr Valley, and Biwa. Why don't these replies satisfy?

Because those factoids are simple and boring. Geography is far deeper than names and places. Consider more flavorful questions. What political compromises caused Bismarck to become the capital of North Dakota? Why isn't Kyoto the capital of today's Japan? What's the history of the Ruhr Valley, and what are the implications of its new Eastern European competition?

Snaggy questions like these branch off into history, politics, economics, and geology. They don't have simple, one-line replies. Their answers are charged with controversy, and they change from year to year as our understanding of geography evolves. These questions require thinking—their importance isn't in the answers, but in what turns up during the research.

Online databases reply readily to the first type of question—simple, direct   45
answers, the kind that show up on multiple-choice exams. It's a black-and-white view of the world, one well-suited to a digital network.

Alas, but our world has no such simplicity. The good questions have no easy answers; likely they have no answers at all. But it's the quest that beckons so seductively! Search the Internet for the pathway to world peace and justice. Find a database telling how to settle the thousand-year-old cross-cultural hatreds in Serbo-Croatia. Create a spreadsheet that balances the federal budget.

That's the problem. Answers are less important than the process of discovery. What else did I uncover in the search? Could I recast my question and run off in a different direction? What are the fallacies in my original assumptions?

The World Wide Web will tell me the volume of water behind Egypt's Aswan Dam—a fact. Far more useful is to know how to calculate this number—a skill. Sure, it's a kick to search out this fact on the Internet, but I find more satisfaction from calculating it myself.

Computer networks return answers—often the right ones—but they emphasize the product over the process. When I'm online, I sense the vast ocean of information available to me. But I'm alone, without a tutor or librarian.

Lisa Kadonaga has spent plenty of hours in the library. To understand climatic   50
change, she studies historical weather data. This is the kind of simple database that ought to be available over computer networks.

And, at first, she found plenty of temperature records from weather stations across North America. These records went back a decade, and covered all the major cities.

But studying global warming means culling through long-term trends, going back centuries. Nobody has ever keyed that data into a computer.

Lisa's research soon took her to stacks in the back of libraries. Turned out that the database isn't simple: weather stations move, urban sprawl changes microclimates, thermometers get recalibrated. News of these crucial alterations doesn't make it onto computer databases—use those numbers at your own risk.

"A student asked me if I used my network account a lot for my thesis work," Lisa said. "Well, I get messages from researchers and from my professors, but most of the notes I send are to friends. Even now, plenty of people in our department are doing just fine without accounts. Who relies on the Internet for all their data? Even if you do find a source, there's no guarantee you'll be able to use it."

Casual users and serious researchers place their trust in the accuracy and complete-   55
ness of data on the network. They're relying upon information of unknown pedigree and dubious quality, since little on the Internet has been refereed or reviewed.

Computer searches are incomplete—they can't tell us what's not yet online. One research group may post their results to the net, another may publish in a journal. The online researcher has thousands of blind spots.

All these factors are hidden from the researcher who relies on the simple string of numbers reported over the Internet. If you're satisfied with clean facts, numeric answers, and institutional reports, then look 'em up on the Internet.

I suspect that most schoolteachers know that there's little value in just getting on the net and retrieving stuff. You might as well walk into a library and randomly pick books off the shelf. A much better educational experience is to gather local data and cooperate with others in analyzing it.

I watched a group of kids measuring how weather patterns move through their town. When a rainstorm blew through, they wrote down when the first raindrops struck their homes. Later, the students compared their data and plotted how the rain clouds traveled.

These high school kids were doing real science—no weather forecaster works at   60
this level of detail. Sure, a network might have helped, but the science came through without the computers. Central to this project were the teachers and students, rather than the technology.

Computers emphasize test scores, rather than accomplishment. Getting the right answer doesn't mean someone has achieved much, nor does messing up an exam mean someone is stupid. These trials measure how well someone can take tests . . . hardly a useful life skill.

Remember sweating through those tired multiple-choice exams? The number-two pencils and electronically graded answer sheets? Computers can't handle anything else.

And the scores from these standardized exams—they have the nerve to report three digits of precision, when their test doesn't justify it. There's no difference between a score of 527 and 523, yet this empty precision hoodwinks the gullible into thinking that one student is smarter than another. It's as if I stuck my hand in a lake and announced that the water is 37.4 degrees.

Every year, the Scholastic Aptitude Test asks graduating high school students, "Which of these sentences is wrong?" They don't ask them to write an essay explaining how the European parliamentary form of government differs from the American congressional system or the Canadian parliamentary.

No, that problem has no right or wrong answer. It measures how well a student   65
knows the subject. Gives her a forum to express an opinion or tell a story. Tells about
her ability to cogently express herself. The testing computers can't even read these
answers, let alone score them.

But you can. I can. A good teacher can.

How well does our new technology fit into the classroom?

Our schools face serious problems, including overcrowded classrooms, teacher
incompetence, and lack of security. Local education budgets hardly cover salaries,
books, and paper.

Computers address none of these problems. They're expensive, quickly become
obsolete, and drain scarce capital budgets. Yet school administrators want them desperately. What's wrong with this picture?

Unlike books, pencils, paper, and chalk, computers have street value. Result: 70
they're routinely stolen from schools, which are notoriously difficult places to secure.
Would you leave your thousand-dollar laptop in a high school locker? Computers
aren't as cheap or as lightweight as books—and the value of portable computers makes
the pupil vulnerable to bullies and thieves.

A few years ago, Apple donated thirty computers to the Oakland Unified School District. Today, perhaps five are still working. Why? All that were not locked down were
ripped off. Someone stole the cables and keyboards to systems that were locked to desks.
And those remaining are used for nothing more advanced than teaching touch-typing.

Computers break down in ways that neither teacher nor student can fix on the
spot. Try rebooting from a cooked hard disk in front of thirty impatient sixth-
graders. Or install a complex piece of software during the ten minutes between
classes. This preparation and overhead isn't considered by advocates for the high-
tech classroom.

And when the computers do work, they're tough to teach with. Stand before a
classroom and everyone looks at you. You can tell when their attention wanders, when
you've made a good point, and when it's time to pack it in. You can scribble a diagram
on the chalkboard, walk around the classroom, or question an individual.

But try speaking to a group that has computers on their desks. First, you can't see
everyone, because those monitors get in the way. The keyboards and screens compete
for the students' attention. And you can't point to the screen so everyone can follow
along. If someone's lost or can't find the control key, you must squeeze behind a row
of students and point to the right place.

Students in these classes have an easier time—they can hide behind the monitors   75
and avoid the teacher's gaze. They have a perfect excuse for not taking notes—there's
a keyboard and monitor where their notebooks oughtta sit.

Incidentally, try taking notes with a computer someday. For a fast typist, it works
OK, though you can't draw diagrams or doodle in the margins. I feel self-conscious,
worried that my typing annoys those around me.

With the exception of well-funded, privileged schools, classrooms lack the most
fundamental infrastructure for computing. They're missing telephone lines and often
have but a single AC power outlet.

Wiring classrooms isn't cheap. The California Department of Education estimates that it would cost almost a half billion dollars to provide telecommunications into every classroom in the state. And that doesn't include adding power outlets. Moreover, today's standard connections, Ethernet and coaxial cable, will be obsolete within a decade.

Schools have few phones, and those they have, teachers are loath to use. Typically, there's zero budget for long-distance telephone calls or online fees. Jack Crawford, active in children's networking, observed that if there are any charges at all, most teachers will avoid the system entirely. A few will use it sparingly, but the only group that will stay online are those who can charge the expense to someone else.

This hits rural school districts especially hard: few of the major communications   80
suppliers have dial-up modems outside of the cities. On top of the online fees, such schools must pay long-distance access charges. In addition, school hours are during the daytime, so phone charges and online fees are highest when classes are in session.

To try to get around these limitations, Jack helped organize the K12net, a low-cost network that uses cheap bulletin boards rather than high-speed Internet links. They begin by assuming that schools have no money, and that individual schools will develop in different ways. They use Fidonet, a slow, unreliable, but utterly cheap way to send messages.

While the Internet is connecting professional computers together, Fidonet is strictly for the hobbyist. It uses ordinary telephone connections between bulletin boards: late at night, modems automatically dial each other, shake hands, and pass the day's messages across. Since mail is compressed and bundled, the system cuts down on long-distance phone charges.

Fidonet offers no guarantees. It might take a week for a message to get across the continent. Addresses may change without notice. Some mail falls through the cracks. If you need essential communications, pick some other pathway.

For tight-budget operations that don't mind slower responses, Fidonet works great and costs a fraction of the Internet. Schools, bulletin boards, and rural community centers are latching on. It's one of those grass-roots systems that works.

Aside from the mechanical problems of using computers in classrooms, I wonder how   85
this digital wizardry will affect the content of schoolwork.

Certainly, college-bound students should know basic computing: enough word-processing skills to write a paper, the ability to use and modify a spreadsheet, and a familiarity with database programs. Remember, though, that plenty of profs still accept handwritten term papers.

Should computer dexterity be taught at the expense of other skills? Hard to say, especially in a time when driver's education is disappearing from many high schools.[1]

Maybe computing should be integrated with other classroom activities? Sounds tempting—combine computing with math, physics, or history. In a sense, we teach students to become information hunter-gatherers. Tell them how to access

_____

[1]"An amusing complaint from a guy who owns five computers but no car," says my editor.

online resources and make sure they're comfortable finding their way around the networks.

This assumes that most everything is available online and that networks use simple, standardized tools. It also assumes that primary source material isn't messy and that students will know how to use the data presented to them. I doubt that any of these assumptions are valid.

There's a deeper assumption: that gathering information is important. These 90
teaching projects magnify the computing side, while making the learning experience seem trivial.

In a well-publicized classroom experiment, a group of fifth-graders from Washington State conducted an online survey. As a geography project, they asked the price of a twelve-inch pizza. Using the networks, they found highs of twelve dollars in Alaska to a low of four dollars in Ohio.

A most appealing project: these students were learning geography, handling the tools of economic research, and meeting others over the Internet. All this from their online classroom.

But hold on. That pizza data could just as readily have been acquired by telephone or letter or fax. There's nothing inherent to the Internet here—it's just the data-transmission vehicle.

More damning: they were learning the wrong-most thing about geography—that data collection is an end in itself. It's usually the easy part of research, and the part requiring the least thought.

Better to hear how the fifth-graders worked with the data further, coming up with 95
hypotheses explaining the trends in pizza prices. Is there more competition in Ohio's pizza market than in Alaska's? Are ingredients cheaper? Are these prices associated with unemployment?

Why not study Spanish, trace the flow of Pacific Rim forest products, or perform a class play? None of these have the same glamour or technological appeal as a class project over the Internet. Yet they're likely to be far more important to the students' future than a survey of pizza prices.

At the 1993 Computer-Using Educators Conference in Santa Clara, California, David Thornburg, director of the Thornburg Center of Professional Development, hooked his computer into the White House section of America Online. From there, he downloaded a dozen press releases, a presidential speech, several proposals to Congress, and hundreds of pages of governmental reports. He turned to the audience and said, "Look at all this research material that these kids now have."

In the back of the room, one teacher quietly remarked, "OK, what's next? I've got one computer and thirty kids. What can they do with this raw data? I'd have to print out a hundred pages, review what's there, then generate a lesson. As it sits, this material is worthless in a real classroom."

✦ ✦ ✦

What do we mean by *computer literacy?* Along with buzzwords like *information superhighway, interactive multimedia,* and *paradigm,* it's a fuzzy term without fixed meaning. Defining these is like trying to nail Jell-O to the wall.[2]

To one person, computer literacy means that a student can type on a keyboard. Another sees it as the ability to use standard tools to send, copy, or delete files. A third expects students to be able to write a simple program in BASIC. One teacher showed me an exam where a student had to describe the functions of different pieces of hardware.

What does computer literacy mean to a child who can't read at grade level and can't interpret what she reads? What does it mean to a teen-ager who can't write grammatically, not to mention analytically?

But what does computer literacy mean to a child who can't read at grade level and can't interpret what she reads? What does it mean to a teenager who can't write grammatically, not to mention analytically?

If a child doesn't have a questioning mind, what good does all this networked technology do?

Have we ever spoken of automobile literacy or microwave-oven literacy? Each of these is important today; yet high schools are shedding their driver's education programs and home economics classes. There's far more need for cooks, drivers, and plumbers than programmers, yet parents and school systems insist on teaching computer skills.

But what are these skills? Over the past decade, we've realized that programming is of little value except to those few who take it up as a career. Word processing is plenty handy, but hardly requires a semester of teaching.

And just because students use computers doesn't mean they're computer-literate. How many couch potatoes know how their televisions work?

Slowly, the term *computer-literacy* is becoming passé, I'm told. In its place, educators speak of computer-aided education, networking, and technology seeding. If computer vendors seem filled with puffery, you haven't heard these people talk.

In physics, you measure the brightness of light with a photometer and voltages with a voltmeter. Bogosity—the degree to which something is bogus—is measured with a bogometer. When listening to these guys, I watch the needle of my bogometer.

It's usually administrators and consultants—not teachers—that give me the heebie-jeebies. Like when Frank Withrow, director of learning technology at the Council

---

[2]Nailing Jell-O to the wall? While a grad student at Princeton, Don Alvarez tried it. I replicated his experiment and discovered that it's not so hard.

The obvious way is to freeze the Jell-O, but we're looking for something with a little more artistry than a tank of liquid nitrogen.

First nail the slab of Jell-O to a horizontal board with a grid of ten-penny nails, spaced an inch apart. Then tip the board up and nail it to the wall.

What won't work is to simply hold the Jell-O against the wall, then pound in nails. It sags under its own weight and tears as fast as you pound the nails. Not enough tensile strength.

of Chief State School Officers, asserts that the network brings us virtual publishing; moreover, the ability to transmit information instantly has brought us to "a major crest of human development and symbolisms."[3]

Symbolisms? My bogometer reads midscale. Then I read David Thornburg's course materials for the fall 1994 Computer-Using Educators Conference. He says that the information age is over, replaced by some sort of communications age. He wants to reshape education because "students are going to primary source materials to research their term papers without leaving their bedrooms. The days of running through the library stacks pulling reference materials are numbered."

Not much need for books and school libraries? The bogometer needle reaches into the red zone.   110

Alan November, a consultant for the Glenbrook high schools in Illinois, believes that today's students are in the test-preparation business. In the May/June 1994 issue of *Electronic Learning,* he says that pupils will soon build information products that can be used by clients around the world. Teachers, in turn, will become brokers "connecting our students to others across the nets who will help them create and add to their knowledge." That one pegged my bogometer.

I'd discount such high-tech mumbo jumbo except that there are so many believers. Parents walk away from schools satisfied if they merely see computers in the classroom. Principals plead for budgets large enough to bring interactive media into their schools. Many teachers are cowed by consultants sporting fancy degrees. School board members apply for grants to bring networks into local districts. Lost in this promotion are students.

← SECOND THOUGHTS

1. How does Stoll support his claim that "only a teacher, live in the classroom" (¶ 3) can inspire students? To what extent do you agree with this argument?
2. Why are computers not essential to most college courses, in Stoll's view? What kinds of learning does Stoll suggest are most important, and why does he think technology can be counterproductive to that learning? How would you compare your own experiences, or those of classmates or fellow readers, in any of the academic fields (from the humanities, sciences, or engineering) that Stoll discusses?
3. Summarize Stoll's views about the high costs of equipping schools with cutting-edge technology. How does he seem to think that money should be spent instead? To what extent do you agree that students get "lost in this promotion" (¶ 112) of computer-aided education and networking?
4. Stoll claims that computers promote "a black-and-white view of the world" (¶ 45). What, if any, value does Stoll seem to find in using computers in education? To what extent do you think Stoll's own arguments about the educational uses of computer technology promote a black-and-white view of this issue?

[3]At Multiple Media: The Next Step, a conference in Atlanta, Georgia, on February 16, 1994. Mr. Withrow was keynote speaker.

The Digital Difference

Kelly A. Zito

Kelly A. Zito (b. 1971) is a business reporter for *The Ithaca Journal* in Ithaca, New York. She graduated in 1994 from Cornell University with a BS in communications. She also contributes to the magazines *Mid-Atlantic* and *Cornell Engineering,* where this article appeared in 1997. *Cornell Engineering* is a magazine primarily for alumni of Cornell's engineering school.

I t's 1 A.M., a few weeks into spring semester, and Thomas Tong '97 CS is sitting at 1
his computer evaluating a classmate's document published on the World Wide Web. This informal critique, which he has to do for about 20 or so other web sites, is required for Computer Science 130: Creating Web Documents. Tong's cursor is on an introductory page, so there are a lot of basics: a brief bio, the student's career aspirations, and links to CNN and Disney—her favorite sites.

But Tong thinks something is missing. He clicks on a little icon at the base of the 2
document and leaves his classmate a note advising her to add more visuals to the somewhat spartan page.

"After all, it's the welcome page, the first thing a person sees," he writes. "If you 3
don't have images and interesting graphics there, who is going to want to continue through your page?"

When the author of the document views her on-line creation—perhaps in the next 4
few minutes—she will see that Tong has left her a comment. If she agrees with his design suggestions, she may decide to digitize family photos or download a cartoon.

The system that allows Tong and his classmate to converse electronically on one of their 5
first assignments in CS 130 is called CoNote. Short for Collaborative Note System, CoNote was developed several years ago by Dan Huttenlocher, associate professor of computer science, and Jim Davis, a researcher with the Design Research Institute, in an effort to improve and expand communication between instructors and pupils.

The system is similar to e-mail or a newsgroup—also known as an electronic bul- 6
letin board—in that students and faculty (or teaching assistants) can send communiqués electronically. The difference is that CoNote can be embedded directly within any online document. In this case, the document was a student's web page, but CoNote is also useful in a computerized problem set, course outline, or lecture transcript.

Like Tong, students can leave questions or comments—officially called "annota- 7
tions" in CoNote-ese—within the page or next to a particularly pesky problem. Periodically, teaching assistants or faculty members check the digitized "handout" and leave helpful hints or corrections.

Huttenlocher, who says more than a thousand students have used the three-   8
year-old system, believes CoNote and systems
like it are the future of engineering education.

"Computers are obviously going to become a
more dominant part of the way we teach," he said.
"In a way, the use of computers in engineering is
evolving. Fewer professors are using computers for calculations—that's what calculators
are for. Now, computers are seen as a way to
communicate."

"Fewer professors are   9

using computers for

calculations—that's what

calculators are for. Now,

computers are seen as a   10

way to communicate."

Huttenlocher's comments reflect a growing
trend. Across Cornell's engineering quad, instructors and students are sitting in front of their screens
more often as a means to connect than to crunch numbers. Sure, there are still the volu-
minous data sets that need to be processed by computer, but educators and administrators are discovering that, whether the final product is a personalized web page or a
bells-and-whistles electronic textbook, computers are a way to contact those hard-to-
reach students and, in some cases, form better one-on-one relationships.

Several factors are driving the evolution, not the least of which is a more cohesive   11
approach to teaching. Huttenlocher's annotation system, for example, is a big improvement over computer newsgroups in which questions and comments are posted in a
chronological list. "With CoNote, a student posts a question within a certain context
and everyone can see it; that way you get very few repeat questions," Huttenlocher
says. "With newsgroups that's not the case."

There are also several learning advantages to CoNote, Huttenlocher says. Problem   12
sets take up much less time. There's no waiting for a teaching assistant's office hours
to get feedback on an assignment. Students and TAs can also work at their leisure
(which may be at 4 A.M. on a Tuesday morning) and still be productive.

As a result, Huttenlocher says, the whole dissemination and learning process is   13
sped up. His colleague and co-instructor in CS 130, Assistant Professor Brian Smith,
says "we're finding that students are answering their classmates' questions before we
can even get to them. Since one of the best ways to learn is to teach someone else,
that's a huge advance."

The teaching assistants who do much of the troubleshooting admit that CoNote   14
does place a certain pressure on them. Andras Ferencz '97 CS, who helped author the
system, is one of five TAs for CS 130. He says that although students answer about 50
percent of their classmates' questions, there is still "some pressure for TAs to respond
pretty frequently." For a recent assignment with a 2 A.M. deadline, all five TAs were up
until the wee hours of the morning answering technical annotations.

"It's definitely a better way of doing things," Ferencz said. "But there are some   15
limitations. Because you're leaving messages that are really broadcast to the whole
class, you have to be thorough, but not give away the answers."

Despite the public nature of such a forum, participants have a sense of privacy that   16
highlights an indirect advantage to CoNote. "In a lecture setting, student questions are
part question, part showing off," Huttenlocher says. "People who are really confused

are not going to ask questions in class. But there is something about posting a message that makes it easier; much easier than stopping a lecture."

Whether it's the sense of anonymity or increased confidence through quicker prob-   17
lem-solving, CoNote users appear to be developing a sense of community around the system. Tong says that while "discussing an assignment in person would be the ideal, CoNote allows you to interact on a pretty personal, private basis."

"For first-year students especially, it's important for them to have communities   18
that they feel a part of," Smith says. "If the computer can help include them, it will enhance their educational experience."

And Smith's assertions are backed up by research. Geri Gay, an associate profes-   19
sor of communication in Cornell's College of Agriculture and Life Sciences, has been studying computer-based collaborative problem solving. Gay is director of the Interactive Multimedia Group (IMG), an interdisciplinary research and design team interested in expanding the role of computers in education and communication. Working with the College of Engineering, the IMG studied a group of engineering students charged with solving a design problem. The study parameters called for students at geographically distributed locations to work collaboratively over a computer network, using audio/visual conferencing, chat boxes, and software that allowed participants to share drawings across the network.

Gay's results show that the wide range of resources encouraged the students to   20
increase the breadth and depth of communication and allowed them to overcome technical difficulties more quickly. But she warns that social and psychological issues surrounding collaborative information systems such as CoNote can't be ignored. Specifically, Gay points out that students may be hesitant to use such systems because of the naturally competitive environment at most universities. In a study of sophomores from several colleges last summer, Gay found that "many didn't want to annotate because they didn't want to leave their best ideas on-line."

Still other students long for the good old days when a pen, paper, and calculator were   21
the only necessities for a prelim. Last summer, Professor David Caughey, director of the Sibley School of Mechanical and Aerospace Engineering, gave his co-op students in a fluid mechanics class the choice between taking an exam on paper or on the computer. Caughey, who taught the course using several chapters of Introductory Fluid Mechanics, an interactive CD-ROM textbook he is authoring with Professor James Liggett in the School of Civil and Environmental Engineering, was surprised at the outcome of his unofficial survey.

"The students weren't as fearless as I thought they might be. They wanted a con-   22
ventional prelim—I think because there was a fear of the unknown to a degree."

Gay says that reaction is natural, especially to a medium that is changing so   23
rapidly. "We're finding that a lot of students aren't using these new communication resources as effectively as they could, almost because there is so much out there. Yes, we can put these tools at their fingertips, but they still need guidance and help finding their way through them."

Caughey says he learned that lesson last summer. "After the course, I realized that   24
there had been no studio time in which the TA and I were available to help students

learn how to use the CD-ROM book. Next time, we'll spend a lot more time working with them, explaining how to best use it."

Still, the book's technical features received good reviews. Not just a digitized text, 25 the chapters include computational utilities, interactive graphs, bits of video, annotations, audio narration, and options to read the material at three different levels of detail.

Caughey says he was motivated by the need to make engineering more dynamic. 26 To demonstrate, he selects one of the book's many magnifying-glass icons. The screen zooms in on a line graph that illustrates a complex problem using oxygen. As Caughey types in the symbol for helium along the graph's vertical axis, the shape of the graph changes dramatically. In another example, he changes the landscape of a diagram showing shockwave patterns by substituting one number.

"This is the kind of thing I want the students to see—the underlying relationships 27 between things. One of the problems with conventional books is that they are so static. This new medium allows students to jump in, play with the numbers, and see the big picture."

Caughey says the book, a project funded by the American Society of Civil Engi- 28 neers, should be finished by the end of this year and will be used when he teaches the Fall 1998 introductory fluid mechanics class in mechanical engineering. Until then, Caughey will be fine-tuning the book with two distinct goals: using every interactive feature available and making learning as enjoyable as possible.

"I literally want it to make homework more fun, so that students spend less time on 29 it, but they get more out of it. I don't want them to be so bogged down with the mechanics of calculating a solution to a problem that they miss the over-arching idea behind it."

But an increasingly computerized learning experience raises other questions— 30 logistical as well as financial. Discourse on web pages, online coursework, and CD-ROM textbooks inevitably leads to the idea of access. In addition to departmental and college resources, Cornell's central support organization has nine public computer labs, including two on the engineering quad. Campus-wide there is a push—with about $4 million behind it—to upgrade classrooms, equipping them with network connections, data-video projectors, and VCRs. Some of the colleges are even creating "smart" classrooms, offering advanced audio and visual link-ups and a computer on almost every desk.

But is that enough in a school where still almost a third of all undergraduates don't 31 own computers? John Hopcroft, the Joseph Silbert Dean of Engineering, believes the number of high-tech classrooms and public labs is sufficient for now, but he admits that pressure is building to create more. In many classes, collaborative problem-solving projects that mimic corporate scenarios are becoming a staple, and increasingly, this means using appropriately designed electronic classrooms. As money from private and public sources becomes available, he says, a larger amount will be spent in the information technology arena.

Paulette Clancy, associate professor of chemical engineering and the chair of the 32 engineering college's Computing Policy Committee, says that her group has talked about requiring all accepted engineering students to bring their own computers. "That's a very thorny issue," she admits.

At this critical point, Clancy sees the role of the college as one of evaluating   33
student and faculty needs for information technology and providing as much guidance and encouragement as possible. Currently the committee is trying to facilitate
faculty initiatives in teaching and attempting to offer standards for hardware and
software.

"This is a really crucial time and the college is trying to prepare for all the   34
changes coming," she said. "As departments are scrambling for money to keep up
with the short life span of computer technology, there is a definite need for central
support, and it's not clear at this point who is going to pay for this. All of these
advances come at a price."

Clancy and Hopcroft both believe that investing intelligently in faculty is a contin-   35
uing priority. Over the last three years, Hopcroft says, the college has hired at least 10
information technology specialists.

Hard-drive capacity and price tags aside, there are quite a few psychological and   36
ideological issues surrounding the computerization of education. Hopcroft emphasizes
that old-fashioned student-teacher interaction shouldn't be overlooked in the tangle of
technical issues. "Yes, we're hiring very forward looking people, people on the cutting
edge of technology. But they also have to be the type of people who engage the undergraduates."

A telecommuter Cornell, where sophomores in Idaho take Computer Science 212, may   37
be farfetched, but educators recognize that the increasing use of computers for communication will change the way faculty members accomplish their mission.

Frank Huband '60 EP, Ph.D. '66, executive director of the Washington, D.C.–based   38
American Society for Engineering Education, suggests that teachers and students at
most universities, including Cornell, will rely on a
mixture of off-campus, computer-based interaction
and on-campus, face-to-face interaction. "I think
it's reasonable to think that as computers become
more integral to the teaching process, computers
will be required for certain functions."

Those who believe strongly in the importance of Cornell's social fabric agree that the computer is an important tool for today's educators, but it's not a substitute for meaningful one-on-one discussion.

Those who believe strongly in the   39
importance of Cornell's social fabric agree that the
computer is an important tool for today's educators, but it's not a substitute for meaningful one-
on-one discussion.   40

"Technology is a good thing, but it won't
replace the classroom," says Hopcroft. "Socrates
and Plato stood in front of a group of people and
that tradition has endured. When television came
along, we thought that would change the face of
education. It hasn't. Interacting with students,
exchanging ideas, understanding the rules of behavior, talking with faculty outside of
the classroom, these are the things that teach students how to acquire knowledge. That
is our job, and I don't see that happening by way of telecommuting."

The Access Issue

How to best provide access to information technology is one of those questions that seems to raise only deeper, more difficult questions at Cornell and peer institutions around the country.

While Cornell has taken some significant steps toward improving existing labs and making Internet access available to residence hall dwellers, demand for technology access continues to grow. And as professors increasingly provide course pages on the World Wide Web and post syllabi on-line, calls for the university to make even greater strides aren't abating.

"Some students believe that there are two Cornells, the haves and the have-nots," says Carrie E. Regenstein, Cornell's associate director for academic technology. "For those who can't afford additional expenses, we have to ensure that their access to technology is as equitable as possible."

But Regenstein says that the multi-faceted issue of access must be studied very carefully before the university makes any sweeping policy decisions.

In January 1995, the Faculty Advisory Board on Information Technology (FABIT) issued a report titled "Planning for Learning Technologies Services." Outlined in the 30-page document were both short- and long-term goals for expanding student access to information resources including wiring residence halls for network communication and providing network IDs and e-mail addresses to incoming freshmen. Both measures have been completed as well as the development of the Travelers of the Electronic Highway workshop in which all incoming students are introduced to information technologies at Cornell during Orientation Week. (Dan Huttenlocher chaired the FABIT sub-committee on Student Access to Information Resources.)

In addition, the university established a line-item in the budget for the upgrade of Academic Technology Services' computer labs each year. The Upson Hall lab is slated for improvements this summer. And since last summer, west and north campus residential areas each have a computer lab open 24 hours, seven days a week.

The number of students who own personal computers has also been advancing rapidly over the past five years. About 66 percent of all undergraduates surveyed in 1995 reported having computers, up from 58 percent, 56 percent, and 48 percent reported in the three previous years. For engineering students, ownership in 1995 was at about 71 percent; for students in arts and sciences, 72 percent.

Regenstein says those figures will most likely keep going up, possibly reaching the 90 percent range. But that doesn't solve all the problems.

"You still have to think about the rhythm of student life," she says. "If students have a two-hour break between classes, they're not necessarily going to want to walk home to do homework. They're going to want to sit down at a computer, and we have to prepare so that they can do that."

The low percentage of students living in university-affiliated housing may be one of the biggest stumbling blocks for Cornell in creating "a port for every pillow," or guaranteeing network access round-the-clock.

At Stanford University, about 95 percent of all undergraduates live in some kind of student housing. There, 24-hour computer clusters—a group of five computers complete with a scanner, laser printer, and network connections—dot dorm floors and university-owned houses and apartment complexes. Jeff Merriman, Stanford's director of residential computing, said that 72 clusters have been in use since the late 1980s, with few complaints.

"Sometimes we do get a call around crunch time that there aren't enough computers. Usually we can set up a few more computers if there's a real problem."

Cornell freshmen get first priority to live in the dorms, which were networked two years ago.

New "express stations"—in campus coffee shops, for example, where students can make a brief stop to send e-mail or check their current bursar bill from a lower-tech machine—have helped reduce some of the traffic in full-service labs.

Mandating computer ownership, as some schools do, is linked to financial aid issues. Potential Cornellians apply directly to individual colleges and—in some cases—departments, where this option might be considered.

Regenstein and others recognize the pressure. The 1995 FABIT report states that if the university does not provide its students with the means and know-how to use information technology, Cornell "runs the short-term risk of having a significant number of frustrated and angry students. . . . In the longer term we will be failing to educate our students for life in the 21st century."

The document also warns that without world-class information technology, Cornell stands the chance of losing the "best and brightest" students—and faculty—to rival institutions.

But despite the occasional newspaper articles and photos depicting long lines of students at campus computer labs, Regenstein says that filling every possible room with networked computers isn't necessarily the answer. "A range of solutions must be explored."

For now, Regenstein says, academic and residential departments, colleges, and the university administration are working together on the challenges of using technology to support innovation while providing adequate access as "standard operating procedure." Regenstein adds that it may be time to update and build on the FABIT report's recommendations.

"The goal of the university is to move forward in a unified fashion so that students can work comfortably anywhere on campus. The best thing we can do is have people come together, share ideas, and plan effective and efficient solutions. The bottom line is that we must provide outstanding service to students—and seamlessly—throughout the university."

SECOND THOUGHTS

1. According to the article, what do engineering teachers and students using CoNotes, Cornell's Collaborative Note System, see as its advantages over more traditional classroom tools? What evidence does Zito present for the success of CoNotes?

2. David Caughey mentions several goals for the interactive CD-ROM textbook he coauthored with James Liggett. What are these goals, and how successfully do they seem to have been achieved? How would you compare any experience you've had with electronic texts or course materials?

3. Zito addresses several problems regarding the uses of instructional technologies, including student resistance, logistical and financial issues, and psychological and ideological issues. Which of these seem most important to you? How would you expand on Zito's analysis of one such problem, and what solutions can you propose?

4. Does your school, company, or organization also divide into the technological "haves and have-nots," as some Cornell students claim in Zito's sidebar on "The Access Issue"? How so? Compare your response with those of other readers.

Computers, Thinking, and Schools in the "New World Economic Order"

Monty Neill

Monty Neill (b. 1948) has written widely on education and assessment issues. He is a member of the Midnight Notes Collective, a group that publishes books about political economy, including *Midnight Oil* (Autonomedia, 1992). This essay appeared originally in *Resisting the Virtual Life: The Culture and Politics of Information* (edited by Iain A. Boal and James Brooks; City Lights, 1995), a collection of essays offering a critical view of technology for an educated audience.

Capitalism is the first productive system where the children of the exploited are disciplined and educated in institutions organized by the ruling class.

> *Mariarosa Dalla Costa and Selma James*

1   Two primary reasons are given for plugging schools into the National Information Infrastructure (NII; called "the information superhighway"). Plugging-in is required to prepare students to be highly skilled, highly paid workers in the economy of the future; and it is essential for reforming schools into institutions that will produce students who can think and solve problems.

2   The "double helix" of high-skill jobs and cognitively complex schooling is presented as liberatory (Berryman and Bailey 1992). But the use of computerization toward a distinctly nonliberatory end is the more likely consequence of the twinning of school and work in the emerging world capitalist economy.

COMPUTERS AND THE JOBS OF THE FUTURE

3   Both conservatives and liberals argue that for the U.S. to "be number 1" in the world economy a more educated working class is needed, one that works harder *and* smarter. The claim is that then corporations will create jobs that utilize the workers' skills. These high-skill workers will be more productive than others and will therefore earn

415

high wages. The alternative, they warn, is low skills and low wages. Schools must therefore educate "all" students to "world-class standards" so that the corporations will be competitive.

This argument is made in the report *America's Choice* by the National Center on   4 Education and the Economy (NCEE 1990), probably the most influential piece on U.S. education since *A Nation at Risk* (fraudulently) maintained that falling school quality endangered national security. The NCEE view can be found in legislation, particularly the recently enacted Goals 2000 school reform bill; in numerous corporate education reform proposals (e.g., California Business Roundtable 1994); and various books and government reports (e.g., Carnevale and Porro 1994). It has become virtually unquestioned conventional wisdom.

The most obvious thing about this claim is that it presumes an uncontrollable and   5 inevitable economy to which "we" must adapt. It demands that educators accept, not challenge—never mind reconstruct—the economy.

Yet two points about the emerging economy suggest that "we" should not accept   6 it. First, continual lowering of wages is already fact and not likely to turn around; second, most new hires are not likely to be doing high-skill work. For U.S. workers, real wages have been declining nearly 1 percent per year for two decades, while the dispersion of the wage—the gap between high- and low-wage work—has simultaneously widened.

As Midnight Notes (1992) argues, this calculated intent of the capitalist system   7 over the past twenty years to reduce working-class power and income around the globe has had substantial success. Its political and technical ability to move products and services rapidly around the world has weakened the capacity of working people to band together at the national level to push up or even maintain wages. Since the competition for jobs cannot be contained by national borders, wages are dropping toward the lowest levels among the competitors even for many high-skill jobs such as computer programmer. This push is, if anything, intensifying. The North American Free Trade Agreement, for example, is organized as a one-way ratchet to continue the lowering of wages in Mexico, Canada, and the U.S. (Calvert and Kuehn 1993), to intensify what Kuehn terms "the race to the bottom." There is certainly no reason to believe that the capitalist system will create a worldwide high-wage system or that the U.S. will remain immune from wages within its borders falling to "world-class standards."

The fallacy that most jobs will be high-skill is also widely accepted. Yet even   8 strong proponents of the claim, such as Bailey (1991), acknowledge that most new hires for at least a decade will be filling old slots that do not require the knowledge and skills that proponents of the "high-skills" argument point to. Moreover, the labor market forecasts that project growth in the U.S. in medium- or high-skill jobs do not consider changes in the world economy that are dispersing skilled employment more widely while driving down wages. At most, the number of middle-level-skill jobs will grow slightly in the coming decade.

Even school reformers whose first interest is not in creating workers to serve the   9 economy nonetheless buttress their reform proposals by pointing to the presumed high-skill information economy. But what are the implications of all this for schools? Lower wages coupled with continuous attacks on public services and increased class and race

stratification—the actually existing U.S. conditions—strongly suggest continuation of the "savage inequalities" so eloquently described by
Jonathan Kozol (1991): sharp class gradation with
immiseration for many.

> **Not only are rich kids more likely to have computers at school, but their schools' machines are more apt to be up to date, drive more sophisticated software, and be connected to the Internet.**

The way computers and paraphernalia have
been distributed already indicates this (Piller 1992;
Pearlman 1994; Ramirez and Bell 1994; SEDLetter 1993). Not only are rich kids more likely
to have computers at school, but their schools'
machines are more apt to be up to date, drive more
sophisticated software, and be connected to the
Internet. Most schools are barely wired—most
classrooms don't have telephone jacks or the electric wiring to run more than a couple of computers.
The less money a school or school district has, the less likely it will be able to ride on
the information superhighway. Presuming that funding can be found for these essentials, schools still must raise money to stay on line and educate teachers in technology
use: over a five-year period, the hardware is only 18 percent of the cost of using technology (Van Horn 1994).

Telecommunications corporations are eager to exploit the school market, some- 11
times offering to wire schools in exchange for controlling the wires that will hook the
schools to the Internet and thus to corporate coffers (Coile 1994; Einstein 1994). Poor
schools in particular are prey for technology profiteers such as Whittle Communications' now-defunct Channel One. Channel One provided satellite dishes, VCRs, and
TV monitors to schools that agreed to force students to watch a ten-minute daily
"newscast" that included two minutes of ads. Schools in poor neighborhoods or those
with the lowest per student annual spending were respectively two or six times more
likely to have Channel One than were schools with the wealthiest students or highest
per student spending (Morgan 1993).

Health and safety issues of computer use are also most stark for poor schools. 12
Children are more susceptible to radiation, including that from computers, and are also
at risk for the same muscular and eye strains as adults (Miller 1992). Schools that can
barely afford computers are least likely to shield them or purchase ergonomically correct furniture.

In sum, the savage inequalities of the past will extend into the wired savagery of 13
the future. There is neither empirical nor theoretical reason to believe this scenario will
change for the better so long as the capitalist system continues. In general, students
from low-wage families and communities need more resources if they are to catch up
in the kinds of skills (technical, academic, and cultural) sought for in high-wage occupations—yet they get substantially less. Why expect the capitalist system and its government to invest extra funds to develop low-income children into sophisticated
problem-solving workers if the jobs don't and won't exist?

In any event, wherever the system does invest in schooling, its purpose is to inten- 14
sify schoolwork by children and to prepare them for future work—while presenting this

as in the students' interest. The call for students to work harder in school is as ubiquitous as the call for schools to produce high-skill workers—and usually comes from the same sources.

Computerization of schools will not contribute to "high wages" or "good jobs." The U.S. class hierarchy will not be ameliorated by computerization, but will be intensified. Indeed, computers have been a fundamental weapon in the capitalist war against the working class over the past two decades. If computer knowledge is required in the economy, it is not because of any capitalist desire for highly paid workers or any great need for highly skilled workers. 15

THINKING MACHINES FOR THINKING STUDENTS?

A strong claim is sometimes made that using computers and related high-tech machinery is *necessary* for a change to a mode of schooling that focuses on thinking. For example, Ramirez and Bell (1994) conclude 16

> It is the position of this paper that if systemic school reform in this country is to succeed it will only do so with the application of telecommunications and information technologies at the classroom level with a simultaneous focus on sustained professional development for teachers.

The argument rests on the purported necessity of computers for enabling all students to engage in higher-order thinking activities such as understanding complex ideas, solving real-world problems, and analyzing critically.

There is an irony in this claim. The emphasis on higher-order thinking in schools rests substantially on the foundation of cognitive psychology. As Noble (1989) has shown, cognitive psychology evolved in large part because the U.S. military wanted to create artificial intelligence—but it had no useful understanding of the genuine thing. The military therefore funded extensive research in cognition, research that ended up largely confirming what progressive educators and psychologists had long maintained, that humans learn actively and by constructing and modifying mental models. 17

The dominant psychological theories in the U.S. have been behaviorist. In the version influencing schooling, humans supposedly learned by passively accumulating isolated bits of information. In time, the bits could be shaped into successively more complex patterns. The impact, however, was that schools presumed students could not think in a given area until they had accumulated enough bits. Those who did not sufficiently grasp the bits were condemned never to do anything interesting in school. This approach still dominates curriculum, instruction, and the ubiquitous standardized tests. Cognitive psychology, however, proposes learning as a fundamentally different process. Recognizing that students think, learn by thinking, and can learn to think better or differently, it calls for a "thinking curriculum" (cf. Resnick 1987). 18

The irony here is that having constructed cognitive psychology in order to develop "thinking machines," the machines are now presumed indispensable for helping students learn to think. But the very existence of thinking in schools without computers shows clearly that machines are not necessary for a thinking curriculum. The reason 19 schools haven't encouraged thinking is not because they have lacked computers, but because the system did not want thinking workers.

A softer claim for the necessity of computers is that because of the way the econ-   20
omy relies on computerization, only via computers will it provide access to materials and knowledge that will facilitate higher-order thinking in academic areas for many more children. Presumably, the NII will enable access to teachers and learned peo-ple, data banks and libraries, analytical tools such as statistical packages, and other software.

Despite the absence of funds, it is claimed that teachers working in poor systems   21
will be able to get this complex operation functioning. However, if teachers had the time, training, and support to do this, they could reorganize their classrooms for inquiry, dialogue, critical thinking, understanding, and problem-solving—with or with-out computers. They don't succeed for a number of reasons: too many students, lack of resources and knowledge, and standardized tests that militate against thinking. Some-how, though, the computer will be the means to make the instructional leap.

Still, the claim of the value of computers has some persuasive aspects, though with   22
many caveats:

- The tools free up time. For example, because of calculators, rather than spend time on arithmetical drill, students can spend time on learning mathematical reasoning and problem-solving.
- Access to information is enhanced. In many schools, the library is outdated or inade-quate. The cost of some information will cheapen, making it more accessible—assuming that poor schools have the money to get and stay on line. Access, however, says nothing about the nature of the materials available on line. In seeking informa-tion, whether on networks or elsewhere, one is limited by one's inquiry framework. Without a strong frame, a student will simply be buried in tons of data. Access to information means little without guidance in learning to use information—which raises questions of whose guidance for what purposes.
- Access to people is expanded. You can use the Internet to dialogue with people all over the planet. (Of course people from all over the planet may now live in your neighborhood.) Computer advocates constantly tout examples of "real" scientists talking with kids from some school, but once millions of students are on line, how many scientists will spend time sorting through hundreds of on-line requests?
- Access to some kinds of computerized tools enable students to work on sophisti-cated problems rather than more basic and boring ones. Working on more realistic and complex tasks, doing so in collaboration with others, proceeding at one's own pace, even having a real-world use for the results, all can help motivate students. Again, much of this does not require computers or the NII. Moreover, once the tech-nology becomes old hat, deeper issues of the purpose for schooling will inevitably reappear for students, for whom lack of control often guarantees lack of interest (Herndon 1972).

The important issues are not ones of technology but of politics: will the funding be   23
there? what kinds of guidance to what ends will students receive? who controls the technology? for whom will the computer ultimately be useful? Class relations that are

played out in technology implementation are also implicated in technology construction. What is done with tools is not determined so much by those who use the tools as by those who construct them. Thus, the ways in which the makers design technology can largely control the structuring and solution of problems by users, to whom the control by the maker remains invisible (Madaus 1993). Computer use is then falsely promoted as a neutral yet liberatory tool.

CONTROLLING SCHOOL AND WORK

The controlling class no more wants problem-solvers and critical thinkers to do most jobs of the future than it did in the past, during the assembly-line era. Computer use in schools *will* fit the economy—not the mythical economy of "high skills and high wages," but the real economy of "the race to the bottom." While following orders, not questioning, being on time, and submitting one's personality to the dictates of the school all prepared workers for jobs in the mass-production era, the schoolwork form directly fit the actual jobs for only a relatively few workers. With computerization, however, form can more closely resemble function.   24

The McDonald's level of familiarity with technology requires no actual knowledge of computers or much thought. Data-entry (with the computer monitoring your speed) and similar work does not require higher-order thinking. Schools will train students to sit in front of computers and do routine work in direct preparation for their jobs. For them, this will be their real-world learning connection.   25

Use of computers at the technician level sometimes does require decision making, but the parameters are usually specified carefully, meaning that the thinking done is not at the order of making definition but of application. (A look at the actual jobs described by Bailey (1990) or Zuboff (1988) reveals this.) These jobs do require more academic—school-based—knowledge and the ability to apply that knowledge, and the number of these kinds of medium-level-skill jobs probably will increase in the coming decade. Controlling the development and nature of the thinking of those who have limited-problem-solving jobs will be another task of schools.   26

Data-entry, monitoring, and limited problem-solving will continue to comprise most computer use by the great majority of employees in the U.S., barring an upheaval against the jobs system. Noble's (1991) critique of Zuboff points out that the "intellective" work she glorifies in fact includes two kinds of work that imply a corresponding schooling: one that is scientific and problem-solving and another that is primarily monitoring the process—a difference that "reflects a cavernous hierarchical division of labor." And, Noble adds, the latter is more "about attitudes and disposition than about 'knowledge' or intellectual abilities." The mind is reduced to the hand. For most, schooling, wired or not, is preparation for routine work, same now as it ever was. However, I suspect that though "the more things change" is still operative, there are yet some important changes in the offing. The changes have to do with capitalist control over thinking.   27

As Noble (1989) explains, behaviorism largely treated thinking as a black box. On the assembly line, it did not matter what, or if, the worker thought, as long as he or she behaved: came to work, did the job, didn't cause trouble. To the extent that thinking   28 was an issue, the concern was how to manipulate the worker into working harder (i.e., to control behavior). Industrial psychology developed as a tool to help organize and ensure the functioning of the productive process. It developed a knowledge base that retains its usefulness for management, because traditional "good worker" characteristics are still those most desired by the bosses (NCEE 1990).

In a system that did not want workers to think too much but needed to control their 29 actions, behaviorist psychology was useful. Thus, corporations, foundations, and government agencies funded research that provided ready tools for shaping schooling and controlling workers.

Cognitive psychology is more useful to today's system, which needs workers to 30 think for the system and to think differently, manipulating abstract symbols. The schools are to provide these skills. Those who use computers to analyze, create, or control will be few in number but important to the system (Bailey 1991; Reich 1992). They too must be programmed, but with allowance for a greater degree of self-regulation.

The danger of progressive education that expects students to think and problem- 31 solve is that it might get out of control, leading students to "unrealistic expectations" and a command of areas of knowledge useful for attacking the system. But as Dalla Costa and James (1975) note, as long as progressive schooling remains within control, it not only presents no danger, it may be a source of yet greater profits (see also Robins and Webster 1989, 218–25). The question for the owners of capital, then, is how to ensure control of the "thinking" curriculum. Revealingly, much of the proposed school reform that rests on cognitive science as the model for instruction still rests on behaviorism for motivation and discipline.

The plans of the New Standards Project are perhaps most illustrative. (The 32 founders of New Standards are leading cognitive psychologist Lauren Resnick and Marc Tucker, head of the NCEE, which produced *America's Choice,* calling for "high skills and high wages.") New Standards, which has signed up sixteen states in its development program, proposes not only a new curriculum, instructional methods, assessments, and professional development for teachers, but also the use of performance levels and tests to measure student progress toward goals that are substantially about workforce preparation. Nonpromotion and nongraduation are the negative reinforcers to complement the presumably more interesting new curriculum.

So what's new? Surely not the drive for control or the use of behaviorism. What is 33 potentially new are the means of control, the computer itself, and the target of control: thinking. On one level this is already quite visible in the use of the work tool to monitor the pace of the work. In schools, however, the issue is more subtle. For example, the application of computers to real-world problems will teach students how to solve problems on terms amenable to the controllers of the system and will sort out those who are most willing and able to do so. The "less able" will be funneled to less cognitively complex computer work to prepare them for lower-skill jobs (or lack thereof), while the less willing will be driven out.

The determination of "less able" is a matter of assessment. While assessment is a 34 necessary part of learning, it is all too likely that emerging cognitive techniques will simply become a more sophisticated method for sorting students. Much of this may be done via computerized exams, enabling a high degree of standardization to "world-class" levels; currently, the same old tests used for sorting by class, race, and gender are being adapted for computer (FairTest 1992). Down the road, this could entail use of sophisticated means of analyzing everything from problem-solving ability to personality constructs to degrees of willingness to work (Raven 1991). This knowledge is used, however, not to help students but to control them (Robins and Webster 1989).

Moreover, the computer itself will be used to shape the personality. The model is   35 the computer—the malleable, controllable, programmable "smart machine." Part of the information-technology agenda is to learn how better to control the thinking of humans. At the crudest level, schools will try to do what they have always tried to do, shape students into workers, but the more subtle strategy is to make the mind *want* to be computerized. Perhaps the child must be caught at a young enough age so that she is less able to resist effectively.

Thinking is redefined as what computers do or what humans do to interact with   36 computers, eliminating the rest of the mind and body from thinking. Zuboff (1988) explains how paper workers historically used smell, touch, and direct sight on the job, and she understands this as a widely generalized use of intelligence, an intelligence destined to be replaced by more abstract modes, tied to symbols on computer screens. Thus, the alienation of the body, long a trend under capitalism (Midnight Notes 1982), leaps to a new qualitative level as the definition of thinking is reshaped to meet new capitalist needs.

Social alienation also intensifies as humans interact via the computer, a form of   37 interaction virtually stripped of emotional and social cues. Already some hints are emerging that extended replacement of in-person interaction by virtual interaction decreases a person's ability to socialize comfortably with other people when in their physical presence. Programs in which students work collaboratively on computer projects will ameliorate this tendency, but the students will still be learning "skills" needed to desocialize themselves. Privatization of schooling will further desocialization because it will increasingly allow schooling at home; contact with others will be only via the wire. (Michigan State has already awarded "charter school" status, and thus funding, to a "school" that is basically an electronic hookup among home-schoolers; the "school" is organized around "Christian" fundamentalist ideology (Walsh 1994).)

> **The computer is the extension of the "white man." Devoid of emotion, disconnected from the body (except during a *work*out), nonnurturing and unmusical, the type of the "white man" excludes all the human traits capitalism has attached to women and people of color (particularly Africans).**

38

In inducing physical and social isolation, the computer is the extension of the "white man." Devoid of emotion, disconnected from the body (except during a *work*out), nonnurturing and unmusical, the type of the "white man" excludes all the human traits capitalism has attached to women and people of color (particularly

Africans). I am not talking genetics but about the historical hierarchical division of labor that associates human qualities with the work one is forced to do and then calculatedly reproduces those qualities in people in order to force them to do the work (James 1975). The "white man"—really, *bourgeois*—qualities are now to be extrapolated and intensified, abstracted into the computer and then used to school the child into being computerlike.

Complex problem-solving can itself be a form of mindlessness. The language of   39
school reform pays some attention to the issue of "habits of mind." On the one side, it suggests that students learn to think about their thinking, learn not to just accept but to probe, question, challenge. Well and good if it happens, but it is more likely that "habits of mind"—that is, "critical thinking"—will be confined to areas defined and controlled by the system.

The computer thus will be used to control how one learns to think in order to sub-   40
sequently control how one thinks. The trajectory of the capitalist use of computers goes from constructing cognitive science for planning artificial intelligence to using artificial intelligence to control thinking as defined through cognitive science. Salomon, Perkins, and Globerson (1991) argue that use of intelligent technologies will make humans themselves more intelligent, provided, however, that these advances are "cultivated through the appropriate design of technologies and their cultural surrounds." The definitions of intelligence, the uses to which intelligence will be put, who is to be made more intelligent and how, and the questions of purpose, design, and control are deferred for "people of different expertise"—academicians all—to debate and plan.

The idea that the capitalist system wants a good many critical thinkers is simply   41
absurd—it can only spell trouble unless the thinkers are thinking for, not against, the boss. Thus the point is to produce the human as puzzle-solver, not really as critical thinker. Puzzles can be entertaining, challenging, require lots of thought, and yet be substantively mindless. The mind is thus habituated to thinking only in limited, even if complex, ways.

The beauty of the computer is not simply the speed with which it computes, nor   42
even all the troublesome work-resistant workers it can replace, but that it can simultaneously powerfully shape the mind and the personality. Thus, if *successful,* computerization will enable the production of the human as computer.

The world has for centuries been dominated by capital, with its exploitation of a hierar-   43
chy of labor power starting with the unwaged (Dalla Costa and James 1975) and interwoven with factors of gender and race. While working-class resistance has pushed the capitalist system to crisis, the working class has not resolved the crisis in its favor (Midnight Notes 1992). Now, as capitalism appears on the advance and recomposes the working class—while incorporating all its old forms, from slavery on—we see the spread of fantastical illusions, from fundamentalist religion to computers, as liberation from the miseries of the world. More mundanely, the use of computers in schools is presented as opening up the possibility of schooling as exciting, powerful learning that leads to "better jobs." Yet the excitement and power will not be for the many—unless the many change society, its economy, politics, and social relations, and how it educates its children.

Only egalitarian, collective, working-class power can assure that any particular   44
technology will be used for its benefit—if it should be used at all. Liberation is not a
matter of technology but of social relations. A first step in the transformation of social
relations is to refuse the inevitability of the economy.

Acknowledgements

Thanks to Shelley Neill, Bob Schaeffer, and Midnight Noters for insights, comments,
and support.

References

Bailey, Thomas. 1990. "Jobs of the Future and the Skills They Will Require: New
    Thinking on an Old Debate." *American Educator* 14 (1).
———. 1991. "Jobs of the Future and the Education They Will Require: Evidence
    from Occupational Forecasts." *Educational Researcher* 20 (2).
Berryman, Sue E., and Thomas R. Bailey. 1992. *The Double Helix of Education and
    the Economy.* New York: Institute on Education and the Economy, Teachers Col-
    lege, Columbia University.
California Business Roundtable. 1994. *Mobilizing for Competitiveness: Linking Edu-
    cation and Training to Jobs.* San Francisco: CBR.
Calvert, John, and Larry Keuhn. 1993. *Pandora's Box: Corporate Power, Free
    Trade, and Canadian Education.* Toronto, Our Schools/Our Selves Education
    Foundation.
Carnevale, Anthony P., and Jeffrey D. Porro. 1994. *Quality Education: School Reform
    for the New American Economy.* Washington: Office of Educational Research and
    Improvement, U.S. Department of Education.
Coile, Zachary. 1994. "'Free' Computer Revolution Now Has a Price Tag." *San Fran-
    cisco Examiner* (January 30).
Dalla Costa, Mariarosa, and Selma James. 1975. *The Power of Women and the Subver-
    sion of the Community.* 3d ed. Bristol, England: Falling Wall.
Einstein, David. 1994. "Pac Bell to Wire State's Schools for High Tech." *San Fran-
    cisco Chronicle,* (February 19).
FairTest. 1992. *Computerized Testing: More Questions than Answers.* Cambridge,
    MA: FairTest.
Herndon, James. 1972. *How to Survive in Your Native Land.* New York: Bantam.
James, Selma. 1975. *Race, Sex, and Class.* Bristol, England: Falling Wall.
Keuhn, Larry. 1994. "NAFTA and the Future of Education." Paper for the annual con-
    ference of the National Coalition of Education Activists (August). Portland, Oreg.
Kozol, Jonathan. 1991. *Savage Inequalities: Children in America's Schools.* New
    York: Crown.
Madaus, George. 1993. "A National Testing System: Manna from Above? An Histori-
    cal/Technological Perspective." *Educational Assessment* 1 (1).
Midnight Notes. 1982. "Mormons in Space." *Computer State Notes.* Boston: Midnight
    Notes.

————. 1992. *Midnight Oil.* New York: Autonomedia.

Miller, Norma L. 1992. "Are Computers Dangerous to Our Children's Health?" *PTA Today* (April).

Morgan, Michael. 1993. "Channel One in the Public Schools: Widening the Gap." A research report prepared for UNPLUG. Amherst, Mass.: Author.

National Center on Education and the Economy (NCEE). 1990. *America's Choice: High Skills or Low Wages!* Rochester, N.Y.: NCEE.

The New Standards Project. 1992. *A Proposal.* Pittsburgh: Learning Research and Development Center & National Center on Education and the Economy.

Noble, Douglas D. 1989. "Mental Material: The Militarization of Learning and Intelligence in U.S. Education." In *Cyborg Worlds.* Edited by Les Levidow and Kevin Robins. London: Free Association.

————. 1991. "In the Cage with the Smart Machine." *Science as Culture* 10.

Pearlman, Robert. 1994. "Can K–12 Education Drive on the Information Highway?" *Education Week* (May 25).

Piller, Charles. 1992. "Separate Realities." *Macworld* (September).

Ramirez, Rafael, and Rosemary Bell. 1994. *Byting Back: Policies to Support the Use of Technology in Education.* Oak Brook, Ill.: North Central Regional Educational Laboratory.

Raven, John. 1991. *The Tragic Illusion: Educational Testing.* Unionville, N.Y.: Trillium.

Reich, Robert B. 1992. *The Work of Nations.* New York: Vintage.

Resnick, Lauren B. 1987. *Education and Learning to Think.* Washington: National Academy Press.

Robins, Kevin, and Frank Webster. 1989. *The Technical Fix: Education, Computers, and Industry.* New York: St. Martin's.

Salomon, Gavriel, David N. Perkins, and Tamar Globerson. 1991. "Partners in Cognition: Extending Human Intelligence with Intelligent Technologies." *Educational Researcher* 20 (3).

SEDLetter. 1993. "Cyberschooling: Fiber Optic Vision? Or Virtual Reality?" *Southwest Educational Development Laboratory Newsletter* 6 (1).

Van Horn, Royal. 1994. "Building High Tech Schools." *Phi Delta Kappan* (September).

Walsh, Mark. 1994. "Charter School Opponents Taking Cases to Court." *Education Week* (October 7).

Zuboff, Shoshana. 1988. *In the Age of the Smart Machine: the Future of Work and Power.* New York: Basic Books.

← SECOND THOUGHTS

1. What ideas about the international capitalist system lie behind Neill's criticism of the educational use of computers? For example, why does he think that working-class power and wages are being reduced or that "the savage inequalities of the past will extend into the wired savagery of the future" (¶ 13)?

2. What is the purpose of our educational system, according to Neill? How does this compare or contrast with other goals of education you have heard or considered?

3. In what ways does Neill argue that school computers are being used to produce "thinking machines" instead of critically thinking human beings? To what extent are you persuaded that computer technology increases physical isolation and social alienation?

4. Neill writes that "the important issues are not ones of technology but of politics" (¶ 23) and "liberation is not a matter of technology but of social relations" (¶ 44). How would you describe Neill's politics, his values, and his definition of liberation? How sympathetic are you with this set of values?

The Giant's Drink

Orson Scott Card

Orson Scott Card (b. 1951) is a science fiction writer and essayist. He has an extensive Web page called "Hatrack River" at <www.hatrack.com/index.shtml>. His novels include *Seventh Son* (Tor Books, 1987), *The Memory of Earth* (Tor Books, 1992), and *Treasure Box* (HarperCollins, 1996); his short story collections include *The Folk of the Fringe* (Phantasia Press/Tor Books, 1989) and *Maps in a Mirror: The Short Fiction of Orson Scott Card* (Tor Books, 1990). This selection is from the novel *Ender's Game* (Tor Books, 1985), based on Card's first published science fiction story by the same name, in *Analog* in 1977. *Ender's Game* begins a trilogy followed by *Speaker for the Dead* (Tor Books, 1986) and *Xenocide* (Tor Books, 1991). Protagonist Ender Wiggin is a boy bred and chosen by military commanders for his potential to save humankind from destruction by a formidable alien species. At this point in the novel, the 6-year-old Ender has been removed from his family and is undergoing training at a special school.

E nder sat on his bed with his desk on his knees. It was private study time, and Ender was doing Free Play. It was a shifting, crazy kind of game in which the school computer kept bringing up new things, building a maze that you could explore. You could go back to events that you liked, for a while; if you left one alone too long, it disappeared and something else took its place.

Sometimes they were funny things. Sometimes exciting ones, and he had to be quick to stay alive. He had lots of deaths, but that was OK, games were like that, you died a lot until you got the hang of it.

His figure on the screen had started out as a little boy. For a while it had changed into a bear. Now it was a large mouse, with long and delicate hands. He ran his figure under a lot of large items of furniture depicted on the screen. He had played with the cat a lot, but now it was boring—too easy to dodge, he knew all the furniture.

Not through the mousehole this time, he told himself. I'm sick of the Giant. It's a dumb game and I can't ever win. Whatever I choose is wrong.

But he went through the mousehole anyway, and over the small bridge in the gar-   5
den. He avoided the ducks and the divebombing mosquitoes—he had tried playing with them but they were too easy, and if he played with the ducks too long he turned into a fish, which he didn't like. Being a fish reminded him too much of being frozen in the battleroom, his whole body rigid, waiting for the practice to end so Dap would thaw him. So, as usual, he found himself going up the rolling hills.

The landslides began. At first he had got caught again and again, crushed in an exaggerated blot of gore oozing out from under a rockpile. Now, though, he had mas-

427

tered the skill of running up the slopes at an angle to avoid the crush, always seeking higher ground.

And, as always, the landslides finally stopped being jumbles of rock. The face of the hill broke open and instead of shale it was white bread, puffy, rising like dough as the crust broke away and fell. It was soft and spongy; his figure moved more slowly. And when he jumped off the bread, he was standing on a table. Giant loaf of bread behind him; giant stick of butter beside him. And the Giant himself leaning his chin in his hands, looking at him. Ender's figure was about as tall as the Giant's head from chin to brow.

This time, instead of running away or standing there, Ender walked his figure up to the Giant's face and kicked him in the chin.   10

"I think I'll bite your head off," said the Giant, as he always did.

This time, instead of running away or standing there, Ender walked his figure up to the Giant's face and kicked him in the chin.

The giant stuck out his tongue and Ender fell to the ground.

"How about a guessing game?" asked the Giant. So it didn't make any difference—the Giant only played the guessing game. Stupid computer. Millions of possible scenarios in its memory, and the Giant could only play one stupid game.

The Giant, as always, set two huge shot glasses, as tall as Ender's knees, on the table in front of him. As always, the two were filled with different liquids. The computer was good enough that the liquids had never repeated, not that he could remember. This time the one had a thick, creamy looking liquid. The other hissed and foamed.

"One is poison and one is not," said the Giant. "Guess right and I'll take you into Fairyland."

Guessing meant sticking his head into one of the glasses to drink. He never guessed right. Sometimes his head was dissolved. Sometimes he caught on fire. Sometimes he fell in and drowned. Sometimes he fell out, turned green, and rotted away. It was always ghastly, and the Giant always laughed.

Ender knew that whatever he chose he would die. The game was rigged. On the   15
first death, his figure would reappear on the Giant's table, to play again. On the second death, he'd come back to the landslides. Then to the garden bridge. Then to the mousehole. And then, if he still went back to the Giant and played again, and died again, his desk would go dark, "Free Play Over" would march around the desk, and Ender would lie back on his bed and tremble until he could finally go to sleep. The game was rigged but still the Giant talked about Fairyland, some stupid childish three-year-old's Fairyland that probably had some stupid Mother Goose or Pac-Man or Peter Pan, it wasn't even worth getting to, but he had to find some way of beating the Giant to get there.

He drank the creamy liquid. Immediately he began to inflate and rise like a balloon. The Giant laughed. He was dead again.

He played again, and this time the liquid set, like concrete, and held his head down while the giant cut him open along the spine, deboned him like a fish, and began to eat while his arms and legs quivered.

He reappeared at the landslides and decided not to go on. He even let the landslides cover him once. But even though he was sweating and he felt cold, with his next life he went back up the hills till they turned into bread, and stood on the Giant's table as the shot glasses were set before him.

He stared at the two liquids. The one foaming, the other with waves in it like the sea. He tried to guess what kind of death each one held. Probably a fish will come out of the ocean one and eat me. The foamy one will probably asphyxiate me. I hate this game. It isn't fair. It's stupid. It's rotten.

> **He stared at the two liquids. The one foaming, the other with waves in it like the sea. He tried to guess what kind of death each one held.**

And instead of pushing his face into one of the liquids, he kicked one over, then   20
the other, and dodged the Giant's huge hands as the Giant shouted, "Cheater, cheater!" He jumped at the Giant's face, clambered up his lip and nose, and began to dig in the Giant's eye. The stuff came away like cottage cheese, and as the Giant screamed, Ender's figure burrowed into the eye, climbed right in, burrowed in and in.

The Giant fell over backward. The view shifted as he fell, and when the Giant came to rest on the ground, there were intricate, lacy trees all around. A bat flew up and landed on the dead Giant's nose. Ender brought his figure up out of the Giant's eye.

"How did you get here?" the bat asked. "Nobody ever comes here."

Ender could not answer, of course. So he reached down, took a handful of the Giant's eyestuff, and offered it to the bat.

The bat took it and flew off, shouting as it went, "Welcome to Fairyland."

He had made it. He ought to explore. He ought to climb down from the Giant's   25
face and see what he had finally achieved.

Instead he signed off, put his desk in his locker, stripped off his clothes and pulled his blanket over him. He hadn't meant to kill the Giant. This was supposed to be a game. Not a choice between his own grisly death and an even worse murder. I'm a murderer, even when I play.

⬅ SECOND THOUGHTS

1. How does Ender defeat the Giant and finally get to Fairyland? In what ways is the simulation game he's playing similar to and different from video or computer games that you've played?
2. What purposes do the designers of this computer simulation seem to have in mind? What could they be training Ender and other students to do?
3. What does Ender learn from the computer game? What other lessons do you think are possible from such a game?

☒☒☒   DISCUSSION THREADS

re: Wallis and Stoll

1. Clifford Stoll says that "real learning means inventing my own ways of solving problems" (¶ 29), and Claudia Wallis offers several examples of "constructivist learning" using computers at Dalton School that would seem to meet or exceed Stoll's definition of "real learning." To what extent do you think Stoll and the teachers at Dalton would agree about the purpose or goals of education? In what ways would they disagree about how to achieve those goals?

re: Wallis and Zito

2. How would you apply the idea of "constructivist learning" from Claudia Wallis's article to the instructional technologies at Cornell's engineering school described by Kelly Zito? What comparisons can you make between specific learning tools or educational software being developed at the Dalton School and Cornell? Based on these two articles and your own experience, how do you think new technologies are changing the relationship between students and teachers? What's your opinion of that change?

re: Wallis, Zito, and Neill

3. Imagine a dialogue between Monty Neill and teachers and students at the Dalton School and Cornell's engineering school about this topic: "Using computer technologies to promote higher-order thinking skills and to facilitate social or collaborative learning." How might Neill criticize the activities in Dalton School's Rooms 711, 608, or 307? What might he say about Cornell's CoNotes or CD-ROM textbook? How might the Dalton and Cornell people respond to each of those criticisms? With whom do you agree more, and why?

re: Stoll and Neill

4. What similarities and differences do you find in the critiques of educational computing offered by Clifford Stoll and Monty Neill? In what ways do you think the social and political values underlying their critiques overlap, and how do they differ?

re: Neill and Card

5. In Orson Scott Card's novel *Ender's Game,* an alien race threatens the survival of the human species. In this context, do you think the authoritarian design of Ender's computer training is more justified, if it's intended to shape him as a potential military commander? How do you think Monty Neill would interpret Ender's educational game-playing as a reflection of today's social and political forces? What other interpretations can you propose?

re: The Classroom of the Future

6. Based on the selections in this chapter, other reading you've done on this subject, and your own experience, consider the social purposes of education and the appropriate methods, media, or technologies for achieving those goals. In terms of those purposes, what do you think are the advantages and disadvantages of particular computer or network technologies for teaching and learning at the dawn of the 21st century?

RESEARCH LINKS

- *For direct links to listed Internet sources, additional reading selections and questions online, plus updates and supplementary Web resources, see* **Composing Cyberspace Online** *at <www.mhhe.com/socscience/english/holeton/>.*
- *For a complete set of research tools for the Internet—including the most useful search strategies, directories, and conventions for documenting online sources—see* **McGraw-Hill English Composition** *at <www.mhhe.com/socscience/english/compde/>.*

1. The equipping of schools with computer technology continues at a rapid pace even in the short time since Claudia Wallis's and Kelly Zito's articles were published (in 1995 and 1997). Research the status of instructional technologies at your own school or a school in your area. What plans are in place? What models for using instructional technologies are being discussed? What funding issues have arisen? If possible, interview administrators, teachers, and students to assess how technology plans are being implemented. What areas of controversy or tension do you detect, such as plans to train and support teachers in the use of technology? (For an overview of the national context, see Richard J. Coley, John Cradler, and Penelope K. Engel, *Computers and Classrooms: The Status of Technology in U.S. Schools* (Educational Testing Service, 1997). The report is available online at <www.ets.org/research/pic/compclass.html>; paper copies can be ordered from the Policy Information Center, Mail Stop 04-R, Educational Testing Service, Rosedale Road, Princeton, NJ 08541-0001.) Choose a particular issue or controversy about your local instructional technology plans and write a proposal to the appropriate authorities, such as the school board or relevant college administrators.

2. Research how computer technology has been used in writing classes. Focus a research paper on a particular issue in computers and writing such as electronic peer review of essay drafts, the use of electronic discussions to replace or supplement face-to-face discussions, or a comparison of traditional textbooks with "online writing labs." Besides articles from mainstream magazines such as *Time* and *Newsweek,* try to include scholarly sources you find in a research library and on the Internet. In the library, you might start with the journal *Computers and Composition* (Ablex Publishing) or anthologies such as *Re-imagining Computers and Composition: Teaching and Research in the Virtual Age* (Boynton/Cook, 1992), edited by Gail E. Hawisher and Paul LeBlanc, or *Evolving Perspectives on*

Computers and Composition Studies: Questions for the 1990s (National Council of Teachers of English, 1991), edited by Gail E. Hawisher and Cynthia L. Selfe. On the Web, starting places include the Alliance for Computers and Writing at <english.ttu.edu/acw/> and *Kairos: A Journal for Teachers of Writing in Webbed Environments* at <english.ttu.edu/kairos/1.1/index.html>.

3. Monty Neill points out gaps in technology between wealthier and poorer schools, and Claudia Wallis, Clifford Stoll, and Kelly Zito discuss a range of ways that computers get used in education from game-playing and simple drills—which might be called "lower order" uses—to more sophisticated research, collaboration, and critical thinking or "higher order" uses. Research lower order and higher order computer use in poor, inner city school districts in the United States or in schools in selected Third World countries. You might compare the uses of instructional technologies in a particular affluent private school, like one of those discussed by Wallis or Zito, with those at a school or district or region with fewer resources. See the Educational Testing Service report *Computers and Classrooms* referenced in Question 1, and look for other studies of school computer use in the education section of your library; ask your librarian about the availability of ERIC (Educational Resources Information Center), a U.S. Department of Education database that includes the Current Index to Journals in Education, which covers hundreds of journals. On the Internet you can look up individual schools through a Web index such as Yahoo! (<www.yahoo.com/>); from a college or university home page, look for links to computer and technology information or to individual courses on the Web. The Dalton School has an extensive Web site at <www.dalton.org/home.html>, including links to the innovative courses and curricula discussed by Wallis. Cornell's College of Engineering has a home page at <www.engr.cornell.edu/>, and information about CoNotes, the Web annotation system discussed by Zito, can be found at <www.cs.cornell.edu/Info/People/aferencz/CoNote/>.

4. Apple Computer <www.apple.com>, which has donated many computers to schools since the 1980s, may be the best-known corporate technology "partner" for public education. Corporate support for schools has accelerated in the 1990s with cuts in federal support and local funding for education, although not without controversy. For example, the short-lived Channel One commercial experiment of Whittle Communications gets discussed by both Clifford Stoll and Monty Neill in this chapter. Channel One broadcast "free" news programs for schools but included several minutes of commercial advertising. Research the background and find out what happened with Channel One in practice, or investigate another case of corporate collaboration with public education and technology. What do you think are the social and educational benefits, costs, or dangers of such collaboration?

5. Economic rationales for educational uses of technology—in particular, the preparation of students for a technological future—are criticized by both Clifford Stoll and Monty Neill. You might compare David Bank's article about corporate "knowledge workers" in Chapter 8, p. 364. One area of controversy is the extent to which the "information economy" will require large numbers of workers with higher order critical thinking skills or merely those with the ability to enter numbers or data into

a computer interface. Neill suggests that the latter, which he calls "the McDonald's level of familiarity with technology," "will continue to comprise most computer use by the great majority of employees in the U.S." Test Neill's claim by researching the latest figures, from the U.S. Census Bureau and other sources, for job growth. Alternatively, research the same topic in a global context.

6. A darker side of video games and virtual reality (VR) is portrayed in Orson Scott Card's "The Giant's Drink," from *Ender's Game*. Consider Card's vision in light of Brenda Laurel's optimistic ideas, expressed in Chapter 7 (p. 328) about the potential of VR. To extend your analysis, evaluate some actual or planned applications of VR in education, taking into account the issues raised by Card and Laurel.

7. Distance education—conducting classes using electronic media only—has been discussed and tried extensively in the 1990s. Many colleges and universities now offer courses by means of TV broadcast, videotape, or the World Wide Web. Distance education has been promoted for its educational and economic advantages, and it's been criticized on both accounts as well, by many others besides Clifford Stoll. Analyze a particular distance learning program or school, or compare two distance learning experiments. Based on these cases, what do you think are the primary advantages and disadvantages of distance learning? On the Web, you can find a directory of online colleges and universities by Lifelong Learning at <homepages.together.net/~lifelong/dlsites.html>. Some pioneers in total distance learning include Virtual Online University at <www.athena.edu/> and the Global Network Academy at <www.gnacademy.org:8001/uu-gna/index.html>.

Cyberspace Glossary

Many of these terms are discussed in more depth throughout *Composing Cyberspace,* and all are discussed extensively on the Internet. This glossary is intended only as a starting place and a way to quickly understand some of the relationships among these terms. Glossary items are cross-referenced in **boldface** type, except for the most common terms such as *Internet, online, software,* and *World Wide Web.* For further information, consult an Internet reference book or one of many online glossaries, such as the ILC (Internet Literacy Consultants) Glossary of Internet Terms at <www.matisse.net/files/glossary.html>, or Patrick Crispen's Internet Roadmap at <www.brandonu.ca/~ennsnr/Resources/Roadmap/>.

Access A social issue often raised with regard to information technologies: who has access to what technology?

Anonymity A common condition in electronic spaces, where the only clues about a person's identity may be textual.

Asynchronous Not at the same time, or not in "real time." **Snail mail** and **e-mail** are both asynchronous communication forms because people send and receive messages at different times.

Bandwidth The amount of data or information that an electronic line or wire can hold. Graphical, video, or multimedia data require more bandwidth than text.

Bits and bytes The smallest form of electronic data, which are measured in a binary system of 0's and 1's. As the building blocks of electronic signals, bits and bytes may be contrasted with atoms and molecules, the building blocks of physical matter. A byte is about 8 to 10 bits; a **kilobyte** (K) is 1024 (2^{10}) bytes; a **megabyte** (MB) is more than 1 million (2^{20}) bytes. The text of a college essay might require less than 20K of computer memory to store, depending on the computer **platform** and program being used, while the word-processing software used to create it may require several megabytes.

Bookmark An electronic placeholder, like a physical bookmark, used to mark a location on the Internet. Web **browsers** can store and customize hundreds of bookmarks, a helpful way for people to organize their online interests and Internet research.

Browser A **client** application program (a kind of software) that allows users to **navigate** the World Wide Web. The two most common browsers are made by Netscape Communications and Microsoft Corporation.

Chat To "talk" electronically—that is, in text—in real time or **synchronously.**

Chat rooms Electronic "spaces," often devoted to particular topics, where people "meet" for conversation or online socializing.

Client A computer or computer program that receives information from a **server** computer across a network. The "client-server" model predominates on the Internet.

CMC (Computer-mediated communication) Any form of communication using computers and computer networks, including **e-mail,** electronic conferences, **newsgroups,** and Web **chats.**

Constructivism Generally, the idea that people and human institutions are socially shaped or "constructed" and that human behavior is determined more by convention than by nature or biology. Social constructivism is one theoretical model for the use of computer networks, such as the Internet, and for educational uses of technology.

Cracker A kind of **hacker** who uses his or her skills maliciously, for example to break into other people's computers and steal, destroy, or corrupt data.

Cyberporn Pornographic or offensive material transmitted across the Internet.

Cyberpunk Can refer to a literary and artistic genre or to a subculture or social movement. The term was coined in the late 1980s to describe the work of William Gibson (see Chapter 1, p. 48 and Chapter 8, p. 369) and other science fiction writers, characterized by a dense, fast-paced narrative and socially marginal characters in a technological future. The cyberpunk counterculture "combines an infatuation with high-tech tools and a disdain for conventional ways of using them," in the words of *Time* magazine's Philip Elmer-Dewitt. That disdain has been associated with online anarchism, rebellious punk music, psychedelic drugs, and rave culture (involving quickly organized, nomadic all-night dance parties).

Cyberspace A general term for any or all electronic "space," or the **virtual** space of **bits and bytes** as opposed to the physical space of atoms and molecules. The term comes from William Gibson's 1984 novel *Neuromancer,* where it refers to a vast electronic matrix of data controlled by powerful corporate entities; Gibson's matrix has a visual, three-dimensional **interface** that specialists **navigate** by "jacking in" or hooking up special equipment.

Cyborg A contraction of the words "cybernetic organism," referring to a human-machine hybrid or a combination of biological and artificial systems. According to Donna Haraway in the Foreword to *The Cyborg Handbook* (ed. Chris Hables Gray, Routledge, 1995), the term was invented by researchers Manfred E. Clynes and Nathan S. Kline in 1960.

Digital Electronic; composed of **bits and bytes**, as opposed to atoms and molecules.

Download To transfer information to one's computer from another computer, usually across a network. See **Upload.**

Electronic democracy A term used by computer enthusiasts, and debated by technology critics, for the potential of electronic technologies to increase opportunities for participatory democracy and social justice.

E-mail Electronic mail, nearly instantaneous messages sent across computer networks. Though fast, e-mail is **asynchronous** because messages are stored on the recipient's computer or mail **server** until she or he wishes to read or reply to them. E-mail is now contrasted with **snail mail,** a term describing the relative slowness or inconvenience of conventional paper mail.

Emoticon Combining "emotion" and "icon," a typographical symbol for an emotional state. Emoticons evolved from widespread use of **e-mail,** a textual medium in which tone and emotion can be difficult to convey. Emoticons are read counterclockwise by turning one's head to the left. The first widely used emoticon was :-) or :), the **smiley face,** used to express a humorous or joking intention; entire dictionaries of other emoticons have evolved for more subtle emotions or purely for entertainment value.

Face-to-face (f2f) In person, "live," or in "real space" as opposed to **digital, virtual,** or electronic space.

FAQ (Frequently Asked Questions) Originally, literally a compendium of the most frequently asked questions, along with answers, about an Internet **newsgroup.** FAQs (pronounced "fax," singular "fak") are published by experienced participants so that **newbies** can quickly get up to speed. Now used more widely, FAQs may be described as documents that summarize the salient facts about any project or endeavor, on or off the Internet (see, for example, the *Composing Cyberspace* FAQ on p. ix).

File server A computer used to store documents and/or to share software applications on a network.

Flame (Verb) To insult someone online or engage in an angry textual exchange, or (noun) the result of that insult or exchange. Flaming has been associated with **anonymity** online, because people can be less inhibited when not using their real names. **Flame wars** are ongoing exchanges of electronic insults.

Gender bending Experimenting with gender identity online, most commonly on **MUDs and MOOs** or in **chat rooms.** The term can describe men posing as women, women posing as men, or either posing as nongendered or "neutral" characters.

Global village Oxymoronic term coined in the 1960s by Canadian media critic Marshall McCluhan to describe how instantaneous communication made possible by electronic technologies could unite the world on a global scale. While McCluhan warned of TV's potential to facilitate a monolithic monoculture, lately the term has been used in constructive ways by enthusiasts of the Internet and other information technologies.

Hacker Originally, someone who illegally breaks into electronic systems such as telephone or computer networks. The first hackers figured out ways to make long-distance phone calls for free. As the term has become more generalized, it can describe any clever computer programmer who enjoys solving problems, especially by less conventional means—as distinct from **crackers,** who use their skills more maliciously.

Hardware Physical computer equipment such as CPUs (central processing units), disk drives, monitors, printers, and scanners and the wires, cables, and hubs that connect them.

Holodeck The Holographic Environment Simulator, an extremely realistic **virtual reality** space imagined by the writers of the "Star Trek" TV series. Holodeck "matter" and even holodeck people look, sound, and feel like the real thing. Star Trek crew members use the holodeck mostly for recreation and training and occasionally for fantasy, intellectual, or artistic expression.

Home page or **homepage** A **hypertext** document on the World Wide Web published by an individual, group, company, or organization. Home pages have proliferated largely because **HTML,** the language of the Web, makes it relatively easy to publish electronic texts and link them to other documents on the Web.

HTML Hypertext Markup Language, the computer code that controls documents published on the World Wide Web. HTML adds "tags"—symbols such as <p> and </p> to indicate the beginning and end of a paragraph—to describe how text, graphics, and other elements should appear. As later versions of HTML have gotten more complex, **WYSIWYG editors** have allowed people more readily to translate other kinds of documents, such as word processing files, directly into HTML.

Hyperlink See **link.**

Hypertext, hypermedia Nonlinear, or multilinear, computerized text. Unlike book pages, which are arranged in a set linear order, hypertexts are arranged in nodes or parts that may be viewed in a variety of orders by following **links.** Hypertext and hypermedia are usually used interchangeably since computer hypertexts often include graphics, sounds, or movies. Some hypertexts, such as a multimedia information kiosk in an airport, are just for reading or viewing; other hypertexts are interactive, meaning that the reader can make changes or add links. The World Wide Web is an interactive hypertext environment because readers with the right hardware and software can publish their own documents and link to others.

Information Highway, Information Superhighway, Infobahn Terms first popularized in the 1980s by then-Senator Al Gore to describe the developing web of communications networks, computers, and consumer electronic appliances. Originally, the "Info Highway" referred more to potential consumer applications such as "movies on demand" than to the Internet, but with the growth of multimedia delivery on the Web, the term has become more generalized.

Instructional technology Broadly, any technology used for teaching and learning, from blackboards and chalk to the Internet. Usually the term refers to the latest electronic technologies, especially computer-aided instruction and the use of instructional software and computer networks.

Intellectual property Current term for information that an individual, group, or company claims legally to own. International copyright laws and agreements governing intellectual property, mostly designed before the advent of electronic publication, are the subject of much debate.

Interface A more general term for the **operating system** or a software program used by a computer or other electronic appliance. Most computer interfaces today are graphical, using the metaphors of "windows," "folders," "menus," and "desktop icons" to help the user control the computer's functions.

Internet, Net A global computer network, actually a network of networks, connecting millions of computers. The hardware of the Internet includes computer **clients** and **servers** along with the various cables and wires, hubs and routers, satellite connections, and phone lines used to connect them. The software of the Internet includes a common communication protocol (IP or Internet Protocol) that allows computers to "recognize" one another, and the **browsers** on individual desktops that allow people to "surf the Web."

Internet Service Provider (ISP) A company or organization that provides hardware (and often software) connections to the Internet. Some commercial ISPs, such as America Online, also provide private network services separate from the Internet.

Intranet Another name for a **local area network (LAN),** especially a corporate LAN that duplicates the data-sharing capability of the Internet but for local or private users only.

IRC (Internet Relay Chat) The first large-scale, real-time electronic **chat** space on the Internet. Analogous to a giant telephone party line, IRC allows participants to join or create separate channels devoted to discussion about any topic of common interest. IRC discussions, which have been popular with college students, are usually fast-paced and largely social in nature.

Keyword A search term used in the most common methods of Internet research. People using **search engines** type in one or several keywords to describe the topic they're researching, similar to searching a traditional library by subject.

Kilobyte See **Bits and bytes.**

Link, hyperlink The hypertext connection between two pieces, or nodes, of electronic information or data. Most links operate with a computer mouse-click: Clicking on linked text (usually underlined or marked by a specific color) or on graphical objects such as buttons leads to another document or portion of the document, which, in turn, may provide further links. Linking is what gives hypertexts—including the vast network of hypertexts comprising the World Wide Web—their complex, three-dimensional, dynamic nature.

Listserv See **Mailing list.**

Local Area Network (LAN) A group of computers and other equipment such as printers and scanners that are linked together for the sharing of information. Many local area networks also are connected to the Internet.

Lurk, lurker (Verb) To read or "listen in" on an electronic forum, such as a **newsgroup** or **mailing list,** without actively participating by replying to others or contributing original messages. (Noun) The majority of participants in most electronic forums are **lurkers.** Good **netiquette** requires new participants in electronic discussion groups to lurk for a while in order to get a feel for the conventions of the group they're joining.

Mailing list, listserv, list server A way for a group of **e-mail** users to share information about a specific topic or shared interest. Mailing list participants subscribe to a **listserv** (or **list server,** an automated program that helps manage the list), allowing them to exchange messages with all other participants by writing or replying to a single e-mail address. Like **newsgroups,** mailing lists may be moderated (with messages filtered by a central facilitator) or unmoderated.

Medium, media General term for method of communication or broadcast, including **face-to-face** and computer-mediated forms. Media may refer to hardware, software, or both. Electronic media include TV, **e-mail,** and the World Wide Web.

Megabyte See **Bits and bytes.**

Modem A device for connecting a computer to a network via a telephone line (a contraction of MOdulator, DEModulator).

MUDs and MOOs MUD stands for Multi-User Dimension or Multi-User Dungeon, from its origins as an electronic version of fantasy games such as Dungeons and Dragons. MUDs are **synchronous** (real-time) **virtual reality** spaces, where participants act out character roles in imaginary worlds, all described in text. The social nature of MUDs can be reflected in elaborate reward and punishment systems. MOO stands for MUD, Object-Oriented. MOOs use software that allows participants more control over constructing the

virtual space. Many MOOs have been devoted to educational, scholarly, or community purposes, as opposed to the game-orientation of the early MUDs.

Multimedia The integration in **digital** form of several media such as text, pictures, sounds, or movies, commonly used on CD-ROMs and the World Wide Web.

Navigate To move through electronic or **virtual** "spaces" or media, especially **hypertext.** Web **browsers** are navigation tools for the World Wide Web. The term arose because the experience of reading or searching hypertexts, which often lack a central or hierarchical organization, differs from the experience of reading a linear paper text or searching a catalogued library.

Net See **Internet.**

Netiquette Network etiquette; conventions that have been asserted by Internet veterans, and that are still evolving, for online politeness. Netiquette "rules" or guidelines have been developed to prevent harassment and **flaming,** to resist **spamming,** and to preserve **bandwidth** on the Internet.

Network A group of computers and peripheral equipment connected for the sharing of information.

Newbie Term, sometimes used derisively by experienced users, for someone new to an online forum, electronic space, or computer technology in general.

Newsgroup An electronic discussion forum on **Usenet,** part of the Internet, where people with a shared interest can exchange information and ideas. There are newsgroups devoted to nearly every topic imaginable. In moderated newsgroups, messages are filtered through a central facilitator who decides what is appropriate and relevant to **post.** In unmoderated newsgroups, participants can post any message they choose. Newsgroups, like **e-mail,** are **asynchronous.**

Offline or off line Not connected to a computer or computer network; see **online.**

Online or on line Usually, connected to or using a network, especially the Internet; often contrasted with **offline.** Alternatively, online means simply on a computer, as in the "online documentation" that may supplement or replace paper manuals for computer programs.

Operating system The software that controls a computer's basic functions and **interface.** Applications such as word processing programs must work in conjunction with a computer's operating system. The two most common operating system **platforms** at educational institutions are Microsoft Windows and Apple Computer's MacOS.

Platform Another term for **operating system.**

Post, posting (Verb) To send a message to a **newsgroup** or other electronic discussion forum. (Noun) A **post** or **posting** is the resulting message.

Search engine A computerized Internet research tool developed for the World Wide Web, such as Alta Vista (<www.altavista.com/>) or HotBot (<www.hotbot.com/>). Typically, users type in **keywords** that the search engine tries to find in Web documents or other Internet sources such as **newsgroups.**

Server A computer that transmits or "serves" information to other computers

called **clients.** The server-client model predominates on the Internet. Web servers, usually shared by a number of individual computers, serve **HTML** documents so that other computers can display them. Other kinds of software and files can also be shared by multiple users on a **file server,** mail server, or **list server.**

Smiley, smiley face See **Emoticon.**

Snail mail Tongue-in-cheek name for traditional mail service, by contrast to **e-mail** or electronic mail, which is much faster.

Social constructivism See **Constructivism.**

Software Any set of codes that work in conjunction with a computer's **operating system** (another form of software) and allow people to do useful things with computers, such as write, manipulate numbers, or communicate on the Internet.

Spam (Noun) Junk mail on the Internet, usually sent to **newsgroups** or via **e-mail.** (Verb) To send junk mail on the Internet. The term originates from a sketch by the comedy troupe Monty Python's Flying Circus, in which a restaurant serves lots of the canned pork product Spam.

Synchronous In real time, at the same time. **Face-to-face** conversation, **MUDs and MOOs, IRC,** and **chat rooms** are all synchronous communication forms.

Thread A topic or subtopic within an electronic discussion group or forum. Discussion threads are often distinguished in the subject header of a message by the "re:" abbreviation for "in reference to" or "concerning." Electronic

.scussion software, such as **e-mail** or **newsgroup**-reading programs, often generate "re: [topic of the original message]" automatically when the sender replies to a message. Other software, such as Web chat programs, can facilitate message **threading** by other means, such as grouping subtopics in the same folder.

Upload To transfer information from one's computer to another computer, usually across a network. See **Download.**

URL Uniform Resource Locator, the addressing convention used for all locations linked to the World Wide Web. Every "page" on the Web has a unique address, usually beginning "http://".

Usenet A network of over 20,000 topical electronic discussion groups called **newsgroups.** Usenet, one of the oldest and most diverse components of the Internet, has a history of democratic and sometimes anarchistic self-regulation.

Virtual Consisting of **bits and bytes** instead of atoms and molecules; electronic as opposed to "real." This distinction is somewhat spurious since electronic information and interaction are still "real," even though they have a different material basis or occur in a different medium.

Virtual community A community that exists in **virtual** space instead of, or in addition to, existing **face-to-face** or in physical proximity.

Virtual rape Rape conducted in virtual space, through words or text instead of by physical force. The existence or seriousness of virtual rape has been debated by critics, especially since the publication of Julian

Dibbell's "A Rape in Cyberspace" (Chapter 2, p. 83).

Virtual reality (VR) Digital simulation of real-life scenarios using computer technology, multimedia, and sensory apparatus such as special helmets and gloves. VR has been used by the military and business community for training purposes and by other people for entertainment or artistic expression. See **Holodeck.**

Web site, website A discrete set of documents published by a person or organization on the Web. In common usage, a website is usually larger or more complex than a **home page.** For example, corporations and universities maintain large organizational websites that may include hundreds or thousands of home pages.

Wired, unwired The state or condition of being or not being hooked up to a computer network, usually the Internet; or more generally, having or not having computer equipment.

World Wide Web, WWW, Web A vast **hypertext** network that comprises the largest and fastest-growing way to access the Internet. It originated as a way for scientists to easily share their research using multimedia. The Web's popularity has derived from its ease of use via graphical-interface **browsers** and the ease of publication using **HTML.**

WYSIWYG editor Computer program for Web publishing that uses a "What You See Is What You Get" **interface,** similar to most word processing programs, so that users don't need to know **HTML** coding to put their work on the Web.

Acknowledgments

Frequently Asked Questions

- Cartoon: BIZARRO © 1996 by Dan Piraro. Reprinted with permission of UNIVERSAL PRESS SYNDICATE. All rights reserved.

Chapter 1

- Cartoon: AUTH © 1996 The Philadelphia Inquirer. Reprinted with permission of UNIVERSAL PRESS SYNDICATE. All rights reserved.
- Sherry Turkle: Reprinted with the permission of Simon & Schuster from *Life on the Screen: Identity in the Age of the Internet* by Sherry Turkle. Copyright © 1995 by Sherry Turkle.
- Charles Platt: "What's It Mean to Be Human, Anyway?" by Charles Platt, *Wired* 3.04 © 1995–1997 Wired Magazine Group, Inc. All rights reserved. Excerpted with permission.
- Iain A. Boal: From "Body, Brain, and Communication: An Interview with George Lakoff" by Iain A. Boal in *Resisting the Virtual Life: The Culture and Politics of Information,* eds. Brook and Boal. Copyright © 1995 by James Brook and Iain Boal. Reprinted by permission of City Lights Books.
- Ellen Ullman: "Come in, CQ: The Body on the Wire," from *Wired Women: Gender and New Realities in Cyberspace,* ed. Lynn Cherny and Elizabeth Reba Wise (Seal Press, 1996). Reprinted by permission of the author.

- William Gibson: "Johnny Mnemonic" from *Burning Chrome* by William Gibson. Copyright © 1986 by William Gibson. Reprinted by permission of William Morrow & Company, Inc.

Chapter 2

- Cartoon: Reprinted by permission of Mike Luckovich and Creators Syndicate.
- Dale Spender: From *Nattering on the Net: Women, Power and Cyberspace* by Dale Spender, published by Spinifex Press, 1995. Reprinted with permission of the publisher.
- Jesse Kornbluth: "{You Make Me Feel Like} A Virtual Woman" by Jesse Kornbluth, *Virtual City,* Winter 1996. Copyright © 1995 by Jesse Kornbluth. Reprinted by permission.
- Barbara Ehrenreich: "Put Your Pants On, Demonboy" by Barbara Ehrenreich from *Time* magazine, October 23, 1995. Copyright © 1995 Time Inc. Reprinted by permission.
- Julian Dibbell: "A Rape in Cyberspace" by Julian Dibbell from *The Village Voice,* December 21, 1993. Reprinted by permission of the author.
- Laura Miller: "Women and Children First: Gender and the Settling of the Electronic Frontier" by Laura Miller from *Resisting the Virtual Life: The Culture and Politics of Information,* eds. Brook and Boal. Copyright © 1995 by James Brook and Iain Boal. Reprinted by permission of City Lights Books.

Chapter 3

- Cartoon: Drawing by P. Steiner; © 1993 The New Yorker Magazine, Inc. Reprinted by permission.
- Charlise Lyles: From "On-line Religion Pews Are Global" by Charlise Lyles as appeared in the *Dayton Daily News,* November 4, 1996. Reprinted by permission of the author and the Dayton Daily News.
- Steve Silberman: "We're Teen, We're Queer, and We've Got E-Mail" by Steve Silberman, *Wired* 2.11 © 1994–1997 Wired Magazine Group, Inc. All rights reserved. Reprinted by permission.
- Max Padilla: "Affirmative Access: A Gay Chicano Lost in Cyberspace" by Max Padilla from *The Village Voice,* September 26, 1995. Reprinted by permission of the author.
- Glen Martin: "Internet Indian Wars" by Glen Martin, *Wired* 3.12 © 1995–1997 Wired Magazine Group, Inc. All rights reserved. Reprinted by permission.
- John Shirley: "Wolves of the Plateau" by John Shirley from *Heatseeker.* Copyright © 1989 by John Shirley. Reprinted by permission of the author.

Chapter 4

- Cartoon: Courtesy of Cory Garfin.
- Howard Rheingold: From *The Virtual Community* by Howard Rheingold. © 1993 by Howard Rheingold. Reprinted by permission of Addison-Wesley Longman, Inc.
- John Perry Barlow: "Is There a There in Cyberspace?" by John Perry Barlow from the *Utne Reader,* March–April 1995. Reprinted by permission of the author.
- Amy Bruckman: "Finding One's Own in Cyberspace" by Amy Bruckman from *MIT's Technology Review,* Jan 1996. Reprinted with permission from MIT's Technology Review Magazine, copyright © 1997.

- Joshua Cooper Ramo: "Finding God on the Web" by Joshua Cooper Ramo from *Time* magazine, December 16, 1996. Copyright © 1996 Time Inc. Reprinted by permission.
- E. M. Forster: "The Air-Ship" from *The Eternal Moment and Other Stories* by E. M. Forster, copyright 1928 by Harcourt Brace & Company and renewed 1956 by E. M. Forster, reprinted by permission of the publisher.

Chapter 5

- Cartoon: *Dilbert* reprinted by permission of United Feature Syndicate, Inc.
- Lawrence Grossman: "The Shape of the Electronic Republic," "Introduction," from *The Electronic Republic* by Lawrence Grossman. Copyright © 1995 by Lawrence K. Grossman. Used by permission of Viking Penguin, a division of Penguin Books USA Inc.
- Jon Katz: "The Netizen: Birth of a Digital Nation" by Jon Katz. Copyright © 1997 by Jon Katz. Reprinted by permission of Sterling Lord Literistic, Inc.
- Langdon Winner: "Mythinformation" from *The Whale and the Reactor* by Langdon Winner. Copyright © 1986 by The University of Chicago. Reprinted by permission of The University of Chicago Press.
- John Schwartz: "The American Dream, and Email For All" by John Schwartz from *Virtual City,* Winter 1996. Reprinted by permission of the author.
- Pamela Varley: From "Electronic Democracy" by Pamela Varley in *MIT's Technology Review,* v94, n8 (Nov–Dec 1991). Reprinted with permission from MIT's Technology Review Magazine, copyright © 1997.

Chapter 6

- Catoon: Copyright © 1993 by Paul Duginski. Reprinted by permission.

- Richard Rodriguez: From "Where Faiths of Many Cultures Flow Together" by Richard Rodriguez, in *The Sacramento Bee,* April 7, 1996. Reprinted by permission of Pacific News Service, San Francisco.
- John Hockenberry: From "Revolution Frees People from Place and Time: Advancing Technology Destroys Borders" by John Hockenberry from *The WorldPaper,* May 1995. Copyright © The WorldPaper, May 1995. Reprinted by permission.
- Dale Spender: From *Nattering on the Net: Women, Power and Cyberspace* by Dale Spender, published by Spinifex Press, 1995. Reprinted with permission of the publisher.
- Rory J. O'Connor: "Africa: The Unwired Continent" by Rory J. O'Connor, *San Jose Mercury News,* May 27, 1996. Copyright © 1997 San Jose Mercury News. All rights reserved. Reproduced with permission.
- John C. Rude: "Birth of a Nation in Cyberspace" by John C. Rude. Reprinted by permission of the author.

Chapter 7

- Cartoon: CATHY © 1997 Cathy Guisewite. Reprinted with permission of UNIVERSAL PRESS SYNDICATE. All rights reserved.
- Jorge Luis Borges: "The Library of Babel" by Jorge Luis Borges, translated by James E. Irby, from Labyrinths. Copyright © 1962, 1964 by New Directions Publishing Corp. Reprinted by permission of New Directions Publishing Corp.
- Dave Barry: From *Dave Barry in Cyberspace* by Dave Barry. Copyright © 1996 by Dave Barry. Reprinted by permission of Crown Publishers, Inc.
- Sven Birkerts: "Into the Electronic Millenium" from *Gutenberg Elegies: The Fate of Reading in an Electronic Age* by Sven Birkerts. Copyright © 1994 by Sven Birkerts. Reprinted by permission of Faber and Faber Publishers, Inc.
- Shyamala Reddy: "The Once and Future Book" by Shyamala Reddy from *Virtual City,* Summer 1996, Vol. 1, Issue 4. Reprinted by permission of the author.
- Brenda Laurel: From *Computers as Theatre* by Brenda Laurel. © 1991 Addison-Wesley Publishing Company Inc. Reprinted by permission of Addison-Wesley Longman Inc.

Chapter 8

- Cartoon: © Tribune Media Services. All Rights Reserved. Reprinted with permission.
- Ann Okerson: "Who Owns Digital Works?" by Ann Okerson from *Scientific American,* July 1996. Reprinted with permission. Copyright © 1996 by Scientific American, Inc. All rights reserved.
- Mark Fearer: "Scientology's Secrets" by Mark Fearer. This article originally appeared in *Internet World* magazine, December 1995, P. 76, 78. Copyright © 1995 Mecklermedia Corporation, 20 Ketchum Street, Westport, CT 06880; http://www.internet.com. All rights reserved. Reprinted with permission.
- Herb Brody: "Wired Science" by Herb Brody from *MIT's Technology Review.* Reprinted with permission from MIT's Technology Review Magazine, copyright © 1997.
- David Bank: From "Know-It-Alls" by David Bank in *The Wall Street Journal,* November 1996. Reprinted by permission of The Wall Street Journal. © 1996 Dow Jones & Company, Inc. All Rights Reserved Worldwide.
- William Gibson: "Burning Chrome" from *Burning Chrome* by William Gibson. Copyright © 1986 by William Gibson. Reprinted by permission of William Morrow & Company, Inc.

Chapter 9

- Cartoon: Reprinted with permission of Chris Suddick.

- Claudia Wallis: "The Learning Revolution" by Claudia Wallis from *Time* magazine, Summer 1995, v145, n12. Copyright © 1995 Time Inc. Reprinted by permission.
- Clifford Stoll: From *Silicon Snake Oil* by Clifford Stoll. Copyright © 1995 by Clifford Stoll. Used by permission of Doubleday, a division of Bantam Doubleday Dell Publishing Group, Inc.
- Kelly A. Zito: "The Digital Difference" by Kelly A. Zito from *Cornell Engineering Magazine,* Spring 1997. Reprinted by permission of the author.
- Monty Neill: "Computers, Thinking, and Schools in the 'New World Economic Order'" by Monty Neill from *Resisting the Virtual Life: The Culture and Politics of Information,* eds. Brook and Boal. Copyright © 1995 by James Brook and Iain Boal. Reprinted by permission of City Lights Books.
- Orson Scott Card: From *Ender's Game* by Orson Scott Card. Copyright © 1992. Reprinted with permission of St. Martin's Press, Inc.

Index

447